Peacock

April 94

The Soul of the American University

Stanford University's Memorial Church. *(Photo courtesy of the Stanford University News Service)*

THE SOUL OF THE AMERICAN UNIVERSITY

From Protestant Establishment to Established Nonbelief

George M. Marsden

New York Oxford
OXFORD UNIVERSITY PRESS
1994

Oxford University Press

Oxford New York Toronto
Delhi Bombay Calcutta Madras Karachi
Kuala Lumpur Singapore Hong Kong Tokyo
Nairobi Dar es Salaam Cape Town
Melbourne Auckland Madrid

and associated companies in
Berlin Ibadan

Published by Oxford University Press, Inc.
200 Madison Avenue, New York, New York 10016

Library of Congress Cataloging-in-Publication Data
Marsden, George M., 1939–
The soul of the American university: From Protestant establishment to established nonbelief / George M. Marsden.
p. cm. Includes bibliographical references and index.
ISBN 0-19-507046-1
1. Education, Higher—United States—Aims and objectives—History.
2. Protestant churches—United States—History.
3. Liberalism (Religion)—United States—Protestant churches—History.
4. Universities and colleges—United States
—Moral and ethical aspects—History.
I. Title. LA226.M34 1994 378.73—dc20 93-25486

2 4 6 8 9 7 5 3 1

Printed in the United States of America
on acid-free paper

For
Henry F. May

Preface

In order to make a complex history intelligible and engaging, I have depicted major themes by recounting especially revealing moments in the histories of key American universities and their collegiate predecessors. Since a fairly limited number of institutions have set the standards for most of the rest of American higher education, I have concentrated on those pace-setting schools.

Such an approach makes the account manageable, I think, for both author and readers, but it also means that many stories are left out. For instance, I say relatively little about the hundreds of small religious colleges that kept a substantial Christian identity through at least the first half of the twentieth century and provided an important alternative to university-style education. My interest has been in the universities which, especially because they trained the teachers in the colleges, eventually shaped the outlooks even of most of the denominational schools.

I have also not concentrated attention on Catholic colleges and universities, since they likewise had little to do with setting the standards that eventually prevailed in American academic life. Women's colleges, African-American colleges, most southern colleges and universities, and conservative Protestant colleges were also long marginalized by those who defined the most respected standards for American intellectual life. While these institutions might be relatively good at what they were doing, they were defined in such a way that they could hardly participate in cutting-edge intellectual activity. Although the histories of the role of religion in such institutions would be fascinating and valuable in their own rights, they are not central to the story of American universities. Nonetheless, I have attempted to take into account the significance of the exclusion of such schools from centrality. Likewise, while I have not looked closely at the few Jewish educational institutions, the attitudes of the Protestant establishment to the rapid growth of Jewish participation in twentieth-century universities is an important part of the story.

Any history of the origins of American universities must take into account that universities were shaped in part by imported models, particularly from England, Scotland, and Germany. A complete history of the role of religion in modern universities would have to deal extensively with the establishments and disestablishments of Christianity in the cultures and the universities of those countries and include comparisons with the American developments. One of my hopes for the present study is that it will generate interest in such neglected subjects. In the meantime, much can be learned by concentrating on the characteristic American developments, while attempting to take into account the overseas influences as they were assimilated into American categories.

Since this is essentially an account of the influence of Protestantism in shaping American higher education, it is limited chronologically to the era when the Protestant establishment was still intact. The account concentrates on the late nineteenth century, when American universities took their basic shape, but it also surveys the colonial and earlier nineteenth-century origins of American higher education and carries the story forward into the 1960s. The last chapter also sketches in broad strokes how these themes have been played out more recently.

For reasons explained in the introduction, my interest in this book has been substantially in how religious perspectives might relate to the *intellectual* life of universities. One of the revealing dimensions of this history is that discussions of such topics have been confined almost entirely to undergraduate education and to university divinity schools. With respect to graduate or other professional education, there is very little story to tell. That in itself is a most significant point; but, since the absence of direct religious influences was hardly contested, it is a point difficult to treat in proportion to its immense importance.

I have also given relatively little attention to the role of divinity schools in universities. My reason for that is that I have been interested in how the currently prevailing dimensions of American intellectual life took their shape in the construction of universities. In effect, one of the ways that religious perspectives were largely eliminated from the intellectual business of the rest of universities was to confine such concerns to divinity schools. In a few cases, such as at Yale, Chicago, and Duke, divinity schools held their own as significant, though secondary, parts of the university through much of the twentieth century. Nonetheless, even at their best, divinity schools have been marginalized. Even where they are academically relatively strong, their presence is an anomaly and a puzzle to much of the rest of the university. Moreover, only a minority of American universities have divinity schools. So while the history of university divinity schools is important in its own right, particularly for the churches that they served,* ministerial and theological education has not had a lasting impact on defining the central features of American academic life.

For similar reasons, I have given only secondary attention to the roles of voluntary religion in serving university communities. While such religious activities may also be of great value, they have seldom touched the main business of the universities. Rather, from a religious perspective,

*The Lilly Foundation has devoted major funding to the study of these institutions, which have been significant in the history of American mainline Protestant denominations. Particularly important are Glenn T. Miller, *Piety and Intellect: The Aims and Purposes of Ante-Bellum Theological Education* (Atlanta: Scholars Press, 1990), and the forthcoming work of Conrad Cherry, who was kind enough to share with me an early version titled "Hurrying toward the Kingdom: Universities, Divinity Schools and American Protestantism, 1880–1980."

they have been significant compensations for arrangements which have effectively excluded religious concerns from the most influential parts of modern intellectual life.

Since, despite these narrowings, this book still covers an immense territory, it is inevitably dependent on secondary sources, although it turns to primary ones whenever feasible. The very point of having secondary historical works, of course, is to make works of synthesis possible. The acknowledgments of so many of them in the notes, which should also serve as bibliographical guides to the topics in question, are signals of my deep debts to my colleagues in the historical community and expressions of my gratitude for their work. This book, more than any other that I have written, makes me aware of how much scholarship arises out of various intersecting communities.

Notre Dame, Ind. G. M. M.
July 1993

Acknowledgments

The Pew Charitable Trusts has been the primary agency that made possible the immediate community of scholarship out of which this book has arisen. Their very generous grant, extending over a four-and-a-half-year term, made it possible to assemble a very talented group of scholars, who provided the groundwork for this volume. Martin Trimble and Joel Carpenter, successive religion officers for the trust, were particularly helpful in initiation and later oversight of the project respectively. I am also grateful to Robert Lynn for his work while at the Lilly Foundation of directing this project to the Pew Charitable Trusts.

Among the team of workers who have contributed to this project, I am most in debt to Bradley Longfield. As my principal associate throughout the term of the grant, he made an immense contribution as a consultant, co-researcher, and friend. Darryl G. Hart, associate for a year and consultant after that, also played a major role in making this book possible. He is to be especially thanked for taking time from his busy schedule for challenging and sometimes apparently aimless consultations at the Duke Golf Club and similar venues. Paul Kemeny was particularly helpful in his years as a research assistant. I am also grateful to Diana Hochstedt Butler, Scott Flipse, Philip Goff, Liz Hutchison, Tony Jenkins, Kathryn Long, Roger Robins, and Jeffrey Trexler for their valuable help as researchers. I would again like to thank those scholars who participated in the scholarly conference held at Duke University in the spring of 1990 and to those who contributed to *The Secularization of the Academy,* edited by George M. Marsden and Bradley J. Longfield (Oxford University Press, 1992). I am particularly grateful to Duke University for its support of the research grant and of this project. Dennis Campbell, dean of Duke Divinity School, was exceedingly helpful and encouraging of this project and to him I owe an especially large debt. Clara Godwin and her assistant, Shelby Wallen, were also always cheerful and efficient in administering the financial details. I am grateful to the History Department of the University of California at Berkeley for opportunity to spend a beneficial year in association with that department while working on this project. My sincere thanks are also due to the University of Notre Dame, the Francis A. McAnaney chair, and the McAnaney family for valuable support in completing this project.

An impressive group of scholars has been willing to comment on a draft of the manuscript. These include Darryl G. Hart, Philip Gleason, Paul C. Kemeny, Bradley Longfield, Henry F. May, Mark Noll, George Rawlyk, Winton Solberg, James Turner and Grant Wacker. I am deeply grateful to them for their advice, encouragement, and editorial comments. Henry May has been a friend and informal mentor throughout much of this project, and a most careful critic and editor of the draft. George Rawlyk also provided invaluable friendship, encouragement, and advice. I also appreciate the helpful comments of Notre Dame graduate students Scott Flipse, John Haas, Michael Keating, and Bill Svelmoe. Cynthia Read of Oxford University Press favored me once again with her superb stylistic suggestions, which go beyond the call of duty for a Senior Editor. I also thank Carole Schwager for her copyediting, and Peter H. Ohlin and Paul E. Schlotthauer of Oxford University Press for their fine help. Greg Marsden helped with typing revisions. Brynne helped by being Brynne. Lucie's role has been inestimable. It is a delight to be part of a loving relationship that has grown with time, and the years during which this book was being written have been some of the best.

"The Ambiguities of Academic Freedom," 1992 presidential address for the American Society of Church History, published in *Church History* 62 (June 1993), is drawn from this study, especially chapter 16 and the postscript.

Contents

Part III When the Tie No Longer Binds, 263

The Soul of the American University

Introduction

This book is about how and why pace-setting American universities are defined as they are. Particularly it is concerned with how and why they are defined with respect to religion. These two questions are closely connected since those who originally set the standards for American universities in the late nineteenth century were shaped by their strongly Protestant heritage. Most of the first generation of university builders were active Protestants and many were ardent believers. Even if they gave up the particulars of the evangelicalism of their mentors' generation, they retained a dedication to liberal Christianity. Through the second and third generations of the evolution of American universities, until the early 1960s, almost all the leaders of the pace-setting institutions were of Protestant stock, had outlooks shaped by a Protestant ethos, and on occasion would honor their Christian heritage.

In the late nineteenth century, when American universities took their shape, the Protestantism of the major northern denominations acted as a virtual religious and cultural establishment. This establishmentarian outlook was manifested in American universities, which were constructed not, as is sometimes supposed, as strictly secular institutions but as integral parts of a religious-cultural vision. The formal strength of such nonsectarian Protestantism was evidenced by the continuing place of religious activities on most campuses. In the 1890s, for instance, almost all state universities still held compulsory chapel services and some required Sunday church attendance as well. State-sponsored chapel services did not become rare until the World War II era. In the meantime, many of the best private universities maintained Christian divinity schools and during the first half of the twentieth century built impressive chapels signaling their respect for their Christian heritages. As late as the 1950s it was not unusual for spokespersons of leading schools to refer to them as "Christian" institutions.

Such vestiges of the Protestant establishment are significant not simply as curious, but largely forgotten, practices. Rather, they provide important clues for unearthing a much larger connection between establishmentarian Protestantism and the construction of American universities. While the United States was formally pluralistic, its cultural centers had never seen a time when Protestantism was not dominant. During the first half of the nineteenth century Protestant leaders consolidated their cultural hegemony. Nowhere was this cultural aggressiveness more successful than in their gaining control over virtually all the influential colleges in the country, including state schools. New Englanders, who drew on centuries of experience in American higher education, were the dominant party in this enterprise, setting national standards that others attempted to emulate. Politically they were Whigs and later Republicans. Heirs to the Puritans, they were national reformers who combined high moral idealism with zeal for modern capitalist and technological progress. For a time after their triumph in the Civil War no other group could challenge their cultural leadership, especially not in education. It was the sons of this heritage—men who came of age during the earthshaking national conflict and who inherited a sense of calling to serve God and nation in a cultural mission—who founded and defined America's universities.

Protestantism was, of course, far from the only factor shaping the founders' heritage or the universities they built. They were responding as well to many practical, technical, professional, and economic forces. Yet it would be remarkable if visionary men reared in an era of such fervent national moral idealism did not view their practical concerns through the lens of their religious heritage. Typically they did not abandon the Christian idealism of that heritage but rather adjusted it to accommodate their commitments to modernity. So while it is possible to look at the shaping of American higher education primarily as responses to practical forces and concerns, it is illuminating to recognize that the ideals for which the universities stood and which helped define practical priorities were also shaped by a powerful and distinctly Protestant heritage. Even major educational ideals that might not seem especially religious, such as scientific standards growing out of the Enlightenment, American republican moral ideals growing out of the Revolution, romantic principles of individual development, or American perceptions of German universities, were mediated through the American Protestant heritage.

If we look at the story from the other side, asking what the universities did with Protestantism, rather than how the Protestant heritage shaped the universities, we immediately see a striking paradox. The American university system was built on a foundation of evangelical Protestant colleges. Most of the major universities evolved directly from such nineteenth-century colleges. As late as 1870 the vast majority of these were remarkably evangelical. Most of them had clergymen-presidents who taught courses defending biblicist Christianity and who encouraged periodic campus revivals. Yet within half a century the universities that emerged from these evangelical colleges, while arguably carrying forward the spirit of their evangelical forebears, had become conspicuously inhospitable to the letter of such evangelicalism. By the 1920s the evangelical Protestantism of the old-time colleges had been effectively excluded from leading university classrooms.

During the next half century the paradox turns into an irony. Many of the same forces set in motion by liberal Protestantism,[1] which rooted out traditional evangelicalism from university education, were eventually turned against the liberal Protestant establishment itself. Now, while it is the spirit of liberal Protestantism that arguably survives, normative religious teaching of any sort has been nearly eliminated from standard university education.

The deep irony in Protestant-dominated American education is highlighted further if we consider dominant attitudes toward Roman Catholicism. On the one hand, the ideals for which the Protestant establishment stood included freedom, democracy, benevolence, justice, reform, inclusiveness, "brotherhood," and service. Education was conceived of as a means of assimilating other traditions into an American heritage that included these ideals. While the cultural leadership often failed to live up to what it professed, these ideals themselves have had a pervasive influence on almost every subgroup in the culture and should not be dismissed lightly. At the same time, as many Catholic educators of the nineteenth and early twentieth centuries could have testified, these universal and inclusive attitudes were also imperialistic and exclusive.

The American Protestant leadership was determined to have a standardized education system and treated Catholics as second-class for persisting in having their own schools. In higher education Protestants insisted on a universal academic ideal, underwritten by Enlightenment assumptions concerning universal science and supported by optimism concerning human nature's ability to progress toward a universal moral ideal. During the era when America's dominant university system was defined, a Catholic university was regarded, as it was popular to remark, as an oxymoron.

Ironically, therefore, Protestant universalism (catholicity, if you will) was one of the forces that eventually contributed to the virtual exclusion of religious perspectives from the most influential centers of American intellectual life. Unlike some other Western countries which addressed the problems of pluralism by encouraging multiple educational systems, the American tendency was to build what amounted to a monolithic and homogeneous educational establishment and to force the alternatives to marginal existence on the periphery. Almost from the outset of the rise of American universities, such universality was attained by defining the intellectual aspects of the enterprise as excluding all but liberal Protestant or "nonsectarian" perspectives. For a time liberal Protestantism also was still allowed to play a priestly role, signaled by the building of chapels, blessing such academic arrangements. Eventually, however, the logic of the nonsectarian ideals which the Protestant establishment had successfully promoted in public life dictated that liberal Protestantism itself should be moved to the periphery to which other religious perspectives had been relegated for some time. The result was an "inclusive" higher education that resolved the problems of pluralism by virtually excluding all religious perspectives from the nation's highest academic life.

Telling the story these ways points out the wisdom of not jumping to evaluative conclusions in considering the role of religion in American higher education. On the one hand, it is a story of the disestablishment of religion. On the other hand, it is a story of secularization. From the point of view of persons with wholly secular values, these two ways of characterizing the history may fit harmoniously, both being laudable. Even for such readers, though, it may be illuminating to reflect on the degree to which many of the things they like as well as those they dislike in contemporary universities may have been shaped by a Protestant heritage. For those who have religious commitments, on the other hand, "disestablishment" and "secularization" are likely to suggest opposed evaluations. Disestablishment is likely to sound like a good thing, while secularization, even if desirable in many of its forms, seems undesirable if it excludes religion from the major areas of public life that shape people's sophisticated beliefs.

Persons concerned about the place of religion in American life might be particularly concerned that the largely voluntary and commendable disestablishment of religion has led to the virtual establishment of nonbelief, or the near exclusion of religious perspectives from dominant academic life. While American universities today allow individuals free exercise of religion in parts of their lives that do not touch the heart of the university, they tend to exclude or discriminate against relating explicit religious perspectives to intellectual life. In other words, the free exercise of religion does not extend to the dominant intellectual centers of our culture. So much are these exclusions taken for granted, as simply part of the definition of academic life, that many people do not even view them as strange. Nor do they think it odd that such exclusion is typically justified in the names of academic freedom and free inquiry.

One of the themes of this book is that there were undesirable features of the American Protestant establishment which have led to equally flawed features of American disestablishment.[2] It has been a particular source of later problems in American higher education that Protestant church-related institutions typically regarded themselves as essentially public institutions as well. From their beginnings, reflecting their European establishmentarian heritages, they made almost no distinction between the ideals that should shape the whole of American society and the particularities of the Protestant faith. After the formal disestablishment of religion, they found ways to perpetuate this identification of religious and cultural heritages. Essentially by broadening the definitions of Protestantism they managed to maintain their cultural hegemony under the rubric of consensual American ideals.

In understanding and evaluating changes in the role of religion in America, it is important to keep in mind that the largest forces involved are by no means unique to the United States. Rather the American developments are part of changes in Western culture that have been going on since at least the Reformation and accelerating since the rise of science, technology, and Enlightenment thought in the early modern era. Such massive transformations as disestablishment, secularization in all its complexities, disenchantment of reality, rationalized approaches to work and other human activities, and revolutions in technology, politics, economics, intellectual life, culture, and in all human relationships were parts of more general Western cultural trends, even if they took distinctive forms in America. Moreover, Americans did not invent universities, even if they reshaped them in their own image. Higher education in the United States was directly influenced by English, Scottish, and German models, which in turn were shaped by the impact of all the overwhelming forces for change in those countries. Nonetheless, if we keep this larger picture in mind, it is possible to see how those forces, as well as particular European models, were refracted though the American experience.

As should be apparent by now, the way in which this story is told is influenced significantly by my own point of view. Since historians when they are candid admit their books are in part autobiographies, I have long thought it appropriate for authors to identify their own points of view, so that readers may take them into account. I am also now pleased to see that, thanks in part to feminist scholars, this has become more customary practice. My point of view is that of a fairly traditional Protestant of the Reformed theological heritage. One of the features of that heritage is that it has valued education that relates faith to one's scholarship. Particularly important is that beliefs about God, God's creation, and God's will and provision for humans should have impact on scholarship not just in theology, but also in considering other dimensions of human thought and relationships. In my own experience I have seen the possibilities for such scholarship demonstrated, often in intellectually impressive ways, particularly at Calvin College where I taught for many years and also among other colleagues, especially in American religious history, who share such convictions.[3] Yet it is also apparent that such viewpoints, no matter what their academic credentials, are seldom given a hearing in American academic life. Most American scholars hardly know that such serious traditional faith-related academic enterprise still persists, or if they do, they write it off as obscurantist. The present study then arises from my puzzlement as to how the dominant American academic life came to be defined in a way that such viewpoints, including their counterparts in other Christian or other religious heritages, have been largely excluded.

Since it is nowhere written in stone that the highest sort of human intellectual activity must exclude religious perspectives, it is helpful, I think, to consider how it came to pass that so many academics believe that such exclusions are part of the definition of their task. Such beliefs are of relatively recent origin. In America they are constructions largely of the late nineteenth and early twentieth centuries, although their roots can be traced further back and to European antecedents. The evaluative question that this historical analysis should raise is, given that many of the original reasons for these beliefs are no longer widely compelling, is it not time to reconsider the rules that shape the most respected academic communities?

One point that I find needs to be underscored is that this book is not a lament for a lost golden age when Christians ruled America and its educational institutions. Rather, if anything, it is a critique of that old regime. Particularly, it critically analyzes the Protestant heritage to which I am closest, the Reformed (such as Congregationalists and Presbyterians), who long set the standards for dominant American education. Nonetheless, this analysis is not first of all a critique of any particular individuals or groups so much as an attempt to understand American tendencies toward cultural homogenization and uniformity with respect to this issue. Those from Protestant heritages, notably the Reformed, who aspired to dominate the culture, are partly responsible for those tendencies. At the same time college and university leaders were responding to broader cultural forces and many legitimate demands. So rather than finding many culprits, what we typically find are unintended consequences of decisions that in their day seemed largely laudable, or at least unavoidable. The evaluative question is whether the unintended consequences regarding religion are desirable. Particularly, in a just society might there not be more room for the free exercise of religion in relation to higher learning?

Now that I have so explicitly identified my evaluative concerns, there is a danger that readers may conclude that what follows is little more than historical partisanship. However, as many historians who do not say much about their own points of view have demonstrated, it is perfectly possible to have strong evaluative interests in a subject and yet treat it fairly and with a degree of detachment. A large part of my motive is to provide a narrative that will illuminate the relationship of dominant American academia to American religion. Moreover, I have attempted to address wider audiences that include many points of view different from mine. My hope is that my somewhat unusual perspective has led me to raise a set of questions sufficiently novel for a wide range of observers to find them intriguing. So while I write from an acknowledged point of view, I have also attempted to tell a story that is fair enough to the evidence and to all parties concerned to be illuminating to others whose interests are very different from my own.

Notes

1. Often in this volume I use the term "liberal Protestantism" rather loosely as a shorthand for the leadership in the major American denominations (such as American Baptist (Northern Baptist), United Methodist, the Presbyterian Church in the U.S.A., United Church of Christ (including earlier Congregational), Episcopal, Disciples of Christ, some Lutherans, and others associated with the Federal Council of Churches and its successor, the National Council of Churches. Although there were many varieties of viewpoints among and within these groups,

the leadership was "liberal" at least in the sense of being theologically inclusive and tolerant. Often leaders from these groups in university education were themselves liberal in theology, though there again there would be many exceptions. Sometimes I refer to these groups synonymously as "mainline Protestants." "Evangelical" also has a number of legitimate meanings. I use it here to refer to Protestant traditions that place a strong emphasis on the authority of the Bible as a reliable historical record of God's saving work centering in Christ and that have at least sympathy for revivalist emphasis on conversion.

2. This observation roughly follows the argument of David Martin that the character of a country's disestablishment will parallel the character of its former establishment. *General Theory of Secularization* (New York: Harper & Row, 1978).

3. I have surveyed both the strengths and the weaknesses of traditional Protestant scholarship in "The State of Evangelical Scholarship," *Christian Scholar's Review* 17 (June 1988), 347–60.

Prologue (I): God and Buckley at Yale (1951)

"I was somewhat concerned," wrote McGeorge Bundy (Yale '40) in the *Atlantic* of November 1951, "lest my readers refuse to believe that so violent, unbalanced, and twisted a young man really existed."

Bundy, a professor at Harvard but speaking on behalf of his alma mater, treated William F. Buckley, Jr., as an upstart who had failed to know the rules at a gentlemen's club. Buckley's infraction was that he had been so ungrateful as to write a scathing attack on the school from which he had just graduated, alleging that it was a hotbed of atheism and collectivism. This ingratitude was compounded by Buckley's failure to recognize that, as a Roman Catholic, he was something of a guest at Yale. "Most remarkable of all," said Bundy near the beginning of his review of *God and Man at Yale,* was that Buckley, while not even mentioning that he was "an ardent Roman Catholic," should attempt to define Yale's religious tradition. "Yale has thousands of Catholic alumni and friends," said Bundy, "who would not dream of such a course."[1] The Rev. Henry Sloane Coffin (Yale '97), chairman of a blue-ribbon committee to report on the spiritual and political condition of Yale, wrote to one inquirer, "Mr. Buckley's book is really a misrepresentation and distorted by his Roman Catholic point of view. Yale is a Puritan and Protestant institution by its heritage and he should have attended Fordham or some similar institution."[2]

God and Man at Yale would have caused a sensation even without the religious issues. Senator Joseph McCarthy was on the loose and at the height of his influence, the United States was in the midst of the Korean War, and at other universities professors had lost jobs over accusations of communism. Buckley did not allege that there were communists on the Yale faculty, but his accusations that traditionally conservative Yale was promoting "collectivism," even if this amounted to little more than New Deal liberalism, threatened to test the loyalty of some of the Old Blue.

In retrospect, however, the religious dimensions of the controversy are the most remarkable, since they are the least remembered. A generation later it seems almost inconceivable that there could have been a national controversy involving the question of whether a major university was sufficiently Christian. Yet not only the responses of Yale, but also those of the reviewers, make it clear that it would have been news to admit that Yale had drifted loose of its Christian moorings.

To be sure, the task of assessing the role of religion in the controversy is complicated by Buckley's conflation of the economic and religious issues. At one point in the book, Buckley even affirmed, "I believe that the duel between Christianity and atheism is the most important in the world. I further believe that the struggle between individualism and collectivism is the same struggle reproduced on another level." Years later Buckley remarked that the words "the same struggle reproduced on another level" were not originally his own but were suggested by one of his conservative mentors. Nonetheless, he let them stand because there was "a nice rhetorical resonance and an intrinsic, almost nonchalant suggestion of an exciting symbiosis."[3] Though Buckley, always the debater, thus acknowledged that his fondness for rhetoric overrode his concern for precision of argument, the explicit equation was implicit throughout the book.[4]

In any case, a substantial section of Buckley's essay dealt solely with the state of Christianity at Yale, and this provides us with a revealing account of both the extent and limits of religious influences at midcentury. Buckley's evidence, as well as Yale's responses, offers clues as to how many American universities of this era could still see themselves as Christian and yet simultaneously, especially from an outsider's point of view, seem essentially subversive of Christianity.

One of the things Buckley was so impolite as to point out was a sizable gap between Yale's rhetoric and reality. His lead quotation was from President Charles Seymour's 1937 inaugural: "I call on all members of the faculty, as members of a thinking body, freely to recognize the tremendous validity and power of the teachings of Christ in our life-and-death struggle against the forces of selfish materialism. If we lose that struggle, judging from present events abroad, scholarship as well as religion will disappear."[5]

The statement was typical of the public philosophy of many universities of the time. The principles of Christianity were identified with the very future of civilization and with what separated the United States from totalitarianism. Nonetheless, at a university, especially a university that served a free nation, these teachings could not be taught by indoctrination but were accepted only by "a thinking body, freely."

On such grounds, Yale claimed to score well. Yale was reputed to be more religious than many universities and Seymour had in the same address called for "the maintenance and upbuilding of the Christian religion as a vital part of the university life."[6] Not only did it have a strong religious heritage, a university chapel, and campus religious programs, but its undergraduate program could point to its large religion department and to many influential faculty who were strongly pro-Christian.

Buckley presented a formidable case that none of these amounted to much and that a Yale education was more likely to shatter a person's commitment to Christianity than to fortify it. The most popular religion course, taught by the university chaplain, was popular because it was easy. Moreover, the professor, despite his personal religious faith, made a concerted effort to teach *about* Christianity, rather than to teach Christianity. The next most popular course, taught by T. M. Greene, a philosopher of religion, though explicitly Christian, was a course in "ethics, not religion." By this Buckley meant that it did not do anything to affirm the essentials of traditional Christianity, such as belief in God and in " 'Jesus Christ as Divine Lord and Saviour.' "[7]

Another well-attended religion course was taught by a man who told his students he was "80 per cent atheist and 20 per cent agnostic." A few other courses were taught by avowed Christians, in Buckley's sense, but were not well attended. In fact, religion, although an option to fulfill some core requirements, enrolled less than 10 percent of Yale students in any given year; its influence thus would not have been pervasive, even if it had been laudable.

Turning from the low Christian influence in religion courses, Buckley documented strong anti-Christian influences in the rest of the curriculum. He did note a few exceptions. A course in European intellectual history and another course in Shakespeare each had avowed Christian perspectives. Professor Robert Calhoun of the Divinity School occasionally taught an undergraduate course on the history of philosophy but kept most of his religious views to himself. Church historian Kenneth Latourette was openly a traditional Christian, but his undergraduate courses were not popular.

Such influences were more than offset by others. In the History Department was a "vigorously atheistic . . . professional debunker . . . who has little mercy on either God, or on those who believe in Him." Two of the leading figures in the Philosophy Department, Brand Blanshard and Paul Weiss, were, respectively, "an earnest and expansive atheist" and "a confirmed debunker of the Christian religion." In the social sciences, where disbelief in God seemed almost a faculty prerequisite, one of the most cynical reputedly declared that "a cleric today is the modern counterpart of the witch doctor" and suggested to Jesuits that they could convert the world overnight if they could "submit the wine to a chemical analysis after consecration and then see if you've gotten hemoglobin out of grape juice."

Noting that most of the texts used in the university were either hostile or indifferent to religion, Buckley summarized the problem at Yale and elsewhere as the triumph of "relativism, pragmatism and utilitarianism," in the spirt of philosopher John Dewey. "There is surely not a department at Yale," Buckley observed, "that is uncontaminated with the absolute that there are no absolutes, no intrinsic rights, no ultimate truths."[8]

Defenders of Yale invariably dismissed any anti-Christian influences in the curriculum as defensible as matters of academic freedom and pointed to the extracurricular religious influences at the university. Catholics had the St. Thomas More Club, Jews had the Hillel Foundation, and Baptists, Methodists, Congregationalists, Lutherans, and Episcopalians had campus ministries; but by far the most important campus organization was Dwight Hall, headquarters of the Yale University Christian Association. This venerable institution began in 1881 as the Yale YMCA when both Yale and the Y were strongly evangelical institutions and still carried considerable social prestige. It sponsored religious retreats, book clubs, and considerable social work in New Haven.

Buckley insisted, however, that "the *religious* influence of Dwight Hall is in no way commensurate with its general importance on campus." Much of its work was not distinctly Christian and Christianity seemed to be regarded by the association as an option (as it would have been at YMCAS generally by this time). In 1949 the editors of Dwight Hall's magazine, *Et Veritas,* stated that they "choose the Christian" philosophy as a matter of "personal conviction" rather than editorial policy. Editors in succeeding years were not even Christian, one being an "avowed agnostic." The Yale Christian Association attitude that Christianity was purely a matter of preference, said Buckley, turned Christianity into " 'my most favorite way of living.' "[9] Buckley's point was that the extracurricular religion promoted at Yale was so bland that, except in rare instances, it had little chance of counteracting the combination of indifference and hostility toward religion displayed in the curriculum and by many professors.

Identifying this problem was easier than proposing a plausible cure. Buckley attacked the ideology of modern universities at a vulnerable point, subtitling his polemic "The Superstitions of Academic Freedom." Academic freedom, he argued, could not be the sacred absolute its proponents were claiming. Universities already ruled out any number of teachings, such as extreme racism. So the question was not whether there were limits on what might be taught, but only what those limits were. The problem remained, however, of how to change those limits.

Buckley's proposed solution was the most heretical part of his essay. Applying principles of free enterprise, he reasoned that if Yale's principal supporters were its alumni and if the alumni were predominantly traditionally Christian and conservative economically, it would be reasonable for alumni to withhold their support until Yale was providing the product they desired. This was a variation on his point about academic freedom. Since Buckley surmised that alumni pressure already limited what might be taught at a university, he was asking only for the more rigorous application of an existing principle.

The idea of substantive external control of universities was, of course, anathema to most educators. McGeorge Bundy dismissed it as simply alien, intimating that Buckley's views reflected "the pronounced and well-recognized difference between Protestant and Catholic views of education in America." The Protestant cultural establishment still cultivated the longstanding view that Catholicism was associated with absolutism while Protestantism had brought the world democracy and freedom.[10] Some

Catholic complicity with fascism during the World War II era had reinforced this view. Freedom of academic institutions from direct control of either church or state was one of the things many educated Americans saw themselves fighting for in the war. As Randolph Crump Miller, a liberal Christian educator, put it, "This is more than an attack on Yale; it is an attack on all liberal education. It is not a plea for more religion, but for a religion of external authority."[11]

Buckley's Catholicism was critical to the debate.[12] Though mainline Protestant leaders frequently condemned Catholic authoritarianism, they also often made special efforts to be tolerant of individual Catholics, especially if they were willing to act like tolerant Protestants. Buckley, however, saw jarring contradictions in the two religious worlds. From his ardent Catholic perspective he could see traits that establishment Protestants took for granted. From his more rigorous religious viewpoint their easy tolerance of unbelief seemed naive, if not hypocritical.

From the inside the claims that Yale was still Christian did not appear hypocritical at all. Mainline Protestantism could genuinely be considered to be flourishing at midcentury and to be holding its own on college campuses. In response to Buckley the standing "Committee on Religious Life and Study" at Yale offered a candid but optimistic internal assessment. Despite religious indifference and "a very active secularism" which celebrated "objectivity" and attempted to exclude value judgments of any sort, Yale was maintaining "a Christian atmosphere which has been accepted as traditional through many college generations." "Students," the committee argued, "are not antagonistic to religion." Even though they were " 'ecclesiastically illiterate,' " the committee had been assured "they believe in God and in the moral and ethical teachings of Christ." Moreover, "they are eager for service which is in the broad sense Christian."[13]

William Buckley and the Yale establishment differed so widely regarding the Christian character of Yale because they were using vastly different definitions of Christianity. Buckley was measuring the religion at Yale against something like traditional Catholicism. Much of the Protestant establishment, on the other hand, was talking about Christianity as "service," "morality," or "high values in living," which was more or less equivalent to faith in God or "religion" and for which formal religious observance was desirable but not absolutely necessary.[14]

So throughout the first half of the twentieth century, despite some obvious decline of Christianity in public life, mainline Protestant religion[15] could plausibly be said to be holding its own, even in the universities. World War II, in fact, had sparked a widespread religious revival. In the 1950s college students were still as likely as the rest of the population to be members of churches and to express religious beliefs.[16] What was not always taken into account in assessing this religious interest, although it was debated among the theologians, was that the low-voltage religion in many of the churches and on the campuses often did little more than impart a warm glow to the best moral ideals of the culture at large. So the disappearance of explicit Christian influences in public culture might be imminent; but at the same time it was possible with the broadened definition of religion to see the situation as the spread of religious enlightenment. Protestantism, also known as "religion," could face the future with confidence.

In response to the furor created by Buckley's book, Yale's president A. Whitney Griswold appointed a committee of distinguished alumni, chaired by the Rev. Henry Sloane Coffin, '97, to review the charges. Not surprisingly, the committee gave Yale a clean bill of health. As to the accusation that Yale was encouraging irreligion or atheism, it was flatly "without foundation." While the committee did not mention Christianity, it affirmed that "there is, today, more than ever, widespread realization that religion alone can give meaning and purpose to modern life." Students particularly needed the wholeness and sense of direction that religion provided. "It is by faith that man sees all things working together in the light of God and gives himself to work with them. To supply such light and truth Yale was at birth dedicated, and to this high aim the University continues." In fact, said the committee, "religious life at Yale is deeper and richer than it has been in many years."[17]

Notes

1. McGeorge Bundy, "The Attack on Yale," *Atlantic* 188 (November 1951), 50–52.

2. William F. Buckley, Jr., "God and Man at Yale: Twenty-five Years Later," in *A Hymnal: The Controversial Arts* (New York: G. P. Putnam's Sons, 1975), 426. An internal Report of the Committee on Religious Life and Study, University Council, Charles P. Taft, Chairman, November 1, 1952, Yale University, A. Whitney Griswold Papers, also notes "some less attractive Catholic qualities" in Buckley's book and that Buckley omitted any mention of his Catholic affiliation.

3. Buckley, "God and Man at Yale," 424.

4. Some reviewers called Buckley to task for this confusion. Peter Viereck observed that it was "humorless, or else blasphemous, . . . to enshrine jointly as sacrosanct 'Adam Smith and Ricardo, Jesus and Saint Paul.' " The book, he thought, was the "product of narrow economic privilege." *New York Times Book Review,* November 4, 1951, 39. *Time,* while taking pleasure at seeing Yale squirm, referred snidely to "the brassy trumpet of a 25-year old alumnus" and also pointed out Buckley's "odd premise that Christianity and capitalism are, if not completely equal, at least inseparable." October 29, 1951, 57.

5. William F. Buckley, Jr., *God and Man at Yale: The Superstitions of "Academic Freedom"* (Chicago: Henry Regnery, 1951), 3.

6. Quoted in Buckley, *God and Man,* 43.

7. Buckley, *God and Man,* 4, 8, the latter quoting a recent World Council of Churches formula.

8. Buckley, *God and Man,* 9, 10, 13, 18–19, 16, 25.

9. Ibid., 29.

10. Paul Blanshard's very popular *American Freedom and Catholic Power* (Bos-

ton: Beacon Press, 1949) was the best-known expression of this. The sentiments, however, often were founded deeply even among the progressives in the Protestant establishment. See chapter 21 below.

11. Bundy, "The Attack on Yale." Randolph Crump Miller, Review of *God and Man at Yale,* in *Churchman* 116 (January 15, 1952), 13.

12. Cf. George Marsden, *Reforming Fundamentalism: Fuller Seminary and the New Evangelicalism* (Grand Rapids, Mich.: Wm. B. Eerdmans, 1987).

13. Report of the Committee on Religious Life and Study, November 2, 1951, 1, 2, 5.

14. This is a summary of the account of "religion" in Merrimon Cuninggim, *The College Seeks Religion* (New Haven: Yale University Press, 1947), 247. Cuninggim was a recent Yale Ph.D. His views are discussed in more detail in chapter 18 below.

15. "Mainline Protestant" is here used in a descriptive, not a normative sense and refers to denominations such as Methodist Episcopal, American Baptist, Presbyterian Church in the U.S.A., Congregationalists, Disciples, Episcopalian, and others associated with the National Council of Churches as distinct from more strictly evangelical, confessional, fundamentalist, pentecostal, or other sectarian groups that remained separatist.

16. Robert Wuthnow, *The Struggle for America's Soul: Evangelicals, Liberals, and Secularism* (Grand Rapids, Mich.: Wm. B. Eerdmans, 1989), 34–35.

17. "Report of the President's Advisory Committee," Henry Sloane Coffin, '97, Chairman, February 9, 1952, Griswold Papers.

Prologue (II): Henry Sloane Coffin's Yale (1897)

The Rev. Henry Sloane Coffin, '97, who chaired the blue-ribbon committee that in 1952 answered William F. Buckley, Jr., with the categorical conclusion that "religious life at Yale is deeper and richer than it has been in many years," could recall more distant student days when Yale's religious life was deeper and richer still. Coffin was a renowned preacher, the president of Union Theological Seminary in New York City (he had once been a leading candidate for the Yale presidency), and had done as much as anyone to shepherd mainline Protestantism from evangelicalism to theological modernism.[1] At Yale he had first come to prominence in his senior year as president of the Yale Christian Association, or Dwight Hall.

To be president of Dwight Hall was reputedly to be only a little lower on the campus scale of being than football captain.[2] This status was remarkable particularly because Yale was known at the time for the "the professional spirit in . . . athletics," which cynics contrasted with "the amateur spirit . . . in Yale scholarship."[3] Yale was one of the first campuses to make football into a major religion. Yet this was also an era of "manly" Christianity when many of the brightest and the best were revitalizing campus Christianity as a first step toward transforming the nation and the world. The Dwight Hall presidency was particularly significant since Yale was a training ground for American elite leadership and the Yale Christian Association was the largest of the burgeoning YMCAs where the campus renewals typically centered. The Yale Christian Association prided itself on being the "conservator of democracy" where "the millionaire and the man who is making his way through college [are] working side by side."[4] Fervent evangelical religion, while far from universal in its influence on Yale students,[5] was nonetheless the dominant religious force and was eminently respectable. Henry Coffin was duly elected to Yale's preeminent secret society, Skull and Bones, and rumor had it the leaderships of the two powerful organizations were closely linked.[6]

One clue to the character of this respectable campus religion was that the person who did most to lend prominence to the Yale Christian Association was Dwight L. Moody. During his student days Henry Coffin cultivated the Moody connection and in later years he still spoke fondly of the evangelist. The Protestant religious situation in the 1890s did not yet include the sharp differentiation between revivalist evangelical missionary fervor and advanced theological opinion, humanitarianism, and social concern. All these could march hand in hand in the heady days when American Christianity, closely allied with its British counterpart, promised to transform and civilize the world. Each summer Yale would send the largest delegation, typically a hundred or more, to Moody's famed college conferences in Northfield, Massachusetts. At Northfield in 1886 Moody had inspired students to form what soon became the Student Volunteer Movement pledged to "the evangelization of the world in this generation."[7] Yale's missionary efforts were so widespread that John R. Mott, chairman of the Student Volunteer Movement, could remark in 1899 that having visited some thirty countries, "I am pained to say I have even been in a country where I did not find the American flag; but I have never been where I did not find the Yale flag."[8]

Moody had first come to Yale in 1878 when he sparked the revival that led to the organization of the campus YMCA. He returned to the campus regularly, and he was instrumental in two other notable revival harvests, in 1890 and in 1899, the year of his death. In that last revival he appeared with biblical critic George Adam Smith and the revival was seen as one point at which "conservatism and higher criticism united in bringing from the same platform the message of Christ to Yale."[9] Henry Drummond, a Scotsman controversial for his progressive views, also made a profound impact both at Northfield and on the Yale campus. The broad-minded Drummond was, like Moody, legendary among Yale Christians. Yale men, however, also fondly recalled preachers at Northfield who would later be thought of as progenitors of fundamentalism, such as Reuben A. Torrey, Arthur T. Pierson, Charles G. Trumbull, and A. J. Gordon.[10] They saw such evangelism as perfectly compatible with "social service," such as proudly evidenced by the Yale mission to the "Bowery of New Haven," founded by Yale sports hero Amos Alonzo Stagg in 1888. In both the goal was "soul saving."[11]

Everyone seemed to agree that the nondoctrinal, activist, accommodating evangelicalism of the day was the best hope for humanity, "an influence that makes for righteousness, and the highest type of civilization."[12] Sectarianism was considered wholly out of place. An effort to found a separate Methodist campus organization was short-lived and tagged as clearly "un-Yale."[13] If Protestants could stand united, proclaiming the best in religion along with the highest ideals of civilization, there were few limits on what they could do for humanity.

Christianity at Yale had become healthier over the past generation by following a familiar American pattern: disestablishment and a shift to a voluntary basis. Lyman Beecher had remarked after formal state religion was terminated in Connecticut in 1818 that it was *"the best thing that ever happened to the State of Connecticut,"* since it threw Christians "on their own resources and on God."[14] Yale Christians at the end of the century could say much the same thing. At mid-nineteenth century religious coercion lingered longer in colleges, where the belief was that boys had to be disciplined, than in most other parts of American Protestantism. Yale in 1850 had two required chapel services daily, the morning one before breakfast. In addition, students were required to attend two lengthy preaching services on Sundays that served as a virtual course in theology. Professors and tutors attempted to enforce strict social discipline.

By the end of the century only one chapel service was required and it remained reasonably popular. Every senior class from 1894 to 1909 voted to perpetuate compulsory service. Aside from the question of piety, the daily services had come to be regarded as important symbols of Yale traditionalism and community.[15] The religious center of the university, however, had shifted from the chapel to Dwight Hall.[16] This was part of the general rise of a semiautonomous student culture, of which the cult of football was the most prominent manifestation. Although campus life was far from predominantly religious, vigorous young men across the country, like Stagg, Mott, Coffin, and many others of equal abilities, had taken command of their own activities and were promising to change the world for Christ. Yale remained, as it always had been in the nineteenth century, the flagship school of interdenominational Protestant evangelicalism. Nevertheless, the progressive evangelical atmosphere among students at Yale was only an accentuation of what could be found on campuses throughout the country.

Observers at the time agreed that respect for Christianity among collegians had increased notably just in the past two decades. During the 1870s and early 1880s agnosticism, fortified by Darwinism and the rising popularity of biblical criticism, had fostered an atmosphere of doubt on college campuses. By the end of the century that era seemed passed. Henry Davidson Sheldon, in a general account of *Student Life and Customs,* published in 1901, could remark:

> The idea so prevalent in the eighties among undergraduates that all forms of aggressive religious endeavour were superannuated survivals of medievalism, out of place in the present enlightened age, is fast giving way either to appreciation or to acute dislike. The movement has stimulated the churches, aroused the religious societies of the colleges to their responsibility, and has extended its influence to foreign countries. Its success in the present age in reviving the ideals of militant Christianity in the same institutions that by subjective criticisms were undermining the foundations of religious belief, is one of the striking signs of the complexity of modern social forces.[17]

Dwight L. Moody, speaking of Yale during 1897–1898, could put it more simply. He was entirely pleased with the broad energetic spirit of Yale's evangelicalism and was happy that his sons studied there. "I have been pretty well acquainted with Yale for twenty years," he remarked, "and I have never seen the University in so good a condition religiously as it is now."[18]

While Moody's enthusiasm for the vigor of the voluntary religion of young men at Yale was understandable, the winds were already blowing that would eliminate Christianity as an effective force at the centers of American academic life. During the next sixty years these winds of modernity would reach gale force, so that even a generation of men dedicated to "evangelization of the world in this generation" could only ride the storm. As a Christian institution, Yale College had originally been designed for far different conditions. The fledgling university had inherited, so far as the interests of Christianity might be concerned, what would prove to be deep structural defects in the face of the forces of modernity. If we step back just a few more years into the history of Yale, to a pivotal contest over its Christian character, we can glimpse some of the obstacles to keeping education at Yale, or other leading American schools, long on a distinctly Christian course.

Notes

1. On Coffin see Bradley J. Longfield, *The Presbyterian Controversy: Fundamentalists, Modernists, and Moderates* (New York: Oxford University Press, 1991), 77–103.

2. Episcopal Bishop Henry Knox Sherrill (Yale '11) made this comparison in recollections quoted in Ralph Henry Gabriel, *Religion and Learning at Yale: The Church of Christ in College and University, 1757–1957* (New Haven: Yale University Press, 1958), 209.

3. Laurence R. Veysey, *The Emergence of the American University* (Chicago: University of Chicago Press, 1965), 235.

4. W. H. Sallmon, "The Young Man's Christian Association," *Two Centuries of Christian Activity at Yale,* James B. Reynolds et al., eds. (New York: 1901), 225.

5. Brooks Mather Kelly, *Yale: A History* (New Haven: Yale University Press, 1974), reports that in 1901 the YMCAs at Yale College and at Yale's scientific school had a total membership of 1000 out of a combined student body of 1800. A count in 1901 revealed that 63 percent of Yale's 1190 undergraduates were "church members," including 44 Catholics and 16 Jews. Of the 610 students at Yale's Sheffield Scientific School, 50 percent were members. Percentages in the medical and law schools were (significantly) 33 percent and 40 percent, while in the graduate school it was 69 percent. In Divinity it was 100 percent. *Two Centuries,* Appendix D (2).

6. George Wilson Pierson, *Yale College: An Educational History, 1871–1921* (New Haven: Yale University Press, 1952), 13.

7. James F. Findlay, Jr., *Dwight L. Moody: American Evangelist, 1837–1899* (Chicago: University of Chicago Press, 1969), 350.

8. John R. Mott, Address at Yale Alumni Dinner, June 1899, quoted in H. P. Beach, "Yale's Contribution to Foreign Missions," in *Two Centuries,* 283.

9. H. B. Wright, "Recent Epochs of Christian Life," in *Two Centuries,* 111.

10. H. B. Wright, "Yale and the Northfield Student Conferences," in *Two Centuries,* 245. Cf. George M. Marsden, *Fundamentalism and American Culture: The Shaping of American Evangelicalism,, 1870–1925* (New York: Oxford University Press, 1980), for an account of this side of the Moody heritage.

11. W. S. Coffin, "Yale and the City of New Haven," in *Two Centuries,* 255–81.

12. Mott, quoted in *Two Centuries,* 283.

13. Wright, "Recent Epoches," in *Two Centuries,* 110. The Methodist group was absorbed in the association. A similar Catholic group was merged into a resident organization under the Dominican Fathers of New Haven.

14. Lyman Beecher, *The Autobiography of Lyman Beecher,* Barbara M. Cross, ed. (Cambridge, Mass.: 1961), I:252–53.

15. George W. Pierson, *Yale: The University College, 1921–1937* (New Haven: Yale University Press, 1955), 84–86. Compulsory chapel continued at Yale until 1926.

16. Gabriel, *Religion and Learning,* 191–203.

17. Henry Davidson Sheldon, *Student Life and Customs* (New York, 1901), 285–86. Cf. Veysey, *The Emergence of the American University,* 280–81, for other evidences of decline in atheism. Veysey attributes this to a growing indifference toward things religious generally. Much indifference toward things religious was indeed present on turn-of-the-century college campuses, as in other eras. However, the successes of counterefforts for voluntary religion were more pronounced during the Progressive era than at any other time.

18. Quoted from Moody (from 1897–1898 school year), in *Two Centuries,* 115.

Prologue (III): A "Christian College"? The Yale of Noah Porter and William Graham Sumner (1879–1881)

On May 27, 1880, Yale College's conservative president, Noah Porter, spoke at Wellesley College on "The Christian College." The setting for this manifesto, which was well circulated as a pamphlet, is in itself significant. Wellesley, a women's college, was founded by Henry and Pauline Durant, ardent evangelical Christians. Henry Durant, who ran the college personally, made sure that everything about the institution proclaimed that, as its first announcement said, "The institution will be Christian in its influence, discipline, and course of instruction."[1] Extensive required Bible study supplemented the regular curriculum. Each of the professors, all women, would have to be able to teach such courses in addition to her regular offering.[2]

Porter was speaking at the laying of the cornerstone of the second building. The ties to the old- college ideal were signaled not only by Porter's presence, but by the choice of the sainted Mark Hopkins of Williams to offer the invocation. Hopkins had already been immortalized by James A. Garfield, who at an 1871 Williams alumni banquet, in response to suggestions that the school was falling behind the times, remarked: "The ideal college is Mark Hopkins on one end of a log and a student on the other."[3] The pious Garfield, himself a model of the old-time college product, was now two weeks away from the presidential nomination.

Prestige and piety converged at the cornerstone ceremony. The Rev. S. F. Smith, author of "America," wrote a hymn, "Founded on Christ," suggesting that Christ was the true cornerstone. Dwight L. Moody, a friend of the Durants who shared their religious style, in 1878 had joined the distinguished board of trustees, made up mostly of leading clergy and clergy-educators, who like the faculty were required to be members of an "Evangelical Church."[4] Noah Porter himself was president of the board.

For the aging Porter, who was approaching eighty years, it was a sign of the times that his strongest allies in concern for Christian colleges were ardent advocates of revival like Moody and the Durants. At midcentury

Porter and other Yale scholars had been progressives who turned away from earlier reliance on college-sponsored revivals toward greater emphasis on cultivating Christian character.[5] Though Porter was still emphasizing building character, his closest affinities were now with those who were renewing the reliance on revivalist piety.

As advocates of gradual change, evangelical Christian educators like Porter and the Durants were up with the times in promoting the new women's colleges with curricula comparable to those of men's institutions. Advocates of women's education could be found across the spectrum of religious views. Intensely revivalist Oberlin under Charles Finney had championed coeducation, but Andrew Dickson White's more secular Cornell University had more recently introduced coeducation to the East. Meanwhile between 1861 and 1875 Vassar, Smith, and Wellesley were founded with varying degrees of explicitly Christian emphasis. Mt. Holyoke Seminary had also been around since 1837 but was more like a Christian training center for teachers and missionaries.[6] Henry Durant wanted Wellesley to be a true college, but with the Holyoke missionary spirit.

Noah Porter thought that women's colleges should be Christian in the same way men's schools should. He shared the dominant middle-class views of his era concerning the two sexes. While on the one hand he affirmed that it was now proven that women were as able in every field as men, on the other he noted that in religious matters their greater sensibilities made them "superior to men." However, "these special endowments of the sex expose them, perhaps more, to unreasoning fanaticism and tenacious bigotry for any cause which they ardently espouse." Hence for Porter the best Christian education for women, even more than for men, should be that which built habits of sound discipline.[7]

Given these views, a woman's college was a particularly appropriate setting for Porter to reiterate his ideas regarding the Christian college. Woman's higher education, like Christian higher education, was widely regarded as strictly an undergraduate concern. Neither one would have much to do with graduate education or with the university as such.

While this setting was revealing of the college culture of the times, the great interest in Porter's address had not so much to do with Wellesley as with the much publicized recent crisis at Yale. Porter's theme was that there was a warfare between Christianity and secularism. This warfare, he was implying, could not be fought simply by extracurricular piety. Rather it centered on a dramatic contest for supremacy over the college classroom. Christians, he announced at the outset, were in a battle with the secular view of education that claimed it "must be free of all alliances with religion." It was crucial therefore that "Christianity must control the college in order to exclude its antagonist, or rival, in the form of some false religion." Atheism and the recently popularized agnosticism "are religious creeds as truly as are theism and dogmatic Christianity."

In this warfare there could be no neutrality. "Ethics, politics and social science suppose a decisive position to be taken one side or the other in respect to both theism and Christianity: even elementary treatises on these subjects teach a positive faith or as positive a denial." Similarly, instructors could not be neutral. Even if they claimed an objective stance, agnosticism might be taught "indirectly by gentle or sarcastic insinuation" or even "unconsciously . . . in subtile ways of impression even by an instructor who may honestly strive to withhold the slightest suggestion of his faith or his feelings."[8]

In the midst of the recent dramatic events at Yale, all this was profoundly loaded. Few in Porter's audience could have missed this significance, since during the previous month Yale College had suffered the embarrassment of having its affairs exposed by the public press. On April 4 and 5 the *New York Times* had published two extensive front-page accounts of recent efforts of President Porter to stop William Graham Sumner, one of Yale's best known younger teachers, from using as a text in his senior course Herbert Spencer's *The Study of Sociology.* As the *Times* put it, Spencer was well known as the "White Czar of Agnosticism," and his iconoclastic book classed Christianity with "the superstitions of the Mohammadans and South Sea Islanders" as the sort of bias that true scientists needed to be rid of. This controversy, the paper proclaimed, divided the Yale faculty down the middle and "involves the whole issue between science and religion and its final settlement will decide the attitude of the college toward the modern spirit of inquiry, which proposes to be guided by reason rather than by faith."[9]

The *Times* followed the next day with a satirical editorial that, mocking Spencer's tone, granted that "no intelligent man in this age of the world will for a moment maintain that there is any truth in Christianity," but that since Christianity still had a strong hold on "the ignorant masses," Yale's giving it up would cause a great outcry. After all, the editorialist sarcastically suggested, if Spencer is right, and everything is relative, then it does not matter whether Spencer and Comte's positivism or Christianity is "the recognized faith to be taught to Yale students." It is all "mere prejudice," so we might as well "rid ourselves of prejudice as well as religion," and let Yale continue to be Christian.[10] At Yale all this was an immense embarrassment. However divided the Yale faculty might be, they all agreed that such matters should be settled privately, among gentlemen.

The Rev. William Graham Sumner had before teaching at Yale been an Episcopal rector in Morristown, New Jersey, and he had been already very much part of the Yale family. Porter had prized him as one of college's promising recent graduates ('63) and Sumner, after a tour in Europe, had served as a tutor at Yale before going to Morristown in 1867. In 1872 he was appointed to the Yale faculty in the chair in political science. At the time he was still a traditional, though broad-minded, Christian who affirmed the full divinity of Christ versus Unitarianism and considered the Bible "a true revelation of spiritual and universal truths."[11]

Early in his Yale tenure, Sumner's religious views began to change rapidly. Although he remained an Episcopal priest all his life, he dropped the "Rev." from his title.[12] Later he made the famous and revealing remark, "I never consciously gave up a religious belief. It was as if I had put my beliefs into a drawer, and when I opened it, there was nothing there at all."[13]

Sumner's conversion to scientific naturalism came in the mid-1870s through the influence of Charles Darwin, T. H. Huxley, and Herbert Spencer, whose work he had not earlier been able to accept.[14] As he explained in a letter to Yale officials in June 1881: "Four or five years ago my studies led me to the conviction that sociology was about to do for the social sciences what scientific method has done for natural and physical science, viz.: rescue them from arbitrary dogmatism and confusion."

Of the few texts available, Spencer's seemed the best, though it was unsatisfactory in some respects. Sumner did not think, however, that Spencer's religious views were even relevant to the question: "Mr. Spencer's religious opinions seem to me of very little importance in this connection, and, when I was looking for a book on sociology, the question whether it was a good or available book in a scientific point of view occupied my intention exclusively."[15]

Since Sumner was a gifted teacher, known for his brusque and forceful manner, his new views that science was the only relevant intellectual authority and religion was at best irrelevant had soon come to President Porter's attention. Recognizing the threat to his Christian humanist citadel, Porter attempted to hold off the alien forces by exercising his presidential authority.

In December 1879, Porter wrote to Sumner that the use of Spencer's *The Study of Sociology* had created "a great deal of talk." Even though Porter himself had used another of Spencer's works in a graduate course, he considered *The Study of Sociology* to be much less solid, "written very largely in a pamphleteering style." Especially he objected to "the freedom and unfairness with which it attacks every Theistic Philosophy of society and of history, and the cool and yet sarcastic effrontery with which he assumes that material elements and laws are the only forces and laws which any scientific man can recognize, seem to me to condemn the book as a textbook for a miscellaneous class in an undergraduate course."[16]

Porter, who in such a small college setting knew the reputations of his teachers, was not confident that Sumner would do anything to correct numerous statements by Spencer that indeed dismissed Christianity as an option for a modern intelligent person. Accordingly, Porter concluded that since "I am presumed to authorize the use of every textbook, I must formally object to the use of this."[17]

At the Yale gentleman's club Porter's ambiguous conclusion left the door open for compromise. Sumner took the point and met with Porter privately to air their differences. The result was that Porter allowed the course to go on in the spring term still using the Spencer text. However, the publicity in the newspapers in the spring of 1880 meant that the matter would now come to the attention of the Yale Corporation. When the corporation met in June, shortly after Porter's Wellesley speech, former Yale president Theodore Dwight Woolsey was prepared to offer a resolution confirming that presidents did indeed have veto power over texts. Porter, however, calmed the waters by assuring the corporation that part of the understanding in December had been that Sumner would not use the text again. Both Woolsey and Porter held the view that discipline of an erring faculty member should be dealt with by the faculty, meaning the president, rather than the corporation.[18]

Again the matter was kept quiet; so quiet, in fact, that it was not until the next December, when the time for offering the course again was near, that Sumner was informed of this resolution. When he learned of it, he was furious that Porter had claimed that he had agreed not to use the text again, when he himself did not think he had endorsed any such agreement. Still the gentleman, however, he was eager to avoid more sensational publicity. So he decided that it would be better for his students to have no course in sociology than to be exposed to such emotionally charged discussion. At the end of the term in June 1881 he addressed his letter to his colleagues and to the corporation somewhat bitterly detailing his discontent and announcing his intention to seek other employment.

The controversy was then successfully kept from the public eye and eventually died down. Sumner was an important asset of the school and was prevailed upon not to resign. In a sense, a compromise had been reached, while the point at issue was left unresolved. Sumner had, on the one hand, stopped using the Spencer text. On the other, he had not conceded the principle that administrative interference in the choice of texts was unacceptable. Most important, just at the moment when its principal competitors were proclaiming themselves scientific research universities, the Yale Corporation could not afford to lose one of its few modern thinkers over what could be construed to be a matter of doctrinal orthodoxy.[19] Sumner's conservative economic views helped secure his position as well. (For our story it is a nice irony that Sumner, who remained at Yale until 1910, taught many who would be among the Yale alumni whom William Buckley would try to enlist on Christian grounds.) The crucial point in 1880, however, was that no matter how much a college leader might be dedicated to defining the academic life of a college as "Christian," there was no way both to retain such a stance and to remain as a leading center of American higher learning. At flagship Protestant schools such as Yale that aspired to be universites, commitments had already been set that would free academic life from the distinctive qualities of its Christian heritage.

Notes

1. Quoted in Alice Payne Hackett, *Wellesley: Part of American History* (New York: E. P. Dutton, 1949), 39.

2. Ibid., 42. For a critical view of Durant, his ties to the old-college ideal, and paternalism, see Patricia Palmieri, *"Insipid Vita Nuova: Founding Ideals of the Wellesley College Community," History of Higher Education,* 1983, 59–78.

3. Frederick Rudolph, *The American College and University: A History* (New York: Vintage Books, 1962), 243. The remark was made at a Williams alumni banquet in 1871 in response to suggestions that Williams was falling behind the times.

4. Hackett, *Wellesley,* 31, 57, 151.

5. For background on Porter see Louise L. Stevenson, *Scholarly Means to Evangelical Ends: The New Haven Scholars and the Transformation of Higher Learning in America, 1830–1890* (Baltimore: Johns Hopkins Press, 1986) and chapter 7 below.

6. See Helen Lefkowitz Horowitz, *Alma Mater: Design and Experience in the Women's Colleges from Their Nineteenth-Century Origins to the 1930s* (New York: Knopf, 1984) for a perceptive overview of these origins.

7. Noah Porter, "The Christian College," address delivered at Wellesley College (Boston, 1880), 29–30.

8. Ibid., 8, 21, 22.

9. "Yale as a Battle Ground," *New York Times,* April 4, 1880, 1; "Two Parties at Yale," April 5, 1880, 1 ("White Czar" quotation).

10. "Yale College," editorial, *New York Times,* April 6, 1880, 4.

11. Harris E. Starr, *William Graham Sumner* (New York: Henry Holt, 1925), 136, 168 (from sermons preached in 1872).

12. *New York Times,* April 4, 1880, 1.

13. Starr, *Sumner,* 543, cf. 541–42. Bruce Curtis, *William Graham Sumner* (Boston: Twayne, 1981), 25–42, provides a clear summary of Sumner's changing religious views. The following account is based largely on Starr, *Sumner,* 345–69, which reprints many of the original documents, and Burton J. Bledstein, "Noah Porter versus William Graham Sumner," *Church History* 43 (September 1974), 340–49.

14. Starr, *Sumner,* 136.

15. W. G. Sumner, "A Private and personal communication to the members of the Corporation and to the permanent officers of Yale College, New Haven, June 1881," reproduced in Starr, *Sumner,* 358–59.

16. Porter to Sumner, December 6, 1879, from Starr, *Sumner,* 346–47.

17. Ibid.

18. Bledstein, "Porter versus Sumner," 341.

19. Academic freedom was not yet established as a principle in American higher education, but its components were emerging as the rights of a professional to regulate his own affairs. See the discussion of this dimension in Richard Hofstadter and Walter P. Metzger, *The Development of Academic Freedom in the United States* (New York: Columbia University Press, 1955), 335–38. Even at Johns Hopkins and Cornell there were cases of faculty not hired because their religious views were considered too radical (340). Hiring and firing were two different matters, however.

I

THE ESTABLISHMENT OF PROTESTANT NONSECTARIANISM

During the seventy years between the William Graham Sumner crisis and the William F. Buckley crisis, leading American schools were transformed almost beyond recognition. Regarding the issue that Noah Porter and William Buckley agreed was pivotal to Christian education, however—that teaching and scholarship should not undermine Christian perspectives—the matter had already been settled in principle by 1881. To his contemporaries who were shaping the new universities Porter's way of protecting Christianity in the classroom seemed hopelessly outdated. The university builders were not, however, opposed to Christianity as such. Rather, the great majority of them were happy both to broaden its definition and to encourage the solution that proved so successful at Yale by the 1890s. Essentially where would be a division of functions. The highest academic pursuits would soon be defined in such a way that the intrusion of specifically Christian concerns would seem irrelevant or prejudicial. Nevertheless, the whole enterprise could be regarded as broadly Christian so long as there was some room for morally uplifting undergraduate teaching and for voluntary commitment as a extracurricular activity.

Such solutions could work for a time, balancing two strong tendencies in American life—trust in scientifically defined technique and concern to be nonetheless spiritual. By the 1950s, however, as Buckley was pointing out, these two dimensions in higher education were drastically out of balance. The substance of the education undermined rhetoric claims to cherish the Christian heritage. Soon even the vestiges of the balance gave way and concerns for Christianity seemed simply out of place at the best universities.

From a historical perspective the most intriguing question is why there was not more controversy over such a momentous revolution in higher education. Dramatic confrontations such as those between Porter and Sumner or between Buckley and the Yale establishment were relatively rare. How was it that distinctively Christian teaching could be displaced so easily from the central and substantive role that it had held in American higher education for over two centuries and in the universities of Christendom for many centuries before that? While such transformations were part of wider changes throughout Western civilization, in America they are best understood in the light of the early dominance of Protestantism and its relationship to the cultural and intellectual life of the emerging republic. The first two centuries of American higher education established some basic patterns that would be perpetuated in shaping the modern universities. Particularly, the early history of American colleges is illuminating if read in the light of this historical question: Why were the fledgling universities of the late nineteenth century, despite their founders' expressed commitments to Christianity, designed in a way that would virtually guarantee that they would become subversive of the distinctive aspects of their Christian heritage of learning?

1

The Burden of Christendom: Seventeenth-Century Harvard

One of the remarkable facts of American history is that only six years after their settlement in the Massachusetts wilderness the Puritans established what soon became a reputable college. Higher education was for them a high priority in civilization building. During its early decades New England had one of the highest per capita concentrations of university-educated men anywhere in the world. By establishing a college so early (in the southern colonies it took a century to do the same) the Puritans laid the foundation for New England's dominance in American higher education for the next three centuries. As late as the era when Americans founded modern universities or transformed their colleges into universities, few of the key leaders lacked New England connections.

The Puritans' commitment to higher education and the tensions that created for such an intensely spiritual movement must be understood in the context of a long history of often uneasy relationships of Christianity to advanced learning. The Puritans of the 1630s, it is helpful to recall, were living as close to the era of Thomas Aquinas as we are to theirs. So while we inevitably refract our understanding of them through what has happened since, we will gain a more balanced appreciation of their own concerns if we think in terms of their own history. They were still in many ways people of the Middle Ages. Their medieval outlook had indeed been modified by what we call the Renaissance, more by the Reformation, and they had been touched as well by glimmers of what was to become modernity. Nonetheless, the problems they addressed were still largely those of medieval Christendom. How could they set Christendom back on its proper course?

So far as university education was concerned, they took for granted some deeply entrenched patterns that for several centuries had defined advanced learning in the Western world; but as reformers they were also ready to bend the patterns to suit their purposes.

Christian and Pagan Learning: The Medieval Pattern

The preeminent theoretical issue inherited from the Middle Ages was the question of how to relate Christian truths to pagan learning. This debate went back to Christian antiquity. Christianity inherited the intellectual standards of the ancient world and for a millennium and a half its thinkers stood in the shadow of the classic achievement. A few could reject the relevance of Athens for Jerusalem, but it was virtually impossible to ignore Athens entirely. Yet the danger was that to honor the pagans for their unparalleled intellectual achievement would seem to dishonor the preeminence of the wisdom revealed in Christ. The rise of the universities within the vigorous medieval civilization of the twelfth century signaled a determination to deal with this paradox. The classical learning had to play a leading role; that was essential to intellectual respectability. The scholar was practically defined as the guardian of ancient wisdom. At the same time leading scholars of each succeeding generation had to address the major intellectual challenge of the epoch. How could they reconcile the pagan authorities with the authoritative theological dogma of the church?[1]

The intellectual dilemma was paralleled by the institutional definition that emerged for the universities. Christian scholars, who earlier had been situated primarily at cathedral schools, established themselves in the twelfth century as self-governing guilds. They were licensed by the pope to grant degrees, meaning that only they could determine who was qualified to be a master, or teacher. Despite the major achievement of some autonomy, these scholars' guilds or universities were ultimately under the control of the church. Masters had to take holy orders as clerics and hence were subject to church control. Their conduct could be a matter of church concern and, very important, their teachings could be condemned.[2]

In this context of limited autonomy Christian scholars perennially debated the relation of reason to faith. No one could seriously challenge the preeminence of faith; the issue was the degree to which the philosophy or science (roughly, knowledge) of the pagans might be of value toward salvation. Did one need to believe in order to understand, as Anselm, following Augustine, had maintained? Or could one say, as Thomas Aquinas did in the thirteenth century, that reason could point toward divine truths, even though it needed to be supplemented by truths known only by faith? In either case it was taken for granted that pagan knowledge of mundane affairs was true knowledge, so far as it went. Education was not conceivable without the pagans. Latin and Greek were the very languages of education. All the practical elements (the trivium of grammar, rhetoric, and logic and the quadrivium of arithmetic, music, geometry, and astronomy) had been established by the ancients.

So from its beginnings Western university education involved a fusion of pagan and Christian elements. The trivium and quadrivium defined the basic liberal arts. Moreover, the consensus prevailing through the early centuries of the universities, was that a proper arts education involved substantial study of Aristotle, especially on logic, metaphysics, and natural philosophy (natural science). While some questioned elements in Aristotle's ethics or metaphysics that contradicted Christian dogma, virtually all recognized a pinnacle of intellectual achievement that must be mastered.

The most practical way of counteracting the prominence of the pagan elements in the curricula was to surround them with a Christian atmosphere. First of all the studies were surrounded liturgically. Christian worship began and ended the university day, signaling that all was to be dedicated to the glory of God. Furthermore, the role of clerics in education inevitably provided Christian perspectives even on pagan authorities. Higher education in this era involved primarily the mastery of texts (as it usually did until the nineteenth century). These texts were presented in the context of commentary or lectures by the university masters, hence providing at least the potential for dealing with issues where Christian and pagan authority conflicted. Since the pagans could not respond, this method of synthesis worked well for centuries. Christian dogma retained its official dominance in academia.

The medieval pattern of surrounding pagan elements with a Christian environment allowed most of university education to be freed from the direct concerns of theology. The half dozen or so medieval universities that shaped Western education included four distinct faculties: the arts, theology, law (canon and civil), and medicine (although each of the universities typically lacked one of the latter three). A master's degree in the arts was normally prerequisite to study of theology, law, or medicine. Theology, then, although queen of the sciences, did not directly rule the other sciences[3] but was a separate, specialized discipline.[4]

Reformation Learning

Within this framework there were many variations over the centuries and many internal debates, but an essential continuity prevailed. Even the Reformation only modified some of the basic structures and emphases. Nevertheless, since the Puritans were first of all a battalion of the international movement for Protestant reform, the Reformation modifications of higher learning were especially relevant to establishing American precedents.

Early in the Reformation, Martin Luther had railed against the universities. "What else are the universities," he complained in 1520, "than . . . 'Places for training youth in Greek glory,' in which loose living prevails, the Holy Scriptures and the Christian faith are little taught, and the blind, heathen master Aristotle rules alone even more than Christ? In this regard my advice would be that Aristotle's [philosophical works] be discarded altogether."[5]

Luther's attack on the Aristotelianism of the Scholastics was not an anti-intellectual attack on universities but rather a critique from within. Luther, after all, was a university man, a doctor on the theological faculty at Wittenberg. The spark that touched off the Reformation thus came from within the university and was, as E. Harris Harbison suggested, a combination of a spiritual struggle and *"a scholar's insight."*[6] In part this insight arose out of longstanding traditions of intellectual tensions between the Aristotelianism of the Scholastics and Augustinianism in which Luther had been tutored. In any case the initial base of the Reformation was a university and one of its first fruits was a curricular revision, increasing the emphasis on Greek and Hebrew in the curriculum.[7]

During the next generations universities remained major centers for the Protestant challenges to Catholic authority. Protestantism was, after all, vulnerable to the accusation that it would open the door to an anarchy of individual opinions. The principal Protestant leaders deeply feared such anarchy. In order to counter it they recognized that it was essential to back up their appeals to the authority of Scripture alone with the firmest scholarship, so as to determine what Scripture actually said. In fact, education at all levels was crucial to the Protestant program. Challenging the exclusive clerical dominance in the church, the Protestant doctrine of the priesthood of all believers encouraged the cultivation of an educated laity, well catechized and instructed in Scripture.

Luther himself was interested primarily in biblical and theological scholarship as they would directly serve the church,[8] but as a professor he recognized the importance of universities to the Protestant program. Philip Melanchthon, who joined Luther at Wittenberg in 1517, was especially important in establishing the models for Protestant universities during the next forty years. The Protestant university curriculum as established by Melanchthon was a mix of progressive and conservative elements. Despite Luther's earlier strictures, Melanchthon persuaded him by the 1530s that Aristotle was useful to the university curriculum, even if not a reliable guide in theology or ethics. At the same time more humanistic classical authors of literary and historical works were being added to the curriculum, as was greater emphasis on the sacred languages (Greek, Latin, and Hebrew) and the study of the church fathers.[9]

Important to understanding the impact of the Reformation on higher education is that the Reformation took place while another critique of scholasticism was already gradually influencing the universities from another direction. Renaissance humanists embraced and revered the classics, but instead of the philosophy of Aristotle their preeminent classics were literary works, like those of Cicero or Virgil, which they saw as God's gifts useful for enriching life in this world. In their view literary texts exemplifying rhetoric, rather than those exemplifying logic, should be foundational in the arts curriculum. Several of the Reformers, including Melanchthon, Zwingli, and Calvin, were well educated in such humanism.[10]

Though the Lutherans under Melanchthon's tutelage established the most important models for Protestant universities,[11] Calvin and Calvinists also played a significant role. Calvinist models would also have the more direct influence in America. Calvin followed Luther in emphasizing the importance of the study of the biblical languages, including Hebrew. Though Calvin did not hold an academic position, one of his major accomplishments was the establishment of an academy in Geneva which functioned as a university for training Protestant leaders. The academy reflected humanist influences in its emphasis on the study of ancient languages and employed texts from Cicero, Virgil, Livy, and Xenophon in teaching grammar, rhetoric, logic, and history.[12]

More generally, Calvin helped develop the broadly Augustinian rationale for the importance of higher learning. Attributing all that is good to God, Calvin's principle of common grace justified learning at least limited truths from the ancients. Though Calvin, like Luther, thought reason of no value on its own in attaining salvation, he considered it competent in things "earthly."[13] Moreover, the Calvinist doctrine of calling emphasized that the vocations of Christians were to serve God in whatever their occupations, not just in special "religious" vocations. Hence university learning, even apart from theological preparation, could be a means of glorifying God.

While there were indeed broad and humanist tendencies in Protestant higher education, these were always tightly fenced in by dogmatic confessionalism. By the middle of the seventeenth century the Western world was sharply divided into cold war camps that followed largely confessional lines. The exigencies of such battles meant that Protestant institutions of higher learning were also militant agents of confessionalism, defenders of the faith, and that their faculties of theology sometimes served as substitutes for pope and councils as the definers of orthodoxy.[14] Until at least the mid-seventeenth century (longer in Puritan New England) the tensions among the claims of the inherited Medieval curriculum, humanism, and theologically oriented confessionalism were the major motifs in Protestant education.

Looking for the broad significance of these developments, we can see that, while curriculum and methods of education evolved more than they were revolutionized under Protestantism, the Reformation brought important changes in the social *function* of education. Protestantism promoted a well-educated clergy, which quickly became the backbone of the international revolutionary movement. Very early in the Reformation, Zwingli and Luther began wearing the scholar's gown for preaching and, although not all Protestant clergy had university training, "the scholar's gown was *the* garment of the Protestant minister."[15] In villages throughout Protestant lands for centuries to come, the clergyman would be the best educated citizen and education would be a key to his authority.

In the Protestant setting the classicist humanist education particularly made sense. In a day before natural science gained intellectual eminence, the key to intellectual expertise and authority was mastery of languages. The claims of the Reformers hinged on the interpretation of texts and on a science of textual interpretation sufficient to challenge church authority. Each Protestant clergyman, accordingly, should ideally have linguistic expertise that would establish him as an authority in the most essential science of the day. Knowledge of the classics helped establish social and intellectual authority, but not for arbitrary reasons. It was an expertise necessary to the highest science of the day. Ultimately linguistic expertise served the cause of theology, still the queen of the sciences in the Protestant (as much as in the Catholic) world and the capstone of Protestant education.

This professionalization of the clergy gave Protestants some advantage over their Catholic rivals. In the Middle Ages clerical education had largely been by apprenticeship and sometimes was minimal. On the eve of the Reformation only about one-fourth of clergy had any university training.[16] After the revolt Catholics countered with more attention to clerical education, including the establishment by the Council of Trent of the innovation of theological seminaries dedicated solely to theological training.

This rivalry contributed to what Lawrence Stone describes as the "astonishing growth" from the mid-sixteenth century to the mid-seventeenth century in which "a staggering number of students were pouring into the universities." At Oxford in England, which Stone investigated, the burgeoning student body of the early seventeenth century was made up of two distinct classes. Most of the growth came from the influx of students from plebeian families, often preparing for theological study for the ministry, for which an arts degree was prerequisite. Others were aristocrats, preparing sometimes for other professions, or more often gaining some university education as a sort of gentleman's finishing school, but not taking a degree. After the English civil wars, the disruptions of the 1640s and 1650s, and subsequent disillusion with religious struggles, English universities hit a prolonged slump in enrollment, with the numbers of plebeians in attendance dropping off dramatically.[17]

Harvard College

It was in the context of the post-Reformation boom that the most important precedents for American higher education were set with the establishment of Harvard College in 1636. The remarkable establishment of a reputable college on the frontier of Western civilization is more understandable in the light of the importance of education to the whole structure of authority in the ongoing Reformation movement. By 1646 one hundred and forty university men had emigrated to New England. Of these the majority were from Cambridge and fully one-fourth were from a single Cambridge College, Emmanuel. About thirty other New

Englanders had been educated at various Oxford Colleges and a few had been educated abroad.[18]

The two English universities had developed as degree-granting federations of colleges. Each college was self-contained, maintaining its own faculties of masters and tutors as well as residential facilities. Hence in practice the colleges were more important than the university, at least for the actual conduct of education.

Oxford and Cambridge colleges had been particularly important to the Puritan movement since the multiple-college system allowed de facto religious pluralism, following the indecisive English Reformation. Puritans, who wished to push the English settlement to a more Calvinistic conclusion, could gain influence in individual colleges or, as in the most important case of Emmanuel, found their own college.[19]

To overstate the case only slightly, in New England the college was the parent of the colony. The New England experiment was largely the product of an old-boy network of Emmanuel graduates, including John Harvard himself, with their close Puritan allies from a number of other colleges. When the founders decided to settle their college in Newtown, the new name they chose for the town was Cambridge.

The essential role of the college in the colony would have been even more conspicuous had the brightest star of Puritan higher education, William Ames (1576–1633), been able to emigrate to the colony as he had intended. Had he lived, Ames almost certainly would have become the head of the new college. One of the most militant of the Puritans, Ames had been suspended from his position at Christ's College in Cambridge in 1609 for refusing to wear a surplice and for delivering a sermon condemning frivolous entertainments. Too uncompromising a Puritan for his bishop to allow him a pastorate in England, Ames found a position in Holland, where he eventually became professor of theology and rector at the University of Franeker. His great prestige in New England can be measured by the fact that his *Medulla Theologica* (Marrow of Theology) became *the* textbook on theology at seventeenth-century Harvard. Symbolic of Ames's influence is one of the early mottoes on the Harvard seal, *Christo et Ecclesiae*—the motto of Franeker University and the text of Ames's inaugural as rector there in 1626.[20]

While the college was first of all in the service of the church, it also was a public institution in the service of the civil government. While this relationship might seem ambiguous in our own terms, it made perfect sense according to the conventions of the time. The church was as much a public institution as was the civil government. "Public" referred simply to the minority who because of rank, land ownership, or other status had a part in running society. The British usage of "public" for schools that Americans would call "private" suggests something of the older usage.[21] So in seventeenth-century Massachusetts, as in seventeenth-century England, a college trained leaders for both church and civil society. In Puritan New England the cooperative relationship between the two was indicated by the fact that Harvard College was created by the civil government and governed by a board of overseers, or trustees, made up equally of clergy and magistrates.

Although universities had served both church and larger society since their beginnings, this specific arrangement represented not the medieval model for universities, which had been created by scholars who gained civil recognition as a guild and degree-granting rights from the pope, but rather the Reformation model, which was one step more secular in the sense of being less directly under church control.[22] The Reformers, who depended on the princes for their success and followed the principle that the state should support one true religion, thereby granted the magistrates greater authority in religious affairs, including higher education. Typically, the princes created the new schools of the Reformation, universities or close equivalents (some Calvinists thought degrees were Romanist trappings), but these were governed by external boards of trustees. For the colonists this was a convenient arrangement, since in English law a charitable trust did not require a royal charter.[23] The balance between clergy and magistrates on the board also reinforced the longstanding point that a college was a distinct entity, not a department of either church or state, though ultimately subject to both.

This Protestant arrangement had several implications for the subsequent history of American higher education. In a strict sense it was more secular because some control was shifted from church to state. It thus created a deep ambiguity for American church-related education, since typically it was state-related as well. However, the picture was complicated by the priority in the colonies of Calvinist models. Calvinists stressed the sacral character of all of life, of the state as well as the church. Hence no major gap was perceived between being a public trust and being under church control. For the first three centuries of American higher education, the dominant view was that such dual functions were easily compatible.[24]

Early Harvard College in fact operated within strict limits set by both church and state. So, for instance, although there was no formal theological test for those who taught at the college, that was only because such a test did not need to be stated. Like other Reformation schools, Harvard served the interests of confessionalism and of the corresponding political principle that an orderly realm should tolerate one religion, the true one. So in 1654 when Harvard's very successful early president, Henry Dunster, questioned the practice of infant baptism, there was no choice but for him to resign. As Samuel Eliot Morison observes, endorsing the views of the radical Baptists in the mid-seventeenth century would be like a Harvard president announcing he was a communist in the mid-twentieth.[25] Or, in the late twentieth, it would be like a Harvard president announcing opposition to equal opportunity for women.

In the seventeenth century, by contrast, theological authority was a mainstay of male social authority. The most striking illustration is that

1636 was the year not only of the legislation establishing Harvard College but also of the turmoil over the Anne Hutchinson case.[26] These two famous events were related since they dealt with two sides of the question of authority. They were establishing who would be allowed to speak publicly in the model Christian society. Anne Hutchinson challenged the leadership's ideas of good order on several counts. First, she was a woman and therefore was regarded as having no right to teach or exercise authority over men in the church. Second, she addressed theological issues (accusing most of the clergy of preaching works rather than grace) and thus defied the principle that formal university education (closed, of course, to women) was the normal prerequisite for exercising theological authority. Third, and ultimately most alarming to the authorities, Hutchison was what we would today call a charismatic Christian who appealed to the direct voice of the Holy Spirit. As a woman, that was her only court of appeal higher than that of the men who legitimated their own authority as the only proper interpreters of Scripture. Had Hutchinson's appeal to a direct voice from God been allowed to stand, the whole Puritan system of hierarchical authority would have collapsed. Anyone, male or female, however unqualified they otherwise might be, would be able to challenge the biblical and theological principles on which the society was being built.

Higher education was thus a keystone of the edifice of social authority. Not only did it separate men from women; just as important, it identified those men who were called by their spiritual and intellectual qualifications to be the interpreters of Scripture and thus those who would maintain the fundamental principles on which the community would run. In 1636 it was urgent not only to eliminate charismatic dissent that challenged the established authority but also to set up the educational link essential for the perpetuation of the system. The primary purpose of Harvard College was, accordingly, the training of clergy.[27]

Nonetheless, as the sacred and the secular were not sharply differentiated in this hyper-Protestant society, the Puritans had no difficulty in maintaining the traditional dual purposes of Christendom's university, serving the temporal as well as the civil order. So the school served a dual purpose, training men for other professions as well. Just over half (52 percent) of Harvard graduates in the seventeenth century became clergy.[28] Though the dual function of the college was comparable to that of English universities, the Puritan emphasis that all vocations were sacred was evident in the religious character that was to pervade. "Every one," said the first college laws of 1646, "shall consider the main End of his life and studies, to know God and Jesus Christ which is Eternal life. John 17:3." Not only did the college have communal religious exercises, but also each student was to give himself to secret prayer ("Prov. 2. 2, 3 etc") and twice a day to reading Scripture ("Psalms 119. 130.").[29]

While the founders emphasized that spiritual principles should pervade the life of the college, most of the actual curriculum inevitably followed the rather traditional lines of the liberal arts. Patterned after that of Emmanuel College (which was also founded primarily for training clergy), the Harvard curriculum in formal respects reflected the amalgam of the theological and the secular that had always characterized Western university education. Latin, the international scholarly and ecclesiastical tongue, was the language of instruction and of formal disputations. In addition to Latin students had to master Greek. Regular disputations balanced the rote learning of much of the curriculum and offered the opportunity to apply basic skills studied in grammar, rhetoric, and logic. Students also read some ancient and some modern authors as parts of their studies of mathematics, geometry, astronomy, physics, metaphysics, history, and geography.[30]

One counterbalance against the strongly classicist patterns was that Saturday and Sunday were, in effect, devoted to theology. Saturday was for formal study of biblical exposition and theology, principally from Ames's *Medulla.* The Sabbath day of rest included two lengthy sermons, each of which had to be repeated to the tutors later in the day. During the week, Hebrew was added to the other ancient languages, since for the Puritans the Old Testament was as authoritative as the New. The twice daily Bible reading was reinforced by a twice daily "logical analysis" of a biblical passage, breaking it down into its major and minor premises and expounding its arguments.[31] The Word might be perspicuous in Protestant eyes, but it also took a sound logical training to be qualified to interpret it plainly.

All this was only part of the regular arts program, which by the 1650s was expanded from three to four years (thus setting a pattern that subsequent Americans have accepted as unassailable). Those training for the clergy took a master's degree, which required an additional three years. This was a far more informal course of reading theology in which residence was optional. A few of the theological students served as the tutors at the college. Others resided at the college, or at home, or occasionally at the home of a clergy mentor.[32]

Christianity and Pagan Learning

Given their commitment to sanctifying every moment of life, New England's Puritans were acutely aware of the issue created by having a major portion of the Christian arts curriculum devoted to the study of pagan authors. The way in which to glorify God in all things, the Puritans argued, was to strictly follow biblical principles. Some radicals challenged them to be consistent with this claim when it came to education. "Humane learning," said these critics, was of the Devil and universities were Antichrists. The Bible alone should be the only basis for education.

Charles Chauncy, successor to Dunster in 1654 as president of Harvard, answered such critics directly in his commencement sermon of 1655.

If, said Chauncy, the radical critics of universities (who were proliferating in Cromwell's Commonwealth in England) meant by "humane learning," which they condemned, simply any study of the arts and science, their position was absurd, since the Bible itself taught principles of ethics, politics, economics, rhetoric, and astronomy, as well as the ancient languages. If, on the other hand, by "humane learning" critics meant "all that learning that the heathen Authors or philosophers have delivered in their writings," then also the critics had failed to note that the Scriptures occasionally cite such humane authors. Moreover, "who can deny but that there are found many excellent and divine moral truths in *Plato, Aristotle, Plutarch, Seneca, etc.?*"[33]

Chauncy was appealing to the familiar Calvinist principle of common grace, which tempered the radical biblicism of their movement. So in typical Calvinist fashion Chauncy appealed to a common light of nature, quoting I Corinthians 11:14: *"Does not nature it self teach you etc.?"*[34]

Such common grace ideals, which in principle said that pagan learning could be sanctified, in practice amounted to much the same thing as the Catholic natural law tradition of Aquinas. In each case there was an assumption that classical learning could be made subservient to the cause of Christ. The resulting tension was, in other words, inherent even in the most successful efforts at maintaining fully Christian learning while still doing justice to pagan science. The biblically informed ideals could well be the dominant first principles, providing the context into which pagan learning was interpreted. Yet the pagan learning was often taken at face value so that it easily could take on a life of its own as the dominant partner. Even though pagan shortcomings on matters pertaining to salvation were often cited, much of pagan thought that implicitly challenged Christian first principles was nonetheless revered. Thus a balancing act was maintained between a strict biblicism and openness to recognizing that mundane aspects of God's truth were revealed in nature or the created order, and therefore could be learned from nonbiblical sources.

The seventeenth-century Puritans resolved this dilemma essentially by surrounding pagan learning with biblical and theological subjects. The difference from some of the earlier precedents in which the arts curriculum had been more detached from the higher study of theology was that the Puritans saturated the arts program with as much Bible and theology as it could contain, thus making subsequent theological study anticlimactic and almost superfluous.[35]

Some Puritan educators, most notably William Ames, wanted to go further and integrate theology into the curriculum, rather than just adding it. If Ames had had his way, as he likely would have had he come to America, both metaphysics and ethics would have been treated as subdisciplines of theology in the arts curriculum. One consequence would have been to remove Aristotle from these parts of the curriculum. Plato, on the other hand, could still be studied since Ames, following Augustine, believed that Plato's teachings could be absorbed into Christian faith.

Ames's curricular puritanism was not dominant, however; at least it did not prevail at early Harvard, where Aristotle was a major text.[36]

Seventeenth-century Harvard inherited all the tensions inherent in Christian higher learning in the West. Perpetuating the medieval ideal of a unified Christendom, American Puritans retained the inevitable tension built into the assumption that the church and the civil state can have common interests. In higher education, where they adopted the Protestant pattern of primary authorization from the state, they accentuated the potential for future conflicts between theological and civil interests. They were also living with tensions that they themselves better recognized, between biblical and pagan authorities. For the time being, in their isolated and strictly controlled environment, they could resolve most of the resulting dilemmas and build a model of Christian learning according to their own standards. In that sense, seventeenth-century Harvard stands as a peak for those who value Christian higher education[37] Nevertheless, the cost of sustaining such an achievement was maintaining a tightly closed environment.

By the end of the seventeenth century total Puritan autonomy in Massachusetts was no longer possible. While clerical influence was still immense by most standards, the long process of adjusting purist biblicist ideals to a gradually more open social and intellectual setting had begun.

While the Puritan legacy set a standard for Christian education, there were major fissures even in these structures. When shaken by the vicissitudes of a less stable sustaining social environment, these fissures would open and reopen as major gaps. Succeeding generations of American educators would live with these gaps, typically plastering them over. Beneath the surface, however, remained perennial faults that would not disappear. How could educators fully serve the church with its particular theological commitments while at the same time serving the whole of society? Closely parallel: how could they be true to the Protestant principle that the Bible alone was the supreme authority yet at the same time gain the respect of the world by being open to the highest other intellectual authorities of the day, whether ancient or modern? As the inherited assumption in Christendom had been that the interests of church and state should coincide, so it was assumed that the truths of Scripture would not contradict the best of science or knowledge which humans had gained on their own. As ideas of Christendom faded, though only slowly even in America, these assumptions were put under increasing strain.

Notes

1. This subject has, of course, been treated by many authors. A suggestive overview of the theme is E. Harris Harbison, *The Christian Scholar in the Age of the Reformation* (New York: Scribners, 1956).

2. This account comes most directly from John Van Engen's fine overview, "Christianity and the University: The Medieval and Reformation Legacies," in *Making Higher Education Christian: The History and Mission of Evangelical Colleges in America,* Joel A. Carpenter and Kenneth W. Shipps, eds. (Grand Rapids, Mich.: Christian University Press, 1987).

3. William J. Bouwsma argues that "Christian education is necessarily secular." Whereas in antiquity education was generally religious in its goal of bringing persons into harmony with themselves and the divine order of the cosmos, "For the Christian, education could neither make man truly virtuous nor unite him to God, and any claims to the contrary were perilous to the soul. The heart of the Christian position was thus a distinction between the aims of education and the end of man." "Models of the Educated Man," in *A Usable Past: Essays in European Cultural History* (Berkeley: University of California Press, 1990), 377.

4. The preceding paragraphs depend most directly on Van Engen, "Christianity and the University," 23–24. Cf. Samuel Eliot Morison, *The Founding of Harvard College* (Cambridge, Mass.: Harvard University Press, 1935), 18–39.

5. Quoted in Van Engen, "Christianity and the University," 27.

6. Harbison, *Christian Scholar,* 121.

7. Ibid., 113.

8. When asked about the usefulness of reason, he replied, "Reason corrupted by the Devil is harmful . . . but reason informed by the Spirit is a help in interpreting the Holy Scriptures. . . . Reason is of service of faith when it is enlightened, since it reflects upon things; but without faith it is of no use." Quoted in Harbison, *Christian Scholar,* 123.

9. Lewis W. Spitz, "The Importance of the Reformation for the Universities: Culture and Confession in the Critical Years," in *Rebirth, Reform and Resilience: Universities in Transition, 1300–1700,* James M. Kittleson and Pamela J. Transue, eds. (Columbus: Ohio State University Press, 1984), 42–67.

10. Perry Miller, *The New England Mind: The Seventeenth Century* (Boston: Beacon Press, 1939), explores the influence of the Renaissance on New England Puritanism.

11. Spitz, "The Importance of the Reformation," 53, points out that Melanchthon was instrumental in the reorganization of Wittenberg and in the establishment of a Lutheran university at Marburg in 1527, both of which became models of Protestant universities.

12. William J. Bouwsma, *John Calvin: A Sixteenth-Century Portrait* (New York: Oxford University Press, 1988), 14.

13. John Morgan, *Godly Learning: Puritan Attitudes towards Reason, Learning, and Education, 1560–1640* (Cambridge: Cambridge University Press, 1986), 43.

14. Spitz, "The Importance of the Reformation," 57.

15. Wilhelm Pauck, "The Ministry in the Time of the Continental Reformation," in *The Ministry in Historical Perspectives,* H. Richard Niebuhr and Daniel D. Williams, eds. (New York: Harper & Brothers, 1956), 147.

16. Van Engen, "Christianity and Universities," 34.

17. Lawrence Stone, "Introduction" and "The Size and Composition of the Oxford Student Body 1580–1900," in *The University in Society,* Vol. I, Lawrence Stone, ed. (Princeton: Princeton University Press, 1974), vii, 3–111.

18. Morison, *Founding of Harvard,* 359–63. One hundred were from Cam-

bridge (thirty-five from Emmanuel), thirty-two were from Oxford, and eight from non-English schools. Trinity College, Cambridge, was also very important, with thirteen graduates in New England, including John Winthrop, Charles Chauncy (later president of Harvard), and John Cotton. Cotton, however, had moved from Trinity to Emmanuel, where he eventually became head lecturer.

19. On early Emmanuel see Morgan, *Godly Learning,* 247–55.

20. Morison, *Founding of Harvard,* 331; this is the motto of the seal of the 1692 charter. The earliest design for a college seal, proposed in 1643, contained the motto *Veritas* but was never used or known again until the nineteenth century. *In Christi Gloriam* appeared on the seal of the 1650 charter.

21. For this point I am indebted to Glenn T. Miller, *Piety and Intellect: The Aims and Purposes of Ante-Bellum Theological Education* (Atlanta: Scholars Press, 1990), 125.

22. Oxford and Cambridge had been to this degree secularized by the Reformation; they passed from the under the aegis of the pope and Crown to the authority of the Crown alone, though they retained some degree of their medieval autonomy. Jurgen Herbst, "The First Three American Colleges: Schools of the Reformation," in *Perspectives in American History* Vol. VII, Donald Fleming and Bernard Bailyn, eds. (Cambridge, Mass.: Charles Warren Center, Harvard University, 1974), 19–20.

23. Ibid., 78–52.

24. This point is illustrated by contrasting the American developments in higher education with that of the German universities arising out of the Lutheran Reformation. German Protestant universities in the nineteenth century were firmly established as agencies of the states, which maintained theological faculties as part of their broader religious establishments. In the United States, by contrast, churches and private corporations of Christians could maintain a controlling role, while colleges still served public functions.

25. Samuel Eliot Morison, *Harvard College in the Seventeenth Century,* Part I (Cambridge: Harvard University Press, 1936), 305–19. Cf. Richard Hofstadter and Walter P. Metzger, *The Development of Academic Freedom in the United States* (New York: Columbia University Press, 1955). 86–91.

26. E.g., Morison, *Founding of Harvard,* 171–80.

27. Puritanism by this time had professionalized the clergy to the point of seldom ordaining men without university training. Morgan, *Godly Learning,* 96. As "New England's First Fruits" put it in 1643, they were "dreading to leave an illiterate Ministry to the Churches, when our present Ministers shall lie in the Dust." From "New England's First Fruits," 1643, reproduced in Morison, *Founding of Harvard,* 432–33. Morison plays down the function of ministerial training, but Winthrop Hudson's response that Harvard was "little more than a theological seminary" seems too strong. "The Morison Myth Concerning the Founding of Harvard College," *Church History* 8 (June 1939), 152.

28. This percentage of clergy was actually below that of Oxford and Cambridge. Morison, *Founding of Harvard,* 247n.

29. "*Statutes of Harvard,* ca. 1646," in *American Higher Education: A Documentary History,* Vol. I, Richard Hofstadter and Wilson Smith, eds. (Chicago: University of Chicago Press, 1961), 8.

30. Morison, *Seventeenth Century,* Part I, 169–266.

31. Ibid., 268–72.

32. Ibid., 272–75.

33. Charles Chauncy, "A Commencement Sermon" (Cambridge, 1655), from excerpt in *The Puritans: A Sourcebook of Their Writings,* Vol. II, rev., Perry Miller and Thomas H. Johnson, eds. (New York: Harper & Row, 1963 [1938]), 706–7. Cf. Norman Fiering, *Moral Philosophy at Seventeenth-Century Harvard: A Discipline in Transition* (Chapel Hill: University of North Carolina Press, 1981), 19.

34. Miller and Johnson, *Puritans,* 706.

35. Cf. Fiering, *Moral Philosophy,* 26.

36. Ibid., 24–29.

37. Cf. Morgan, *Godly Learning,* 261–63.

2

The New Queen of the Sciences and the New Republic

God's Way in Nature

For what is still one-fourth of the era of English-speaking people in America, from the mid-seventeenth to the mid-eighteenth century, Harvard and eventually its Connecticut counterpart, Yale, were almost all there was to American higher education. Only toward the end of the period was the Anglican college in the South, William and Mary, fully functional. With a head start of nearly a century, New England thus achieved the dominance it would long maintain.[1]

The unresolved tensions between the realms of common grace and the realms of theology in Puritan learning helped stimulate the major developments in the content of Puritan college education during this first century. The American colonies were still marginal outposts of European culture. On the one hand, this gave colonists the freedom to preserve much of their distinctive traditions. On the other hand, it also meant a provincial mentality in which they were always reassuring themselves that they were keeping up with British and European standards, particularly those that accompanied the scientific revolution.

Puritanism was congenial to the study of the natural order. The Reformed emphasis that the creation could be known through reason, combined with the broader Protestant ideal that one could serve and glorify God in the mundane as well in special spiritual vocations, stimulated scientific study. Certainly there was no intimation of a warfare between science and religion in New England. Rather the Puritans assumed that natural philosophy (natural science) would serve the interests of religion and point toward the glories of God in creation.

It is not surprising then that the curriculum of early Harvard kept somewhat up-to-date in natural philosophy, considering its location in a distant province. The principal issue in the seventeenth century was not natural science versus the Bible; rather it was the new natural philosophy versus the "peripatetic" philosophy of Aristotle. By the end of the century Aristotle's long dominance in Western university education was finally being ended in all fields, including natural philosophy. So at Harvard President Increase Mather could commend the students in a commencement address because they "seem to savour a liberal mode of philosophizing, rather than the Peripatetic." After a few swipes at Aristotle for his pagan denials of creation, resurrection, and immorality of the soul, Mather ended with a tribute to the new philosophy, while honoring the old: "You who are wont to philosophize in a liberal spirit, are pledged to no particular master, yet I would have you hold fast to that one truly golden saying of Aristotle: *Find a friend in Plato, a friend in Socrates* (and I would say a friend in Aristotle), *but above all find a friend in* TRUTH."[2]

Shortly after the turn of the century, Mather's control of Harvard was displaced by a rival faction, slightly more progressive. The champion of the new party, John Leverett, elected president in 1707, enunciated in the 1711 commencement what would be the prevailing opinion in most eighteenth-century American college education:

> In philosophical [scientific] matters, Harvardians philosophize in a sane and liberal manner, according to the manner of the century. . . . [After a nod to Aristotle and others] For what is Natural Philosophy, unless a system in which natural things are explained; and in which that hypothesis is certainly the best by which the greater part of natural phenomena are most fully and clearly explained; these things are to be sought and acquired. Without any manner of doubt whatever, all humane matters must be tested by Philosophy.
>
> But the same license is not permissible to Theologians. . . .[3]

A number of points are significant in such resolutions of the issues of Christianity and higher learning as the Western world shifted to the modern era of scientific dominance. First, in both Mather and Leverett, there is a general shift to the "liberal" spirit of truth-seeking, rejecting (though still respecting) the ancients as authorities in favor of modern scientific method. Nonetheless, the new learning like the old is still to be surrounded by Christian liturgical, behavioral, and theological dictates. Theology is still assumed to be the queen of the sciences and the crucial component added to the arts curriculum. Even while Harvard was determined to keep up with the currents from abroad, theology there was still based on the authority of the ancient texts and assumed to serve the interests of a particular church group.[4]

This emphasis on dogma was appropriate since dominant New England opinion was that their theological tradition embodied universal truth. The traumatic events of the 1680s, the reorganization of the colonies under the Crown, and the enforcement of religious toleration even after "the Glorious Revolution" of 1688, had undermined some of the institutional support for such dogmatism. Yet the spirit of the theological age persisted in New England. The idea of the modern age that a church was a denomination, just one among many equal religious groups, had not yet blossomed. In higher education theological exclusivism was firmly entrenched institutionally throughout the Western world. As a matter of course, schools were defined by church loyalties. In England, one had to subscribe to the Thirty-nine Articles in order to matriculate in Oxford and Cambridge universities, so that members of dissenting churches, such as Congregational, Presbyterian, and Baptist, were effectively barred. Confessional exclusivism, therefore, did not set New England apart from the rest of the Western world, even if theological dogmatism was particularly strong there.

Relating faith and science was a matter of relating two approaches to universal truth within this dogmatic context. The truths learned from Scripture and those learned from nature were assumed to be complementary. Christians who had long learned from the pagans could learn even more from their own natural philosophers. And since the creator of heaven and earth was also the author of Scripture, truths learned through the methods of philosophy and those learned from biblical authority would supplement each other and harmonize in one curriculum.

The New Moral Philosophy

Though we might assume that the introduction of the new science was the major transforming factor that brought higher education into the modern era, the more immediately revolutionary force was the introduction of a new concept of moral philosophy. The new natural science was, of course, immensely important, especially because it suggested that there must be a universal mechanics that would explain all physical phenomena, thus underscoring questions as to what room there was for spiritual forces and divine causality once the creator had set the system in motion. Since such questions could be plausibly resolved, however, the new scientific outlook did not necessarily replace Christianity as a factor for understanding the physical world, so much as make it, at least potentially, superfluous. Issues raised directly by the new mechanics, however, were likely to be met head on by Christian apologists.

Less obvious was the challenge of the new ethics. By purporting to discover a universal set of rationally based moral principles, the new ethics was presuming to do for core elements in human experience what the new physics did for the periphery. This audacious yet plausible project seemed entirely complementary to Christianity, since most of the moralists assumed that such a rationally discovered ethic had to originate with the creator, and so could not contradict truly revealed religion. Reinforcing a divinely sanctioned ethic with the authority of universally valid rationality seemed obviously a good thing for civilization. It was hence more difficult to see that this project, at least when it was conducted by pious confessing Christians, also had the potential for making Christian revelation superfluous.

The new moral science had many obvious merits. One was that the idea of finding a rationally based universal ethic promised a way for shoring up Christian civilization. The Reformation and the ensuing century of religious warfare had precipitated a crisis in authority. By the eighteenth century religious dogmatism was coming to be widely questioned in sophisticated circles. Mutually exclusive claims of religious authorities threatened to undermine morality and hence political stability. Universal reason, on the other hand, offered to provide a new rock-solid foundation of authority on which a consensus of enlightened humanity might at last be built. Such principles, so it seemed, would only undergird true Christianity.

Since most eighteenth-century Christians saw the support of civilization as among their major goals, a shift from emphasis on contemplation of God to the contemplation of humans, the apex of God's creation, could be made without intending an assault on piety.[5] Christians of many shades could unite in this new veneration of the divine through rational explication of God's crowning work.

In Protestant collegiate curricula we can trace a corresponding shift during this century in which moral science emerged as their integrating feature. This theme provides a window through which we can view the subtle change in the role of religion in American higher education during this era.[6]

The practical payoff of the eighteenth-century shift toward explorations of humanity as a way of knowing God was that it would produce "virtue."[7] Virtue was one of the key words of the era. Moreover, it was an ideal with which few Christians were likely to quarrel. Particularly with the emergence of the American republic it seemed almost self-evident that the goal of education should be to produce "virtuous citizens." Correspondingly, by the end of the century American colleges were instituting courses in moral philosophy, taught by the clergyman-president, as the capstone and integrating feature of their curricula. Rigorous theology still might be preached in required Sunday services and students might still study the Westminster Catechism at many New England and Presbyterian colleges, but moral philosophy provided a common ground for building a republic of virtue.

Since Aristotle's ethics had played a large role in Western education for so many centuries prior to the eighteenth, it is fair enough to ask what was so different about the new science of morality. The difference may be compared to the difference between Aristotelian and Newtonian physics. In Aristotelian physics, qualities like impetus, levity, or gravity could be acquired dispositions of objects. So one can impart impetus to a stone, but when the impetus wears out, it will come to rest. The Aristotelian physical universe was thus wide open to the interposition of external personal agencies, including supernatural miracles. The Newtonian universe, on the other hand, despite the piety of Newton and most of his immediate heirs and despite the faith in a creator it presumed, was for practical purposes a closed system of universal physical laws. The difference in the ethics was similar. In Aristotle virtue was conceived as an acquired skill, developed by practice. Hence one could benefit from the wisdom of Aristotle in the principles of acquiring the habits of virtue, but the door was wide open for adding Christian content in defining the content of the virtues. Aristotle's ethics thus could be presented with Christian commentary that would correct his misconceptions, for instance, concerning the human soul or immortality.[8] The new moral philosophy, on the other hand, was conceived of as a potentially closed system, which eventually would make special revelation superfluous, at least for ethics.

Add to this an advantage that the new moral philosophy had over Aristotle: like Newton's physics, it was a broadly Christian philosophy in the sense of arising out of Christian civilization. In its earliest forms, such as in the Cambridge Platonism originated in the mid-seventeenth century, the Christian dimensions of the enterprise were quite explicit. Already by the 1690s such texts replaced Aristotle at Harvard. By the next generation, broadly Christian moralists such as Samuel Clarke, Francis Hutcheson, and the third Earl of Shaftesbury were well known to virtually every educated American.[9] So the view gained ground that, as Clarke put it in 1708, "Moral Virtue is the Foundation and the Summ, the Essence and the Life of all true Religion; For the Security whereof, all positive Institution was only designed; For the Restoration whereof, all revealed Religion was ultimately intended."[10] Or as an admirer of Shaftesbury and Hutcheson put it in 1740, "religion and virtue are the same thing."[11]

Yale College

We can gain some sense of both the extent and the limits of these developments by looking at the origins of Yale College. When Connecticut clergy founded Yale in 1701 it was in the context of, even though not explicitly a response to, a perceived decline in theological orthodoxy at Harvard.[12] This was the year that Increase Mather was ousted from his post at Harvard, and for Increase and his son Cotton, at least, the change in the Harvard presidency signaled the demise of Massachusetts orthodoxy.[13] In letters of advice to the Connecticut college founders, the Mathers indicated that they were ready to support their Connecticut brethren in taking a firm stand for orthodoxy. They suggested that they follow a continental rather than English model for Reformed colleges by requiring faculty to subscribe to the confessions of the church as a guarantee of orthodoxy. Increase had failed to get such a provision approved by the Crown in a proposed Harvard charter, but he hoped for better in Connecticut, where the college, despite local government support, was doing without a charter.

Connecticut clergy, despite the concern for orthodoxy that often characterizes those in outlying provinces, were at first disinclined to demand formal subscription to creeds.[14] The issue, however, was soon forced on them. In 1722, Timothy Cutler, the capable rector who had recently brought stability to the fledgling college, declared himself Anglican. This was truly shocking for a Connecticut clergymen. It was as though an elder in a Mennonite community had announced he was joining the army. Anti-Anglicanism had been an integral part of the definition of the Connecticut colony. Anglicanism signaled broad-mindedness and "Arminianism," the code word for the increasingly popular optimistic views of human nature as opposed to strict Calvinism. Further, Cutler was not alone among Connecticut clergy in his apostasy, a fact that sent up choruses of laments from the orthodox. The Yale trustees promptly dismissed Cutler and an offending tutor. To ensure continued orthodoxy, they now required all officers of the college to subscribe to the Westminster Confession of Faith, as stated in the Congregational Saybrook Platform. They even asked Cotton Mather to take over as rector; but Mather, who spent his life compulsively writing tomes proving that he was not a provincial, was not ready to leave Boston for the Connecticut hinterlands.[15]

Concern for orthodoxy, however, was set as part of the early Yale's identity. The young Jonathan Edwards is a well-known example of the early orthodox spirit. Edwards's father, Timothy, was of the orthodox party, and young Jonathan was student at Yale under Cutler. Though one should not be blamed for one's traits as a teenager, Edwards as a student may have been a little too good to be true. Most college students in the eighteenth century found release from the strict discipline of the campus by occasionally raising hell. Young Edwards, always in the throes of strict Puritan self-discipline, would have none of it. He complained of "Unseasonable Nightwalking, Breaking People's windows, playing at Cards, Cursing, Swearing, and Damning, and Using all manner of Ill Language." At age fifteen (younger than average, but not unusual for college students of the time) Edwards wrote to his father about a fellow townsman, Isaac Stiles, aged twenty-one. Stiles had joined in a rebellion protesting the quality of the college food. "As soon as I Understood him to be One of them, I told him that I thought he had done exceedingly Unadvisedly, and told him also what I thought the Ill Consequences of it would be, and quickly made him sorry that he did not take my advice in the matter." Edmund Morgan may be correct that most students thought young Edwards "a hopeless prig."[16] On the other hand, Edwards was brilliant and admired at least by adults and perhaps by some of his peers as well. Shortly after the Cutler defection he was named tutor and served for a year, no doubt firmly defending orthodoxy, even as he was privately developing some of his breathtaking insights into orthodoxy's implications for the modern era.

Edwards aside, Yale College was set on a path of sectarianism that would characterize it until the American Revolution. The most notorious sectarian was Thomas Clap, an exact contemporary of Edwards (though Clap graduated from Harvard) who became rector in 1739 ("president" after Yale received its charter in 1745). Clap's tenure at Yale illustrates most of the hazards of taking a strict sectarian stance, especially for a school that had a monopoly on higher education. Clap himself, of course, saw the issue as a simple one of maintaining a traditional orthodox basis for a responsible state establishment of religion.

The issue was being much debated in Great Britain and its colonies. The presumption still was that colleges were established state religious organizations. Since Oxford and Cambridge excluded members of dissenting sects, Nonconformists in England were forced to found "dissenting academies" for the equivalent of college training. In the Anglican colony of Virginia, the Oxbridge pattern was followed, though only in a general way. The College of William and Mary—chartered in 1693, opened in 1707, and only gradually becoming a full-fledged college—was an integral part of the Anglican establishment. Seated facing the statehouse in Williamsburg, it was supported by state revenues while its faculty were required to be Anglican and were almost all clergymen. By midcentury William and Mary was comparable to the New England colleges and included as well a divinity school for the training of Anglican clergy.[17]

Thomas Clap and most of Connecticut took for granted that Yale should have the equivalent privileges in Congregationalist Connecticut. Just about half the college's graduates had become Congregationalist clergy and it seemed sensible that such a vital function should be governed as strictly as the church itself.

The issue became complicated almost immediately after Clap took office as the convulsions of the Great Awakening shook New England. George Whitefield was welcomed at Yale during his grand tour of 1740, but his more extravagant successors and imitators, including the most extreme, James Davenport, a Yale graduate, began to disrupt Congregationalist unity. Soon it was one orthodoxy versus another.

At a crucial juncture in the controversy, at the commencement of 1741, Jonathan Edwards, already renowned for his account of the revival in Northampton, was brought in to preach. Many of the audience had heard James Davenport preaching in the vicinity the night before his "indecent mad and blasphemous religion," as the Old Lights typically put it. Edwards, preaching on "The Distinguishing Marks of the Works of the Spirit of God," made clear that extravagances such as Davenport's were not necessarily evidence of the Spirit of God; but he made just as clear (as only he could) that emotion and enthusiasm were no signs of the lack of the Spirit either.[18]

David Brainerd was a Yale student at the time and a great admirer of Edwards. Young Brainerd, following the pattern set by some of the less cautious New Lights such as Presbyterian itinerant Gilbert Tennent, was quick to make dogmatic pronouncements about the spiritual condition of those in the establishment who were cool to the awakening. Already at commencement time in 1741 the trustees had passed a college law forbidding students to call college officers "carnal" or "unconverted." When Brainerd soon remarked that one of the Yale tutors "has no more grace than the chair I am leaning upon" he was expelled. Yale was now firmly in the Old Light camp. In 1742 the commencement speaker was Isaac Stiles, who accused Edwards and company of leaving "the Pole-star to follow Jack with a Lanthorn."[19]

The awakeners were claiming that New England's colleges were already hopelessly secularized (which underscores the point that it just depends on the standard one is measuring from). The most notorious accusations came from George Whitefield. In 1740 the Grand Itinerant had been warmly welcomed both at Harvard and at Yale. Whitefield, however, was keeping a journal of his travels. Relying on the characterizations of his New Light informants,[20] Whitefield characterized the schools as "not far superior to our Universities in piety." This was a scathing insult, especially since in the same journal Whitefield wrote that Oxford and Cambridge were "sunk into *meer Seminaries of Paganism. Christ or Christianity* is scarce so much as named among them." Whitefield, who was not a private man, soon published his journal. His former hosts at the New England schools were in a rage.

Harvard, though still professing orthodox Calvinism, was more vulnerable than Yale since it was slightly more open to fashionable British opinion. Whitefield claimed that discipline there was at a low ebb and that students and teachers were reading latitudinarians such as John Tillotson and Samuel Clarke rather than the old evangelical Puritan authors. In 1744, when Whitefield was back in New England, the Harvard faculty replied indignantly, characterizing Whitefield as "an uncharitable, censorious and slanderous Man," and, worst of all, an *"Enthusiast,"* meaning he claimed direct guidance from the Spirit of God. "Enthusiasm" had been a damning accusation in Massachusetts since Anne Hutchinson's time. Indeed the issue was similar. Some New Lights were suggesting that persons might be called to preach directly by the Holy Spirit, without the benefit of a classical education. Harvard professors and their clerical supporters correctly perceived that Whitefield was a threat to their whole system of social authority.[21]

Though the Yale faculty also issued a rejoinder, Whitefield's characterizations of spiritual laxity were less plausible there. While Harvard was combating the Awakening from a moderate Calvinist position, Thomas Clap's Yale opposed it from a position of strict orthodoxy. Clap was an imposing and domineering character who thought to ride out the turmoil by standing firm against the pluralism of the age. The extent to which he was willing to go was suggested in 1744 when Clap expelled two students, John and Ebenezer Cleveland, because while home on vacation they had attended a New Light church service conducted by a lay exhorter, rather than attending the Old Light church in their town.[22]

By the 1750s, however, Clap had forged a political alliance with the New Lights, who he may have decided were, in the long run, less prone to tolerance than some of the moderate Old Lights. Yale was also now in competition with the new College of New Jersey (Princeton), which was New Light.[23] In any case, Clap successfully resisted any trend of his time to see tolerance as a virtue. In 1753 he denied the request of New Haven's recently settled Anglican minister to allow his sons to attend their own church instead of the college services. In reply to the irate Anglican's rejoinder, Clap spelled out the case for the old order of narrow religious establishments. First of all, alluding to the exclusions of dissenters at Oxford and Cambridge, he remarked that while Yale College "does not come up, to the Perfection, of the Ancient Established Universities," it still "would endeavour to Imitate them in most things." And, said Clap, "Religious Worship, Preaching, and Instruction on the Sabbath, being one of the most important Parts, of the Education of Ministers," it was the part of education that should be most under the authority of the college. No outside agency, whether parent or church, should be controlling the part of education which the college was set up most to preserve. And if students were simply required to attend the worship of their choice, what would happen, asked, Clap, if "there may be an Assembly of *Jews,* or *Arians,* in *New Haven,*" then the college would be requiring "such a Worship, as they esteem, to be *worse than none.*"

As to the objection that since Anglicans, such as Bishop Berkeley and Eli Yale himself, had made large contributions to the college, they should have some influence over college laws, Clap had an answer that probably every college president since would have appreciated. "If it were so; it seems, as if they intended to *Buy* the College rather than to make a *Donation* to it."

To the more difficult objection that Anglicans paid taxes to support the college, Clap had a feebler reply. Anglicans, he said, were free to send their children to the college so long as they abided by its rules; furthermore, Yale had trained enough Anglican clergy (Clap did not mention that these were mainly Cutler and his friends) to make their tax donations a bargain.[24]

During the next decade, Clap's narrow partisanship managed to alienate almost everyone. He insisted that everyone having to do with the corporation be subjected to tests of orthodoxy. He alienated former Old Light allies and never gained the full confidence of New Lights. He fired tutors on suspicions of heterodoxy. He refused a contribution of books because it contained some heretical volumes. Meanwhile the legislature was threatening to cut off funds, the college was losing students, tuition was rising, and the food was bad. Only the unusual force of Clap's personality kept the college running. Finally in 1765 the situation collapsed. A mob of students and townspeople rioted and damaged his home. Student dissension, rebellion, and calls for Clap's ouster continued through the next year. Finally in 1766, exhausted and in ill-health, Clap resigned.[25]

New Light and Enlightenment

The intensity of such mid-eighteenth-century controversies should help us to understand the religious dimension of the founding of the other colonial colleges. Most of these colleges—The College of New Jersey (Princeton, 1746), Brown (1764), Queen's (Rutgers, 1766), and Dartmouth (1769)—were founded by the activist New Light clergy, respectively among Presbyterians, Baptists, Dutch Reformed, and Congregationalists. The two exceptions were King's (Columbia, 1754) in New York City and the College of Philadelphia (Pennsylvania, 1755), more broadly supported by non–New Light coalitions with Anglican leadership and Presbyterian support.

Of the New Light colleges the College of New Jersey located at Princeton proved to be the most significant, especially since Presbyterians would be the chief college founders during the next century and their college became the only major rival to the older New England colleges as a national model. The Princeton charter, granted in 1746 and revised in 1748, originally designated as trustees only New Side Presbyterian ministers, but to ease public unrest, the sympathetic royal governor persuaded the trustees to add the governor and four members of his council and three Presbyterian laymen to the board, though the board remained overwhelmingly Presbyterian and clerical and was self-perpetuating. More notably, the charter guaranteed that students "of any religious Denomination" could enjoy the full privileges of the college, regardless "of his or their Sentiments in Religion, and of his or their being of a Religious profession Different from the said Trustees of the College." Princeton was founded immediately in the wake of the exclusions of the New Lights at Yale and the connections were close.[26] Gilbert Tennent and Aaron Burr, Jonathan Edwards's son-in-law, were on the original Princeton board. In New Jersey, where there was more diversity, there was also greater sensitivity to the rights of dissent.

With the exception of Queen's College, where ethnicity sharpened Dutch Reformed standoffishness, all the colonial colleges founded in this period resolved the problem of interdenominational rivalries by allowing minority denominations some representation on their boards.[27] Also, with the exception of Yale, all the boards were or became mixes of clergy and laymen, even if clergy usually retained their traditional dominance. Most had the colonial governor and members of his council as ex officio members; but unlike the first three colleges, they received little, if any, tax support. Interdenominational rivalries were again the crucial factor. Politics and religion were inextricably linked in the mid-eighteenth century. Despite growing tolerance forced by the public functions of the colleges, they were still essentially under the control of a dominant religious group.

Even the College of Philadelphia, the most secular of the schools, and the only one with an entirely lay board, was beset by rivalries between Anglicans and Presbyterians for control. Similarly, King's College in New York City, the only other new college not a direct product of the Awakening, was the focus of intense rivalries between the Anglicans, who by charter held the presidency, and the powerful Presbyterians, who countered any Anglican sectarianism. Samuel Johnson, the first president, was himself no friend of sectarianism. He had been one of the tutors who joined

Cutler in defecting to Anglicanism and were forced to leave Yale. In 1754 he formulated for Protestant colleges serving the public the creed that in substance would be repeated at almost every such college for the next two centuries. It is so typical as to be worth italicizing: *"As to religion, there is no intention to impose on the scholars, the peculiar tenets of any particular sect of Christians; but to inculcate upon their tender minds, the great principles of Christianity and morality in which true Christians of each denomination are generally agreed."*[28]

Maintaining a moral order was a major challenge for eighteenth-century British society, as it is in every era. So far as young people were concerned, the traditional way to promote habits of good behavior was coercion. At King's College, for instance, monetary penalties were used. Absence from chapel brought a fine of two pence, one pence for tardiness. Students caught at fighting cocks, playing cards, or dice were fined up to five shillings. The lesser offense of "fighting, maiming, slandering, or grievously abusing any person" drew a three-shilling penalty.[29] Traditional methods of controlling youth by strict regulation and discipline often fostered between faculty and students a cold war atmosphere, punctuated by student rowdiness and occasional riots.

Those in control seldom questioned the well-tried authoritarian methods, but one trend in the eighteenth century was to look more to the individual as a self-regulating force. Inner discipline could supplement external authority. Puritan and other religious disciplines anticipated this emphasis on internalizing a moral order. The problem for Protestantism, however, was how to apply this to entire societies.

The two major eighteenth-century solutions to this problem were those associated with pietism and the Enlightenment. Despite some striking parallels between these movements (such as individualism, challenging old authorities, and concern with morality), they moved in essentially opposite directions regarding the crucial question of human nature. Pietism and the associated revivals emphasized the need for a dramatic change in the individual through conversion experience, suggesting a fundamental gap between the saved and the lost. So far as the social order was concerned, the redeeming feature was that revivalism offered the hope that vast numbers might be saved, thereby infusing society with Christian virtue.[30] The Enlightenment approach, on the other hand, emphasized human commonality and ability to internalize the findings of a universal moral science, once people correctly apprehended them.

For the next century, these two programs, the revival and moral philosophy, were the chief collegiate supplements to traditions of regulated worship, required church services/theological study, and discipline of personal behavior. The tension between the Christian particularism of the revival and the scientific universalism of the Enlightenment was a source of potential conflict between the two outlooks. Remarkably, in the late eighteenth and the early nineteenth centuries, however, these two programs generally were not seen as in conflict, but more often as complements in the task of Christianization.

The experience that bonded these two disparate trends was the American Revolution. Protestant dissenters, among whom New Lights were the most vigorous party (as their college founding illustrates), gained cultural influence in alliance with more broadly enlightened opponents of the Anglican and British establishment. Enlightenment moral philosophy, which British dissenters for over a generation had been using to challenge Anglican and royal authority,[31] provided the common language for the revolutionary enterprise. Hence moral philosophy became a fixed part of the American New Light or evangelical tradition.[32]

The Scottish Connection

American colonial educators were provincials intellectually dependent on sophisticated Great Britain. Their primary models in the eighteenth century were the Scottish universities. While Anglican gentlemen's education at Oxford and Cambridge had fallen into the doldrums, the Scottish universities suddenly blossomed into a golden age of the Scottish Enlightenment. The Enlightenment in Scotland was as brilliant as anywhere in the world, boasting scholars such as Francis Hutcheson, Thomas Reid, David Hume, and Adam Smith, as well as a formidable second rank almost as well known in their day. Unlike its more renegade French counterpart, the Scottish Enlightenment was situated primarily in the universities. In part this was possible because the Scottish universities were dominated by Presbyterian Moderates who combined Presbyterian zeal for learning with a determination to demonstrate the compatibility of Christianity with the latest cultural and scientific trends.[33] Their prestige virtually guaranteed that they would set the standards for the fledgling American schools.

Scottish universities were especially important to American dissenters because they stood at the apex of the vigorous network of non-Anglican education in Greater Britain. To combat the Anglican monopoly dissenters in England had developed "dissenting academies," which provided precollegiate and collegiate education. The Scotch-Irish in Ireland, many of whom were migrating to America, had built similar Presbyterian academies and soon imported the system to the colonies. The most famous of these was William Tennent's "Log College" at Neshaminy, Pennsylvania, founded in 1727, out of which eventually grew the College of New Jersey. During the next seventy-five years at least sixty-five other academies were founded by Presbyterian minister-teachers, largely in new settlements of the West and South. These provided mostly precollegiate work but also some college-level instruction, and the ministers might also tutor some college graduates reading divinity. A few such schools evolved into colleges.[34]

So extensive was the Presbyterian educational program that it is not much of an exaggeration to say that, outside of New England, the Scots were the educators of eighteenth-century America. Even Thomas Jefferson, who studied at William and Mary, found the one stimulating teacher to be a Scotsman, William Small. Small, the only layman at the school, was professor of mathematics but also taught the moral philosophy of Francis Hutcheson. Jefferson attributed to Small his own intellectual awakening to modern science and learning.[35]

By the end of the Revolutionary era, Scottish moral philosophy was well on the way to becoming the integrating crown of American collegiate education. In the New England and New Light colleges that still used Saturdays and Sundays for theological study (which was as integral as anything else in the curriculum, since there were recitations but no grades), moral philosophy might share its rule with theology. In the less sectarian schools that did not have a fixed theological program, the emerging science could aleady stand alone as the chief embodiment of the best of modern, scientifically based, and broadly Christian ideals.

A Dissenting Alternative

The total autonomy of morality as a science did not go entirely uncontested, especially by some New Englanders. Particularly, a number of Christian thinkers recognized the tension between the exclusivism of conversionist theologies and the universal claims of the new moral science. Most formidable were Jonathan Edwards's attacks on Arminianism, a catchall term he used to designate most of the theological and ethical trends of the era. In his most purely philosophical work, *The Nature of True Virtue,* for instance, he attacked Francis Hutcheson's view of a reliable universal moral sense. As an ardent Calvinist and a luminously clear thinker Edwards recognized that modern claims to establish a universal ethics rested on optimistic views of human nature that denied the severity of original sin and affirmed the free ability of persons to choose the good simply by putting their minds to it. Such moral systems, he argued, would ultimately undermine a sense of total dependence on God.

In 1757 Edwards became president of the college at Princeton, already a contender for the position of leading colonial college. Early in the next year he died from a smallpox inoculation. We can only speculate as to what his rigorous challenge to the autonomy of the new moral philosophy would have done for Presbyterian collegiate education.

Perhaps it would not have been much different from what happened at Yale, where a similar stance by Thomas Clap simply slowed the transition to the new philosophy for a generation or so. Clap's ethical principles, though less brilliantly argued, were not far from Edwards's. In Clap's lectures to Yale students he insisted that moral philosophy was learned not by examining human nature, but from the perfections of God. Moreover, "the divine Revelation is the only Way and Means whereby we can know what the Perfections of God are, and what Dispositions and Conduct in us, are a Conformity to these Perfections." Clap summarized and refuted each of the contenders for alternative moral foundations, such as self-interest and happiness, moral taste or sense, or conformity to reason. He conceded, for instance, that humans had a moral sense, but then pointed out in rigorous Calvinist fashion that "since the Fall, his Understanding is darkened, his Judgment is perverted, his Taste and Relish is defiled. . . ."[36]

Edwards and Clap, seeing that the orthodox Puritan heritage was going to be out of step in the modern world, were raising the disturbing theoretical issue that Christian education must be distinctive, not only in theology, but in the most crucial practical philosophical understandings of human behavior and morality. Theoretically this argument looked formidable; in practice it created the huge problems, already considered, of sectarianism for essentially public institutions. It implied also a practical moral rigor in college that would be difficult to sustain. Clap's efforts almost killed Yale and finally had his presidency effectively ended by an uprising. Edwards, for all his theoretical brilliance, was not known for his tact when it came to enforcing the moral order. If the good citizens of Northampton ran him out of town, one wonders how long he would have lasted with the students of Princeton had he lived into the revolutionary era.

Moral Philosophy in the Service of the Republic

On the other hand, in the long run the more usual solution was for orthodoxy to make peace, as it usually had done through the centuries, with a broader moral philosophy that could be taught without distinguishing between true and nominal Christians. For instance, Francis Alison, the leading figure among the theologically conservative but antirevivalist Old Side Presbyterians, was also the most influential early proponent of Francis Hutcheson's views in America. Alison was educated at Scottish universities, in part by Hutcheson himself. In America he founded one of the more advanced Presbyterian academies in Chester County, Pennsylvania, in 1742. Alison was highly regarded by most of the colonial intellectuals, including Benjamin Franklin, and with William Smith became co-founder in 1755 of the College of Philadelphia. He participated in some of the practical and scientifically oriented educational reforms of the Pennsylvania college and taught Hutcheson's moral philosophy there until 1779. That Alison was no theological liberal is suggested by the fact that in 1755 Clap's Yale awarded him an honorary doctorate.[37]

Alison's principal influence on Yale, however, came through his close friendship with Ezra Stiles, with whom he corresponded for years. Stiles was a tutor under Clap and eventually served as Yale's president from 1778 to 1795. Alison certainly helped foster in Stiles an appreciation of Scottish universities and methods, and Stiles in fact obtained an honorary doctorate from Edinburgh in 1765.[38]

Even though Stiles was a model of the broad intellectual of his era, interested in mastering all human learning and sciences and of a tolerant, open spirit, he was a conservative in his religious allegiances. When, for instance, in 1792 some state officials were made ex officio members of the Yale Corporation in exchange for tax support, Stiles reflected on the disaster it would be to the religious interests of the college if the Corporation ever became all laymen. First, he said, there would be terrible fights for balance among all the religious sects. Then they would have to drop all religious tests for the board and admit "Deists & enemies to all Sects of Xtians." Soon even theistic tests would be removed for the faculty. "In short," Stiles concluded (in a dim prophecy of *God and Man at Yale*), "the Religion & that good Order which arises from the Religion of the original Institution must be laid prostrate."[39]

Stiles nonetheless managed to synthesize strong concerns for a continuing Christian identity with the catholic spirit of the Enlightenment.[40] So on the one hand, out of respect for his mentor, he continued to include Clap's text as a brief part of his senior course on moral philosophy. Nonetheless, by 1790 he had added to the senior requirements William Paley's *Principles of Moral and Political Philosophy* and Montesquieu's *Spirit of the Laws.* Theology was still a formidable presence at Yale; but what was most significant in these changes was that the subject of political philosophy had now risen to prominence as part of moral philosophy. Following the Revolution and facing the traumas of nation building, the overwhelming priority in collegiate education was shaping good citizens.[41]

The most dramatic shift, however, came at Princeton. Within less than a generation its atmosphere seemed vastly different than when it was a New Light and New Side stronghold with Jonathan Edwards as president.

Crucial to the change was the Scotsman John Witherspoon, who was Princeton's president from 1768 to 1794. The college trustees, having suffered one after another early death of New Light presidents, turned abroad to find Witherspoon, who might offer some added prestige. Although Witherspoon had been an outspoken opponent of liberal tendencies among Scottish Presbyterians, in American categories he turned out to be closer to moderate Old Lights than to the New Lights. Francis Alison in Philadelphia and Charles Chauncy (an old opponent of Edwards) in Boston took delight in discovering that they suddenly had an ally at Princeton. As Chauncy put it, "He is no friend to the grand and distinguishing Tenets of Mr. Edwards wch. have been almost universally imbibed in that part of the Country."[42]

Upon arriving in Princeton, Witherspoon immediately took the situation in hand: he cleared out the tutors who were champions of Edwardsean philosophy and introduced the principles of Francis Hutcheson. Disagreement with Hutcheson's moderate theology was to Witherspoon no reason to reject his philosophy. Witherspoon's lectures, in fact, followed Hutcheson closely with little real criticism. Ethics, he emphasized, must be a natural human science. The foundational facts could be discovered by examining human nature. "The principles of duty and obligation must be drawn from the nature of man." So human consciousness became a source of scientific data. Such self-examination led to a moral sense of good and evil, principles from which a universal ethical system could be derived. Witherspoon, like the other Scots, was hopeful that "a time may come when men, treating moral philosophy as Newton and his successors have done natural, may arrive at greater precision." Though Witherspoon spoke of his views as a Christian philosophy, and backed them with appeals to Scripture, he regarded them as ultimately part of an inductive science.[43]

Scientific method could thus both confirm Christianity and support the moral foundations necessary to the republic. Science and religion were in no way seen as in conflict. Witherspoon, accordingly, like Alison in Philadelphia or Stiles in New Haven, took pride in acquiring scientific equipment and adding doses of practical natural philosophy to the classical curriculum.[44]

One striking index of the change was that from the early years of the presidency of John Witherspoon (1768–1775) to his last years (1784–1794) the number of the college's graduates entering the ministry fell from nearly one in two to little more than one in eight. Clearly this was a reflection of the revolutionary times. Princeton was particularly susceptible to the political fervor; nearby Philadelphia, where some of its best known trustees resided, was the center of American national political life. The College of New Jersey itself, which boasted the largest building in the colonies, even served as the seat of the Continental Congress for five months in 1783. President Witherspoon, the only clergyman to sign the Declaration of Independence, was among the most active leaders in organizing the new government. His student James Madison was a leading figure in drafting the Constitution. During the national era Princeton produced so many leading public officials that it eventually characterized itself as "the school of statesmen."[45]

Service to the Republic had emerged as the preeminent goal. For this there was hardly any distinction between the benefits of religion and the benefits of the science of morality. The two supported each other. As Witherspoon's successor, President Samuel Stanhope Smith of Princeton, put it in a conventional statement, "the truths of religion . . . [are] the surest basis of public morals." "Every class of the people" needed to be trained in their "moral and social duties."[46]

Dr. Benjamin Rush of Philadelphia, a Princeton graduate and friend of the college, with sincere though broad Christian sensibilities, made a similarly conventional point in 1798, saying that "the only foundation for a useful education in a republic is to be laid in Religion." Rush was one of the principal champions of educational reform, including the establishment of a national university. Like most leaders of the American Enlightenment, he favored more practical scientific education; but moral education was the most practical subject of all. Education was crucial to the republic because citizens needed to be shown their moral duty in order to act upon it.[47]

Christianity was crucial to the equation that led to republican virtue.

Rush admitted that rather than no religion, he would prefer "the opinions of Confucius or Mohamed inculcated upon our youth." Christianity, however, according the old "real Whig" or British dissenter tradition of the American revolutionaries, had unique civil benefits. The Old Testament teaching of a common creation was "the strongest argument that can be used in favor of a natural equality of all mankind." In fact, Rush insisted, in a revealing summary of how Gospel and republic had been fused:

> A Christian cannot fail of being a republican, for every precept of the Gospel inculcates those degrees of humility, self-denial, and brotherly kindness, which are directly opposed to the price of monarchy and the pageantry of a court. A Christian cannot fail of being useful to the republic, for his religion teacheth him, that no man "liveth to himself." And lastly, a Christian cannot fail of being wholly inoffensive, for his religion teacheth him, in all things to do to others what he would wish, in like circumstances, they should do to him."[48]

Notes

1. Disestablishment at the time of the American Revolution and defeat in the Civil War both severely limited the influence of Anglican William and Mary.

2. Increase Mather, Commencement Address (before 1697), quoted in Samuel E. Morison, *Harvard College in the Seventeenth Century* (Cambridge, Mass.: Harvard University Press, 1936), 167, cf. 224–27.

3. Quoted in Morison, *Harvard College,* 168.

4. Cf., Rick Kennedy, "The Alliance between Puritanism and Cartesian Logic at Harvard, 1687–1735," *Journal of the History of Ideas,* 51 (October–December 1990), 549–72.

5. As the eighteenth-century Scottish moral philosopher Thomas Reid, who became very popular in America, later put it, "We ought never to despair of human genius, but rather to hope, that in time it may produce a system of the powers and operations of the human mind, no less certain than those of optics or astronomy." Such certain principles would provide a firm foundation for moral judgments. Since, however, "the mind of man is the noblest work of God which reason discovers to us," focus on humanity was not the least bit impious. Rather, "we may be admitted . . . into the councils of the Almighty by a consideration of his works." Thomas Reid, *Essays on the Intellectual Powers of Man* (Cambridge, Mass.: M.I.T. Press, 1969 [1785]), xxxvii, xxxv, xxxix.

6. The best general account of religion in higher education of this era is found in Howard Miller, *The Revolutionary College: American Presbyterian Higher Education, 1707–1837* (New York: New York University Press, 1976).

7. Norman Fiering, *Moral Philosophy at Seventeenth-Century Harvard: A Discipline in Transition* (Chapel Hill: University of North Carolina Press, 1981), 42. This volume and its companion, *Jonathan Edwards's Moral Thought and Its British Context* (1981), provide a marvelously sophisticated account of these developments.

8. Fiering, *Moral Philosophy,* 102 and passim; *Jonathan Edwards,* 3.

9. Fiering, *Moral Philosophy,* 296.

10. Quoted in Fiering, *Moral Philosophy,* 297.

11. Fiering, *Jonathan Edwards,* 8.

12. Richard Warch, *School of the Prophets: Yale College, 1701–1710* (New Haven: Yale University Press, 1973), 10. I am relying on Warch as the most complete of many accounts of these developments.

13. Miller, *The New England Mind: From Colony to Province* (Cambridge: Harvard University Press, 1953), presents a compelling dramatization of this crisis.

14. Warch, *School of the Prophets,* esp. 36. Their kin in the middle colonies, in fact, soon found that their harmony with their Scotch-Irish brethren in organizing a Presbyterian denomination was disrupted by differences of their English dissenter views of the place of creeds compared with the Scottish view, which was closer to the continental matter of requiring strict subscription.

15. Ibid., 96–117. Part of Increase Mather's problem as Harvard president was that he refused to move from Boston to Cambridge.

16. Edmund S. Morgan, *The Gentle Puritan: A Life of Ezra Stiles, 1727–1795* (New York: W. W. Norton, 1962), 36–37. Perhaps this incident cast light on the speculation concerning where Edwards would have stood concerning the American Revolution.

17. Frederick Rudolph, *The American College and University: A History* (New York: Vintage Books, 1962), 14. Richard Hofstadter and Walter P. Metzger, *The Development of Academic Freedom in the United States* (New York: Columbia University Press), 133–34, make the point that the faculty lost the autonomy enjoyed by the English schools and the college was controlled by a board divided between clergy and lay members, reflecting its dual obligations to church and state.

18. Morgan, *Gentle Puritan,* 34–37, has a fine account of this episode.

19. Ibid., 39–40. Hofstadter and Metzger, *Academic Freedom,* 168–69.

20. Edwards, for instance, retained the dim view of his student days concerning the benefits of college education for piety. See *Some Thoughts concerning the Present Revival of Religion in New England (1740),* excerpt in Sol Cohen, ed., *Education in the United States: A Documentary History,* Vol. II (New York: Random House, 1974), 680–81.

21. Whitefield replied, saying that he was sorry, but he conceded nothing. Edward Wigglesworth, Hollis Professor of Divinity at Harvard, issued a careful rebuttal to Whitefield in 1745. Wigglesworth pointed out, for instance, that Tillotson had not been taken out of the library for nine years prior to Whitefield's first visit. Cohen, *Education,* 681. See also Hofstadter and Metzger, *Academic Freedom,* 161–63.

22. See documents in Richard Hofstadter and Wilson Smith, eds., *American Higher Education: A Documentary History,* (Chicago: University of Chicago Press, 1961), 64–72. Clap obtained a charter for the college in 1745 and formulated at the same time the strictest laws for regulation of students lives. Ibid., 49–61.

23. Morgan, *Gentle Puritan,* 104. The term Presbyterians used was "New Side."

24. Thomas Clap, *The Religious Constitution of Colleges* (New London, Conn., 1754), excerpt in Cohen, *Education,* 687–91.

25. Morgan, *Gentle Puritan,* 316–18. Louis Leonard Tucker, *Puritan Protagonist; President Thomas Clap of Yale College* (Chapel Hill: University of North Carolina Press, 1962), 232–62. Hofstadter and Metzger, *Academic Freedom,* 170–77.

26. Nine of the twelve clergy on the original board (of twenty-three total) were New Englanders. Douglas Sloan, *The Scottish Enlightenment and the American College Ideal* (New York: Teachers College Press, 1971), 58.

27. Hofstadter and Metzger, *Academic Freedom,* 116–17. At Rhode Island College, for instance, while Baptists were ensured control, an elaborate scheme was

worked out to include fixed numbers of Quakers, Congregationalists, and Anglicans. "Charter of Rhode Island College (Brown University), 1764," in Hofstadter and Smith, *Documentary History,* 134–36.

28. "Samuel Johnson Advertises the Opening of King's College (Columbia), 1754," in Hofstadter and Smith, *Documentary History,* 110. Cf. 99–136 for valuable documents on sectarian rivalries of the era. Cf. Hofstadter and Metzger, *Academic Freedom,* 115–17, 144–51.

29. "Laws of Kings College, 1755," in Hofstadter and Smith, *Documentary History,* 117–21. Students at Kings were required to attend morning and evening prayers daily and on Sunday they had to be present at the church designated by their parents or guardians.

30. Miller, *Revolutionary College,* 79–86, provides a helpful account of efforts to implement this approach.

31. See, for example, Gordon S. Wood, *The Creation of the American Republic, 1776–1787* (New York: W. W. Norton, 1969).

32. See Henry F. May, *The Enlightenment in America* (New York: Oxford University Press, 1976), for a particularly valuable account of the era.

33. Sloan, *Scottish Enlightenment,* 1–35. David Hume, of course, was an exception, neither defending Christianity nor gaining a university position.

34. Ibid., 36–72.

35. Garry Wills, *Inventing America: Jeffersons' Declaration of Independence* (Garden City, N.Y.: Doubleday, 1978), 176–80, 200–201. Wills also documents some of the other extensive Scottish influence. Small followed the Scottish method of vernacular lectures, rather than commentary on Latin texts. In addition he helped add some new practical subjects and belles lettres to the curriculum.

36. Thomas Clap, *An Essay on the Nature and Foundation of Moral Virtue . . . for the Use of the Students at Yale-College* (New Haven, 1765), 41, 24, and passim. Cf. Tucker, *Puritan Protagonist,* 144–74. Lawrence A. Cremin suggests that Samuel Johnson, president of Kings, held a similar view. Johnson, a Yale graduate, was a leading tutor who joined Timothy Cutler in defecting to Anglicanism. He was an admirer of the philosophy of George Berkeley, which may have put him in a differing camp from the Scottish philosophers; but he was also an Arminian open to an expanded view of human ability. *American Education: The Colonial Experience, 1607–1783* (New York: Harper & Row, 1970), 461. Cf. Warch, *School of the Prophets,* 294.

37. Sloan, *Scottish Enlightenment,* 73–102, provides a most valuable account of Alison.

38. Ibid., 86–88.

39. "Ezra Stiles on Changes in the Yale Corporation, 1792," in Hofstadter and Smith, *Documentary History,* 164.

40. Hofstadter and Smith say, "No man then in academic life displayed more admirably the viewpoint of the American Enlightenment." Ibid., 159.

41. Morgan, *Gentle Puritan,* 318, 376–403.

Paley's work was recently published (London, 1785). Paley was a Lockean who rejected the "moral sense" of the Scots and his influence in collegiate education paralleled that of the Scots. Paley was a "rational Christian" (of a broad nonsectarian sort) who saw Scripture as an important supplemental guide in making moral judgments, but he was also optimistic as to human ability to find moral truth though rational calculation. This combination of piety and reason, as well as Paley's simple, engaging style, contributed to the popularity of his text during the next half century. Eventually, by the pre–Civil War era, the rival Scottish moral philosophers had triumphed, though Paley's *Natural Theology; or, Evidences of the Existence and Attributes of the Deity collected from the Appearance of Nature* (London, 1802) remained a standard text until the Darwinian era.

It is important to keep in mind also that college teachers often used texts with which they disagreed as occasions for developing their own critical viewpoints. Stiles's successor, Timothy Dwight, for instance, used Paley but criticized him from a Calvinist perspective. Stephen E. Berk, *Calvinism versus Democracy: Timothy Dwight and the Origins of American Evangelical Orthodoxy* (Hamden, Conn.: Archon Books, 1974), 84–85.

42. Quoted in Mark A. Noll, *Princeton and the Republic, 1768–1822: The Search for a Christian Enlightenment in the Era of Samuel Stanhope Smith* (Princeton: Princeton University Press, 1989), 43.

43. Ibid., 41, from Witherspoon's lectures. For an engaging explanation of Hutcheson's analysis of how human moral principles worked, see Wills, *Inventing America,* passim.

44. Helpful for understanding the changing spirit of eighteenth-century education is Robert Middlekauff, *Ancients and Axioms: Secondary Education in Eighteenth-Century New England* (New Haven: Yale University Press, 1963).

45. Quotation from Thomas Jefferson Wertenbaker in Noll, *Princeton and the Republic,* 52. Statistics from 171–72. Public service, 135, 216–17.

46. Ibid., 203.

47. Benjamin Rush on Republican Education, 1798, in Hofstadter and Smith, *Documentary History,* 170–71. Cf. Noll, *Princeton and the Republic,* 201 on Stanhope Smith's similar views.

48. Rush in Hofstadter and Smith, *Documentary History,* 171.

3

Two Kinds of Sectarianism

The "ambition and tyranny" of the Presbyterians, Thomas Jefferson fumed to his friend Thomas Cooper in 1822, "would tolerate no rival if they had power." Jefferson's contempt for the Presbyterians assumed Voltairian proportions. "Systematical in grasping at the ascendancy over all the sects, they aim, like the Jesuits, at engrossing the education of the country, are hostile to every institution which they do not direct, and jealous at seeing others begin to attend at all to that object."[1] Presbyterians, Jefferson was convinced, yearned to reinstitute a Protestant inquisition that would, as Calvin had done to Servetus, "exterminate all heretics to Calvinistic Creed." As it was, they controlled by manipulating "public opinion, that Lord of the universe." Jefferson was convinced nonetheless that he had reason on his side. Despite Presbyterian "fulminations against endeavors to enlighten the general mind, to improve the reason of the people, and to encourage them in the use of it," he assured another correspondent, "the liberality of this State will support this institution [the University of Virginia] and give fair play to the cultivation of reason."[2]

The aging revolutionary had cause to resent the Presbyterians. For over forty years he had been attempting to found a first-rate nonsectarian university in Virginia, a step he considered essential for the health of the republic. By now, however, the Presbyterians had emerged as the principal rivals to his republican dreams for higher education. Demanding an educated clergy, the Presbyterians, although no longer as numerous as the more populist Baptists and Methodists, were by now the leaders in American higher education and gaining in strength. Although Jefferson persisted in his plans to found a revolutionary university and the Jeffersonians were holding on in educational influence, Jefferson had reason to fear that Presbyterians might represent the wave of the future.

On the eve of the American Revolution, the major contenders for control of American higher education (outside of New England) had been the Anglicans and the Presbyterians. Schools, however, were not solely church organizations but also quasi-public institutions that depended on the colonial governments for the privilege of charter and sometimes support. In the South Anglicans controlled William and Mary; in New Jersey Presbyterians controlled the more private College of New Jersey. In the pivotal cities of New York and Philadelphia, the two parties had vied for control, debating the issues of the propriety of government favoritism to one sect over all others. In New York, King's College was Anglican but had to make concessions in the face of constant Presbyterian accusations of public favoritism. The College of Philadelphia, the most nonsectarian of the colonial schools, balanced interests by having an Anglican provost and a Presbyterian vice-provost.

Since the Presbyterians had been overwhelmingly on the side of the Revolution, whereas the Anglicans were badly divided, independence gave the Presbyterians the advantage. Although dependent on a primary Scotch-Irish ethnic base that made them something of outsiders, they were now in a position to play insiders' roles in shaping the ethos of the new republic. Some Presbyterians cultivated a continuing alliance with Calvinist Congregationalists of New England, primarily Connecticut, and in 1801 established a formal alliance, the Plan of Union, for joint work in frontier settlements, primarily in New York State.

While the Revolution had strengthened the Presbyterian hand and weakened the Anglican, it had also brought onto the scene a new major contender for shaping American education—liberal Christian and Deist champions of freer thought. The American Revolution had been supported primarily by an alliance of Calvinists and such enlightened liberal Christians. Since American revolutionary theory had grown largely out of the dissenter tradition, which traced its lineage to the Puritan revolution and commonwealth, these two heritages were related and had much in common. Each opposed Anglican establishments and each believed that scientific thinking could discover universally valid first principles of morality. Nonetheless, once the smoke had cleared from the Revolution, it soon became apparent that they also had sharply opposed visions for the new nation.

Agreeing that the new nation should not have an established church, both sides saw education as crucial to founding common values and beliefs. The Jeffersonians, who had worked to make the federal government largely secular in definition, envisioned secular government, either federal or state, as the best agent for organizing a common educational system. Often, especially immediately after the French Revolution, this was based on French models and involved a recognition that, as Rousseau had pointed out, without an established church the state would have to provide some sort of common moral teaching. During the first years of the Republic the Jeffersonians wrote much about the necessity of state educational programs and through the Jeffersonian era there were regular proposals to found a national university.

Although the involvement of the states in education was nothing new, the initial enthusiasm for such ideals in the revolutionary era soon ran into the related questions of how centralized and how secular such systems should be. Church groups, especially the Presbyterians and the Anglicans (who were down but not out), inevitably were to be the chief opponents of such state educational schemes—unless, of course, they saw prospects of taking them over.

New York State provided an early example. In the wave of revolutionary enthusiasm, the legislature in 1784 established a state "university," meaning a centralized board of regents who would establish schools and colleges in the state. The legislature also changed the name of King's College, the only actual college in the system, to the appropriately patriotic Columbia. At the reorganized college, no "preference" would be given to any religious group. Each religious denomination could name a regent, but these would be considerably outnumbered by representatives of the state's counties and major cities. In order to establish a theological faculty, any "religious body or Society of Men" could endow a professorship for the "Promotion [of its] particular religious Tenets." The progressive outlook of the reorganizers is suggested by their committee's initial nominees for president, Joseph Priestley, Richard Price, and John Jebb, three Englishmen known for their liberal religious views. These presidential nominations were quickly tabled, ostensibly because of financial concerns. In fact the whole system was unwieldy and unrealistic and soon collapsed in the face of widespread opposition. In 1787 control of colleges was returned to local hands. In New York City this meant a resumption of control of the college by competing religious interests. By 1800 Columbia once again had an Episcopal clergyman as president, though it also had a cross section of laity and clergy of other denominations, especially Presbyterian and Dutch Reformed, on its faculty and board.[3]

Jefferson ran into similar dynamics in Virginia. In 1779, when he was governor of revolutionary Virginia, Jefferson had proposed that the state take over William and Mary as part of a general system of public education. In Jefferson's view, since the church college always had been a state agency anyway, it now should conform to revolutionary principles. Jefferson's bill was not adopted. Nonetheless, in 1780 he did manage to get the college to drop its two professorships of divinity. The school, however, remained in Episcopal hands and by about 1800 it was clear to Jefferson that he would make no more progress in deflecting it from its ecclesiastical course.[4] In the meantime, the Presbyterians were in the midst of their own campaign to educate the republic. In Virginia they founded their own college, Hampden-Sydney (1783), as well as a couple of academies, making centralization of education under the state even less likely.[5]

South of Virginia, in states that previously had been largely innocent of institutions of higher education, it was easier for governments to move to fill the gap. Georgia (1785), North Carolina (1789), and South Carolina (1805) each established a state university. Even in such instances, the Jeffersonian liberal program was not unopposed. In North Carolina, for instance, Scotch-Irish Presbyterians took the lead in founding the state school. The two most influential trustee organizers were both Princeton graduates, although one of them, William Davie, was a Deist and a rationalist while the Rev. Samuel F. McCorkle was an orthodox Presbyterian.

The curriculum and regulations were patterned closely after Princeton and in 1799 another Princeton graduate, Joseph Caldwell, became head of the school. The original regulations provided for morning and evening prayers, "divine Services" each Sunday, and Sunday evening examinations "on the general principles of morality and religion," all strictly required.[6] Caldwell used the Bible as a text and the senior course in moral and mental philosophy followed closely Witherspoon's syllabus of lectures.[7] In Georgia, after a more liberal start, Presbyterians soon became entrenched on the board of trustees and that school also was run by a succession of men with Princeton connections. The strongest of these was the Rev. Moses Waddell, who became president in 1819. Waddell was dedicated to communicating "to the system of public education *the spirit of Christianity,* and insisted on "the Bible as the source and fountain of all true wisdom and government."[8]

By the early 1820s, when Jefferson was complaining about the influence of the Presbyterians, an all-out war was going on over whether American higher education would follow the Jeffersonian revolutionary model of liberal Christian leadership or be controlled by more traditional denominational interests.[9]

The most celebrated instance was the Dartmouth College case. Dartmouth had been founded in 1769 under the control of Congregationalists. In 1799 John Wheelock, the son of the founder, became president. The younger Wheelock moved away from his father's conservative religious views, and in 1815 the Board of Trustees took the drastic step of removing him and appointing a Congregational minister in his place. Wheelock's Democratic political views were apparently also at issue and Democrats hurled accusations that the old-guard Congregationalist minority was wielding unfair power by preserving the college for their own interests alone. In retaliation the state legislature, which had recently gained a Democratic majority, voted to revoke Dartmouth's charter and to make it into a "university," following the Jeffersonian revolutionary model. Jefferson himself wrote to William Plumer, the Democratic governor, congratulating him on the act. In Jefferson's view, "The idea that institutions established for the use of the nation cannot be touched nor modified, even to make them answer their end . . . may perhaps be a salutary provision against the abuses of a monarch, but is most absurd against the nation itself."[10]

The suit went to the United States Supreme court, where Daniel Webster (Dartmouth '01) pleaded his first case before the high court. Webster concluded his defense with the famed oratorical flourish: "It is, Sir, as I have said, a small College. And yet *there are those who love it.*" More to the point, Chief Justice John Marshall was a Federalist and his court ruled against the Jeffersonians. "Is education altogether in the hands of government?" Marshall asked rhetorically. "Does every teacher of youth become a public officer, and do donations for the purpose of education necessarily become public property, so far that the will of the legislature, not the will of the donor, becomes the law of the donation?" While the distinction between public and private colleges would not be fully clarified for another generation, Marshall's landmark decision was a major step in establishing the immunity of charitable corporations from state control and struck a blow in an ongoing contest for sectarian versus state higher education.[11]

The contest was proceeding on other fronts with more openly partisan religious dimensions. In Kentucky, Transylvania University at Lexington, founded in 1799, had long been the focus of an open battle between Presbyterians and liberals for control. In 1817 Presbyterian dominance came to an end with the election of Horace Holley, a Yale graduate who, however, had become a Unitarian minister. Under Holley the institution flourished, but the Presbyterians, who represented only a small minority of the state's population, were in the midst of a fierce campaign (eventually successful in 1827) to drive the Unitarian (who had an even smaller ecclesiastical constituency) from office.[12]

Thomas Jefferson and Thomas Cooper were painfully aware of what such campaigns involved. Since his retirement from national politics, Jefferson had been carefully shepherding Virginia toward accepting a state university. He began by establishing Central College; although it existed on paper only, the organizing board in 1817 invited Thomas Cooper to be its first professor. When in 1819 the Virginia Legislature finally adopted Jefferson's plan to take over Central, the question of the status of Cooper immediately arose. Though questions were raised about his drinking habits and temperament, the substantial issue was Cooper's religious beliefs. Cooper, English by birth, was a friend and protégé of Joseph Priestley and was known for his skepticism regarding traditional theology. As editor of Priestley's *Memoirs,* he had remarked, "The time seems to have arrived, when the separate existence of the human soul, the freedom of the will, and the eternal duration of future punishment, like the doctrines of the Trinity and transubstantiation, may no longer be entitled to public discussion."[13]

The Presbyterians, led by the Rev. John Rice, raised such an outcry against Cooper's beliefs that, much to Jefferson's embarrassment, they forced Cooper's resignation from the promised post. Cooper in the meantime had taken a temporary position at the University of South Carolina, which was eager to keep him on. The destruction of the keystone in his effort to build a university faculty, however, brought Jefferson's anti-Presbyterianism to full boil.

Joseph Cabell, who was Jefferson's right-hand man in the legislature managing the efforts to build a university, attempted repeatedly to explain to Jefferson that the Presbyterian objections to Cooper were not part of a general opposition to the university. What the Presbyterians were objecting to was the virtual establishment of Jefferson's own unitarian religious views. "They believe," Cabell wrote in a letter, "that the Socinians are to be installed at the University for the purpose of overthrowing the prevailing religious opinions of the country."[14] Jefferson had difficulty seeing this point. From his perspective liberal religious views appeared objective and scientific and only traditional ones appeared sectarian. Hence he saw nothing wrong with using the state to enthrone his objective scientific views.[15]

In Jefferson's principal blueprint for the university, the Rockfish Gap Report of 1818, he and his associates, while alluding to a room that might be used for worship (presumably by approved religious groups), had stated that at the state school a professor of divinity would be constitutionally inappropriate, since that would be inevitably sectarian. The report did allow, however, that principles which they regarded as common, such as proofs for the existence of God and for moral obligations "on which all sects agree," could be taught by the professor of ethics. Study of Hebrew, Greek, and Latin would also be useful to all religious groups.[16]

Cabell explained to Jefferson that these provisions also were raising the ire of Presbyterians against what they saw as an unfriendly establishment, since their own more particular theological views were being specifically excluded.[17] Jefferson, who did believe that each religious group should have the freedom to promote its own views, was apparently more sympathetic to this objection. Eventually he agreed to what he thought would be a constitutionally acceptable solution. In 1822, the report of the university's Board of Visitors suggested that each sect might build a divinity school "on the confines" of the university. Divinity students could then take courses in other disciplines at the university as well as enjoy specialized training from their sectarian theological professor. Divinity faculty could also lead worship for the various denominations within the university facilities. According to Jefferson, this remedy, "while it excludes the public authorities from the domain of religious freedom, would give to the sectarian schools of divinity the full benefit of the public provisions made for instruction in other branches of science."[18]

This solution, though not taken advantage of by the denominations, was much like that later adopted in Canada[19] and had much to recommend it in resolving the dilemma of how to have public education without either having discriminatory sectarian religious teaching or excluding religion entirely and thus discriminating against all religious views. It did nothing to address the problem of sectarian or antisectarian bias in undergraduate training, except that it did provide for some denominational worship. However, it did recognize that theology was among the sciences that belonged at a university and provided a means for its practitioners to enjoy benefits of the state-supported academic center without being directly supported by the state.[20]

The proposal to have theological seminaries on the grounds was in tune with one of the latest developments in American higher education. Prior to the nineteenth century theological training beyond what everyone received on Saturdays and Sundays at colleges had been largely a matter of informal study or apprenticeship. By the end of the revolutionary era, however, many colleges were no longer attracting and graduating ministerial candidates. Moreover, the broadening religious sentiments of the era were creating tension between the beliefs of the orthodox and what was being taught in some of the colleges. The most celebrated case was at Harvard where Henry Ware, a Unitarian, was elected Hollis Professor of Divinity in 1805. Orthodox Congregationalists of Massachusetts responded by establishing Andover Theological Seminary in 1808, dedicated by its charter to be forever committed to orthodox Calvinism. At Princeton the struggle was more subtle. The college at the turn of the century, under Samuel Stanhope Smith, was still firmly in Presbyterian control but fused Presbyterian doctrine with an enlightened spirit. The students were riotous (in 1802 they burned down the great Nassau Hall and a rebellion in 1807 brought the suspension of most of the student body) and the number of ministerial candidates was down alarmingly. In response some of the more orthodox trustees in 1812 established a theological seminary, located at Princeton, but separate from the college, and under the auspices of the Presbyterian Church.[21] Thus an important pattern of division of labor was established or reestablished. Theological seminaries could perform distinctly ecclesiastical functions, thereby making it easier for the colleges to continue in their more problematic dual role as both denominational and public institutions. During the next decade or so Episcopalians, Lutherans, Presbyterians, Congregationalists, and Unitarians all founded additional seminaries or college-related divinity schools.[22]

When the plan to encourage denominations to found seminaries on the premises of the state university was suggested to Jefferson by some "pious individuals," he adopted it both as a constitutionally viable compromise that might pacify religious opponents and also with the hope that it might help neutralize sectarianism. In his letter reporting the development to Thomas Cooper in 1822 he prefaces the report with his tirade against Presbyterian aggressiveness, quoted at the opening of this chapter. Then, after describing the plan to Cooper, he reassures his friend that the arrangement might alleviate sectarianism, "by bringing the sects together, and mixing them with the mass of other students: we shall soften their asperities, liberalize and neutralize their prejudice, and make the general religion a religion of peace, reason and morality."[23] Jefferson never lost confidence that reason would triumph over prejudice.

The tide, however, was turning against him. Thomas Cooper found this out in South Carolina in the years following Jefferson's death. Cooper, who had become president of the College of South Carolina in 1820, kept up his mentor's bitter attacks on Calvinism, differing from Jefferson only in making them fully public. In 1830 he published a pamphlet titled, *An Exposition of the Doctrines of Calvinism,* alleging of Presbyterian doctrine that there was not "from ancient or modern times, a set of tenets so absolutely, so unprovokedly cruel, blasphemous, and devilish." The Presbyterians, he said, echoing Jefferson's sentiments, were an arrogant priesthood, much like the Jesuits, who were attempting to control all the educational institutions of the land and thus become the established religion.[24]

Presbyterians and other Protestants responded true to form by organizing a campaign in 1832 to oust Cooper from the college on the charge of infidelity and undermining the faith of Christian students. Cooper answered with an eloquent plea for academic freedom, arguing that the freedom of speech guaranteed by the constitution of the South Carolina should not cease at the college doors. Moreover, he argued forcefully, it was unconstitutional for the state to impose a religious test on its college president. No doubt, he admitted, his views were unpopular with much of the school's constituency; but similar objections had been raised to the teachings of Socrates, Jesus, Wycliffe, Galileo, and others.[25]

Politics was involved in as well. Cooper was proslavery and for state's rights and the South Carolina Nullification movement. For the moment, his political allies in these locally popular stands saved him from dismissal.[26] Nonetheless, because of the adverse publicity, enrollment at the college declined sharply and the next year Cooper, now seventy-four, resigned. Technically he was a winner but in fact the religious climate in the South had so turned against the Jeffersonian outlook that a stance of open hostility to Christianity could not be sustained. As Richard Hofstadter observed, "It is perhaps significant that the boldest and most advanced argument for academic freedom to be made in the United States during the pre–Civil War period should have been made by a man in his seventies."[27] The skeptical Enlightenment's hopes for a age of reason seemed near an end.[28]

Jefferson's prediction that the work of revolutionaries might last only one generation also proved more prescient than he would have liked at the University of Virginia. Within two decades of the founder's passing, the best known professor at the university was a stalwart Presbyterian, the Rev. William H. McGuffey, elected professor of moral philosophy in 1845. McGuffey was know for his *Eclectic Readers,* which in their early editions taught explicitly Protestant principles to the nation's schoolchildren. His election at Virginia had been in response to continued attacks on the school for alleged infidelity, including objections to hiring both a Catholic and Jew. Also by this time the university was facing competition for students from seven church colleges in the state, which together enrolled a total of 550 students to the university's 122.[29] So the university was capitulating to a trend. Much as Jefferson had feared, once the Presbyterians had a firm foothold on the faculty, they could back up their stance with the weight of a strong supporting constituency in an increasingly conservative society. McGuffey instituted a successful voluntary morning prayer meeting to supplement the voluntary chapel services. In 1849, the Presbyterian chaplain for that year organized a series of lectures by an impressive group of Presbyterian divines on the scientific evidence for Christianity, in what became an important volume on the subject. For the generation of Stonewall Jackson and his ilk the Presbyterians had thus successfully placed their batteries on the high ground of Virginia infidelity. In 1859 the Presbyterians scouted the prospects for consolidating their position by being the first to establish a theological seminary on the premises. The War between the States, however, interrupted the cultural scrimmages and, for the time being, left the university simply a desolated enterprise.[30]

The cases of Thomas Cooper and of the University of Virginia epitomize the roadblock that the Jeffersonian version of American public education faced. The Jeffersonians had on their side the revolutionary principles of freedom from religious tests, even though these had not been at all consistently applied to states. At least if states had one centralized educational establishment, rather than attempting equally to encourage sectarian varieties, a religious test seemed inappropriate. Yet as opponents of the Jeffersonians were pointing out on all sides, their own views were just as sectarian and repressive of opposing opinions as anyone's else.[31] So long as Americans were deeply divided on religious opinions, equity could not be served by having any one of the minorities in a dominant role. Liberal unitarian Christian moralists were not any less a religious party than were conservative Presbyterians. At least so the Presbyterians successfully argued. Furthermore, the public would not support a takeover by one religious group. Lacking any consistent alternative, the only solution was to find a compromise of views sufficiently inoffensive to avoid alienating any major segment of prevailing public opinion. In the case of nineteenth-century America this would have to be some sort of awkward blend of Christian and Enlightenment views. Traditionalist Protestants would have to demonstrate that they were just as enlightened and nonsectarian as the Jeffersonians claimed to be. To do so they would have to borrow pages from the Jeffersonian book.

Notes

1. Thomas Jefferson to Thomas Cooper, November 1, 1822, from selection in *American Higher Education: A Documentary History*, Vol. I, Richard Hofstadter and Wilson Smith, eds. (Chicago: University of Chicago Press, 1961), 395–96.

2. Jefferson to William Short, April 13, 1820, from excerpt in Robert M. Healey, *Jefferson on Religion in Public Education* (New Haven: Yale University Press, 1962), 236. Cf. equally vitriolic remarks to Cooper, March 13, 1820, excerpt on 235.

3. David C. Humphrey, *From King's College to Columbia 1746–1800* (New York: Columbia University Press, 1976), 269–82. A similar development took place in Pennsylvania in 1779, when the state took over the College of Philadelphia, renaming it the University of Pennsylvania. In 1789 the school was returned to its original trustees under the direction of the Anglican provost William Smith, who had been displaced in 1779. The religious dimensions of this conflict, how-

ever, were less clear, since the college was always more secular than its counterparts, a factor that may have contributed to its languishing for a half century after the Revolution. Edward Potts Cheyney, *History of the University of Pennsylvania, 1740–1940* (Philadelphia: University of Pennsylvania Press, 1940), 129–216.

4. Healey, *Jefferson on Religion,* 210–13. Philip Alexander Bruce, *History of the University of Virginia, 1819–1919,* Vol. I (New York: Macmillan, 1920), 45–55.

5. On Presbyterian college founding see Howard Miller, *The Revolutionary College: American Presbyterian Higher Education, 1707–1837* (New York: New York University Press, 1976), esp. 123–28, 145–49.

6. University of North Carolina, Trustee Minutes, February 6, 1795. I am grateful to Roger Robins for his research on this topic. See also Donald Robert Come, "The Influence of Princeton on Higher Education in the South before 1825," *William and Mary Quarterly,* 3rd ser., 2 (October 1945), 378–87.

7. Kemp P. Battle, *History of the University of North Carolina,* Vol. I (Raleigh: Edwards & Broughton, 1907), 42, 240.

8. Quoted in Come, "Influence of Princeton," 395. By the end of Waddell's administration, even the Baptists were complaining that the school had been turned into a sectarian Presbyterian enterprise. Thomas G. Dyer, *The University of Georgia: A Bicentennial History, 1785–1985* (Athens: University of Georgia Press, 1895), 31–32.

9. When the Presbyterians asked for state support they emphasized the inclusive and nonsectarian nature of their enterprise. Miller, *Revolutionary College,* 149–59.

10. Jefferson to Plumer, July 21, 1816, quoted in *The Colleges and the Public, 1787–1862,* Theodore Rawson Crane, ed. (New York: Teachers College Press, 1963), 64. See also the views of Isaac Hill and William Plumer, in excerpts, 61–66. Also see Donald G. Tewksbury, *The Founding of American Colleges and Universities before the Civil War: With Particular Reference to the Religious Influences Bearing upon the College Movement* (New York, 1932), 148–52. Richard Hofstadter and Walter P. Metzger, *The Development of Academic Freedom in the United States* (New York: Columbia University Press, 1955), 219–20.

11. Hofstadter and Smith, *American Higher Education,* 202–19, for Webster defense and Marshall decision, quotation, 216. Historical debate about interpretations of the Dartmouth decision have centered around whether it was clearly a private versus public issue and about whether concerns for religious orthodoxy were primary in the dispute. See the "Forum" between John S. Whitehead and Jurgen Herbst, "How to Think about the Dartmouth College Case," *History of Education Quarterly* 26 (Fall 1986), 333–49.

12. Hofstadter and Metzger, *Academic Freedom,* 248–51. Cf. Miller, *Revolutionary College,* 236–44.

13. Quoted from Priestley's *Memoirs,* I:335, in Healey, *Jefferson on Religion,* 233. See also Dumas Malone, *The Public Life of Thomas Cooper, 1783–1839* (New Haven: Yale University Press, 1926), 234–47.

14. Cabell to Jefferson, August 5, 1821, quoted in Healey, *Jefferson on Religion,* 237.

15. Healey, *Jefferson on Religion,* argues for this interpretation, describing Jefferson as a "Unitarian evangelist" (244). Jefferson was convinced that religion was important to a republic but wanted it to be the right sort of religion, which he regarded as nonsectarian (257).

16. Jefferson et al., Report of the Rockfish Gap Commission (1818), reprinted

in Hofstadter and Smith, *American Higher Education,* 193–99, quotation, 198. Cf. discussion in Healey, *Jefferson on Religion,* 217–19.

17. Healey, *Jefferson on Religion,* 239.

18. Report of Board of Visitors, University of Virginia, October 7, 1822, quoted in Healey, *Jefferson on Religion,* 220.

19. See D. C. Masters, *Protestant Church Colleges in Canada: A History* (Toronto: University of Toronto Press, 1966). The most notable example of this arrangement is at the University of Toronto.

20. As an alternative, James Madison, Jefferson's successor as rector, suggested a plan, eventually adopted, of having chaplains appointed yearly rotating from the four major Protestant denominations.

In 1859 Presbyterians explored starting a theological school at the university, but the Civil War deflected the plan. Philip Alexander Bruce, *History of the University of Virginia, 1819–1919,* Vol. II (New York: Macmillan, 1920), 368–71.

21. Mark A. Noll, *Princeton and the Republic, 1768–1822* (Princeton: Princeton University Press, 1989).

22. For an interpretive overview see Glenn T. Miller, *Piety and Intellect: The Aims and Purposes of Ante-Bellum Theological Education* (Atlanta: Scholars Press, 1990). By 1832 there were already twenty-two theological seminaries. Lawrence A. Cremin, *American Education: The National Experience, 1783–1876* (New York: Harper & Row, 1980), 400.

23. Jefferson to Cooper, November 2, 1822, quoted in Healey, *Jefferson on Religion,* 224.

24. Quoted and summarized in Malone, *Cooper,* 342–43.

25. *Dr Cooper's Defense before the Board of Trustees of South Carolina College* (1832), reprinted in Hofstadter and Smith, *American Higher Education,* 396–417.

26. Malone, *Cooper,* 360.

27. Hofstadter and Metzger, *Academic Freedom,* 269.

28. Henry F. May, *The Enlightenment in America* (New York: Oxford University Press, 1976), 307–36, provides an account of the decline of the skeptical Enlightenment, especially in the South.

29. Albea Godbold, *The Church College of the Old South* (Durham, N.C.: Duke University Press, 1944), 162.

30. Bruce, *University of Virginia,* III:133–37; II:368–69.

31. E.g., Malone, *Cooper,* 345 and passim.

4

A Righteous Consensus, Whig Style

By midcentury Jeffersonian "infidelity" was being outgunned across the entire front of American higher education. One index was that the most formidable intellectual strongholds of the day were theological seminaries. These schools were in the forefront of American professional education and offered about the only American opportunity for anything resembling graduate education. The leading seminaries, especially those in the Presbyterian-Congregationalist axis, published redoubtable and well-edited theological quarterlies which were the forums for most of the nation's major academic debates. The momentous struggle over Calvinism and its various modifications overshadowed everything else and preoccupied most of the ablest academic minds of the era.

Despite the strengths of the theological enterprise, the perennial debates over Calvinism nonetheless signaled an intellectual sea change. Except within the Reformed (Calvinist) denominations themselves, it seemed as though everyone from Unitarians to populist revivalists was trashing Calvinists doctrines as absurd and unreasonably harsh in an enlightened and benevolent age.[1] Even within the Reformed churches the shifting cultural sentiments were taking their toll by midcentury. The tradition's most exclusivist versions, which had emphasized the totality of God's sovereignty, were under widespread attack and beginning to give way to modifications more congenial to democratic ideals of free choice and moral responsibility.[2] Some critics were challenging the theological profession as such. Harriet Beecher Stowe is a striking example. Tied to the theological heritage by birth and by marriage, yet as a woman excluded from formal theological education, Stowe did more than anyone to establish the novel as an alternative forum for religious debate. In *The Minister's Wooing* (1859), for instance, she directly attacked not only Calvinism but any teachings that tied eternal salvation to correct theological belief. Like many of the middle class of her generation, she was becoming convinced that the essence of Christianity was moral character, not divisive doctrines.

The proliferation of American colleges during this era can be better understood in the context of such theological debates and debates about theology's place. For one thing, the professionalization of theology in theological seminaries and divinity schools helped free colleges to emphasize other concerns, such as morality. This trend was reinforced by American social realities. While most of the new colleges were church-related, each typically had to serve a public beyond its own denomination. The very religious diversity of the American context thus was pushing American collegiate education in seemingly contradictory directions. On the one hand the decentralized atmosphere was conducive to free enterprise and sectarian rivalry. Each denomination started its own colleges. At the same time this centrifugal force toward fragmentation was always being countered by centripetal forces which fostered a degree of uniformity. No matter what the denominational identity and the theological issues in its background, each Protestant college had to deal with more or less the same American market. In such a free enterprise system a strong emphasis on theological distinctions could limit a college's constituency and be a competitive disadvantage. Hence each college was more likely to emphasize the socially unifying aspects of its Christian tradition, especially its moral benefits, rather than theological peculiarities.

The pace of American college founding during this era was phenomenal. Many of the new enterprises were like the seed that fell on rocky ground in the biblical parable, which sprouted quickly but soon withered in the sun. Fledgling colleges or collegiate institutes were planned everywhere. In the pre–Civil War era over five hundred were founded or at least founded on paper, although perhaps only two hundred survived into the twentieth century. Determining what to include in a count of colleges is difficult, since some of the schools offered primarily, or sometimes exclusively, precollegiate training. Still the total by 1860 was remarkable when compared to the nine colonial institutions. Probably two-fifths of the surviving institutions were founded under either Presbyterian or Congregationalist auspices. In Jefferson's day, such Calvinist schools had been well over half, but since then the larger Methodist and Baptist denominations had advanced socially and were taking an interest in higher education, adding to the craze for college founding, which accelerated sharply after 1830. Catholics also became active founders, especially after 1850.[3]

The typical educational patterns that emerged fit the unique American situation. Free enterprise was triumphing over earlier efforts toward centralization. In part the predominant decentralization was a matter of geography and the frontier conditions in the vast, new, and sparsely settled nation. Transportation was poor and colleges were objects of local community pride. Every town, it seemed, wanted one. Churches were well prepared to move into this vacuum, performing their traditional functions as educational leaders, providing community service, and accruing some advantages to their denomination. As was traditionally the case, colleges did not have religious tests for their students and the lines between church-private and public were not clearly drawn. This broader inter-Protestant nonsectarianism was necessitated by localism. Denominational identifications, in fact, may have become more significant later in the century as transportation improved and each school could cultivate wider regional loyalties from its own group.[4]

Though oriented to community as well as to church, the schools clearly were religious institutions. In 1840 four-fifths of the college presidents of denominationally related colleges were clergymen, as were two-thirds of state college presidents. Other faculty and tutors might be clergy as well, although clerical dominance was not nearly as overwhelming as in colonial days. The professoriate had only begun to be differentiated as a distinct profession. Natural sciences were being added to curricula and some specialists were appearing in those fields. Most faculty members, however, were expected to be generalists who could teach almost anything. Even if they were not clergymen, they were expected to be pious. Faculty members, particularly residential tutors, were supposed to keep a close eye on the students since the college was expected to act in loco parentis in maintaining Christian behavior among its charges. The most explicitly religious requirements were attendance at daily chapel and Sunday religious services.[5]

Broadly Christian concerns were also worked into parts of the curriculum. The natural sciences, for instance, were typically taught "doxologically," emphasizing the design in nature for which one should praise the creator. Students typically learned "evidences of Christianity" or "natural theology" which reinforced this point. William Paley's *Natural Theology* (1802), containing the famous argument that if we discovered a watch we could be sure there was a watchmaker, was a popular text. Since belief in the deity was essential to establishing a moral order, such apologetic concerns were closely related to courses in moral philosophy, taught usually by the president in the senior year. Moral philosophy now was firmly established as the capstone of the program, providing without apparent sectarian bias a moral base for Christian civilization building.[6]

The moral philosophy courses were attractive, wide-ranging, and long-lived. One of the most vivid accounts comes from the latter days of their dominance, from a survey of American colleges by G. Stanley Hall, published in 1879:

> The most vigorous and original philosophical instruction is almost everywhere given in ethics, though like nearly all other subjects it is taught from text-books. . . . The work with text-books is commonly supplemented by lectures where ethical principles are applied to law, to trade, art, conduct, &c., in a more or less hortatory manner. The grounds of moral obligation are commonly deduced from Revelation, supplemented by the intuitions of conscience, which are variously interpreted. The practical questions of daily life are often discussed in the class-room with the professor with great freedom, detail and interest. Current social or political topics are sometimes introduced, and formal debates by students appointed beforehand by the professor, and followed by his comments, may occasionally take the place of regular recitations and lectures.[7]

While moral philosophy had established its popularity in American collegiate studies in the first half of the nineteenth century, the classics still made up most of the curriculum. The rationale for this continuing emphasis was consistent with broadly Christian moral concerns. The classics were useful for development of human faculties, both intellectual and moral.

This ideal was definitively expressed in the famous Yale Report of 1828. Not only was Yale one of the oldest colleges, its several hundred students also made it one of the largest. During the national era it had emerged as the leading model for colleges with evangelical ties.

The premise of the Yale Report was that the human personality was made up of various faculties of which reason and conscience were the highest.[8] These faculties could be developed by exercise, much like physical strength. At the same time the development of these faculties must be balanced. So the goal of education was "to maintain such a proportion between the different branches of literature and science, as to form in the student a proper *balance* of character." Drawing on the analogy to physical development, the report argued that "as the bodily frame is brought to its highest perfection, not by one simple and uniform motion, but by a variety of exercises, so the mental faculties are expanded, and invigorated, and adapted to each other, by familiarity with different departments of science."

The classics formed the core of this balanced character-building education. While they needed to be supplemented with modern natural science and moral science, they contained wisdom, elevated tastes, and exercised a variety of mental faculties. "It must be obvious to the most cursory observer," the report argued, "that the classics afford materials to exercise talent of every degree, from the first opening of the youthful intellect to the period of its highest maturity. The range of classical study extends from the elements of language, to the most difficult questions arising from literary research and criticism."[9]

Most American college builders, however, were heirs to the Great Awakening as well as to classicism, Enlightenment moralism, and formal Christian practice. In the New Light tradition colleges were also part of a larger missionary and evangelistic enterprise. So it was natural for evangelical clergymen at these colleges to seek revival among their students, and during the era from the Revolution to the Civil War many college revivals took place. These revivals, however, were not routine. Even at the institutions where they were most frequent, they were likely to occur no more than once in a given student's career. When they did, classes might be canceled for days as the time of prayer and renewal continued. Annual days of prayer, however, were common parts of the college year, always with the hope for spectacular spiritual outpourings.[10]

Yale was also the leading model of this New Light missionary spirit in American collegiate education. In 1802 President Timothy Dwight, grandson of Jonathan Edwards and successor to Ezra Stiles, preached a series of sermons refuting Enlightenment infidelity. Unexpectedly, a major revival broke out, in which a third of the Yale students professed conversion. The Yale revival had symbolic importance for sparking the New England wing of what became known as the Second Great Awakening. During the next decades Yale and Connecticut became major staging grounds for organizing a formidable phalanx of agencies, missionary and reform societies, that set out to evangelize and transform the nation.[11] Such efforts were closely related to Yale's strategic social position. Connecticut Yankee emigrants were in the forefront of settling western New York State and the upper Midwest. Not only did they take with them the New England Puritan heritage; they did so with a missionary zeal to shape the West in their own image.

In such efforts New Englanders were in close alliance with like-minded Presbyterians. Many New Englanders, in fact, became Presbyterians when they moved west. New York City, where Congregationalism had long since merged into Presbyterianism, was also a center for many of the national agencies. By the 1830s the combined budgets of the agencies of this "united evangelical front" rivaled that of the federal government. In an era when voluntarism reigned, New Englanders and their allies had appropriated for themselves the role of chief religious and moral agents in civilizing the nation.

Educational leadership was one service that New Englanders had to offer the new settlements and college revivals were crucial to producing and motivating educated leaders for the missionary enterprise. Conversion of young men was, in fact, one of the common rationales for promoting and sustaining colleges. For instance, the Society for the Promotion of Collegiate and Theological Education at the West (SPCTEW), which with its founding in 1843 became the principal agency in the Presbyterian-Congregational network for college founding, always kept the well-documented benefits of college revival prominent in its promotional literature.[12]

The larger mission of the colleges was the civilizing task of spreading Protestant Christendom into the untamed wilds. Lyman Beecher, a protégé of Dwight's and a founder of the SPCTEW, is justly famed for articulating this motive in his *Plea for the West* of 1835. Noting that the millennium was likely to start from America, Beecher urged that "if this nation is, in the providence of God, destined to lead the way in the moral and political emancipation of the world, it is time she understood her high calling, and were harnessed for the work." The West was the key to the American empire and hence the territory to which its religious and civil ideals must be transmitted. Specifically, what the West most needed was "universal education, and moral culture, by institutions commensurate to the result." Education, Beecher argued to audiences who were facing the uncertainties of the Jacksonian revolution, was essential if republican institutions were to survive universal suffrage. Moreover, the education of the West could not be achieved simply by sending an army of teachers from the East. It must be accomplished through western institutions themselves, colleges and theological seminaries. Schools such as Lane Theological Seminary in Cincinnati, where Beecher was president, would train the most talented men in the region.[13] Educational institutions, in Beecher's view, would determine who controlled the West.

The great fear, the flames of which Beecher did his best to fan, was that Catholics would take over the West. Much of his *Plea* was a fervid effort to document a conspiracy of the alliance of Catholic ecclesiastical power and Romanist European despots to capture the American West through massive Catholic immigration, fortified by Catholic centers for higher education. Disclaiming any intention to discriminate against Catholics, Beecher assured that he would welcome them if they just acted like other American denominations. "Let the Catholics mingle with us as Americans, and come with their children under the fell action of our common schools and republican institutions, and we are prepared cheerfully to abide the consequences." The problem with the Catholics, Beecher insisted, was political. They were determined to unite church and state into a single antirepublican despotism.

Recognizing that some Americans had alleged similar ambitions of Presbyterian and Congregationalist Calvinists (even comparing them to Jesuits, he might have added), Beecher argued that the record demonstrated the opposite. Calvinists, he said, had since the Reformation and the days of the Puritans always been on the side of liberty. Catholics, on the other hand, were almost invariably associated with tyranny and opposed to republicanism. One only had to look at the antirevolutionary, antirepublican Catholicism of contemporary Europe to confirm this. On the other hand, so long as Americans retained separation of church and state, said Beecher, it was impossible that they had anything to fear from Calvinists.[14]

The Whig Ideal

Beecher's outlook was a typical expression of the Whig cultural ideal of mid-nineteenth-century New England. Such "conscience Whigs," who played an important role in the Whig political party and in later Republicanism, were both heirs to the Puritan heritage and builders of modern civilization. Civilization building, in their view, was as much a moral task as a material one. It required both principled leadership from government and the training of strong, disciplined individuals.[15]

This outlook was closely related to their Protestant and republican heritage. In New England republican and Whig rhetoric dating back to the American Revolution, Protestantism was identified with the advances of civilization and the cause of freedom. Freedom in this outlook meant not only political freedom and personal liberties derived from higher moral law but also the free inquiry necessary for modern science. Catholicism, by contrast, represented absolutism, suppression of individual development, and suppression of free inquiry.

The advance of morally responsible education was accordingly part of the Protestant and Whig program, so that Whigs became the educators of the nation. Such New Englanders, Unitarians as well as Trinitarians, wrote most of the nation's textbooks, championed public schools, and with a missionary spirit helped carry the zeal for founding colleges to towns and hamlets through much of the nation. Next to religion, education was the best means of taming an unruly populace and assimilating diverse peoples into a common culture with shared ideals. Education would develop the individual sense of duty and a national conscience.

Science and Protestant religion went hand in hand, since both stood for free inquiry versus prejudice and arbitrary authority. Francis Bacon, the seventeenth-century progenitor of the ideal, was high among the saints in the American Protestant hierarchy. Praise for Bacon's nonspeculative, nonmetaphysical down-to-earth methods knew few bounds.[16] Neither the natural order nor the moral order was a matter of sectarian doctrine; rather, both were of divine creation, open for all to see. The candid inquirer had nothing to fear from a disciplined search for the truth.

What is fascinating is that Calvinist educators like Lyman Beecher, who embodied this Whig outlook, insisted just as much as had the Jeffersonians before them that they were not a sect. They represented, rather, in their own view, simply the essence of Americanism, combining its highest political, moral, and religious ideals to which others might be fairly expected to conform.[17]

Whig educators could thus take over the Jeffersonian agenda of building a public educational system. In the Midwest, for instance, there was much discussion, for many of the same reasons that Beecher had raised, of the need for the states to organize educational systems to help bring order to the frontiers. State colleges or "universities" were to be the capstones of such state systems. Between 1828 and 1848 Indiana, Michigan, Kentucky, Missouri, Iowa, and Wisconsin chartered such publicly supported institutional higher learning. With the secular Jeffersonian ideology by this time battered and on the defensive, and the Methodists and Baptists still seen as poor relations just beginning to value education, the obvious, experienced, and well-qualified candidates for leadership in such state-sponsored enterprises were the moderate Presbyterians and Congregationalists.

In Michigan, for example, the founders of the new university addressed the question of sectarianism directly, and in a way that would hardly have pleased the Jeffersonians. Rather than excluding Christian teaching, they decided to try to rotate professorships among the major Protestant denominations.[18] This they saw as fairer than establishing irreligion. By this time it had become commonplace to point out, as the Presbyterians had in Virginia, that, as the Michigan Regents put it in 1841, "Attempts made to exclude all religious influence whatever from the college, have only rendered them the sectarian of an atheistical or infidel party or faction." Since, on the other hand, "the great mass of the population profess an attachment to Christianity," there "is common ground occupied by them, all-sufficient for cooperation in an institution of learning, and for the presence of a religious influence, devoid of any sectarian forms and peculiarities." All that was needed was "men to be found in all different Christian sects of sufficiently expanded views, and liberal spirit, and enlightened minds, devoid of the spirit of bigotry and narrow prejudices of sect." The guarantees would have to be informal. Such men of open-minded spirit would "furnish the best and only true guarantee against the evils of sectarianism."[19]

The statement was drafted by the Rev. George Duffield, a prominent Presbyterian pastor in Detroit. Duffield was typical of the shapers of American education. He was from among the first families of Presbyterians, being the grandson and namesake of the chaplain to the Revolutionary Army. He was also a "New School" Presbyterian. New School Presbyterianism had been shaped largely by its alliance with Congregationalists in the campaigns to create a nonsectarian Protestantism that could serve to shape the national ethos.

In 1837 and 1838 the New School had separated from the Old School Presbyterians, resulting in two denominations of comparable size, each claiming the same name, the Presbyterian Church in the U.S.A. Duffield, along with Lyman Beecher and others, had been prominent in the bitter controversies that preceded the schism. Though a number of points had been at issue, they all involved the question of how American as opposed to how distinctly Presbyterian the denomination would be. The New School, which had its strength in the Yankee alliance with the Congregationalists, prided itself on representing "American Presbyterianism." It softened Calvinist doctrines and had built the empire of agencies that were to evangelize, reform, and educate the nation. The Old School, predominantly Scotch-Irish in constituency, insisted on maintaining distinctive Presbyterian traditions, regardless of American trends. They brought New School leaders to trial on charges of heresy and insisted that the only proper agency for missions, education, and reform was the denomination itself. The Old School, which had much more strength in the South than did the New School, resisted especially cooperation in antislavery societies. Most Old Schoolers were Democrats, most New Schoolers were Whigs. Politics, however, was far from the only divisive issue. Americanism, of the New England Whig variety, was at stake. And in 1841 New School leaders like Duffield could see themselves as having resisted sectarianism, thus putting themselves in the forefront for building a broad Protestant America.

Whig Educational Ideals: The Common School

The questions at stake for the colleges are illuminated if we put them in the broader context of the major educational reforms of the era, the quest for common schools. Often as in Michigan the two educational levels were directly related, as state higher education was expected to be part of a more comprehensive state-run educational system.

The model for state-regulated common schools came from Massachusetts under the leadership of Horace Mann, secretary of the new state board of education from 1837 to 1848. Mann had been raised in a strict Calvinist environment under the preaching of the rigorous Edwardsean Nathaniel Emmons. In reaction, he had become a Unitarian and considered Calvinist education an "unspeakable calamity."[20] As a crusader for the benefits to the republic of universal public education, Mann sounded much like Jefferson. In his reforms Mann succeeded in centralizing and standardizing the previously localized and uneven Massachusetts common schools.

At first orthodox Calvinist critics in the state raised the standard cry against the Jeffersonians that Mann was attempting to establish irreligion. Mann, however, disarmed many of his critics by emphasizing the religious and moral dimensions of the common schools. He insisted on the importance of "daily reading of the Bible, devotional exercises, and the constant inculcation of the precepts of Christian morality in all the Public schools."[21] Such religious training, he was convinced, could overcome the charges of both sectarianism and irreligion. After all, the Bible could "speak for itself" and "if this bible is in the schools, how can it be said that Christianity is excluded from the schools?"[22]

While some of the stricter orthodox continued to point out that religion with Christ and a doctrine of salvation left out was different from traditional Christianity,[23] Mann continued to outflank them with his insistence on the Bible and morality in the schools. In a public forum, how could such pieties be construed as impious?

Mann indeed saw a religious role for the schools and could wax eloquent, drawing on the millennial expectations of the day; for example, "the universal diffusion and ultimate triumph of all-glorious Christianity itself must await the time when knowledge shall be diffused among men through the instrumentality of good schools."[24] The goals of civilization, education, and Christianity were thus fused into a public piety. As many have pointed out, with the disestablishment of the church in the United States, educational reformers looked to the school to assume its civilizing function. The religion they would teach would blend the history and ideals of the Christian republic, the Bible, and English literature, inculcating a broadly Christian morality.[25]

Transparent in the common school enterprise was its anti-Romanism. Mann as much as Lyman Beecher feared the Catholic threat, but in the East the urgency was heightened by the prospect of social disruption created by the rapidly rising urban masses of the poor and uneducated, mostly Catholics. The leaders of American educational reform were, in short, determined to have unified public educational systems in which solid citizens (i.e., Protestants, especially Whigs) would be in control. The issue became perfectly clear as Catholic leaders in both Massachusetts and New York bitterly opposed Protestant efforts to impose a single educational system. Catholics not only objected to such practices as the reading of the Protestant version of the Bible or reciting the Ten Commandments in Protestant form but also, more substantially, to the idea that the Bible could "speak for itself." Catholic doctrine said just the opposite. The Bible was to be understood under the guidance of church authority. The idea that children should "judge for themselves" was not neutral, as it sounded, but a sectarian Protestant doctrine.[26]

The issue of whether governments might encourage multiple school systems, including those under denominational control, had been well tested and rejected by the Protestant majorities. In New York City, for instance, the practice until the early nineteenth century had been for the state to help fund schools regardless of their denominational attachments. In 1825 the practice was terminated in reaction to the granting of funds to an aggressively sectarian Baptist school. The city-funded schools, still primarily for the poor, were, however, declared Christian and nonsectarian. Soon the increasingly formidable Catholic population raised the issue again, asking for state funds for Catholic schools. Amid much controversy, heightened by the anti-Catholic agitations of the 1840s, Protestants rejected the suggestion, insisting all the more adamantly on the nonsectarianism of the emerging state school system.[27] Massachusetts experienced similar controversies.

Among the Whig Protestants, the alternative of giving equal privilege to Catholics was hardly given serious consideration. Their most admired model for education at all levels was Prussia, a Protestant state. Professor Calvin Stowe, Lyman Beecher's son-in-law, traveled to Prussia in 1837 and issued the most influential account of the virtues of Prussian education. His account of the moral and religious character sounded the old refrain: "Its morality is pure and elevated, its religion entirely removed from the narrowness of sectarian bigotry. . . . If it can be done in Prussia, I know it can be done in Ohio."[28] Stowe was impressed by the nonsectarianism of the successful Prussian merger of Lutheran and Reformed churches. What he left vague, however, was that Prussian state schools could explicitly be either Protestant or Catholic.[29]

At the national level the most formidable Protestant dissent from the growing nonsectarian educational consensus came from the Old School Presbyterians. In 1847 the Old School General Assembly urged its congregations to establish parochial schools. By 1855 Old School Presbyterians had built a system of one hundred schools in twenty-six states.[30] In the debate that led to the establishment of the Old School system, Charles Hodge, the Achilles of Old School theologians, observed that the Presbyterian opponents of parochial schools typically claimed that the spirit of the age favored common schooling and that Presbyterians could be leaders in shaping it. The sectarianism of a separate school system, the opponents further alleged, would be disastrous to national influence. Hodge countered these arguments, however, by pointing out that a common school system would not be able to teach the distinct doctrines of Christianity but "merely natural religion" or "religion in general." The new public system, said Hodge, was leading schools to concentrate on secular subjects and ultimately was "infidel in its whole tendency" and hence discriminatory against those who wanted distinctly Christian education for their children.[31]

The Old School Presbyterians were fighting a losing battle. Pious nonsectarianism seemed to most Protestants ideally suited to resolve the impasse between infidelity and sectarianism in the republic. The New School Presbyterians and their allies, for instance, led in promoting the compromise. Most of the "friends of education" who organized common schooling in various states during the middle decades of the century were Congregationalists or Presbyterians, and many were clergy.[32] The fact that Horace Mann, one of the initiators of the ideal, was a Unitarian was not a major concern. Mann, after all, was in Massachusetts. What was not much noticed, except by critics such as Hodge, was that the religion that was taught was essentially Unitarian dogma, emphasizing the commonly held doctrines of God as creator and Christian morality.

The public schools thus became part of the united Protestant mission to the nation. Catharine Beecher, one of Lyman's renowned daughters, envisioned an army of single women teachers, the Protestant equivalent to Catholic nuns, civilizing the nation. Her leadership did much toward transforming elementary teaching into a woman's profession. The doctrines of the younger Beechers, including Harriet and Henry Ward, were more moderate than Lyman's. Conversion was less of an issue, and growth in Christian morality and American civility were more central concerns. Horace Bushnell's *Christian Nurture* (1847), which argued for these values, was characteristic of progressive views of Congregationalist and New School leadership by the 1850s. Such leaders were cultural imperialists, who nonetheless stood on high moral ground, as on the slavery issue. They could say with Bushnell in 1853: "We have had the common school as a fundamental institution from the first—in our view a Protestant institution. . . . We are still, as Americans, a Protestant people." To those who demanded their own schools, he retorted, "No! take your place with us in our common schools, and consent to be Americans, or else go back to Turkey, where Mohammedans, Greeks, Armenians, Jews are walled up by the laws themselves, forbidding them ever to pass over or change their superstitions." Lack of acquaintance among diverse religious groups, Bushnell feared, would only perpetuate the religious-ethnic animosities so prevalent in Old World cultures.[33]

Such assimilationist ideals necessitated the steady toning down of distinctly Christian teachings in the public sphere. The history of William McGuffey's readers provides a succinct illustration. Prior to his professorship in Virginia, McGuffey had been an ordained Presbyterian college educator in Ohio and promoter of a common school system there. Among his close associates were the Beechers and the Stowes. In the mid-1830s a textbook publisher asked Catharine Beecher to compile elementary readers for common schools. Catharine, who was preoccupied with female education at the time, apparently suggested McGuffey for the task. In 1837 he produced the first edition of his books. These spoke of God's creation and Providence, the insignificance of the world, the sinfulness of humans, the primacy of salvation through Christ for the next life, and the necessity of righteousness and piety in this life. Though McGuffey's early volumes sold widely, they were far surpassed by later editions, which he no longer controlled. By the 1879 editions all the earlier emphases on Christian salvation and piety had disappeared. The stories now emphasized the rugged Victorian virtues of hard work and self-denial as keys to success. Of biblical selections, only the Sermon on the Mount and the Protestant version of the Lord's Prayer remained.[34]

The Colleges

The American college situation was, of course, different from that of the common schools. American higher education was more thoroughly diverse and decentralized and likely to remain so. Most Protestant colleges sought to evangelize their students and retained some sectarian religious practice. Pressures to drop such distinctive practices in favor of exclusive emphasis on broad Christian moralism were not as immediate or as sweeping as in common schools and counterefforts were more apparent.

Nevertheless, the rise of the common schools casts light on the outlook of those who were shaping American education. The most immediate analogues to the common schools' ideology were in the emerging state universities. Protestant educational leaders presumed that such state institutions could be both Protestant and nonsectarian, much like public schools. More or less the same type of people were involved in building most of the private colleges. While one force shaping such colleges was indeed the impulse to promote denominational loyalties, another contrary force was a deep commitment among the leadership to establish a nonsectarian public philosophy, much as in the common schools.

Common Sense

Such a public philosophy required an intellectual rationale. This was essential to an age that revered science and reason. And such a rationale arose out of the peculiar American revolutionary synthesis of evangelical Christianity, the Enlightenment, science, republican principles, and morality. The moral science of the eighteenth century had emerged as fundamental dogma built on appeals to self-evidence. This outlook, taught in college moral philosophy courses, was closely tied to the broader development of Scottish philosophy, known collectively as the philosophy of Common Sense. This philosophy was considered supremely scientific and universal and hence ideally suited to producing good citizens whose fundamental beliefs went beyond sectarianism. "Common sense" was also a revolutionary slogan and so could be popularized as a appeal to democratic sentiments. By 1830 Common Sense philosophy seemed to have swept everything before it in American intellectual life.

The character of the American Revolution, which wed Enlightenment ideals and dissenting Protestantism, best accounts for this triumph. The revolutionary principles, to which all major parties in America were in one way or another dedicated, were viewed as embodying the epitome of human morality grounded in universal self-evident, or commonsensical, principles. These principles were not only seen as supremely rational or scientific; they were also assumed to be congruent with true Christian morality. Behind such assumptions was the premise that God's revelation in Nature and Nature's law must be consistent with any true revelation in Scripture.

In postrevolutionary America, then, it was a widely shared article of faith that science, common sense, morality, and true religion were firmly allied. Various parties disagreed on exactly how the argument concluded. All the major Protestant parties agreed that commonsensically based scientific understanding of God's revelation in Nature confirmed his revelation in Scripture. They disagreed sharply, however, on how much weight to give to reason and to Scripture when there was apparent conflict. Nonetheless, everyone, it seemed, from Campbellites to Unitarians, from Old School Presbyterians to Jeffersonians, was in the same debate. Moreover, all were convinced that in fair controversy universal truth would eventually flourish.

The first principles for this scientific worldview were derived largely from the Scottish Enlightenment, especially in its later, more intellectualist formulation provided by Thomas Reid (1710–1796). Reid, in answering David Hume's skepticism, emphasized that there were a host of foundational beliefs, such as one's personal identity, the existence of other minds, consistency of nature, verifiable empirical data, and beliefs based on reliable testimony, as well as necessary truths of mathematics and logic, that all normal people (i.e., except philosophers and the insane) could not help believing. A firm science of human behavior could be founded on such unquestionable principles and eventually, through careful inductive reasoning, all philosophical disputes should simply be settled.[35]

Such views found fertile soil in the new nation. For one thing, they appealed to the practical and antimetaphysical bent of popular American thought and conceptions of science. For another, since the new nation was cut off from England and suspicious of France after its revolution, Americans found in Scotland the most congenial resources for defining a national outlook. This dependence on Scotland was strongest until about the 1820s, after which a few younger Americans began looking to Protestant Germany for alternatives. By that time, however, Scottish models had a firm hold on American higher education.

In the colleges, Common Sense philosophy combined with celebrations of the inductive methods of Bacon, was especially useful as a tool of apologetics. Those who won the battle to dominate American higher education had won against the forces of the skeptical Enlightenment.[36] In their own view, this victory was through force of argument. Modern science and rationality, they argued at length to their students, were really on the side of Christianity and the Bible. Scottish epistemology reinforced strategies that had already taken firm hold. The two most common texts were Bishop Joseph Butler's *The Analogy of Religion, Natural and Revealed* (1736) and William Paley's *Natural Theology* (1802). Both authors were ardent empiricists. Each argued, as was common to the era, that empirical questions must be settled by accumulating evidences that, like the many strands that make a rope, would establish an inescapable probability that amounted to virtual certainty.[37]

Mark Hopkins, famed teacher at Williams College in Massachusetts, provides a classic compilation of such arguments in his own textbook on *Evidences of Christianity* (1846). "If God has made a revelation in one mode," he says, echoing Bishop Butler, "it must coincide with what he has revealed in another." If Christianity was true, it would harmonize with the other facts of the universe. Standing on this ground, Hopkins claimed to show that "the Christian religion admits of certain proof." Human sinfulness, which creates a moral resistance to Christianity's claims, can blind us or at least incline us toward skepticism, but such prejudices can be put aside if we look at the evidence "in the position of an impartial jury." "This course alone," says Hopkins in typical Baconian rhetoric, "decides nothing on the grounds of previous hypothesis, but yields itself entirely to the guidance of the facts properly authenticated."[38]

Hopkins proceeds with a long series of arguments, both from Nature and from Scripture, cumulatively strengthening the case for Christianity. The moral nature of humans, for instance, makes it as unlikely that the Creator would not provide a revelation that speaks to our moral needs as it would be to create an "eye without light." So, says Hopkins, just as a key is adopted to a lock, the wing to a bird, or a fin to a fish, "Christianity, I hope to show, is adapted to man." Such proofs are confirmed by evidences such as the miracles of Scripture, prophecy fulfilled, and the high moral character of the patriarchs and Apostles who witnessed these things. These, and much other evidence, creates a "moral certainty" of the truth of Christianity, that is, a conclusion based on empirical grounds as compelling as those that could settle matters of life and death in a court of law.[39] Objective science, then, was the best friend of the faith.

In the short run, the defense of traditional interpretations of Scripture on the grounds of a science built on universal common sense proved something of a triumph in the intellectual life of Protestant America. Evangelical Protestants had effectively taken over the Jeffersonian claims to scientific authority and had also captured the initiative in shaping national educational standards. Biblicist Protestantism and enlightenment, they boldly affirmed, went hand in hand.

This intellectual stance fit exactly with evangelical Protestant efforts to

Christianize America. In the absence of state establishments of religion, evangelicals were entrenching themselves as a voluntary religious establishment. Standing for republican values, Christian morality, and in the forefront of industrial and economic progress, they presented a cultural outlook to which all Americans might be expected to assimilate. With objective science seemingly on their side, their case could be overwhelmingly persuasive. Science, moreover, promised to be a powerful force for cultural unity, since eventually all educated persons should agree with its conclusions.

In the long run, however, the claims to ground the distinctive aspects of biblicist Christianity on science and a universal commonsense epistemology put traditional Protestantism in a most vulnerable position. While evangelical Christians controlled much of the culture's intellectual life, they also confidently proclaimed that they would follow the scientific consensus wherever it would lead. Yet the Western European intellectual community was fast moving in reaction to the hegemony of Christian establishments.[40] Once natural science took the step of operating without the implicit assumption of a creator, its findings would be as uncongenial to traditional Christianity as were its new premises. The American evangelicals' faith in the objectivity of empirical science provided no preparation for such as shift. While in 1850 Mark Hopkins could make compelling statements about how scientific findings would always confirm biblical revelation, within a generation such claims would look like bravado.

Yet the Protestant establishment was too committed to its course of cultural dominance to turn away from claims to stand for an objective, universally compelling science. Even if Common Sense went out of style, as it soon did, their dedication to the objectivity and scientific empiricism would persist. Christian teaching itself would have to be adjusted to meet the demands of a scientific age.[41] The spirit of Jefferson's broadly Christian enlightenment would live on, but it would be embodied in the sons of New Englanders.

Notes

1. On the populist attacks see Nathan O. Hatch, *The Democratization of American Christianity* (New Haven: Yale University Press, 1989), especially the appendix of anti-Calvinist verse, 277–43.

2. George M. Marsden, *The Evangelical Mind and the New School Presbyterian Experience* (New Haven: Yale University Press, 1970), discusses many of these trends.

3. The standard source is Donald G. Tewksbury, *The Founding of American Colleges and Universities before the Civil War: With Particular Reference to the Religious Influences Bearing upon the College Movement* (New York, 1932), e.g., 16–28, 69. Tewksbury tabulated "permanent colleges" and their denominational affiliations. Natalie A. Naylor, "The Ante-Bellum College Movement: A Reappraisal of Tewksbury's Founding of American Colleges and Universities," *History of Educa-*

tion Quarterly 13 (Fall 1973), 261–74, shows that Tewksbury's statistics, although useful for relative comparisons, are not complete. Also she shows that the often-cited 81 percent failure rate that Tewksbury reported is misleading since most of the failed colleges existed only on paper.

4. David B. Potts, "American Colleges in the Nineteenth Century: From Localism to Denominationalism," *History of Education Quarterly* 11 (Winter 1971), 363–80. Cf. Potts, *Baptist Colleges in the Development of American Society, 1821–1861* (New York: Garland, 1988).

5. On the general character of these colleges see Douglas Sloan, "Harmony, Chaos, and Consensus: The American College Curriculum," *Teachers College Record* 73 (December 1971), 221–51. Lawrence A. Cremin, *American Education: The National Experience, 1783–1876* (New York: Harper & Row, 1980), 406–7. William C. Ringenberg, "The Old-Time College, 1800–1885," in *Making Higher Education Christian: The History and Mission of Evangelical Colleges in America,* Joel A. Carpenter and Kenneth W. Shipps, eds. (Grand Rapids, Mich.: Christian University Press, 1987), 77–97, is a useful overview. Also Albea Godbold, *The Church College of the Old South* (Durham, N.C.: Duke University Press, 1944).

6. Sloan, "Harmony, Chaos, and Consensus." Godbold, *Church College,* 126–27. On doxological science see also Theodore Dwight Bozeman, *The Baconian Ideal and Antebellum American Religious Thought* (Chapel Hill: University of North Carolina Press, 1977), and Mark A Noll, "The Revolution, the Enlightenment, and Christian Higher Education in the Early Republic," in Carpenter and Shipps, *Making Higher Education Christian,* 56–76.

7. G. Stanley Hall, "Philosophy in the United States," *Mind* 4 (January 1879), 93.

8. Cf. Daniel Walker Howe's account of faculty psychology, *The Political Culture of the American Whigs* (Chicago: University of Chicago Press, 1979), 29.

9. "The Yale Report of 1828," reprinted in *American Higher Education: A Documentary History,* I, Richard Hofstadter and Wilson Smith, eds. (Chicago: University of Chicago Press, 1961), 279, 289.

10. Godbold, *Church College,* 128–39. Frederick Rudolph, *The American College and University: A History* (New York: Vintage Books, 1962), 79–84.

11. Cremin, *American Education,* 56–74, provides a convenient summary of the predominantly Presbyterian and Congregationalist voluntary crusades and their wide implications for both schooling and education at all levels.

12. James Findlay, "The SPCTEW and Western Colleges: Religion and Higher Education in Mid-Nineteenth Century America," *History of Education Quarterly* 15 (Spring 1977), 37–38.

13. Lyman Beecher, *A Plea for the West* (Cincinnati: Truman and Smith, 1835), 10–11, 17, and passim.

14. Ibid., 79–81, 124n.

15. For the best account of this outlook see Daniel Walker Howe, *The Political Culture of the American Whigs* (Chicago: University of Chicago Press, 1979) and "The Evangelical Movement and Political Culture in the North during the Second Party System," *Journal of American History* 77 (March 1991), 1216–39. Louise Stevenson, *Scholarly Means to Evangelical Ends: The New Haven Scholars and the Transformation of Higher Learning in America, 1830–1890* (Baltimore: Johns Hopkins University Press, 1986), makes some of the same points.

16. Bozeman, *Baconian Ideal,* esp. 3–31, 71–86.

17. The question of sectarianism was being sharply debated during this whole era. For instance, Philip Lindsley (1786–1855), president of the University of Nashville and a protégé of Princeton's Samuel Stanhope Smith, decried the pretensions of the scores of sectarian schools that were springing up in his region, because of both their educational superficiality and their claims to be nonsectarian. "I do not object to any sect's being allowed the privilege of erecting and maintaining, at their own expense, as many schools, colleges and theological seminaries as they please. But then, their sectarian views should be openly and distinctly avowed. Their purpose should be specified in their charters: and the legislature should protect the people from imposition. . . . Hitherto, almost every legislature has pursued an opposite policy, and has aided the work of deception, by enacting that, in the said sectarian institution, youths of all sects should be entitled to equal privileges." Philip Lindsley, Baccalaureate Address, 1829, in Hofstadter and Smith, *Documentary History,* 234.

Howard Miller, *The Revolutionary College: American Presbyterian Higher Education, 1707–1837* (New York: New York University Press, 1976, 242–46, 257–58, documents the constant debate over sectarianism, particularly when public funding was involved. Miller also argues, however, that the Presbyterians of the early nineteenth century had lost their broader nonsectarian version of the colonial era (284–85). It is probably more accurate to say that they *continued* to experience a deep tension between their sectarianism and their aspirations to lead in shaping a righteous republic.

18. Victor Roy Wilbee, "The Religious Dimensions of Three Presidencies in a State University: Presidents Tappan, Haven, and Angell at the University of Michigan," Ph.D. dissertation, University of Michigan, 1967, 24.

19. George Duffield et al., Report of Michigan Regents, December 20, 1841, Hofstadter and Smith, *Documentary History,* 437–38. Cf. Howard H. Peckham, *The Making of the University of Michigan, 1817–1867* (Ann Arbor: University of Michigan Press, 1967), 23–24.

Political sectarianism complicated the issues at Michigan. The religious and political mix is illustrated through the case of the Rev. Daniel Denison Whedon, of the Methodist Episcopal Church (and later a prominent biblical commentator), who in 1851 was dismissed by the regents of the university for opposing the extension of slavery. Specifically, Whedon was condemned for having "advocated the doctrine called, 'The Higher Law,' a doctrine which is unauthorized by the Bible, at war with the principles, precepts, and examples of Christ and His Apostles, subversive alike of Civil Government, civil society, and the legal rights of individual citizens, and in effects constitutes in the opinion of this Board a species of moral treason against the Government." From I. N. Demmon, ed., *University of Michigan Regents' Proceedings, 1837–1864,* 501–503, excerpted in Hofstadter and Smith, *Documentary History,* 439.

20. Quoted from a later letter of Mann in Charles Leslie Glenn, Jr., *The Myth of the Common School* (Amherst: University of Massachusetts Press, 1987), 143.

21. Quoted from Mann's *Eleventh Annual Report, 1848,* in Glenn, *Myth,* 166.

22. Quoted from Mann's *Twelfth Annual Report, 1849,* in Glenn, *Myth,* 169.

23. For examples see Glenn, *Myth,* 125 and passim.

24. Quoted from an 1839 speech by Mann in Glenn, *Myth,* 138.

25. Cf. Cremin, *National Experience,* 140, for summary of emphases.

26. Glenn, *Myth,* 199.

27. Rockney M. McCarthy, James W. Skillen, and William A. Harper, *Disestablishment a Second Time; Genuine Pluralism for American Schools* (Grand Rapids, Mich.: Christian University Press, 1982), 60–70.

28. Calvin E. Stowe, *Report on Elementary Public Instruction . . . March 29, 1838* (Boston, 1838), 42, quoted in Glenn, *Myth,* 108.

29. Glenn, *Myth,* 108. In Prussia pastors also were required by the state to provide two years of religious instruction to all teenagers. Charles Hodge, "Parochial Schools," *Princeton Review* 18 (July 1846), 437.

30. Cremin, *National Experience,* 170.

31. Hodge, "Parochial Schools," 443–41.

32. Cremin, *National Experience,* 176. Robert Breckinridge, who shaped the educational system in Kentucky, was an Old School Presbyterian who opposed the parochial alternative. Cf. Hodge, "Parochial Schools," 434.

33. Horace Bushnell, *Life and Letters of Horace Bushnell* (New York, 1880), ca. 299–303, quoted in Glenn, *Myth,* 229. Bushnell was also active in the Society for the Promotion of Collegiate and Theological Education at the West (SPCTEW).

34. John H. Westerhoff III *McGuffey and His Readers: Piety, Morality, and Education in Nineteenth-Century America* (Nashville: Abingdon Press, 1978), 36–105.

35. Thomas Reid, *Essays on the Intellectual Powers of Man* (Cambridge, Mass.: M.I.T. Press, 1969 [1785]), esp. xxxix, 614–43.

36. Cf. Henry F. May, *The Enlightenment in America* (New York: Oxford University Press, 1976).

37. For a fuller discussion of these views and their implications see George M. Marsden, "The Collapse of American Evangelical Academia," in *Faith and Rationality: Reason and Belief in God,* Alvin Plantinga and Nicholas Wolterstorff, eds. (Notre Dame, Ind.: University Notre Dame Press, 1983), 219–64.

38. Mark Hopkins, *Evidences of Christianity* (Boston, 1876, [1846]), 97–98, 39.

39. Ibid., 75 and passim.

40. Adrian Desmond and James Moore, *Darwin: The Life of a Tormented Evolutionist* (New York: Warner Books, 1992), provides a compelling account of this motive and of the social dynamics associated with it in England.

41. See Marsden, "Collapse," for elaboration of this argument. A similar version of this point is found in James Turner, *Without God, Without Creed: The Origins of Unbelief in America* (Baltimore: Johns Hopkins University Press, 1985).

II

DEFINING THE AMERICAN UNIVERSITY IN A SCIENTIFIC AGE

The Protestant colleges of the mid-nineteenth century would have been readily recognizable to the founders of Harvard two centuries earlier. Chapel services were still regular parts of the day. Classical texts shaped much of the curriculum. Clergy dominated college leadership. Professors and tutors taught a variety of subjects. They were concerned for student piety and attempted to control student behavior largely by coercion. Almost all colleges were for white boys only.

Despite these striking continuities, American collegiate education had also evolved in substantial, though subtle, ways. The subtlety of these changes within the inherited institutional framework hid the potential for the quantum leap from old-time college to modern university within one generation following the Civil War. Pressured by a changing environment, the potentiality for transformation into a whole new species had been building for at least a century within the apparent equilibrium of the old system. During that time gradual but momentous shifts taking place in essential commitments made the modern colleges of the 1850s far different from their premodern, almost medieval, Harvard predecessor two centuries earlier.

With respect to religion the most obvious modification was that the training of future clergy had been the strongest reason for maintaining colleges in early New England, but by the mid-nineteenth century concern for clerical education no longer was a primary defining feature. By far the majority of collegians were preparing for other professions, and ministerial education itself had been shifted to divinity schools or separate theological seminaries.

The other more subtle major changes all had to do with accommodations to the demands either of Enlightenment thought or of the culture of the first modern nation. The reverence for scientific authority was the major intellectual manifestation of the new commitments. The corollary was that moral philosophy replaced theology as the primary locus for defining collegiate Christian intellectual life. Theology, while never well integrated into collegiate curricula, long had played an important role in defining intellectual boundaries and in providing a point of reference for some intellectual inquiry. By the late colonial era, however, the demands to serve several Protestant constituencies had bought pressures against theological definitions of the enterprise. Theology remained a point of intellectual reference at most colleges, but often in a residual capacity. So the potential was already there for the distinctly Christian aspects of the intellectual enterprise to be jettisoned, or broadened into vestigial platitudes, without threatening any of the fundamental functions of the educational enterprise.

The intellectual changes were thus intimately related to the colleges' commitments to the American public. Colleges had to serve their immediate communities or regions and be responsive both to popular American ideologies and to practical needs. They were competitors in a free market economy in which by midcentury the struggle for survival was fierce.

While American colleges always had served both church and community, the character of public life had changed. In the seventeenth century the distinction between church and community was not always clear. An established church was part of public life and a college was an extension of the church's public role. In nineteenth-century America such assumptions persisted among collegiate leaders, but in fact the constituencies that they were expected to serve were far more diverse than those of any one supporting church. Churches were only one component in an increasingly market-oriented cultural ethos in which the churches' public role was becoming superfluous.

The institutional framework—the old-time college—that contained these potentialities and commitments was ready to give way to dramatic change. The old classicist education was outmoded and served a limited constituency. Not even all the presidents of the United States were college graduates. Americans were eager to be practical and up-to-date and the colleges were scrambling to keep up, adding this and that scientific or practical offering into the cumbersome classicist curriculum. Only so much could be added, however, within the old structures. Little in the old system allowed for professional or specialized development. For graduate training one had to go abroad. The colleges were also saddled with a tradition of attempting to control student behavior by strict oversight and regulation, a system uncongenial to emerging nineteenth-century ideals of cultivating self-regulating character. In an age of reform, as the middle decades of the century were for many middle-class Yankees, the golden age lay in an American future of prosperity and virtue. Some visionaries could foresee a reformed higher education as part of that promising future.

The American Civil War released the energies necessary for these potentialities that had been building in American higher education toward a dramatic metamorphosis. The Southern secession and the war cleared the way for the dominance of Republican reformers who combined commitment to industrial expansion with moral idealism. A generation of younger men, almost all from the Northeast, had visions of replacing colleges with universities as the dominant structure of American higher education.

As in many American developments, there was no central plan. Although the founders of the major universities knew each other well, each of their universities had its distinctive character. Typically these schools reflected the personalities of their founders, the "captains of erudition" as they were later called. By surveying the outlooks of the foremost designers of American universities, their schools, and leading faculty, as do the chapters that follow, we can piece together a variety of crucial traits that converge in the dominant university culture that emerged by the early twentieth century.

5

American Practicality and Germanic Ideals: Two Visions for Reform

Prophet of the Practical

The evangelicals who dominated American higher education at midcentury confidently awaited the arrival of millennial days. One of the ways they resolved the problem of Christian particularism and American pluralism was with the promise, popular since the era of Edwards, that in the last days almost everyone would be converted to Christianity. History, then, would end with a final golden age, "the millennium." This outpouring of the spirit in the greatest of all awakenings would be accompanied by human progress on every front, in science, technology, politics, and especially in morality. Nations of the world would learn liberty and justice for all, which was already best exemplified in Protestant lands. Oppression, slavery, and warfare would come to an end. Many of the signs of this millennial age were already present, and common speculation was that the new era might dawn soon after midcentury.[1]

"Our last thought is that the world is growing *better,*" wrote the famed New School Presbyterian pastor Albert Barnes, in "The Position of the Christian Scholar." The advance of knowledge was one of the signs of the approaching golden age. During the Middle Ages, Barnes explained, science had been subordinated to theology. The Reformation, however, "broke the shackles which had bound the human intellect; [and] made men more independent in their scientific investigations." The nineteenth century was now reaping the benefits. "[The Christian scholar's] religion is accompanying the march of science around the world." And "where Christianity prevails, there also civil liberty prevails."[2] Christian scholarship, including scholarship in political and natural sciences, promised to advance a new world order, and hence the kingdom.

The increase in knowledge, however, was worth nothing without an increase in virtue. Otherwise, explained Francis Wayland, in the era's most popular college text on *Political Economy,* "intellectual cultivation" will only "stimulate desire, and this unrestrained by the love of right, must eventually overturn the social fabric which it at first erected." Religion was, of course, crucial to the equation. "No nation can rapidly accumulate or long enjoy the means of happiness, except as it is pervaded by the love of individual and social right; but the love of individual and social right will never prevail, without the practical influence of the motives and sanctions of religion; and these motives and sanctions will never influence men, unless they are, by human effort, brought to bear upon the conscience."[3]

Wayland's views are especially significant because he was a leader in the midcentury era in calling for extensive reform of higher education. A New England Baptist and president of Brown University, Wayland was thoroughly connected with the network of Presbyterian and Congregational educators. A graduate of Andover Theological Seminary, he had earlier studied at the "Presbygational" Union College in New York under the tutelage of the legendary Eliphalet Nott. Nott, who served an incredible sixty-four years as president of Union, from 1802 to 1866, was renowned for his extraordinary influence as an advocate of college reform. At Union he pioneered the idea of developing a parallel science-oriented track for the bachelor of arts degree. Wayland, as a protege of Nott, likewise championed more practically and scientifically oriented options in the curriculum.[4]

Wayland combined science and revelation in the way that was typical of the era, as complementary avenues to truth. Scientific observation was reliable, but truths of special revelation needed to be added. Wayland connected these through repeated reminders that all truth, as well as our ability to apprehend it, came from the Creator. The laws of the universe, whether physical or moral laws, were simply matters of cause and effect, "sequences connected by our Creator." From careful science, therefore, we could derive principles, not only for personal morality, but for sciences like political economy. Personal industry, for instance, should be rewarded. Laws of the market should be allowed to operate freely, rewarding people duly for their labor. Such economic laws could be discovered simply by scientific observations, that is, "on merely economical ground." Ultimately, however, the reason our science could discover such truth was that both our minds and the economic laws were part of a created order.[5]

On precisely such grounds, then, Wayland spoke for collegiate reform. Consistent with his market-reward approach, he argued that since churches had founded the vast majority of American colleges, religious leaders should continue to control them.[6] More critically, however, he pointed out that the particular structures of the colleges were based on ancient and outmoded traditions borrowed from England and were no longer in a natural relationship to the economy. Colleges were small and had to be artificially supported by scholarships because the product they had to offer was so little in demand. What had happened was that the classical curriculum was of benefit only to those training for the professions of ministry, law, and medicine. In the meantime, because of demands to add modern subjects, the whole curriculum had become increasingly superficial. Except for the ministry, which was artificially supported by scholarships, even members of the professions were depending less on collegiate education. Furthermore, some of the wealthiest and most productive segments of society, the business classes, the mechanics, and farmers, were being neglected. "Nothing would tend so much to the progress of wealth among us as the diffusion throughout the whole people of a knowledge of the principles of science, and the applications of science to the arts."[7]

While arguing that preprofessional courses should be strengthened, Wayland also insisted that other practical programs should be added. Furthermore, collegiate education should not be an arbitrary set length but should be tailored to the particular needs of its constituents.[8]

Wayland anticipated some of the most important principles that would soon reshape colleges into universities. Particularly he saw that in a rapidly diversifying economy a chief function of higher education would be to serve the technological needs of society. Moreover, his ideas suited practical American sentiments. The Yale Report of 1828 had defended the classics on the practical grounds that the discipline was simply good exercise for the mind. Wayland saw that ultimately American university education would have to play a more vital social role and thus have a more tangible cash value on the bottom line. The outmoded colleges, which few Americans attended, were hardly going to lead the nation into a golden age of prosperity and moral and intellectual progress.

Ironically, Wayland's attempted reforms at Brown, after a promising start, were thwarted in the 1850s by the realities of the market. He could not offer the full-fledged diversity that he had promised.[9] Such changes would have to wait another half generation until both government grants and vast private endowments were available to redirect the educational enterprise.

Typical of the Whig reformers, Wayland combined moral concern with desire to serve the nation by serving the interests of business. While the details of his moral philosophy may have fallen out of academic favor, his practical concerns, grounded in down-to-earth commonsense outlooks, have persisted as one of the major themes in American higher education ever since.

The "John the Baptist" of the German University Ideal

While Francis Wayland may have been the prophet of the practical orientation that eventually shaped so much of American university education, Henry P. Tappan (1805–1881), chancellor of the University of Michigan from 1852 to 1863, is rightly called "the John the Baptist" of the age of the American university.[10] Although Tappan did not see all his ideals realized in the Michigan wilderness, he did establish the university's reputation as the leader in the American West.

What Tappan had that the hardheaded Wayland lacked was romantic idealism. The new American universities of the next generation would arise in a romantic age and their academic founders would be inspired by a vision of making America a land of great scholars, even while their financial support came mostly from the more practically minded realists. A monumental difference was that, whereas Wayland stood firmly in the British philosophical tradition of empiricism and common sense, Tappan was among the first major educational reformers to have studied in Germany. Between 1815 and 1914 about nine to ten thousand Americans studied in Germany. In Tappan's day the trend had barely begun; yet Tappan's generation established an immensely important precedent. Throughout the rest of the nineteenth century German universities would serve as America's graduate schools. It would be rare to find either a university leader or a major scholar who had not spent some years studying in Germany.[11]

The impact of Germany in reshaping American education is difficult to measure precisely. One thing that most interpreters agree on, however, is that neither German ideals nor educational models were imported without major adjustments to the American setting.[12] Germany nevertheless had overwhelming symbolic importance. Americans stood in awe of the Germany universities. Eighteenth-century German universities had taken the lead on the European continent and, especially after the establishment of the University of Berlin by Prussia in 1810, had moved to world preeminence. For Americans, who in university building were behind just about every European country, an appeal to a German precedent could be an intimidating argument.

The rise to preeminence of German universities coincided with the rise of German idealism and must be understood in terms of that broader romantic movement. So, for example, while a scientific research ideal came to be associated with the German universities, its leading traits developed not simply in the natural sciences but largely in the humanities. In the late eighteenth and early nineteenth centuries the flagship scientific discipline was philology, which explored the history of ancient languages. This emphasis, in turn, reflected a growing historical consciousness, or a sense that things could be understood best in terms of their development. The broad implication was that intellectual inquiry was not directed primarily to the discovery of fixed verities but rather to ideals as they developed in a cultural context. While such ideals might be attributed to the divine, as in Hegel's philosophy, human history had a lot to do with creating and shaping them.

Such developments were also related to Immanuel Kant's "Copernican Revolution" in more abstract philosophy, which suggested that the human mind be thought of not as a passive receiver of truth but as an active creator of the categories that made sense out of reality. "Discovery" took on a creative dimension, so that original discovery became essential to an emerging research ideal. Yet the German version of the scientific ideal was not a celebration of cold abstract analysis as the model for all thought. Rather German science, or *Wissenschaft,* was to take place within the context of philosophical idealism and could contribute to the larger humanistic goal of *Bildung.* Sometimes translated as cultivation, *Bildung* suggested the ideal of education as building character or "untrammeled personal development of personal powers and faculties to some kind of transcendental fulfillment."[13]

The new learning and the universities that embodied it were thus truly liberating to the race. They were the keys to the progress of humanity, especially spiritual progress. In the new idealist philosophy learning took on a redemptive quality. Johann Gottlieb Fichte, the most influential of the university theorists associated with the model university established at Berlin in 1810, made this implication explicit:

> The University . . . is the institution . . . where each generation hands on . . . its highest intellectual education to the succeeding generation. . . . All this, however, is solely with the intention that the divine may ever appear in the human in fresh clearness. . . . Now if the university is this, it is clear that it is the most holy thing which the human race possesses. Since the education given there preserves . . . and hands on everything divine that ever burst forth in mankind, the real nature of mankind lives there in its uninterrupted life, far above everything transitory; and the University is the visible representation of the immortality of our race.[14]

This rhetoric went beyond most American counterparts, although by Tappan's day one could find approximations of it among the Transcendentalists. Emerson's "The American Scholar," for instance, is an individualized variation on such themes. Character and scholarship were to be united; the great scholar was to be a great individual, not the withdrawn laboratory scientist. Most American academic scholars, of whom Tappan would be a fairly typical example, were more restrained in appropriating German ideals, blending them in various degrees with British-American philosophical and theological traditions. Nonetheless, German scholarship and the many stars at the German universities helped promote the idea in America that scholarship should be a profession in its own right. This development had important implications for America, where theology had often been the preeminent intellectual profession. After the mid-nineteenth century, it could no longer be presumed that many of the strongest American intellects would be dedicated to theology.

By Tappan's day German trends were having an impact on the mainstream of American Protestant theology itself. During the early decades of the American student migration, prior to 1850, many Americans, over one-fourth of the total, studied with the Protestant theological faculties of the leading German universities.[15] German theology, while still within the general bounds of Protestant orthodoxy, was also being reshaped by idealism. The more conservative Americans, typically trained in Calvinist orthodoxy supported by Scottish Common Sense philosophy, often found the German outlooks difficult to assimilate. Nonetheless, by the mid-nineteenth century, imported German traits were beginning to modify the dominant Calvinist heritage. These involved a growing historical consciousness, implying that theology was a historical development. Less palatable to most Americans was the controversial German view that the Bible should be subjected to historical criticism. Nonetheless, the Common Sense foundations for the eighteenth-century defenses of the old theology were being undermined. Subjective approaches to truth were being credited with more validity. Trends (found in the British-American traditions as well) toward making morality and character-building the tests for theological truth were being reinforced as well.

For the time being the old and the new could be held together in creative tension. After the Civil War, however, when the advanced German theological views became commonplace in American educational circles, these theological changes played an important role in allowing adjustments to the latest academic trends, such as scientific historical investigation and emphasis on the development of character.

Henry Tappan, while holding an almost mystical reverence for the educational ideals of Prussia and the University of Berlin, nonetheless was typical of those who were holding a creative middle ground between Germany and their American heritage. Tappan had the full pedigree of the dominant circle of educational leaders of his era. He was another of the distinguished protégés of Eliphalet Nott at Union College, a graduate of Auburn Theological Seminary, and an ordained New School Presbyterian minister. Though an advocate of Common Sense philosophy, Tappan was a representative of the popular midcentury variant, which fused trust in Common Sense with idealism. Like many American thinkers of his day, Tappan rhapsodized about Scotland's Sir William Hamilton, who had forged what was thought to be a compelling synthesis of Scottish and German thought, especially that of Kant.[16] Tappan's own major scholarly work was a treatise attempting to refute Jonathan Edwards's on *The Freedom of the Will.* Tappan was relatively optimistic about natural human powers and human freedom was a central motif of his thought.[17]

Tappan's described his educational goals, which he contrasted directly to Wayland's practicality, as "philosophical and ideal."[18] Rather than "fitting our colleges to the temper of the multitude,"[19] education needed leadership from wise men at the top, who could cultivate the best of human potential. "This conception of education is not that of merely teaching men a trade, an art, or a profession; but that of quickening and informing souls with truths and knowledges *[sic],* and giving them the power of using all their faculties aright in whatever they choose to exert them."[20] Or even more ideally, and seeming to echo Fichte, "the true end of Learning, the genuine fruit of knowledge is the development of the human soul that it may become wise, pure and godlike—that it may reach that perfection which is the ultimate ground of its existence."[21]

Another lesson which Tappan brought from Prussia was that educational reform should come from the state. German universities were strongly controlled by the various German states. Rather than being restrictive, state control could be seen as a way of guaranteeing a measure of academic freedom, that is, freedom could be limited by the interests of the state, rather than by more local or sectarian interests. In Prussia, for instance, professors, by being designated as civil servants, gained an immunity against arbitrary dismissal, which amounted to academic tenure. An enlightened state ministry could also promote excellence in universities, and hence promote the interests of the state, by appointing distinguished professors who would attract students. In Prussia, idealism played a role in this state leadership. The state existed for the development of the culture, or of the spiritual essence of a people. Universities symbolized this grand cultural ideal. Such idealism ultimately was not impractical. The universities strengthened the state by training bureaucrats, professionals, and researchers who would serve society.[22]

Tappan immensely admired the Prussian model, which he hoped would be applied to Michigan. The current American four-year college degree, he thought, was roughly equivalent to the German gymnasium course and should be so designated. This preliminary education ought to be completed by three more years of true "university" study in which students attended the lectures of advanced faculties, who were truly specialists in their fields. The analogy to Prussia could hardly be made exact in the American setting, but Tappan did establish a foothold for the ideal in Ann Arbor.[23]

While Tappan's proposals for major structural reforms met many obstacles, he did succeed in planting at Michigan the ideal that he saw as the key to European universities—a great university was made up of a great faculty. What is needed for a great university, asked Tappan. "There is but one reply—scholars and books." "Of all mere human institutions there are none so important and mighty in their influences as Universities; because, when rightly constituted, they are made up of the most enlightened, and the choicest spirits of our race."[24] Tappan had a great man view of history and thought that he was one.[25] He also worked hard at bringing other scholars to Michigan. The essential criterion was that they had to be professionals. This was the most fundamental lesson that Americans absorbed from studying in Germany, and Tappan was one of the first to attempt to implement it consistently. "However amiable his character, however pure his religious or political creed according to the judgement of any sect or party, if he have not the requisite literary or scientific qualifications, he is of no account."[26] Though Tappan did not immediately make Michigan into a great university, his ideals had wide influence. Four of his faculty later became college presidents. The best known is Cornell's founder, Andrew Dickson White, who attributed many of his views to Tappan's influence.[27]

The University of Michigan under Tappan also had striking success in attracting students. By the eve of the Civil War well over six hundred were enrolled, tripling its size from when he had arrived and making it one of the largest schools in the nation.[28]

Tappan had definite ideas about the relation of religion to the university. Essentially a broad-minded evangelical, Tappan assumed that the university would be broadly Christian and even Protestant, as was his Prussian model. He supported the university requirement that all students attend a Sunday service, he regularly led the required daily university chapel, and he offered voluntary Sunday afternoon lectures, open to the public, on moral philosophy or natural theology. He supported voluntary student religious organizations at Michigan,[29] which had one of the nation's first collegiate YMCAS. He further hoped that various denominations would establish theological faculties in Ann Arbor, since he believed that theological faculties were integral to a true university and denominational differences at the state school itself could be avoided in this way.[30]

Tappan was vehemently opposed to any sectarianism at the university. When he arrived at Michigan he was appalled to discover that there was an informal agreement among the leading Protestant denominations to keep a balanced representation on the faculty by having various "chairs" that should be filled from each denomination. This arrangement was apparently an effort to compensate for the fact that the state, reflecting some earlier Jeffersonian influences, attempted to discourage the proliferation of sectarian colleges by not granting them the formal power to grant degrees. Tappan agreed that there was no need for sectarian colleges. The American majority, he argued, should be consistent in its educational views. Since they were insisting against Catholics that the common schools could be nonsectarian, how could they turn around and demand that they must have sectarian higher education? University policy should be consistently nonsectarian. So Tappan brought an end to the denominational chair scheme, pointing out that Catholics, Unitarians, Universalists, and others, would soon be claiming chairs as well. In his view, except where there were theological faculties, sectarian teachings simply had no place in a university.[31]

Tappan held a two-realm view of scientific and biblical truth. He was a believer in the Bible, but he also emphasized that scientific thought demanded complete freedom of inquiry. Like most of the evangelicals of midcentury, he assumed that the conclusions of free science and of proper bibilical interpretation would eventually harmonize. In the meantime one could live with some apparent differences.[32] The overriding point in his mind was that neither the Bible nor theological dogma should be the starting point for philosophical or scientific inquiry. Nonetheless, he reassured, Christianity could still come into the college experience in less formal ways. It could appear "by graceful and apt episodes in the class room when the subject naturally suggests them; by employing scientific truths to illustrate natural theology; by the easy familiarity of daily converse opened by the relation of the teacher to the pupil; . . . [various displays of personal concern or counselling;] . . . and by the exercise of all those tender charities which are as remote from sectarian bigotry, [as] they are near the vital heart of Christianity."[33]

Tappan's opposition to sectarian bigotry was reinforced by historical analysis, always a prominent aspect of his educational discourses. Tappan had been originally recommended to the Michigan regents by George Bancroft, the first American historian with German training. Like Bancroft's celebrations of the rise of democracy in his *History of the United States,* Tappan's educational history was the story of the rise of freedom. "Freedom," he proclaimed, "—this is the grand characteristic of University Education, as it is the essential attribute of manhood."[34]

Universities played a leading role in the history of human freedom. The "Scholasticism" of the founders of European universities "was really a struggle of the human mind for freedom and enlargement of thought against the authorities of the Church and the State." But they did not go far enough. "The great error of the Schoolmen lay in receiving both their religious dogmas and their philosophical systems upon authority." The evils of scholastic dogmatism survived even to the present day. For instance, the English universities were still "paralyzed by high-church influence" and "still feel the incubus of the old Scholasticism, and reap the effects of the changes introduced by the Chancellorship of Laud."[35]

Where universities had succeeded, on the other hand, was primarily in the Protestant lands. In "Protestant Germany" and to some extent Scotland, "freedom and independence" were coming to prevail.[36] Although Luther was a contributor to freeing people from the tyranny of church dogma, Protestantism by itself did not press the principle to its conclusion. Rather it was one great man, Francis Bacon, who was at first the solitary prophet of the new ideal. Just as "the divine religion made its advent in the solitary Jesus of Nazareth," so Bacon's views progressed from a few admirers to the current era of "the beginning of association preparatory to the universal diffusion of knowledge." A great new era of intellectual freedom was about to dawn. "The third period is that in which association will be perfected, and the universal diffusion of knowledge take place. In Universities we have the association which in the end creates common schools, or schools for the people."[37] The kingdom of God was at hand.

Though Tappan's fate was not as dramatic as John the Baptist's, his demise as an educator was almost as sudden. The state regents had long been struggling with the chancellor for control. On June 24, 1863, they caucused secretly and the next day in regular session voted Tappan's dismissal. Tappan's pretensions to greatness apparently had alienated many people. The Democratic press relentlessly accused him of being an elitist, which he was. The religious denominations resented him because he had attacked their influence in the university. To make matters worse, Tappan, true to his European tastes, served wine with meals and did not object to students drinking beer (thus anticipating another basic component of the modern university). This stance, in days of ardent temperance sentiments, lost him Republican friends. The result was that he had few allies. Tappan accepted his defeat quietly and retired to Europe, where he spent his last two decades in exile. His last words to the Michigan regents were: "The pen of history is held by the hand of Almighty Justice, and I fear not the record it will make of my conduct."[38]

Notes

1. See George M. Marsden, *The Evangelical Mind and the New School Presbyterian Experience* (New Haven: Yale University Press, 1970), 182–98, for a discussion of millennial views.

2. Albert Barnes, "The Position of the Christian Scholar," *Biblical Repository,* 3rd ser., 6 (October 1850), 625, 604, 608, 609.

3. Francis Wayland, *Elements of Political Economy,* 2nd ed. (1852 [1837]), quoted in William G. McLoughlin, ed., *The American Evangelicals, 1800–1900: An Anthology* (New York: Harper & Row, 1968), 126.

4. On Nott and Wayland see Frederick Rudolph, *Curriculum: A History of American Undergraduate Course of Study since 1636* (San Francisco: Jossey-Bass, 1977), 85–87, and Lawrence A. Cremin, *American Education: The National Experience, 1783–1876* (New York: Harper & Row, 1980), 273–79.

5. Wayland, *Elements of Political Economy* (Boston, 1860 [1837]), iv and passim.

6. Francis Wayland, *A Discourse Delivered at the Dedication of Manning Hall, the chapel and Library of Brown University, Feb. 4, 1835* (Providence, 1835), 20–21, in *American Higher Education: A Documentary History,* Richard Hofstadter and Wilson Smith, eds. (Chicago: University of Chicago Press, 1961), I, 242–243.

7. Francis Wayland, *Thoughts on the Present Collegiate System of the United States* (Boston, 1842), 153–55, quotation from 154.

8. Ibid., 155–56. On Wayland see also William G. Roelker, "Francis Wayland: A Neglected Pioneer of Higher Education," *American Antiquarian Society* 53 (April 1943), 27–78, and Theodore Rawson Crane, "Introduction," in *The College and the Public, 1787–1862,* Crane, ed. (New York: Teachers College Press, 1963), 1–33.

9. Frederick Rudolph, *Curriculum: A History of the American Undergraduate Course of Study since 1636* (San Francisco: Jossey-Bass, 1977), 109–12.

10. Lois Mayfield Wilson, quoted in Victor Roy Wilbee, "The Religious Dimensions of Three Presidents of a State University: Presidents Tappan, Haven, and Angell of the University of Michigan," Ph.D. dissertation, University of Michigan, 1967, 81

11. Carl Diehl, *Americans and German Scholarship, 1770–1870* (New Haven: Yale University Press, 1978), 50–69, 148.

12. E.g., Diehl, *Americans and German Scholarship;* James Turner, "The Prussian Road to University? German Models and the University of Michigan, 1837–c. 1895," *Rackam Reports* (Ann Arbor: University of Michigan, 1989), 6–52; Laurence

Veysey, *The Emergence of the American University* (Chicago: University of Chicago Press, 1965), 126–33.

13. Diehl, *Americans and German Scholarship,* 18. Cf. Konrad H. Jarausch, *Students, Society, and Politics in Imperial Germany: The Rise of Academic Illiberalism* (Princeton: Princeton University Press, 1982), 9. R. Steven Turner, "The Prussian University and the Research Imperative, 1806–1848," Ph.D. dissertation, Princeton University, 1973, 259–67, 273–77. Turner's is the best work in English on the rise of the German universities.

14. Fichte, "Concerning the only Possible Disturbance of Academic Freedom," Rector address at Berlin University, October 19, 1811, quoted in Turner, "Prussian University," 268.

15. Diehl, *Americans and German Scholarship,* 56–57. After 1850 this percentage dropped off sharply, paralleling a decline in the popularity of theological education in Germany itself.

16. He considered Hamilton, for instance, "the very highest authority on the subject" of educational reform. Henry P. Tappan, *The University: Its Constitution and its Relations, Political and Religious: A Discourse, June 22, 1858* (Ann Arbor, 1858), 8.

17. Wilbee, "Religious Dimensions," 52–70.

18. Henry P. Tappan, *University Education* (New York, 1851), 61. Cf. 54–56 and 75 on Wayland's views.

19. Ibid., 65.

20. Ibid., 13–14.

21. Tappan, "John Milton," unpublished manuscript, Tappan Papers, Michigan Historical Collections of the University of Michigan, 63, quoted in Wilbee, "Religious Dimensions," 75.

22. Turner, "Prussian University," 358, 429–30.

23. Turner, "Prussian Road to University?"

24. Tappan, *The University,* 5.

25. Wilbee, "Religious Dimensions," 59.

26. Tappan, *The University,* 20. Harvard, for instance, by this time was hiring some faculty on this basis but others on the more traditional informal and local criteria. See Robert A. McCaughey, "The Transformation of American Academic Life: Harvard University, 1821–1892," *Perspectives in American History* 8 (1974), 239–332.

27. Wilbee, "Religious Dimensions," 99, 108.

28. Howard H. Peckham, *The Making of the University of Michigan, 1817–1967* (Ann Arbor: University of Michigan Press, 1967), 38, 47.

29. Tappan, *The University,* 32–33.

30. Wilbee, "Religious Dimensions," 99. Tappan had already proposed such an arrangement before he went to Ann Arbor. *University Education,* 94.

31. Tappan, *The University,* 23–25. By the 1850s other colleges were being allowed formally to grant degrees as well. On background of religious issues see Wilbee, "Religious Dimensions," 1–51, 99, 120, and passim.

32. Wilbee, "Religious Dimensions," 61.

33. Tappan, *The University,* 32. The question of whether science might start with biblical data was being sharply debated at midcentury with respect to the science of geology, for instance, regarding the work of Taylor Lewis at Union College. See George Marsden, *The Evangelical Mind and the New School Presbyterian Experience* (New Haven: Yale University Press, 1970), 142–56.

34. Tappan, *The University,* 6.

35. Tappan, *University Education,* 27, 42, 39.

36. Ibid., 40.

37. Henry P. Tappan, *The Progress of Educational Development: A Discourse . . . , June 25, 1855* (Ann Arbor, 1855), 22.

38. Peckham, *The Making of the University of Michigan,* 39–52.

6

The Christian Legacy in the Epoch of Science

Tappan's work would be carried on by disciples, even if not always in precisely the way he had envisioned. The best known of his protégés was Andrew Dickson White, whom Tappan had brought to Michigan to teach history in 1857. In the fall of 1863, during a long leave of absence to care for his health, White was elected to the New York Senate. He immediately took an interest in education in New York, his home state, and especially hoped to implement a longstanding dream of building a model university. White always revered Tappan as the founder of the modern American university and honored some of his ideals. In other respects, however, he was as much a disciple of Francis Wayland. Tappan had the professional scholar's faith in the triumph of pure intellect. White was more the nineteenth-century gentleman scholar, who was just as interested in practical affairs, and also resembled Wayland in his commitment to egalitarian ideals. His university was thus substantially more dedicated to practicality than was Tappan's.

Nonetheless, White followed Tappan closely in one major respect. Like Tappan he was intensely dedicated to science and saw it as opposed to sectarianism and as the key to human freedom. White viewed Tappan as having been destroyed by sectarian attacks at Michigan,[1] and the younger man would be preoccupied throughout his career by the horrors of sectarianism.

White, like Tappan, opposed sectarianism in the name of Christianity, but with an important difference. While Tappan was a more-or-less orthodox New School Presbyterian, White always had a broader conception of Christianity. Reared in the Episcopal Church, White retained something of the high-church disdain for evangelicals. Yet he rejected Episcopal sectarianism just as firmly. His father had insisted that he attend tiny Geneva College (now Hobart) in New York State. Andrew found the churchly atmosphere intolerably stifling. Early in his sophomore year he walked out of Geneva and soon transferred to Yale. Though he was more satisfied with Yale, he viewed it as far from ideal educationally and essentially sectarian. Rather than rejecting Christianity, White adopted a liberal version of it, crediting Unitarians William Ellery Channing and Theodore

Parker with strengthening his faith.[2] Parker taught, for instance, that whereas the external forms of religion might change, a permanent essence of pure religion and pure morality underlay all particular dogmas.

As a gentleman with no clear plans upon graduation in 1853, White settled on accompanying his Yale friend Daniel Coit Gilman as an unpaid attaché to the American diplomatic mission in Russia. While abroad, White enrolled for lectures in history, art, and literature at the University of Berlin, thus sampling the renowned German universities, an enterprise that was becoming almost mandatory for aspiring American scholars. The experience was sufficient for him to decide on a scholarly career.

Apparently hoping to improve his chances for employment at Yale, White returned to New Haven to receive a master of arts degree, which was still a perfunctory degree granted after three years to virtually any graduate who paid a fee.[3] While there he was inspired by a remark of the visiting Francis Wayland (who by then had been largely frustrated in his attempts at grand reforms in the East) that the future of American education lay in the West. White applied to Tappan's Michigan and was hired.

It is worth noticing that while at Michigan, White, who favored abolition of slavery, attempted to have published a scholarly article on Jefferson and slavery, in which he sought to prove that Jefferson was actually a free-soil politician. He sent this to the *New Englander,* the Yale house organ. After initial interest the editor eventually responded that the problem was not with White but with Jefferson. "Ninety-nine out of a hundred of the readership," he explained, "have a strong dislike for the man, in which I must be free to confess I share to almost any extent."[4] Though Jefferson's educational opinions were not at all in immediate view, White's interest in rehabilitating Jefferson in the North can hardly be unrelated to his evident affinities to Jefferson's views on both education and religion. In fact, White's effort on behalf of American education might be seen as an assumption of the mantle of Jefferson and an attempt to counter the effects of the fifty years of evangelical dominance that had intervened.

In the New York Senate White found a congenial spirit in the wealthy Ezra Cornell. Cornell, a self-made man, had drifted from the Quakerism in which he had been reared and developed a sort of home-grown deism that limited his formal religious options to the Unitarian Society, which he attended as a nonmember. He had, if anything, more antipathy than White to evangelical religion, which he considered the height of unreason. Nonetheless, he also believed in a deity who guaranteed and affirmed human progress. "I have no doubt," he wrote in a letter to his wife, "that God's first and unalterable design was good will to man." "But the gospel as it is preached," he wrote in another letter, "falls more like a mildew upon a benighted world, and tries to shield the deformities of the dead and putrid carcass of 'the Church' from the penetrating eye of advancing science and humanity. . . . The steam engine, the railroad and the electric telegraph are the great engines of reformation, and by the time we enter upon the twentieth century the present will be looked back to as we now look back to the dark ages. . . . A new era in religion and humanity will have arrived."[5]

White and Cornell found the opportunity to join their somewhat disparate ideals for the modern university as a result of the momentous Morrill Land Grant Act of 1862. This act represented the culmination of popular agitation for higher education in the mechanical and agricultural arts, a proposal that promised to help make the United States competitive in economic and industrial development. The cause was part of the emerging Republican agenda to develop the nation industrially and morally. "We want a seminary," inveterate reformer Horace Greeley declared in 1858, "which provides as fitly and thoroughly for the education of the Captains of Industry as Yale or Harvard does for those who are dedicated to either of the Professions."[6] In 1858 the act had been passed by Congress but vetoed by President Buchanan as an unconstitutional infringement of the federal government. With the southern states absent in 1862, the way was cleared for passage of the act, which was signed by Lincoln on July 2, 1862. The act provided for the proceeds from large tracts of public land to go to the establishment and support of colleges of agricultural and mechanical arts.[7]

Initially it was not at all clear precisely how the funds should be distributed, whether they should go to one or to several institutions, and whether they should go to existing schools or to newly established ones. Nothing prevented the funds from being used at schools with liberal arts programs as well as the more utilitarian ones. States handled the issue in various ways, many eventually establishing a separate state agricultural and mechanical school, others funding existing programs or scientific schools.

Andrew White was convinced that New York needed to concentrate its university-building energies in one place and persuaded Ezra Cornell to fund such a school in Ithaca. The new university would have both liberal arts and practical programs. By 1868 it was ready to open with over four hundred students. White had designed multiple degree tracks for practical subjects, such as agriculture, mechanical arts, engineering, mining, and medicine. There also was a general track, with or without classics. All programs were treated as equal. Under some pressure from Catharine Beecher and others to prove their liberality, White and Cornell agreed to include women on a regular basis beginning in 1872.[8]

From the outset, opposition to sectarianism was a major theme of the university. As soon as the Cornell plan was formulated, denominational colleges led the opposition in the New York legislature, hoping to gain the public funds themselves. When Cornell announced its opening they quickly tagged it as "godless." White immediately counterattacked, claiming the now venerable distinction between Christian and sectarian. "We will labor to make this a Christian institution," he proclaimed in his inaugural, "—a sectarian institution it may never be." In what was to become his characteristic manner, White recounted the evils of sectarianism. As was already common in Massachusetts, White used the evils of the Puritan heritage to batter sectarianism. "From the days when Henry Dunster, the first president of the first college in America, was driven from his seat with ignominy and with cruelty because Cotton Mather declared him 'fallen into the briars of anti-paedo-baptism,' the sectarian spirit has been the worst foe of enlarged university education." Anticipating words later enshrined as the shibboleth of the movement by Harvard's Charles Eliot at the Johns Hopkins inaugural in 1876 ("A university can not be built upon a sect"), White proclaimed, "I deny that any university fully worthy of that great name can ever be founded upon the platform of any one sect or combination of sects."[9] Ezra Cornell made the same point with succinct railroad imagery: "It shall be our aim, and our constant effort to make true Christian men, without dwarfing or paring them down to fit the narrow gauge of any sect."[10]

White seldom missed an opportunity to point out that Cornell was indeed a Christian institution. Concerns about public relations no doubt provided the immediate motives for such expressions, yet they were not entirely alien to White's personal outlook. Although he was never confirmed, White attended Episcopal services and often professed a broad religious commitment. He wrote in a private letter, for instance, that "whatever my heterodoxies I do believe in a higher power who controls human affairs for good."[11]

This broad identification of Christianity with humanism, in the sense of whatever promotes human welfare, was reflected in university policy. Chapel was not required at Cornell (though, as at all land grant colleges, military training initially was), but White was proud to point out that religious services were held daily. Moreover, he welcomed the Christian Association and gladly accepted a gift to build a substantial chapel on campus and to introduce the novelty of filling the pulpit with leading preachers from a variety of denominations. In 1872 White offered a pamphlet, "The Cornell University: What it is and What it is not," in which he argued at length for its Christian character. Again the definition was broad. "The Cornell University is governed by a body of Christian Trustees, conducted by Christian Professors, and is a Christian Institution," wrote White, "as the Public School system of the State is Christian."[12] The analogy in the last clause was revealing.

There were limits to what public relations could stand. In 1874, the university accepted a gift for the purpose of hiring Felix Adler to teach Hebrew and Oriental literature. It was indeed a progressive move to hire a Jew, though there had been precedents at American colleges for the teaching of Hebrew. Adler, who founded the Ethical Culture Society in 1876, however, was a different case. Adler used his courses directly to attack religious beliefs. In 1877 his contract was not renewed, ostensibly on the grounds that the university did not want to be controlled by donors who endowed chairs. In fact, whatever the sympathies of the university administration toward Adler, it could not afford to allow the accusation of harboring skepticism to be so openly confirmed.[13]

White regarded the university as having a moral mission and regarded "the sickly cynic" as the "most detestable" product of college life. To his friend Daniel Coit Gilman he wrote in 1884, "Why is it not possible in this country to have the great fundamental principles of . . . ethics . . . presented simply and strongly, so that we can send out into the country men who can bring simple ethical principles to bear upon public instruction everywhere?" Early in 1886 he received the endowment of a professorship from Russell Sage which included the provision that the teacher "shall instruct students in mental philosophy and ethics from a definitely Christian standpoint." White did not object to Christianity being represented in the university, but only to traditional Christian dogmatism. In his 1885 *Annual Report* he remarked, "Even error honestly arrived at will do more for religion and for science, than truth merely asserted dogmatically. . . . No talk about the *tendency* of any man's teaching should have any weight against him if he be capable and honest."[14]

By insisting that Cornell was Christian, nonsectarian, dedicated to high moral values, yet free, especially free for scientific inquiry, White was effectively taking over the rhetoric of the evangelical establishment. White particularly emphasized a Whiggish version of the rise of science, free inquiry, moral advance, and human betterment. In insisting on the importance of free inquiry for scientific progress White sounded essentially like his mentor, Henry Tappan. But in White's version nonsectarian Protestantism had been quietly dropped from the story and replaced by a broader Christianity or religion of humanity.

White underscored this point in what became his life's intellectual work, *A History of the Warfare of Science with Theology in Christendom.* Though not published in its final form until 1896, this work originated as part of the immediate counterattack on sectarianism connected with the establishment of Cornell. The year after the founding, in December 1869, White delivered the initial version as "The Battlefields of Science," at the Cooper Union of New York; it was published the next day in the *New York Tribune* by White's friend Horace Greeley.[15] Over the year it went through various forms as White added more and more evidence of what he saw as a perennial problem.

White's emphasis on the military metaphor may reflect the influence of the English debates which had surrounded the advent of Darwinism. White kept in close touch with the English scene where in the early 1860s there was something akin to warfare between the clerics who controlled the universities and a rising contingent of religious liberal freethinkers who were a more formidable force in their nation's intellectual life than were their American counterparts. Part of the reason for the deeper antagonism was that as late as the 1860s Oxford and Cambridge were still under the domain of the church, with assent to the Thirty-nine Articles required for matriculation and university positions limited to Anglicans.

While reform was in the air, the atmosphere was also charged with resentments of those who wished to wrest intellectual hegemony from the conservative religious establishment. In this setting the antibiblicist implications of Darwinism were enthusiastically hailed for their liberating qualities. T. H. Huxley, the self-styled "gladiator-general" of Darwinism, sounded the warfare theme in 1860 against the "Bibliolaters." It was remarkable, he said, that opposition to scientific truth, even "after a hundred defeats . . . is at this day as rampant, though happily not so mischievous, as in the time of Galileo."[16] In post–Civil War America, where military images were poignant but the lines between science and religion were usually less sharply drawn, White was introducing a polarizing metaphor for interpreting the ongoing debates.

White always insisted that he was working in the true interests of religion, not against it. While time and again free scientific inquiry has been thought to be opposed to the interests of religion, in fact it "has invariably resulted in the highest good of Religion and Science." This was so, White reassured his 1869 audience, because "God's truth must agree, whether discovered by looking within upon the soul or without upon the world." This sounded much like the conventional formula that there were two revelations, nature and Scripture. The difference was that White left out Scripture, substituting a transcendental "looking on the heart within." In any case White affirmed that the best men in the church agreed that "searchers for truth, whether in Theology or Natural Science shall work on as friends, sure that no matter how much at variance they may at times seem to be, the truths they reach shall finally be fused into each other." The crucial point was that science must be free. Employing idealist language that indentified God with the vindicating progess of knowledge, White declared, "The very finger of the Almighty has written on history that science must be studied by means proper to itself, and in no other way."[17]

Most significantly, White argued, in what might be seen as an elaboration on Henry Tappan, science and Scripture must be kept in separate compartments. "There has never been a scientific theory framed from the use of Scriptural texts which has been made to stand." As to specifics, White picked relatively safe examples in his 1869 version of the argument. The Bible had been used to argue for a flat earth and against Galileo for a geocentric universe. Spiritual and demonic explanations of human ills had blocked early medicine and study of anatomy. In the field of political economy, biblical prohibitions had been used in the Middle Ages to forbid usury. More recently Genesis had been used as a basis for determining the age of the earth, and "strange as it may at first seem the war on geology was waged more fiercely in Protestant countries than Catholic, and of all countries England furnished the most bitter opposition." The culmination of this recent abandonment of the Protestant and Whig tradition of support for freedom, White intimated, was that even in America founders of a university "earnestly devoted to building up Christian civilization" were accused of being "godless" "infidel," and "irreligious" because they were not sectarian.[18]

True religion, White insisted, did not interfere with scientific freedom; only sectarianism and theology did. In later versions he elaborated this theme. In the 1876 edition of his small book, *The Warfare of Science,* White described true religion as simply truth seeking plus virtue. " All history" he proclaimed, "shows that the first article of a saving faith, for any land or time, is faith that there is a Power in this universe strong enough to make truth seeking free." True Christianity, he wrote in words that echoed Theodore Parker and Thomas Jefferson, was found only by those who preached and practiced the righteousness of the prophets, the psalms and the Sermon on the Mount, that is, " 'pure religion and undefiled.' " The choice was between "the living kernel of religion" and "the dead and dried husks of sect and dogma."[19]

In the final massive two-volume 1896 version of his opus White clarified his thesis with his title: *A History of the Warfare of Science with Theology in Christendom.* The warfare was with *theology,* not with true religion. By now, however, the tide had turned decisively in his favor, and White felt free to launch a frontal attack on all traditional Christian and biblical belief. No longer did he stick to the safe examples of questions long since settled. Opening with a cannonade drawing on the prestige of Darwinism, he argued that "the old theory of direct creation is gone forever," and that we now understand the creation stories themselves as products of the evolution of humanity. Given all the evidence of human progress, it was incredible that any religion still taught the fall of humanity. White proceeded to furnish a complete handbook for turn-of-the-century skepticism regarding traditional Christianity, his assault culminating in expositions of the incredibility of biblical accounts of miracles, the superiority of modern medicine and psychology over biblicist supernatural explanations, and of how higher criticism had altogether demolished biblical credibility in scientific and historical matters.

All this was in the name, however, of saving pure religion. "The divine revelation of science," he still assured, had not done harm to the Bible, but rather "made it all the more precious to us." As to the clergy, "among them are some of my dearest friends," and "no one honors their proper work more than I do," with "proper" the functional word. White pointed once again to the vigorous chapel program and Christian Association at Cornell, and he argued that despite the rise of science "there has been no sign of any tendency toward irreligion. On the contrary, it is the testimony of those best acquainted with the American colleges and universities during the past forty-five years that there had been in them a great gain, not only as regards morals, but as regards religion in its highest and best sense."[20]

When White's polemic appeared in 1896 it was very nearly forty-five years since Henry Tappan had gone to Michigan. White had indeed carried on the mission that he and his generation saw as necessary for the completion of the work of establishing American science and the university. "Ye shall know the truth and the truth shall make you free" was still their motto, and there was still a place for Christianity in a broad sense, but only with its narrow ecclesiastical and theological functions kept to a strictly limited place.

Ultimately, the question was one of authority. Science and Scripture had in the previous generation been, in effect, co-equal authorities. Now science was supposed to rule alone. White, however, saw the advantage in describing the conflict as one between science and *theology,* which had a much lower public rating than the Bible. The conflict, said White, had been "between two epochs in the evolution of human thought—the theological and the scientific." Since the process was progressive and evolutionary, there was no turning back. In Tappan's day Protestant leaders had to respect boundaries set by Scripture and pursue their inquiries within a broad Christian framework. Francis Wayland was a good example, constantly relating political economy and moral philosophy to the creation order. Forty-five years later, not only was science freed from Scripture, it was proclaimed the unsurpassable judge of Scripture itself.

Evangelicals of Tappan's day had made a tremendous investment in "free inquiry." To win the battle against Jeffersonian skepticism, they had adopted Jeffersonian rhetoric. Now that same rhetoric was being reclaimed and turned against them, and there was little ground on which to reply. No one had celebrated more than they the virtues of Baconian science, which they assumed would never subvert biblical truth. Now that the best respected science had suddenly turned to naturalistic and evolutionary premises, they could hardly turn around and say that science should not be quite so free.

Moreover, the champions of science claimed morality on their side. Free inquiry, after all, seemed to amount to simple honesty and cultivating such habits seemed the essence of intellectual integrity. The progress from the theological to the scientific stage in human evolution could thus be seen as moral progress, an emancipation from the slavery of the mind. This was the destiny of Western civilization, to free humanity.

As historian David Hollinger and others have pointed out, the reverence for science often assumed cultic proportions. By White's day the metaphor of the temple was common and proponents of science might depict themselves of the '"priests" who guard the shrine, or the "worshippers" who would enjoy "sweet communion and peace of mind."[21]

White, who relished military training and quasi-military discipline at early Cornell,[22] preferred the masculine image of warfare, and indeed there was much to the suggestion that the new universities, even if women might be present, with their professional schools, technology, and mechanical and practical arts, were male domains par excellence. There would be no women's universities. The description of the scientific ideal in 1888 by another Tappan protégé, geologist and college president Thomas C. Chamberlain, for instance, fits just as well with the masculine images of the time:

> The supreme love of truth is . . . not a mere passive, receptive love of truth when truth is forced in upon the mind. It arises in its own strength and in its own inspiration, and goes forth to search for specific, positive, demonstrative truth. It is moved by a controlling thirst for truth, the naked, the innermost, the vital, the fundamental truth.[23]

University building in the late nineteenth century was part and parcel of the victorious Republicans' efforts to harness American technological potential. The practical promises of a first-rate educational system were essential to gaining financial and legislative support. The Morrill Act fit well with Republican efforts to strengthen the economy and the nation. Andrew Dickson White and Ezra Cornell were meant for each other. White remained active in Republican politics and was rewarded several times with major ambassadorships. He was a leading figure in the generation for whom the Civil War provided a model for the mobilization of American power. The cause of the Union had combined high ideals with increasingly professionalized organization and mastery of technique. There was no contradiction, therefore, in the minds of reforming Republicans in wedding rationalized material force to high ideals any more than there was in freeing the slaves through the awful power of the organization of Grant and Sherman. Nor was there a contradiction after the war between their continuing millennial dreams and their championing of business, industrial, intellectual, and scientific expansion. All could be seen as part of a single Protestant hope to uplift humanity and usher in an age of redemption.

Notes

1. White, *Autobiography of Andrew Dickson White,* 2 vols. (New York, 1906, I:279.

2. Earl Hubert Brill, "Religion and the Rise of the University: A Study of the Secularization of American Higher Education, 1870–1910," Ph.D. dissertation, American University, 1969, 50; Glenn C. Altschuler, *Andrew D. White—Educator, Historian, Diplomat* (Ithaca: Cornell University Press, 1979); Morris Bishop, *A History of Cornell* (Ithaca: Cornell University Press, 1962); Walter P. Rogers, *Andrew D. White and the Modern University* (Ithaca: Cornell University Press, 1942); and White, *Autobiography.*

3. Altschuler, *White,* 56.

4. William Kingsley to White, February 10, 1858, quoted in Altschuler, *White,* 46.

5. Cornell to his wife, August 20, 1843; April 2, 1854, quoted in Bishop, *Cornell,* 26–27.

6. Horace Greeley, *Address at the Laying of the Cornerstone of the People's College* (1858), quoted in Rogers, *White,* 9.

7. Rogers, *White,* 54–60.

8. Beecher, who was in her seventies, decided to enroll in a course at Cornell. When White informed Beecher that Cornell had no course open to women, she replied, "Oh that is quite all right Doctor White, in fact I prefer to take it with

men." Kathryn Kish Sklar, *Catharine Beecher: A Study in American Domesticity* (New York: W. W. Norton, 1878), 258–59.

9. White, "Inaugural Address," in *Account of the Proceedings of the Inauguration, October 7, 1868* (Ithaca: Cornell University, 1869), quoted in Bishop, *Cornell,* 190–91; Rogers, *White,* 73; and Brill, "Religion," 152.

10. Ezra Cornell, *Address at the Inauguration of Cornell University,* quoted in Rogers, *White,* 73.

11. White to Willard Fiske, October 19, 1880, quoted in *White,* Rogers, 81.

12. Quoted in Bishop, *Cornell,* 191. Cf. 190–96.

13. Ibid., 192–39; Richard Hofstadter and Walter P. Metzger, *The Development of Academic Freedom in the United States* (New York: Columbia University Press, 1955), 340–41. Firing a Jew was, of course, easier than firing someone of Christian heritage, such as William Graham Sumner at Yale. On the other hand, White insisted that he would be glad to hire an academically qualified Buddhist. Laurence R. Veysey, "The Emergence of the American University, 1865–1910: A Study in the Relations between Ideals and Institutions," Ph.D. dissertation, University of California, Berkeley, 1961, 373n.

14. Quotations are from Veysey, "Emergence," 372–73, except for Sage proviso from Robert S. Shepard, *God's People in the Ivory Tower: Religion in the Early American University* (Brooklyn: Carlson Publishing, 1991), 19. In 1890 Sage also endowed an entire School of Philosophy, which included a professorship in the history and philosophy of religion and Christian ethics. This was one of the first positions in comparative religion in an American university. Christian ethics was added to accommodate the training of the first incumbent, the Rev. Charles Tyler, who had been pastor of Sage's Congregational church in Ithaca. Ibid., 18–20.

15. See Bishop, *Cornell,* 191.

16. James R. Moore, *The Post-Darwinian Controversies: A Study of the Protestant Struggle to Come to Terms with Darwin in Great Britain and America 1870–1900* (Cambridge: Cambridge University Press, 1979), 59–60, cf. 19–100. On the cultural dynamics contributing to the development and acceptance of Darwinism see also Adrian Desmond and James R. Moore, *Darwin: The Life of a Tormented Evolutionist* (New York: Warner Books, 1991).

17. "Prof. White on "The Battle-fields of Science," *The New York Tribune,* December 18, 1869, 4. Cf. Henry Tappan's similar language when he was ousted at Michigan, quoted at the end of chapter 5.

18. White, "Battle-fields of Science," 4.

19. Andrew Dickson White, *The Warfare of Science* (New York, 1876), 148, 151. White's missionary zeal may be indicated by the fact that he personally donated an early copy to the University of California, where it is still on the shelves.

20. Andrew Dickson White, *A History of the Warfare of Science with Theology in Christendom,* 2 vols. (New York, 1896), I:86, 24; II:207; I:xi, viii, 414. Altschuler, *White,* 202–16, provides a useful analysis.

21. David Hollinger, "Inquiry and Uplift: Late Nineteenth-Century American Academics and the Moral Efficacy of Scientific Practice," in *The Authority of Experts: Studies in History and Theory,* Thomas L. Haskell, ed. (Bloomington: Indiana University Press, 1984), 147.

22. Veysey, "Emergence," 374.

23. Thomas C. Chamberlain, *The Ethical Functions of Scientific Study* (Ann Arbor, 1888), 6–7, quoted in Hollinger, "Inquiry," 148. Hollinger suggests the masculine character of the specifically military metaphors of the day (150–51).

7

Positive Christianity versus Positivism at Noah Porter's Yale

The announcement in the late 1860s that Yale's president Theodore Dwight Woolsey would retire in the spring of 1871 sparked excited talk of turning the college into a university. Yale was the flagship evangelical college and long had been in the forefront of national trends. Cornell had opened its doors in 1868 and in 1869 Harvard inaugurated President Charles Eliot, a relatively young man clearly in the progressive camp. Yale alumni started a "Young Yale" movement centered in New York[1] and called for a similar choice at their alma mater. The leading progressive candidate was Daniel Coit Gilman,[2] a Yale graduate and the principal administrative officer at Yale's Sheffield Scientific School. Gilman had already turned down two college presidencies and was known to favor transforming the college into a true university. The conservative Yale Corporation, still virtually all Connecticut clergymen, chose instead Noah Porter, the college's professor of moral philosophy. Porter (1811–1892) had been one of the leading figures during the recent decades of Yale's preeminence, was a champion of the classical curriculum, and promised to preserve the old-time college ideal.

Modernization at Midcentury Yale

Although in the 1870s Porter looked like a conservative, at midcentury he had been part of a generation of New Haven scholars who had fostered some important modernizing trends within the old-time college structures. Most significantly the midcentury Yale scholars were part of the first generation of Americans to define scholarship as a profession. In New England, theology had long dominated intellectual life. Theology in turn had led the way toward professionalization, signaled by the establishment of theological seminaries, such as Andover (1808), or separate divinity schools at colleges, such as the Theology Department of Yale (begun in 1822). The next generation of New Haven scholars, coming on the scene around midcentury, marked a new stage in professionalization. Although many of them, such as Noah Porter himself, were clergymen, they also developed specialties in disciplines. They were also shaping subcommunities of scholars who shared findings, set scientific standards, defined conventions of style, and founded some of the first American scholarly societies. Yale professors also established their own scholarly journal, the *New Englander,* a quarterly of lengthy essays and reviews directed toward a general literate audience, which marked a transitional form from the theological reviews that dominated American academic thought in the first half of the century to the more specialized journals that would emerge by the end of the century.

The new tendencies were reflected in some gradual modifications of the still predominantly classical tradition. Under President Woolsey history was added as a separate subject in the undergraduate curriculum in 1847 and a professorship of history was established in 1865. In natural science the college established two professorships in 1846, a separate degree in science in 1852, and in 1860 founded the satellite Sheffield Scientific School with its own curriculum and student body. In 1860 the college also inaugurated the first American Ph.D. program for work in its graduate Department of Philosophy and the Arts. Three candidates met the relatively modest requirements for the degree as early as 1861. No one pretended that awarding a Ph.D. made Yale into a university, but it was another sign of the new professional orientation.[3]

These professionalizing tendencies among the New Haven scholars were direct reflections of the influence of Germany, where most of the leading Yale professors had studied.[4] Like other Americans making the trek to the Continent, what they brought home was not so much the particulars of the German academic system as the inspiration of the ideal of the professional scholar as a cultural leader.

The New Haven scholars of Porter's generation also found German romanticism and philosophical idealism liberating from some of the strict dogmas of their Calvinist heritage.[5] Like his contemporary Henry Tappan, Porter spent a good bit of his intellectual energy in attempting to reconcile German philosophies with the inherited American traditions of Baconianism and Scottish Common Sense.[6] While he was still a student in Germany, for instance, Porter wrote back to President Woolsey that he was enthusiastic "to lay the philosophy of Schleiermacher and its basis before the American public and have it understood."[7] Friedrich Schleiermacher's theology represented for the New Englanders not a repudiation of Calvinism but a shift toward experiential verification by way of truths known to the heart which undercut some of the harshest emphases of the old creed. Also important were changing views on cultivating character. Rather than relying on conversion, as had the generation of Timothy Dwight, they emphasized the goal of fostering growth toward wholeness in the human personality. In theology such emphases were most fully developed by Hartford pastor Horace Bushnell, a close associate of the New Haven group. At Yale College the longstanding commitment to the ancient classics, underscored by the Yale Report of 1828, could be defended as advancing this modern ideal for the balanced development of human character.[8]

The Yale scholars also reflected the modern Whig ideals so prominent in midcentury New England.[9] They were forward-looking in favoring the advance of industry and science, yet they emphasized balancing material advance with simultaneous efforts to develop American character, both individually and communally. Building civilization was, as much as anything, a moral task. Morality, in turn, was essentially a matter of duty. So when Noah Porter taught moral science, he organized it around the subject of duty including coverage of theories of duty and practical subjects such as various duties of self-discipline, duties to others, to friends, family, the state, even to animals and to the physical world, and of course, duty to God.[10]

The Idea of a Christian College

In this context we can understand one of the era's most significant reflections on Christianity and American higher education. In 1869 Noah Porter, who was well known to be a candidate for the Yale presidency, published what amounted to his campaign platform in a series of lengthy articles in the *New Englander,* titled "The American Colleges and the American Public," later to be published as a book. Although some disagreed with Porter's curricular conservatism, he was widely respected as a leading philosopher. He has even been characterized by one historian of American philosophy as "in many ways the greatest and most erudite of the professors of philosophy" of his day.[11]

Porter's principal concern was to preserve what he thought was excellent about the American undergraduate college at it was exemplified at midcentury Yale. So, for instance, he defended the classicism of the Yale Report of 1828, arguing on the broad grounds that the primary purpose of college education was "to give power to acquire and to think rather than to impart special knowledge." College was a place to learn valuable habits that would foster growth in later life. It would promote cultural development. Specialized information concerning physical or practical sciences had proper places in preparatory and graduate education. But there was a danger that these would crowd out the character-building purposes of undergraduate training. By now, he said, most colleges had made sufficient—"perhaps excessive"—concessions in the direction of the immediately practical.[12]

In his culminating essay Porter defended the proposition that "American Colleges should have a positively religious and Christian character." Some persons, he noted, said that since the goal of education is to inculcate culture, religion should be relegated to an indirect and incidental role. At the opposite extreme, others argued that religion was supreme, and culture might therefore be sacrificed to religion. Porter insisted that there need be no such tension. Religion and culture were perfectly complementary.

Porter characterized the contributions of Christianity to enlightened, tolerant, and civilized culture, essentially summarizing the Whig ideals. Christianity contributed to *"industry,"* it was *"truth-loving,"* and it was *"refining"* of culture. Culture could indeed refine Christianity also, but "culture itself is exposed to certain excesses for which Christianity is the only adequate counterpoise and remedy." It was needed "as a corrective against the one-sidedness, the Philistinism we might call it, of modern science and literature."

On the subject of modern science Porter seemed to be responding particularly to his former student Andrew Dickson White. In his recently published inaugural address White had depicted the evils of Christian dogmatism and proclaimed that no university "fully worthy of that great name can ever be founded upon the platform of any one sect or combination of sects." Porter, however, turned the tables on White by quoting the Cornell president's *Report on the Organization of Cornell University* in which White mentioned that science itself had sectarian divisions. Porter, who emphasized that the sort of Christianity he stood for was "nonsectarian," suggested that such Christianity could help scientists rise above the narrow perspectives of their specialized disciplines. So to the claim that science was the highest road to nonsectarianism he retorted that in fact "Christian science furnishes the natural and most efficient prophylactic and cure for . . . sectarian narrowness and embitterments."[13]

Like other evangelical apologists Porter could proclaim that Christians had nothing to fear from modern science. Since truth-seeking was all they were interested in, they could affirm open inquiry.[14] Such assurances grew out of the evangelicals' experience of having been part of a cultural and intellectual establishment. It was an optimistic mood related to their Whig heritage of cultural reform and their assurance that Christianity would lead to cultural progress.[15]

Porter, however, was sounding a more ominous note as well. He was well enough informed about British and German trends to recognize that modern culture might be turning against Christianity. The world of the 1840s and 1850s when for Americans evangelicalism seemed to hold firm intellectual sway might be disappearing. Christianity therefore had to play a new kind of defensive role. "Religious influences and religious teachings," he wrote in his *New Englander* essay, "should be employed in colleges, in order to exclude and counteract the atheistic tendencies of much of modern science, literature, and culture." Powerful currents from the international community of which Yale was just an outpost were threatening to overwhelm the comfortable consensus. "Every educated man now a-days," Porter warned, "must either accept or reject the ill-disguised materialism of Huxley, the cerebralism of Bain, the thin and vacillating metaphysics of Mill, the evolutionism of Herbert Spencer, with its demonstrated impossibility of a positive theism, and the serene fatalism of the devotees of Nature or of the Absolute."

Faced with the practical atheism of much of modern culture there could be no middle ground. These teachings, Porter pointed out, were not neutral regarding religion, but took definite theological positions. "The question is not whether the college shall, or shall not, teach theology, but what theology it shall teach,—theology according to Comte and Spencer, or according to Bacon and Christ, theology according to Moses and Paul, or according to Buckle and Draper."

The question of the openness of higher education looked entirely different in this light. "The plea of freedom and tolerance is put in on every quarter," said Porter, but if that meant that these atheistic views were to be presented without Christian refutation, the plea was deceptive. Not to answer atheistic views was practically to promote them, which was beyond the pale of the Christian college.

Surely advocates of anti-Christian outlooks should not be teaching impressionable young people. "If all opinions should have a hearing, as they ought," Porter suggested, still claiming to stand for openness, "let theistic teachers be selected who will represent fairly all the atheistic and anti-Christian objections and difficulties, but let not atheism or anti-Christianity be taught in any of its chairs, either directly or indirectly." This raised a question "of the greatest delicacy." What should be the religious tests for teachers? The inability to resolve this issue was the point on which Porter's presidency would founder in his famous encounter with William Graham Sumner.

We can understand the limitations built into Porter's position if we see that he was caught between his two views of the relationship of Christianity to culture. On the one hand lay his Protestant-Whig view that there was no conflict between Christianity and the highest culture and that Protestantism stood for openness and free scientific inquiry. This was the establishment side of the ruling New England culture. To retain hegemony it had to be open enough to embrace and absorb all relevant views. On the other hand, the ominous turn that Porter saw advanced culture taking suggested that Christians would have to hold a more closed sectarian stance if they were to retain their distinctiveness.

Another way of putting it is that Porter was faced with a latter-day version of the Puritan dilemma of how to live in the world but not of it.[16] On the one hand, he had inherited the establishmentarian side of Puritanism, which assumed that Christians should dominate the culture. In the republican context of the nineteenth century such tendencies had merged with Whiggish ideals of liberty, moral reform, free scientific inquiry, and progress. On the other hand, Porter was heir to the sectarian side of Puritanism, which was still vigorous in New England theological debates. This side of the heritage emphasized the distinctiveness of Christian thought in opposition to all rivals. On this reading of the tradition New England provided a haven of purity against the corruptions of old-world rivals. The sectarian side of the heritage said that colleges should be bounded by doctrinal orthodoxy; the establishmentarian side said that they could not.

Porter attempted to resolve this dilemma by maintaining that there should be religious tests, but that they should be informal, left to the discretion of the college president who did the hiring. Sometimes the teacher with "honest doubts" would be preferable to the overbearing orthodox dogmatist. In some chairs, Porter thought, the religious views of the incumbent could not affect the teaching. In others, however, "an anti-Christian sophist or a velvet-footed infidel might pervert [it] to the most disastrous uses."

By thus making religious tests a matter of judgment of character more than of creed, the New Haven scholars could retain their stance of having moved beyond dogmatism. They could also claim to be "nonsectarian," meaning that the college should not stand narrowly for the views of one Protestant denomination as opposed to the others. They remembered well bitter controversies with rock-ribbed conservatives who insisted on creedal tests. So they could hardly turn around and impose such tests, even if Christianity itself became culturally beleaguered. The only checks on infidelity would be the power of personal influence. That power, it seemed, would serve well enough for a time, so long as the right individuals remained in control.

Porter correctly recognized that the campaign for transformation from college to university threatened the maintenance of such personal control. The ideal of freedom, even if vague in its implications, was essential to the university. Porter, who had studied two years at the University of Berlin, conceded that wider room for free inquiry might be appropriate to a true university. However, he called for a sharp distinction between colleges and universities. Much of the current confusion in America, he thought, came from conflating the two and applying university standards to colleges. Colleges were for the training of "immature" boys.[17] Porter had devoted one of his articles to the college as a community, an ideal threatened by the individualism of university freedom. Even in a university, Porter was not prepared to concede that every shade of opinion and "antireligious philosophy" should have a chair to represent it. At a Christian college, however, it was entirely inappropriate to hire people to teach anti-Christian viewpoints.[18]

Porter, who was one of the ablest defenders of the centrality of positive Christianity in America's influential nonsectarian colleges, thus backed himself into a corner. It was a corner that advocates of distinctly Christian education could defend, but only temporarily. Even though they proclaimed that Christianity stood for freedom, the only way they could retain a semblance of free inquiry without opening the door to atheism was by maintaining a setting in which they could hold close personal control. They could defend what they already had, the disciplined undergraduate college as a haven against secular intrusion, but they had no real plan for the university as a graduate, professional, or specialized scientific institution. This line of defense thus had momentous implications in that it simply failed to address the issue of the relationship of Christianity to the emerging universities.

This strategy also had the side effect of tying the defense of Christianity to the prescribed classical curriculum. There was, of course, no logical necessity for this alliance; the Greek and Latin writers were not Christian. Of course, a millennium and a half of incorporating these "spoils of Egypt" (as Augustine had said) into Christian thought made this a moot point. Moreover, the millennium of precedent since the dawn of Western universities made the continuation of the strategy seem the more sage. It was also proven safe, which could not be said for Comte, Buckle, Mill, Huxley, Spencer, and their crowd.

At the same time Porter was implicitly tying the defense of Christian higher education to the continued dominance of the clergy. One of the articles in his series argued that colleges should be built around teachers rather than researchers. The ideal scholar in his view was a renaissance person who had developed a specialty but still was essentially a well-rounded gentleman. It fit the mid-nineteenth-century model of the gentleman-scholar or the clergyman-scientist. Porter and the New Haven scholars might be promoting professionalism, but they were still doing it largely as clergy. One of the ways that clergy had ensured their status as an intellectual elite, especially in the Reformed traditions that shaped so much of higher education, was with their extensive skills in ancient languages. This dominance was breaking down within American Protestantism as popular sects such as the Methodists and Baptists, who typically sidestepped classical training for clergy, far surpassed the Reformed numerically. Now, however, in the college, one of the last bastions of classically trained clergy, their dominance was threatened as well. Predictably, they defended the curriculum in which they had true expertise as professionals. And inevitably this became tied to their defense of positive Christian education.

The Problem of a Christian College

The crisis precipitated in 1879 by Porter's attempt to stop William Graham Sumner from using Herbert Spencer's *The Study of Sociology* brought these principles to the test and proved that ideals that might have seemed viable in the middle decades of the century were not going to survive its later years. The forces of professionalization and scientific ideals which Porter and his generation had helped nourish in America now had emerged with the self-assurance of adolescence. Long-held standards of submission to duly constituted authority were crumbling and proclamations of individual autonomy were taking their place. William Graham Sumner's rugged "dog-eat-dog" social Darwinist *laissez-faire* sociology not only fit the economic realities of the day but was just one expression of the watchword of "freedom" heard on every front. In practical terms for higher education it meant that the rules that had prevailed among clergy, where boundaries were set on the basis of doctrinal orthodoxy, would no longer apply. Science would be the new orthodoxy. Whatever the theoretical concerns, the institutional realities were that colleges were becoming universities and universities were being defined as scientific institutions, free from traditions. The newest institutions were on this basis threatening to displace the old colleges. In addition to Andrew Dickson White's Cornell, the intellectually formidable Johns Hopkins University opened in 1876, headed by Porter's principal progressive rival for the Yale presidency, Daniel Coit Gilman. In the contest between Sumner and Porter, time was on the side of Sumner.

Science and Christianity

Had the issue been purely intellectual, Porter's emphases on the threats to Christian distinctiveness might have received wider hearing. It was not a question of a warfare between science and clerical dogmatism as Sumner, Andrew Dickson White, and others, represented it.[19] Nor was it, as is often thought, primarily a debate over Darwinism; Yale, like almost all leading colleges in the North, was teaching biological evolution by 1880.[20] Rather, the crucial issue was the assumptions on which natural scientific inquiry would be founded. As Charles Cashdollar has shown, the underlying challenge to Christian thought in this era was the challenge of positivism.[21] Positivism, arising from the views of Auguste Comte (1798–1857), the founder of the field of sociology, asserted that true science precluded religious considerations. In Comte's construction of history, humans were rising from a religious stage in which questions were decided by authority, through a metaphysical stage in which philosophy ruled, to a positive stage in which empirical investigation would be accepted as the only reliable road to truth.[22]

Noah Porter, like some other thinkers of the era influenced by idealism, recognized that the question concerned the assumptions that would determine the context in which science would take place. In his substantial text, *The Human Intellect* (1868), he concluded with a purely philosophical (that is, not directly Christian or biblical) argument for "the absolute." Belief in the absolute, Porter argued, was a presupposition necessary to explain how we can know anything.

> We assume that this absolute exists, in order that thought and science may be possible. We do not demonstrate his being by deduction, because we must believe it in order to reason deductively. We do not infer it by induction, because induction supposes it; but we show that every man who believes in either, or in both, must assume it, or give up his confidence in both these processes and their results. We do not demonstrate that God exists, but that *every man must assume that He is.*[23]

The objection to Spencer was that he a priori excluded any absolute and asserted that observable phenomena are all we can know about. As Porter put it in a sharply worded review of Spencer's *The Study of Sociology* in the midst of the Sumner controversy, Spencer's iconoclasm was based simply on arguing in a circle. Having defined science in such a way as to exclude all absolutes, he then triumphantly concludes that science shows there are no absolutes: "And so he ends this long discussion with the assumption with which he begins, that in social phenomena we can only recognize natural causation, because, forsooth, if Sociology is a science it cannot admit any other agencies."[24]

In retrospect, Porter does not appear obviously to have had the worst of the argument, as sometimes is assumed.[25] He recognized, as is largely granted today, that both natural science and sociology always take place within a framework of assumptions. Sumner's view that religion could not be relevant to social science seems indeed to be built on uncritical acceptance of the Comtean positivist claim that science must be defined outside any theistic context. Clearly both natural science and social science investigations could take place either within or without theistic assumptions. In fact, in Porter's day Sumner represented a tiny minority of American academics who explicitly rejected the relevance of theism. Even many American sociologists for the next generation attempted to relate their sociology to their Christianity, at least to Christian ethics.

The significance of the episode, however, is that even on the limited ground of undergraduate education Porter could find no acceptable way to establish effective institutional safeguards against Christian theism being undermined in the name of positive science. Sumner remained at Yale and continued there into the twentieth century as a formidable alternative to popular evangelical influences. Given Yale's history of commitment to serve the public as well as the church, there was much to be said for this solution. Porter looked like an obscurantist because he was attempting to impose standards of the church on an institution that had more than church loyalties. And for the time being there was little danger that Yale as a whole would lurch off into agnosticism. In the short run it had enough ties to its evangelical past to absorb some diversity of opinion and to be all the more stimulating a place for it. During the next generation most Christian academics came to believe that wide freedom of expression for faculty and opportunities for students to encounter representatives of a variety of viewpoints were essential to the best education. Despite the evident merits of these considerations, however, Porter should be credited with recognizing that there was a dilemma involved. In the long run Porter was correct that the Sumners would win. Standards for science that a priori excluded considerations of faith would become the norm. Within two generations Porter would look like something out of the Dark Ages, and it would be difficult to remember what the question of the relationship of Christianity to collegiate academic life was all about.

Notes

1. Louise L. Stevenson, *Scholarly Means to Evangelical Ends: The New Haven Scholars and the Transformation of Higher Learning in America, 1830–1890* (Balti-

more: Johns Hopkins Press, 1986), 63–65. Much of the following account is indebted to Stevenson's insightful study.

2. Earl Hubert Brill, "Religion and the Rise of the University: A Study of the Secularization of American Higher Education, 1870–1910," Ph.D. dissertation, American University, 1969, 60–61, 248. See 229–51, which provides an excellent account of the Yale struggles.

3. Stevenson, *Scholarly Means,* 2, 24–25, 38–39, 43–45, 87–88. Frederick Rudolph, *The American College and University: A History* (New York: Vintage Books, 1962), 335.

4. Stevenson, *Scholarly Means,* 36.

5. Ibid., 1–13 and passim.

6. See, for instance, Noah Porter, *The Human Intellect: with an Introduction upon Psychology and the Soul* (New York: Charles Scribner's Sons, 1891 [1868]).

7. Quoted in Stevenson, *Scholarly Means,* 36, from letters of February 22, 1854, and December 13, 1853.

8. Stevenson suggests these views were influenced by the German concept of *Bildung.* Ibid., 58–59.

9. Ibid., 5–6.

10. Noah Porter, *The Elements of Moral Science: Theoretical and Practical* (New York: Charles Scribner's Sons, 1885).

11. Herbert W. Schneider, *A History of American Philosophy,* 2nd ed. (New York: Columbia University Press, 1963), 215.

12. Noah Porter, "The American Colleges and the American Public," *New Englander* 28 (January 1869), 81, 76, and passim, as summarized by Brill, "Religion," 238.

13. Noah Porter, "The American Colleges and the American Public, Part IV," *New Englander* 28 (October 1869), 753–60.

14. Cf. Porter, "Inaugural Address," Yale College, October 11, 1871, quoted in Stevenson, *Scholarly Means,* 69.

15. For instance, President Theodore Dwight Woolsey of Yale in "The Religion of the Future," *New Englander* 28 (July 1869), 463–88, argued that, contrary to some recent claims, Christianity is the only religion capable of leading humanity to its ultimate progress.

16. Cf. Edmund S. Morgan, *The Puritan Dilemma: The Story of John Winthrop* (New York: Little, Brown, 1958).

17. Brooks Mather Kelley, *Yale: A History* (New Haven: Yale University Press, 1974), 241, points out that the disciplinary model of the Yale Report of 1828 to which Porter appealed was designed for an era when boys might enter college earlier and when some were graduating by age eighteen. By the 1870s the average entrance age was over eighteen.

18. Porter, "American Colleges," 762–67.

19. For example, David Starr Jordan, who became president of Stanford, described the clerical mind as irrevocably committed to untestable assumptions. From "The Church and Modern Thought," *Overland Monthly* 18 (1891), 392, cited in Richard Hofstadter and Walter P. Metzger, *The Development of Academic Freedom in the United States* (New York: Columbia University Press, 1955), 348. During the 1870s the *Index,* the journal of the American Liberal Union, edited by Francis E. Abbott, also pushed this interpretation. See Hofstadter and Metzger, *Academic Freedom,* 348–51.

20. In 1879 G. Stanley Hall wrote that "with comparatively few exceptions all

the most competent teachers of natural or physical science either tacitly accept or openly advocate the fundamental principles of evolution. Even the most orthodox institutions are often no exception to this rule." "Philosophy in the United States," *Mind* 4 (January 1879), 101. On Yale see Hofstadter and Metzger, *Academic Freedom,* 332–33. Stevenson, *Scholarly Means,* 76–79.

21. Charles D. Cashdollar, *The Transformation of Theology, 1830–1890: Positivism and Protestant Thought in Britain and America* (Princeton: Princeton University Press, 1989), esp. 446.

22. Ibid.

23. Porter, *The Human Intellect,* 661–62.

24. Noah Porter, "Herbert Spencer's Theory of Sociology," *Princeton Review,* ser. 4, 6 (September 1880), 295

25. This is the tone implied by Hofstadter and Metzger, who lump the Porter–Sumner controversy with repression of teaching of biological evolution (*Academic Freedom,* 336–38).

8

California: Revolution without Much Ideology

Rather than warfare, the typical motif in the transition from the old-time colleges to the new universities was peaceful revolution. Few of the old guard were willing to take a stand, as Porter did, that would risk looking sectarian. On the other side, most of the revolutionaries were sons of the evangelical college tradition and wished to emphasize that they were the true heirs to its ideals. While they were well aware of a need for a break from the past, they also saw continuity between the old colleges and the new universities.

Nowhere were such continuities suggested in a more intriguing way than in the origins of the University of California out of the College of California. On October 9, 1867, the trustees of the College of California, a private college, voted to cede all its assets to the proposed new state university. The College of California, which had opened its doors in Oakland in 1860, was a typically New England enterprise, conducted by New School Presbyterians and Congregationalists, aspiring to establish the "Yale of the West." Although the college was struggling and had few students, it was not entirely impoverished. Its most valuable tangible asset, which it donated to the state, was a magnificent tract of land in a nearby area that the college leaders had named Berkeley.

The name, honoring the eighteenth-century philosopher Bishop George Berkeley, suggested the founders' broad religious sensibilities. Bishop Berkeley had taken a strong interest in education in the American colonies, had made a substantial donation to Yale, and was best known in California for "Westward the course of empire takes its way," which he, like the New Englanders, connected with the advance of Christian higher education. As though to symbolize the American harmony of Christianity and learning, the streets of the proposed town were laid out in alphabetical order, those running north–south named for American inventors and scientists, and those running east–west, for American (mostly New England) cultural figures, including theologians (Allston, Bancroft, Channing, Dwight, Everett, etc.)

What is most striking about the story is that the college trustees saw so much continuity between their own goals and those of a state university that they would donate their entire enterprise to the state institution. This is especially striking if one notices that the university which took over the college facilities and began its own operation in 1869 was from its outset one of the most secular such enterprises in the country. Thus in California the transition from the old order to the new took place almost overnight. And while there was some outcry from those of offended religious sensibilities and one serious defection, the revolution was nearly bloodless.

The story of how this quiet revolution was effected and of the intrareligious debate that preceded it illuminates many of the critical themes being considered. Since the developments took place in California, where there were no established traditions to take for granted, the issues at stake could emerge vividly.

Even before the Gold Rush, the American Home Missionary Society, a cooperative agency of New School Presbyterians and Congregationalists, had turned its attention to bringing the Gospel and civilization to California. The Rev. Samuel Hopkins Willey, a Dartmouth graduate whose name signaled a solid Congregationalist pedigree, arrived as the AHMS missionary at Monterey early in 1849, just as the rush was beginning. Willey immediately recognized that education would be essential to bringing any order out of the violent and materialistic frontier chaos. He organized an attempt to found a New School and Congregationalist "College of California" in San Jose in 1850, but the plan failed. Methodists and Catholics did manage in 1851 to start fledgling schools, essentially precollege academies, in San Jose and Santa Clara, respectively. At the time California had almost no schools of any sort and the Presbyterian-Congregationalist coalition turned its attention to supporting the beginnings of a public school system.[1]

The New Englanders' college plans were revived with the arrival in 1853 of the Rev. Henry Durant, who had come west in hope of founding a college. Durant, who had been a pastor and a high school teacher, was a graduate of Yale in 1827 and afterward a tutor there for four years, in the era of the Yale Report of 1828. The New School Presbyterians and Congregationalists proceeded immediately to establish a precollege academy in Oakland, which in 1855 became the College of California. The school remained a preparatory school until 1860, when it offered its first college-level classes, with Durant and the Rev. Martin Kellogg, a younger Yale graduate, serving as the faculty. Although Oakland at the time was referred to as "the New Haven of the Pacific"[2] (supposedly a compliment), the site was too crowded for much expansion. Horace Bushnell, the famed Hartford theologian, on a visit for his health, spent most of 1856 personally touring northern California in search of a larger site for the college, though eventually the trustees turned back to a spectacular nearby site in what became Berkeley. Bushnell and the trustees had grandiose hopes for "the founding of a University for the State."[3] The school, though "under the pervading influence and spirit of the Christian religion,"[4] was not under ecclesiastical control, and was, of course, billed as thoroughly nonsectarian.

By the late 1850s the problems inherent in New Englanders' claims to be nonsectarian in a region where they had not yet established cultural hegemony were becoming increasingly apparent. Methodists, who had often been looked down upon as poor relations, were becoming increasingly respectable, and Catholics were more numerous. Denominations were consolidating institutionally and rivalries were increasing; even New School Presbyterians and Congregationalists had been drifting apart in much of the nation. And the bitter sectional debates over slavery were critical in sharpening religious tensions. In the highly charged political atmosphere, claims to stand for a nonsectarian Protestantism sounded, at least for the time, rather hollow.

As the time approached for the school in Oakland to open as a true college, the rival Old School Presbyterians, led by the Rev. W. A. Scott, editor of the *Pacific Expositor,* launched a journalistic barrage against its pretensions to be nonsectarian. Christian teaching, the Old School insisted, had to have a distinctive theological slant if it amounted to anything. For that reason Old Schoolers opposed agitation to have Bible reading and instruction in state schools, since this would necessarily discriminate against Roman Catholics and Jews and jeopardize separation of church and state. In their view, which was a minority one, there should be two distinct classes of schools, both of which they would support, secular state institutions and sectarian ones.[5]

The vague nonsectarianism of interdenominational Protestantism, argued the Old School, simply opened the door to liberal religious opinion. If the so-called Yale of the Pacific simply relied on informal good will to preserve the Christian character, argued the Old School journal in 1859, then there was no guarantee

> against the total perversion of the funds now to be invested—the history of Harvard is not to be forgotten—nor is it a solitary one—there is no surety, that a Puseyite, or a Jesuit may not control the religious instruction of the College of California in the next generation—there is no surety—there can be no guarantee on the plan proposed for the Oakland College that such a man as Mr. Theodore Parker, of Boston, may not be at its head within less than thirty years.[6]

In response to such criticism the college adopted a more definite statement of its religious position in "Organic Basis," of March 1860. Concerning the trustees it specified that "(1) A Majority of them shall always be members of evangelical Christian churches, and (2) Not more than one-fourth of the actual members shall be of one and the same Christian denomination."[7]

The Old School critics were no happier with this position, since it just proved their point that one could not avoid being sectarian. "Now," they railed, "who is to sit in judgment, and decide what constitutes an evangelical church?" And even if the college was to have Unitarians and others on the board (which it did), why were they not willing to have a Unitarian professor (which they did not)? What the college trustees were after, the Old School alleged, was Unitarian, Episcopalian, Baptist, and Old School Presbyterian *support,* without offering any corresponding control.[8] The Old School Presbyterians, unwilling to accept any of this, in 1861 opened their own grammar and preparatory school, City College, initially meeting in Scott's own Calvary Church in San Francisco.[9]

Henry Durant published in pamphlet form a scathing reply, lashing out at the *Pacific Expositor* for speaking with "a forked tongue," accusing it of "great Humbug," of fulminating its "old trash," and of promoting the "old cant of the Infidel and the Jesuit," with a list of similar epithets which it took the *Expositor* a third of a page to compile in its rebuttal.[10]

Feelings were running extraordinarily high when the Civil War broke out. Scott, the Old School spokesman, was a Democrat and favored a "peaceful separation" in the national crisis.[11] The New Englanders were Republicans. These sharp political differences exacerbated religious rivalries in the new settlements. To the New School party it was bitterly disappointing not only to be unable to obtain inter-Presbyterian cooperation, but to have the Old School attempt to build a rival school across the bay.

City College lasted only about a decade and never became more than a preparatory school.[12] Nonetheless, the debate left two significant legacies. First, the Old School articulated in its characteristic fashion problems which its adherents and others, such as Methodist sectarians, had with the claims of "nonsectarian" Protestants to represent all of Protestant civilization. Second, the bitter rivalry left a legacy that gave a peculiar twist to the merger of the Christian College of California into the state university.

The Morrill Land Grant Act of 1862 had an effect in most states something like the gift promised in Mark Twain's "The Man That Corrupted Hadleyburg." Competition for educational leadership was intensified and schools were willing to sell their souls to demonstrate that they were great friends of the agricultural and mechanical arts, which the act was designed to support. The College of California, numbering its students only in the dozens and unsuccessful in finding a major benefactor, very quickly announced the creation of a "Mining and Agricultural College" as a department within the institution and informed the state that it would be quite happy to accept the Morrill endowment. Since the mining and agricultural division existed only on paper, and the College of California was self-evidently a typical classicist and, in the minds of most Californians, impractical enterprise, the offer, though taken seriously, was not accepted. In 1866, the state itself, in order to secure the funds, created its own Agricultural, Mining, and Mechanical Arts College, which also existed only on paper. The state had been committed by its institution to establishing a university; but without much of a school system of any sort, and without highly educated leadership, this was not easily done.

There were still possibilities for combining the enterprises. Henry Durant of the College of California apparently hoped to foster at least informal ties by offering to sell to the proposed state technical school land near the college's property in Berkeley. Nothing came of this offer and a more ominous possibility loomed that the state soon might simply start its university in the Bay area as a rival to the college. On the other hand, the state governor, Frederick Low, was a Republican, a friend of the College of California, and favored some cooperation. Low's views were apparently solidified at the commencement exercises of the college in the summer of 1867 at which Benjamin Silliman, Yale's famed scientist, was the speaker. Silliman chided Californians for prematurely starting a polytechnic school instead of a real university, including an arts college. On the same day, Governor Low reportedly remarked to Samuel Willey, acting president of the college, that the college had "organization, enthusiasm, scholarship, and reputation," and the state had money. "What a pity they could not be joined together."[13]

With this encouragement in mind and faced with a perennially bleak financial and enrollment picture, the college trustees made their bold move. Governor Low on October 8, 1869, had assured them that the merger of the college and the state university was always "a favorite idea" with him. They, in turn, avowed that they had "the *object* for which it [the college] was established more at heart than its corporate existence."[14] The next day they donated their site and assets to the state school with the "earnest hope and confident expectation" that the state would establish on the site "a University of California, which shall include a College of Mines, a College of Agriculture, and an Academical College, all of the same grade, and with course of instruction equal to those of Eastern Colleges."[15] Low was convinced that the new university should be modeled after the University of Michigan, which was the most successful of the state universities, and which kept liberal learning at its core.[16]

Clearly the assumption of everyone present was that the College of California would, in effect, become the arts college of the new university. Though the trustees would lose their formal control, the continuities inevitably would be so substantial that the college's long-term goal to shape the state's higher education would be fulfilled. As Samuel Willey later explained to a correspondent, "They (i. e. the resolutions) were so unreserved, because it was thoroughly understood that the college should be the germ, in its spirit and organization, and the University should be the outgrowth. Even then the old friends and all of us main workers in the college, held back to the last. But when the thing was done we thought we would try and save the spirit of the college, in the University, if we could."[17]

Demand for an "eastern" education in Greek and Latin had not been high on the rough California frontier, and the friends of the college were desperate to save something. They had been graduating only three or four students per year and the inauguration of a nearby state university was bound to cut into their nonsectarian clientele. There was good reason to hope that their goals could be blended into those of the state. Given the touchiness of the subject, their religious interests were not something that could be mentioned; but they surely could be taken for granted.

The very next month the plan began to go awry. The Republican party split and the Democrats elected their candidate for governor, Henry Haight of San Francisco. From the point of view of the College of California man, Haight had a number of attractive qualities: he was a Yale graduate, formerly a Freesoiler and Republican supporter of Lincoln, and a professing Presbyterian church member. The drawbacks were that he had turned against Lincoln, had supported George McClellan in 1864, was now a Democrat, and was a member of Calvary Presbyterian Church, Old School, where the polemical W. A. Scott had formerly presided. Even though by this time there was serious talk in the East, that the Old School and the New School would reunite, old differences were not yet healed. For the college there was little to do but go on with the plans to dissolve into the state university and hope that the interests of the college would be dealt with "honestly and fairly."[18]

John W. Dwinelle of the college trustees proceeded to manage the bill reconstituting the university, now including an arts college, through the legislature. The Methodists, who were concerned regarding the future of their College of the Pacific in Santa Clara, raised some objections concerning possible Presbyterian-Congregationalist influence, especially as symbolized by designating College of California graduates as university alumni, but the vote taken on May 21, 1868, was without dissent.[19]

To the consternation of most College of California men, Governor Haight's idea of dealing "honestly and fairly" was a quite literal one of reducing their influence to little more than that of any other group. When the regents were appointed, the only carryover from the college trustees, aside from Dwinnelle, was the Rev. Horatio Stebbins, the Unitarian on the board, and the only other ordained man was the superintendent of public instruction, a Methodist no longer serving a church. The board also included a Jew and a Catholic and several regarded as "indifferents and skeptics."[20] Governor Haight reportedly told the Rev. William Alexander, an Old School Presbyterian who had recently arrived to take over the City College, "those gentlemen expected to have a good deal to say about organizing the University, *but I'll see that they don't.*"[21]

The atmosphere was still charged with partisanship. In what amounted to a flat declaration that a revolution had taken place against the New Englanders, the new regents voted in the fall to invite as the first president of the university none other than General George McClellan, the bitter opponent of Lincoln in 1864. McClellan's academic qualifications were not readily apparent and the invitation sparked a furor of accusations of crass party politics that died down only early in 1869 when the news arrived that McClellan (never one to take chances) had declined the honor.[22]

As to the faculty, the only carryover was Martin Kellogg, a thoroughly tolerant friend of the university ideal, who would teach the classical courses at the university.[23] The centerpieces of the new faculty were southerners, John and Joseph LeConte, distinguished scientists of the University of South Carolina, who were fleeing from carpetbaggers.

In the meantime, the regents had asked the college to operate for one more year while they made adequate preparations. The college did so but also was exploring whether the cession might be illegal on the grounds that money donated for one sort of enterprise was now being used for something quite different. Only the Western College Society (the Society for the Promotion of Collegiate and Theological Education at the West), which was explicitly designed to promote Christian education, asked for its funds back; but it was not willing to press the point. The college also hoped to use funds from its excess land to endow a chair that would "save something of the influence of the College in the Institution it had brought into being."[24] This too was blocked. The university opened in the fall of 1869 with John LeConte as acting president. The college disappeared with no guarantees for the future.

Samuel Hopkins Willey, progenitor of the college and its vice president since 1862, was especially outraged. In a letter to the head of the Western College Society in September 1869, he complained bitterly that the understanding with Governor Low had been betrayed by the secular and nonevangelical trustee appointments of Governor Haight. Most of the trustees were Democrats and few had any experience in running a college. The primary issue for Willey, however, was religious. From the day of the trustee appointments "the discerning friend of the college and Christian education" had "small hopes for the university." Resigning his post, Willey lamented. "I took on this work seven years ago, as a Christian minister . . . but it looks like not a well expended seven years."[25] Twenty years later he was still complaining bitterly about the betrayal.

A Place for Religious Ideals

The revolution that displaced the New Englanders from educational leadership, however, was soon followed by a Thermidor that restored some of their influence. Apparently once the point had been made decisively that the University of California was a new entity of the state, and not an outgrowth of the College of California, some College of California and New England influences could be brought in.

The trustees found an ideal candidate for effecting such a compromise between the old and the new in Daniel Coit Gilman, whom they invited to the presidency in June 1870. Gilman was at the time still in the running for the Yale presidency against the "old-fogeyism" (as one California trustee put it)[26] of Noah Porter and company. Gilman was a close friend of Andrew Dickson White and eager to take on a similar project of university building. He thus combined impeccable New England credentials with the ideals of the new university.

Gilman turned down the offer, pleading his interest in Sheffield College and also noting that his wife had recently died and his two young daughters could be better cared for by relatives in New Haven. He nonetheless kept the door open, mentioning his strong interest in the prospect of shaping almost from its start a university in California.

In the meantime, rather than go another year without a president, the fledgling university called the nearby Henry Durant out of retirement to head the school. Expediency thus temporarily restored some of the old college influence, though the president had little power. While there seem to have been no formal religious exercises except on ceremonial occasions, the one clear religious influence was that Seniors under Durant were required to take three hours of mental and moral philosophy, with texts by Joseph Haven, Mark Hopkins, and Noah Porter.

Durant was serving in a stopgap capacity and after two years the trustees renewed their invitation to Gilman. By now Porter had been selected to head Yale and Gilman thought that the California climate might be favorable to the delicate health of one of his daughters. So this time he quickly accepted, full of hope for the promising California situation.

California, however, proved to be less than a paradise. The main problem was that anti-intellectualism was strong among the state's rough-hewn population and Gilman was perceived as a New England elitist. The Grangers, a rising political force, insisted especially strongly that the university was supposed to be for mechanical and agricultural arts only. As Henry George, then a San Francisco newspaper editor and spokesman for populist sentiments, put it, "The Regents . . . have perverted the University from its original design into a college of classics and polite learning."[27] Gilman soon was spending all his time defending the university's independence. "The University of California is . . . nominally administered by the regents" he wrote to his principal confidant, Andrew Dickson White, but "it is virtually administered by the legislature."[28]

Gilman's handling of the religious issue in California, although less well known and less central to his concerns, is nonetheless revealing both about him and about the tensions of the time. Gilman was not irreligious. Andrew White, with whom he had traveled to Russia and Europe, was probably his best friend, but their views were not identical. Gilman shared White's distaste for all sectarianism and his faith in free scientific inquiry as the best hope of humanity, but he combined these with conventional enough Christian concerns to fit in at Congregationalist Yale. In 1854 during his travels in Europe he had spent three days with Noah Porter and had discussed going into the ministry.[29] In 1860, while working at Yale, he attended Porter's lectures on theology and obtained from the Congregationalist Association a licence to preach. Though he did not pursue this avenue any further, he retained active lifelong religious interests.

Gilman's religious outlook, however, was broad in the midcentury

Congregationalist context. He considered Bushnell (who later encouraged him to go to California) the great "theological emancipator."[30] Notably absent from Gilman's later theological pronouncements, however, was any reference to Christ, except as "the Master" and moral teacher. Gilman typically talked of religion as a promoter of morality and character. In this respect, his gospel of science and education was fully compatible with his understanding of the Christian Gospel. Both had the goal of uplifting humanity.[31]

Recognizing these genuine loyalties in Gilman, it is not so surprising to find that he had a well-thought-out program for relating religion to the university. In fact, at his inaugural at California, fresh from Yale, and well aware of the sensitivities of some of the friends of the College of California, he addressed the vexing question at length.

Gilman was well aware that the formally secular direction the new university had taken was atypical for the times. At the University of Illinois, for instance, a land grant school opened in 1868, one year before the University of California, not only was daily chapel required but students were also expected to attend Sunday morning worship services and required to attend a Sunday afternoon worship and a lecture by the president, John M. Gregory, on such topics as Is there a God? Is the human soul immortal? Is the Bible of divine authority? Was Jesus more than a man? Is Christianity true?[32] At the University of Michigan, one of the principal models for the University of California, the president James B. Angell, another friend of Gilman, openly spoke of the school as a "Christian" university. At California, however, the school apparently did not include even voluntary chapel, thus making it in a formal sense the most secular college in the land.

Addressing the religious question in his inaugural in 1872, Gilman first of all pointed out California's remarkable religious pluralism. Not only did it have all the Protestant sects, but Catholicism had long had a foothold there, and Oriental religions were represented as well. How could the state and its university protect all these, while favoring none? First it could be open to "a religious spirit no one objects to"—that is, a spirit of truth and charity. That was safe enough. Gilman, however, went further to suggest that "if the body of teachers and students, imbued by this spirit of truth and charity, will daily assemble of their own accord to acknowledge their dependence upon divine wisdom, to chant the psalms of David, and to join in the prayer which the Master taught his disciples, who can doubt that such communion of worship will elevate the character of all who engage in it, and of the institution to which they belong?"[33]

But even if the university had such voluntary chapel, which it apparently never did,[34] Gilman recognized that the true friends of religion would want "positive, outspoken, and persuasive religious influences." Following a suggestion of President James McCosh, recently installed at Princeton, Gilman presented his solution of churches providing religious training in the houses in which students reside. This was a variation on the Jeffersonian proposal of surrounding theological faculties and seemed a promising practical approach to the same issues.

Despite this recognition of sectarian interests, when Gilman got down to it, he saw little to distinguish the role of a university from the civilizing role of Christianity itself. So he suggested in his California inaugural that a university "must show how Christian civilization has overcome pagan practices and beliefs, and has purified the home, the state, and the relations of nations, modifying laws, usages, manners and languages, establishing charities, reforming prisons, securing honesty, virtue, and justice."[35] He spoke also of how the University of California might especially serve for "the enlightenment of Asiatic nations" and of "a new epoch in history [which] seems to be opening before us." Gilman closed his inaugural by quoting, of all people, John Henry Newman. Two decades earlier, in connection with the founding of his new Catholic university in Dublin, Newman had argued that the idea of a university as the embodiment of all knowledge implied the inclusion of theology. The science of God was integral to any claim to universal knowledge. Gilman, typical of the broad Protestantism emerging at the time, saw science and morality explicitly *without* theology as the only true hope for universality. So, having taken for granted this major reversal in emphasis, Gilman could apply Newman's vision directly to the University of California.

> Thither, as to a sacred soil, the home of their fathers, and the fountain-head of their Christianity, students are flocking from east, west, and south, from America and Australia and India, from Egypt and Asia Minor, with the ease and rapidity of a locomotion not yet discovered, and last, though not least, from England—all speaking one tongue, all owning one faith, all eager for one true wisdom; and thence, when their stay is over, going back to carry over all the earth, "peace to men of good will."[36]

Newman's prediction was actually quite different with respect to Protestant universities that were removing all reference to theology in defining the intellectual enterprise. The banishment of theology, he argued, was symptomatic of losing a unified vision of knowledge as all part of one integrated whole. In place of unity, he predicted, each of the special sciences would emerge with its particular angle of vision for which it would claim universality. Each science, having declared theoretical sovereignty, would demand total autonomy. Under Protestant auspices universities were likely to emerge as a conglomeration of special sciences, united most by their common resolve to be free from each other and any external authority.[37]

While essentially Protestant, the University of California was committed to a nonsectarian course. The state political code stated directly that "no sectarian, political, or partisan test must be ever allowed . . . in the selection of Regents, faculty, or students . . . nor must the majority of the Board of Regents be of any one religious sect or of no religious sect." Gilman had this statement printed in the university catalogue.[38]

Critics, of course, continued to snipe at the supposed irreligion of the university. A small scrimmage took place concerning the first commencement of the university, held in July 1873. While the former New School Presbyterian paper, the *Pacific,* reported the ceremonies with approval,[39] the Rev. Robert Patterson, a Presbyterian in Oakland still trying to raise funds for the dying City College of San Francisco, used the occasion to attack the university in a well-known eastern religious newspaper, the *New York Evangelist.* Pointing out that the state constitution barred the university from supporting religion, Patterson claimed that at the lengthy ceremonies (in which, apparently as a vestige of New England graduations, students presented excerpts of theses)[40] "the name of God was not spoken; no prayer was offered; nor any reference made in any of the young men's speeches to moral or religious ideas." He added that "even an atheist does not desire his boy to be trained a materialist."

Gilman felt it necessary to publish a brief reply. Patterson, who (oddly) described Berkeley to the easterners as "away out on the prairie," may have been guilty of some hyperbole and chose to mention only the secular character of the student presentations. In any case Gilman could point out that the ceremonies themselves were opened and closed with prayer by clergymen. In fact, none other than Samuel Hopkins Willey had offered the opening blessing. Gilman pointed out furthermore that he was on record as encouraging denominations to found residential houses for their students. Moreover, his own remarks to the students had invoked "the blessings of Almighty God" and had warned them against "dishonesty, selfishness, and sloth." While the university, he argued in summation, "is so conducted that neither Protestant, Catholic, nor Jew can claim that it is a 'sectarian' or 'ecclesiastical' foundation; it aims to promote the highest development of character."[41]

Gilman's frustrations with the California legislature soon convinced him that he would not have the freedom to shape the institution the way he wanted. By contrast, an opportunity to found a university without financial constraints presented itself in 1874 when the will of Johns Hopkins, a Quaker businessman, provided funding for such an enterprise in Baltimore. Gilman let it be know to his friends in the East that he would be interested in the presidency and quickly accepted it when offered.

Despite Gilman's discouragement during his brief stay in California he had helped set the university on a track toward success. The school soon gained a measure of independence from the legislature and gained strength academically. Within a couple of decades the school had one of the respectable faculties in the nation and a thriving coeducational student body.

The religious character of the enterprise was much like that of most other state universities of the era: broadly but vaguely Protestant. The best known professors were Joseph LeConte and George Holmes Howison. LeConte, a geologist, was a leading reconciler of Darwinism and the divine, who explained that natural phenomena were "naught else than objectified modes of divine thought" and the forces controlling evolution, "naught else than different forms of one omnipresent divine energy."[42] Howison, a philosopher, was a leading promoter of a theistic philosophical idealism. Like LeConte and many others of their generation he had moved far from the evangelical orthodoxy in which he had been reared but still was eager to preserve the essence of the Christian heritage while accepting the claims of modern science.[43]

More orthodox Protestants continued to complain from time to time. The most publicized case was a controversy in 1888–1889 sparked by the endorsement by a local Unitarian minister of the novel *Robert Elsmere,* by British writer Mrs. Humphry Ward. The novel told of a young man's loss of faith and openly ridiculed evangelicalism. A local Presbyterian pastor, the Rev. Francis Horton, used the incident to condemn what he saw as the Unitarian takeover of the university. The recently elected president, Horace Davis, was a Unitarian. Davis was furthermore a member of the congregation of the Rev. Horatio Stebbins, the most influential member of the Board of Regents, and the only clergyman among the regents. Horton claimed that "the Board of Regents is closed against any orthdox clergyman." He also alluded to the "open secret" that with the transfer from the College of California in 1867 the Presbyterians had been denied the influence they expected. Horton proposed that to counter the infidelity at the university the Presbyterians found a college associated with the university, which would offer its own course in moral philosophy and biblical languages.[44]

Dominant opinions regarding American education were too dedicated to uniformity for anything to come of this proposal to introduce collegiate pluralism into American higher education,[45] and after a considerable flurry the controversy died down. Whether by design or coincidence, the next president, chosen in 1892, was the Rev. Martin Kellogg, a Congregationalist. Kellogg was the one faculty carryover from the old College of California. He was a Yale graduate of 1850 and was tolerant and noncontroversial in his religious opinions.[46] The dominant attitude toward religion in the 1890s was probably well reflected in a student address by Mary Hawes Gilmore at the commencement of 1894. Religion, said Gilmore, was all influence that is uplifting "from the sordid, the partial, the insignificant [toward] the absolute, be it called Beauty, Truth or Goodness." "The fundamental idea of a University," in turn," is universal truth-seeking, fair-mindedness, and impartial reception and scrutiny of all views—the enforced acceptance of none." It followed then, she argued, that to "enforce religious doctrines by direct methods would be subversive to its very nature—would be a return to medievalism." None of this, however, entailed opposition to traditional religious teaching. "Direct inculcation of divine truth and of practical moral precepts is necessary indeed, but the proper instrument and institution for that duty is surely the church."[47]

Such a division of labor seemed to resolve the issue, at least for those of the dominant social classes and religious sentiments. The universities could be practically unitarian with lots of room for liberal Christian opinion, religious indifference, or skepticism. The specifics of traditional Christianity could also flourish, but as an encouraged voluntary activity. From the dominant Protestant perspective, the university then should hardly look subversive to Christian interests. As one Berkeley professor pointed out in 1900, church membership at the university was actually higher than in the state generally. So he could argue that "of all the forces which make for righteousness as Christian forces, I think a strong case might be made out for our state institutions of higher education."[48]

Notes

1. Verne A. Stadtman, *The University of California, 1868–1968* (New York: McGraw-Hill, 1970), 4–7. This and the following accounts of the early history are drawn from Stadtman and Samuel H. Willey, *A History of the College of California* (San Francisco, 1887), and William Warren Ferrier, *Origin and Development of the University of California* (Berkeley, 1930).

2. Ferrier, *Origin,* 138.

3. Bushnell report to trustees, January 1857, reprinted in Willey, *College of California,* 21.

4. "Organic Basis," of College of California, 1859, quoted in Stadtman, *California,* 15.

5. "Church Schools and State Schools: The True Policy of the Presbyterian Church," *Pacific Expositor,* January 1861, 280–84.

6. "The Synod and Its Schools," *Pacific Expositor,* November 1859, 237. The next month, the *Expositor* quoted approvingly from an 1845 speech from President Hitchcock of Amherst: "We are all sectarians . . . and to exclude sectarianism from a literary institution is to exclude all religion from it. . . . But really, of all the kinds of intolerance, that is the worst which is furious for toleration." December 1859, 264. It added to the case, of course, that Hitchcock was prominent in New School Presbyterian and Congregationalist circles. Presumably, as president of Amherst, he had Harvard in mind.

7. Quoted in Ferrier, *California,* 205. See 196–204, where the controversy is discussed.

8. "The Catechism and the College of California," *Pacific Expositor,* April 1860, 446.

9. *The Pacific,* a religious paper supporting the College of California, published a derogatory report of its opening suggesting that it was not a college at all and that most of its seventy-four students were under ten years of age. February 7, 1861. A subsequent correction indicated the students were mostly fifteen to twenty.

10. *Pacific Expositor,* May 1861, 495.

11. Ibid., 497.

12. Ferrier, *Origin,* 204n–205n.

13. Willey, *History,* 207. Willey apparently reported this on earlier occasions. Ferrier, *Origin* 263n. For general account of background see Stadtman, *History,* 24–30.

14. Minutes, October 8, 1867, in Transfer of the College of California book, archives of University of California, Bancroft Library, University of California, Berkeley (hereafter cited as UC archives).

15. Trustee resolutions, October 8, 1867, Stadtman, *History,* 31.

16. Ferrier, *Origin,* 270.

17. Samuel Hopkins Willey to the Rev. Theron Baldwin, September 1, 1869, College of California Documents, UC archives.

18. Ibid. Cf. Ferrier, *Origin,* 281–82.

19. Ferrier, *Origin,* 267, 272–73, 286. The files of the principal Methodist journal, the *California Christian Advocate,* were lost in the San Francisco fire of 1906 (286n).

20. Willey to Baldwin, September 1, 1869, in Stadtman, *History,* 36.

21. Samuel H. Willey, Memoranda re founding of University of California, 1888, College of California Documents, UC archives. Alexander reportedly told this to Willey in 1888.

22. Stadtman, *History,* 48.

23. Freshmen were required to take twelve hours of Latin and Classical Greek in their first three years. Except for five hours of mental and moral philosophy, the rest of the curriculum was modern, including requirements in English, modern languages, mathematics, science, geography, drawing, and military science. "Schedule of Studies Pursued in University and Text Books used. Reported to President Durant, April 7, 1871," UC archives, Box 12:2.

24. Samuel H. Willey, memoranda re founding of the University of California, 1888, College of California Documents, UC archives.

25. Willey to Theron Baldwin, September 1, 1869, UC archives.

26. Edward Tompkins to Daniel Coit Gilman, ca. June 1870, in Ferrier, *Origin,* 326.

27. Henry George, *Daily Evening Post,* quoted in Fabian Franklin, *The Life of Daniel Coit Gilman,* 146. See Stadtman, *History,* 61–83, for a useful summary.

28. Gilman to White, 1874, quoted in Stadtman, *History,* 79.

29. Earl Hubert Brill, "Religion and the Rise of the University: A Study of the Secularization of American Higher Education, 1870–1910," Ph.D. dissertation, American University, 1969, 52–53.

30. D. G. Hart, "Faith and Learning in the Age of the University: The Academic Ministry of Daniel Coit Gilman," in *The Secularization of the Academy,* George M. Marsden and Bradley J. Longfield, eds. (New York: Oxford University Press, 1992), 16–17.

31. As D. G. Hart points out in "Faith and Learning," 107–45, Gilman and the persons in his generation whom he represented could be seen as harmonizers of science and religion in continuity with the antebellum evangelical harmonizers, as genuine affirmations of the Christian heritage, broadly conceived.

32. Winton U. Solberg, "The Conflict between Religion and Secularism at the University of Illinois, 1867–1894," *American Quarterly* 18 (1966), 189–90.

33. Daniel Coit Gilman, "The University of California in Its Infancy," Inaugural, November 7, 1872, in *University Problems in the United States* (New York, 1898), 178.

34. I have been able to find no evidence that there ever was such a voluntary chapel at the university. The *Register* of 1872–1873, Gilman's first year, announces "weekly assemblies will be held for lectures and other literary exercises." The first assembly at the new campus at Berkeley was opened with a religious ceremony, including a reading by a Presbyterian pastor from a favorite passage of Gilman from Proverbs 9 on wisdom. Ferrier, *Origin,* 349–50. (Cf. Gilman, Inaugural, 183, in which he suggests that the biblical verse "Give instruction to a wise man, and he will be yet wiser" in an endorsement of postgraduate education.) At Johns Hopkins, Gilman regularly led voluntary chapel services, speaking primarily on topics related to cultivating good character. Hart, "Faith and Learning," 19. At UC, Berkeley, prayers and religious hymns continued to be used on ceremonial occasions into the 1950s. Comment on this manuscript of Henry F. May, January 1993.

35. Gilman, Inaugural, 178–97.

36. Quoted from Newman in Gilman, Inaugural, 185.

37. John Henry Newman, *The Idea of a University* (Notre Dame, Ind.: University of Notre Dame Press, 1982 [1873, 1858]), 38–39, 53–74.

38. *Register of the University of California,* 1874, 105, from California Political Code (1874).

39. *The Pacific,* July 24, 1873.

40. Ibid.

41. Gilman reply to Patterson (two printed pages) [1873]. Gilman cover letter of April 15, 1901, says he is not sure where it was published. Historical Pamphlets, vol. 1, UC archives.

42. Joseph LeConte, *Evolution and Its Relation to Religious Thought* (1881), quoted in James R. Moore, *The Post-Darwinian Controversies: A Study of the Protestant Struggle to Come to Terms with Darwin in Great Britain and America, 1870–1900* (Cambridge: Cambridge University Press, 1979), 225. On LeConte's religious evolution from orthodox Presbyterianism to idealism see Lester D. Stephens, *Joseph LeConte: Gentle Prophet of Evolution* (Baton Rouge: Louisiana State University Press, 1982).

43. On Howison see Bruce Kuklick, *The Rise of American Philosophy: Cambridge, Massachusetts, 1860–1930* (New Haven: Yale University Press, 1977), 56, 135–36. Howison is usually classed as a Hegelian. At one point Howison, who belonged to no church in California, was wrongly accused of being an atheist. *Oakland Inquirer,* January 4, 1889, Newspaper Clippings Relating to the University of California, vol. 5, UC archives. Howison's correspondence, e.g., January 1, 1883, to Mrs. Susie Lockwood, and January 28, 1884, to President l. Clark Seelye of Smith College, suggests that he was a sensitive liberal Christian, struggling with the vestiges of the evangelical heritage, who saw biblical miracles as symbolic, but who could still claim to be a trinitarian. George Holmes Howison Papers, Bancroft Library.

44. "A Dissolving View; Rev. Dr. Horton's Opinion of Unitarianism," *Oakland Tribune,* December 17, 1888. "Dr. Horton's Scheme of a Presbyterian College," *Enquirer,* July 29, 1889.

45. In William Carey Jones, *Illustrated History of the University of California* (San Francisco, 1895), 103–4, the Canadian model is cited in favor of a similar proposal. "In the province of Ontario, for instance, the design is to remove all the denominational colleges to the seat of the University of Toronto. . . . The movement [in Ontario] was initiated by the Methodists and in the words of Dr. Withrow . . . '[The church college will] no longer hold itself aloof as a denominational college, but enter into intimate association with the national university in the en-

deavor to develop one of the broadest and best-equipped institutions of higher learning on the continent.' "

46. Kellogg's surviving statements on religion are uniformly vague.

47. Quoted in Jones, *Illustrated History,* 101–2.

48. Elmer Ellsworth Brown, "Religious Forces in Higher Education," *Pacific Theological Seminary Publications,* No. 3, 4, quoted in Merrimon Cuninggim, *The College Seeks Religion* (New Haven: Yale University Press, 1947), 81. Brown's views of religion and its place in the university (Cuninggim, 81–82) are very similar to those expressed by Mary Gilmore.

The architecture of Berkeley that emerged in the first half of the twentieth century argued for the same ideal. While the university itself was built in a massive classical style, it was surrounded by an array of churches, Y's, and theological seminaries.

9

Methodological Secularization and Its Christian Rationale at Hopkins

In the meantime Daniel Coit Gilman had made the most of his opportunity back East. The Johns Hopkins University opened it doors in 1876 and remained under Gilman's leadership until his retirement in 1901. Unlike his situation in California, Gilman had almost complete control over his institution. One of the legacies of the old-time colleges that the founders of the new universities typically retained was the wide discretionary power of the president. With a relatively free hand to implement his dream for a university, Gilman quickly built Johns Hopkins into America's leading graduate university, setting the standards for others to emulate.

Johns Hopkins is often thought of as a thoroughly secular institution and in many respects it was. Yet Gilman's background of religious concerns, both at Yale and in California, cast a light on the character of that secularity. Gilman was, as we have seen, a moderately liberal Congregationalist, who had studied theology and seriously considered the ministry. If he had entered that profession, he would have been a colleague congenial to Horace Bushnell, or Henry Ward Beecher, or perhaps in later years to Beecher's successor in Brooklyn, Lyman Abbot. As a candidate for the Yale presidency, his orthodoxy had apparently not been at issue. Subsequently he had taken as his second wife Elizabeth Dwight Woolsey, niece of Yale's former president Woolsey, thus retaining a full Yale pedigree. He always remained active in Christian concerns, and he approached what D. G. Hart calls his "academic ministry"[1] at Hopkins with a New Englander's sense of Christian calling.

The question of what role religion would have at the new Johns Hopkins University was relatively open. Seven of the original twelve trustees were Quakers, as had been Johns Hopkins (d. 1873). Three of these were also on the board of Haverford College,[2] suggesting serious Quaker educational concerns. To Gilman they affirmed that there should be a spirit of "enlightened Christianity" at the university, an ideal with which he could readily concur.[3] The only provision was for "the absence of all sectarian bias, and of political spirit on the part of the President of the University," a point especially important to the Quaker trustees because of "the position of our community during the troubles of the war, and its sensitiveness even to this day, in relation to those issues." Such sentiments, received in 1875, must have been music to Gilman's ears, when he was still reeling from attempts of the California legislature to run the university via public opinion. In responding he set forth his own credo eloquently.

> The Institution we are about to organize would not be worthy of the name of a University, if it were to be devoted to any other purpose than the discovery and promulgation of the truth; and it would be ignoble in the extreme if the resources which have been given by the Founder without restrictions should be limited to the maintenance of ecclesiastical differences or perverted to the promotion of political strife.
>
> As the spirit of the University should be that of intellectual freedom in pursuit of the truth and of the broadest charity toward those from whom we differ in opinion it is certain that sectarian and partisan preferences should have no control in the selection of teachers, and should not be apparent in the official work.[4]

In Baltimore Gilman's efforts to take a stand for a thoroughly nonpartisan quest for truth soon drew sniper fire from the religious orthodox, similar to that which he had experienced in California. The East Coast version of the controversy, however, became much more celebrated, especially because of interest in the auspicious beginning of the new university and the notoriety of the participants.

In conjunction with the opening of the university to students, Gilman had invited Thomas Huxley, then on tour in the United States, to deliver a public lecture during September 1876. Huxley was notorious not simply as a leading proponent of Darwinism but as a militant in using the prestige of Darwinism to champion the recently invented concept of "agnosticism." This idea that a scientific thinker was in principle unable to settle questions about God was currently making a major intellectual stir in Britain and the United States and contributing to skepticism among some college students. Huxley was also a leading champion in the campaigns to combat Anglican dominance in English academic life. While Gilman did not share all of Huxley's views, he considered that having Huxley speak represented just the sort of openness in the scientific search for truth to which the university was most dedicated. The lecture was presented to a packed house at the Baltimore Academy of Music. Contrary to Gilman's suggestion, the trustees felt the event should be kept professional and not opened by prayer.[5]

The predictable happened. As usual the Presbyterians were first into the field. The Presbyterian *New York Observer* accused the university of opening with honor to "evolutionism" while "honor . . . was refused to the Almighty." Gilman, they surmised, must have been well aware of this anomaly. "But if the neglect was due to the unchristian or materialistic sentiments of the authorities, then we can only say, God help them, and keep students away from the precincts of the young institution."[6] The Methodist *Christian Advocate* followed with similar sentiments, suggesting that "if reports are correct, the Johns Hopkins University has started wrong." The Methodist editors, in good evangelical form, suggested the Hopkins board should perhaps "retrace their steps, repent of their sins, make their peace with God and give their university a Christian management."[7]

Reports, however, were not entirely correct. The religious journals had mistakenly assumed that Huxley's speech constituted the opening of the university and hence that the enterprise was begun without prayer. Huxley's speech had sometimes been referred to as an "opening address," but in fact the university had been formally opened with ceremonies the previous February when Gilman had been inaugurated as president. At that time there had been the full requisite of prayers and a good bit of talk about the religious character of the enterprise. The critics were forced to publish corrections. Nonetheless, in the considerable controversy that surrounded the event, the image of a godless institution was what stuck. As one New York clergyman put it, in the best remembered quip from the controversy: "It was bad enough to invite Huxley. It were better to have asked God to be present. It would have been absurd to ask them both."[8]

Gilman, however, was sincerely convinced that one could have both. In his dealings with the religious questions, he was of course also dealing with a public relations crisis, so it is sometimes difficult to distinguish the two. Yet Gilman had raised the religious issues in California when he probably did not have to and his efforts to relate his religious interests to university life were substantial enough to indicate that they were not only for public consumption.

The most conspicuous expression of Gilman's Christian interests in his administration of the university was his establishing voluntary chapel, which he himself conducted for many years. He also encouraged the presence of the YMCA and often spoke at its meetings as well as at voluntary assemblies instituted for undergraduates in 1883. His taking on these tasks suggested the seriousness with which Gilman took the ideal of preserving what he saw as the best of the old Christian college heritage. He still was willing, at least for undergraduates, to play something of the role of the old-time college president. Yet he did so in a way that could hardly offend the sensibilities of the Quaker trustees or anyone else (except perhaps some theological hard-liners). When he spoke to the assembled undergraduates, he spoke on topics such as "Bodily Discipline," "The Training of the Will," or "A Lesson on Truth" (against lying). These were consistent with one of the expressed aims of the new university, "to develop character—to make men."[9] On this front, the old-college ideal persisted.

Yet if we look at the university as a whole, it becomes clear that such efforts had little to do with the heart of the enterprise. Crucial to the revolution that was being effected was the sharp distinction that Gilman made between the undergraduate college and the university as a whole. The college, in his view, was still a steppingstone to the perfect freedom of the university. Vestiges of in loco parentis might still be appropriate to it,[10] and hence there was direct concern to provide for spiritual and moral welfare. The college, for instance, included a course called "Logic, Ethics, and Psychology," that is, moral philosophy. It took years to find a professor pious enough to teach it. George Emmott, the man who was found, used as the first textbook Noah Porter's *Elements of Moral Science.*[11]

What made Johns Hopkins immediately famous among American universities, however, was that it was the first school to make graduate and professional education the center of the enterprise. Gilman, in fact, initially wanted to make it purely a graduate and professional institution, including a projected medical school, but added the undergraduate college as a concession to the local Baltimore constituency.[12] At the graduate and professional level, he wanted freedom to prevail. Freedom was essential to the scientific search for knowledge, which was the overarching function of the university. The natural sciences and methodologies patterned after the natural sciences were therefore emphasized in the early design of Hopkins. The Baltimore university was renowned for following German models, for instance, in the introduction of graduate seminars. Such models were always translated and modified in American settings, but the appeal to German precedents served as a powerful symbol of an ideal of value-free scientific inquiry.

The symbolic meaning of the German model had thus shifted somewhat since Henry Tappan's day. Idealism and the humanistic shaping of character were still essential to the educational outlook; but since midcentury in Germany, meticulous research had become increasingly important to defining educational ideals. At the same time the number of American students traveling to Germany for graduate education was rapidly increasing by the 1870s. What they most often brought back with them was a reverence for the "German method," by which they meant rigorous empirical investigation. As the Americans appropriated it, in fact, it bore the deep impress of their own traditions of British empiricism[13] and of the Baconian rhetoric that had dominated earlier American science. German *Lehrfreiheit*—the freedom for the guild of professors independently to pursue its inquiries, publications, and teachings—became a symbol for an emerging ideal of academic freedom.[14] This ideal, in the minds of American reformers such as Gilman, was inextricably mixed with the simple ideal of pure scientific investigation, or the pursuit of truth. The graduate seminar was an important forum in which such investigation could take place. The seminar had developed in Germany as a model of how the research ideal and the humanistic ideals could be combined. It simultaneously stressed individual attention from professors, original scientific research, individual creativity, and honing of critical skills.[15]

Just as important as any specific model or technique was a broader assumption borrowed primarily from the German experience. Longstanding in Germany was the tradition of freedom for university students, or *Lernfreiheit.* Such freedom was premised on a strong distinction between preparatory education in the gymnasium and university education. The gymnasia, in which the abilities were "exercised," much as in the old American college ideal, were known for their discipline. Universities, on the other hand, were places for the expression of student freedom. Students, who were now adults, had freedom both in how they regulated their own lives and in what they learned. American colleges, which had developed their style when many of the boys they educated were only in their mid-teens, had retained the disciplinary model, both in regulating personal life and in what was learned. As a clearly new level of education emerged, with the introduction of graduate education and the expansion of professional education, especially medicine, almost all American educators accepted the child versus adult distinction including the idea that the higher levels of education (except in theology) should be freed from the old restrictions, including theological concerns.

This definition of the theoretical basis for graduate and professional education marked a momentous step in American higher education. Given its immense repercussions, it is breathtaking to realize that the step was taken almost without dissent or criticism. Even Noah Porter, as we have seen, acknowledged essentially this same distinction between graduate and undergraduate education. While Porter recognized theoretical differences between Christian and non-Christian thought, his institutional conservatism extended only to preserving the Christian undergraduate college. For graduate education "freedom" seemed a compelling ideal, and in light of the cultural dominance of Protestantism there was little reason to suppose that Christianity would be discriminated against in a free exchange. It was so commonplace for Protestants to claim that science was on the side of nonsectarian Christianity that even someone like Porter seems to have seen no threat to his ideals in defining the methodology of graduate education as value-free science.

Rather, the Porters as much as the Gilmans seemed oblivious to the broader theoretical issue of what would be central to universities, while concentrating on the more immediate and personal question about the religious and moral welfare of undergraduates. As important as that issue might be, it almost totally distracted attention from the innovations, and the assumptions behind them, that would determine the soul of the university. Not only graduate education, but also professional education and technical institutes were being established on a new professionalized basis with almost no reference to religious concerns. The value-free ideal declared religion irrelevant to scientific inquiry. At the same time, however, administrators could refer religious supporters to their concern for the morality and even the religious life of undergraduates. So far as the denominations were concerned, though a few experimented with universities, none seriously challenged the undergraduate versus graduate and professional distinction. Rather, their overwhelming response was to concentrate on undergraduate colleges and perhaps on university divinity schools. For constituents who might be deeply concerned about religious issues, church colleges provided an alternative that further could allay concern about the larger trends in higher education.[16]

Thus, even though the story of religion and higher education continued long after the days of Gilman and his peers, a major portion of it had been settled from day one of the design of the modern American university. Religion would have virtually nothing to do with the vast majority of the enterprise, including graduate, professional (except theoogy), and technical education. Since virtually all university teachers eventually would be trained in graduate schools built on the purely naturalistic assumptions of the new science and professionalism, the forces eroding Christian influences even in the undergraduate classrooms were destined to be immense as well.

Christian scholars were hardly likely to see such developments as a threat to the faith, not only because of the assumptions most of them shared concerning the objectivity of the scientific method, but also because of educational precedents. In the longer history of universities, theology had seldom been well integrated with the arts or the other professional faculties. Similarly, the old-time colleges had treated most of the sciences as well as the classical arts as essentially autonomous disciplines, even though working within a broad framework of theological assumptions and tying together some theological and practical issues in moral philosophy. For the first generation of the universities, much the same practice continued, so that there was a transitional period when there was enough continuity with the past not to cause alarm. In philosophy itself, and in the various fields growing out of moral philosophy, such as psychology, sociology, and economics, some religious or at least moral concerns persisted. The study of literature also picked up some of the functions of moral philosophy, encouraging students to explore the deeper issues of life.[17] Since the college and the graduate schools had the same faculties, some of these concerns survived for a time in graduate education and in professional publications as well. Nonetheless, given the scientific-technical definition of the professional scholar, such functions were vestigial and soon disappeared.

The bottom line was that the new universities were designed to serve an emerging industrial technological society. The professionalization of the universities was part of the much larger process of differentiation and specialization necessary for industrial and commercial advance. As Burton J. Bledstein argues at length, "By and large the American university came into existence to serve and promote professional authority in society." In the new middle-class society, which the universities were designed to serve, "success increasingly depended on providing a service based on a skill, elevating the status of one's occupation by referring to it as a profession."[18] Such emerging professions were legitimated on a technological or scientific basis. Technical specialization almost inevitably meant that there would be vast realms separated from direct religious influences. American universities emerged just when these cultural processes were taking place on a massive scale and were an integral part of these processes. That meant that the universities themselves, as well as the vast majority of their disciplines, were defined according to the new professional scientific basis for which religion was considered irrelevant. Religion also could be regarded as a specialized leisure-time activity to which universities might give their blessings as a healthful option for individuals.

Christians and Methodological Secularization

Why pious Christians, like Gilman and his counterparts in business, the professions, science, and technology, did not see such developments as threats to the faith can be explained in terms of a larger tendency of modernity which we can call "methodological secularization." One of the major dynamics of complex modern societies arises from the principle that many tasks are done most efficiently by isolating and objectifying them. This methodology works particularly well in technical tasks, both those that demand large-scale organization and those that demand intensive analysis. In effect, one creates a mechanism for addressing the issue and applies this to a practical problem. Religious considerations play little if any role in the mechanism itself. Hence if one is considering how to improve the efficiency of the steam engine, information derived from religious belief would not be expected to affect the construction of the mechanism. In the late nineteenth century this scientific-technological principle, which paid momentous dividends, was being extended to almost all areas of life. The new universities were especially devoted to the service of this technological ideal and were among its major proponents. Thus, when entering the laboratory, pious Christians were expected to leave their religious beliefs at the door, even if they had prayed God to bless their work and came from their discoveries praising God for his work. Diversities of religious beliefs also made it particularly important for scholarly cooperation that their substance be kept out of the laboratories. Since the laboratory became a key metaphor and model for all advanced intellectual work, this ideal was extended throughout the university.

Pious Christians were hardly likely to protest this methodological secularization. Since scientific activity might take place within the context of piety and be an expression of the highest moral ideals of service to humanity, there was nothing about the method that seemed inherently antagonistic to Christianity. Moreover, if serving humanity was indeed the goal, then the scientific-technological method was unquestionably a good, since it provided unprecedented means to help one's neighbors, ease their lives, and help them better to understand themselves, their culture, and their environment. Besides, Christians had little reason to quarrel with a methodology that had so often, regarding concrete issues, demonstrably improved human ability to discover the truth.

Liberal Christians like Gilman were deeply convinced, as he said at his Johns Hopkins inaugural and often repeated, "Religion has nothing to fear from science." "Religion," he explained, "claims to interpret the word of God, and science to reveal the laws of God." "The interpreters may blunder," he continued, implying that theologies may change, "but truths are immutable, eternal, and never in conflict."[19] If Christians took seriously the antebellum dictum that science and religion must necessarily harmonize, how could Christians fear the scientific advance of truth?

Gilman thus saw his work at Johns Hopkins as essentially a Christian ministry. This is suggested further by an invitation he accepted in 1887 from the Evangelical Alliance, a leading mainstream Protestant group, to address them on the role of the universities in the evangelical mission to the nation. Indeed Gilman was one of the signers of the call for this special ecumenical gathering of evangelicals on "National Perils and Opportunities" faced by the increasingly industrialized and urbanized world.

After rehearsing how universities had long served the churches, Gilman justified their continuing service exactly on the grounds of the virtues of methodological secularization, or of the argument that the methods of science were the best means to advance the goals of Christianity:

> The methods they [the universities] employ are particularly directed to the ascertainment of truth and the detection of error; and these methods are those which all men everywhere can make use of. Moreover, the end in view—the ultimate end of all educational and scientific effort, as well as of all legislation and statesmanship—is identical with that at which Christianity aims . . . , "Peace on earth, good will to men."

Gilman illustrated this point by enumerating the recent discoveries in universities that had benefited humanity in "the age of electricity." Such discoveries had benefited commerce, diplomacy, missionary efforts, medicine, understanding human behavior, and even theology itself. All this achievement should assure us that "in the long run, in the progress of centuries, even in the progress of decade after decade, the world grows better." Gilman was convinced that "as misery, vice and sin grow less, religion has a freer field, and Christianity extends its invigorating and uplifting influence." So he said that he often asked which branch of the church would be the first to "assert everywhere that Science is the handmaid of Religion, that every effort made to extend the domain of human thought, and to interpret the plan of creation, is an effort to extend the reign of righteousness and truth."[20]

Gilman's appropriation of postmillennial language was to some extent rhetorical flourish; yet at the same time there is no reason to think that he did not believe what he said. In his view science simply *was* an expression of Christianity. As far as the design and conduct of the university was concerned this meant that, although he had to be solicitous of the spiritual and moral welfare of undergraduates and to keep some regard for public opinion, by far the overwhelming duty was to follow the scientific method wherever it led.

For the generation of university builders reared during the heady days of antebellum and Civil War millennialist evangelicalism, it was important to insist that methodological secularization in the universities was not secularization at all. Rather what they were doing illustrated the principle that secularization often proceeds at first not by the contraction of areas that religion touches but by what may be regarded as their expansion. Midcentury evangelical orthodoxy had anticipated this sacralization of science, celebrating its theories as discoveries of the revelations of God and its applications as signs of the millennium. University reformers typically extended such rhetoric to maintain that scientific investigation simply was a Christian enterprise. Hence its autonomy could not be challenged on either rational or religious grounds.

The degree to which commitment to this principle would lead to secularization was obscured also by the simultaneous liberal Protestant redefinition of Christianity as broad ethical ideals or even as just the highest principles of civilization. In such form explicit Christianity could linger in the curriculum, especially in the humane and social scientific disciplines that were the successors to moral philosophy. In this sense, Johns Hopkins of the 1880s could be seen also as a haven for Christian thinking, including among its faculty and graduate students such figures as Henry C. Adams, John Dewey, Richard T. Ely, G. Stanley Hall, and George Sylvester Morris, all of whom were intensely interested in relating the new science to their Christian heritage.

Thus the emphasis on the broadly Christian uses of science ironically contributed to establishing the sanctity of the scientific method and hence its autonomy. Science did not have to be conducted with any reference to theological formulae, not even with reference to the crucial doctrine of the previous era, that God had created the universe and its laws. Instead science typically was absorbed into a broader framework of philosophical idealism. Science was part of a more general spiritual progress, an expression of God's ongoing creativity. Idealism was the answer to the grim materialism of some of the most aggressive secularists and free thinkers.

While Gilman was open to having Huxley lecture at the university, he seems to have been genuinely concerned to counter pure agnosticism and the practical materialism it might imply. At least he made a vigorous effort in 1880 to hire as his principal professor of philosophy Robert Flint, a Scottish professor of divinity at Edinburgh who the same year had impressed orthodox and progressives alike by his critique of agnosticism, given as the Stone Lectures at conservative Princeton Theological Seminary. Flint's presence would have detoxified the atmosphere after the Huxley controversy and perhaps changed Hopkins's image.[21]

These events took place just at the time when the furor of the Sumner-Spencer controversy was causing such embarrassment at Yale and suggest that there might not have been as much difference between Porter and Gilman, or as much discontinuity in principle between the old and the new ideals, as might at first appear. Public relations were surely a concern for Gilman; but his faith that science was an expression of Christianity was consistent with a genuine aversion to materialism. That such issues weighed heavily on Gilman's mind is indicated by a letter early in 1881 from G. Stanley Hall, who for years had been hoping to get the appointment in philosophy at Hopkins. Hall, a graduate of Union Theological Seminary in New York, was well known to have turned far from earlier evangelical orthodoxy. Gilman, who was on the verge of hiring Hall, may have wondered if he would have a Sumner on his hands. In any case, Hall wrote in apparent response to a specific inquiry:

> I am as far as *possible* from materialism in every form. My physiological studies of the nervous system bring me incessantly before the question of the identity of thought and matter and I can only say that my deepest private feeling . . . is that materialism is simply want of education. As to my religious sentiments, I am a graduate in divinity, and without agreeing entirely with all I hear, am in the habit of church-going, and indeed am still a nominal church member I believe. I do not think it is possible for any one to become deeply interested in philosophy without a devout respect for religion growing more profound at every step.[22]

Such apparent questioning of a candidate concerning his religious belief[23] might appear to counter the notion that methodological secularization was shaping the university. Nonetheless, it appears that, even though such concerns persisted, they touched only parts of the university. G. Stanley Hall himself had noted that in the eight or nine most advanced American universities natural scientists were "allowed to teach the principles of Huxley and Haeckel if they wished, unmolested."[24] Philosophy was quite another matter since it was the traditional locus for religion in colleges. So even at Hopkins the professor of philosophy was expected to teach the "Logic, Ethics, and Psychology" course. "L.E.P." was an upgraded name for moral philosophy. The problem for Gilman, which it took him a decade to resolve, was to find someone who was both scientific enough to meet his university ideals and enough of a Mark Hopkins to serve the undergraduates and the religious constituency. Eventually Gilman, in effect, gave up and under pressure from the trustees agreed to the appointment of a capable but undistinguished pious Quaker to teach the L.E.P. course.[25]

G. Stanley Hall: Science Applied to Religion

The career of G. Stanley Hall, who arrived at Hopkins in 1881 and for a time attempted to teach the L.E.P. course, illustrates both the extent and the limits of religious concerns as they touched the definition of the university.

When Hall came to Hopkins he was preeminently a champion of professionalization and of the experimental science method. He had studied physiological cognitive psychology with Wilhelm Wundt in Germany and had also studied and worked closely with William James. He and James, in fact, were championing the formation of psychology as a field separate from philosophy. While at Hopkins, Hall staked a claim to be the principal founder of professional psychology in America, establishing in 1887 the first professional journal, the *American Journal of Psychology,* and the American Psychological Association five years later. The *Journal* stood for "a standpoint which is scientific, without mystic infiltration."[26] This was a model of the sort of scientific professionalism that was supposed to come out of Johns Hopkins.

In order to establish psychology as a true science free from philosophy, the first step, as both James and Hall had emphasized in the 1870s, was to free philosophy from theology. In 1879 Hall made a memorable contribution to this campaign with an analysis of "Philosophy in the United States," written for the British journal *Mind.* Hall, who had visited some thirty colleges and looked at the catalogues of many more, provides a valuable picture of American education in the last days of the old-time college. According to his estimate, of the nearly three hundred non-Catholic colleges in the country more than two hundred were "strictly denominational, and the instruction given in philosophy is rudimentary and mediaeval." Of more than sixty others that claimed to be nonsectarian most were in fact strictly evangelical. "Indeed there are less than half a dozen colleges or universities in the United States where metaphysical thought is entirely freed from reference to theological formulae." Many teachers of philosophy, Hall went on, were trained only in theology "and their students are made more familiar with the points of difference in the theology of Parks, Fairchilds, Hodges, and the like, than with Plato, Leibnitz, and Kant." While Hall acknowledged that there were some brilliant teachers such as Mark Hopkins (he had studied at Williams), he still complained that "the idola of orthodoxy" were such that "all these institutions unite in impressing upon their students the lesson that there is an abyss of skepticism and materialism into which, as the greatest of all intellectual disasters, those who cease to believe in the Scriptures as interpreted according to the canons of orthodox criticism, are sure to be plunged."[27]

The cause of providing a professional scientific alternative was profoundly personal to Hall, as it was to most of the first generation of university founders. Hall's case is particularly vivid because he was introspective and his own adolescent religious crisis remained an overshadowing episode in his life and thought. He articulated the experience of a vast number of influential Americans who grew up in an intensely Christian home in the antebellum era when evangelicalism was at the height of its confidence and intellectual prestige. As adults these men found themselves living in a world where the certainties of their youth had been undermined and where there was always the lingering dread of the abyss of a meaningless universe.

Born in 1844, Hall grew up on a farm in western Massachusetts, the heartland in which Edwardsean orthodoxy had left its deepest mark. Hall, for example, was plagued by guilt over masturbation, a subject that played a conspicuous role in his later ground-breaking analysis of adolescence. As a youth, Hall's major ambition was to leave the farm and to have an impact on the world. During his first year at Williams there was a campus revival and Hall had a classic conversion experience. Though he admired Mark Hopkins, the stronger influence during his later college years was the more open-minded John Bascom (later president of Wisconsin), who favored a romantic Christian idealism. In the meantime Hall was inspired by visits of Emerson and by reading romantic poets, though he was impressed as well by John Stuart Mill's empiricism.

Unable to afford graduate study in Germany, Hall in 1867 went to Union Theological Seminary instead. Although Union was a relatively orthodox evangelical institution, Hall there learned more about the alternatives. He was convinced by the radical biblical criticism of Ernest Renan and David Friedrich Strauss, which made it impossible for him to hold on to the tenets of evangelical orthodoxy. His position now was influenced by Hegelian idealism, an increasingly popular alternative to conventional Christianity. Aided in his seekings by Henry Ward Beecher of Brooklyn, Hall joined Beecher's church, which had the attraction of not demanding exact beliefs. Beecher also found financial support for Hall to make his long-delayed trip to Germany. In Germany he was impressed that "Comte and the Positivists had pretty much made out their case and that the theological, if not the metaphysical, stage of thought should be transcended."[28]

Nonetheless, the indelible religious sensibility that had been focused in his conversion experience did not allow him to drift into a positivist materialism. Rather, again like most of his generation who were associated with universities, he needed to believe there was more. For the time being the solution was a Hegelian one adapted to the sanctification of Darwinism, so that the ideal of the laws of thought might be revealed in developing laws of matter.[29]

Hall had, however, to pay for his unorthodoxy. He later claimed that he was turned down for several teaching positions, including one at the University of Minnesota, because of his religious beliefs. In 1872 he did gain a position in Ohio at Antioch College, a Unitarian school, where he remained four years.

The next stage in Hall's quest eventually brought him to Hopkins. In 1876 he went to Harvard where he studied with James and then to Germany to learn psychological empiricism from Wilhelm Wundt, its founder. Hall's philosophical outlook now became much like that of James. Hegelianism and similar formal idealisms appeared too soft-headed.[30] The mind should be regarded as an adaptive mechanism in an evolutionary framework. For Hall, rigorous experimentation was the key and should provide the clues to resolve some of the questions of knowledge that were plaguing nineteenth-century philosophers. Nonetheless, he refused to let his practical agnosticism lead toward a materialism, always insisting that there must be more.

Thus, on the one hand, Hall was a great champion of empiricism and experimentation. He had a virtually religious faith in pure science and could readily speak of "facts which are allowed to speak out for themselves."[31] Among the remarkable group of philosophers contemporaneous with him at Hopkins, he was most impressed philosophically by the brilliant but eccentric logician and pragmatist Charles Sanders Peirce, who championed rigorous scientific methods of inquiry.[32] Peirce, who was hired as a lecturer at Hopkins about the same time as Hall, was abruptly dismissed in the spring of 1884, apparently because of mysterious derogatory personal information.[33] In the meantime, John Dewey, a Hopkins graduate student, had filled in, teaching the history of philosophy in the spring of 1883, supplementing the work of George S. Morris, Hall's junior colleague in the history of philosophy. Morris was, like Dewey at this time, a Hegelian, and Hall seemed not at all unhappy to see them both go to the University of Michigan.

On the other hand, for all his professionalism, Hall was still haunted by his evangelical heritage and was still ready to address the religious issues directly. In fact, in his inaugural as professor of psychology in 1884, he made the religious question his principal theme. Essentially he took the same tack as Gilman. Science simply *was* Christian. So he declared:

> The new psychology, which brings simply a new method and a new standpoint to philosophy, is I believe Christian to its root and center; and its final mission in the world is not merely to trace petty harmonies and small adjustments between science and religion, but to flood and transfuse the new and vaster conceptions of the universe and of man's place in it—now slowly taking form, and giving to reason a new cosmos, and involving momentous and far-reaching practical and social consequences—with the old Scriptural sense of unity, rationality, and love beneath and above all, with all its wide consequence.[34]

Hall thus lamented the loss of the overarching intellectual unity that Scripture had provided and explicitly dedicated himself to finding its replacement as a basis for a new world order. Science, particularly psychology, which he viewed as simply experimental philosophy, was the basis for the new order. Rather than challenging religious instincts, it could "rescue the higher mythopoetic faculties from the present degradation to which prejudice and crass theories have brought them."[35]

Hall hoped that the science of psychology would help deliver the younger generation from the religious crisis that they and he had experienced. During the late 1870s and the early 1880s, agnosticism was at its height on campuses, shaped particularly by current British fashion.[36] Hall reported in his inaugural that he had conducted a survey of between three and four hundred seniors in six of the largest American colleges concerning their interest in philosophy. Over four-fifths described their interests in ways that, according to Hall, "are now unmistakably recognized as adolescent crises and readjustments." Students were asking questions such as " 'Why does the world exist?' " " 'Who or what am I?' " " 'What should I do, be, know?' " "They had 'doubted nothing and now suddenly doubted all things.' "[37]

Hall was evidently evaluating how he should approach teaching the Logic, Ethics, and Psychology course at Hopkins and maintaining that in the long run his putting of religion on a scientific basis was the best response to the collective crisis of faith. In the short run, however, he admitted that college students might need a more fatherly mentor of the old college president variety. Hall himself was not suited for that role, as he and the trustees soon realized. His strength and interests were in graduate and professional education.

In 1888 Hall's efforts to professionalize American scholarship took another step forward with the sudden opportunity to establish his own university. Jonas Clark, a businessman who had made a fortune as a San Francisco merchant during the gold rush, came back to his native Worcester, Massachusetts, offering to endow a great university. He choose Hall to be the founding president. Hall, in turn, convinced Clark that the university should be essentially a Johns Hopkins without undergraduates, apparently to Hall the best of possible worlds.

Although Clark University started with great promise as the nation's first purely graduate institution, it soon fell upon hard times. Jonas Clark, after showing somewhat too much personal interest in the enterprise during its first years, in 1892 lost interest entirely. Philanthropists were not likely to be deeply interested in pure academic research, without undergraduate colleges to provide both a justifying moral purpose and more immediate community service.[38] Much of Hall's fine faculty abandoned Clark for the new University of Chicago, more securely endowed with Rockefeller money. Hall was left with little more than a graduate program in psychology.

Hall's unending intellectual quest took some further turns as well. While remaining a champion of experimentation, in the 1890s Hall was much more open to varieties of psychological methodologies. William James criticized him for embellishing his psychology with "religious cant."[39] Religion indeed remained a major concern and Hall directed a number of his students in studies of religious conversion, published in the *American Journal of Psychology.* The import of these studies was, as Hall himself advocated, that religious impulses, although important, should be understood not through categories of theology but on the basis of science, especially comparative anthropology, like any other data.[40] As Hall himself put it, psychology should study religion as

> the anthropology of myth, custom, religious belief, symbols, etc., among savages and ethnic stocks; rites, ceremonies and all products of the mythpoeic faculty. . . . The grand old cult sometimes spoken of as conversion, the new life, regeneration, which in the old American college was central in all instruction in ethics . . . as it has been in some form for adolescence in every religion, savage or civilized, can only be rescued from its present degeneration by such studies.[41]

Such studies, of course, kept religion an ongoing concern even at the graduate research level. Despite their religious rationale, they were hardly any comfort to those who subscribed to anything like traditional Christianity. Rather such interest in religion was truly an instance of applying methodological secularization to religion itself. Studies *about* religion, as well as proclamations about the religious qualities of science, could ease the transition for a generation suffering the loss of evangelical verities.

Notes

1. I am indebted for to D. G. Hart, "Faith and Learning in the Age of the University: The Academic Ministry of Daniel Coit Gilman," in *The Secularization of the Academy,* George M. Marsden and Bradley J. Longfield, eds. (New York: Oxford University Press, 1992), 107–45, for his valuable research and insights on Gilman.

2. Hugh Hawkins, *Pioneer, A History of the Johns Hopkins University, 1874–1889* (Ithaca: Cornell University Press, 1960), 4–5. Four of the other trustees were Episcopal and one was Presbyterian.

3. Gilman, "The Johns Hopkins University in Its Beginnings," in *University Problems in the United States* (New York, 1898), 39.

4. Reverdy Johnson, Jr., to Gilman, January 4, 1875, and Gilman to Johnson, January 30, 1875, quoted in Hawkins, *Pioneer,* 22.

5. Hawkins, *Pioneer,* 69–71.

6. *New York Observer,* September 21, 1876, quoted in Hawkins, *Pioneer,* 71.

7. *Christian Advocate,* September 22, 1876, 308, quoted in Earl Hubert Brill, "Religion and the Rise of the University: A Study of the Secularization of American Higher Education, 1870–1910," Ph.D. disssertation, American University, 1969, 166.

8. Quoted in Hawkins, *Pioneer,* 71.

9. Hawkins, *Pioneer,* 252. Gilman, "The Johns Hopkins University," 19.

10. Gilman, "The Johns Hopkins University," 14–15.

11. Hawkins, *Pioneer,* 253.

12. Ibid., 238–39

13. Laurence Veysey, *The Emergence of the American University* (Chicago: University of Chicago Press, 1965), 127.

14. See Richard Hofstadter and Walter P. Metzger, *The Development of Academic Freedom in the United States* (New York: Columbia University Press, 1955), 367–412, on similarities and difference to the German model.

15. Roy Steven Turner, "The Prussian Universities and the Research Ideal, 1806 to 1848," Ph.D. dissertation, Princeton University, 1973, 387–90.

16. In England the issue was resolved with the same distinction. The universities were declared public and formally secularized by legislation in the latter half of the nineteenth century, while colleges were designated as private and thus free to continue religious practices and to be the loci for building character, manliness, and other Christian virtues. The difference was that in England there was a real institutional distinction between a college and a university. A university was a degree-granting agency, whereas a college was a community of teachers and students and traditionally the principal locus for instruction. In the United States, on the other hand, the university was almost always considered the extension of a college so that it was more difficult for the character of the two to remain distinct. I am grateful to Sheldon Rothblatt for clarifying for me the English analogy. See also his *The Revolution of the Dons: Cambridge and Society in Victorian England* (London: Faber and Faber, 1968).

17. James Turner, "Secularization and Sacralization: Speculations on Some Religious Origins of the Secular Humanities Curriculum, 1850–1900," in Marsden and Longfield, *Secularization of the Academy,* 74–106.

18. Burton J. Bledstein, *The Culture of Professionalism: The Middle Class and the Development of Higher Education in America* (New York: W. W. Norton, 1976), x, 34.

19. Gilman, "Johns Hopkins University," 18.

20. "Address by President D. C. Gilman, LL.D., of Baltimore," in *National Perils and Opportunities: The Discussions of the . . . Evangelical Alliance for the United States* (New York, 1887), 281, 283, cf. v–x. In an address before the Phi Beta Kappa Society of Harvard University, July 1, 1886, Gilman makes similar points. "The Characteristics of a University," in *University Problems,* 97.

21. Hawkins, *Pioneer,* 188.

22. G. Stanley Hall to Gilman, January 5, 1881, quoted in Dorothy Ross, *G. Stanley Hall: The Psychologist as Prophet* (Chicago: University of Chicago Press, 1972), 138–39.

23. Another candidate for the position, James Ward of Trinity College, Cambridge, claimed some years later that when a Quaker trustee had visited him, "he told me frankly that I was not orthodox enough—and then went back and appointed Stanley Hall! 'At Baltimore,' he said 'we are a church going people'; and had awful stories of the consternation [over] Huxley." James Ward to Mark Baldwin, September 15, 1903. Hawkins, *Pioneer,* 189n.

24. G. Stanley Hall, "Philosophy in the United States," *Mind 4* (January 1879), 101.

25. Hawkins, *Pioneer,* 204–5.

26. G. Stanley Hall, Editorial, *American Journal of Psychology* 7 (October 1895), 4.

27. Hall, "Philosophy in the United States," 89–91.

28. G. Stanley Hall, *Life and Confessions of a Psychologist* (New York, 1924), 222, quoted in Ross, *Hall,* 44. This account of Hall's biography is drawn from Ross.

29. Ibid., 47.

30. Hall, who was not always tactful and was often preoccupied with his adolescent crisis, reportedly told Josiah Royce at a professional meeting in 1894 that his idealism was similar to, and no better than, masturbation. Hall wondered why Royce became furious. Ross, *Hall,* 254.

31. G. Stanley Hall, "Psychological Literature," *American Journal of Psychology* 1 (November 1887), 159–60, quoted in Ross, *Hall,* 173.

32. Hall presents Peirce as the most advanced example of American philosophy. "Philosophy in the United States," 101–3.

33. Ross, *Hall,* 136n.

34. G. Stanley Hall, "The New Psychology," *Andover Review* 3 (March 1885), 247–48.

35. Ibid., 134.

36. John Bascom, Hall's former teacher, now president of the University of Wisconsin, expounded on this point in "Atheism in Colleges," *North American Review* 82 (January 1881), 32–40.

37. Hall, "The New Psychology," 241.

38. Veysey, *Emergence,* 165–71.

39. Ross, *Hall,* 269.

40. E.g., Arthur H. Daniels, "The New Life: A Study of Regeneration," *American Journal of Psychology* 6 (October 1894), 61–103; James H. Leuba, "A Study in the Psychology of Religious Phenomena," *American Journal of Psychology* 7 (April 1896), 308–71; Edwin Diller Starbuck, "A Study of Conversion," *American Journal of Psychology* 6 (January 1897), 268–307.

Franz Boas, one of the founders of the field of anthropology, was on the early Clark faculty.

41. Hall, Editorial, 7. Hall later became renowned for his ground-breaking study, *Adolescence: Its Psychology and Its Relations to Physiology, Anthropology, Sociology, Sex, Crime, Religion and Education,* 2 vols. (New York, 1904), and for hosting the visit of Freud to the United States in 1909, an event important in boosting Freud's scientific reputation.

10

Liberal Protestantism at Michigan: New England Intentions with Jeffersonian Results

When in 1888 the Rev. Francis Horton of Oakland attacked the University of California for its religious heterodoxy, the contrast he cited was the University of Michigan. "That institution does not teach religion any more than does ours, but its prevailing sentiment is favorable to revealed religion, as here it is against it."[1] Horton's reference was typical. Michigan was often mentioned hopefully as a model for the future of religion in higher education. The Ann Arbor example showed not only that a state school could be openly sympathetic to Christianity—the same could be said of most state universities[2]—but also that such sympathy was in fact displayed by a leader among the new research universities.

In this era when presidents ran institutions almost singlehandedly, Michigan's reputation as a Christian university was closely related to the express Christian piety of James Burrill Angell, president from 1871 to 1909. Angell was from Rhode Island and had studied at Brown under Francis Wayland and subsequently taught there. Like most university reformers, he had been ardently pro-Lincoln. During the Civil War he edited a Republican newspaper. He then served as president of the University of Vermont before going to Michigan. As a student he had thought seriously about a ministerial career and clearly carried that sense of calling into his work in higher education. When Angell was being considered for Michigan, Professor George P. Fisher of Yale described him as "a religious man, without the least taint of bigotry."[3] In Angell's case, this was no pro forma stance. Unlike some of his peers who largely kept their piety under wraps, Angell made Christianity in the university a major cause. He spoke about it, conducted surveys on it, wrote articles and edited a book on Christianity, facilitated the growth of campus ministries, and continued through the first decade of the twentieth century to preach Christ to Michigan.

Angell liked to quote Article III in the Northwest Ordinance: "Religion, morality and knowledge being necessary to good government and the happiness of mankind, schools and the means of education shall forever be encouraged." At his inauguration Angell interpreted "religion" to mean explicitly Christianity, announcing that "the Christian spirit, which pervades the law, the customs, and the life of the State shall shape and color the life of the University, that a lofty, earnest, but catholic and unsectarian Christian tone shall characterize the culture which is here imparted."[4]

This endorsement of a broad Christianity was hardly less controversial in Michigan than it would have been in California, except that a different group held control. Already in 1841, as we have seen, the Michigan regents had made very similar statements and the university had been attacked from both sides ever since. On the one hand, denominations that had their own schools accused the university of being pagan. Methodists, who never felt quite fairly represented by New England nonsectarianism,[5] complained the most. On the other hand, non-Christians, especially secularists, were insistent that the university was *too* Christian and thus violating separation of church and state.

Angell's explicit Christianity brought the latter issue to a head. In 1873 Stephen B. McCracken of Detroit made a formal complaint about the statement in the inaugural and Angell's expressed intent to hire faculty "whose mental and moral qualities will fit them to prepare their pupils for manly and womanly work in promoting our Christian civilization." McCracken pointed out that the population of Michigan included Jews, spiritualists, and various types of free thinkers and alleged that treating Christianity as an "exclusive or privileged opinion" violated the state constitution. He also observed that claims to be nonsectarian were hollow when everything but Protestantism was excluded. Angell's university, he argued, intimating Celtic resentments against New England imperialism, really stood for "puritan sectarianism."[6]

The state senate, after some reluctance to take the complaint seriously, appointed a committee to visit the university and investigate. There the senators were instructed on the true meaning of nonsectarianism. Some of the transcript is well worth a close reading as a window into the state of the discussion of the time:

STATEMENT OF PRESIDENT ANGELL

. . . .

Question. Please explain to the committee what you deem religious or denominational sectarianism.

Answer. The ordinary acceptation of the term is well known. I consider it a spirit of special devotion to some one denominational system of belief in some branch of the Christian church.

Question. Do you construe it to mean denominationalism and Christianity generally, as the opposite of infidelity, materialism, spiritualism, or any other unorthodox "isms"?

Answer. No, sir, that is not my idea. I should think sectarianism was devotion to one system of Christian belief in opposition to another,—not going outside of Christian beliefs.

. . . .

Question. By the committee: Do you inculcate Christianity as a system of religious belief as a teacher and professor in the University? and, if so, do you regard that as sectarian?
Answer. To the first part of the question I should say indirectly, Yes; to the second, No. I will explain as to the first answer that I believe it to be necessary for any Christian to state, if he is honest, what his beliefs are, and to honestly state opposing beliefs, if he knows what they are; for example, I don't think you can teach the History of the Reformation without stating your beliefs, while stating the opposing ones also, and, if a man of any power over your students, without impressing them besides. But I have never tried to enforce my beliefs.

. . . .

Question. Is there any restraint whatever laid upon the investigation or discussion of infidelity, spiritualism, materialism, or rationalism by the students?
Answer. Not at all. On the contrary, I think Dr. Cocker has explained those things to them.
Dr. Cocker. No, but there's been a Radical Club here, which talks over all sorts of things.

. . . .

STATEMENT OF DR. COCKER

Dr. Cocker: My name is Benjamin F. Cocker, and I have been Professor of Intellectual and Moral Philosophy for four years.

. . . .

Question. I wish to ask if your teaching is founded on what is known as Christian theology?
Answer. If by "theology" you mean the doctrine concerning God,—yes.
Question. Including the theological basis of ordinary Christianity?
Answer. Yes. My definition of Christianity is "to yield one's heart to the teachings and spirit, and to follow the example of Jesus Christ, who went about the world doing good." I urge all the boys to follow Christ as hard as they can in that way.

. . . .

Question. By the committee: You speak of Theology as a teaching of God, or of his attributes. Do you, or do you not, teach the miraculous birth, and redemptorial office of Christ as a necessary part of the "Christian Theology," and do you, or do you not teach, the "Christian Theology," so called, as the true religion?
Answer. I have never made an allusion to that subject since I have been in the University. I believe it. It is my private view, but I don't teach the doctrine in my class.
Question. By the committee: What do you mean by Christianity in the University?
Answer. I mean the spirit which pervades the University as Christian; there is Christianity in the observance of the Sabbath, in the date of the year, in the intercourse of the professors, in the repetition of the Lord's Prayer in chapel, in the bricks and mortar of the walls, in everything connected with the institution.

The senate committee cleared the university, concluding:

> The teachings of the university are those of a liberal and enlightened Christianity, in the general, highest and best use of the term. This is not in our opinion sectarian. If it is, we would not have it changed. A school, a society, a nation devoid of Christianity, is not a pleasant spectacle to contemplate. We cannot believe the people of Michigan would denude this great university of its fair, liberal and honorable Christian character as it exists today.[7]

President Angell and his faculty (such as Benjamin Cocker) had resolved the question of Christianity in the university in the way that Christian leaders of the era typically did. While they supported evangelical Christianity personally, in the classroom they limited what they said to essentially unitarian Christianity, advocating the ethics of Jesus and celebrating a "Christian spirit" within the civilization.

James Angell recognized that the Christian spirit in a modern state university would have to be cultivated differently than Christianity had been sustained in the old colleges. One of the first things he did was to shift chapel, which had been required for undergraduates, to a voluntary basis. When Angell arrived, the rebellious student spirit of the old-time college survived in a tradition of creating bedlam before, after, and sometimes during chapel. During his first weeks, Angell managed to quiet the multitude, but by the next year he had permanently resolved the issue by dropping compulsion. He also made moral philosophy and history of philosophy electives.[8]

Angell also moved to broaden the university's religious base. Early in 1873, while the agitation over McCraken's complaint was at its height, he proposed appointing a Roman Catholic, E. W. Hilgard, to the faculty. He felt, however, that he had to solicit the approval of the regents before taking such a step. Their reactions were mixed. One said an orthodox Catholic would be preferable to an infidel; another said that one moderate Catholic might be acceptable, another was not sure what the people would think. In general, however, they approved and Hilgard was appointed.[9]

Angell saw these moves to disestablish Protestantism as of a piece with his efforts to build Christianity at the university on a healthier voluntary basis. In 1890 responding to a request from the editors of the *Andover Review,* an influential progressive Congregational journal, Angell attempted to disabuse easterners of the impression that, because "we have such a complete separation of church and state," the state universities were "devoid of the religious spirit." The evidence proved the contrary, Angell argued. For instance, in a survey he had conducted of twenty-four state schools of learning, chapel services were held at twenty-two and at twelve were compulsory for undergraduates. The old type of chapel requirements enforced by a monitor, he suggested, were inappropriate when, as at Michigan, the entering age for freshmen was nineteen and a half years. Besides, he pointed out, those who were so solicitous about required chapel for undergraduates made no objection when such services were typically neglected at scientific schools in the East, such as the Massachusetts Institute of Technology or the Sheffield Scientific School at Yale.

More important than formal requirements was the general Christian spirit that pervaded institutions. The faculty was, of course, crucial. Of the schools surveyed, 71 percent of the teachers were church members and many others were actively religious despite not having formally joined churches. Angell did not mention it, but these church membership figures were far above national averages, especially for men. True, there were a few teachers at state schools, as at others, who might undermine Christian faith, but the majority were models of earnest and reverent men. In fact, in cities where state universities were located one could find members of university faculty teaching Sunday schools, conducting Bible classes, and engaged in every other sort of exemplary Christian activity.

Angell, no doubt, had his own faculty in mind as a model of such activity. He himself took care, especially in the fields that were replacing moral philosophy, to seek Christian teachers. "In the chair of History," he wrote to Daniel Coit Gilman in 1885, "the work may lie and often does lie so close to Ethics, that I should not wish a pessimist or an agnostic or a man disposed to obtrude criticisms of Christian views of humanity or of Christian principles. I should not want a man who would not make his historical judgments and interpretations from a Christian standpoint."[10]

At the University of Michigan, Angell could point out as well, such positive faculty influences were coordinated with growing opportunities for extracurricular religion. Michigan like every other state university had a Christian Association or the equivalent. These usually were affiliated with the YMCA or the YWCA. The university provided rooms for meetings and faculty spoke regularly at these. Dwight L. Moody had recently conducted revival services at the University of Michigan and Angell pointed with pride to the number of missionaries the university had sent to the foreign field. State universities, of course, did not have the percentages of ministerial graduates that denominational colleges had. But this was because denominational colleges typically offered scholarships for students preparing for ministerial study. It would be a mistake, Angell felt, however, if denominations neglected state schools where they could have considerable influence as well.

In fact, with Angell's encouragement Ann Arbor was becoming the model for denominational work at state schools. In 1887 Episcopalians and Presbyterians had established student centers or guilds near the university, and they were very soon followed by the Methodists, Catholics, and Unitarians. The Tappan Presbyterian Guild, for instance, had a library of some four thousand volumes, a gymnasium, social rooms, and study rooms. Guilds offered courses of lectures on religious topics and sponsored prominent religious speakers.[11] Eventually denominations imitated this Ann Arbor model in most state universities' towns, although it took several decades for denominational centers to emerge as the typical pattern.

Religious Thought at the University of Michigan (1893)

While recognizing that Christianity would not play much of a role in the classroom of a modern state university, James Angell wanted to make sure that the voluntary religion proclaimed by the surrounding institutions could offer the same benefits as had moral philosophy at the old colleges. One evidence that this concern was widely shared was a volume published in 1893 by the Student Christian Association, *Religious Thought at the University of Michigan.* The volume contained twenty addresses, two by Angell and the rest by university faculty members, delivered on Christian themes at the Sunday morning services of the Christian Association. The reason for the lectures, the editors explained, was that it had been pointed out to them that "most of the University instructors . . . were interested speculatively as well as practically, in matters of religion." However most of what went on intellectually was "a great deal of quiet but active thinking about religious questions . . . of which students had but occasional intimations."[12]

The lectures touched on a wide range topics including assurances that Darwinism did not challenge essential Christianity, discussions of the impact of Christianity on history and society, and questions of the relationship of Christianity to teaching, medicine, music, and missions.

The overwhelming impression offered by these lectures is of an aggressively liberal Christianity. Repeatedly the lecturers urge students that the way to resolve the apparent tensions between faith and learning is to see that Christianity is in essence simply a life of morality which science can only enhance. Thus in addressing the much discussed topic of "How has Biological Research Modified Christian Conceptions?" Professor V. M. Spalding assured his audience that the essence of Christianity was the "absolute unselfishness of Christ," which presented us with a "sublime gospel" that we could know to be eternal. "Has the onward march of scientific discovery," he asked, "has the development of philosophical thought in any form affected by so much as a shadow the great central figure of Christianity?" Nothing had "come to light that prevents any one of us from being his disciples, learning of him, catching his spirit."

On the other hand, said Spalding, the "venerable structure" of theology offered a great heritage of "men who walked with God." "Yes, but of *men!*" he immediately added. "And no work of man has ever stood unchanged through any long period of time." So, the entire history of Christian theology, much as it should be revered, would be dismissed. There would be, "to use Prof. LeConte's expression, the necessity of a complete reconstruction of Christian theology," based on scientific principles. Most important, Scripture as a dogmatic authority would have to go. "An increasing number of the most conscientious and intelligent leaders of Christian thought are looking upon the Bible simply as the lamp through which the light of God shines." So the Bible was "a book written for men and by men, but full of sublime, holy and divine truth." Regarding the Bible "as an infallible oracle," on the other hand, "tends directly to encourage indolence and superstition." More and more thinkers were coming to recognize that "the search for truth is God's ordained means of obtaining it." Christians were "coming to understand that religious truth is no exception to this rule."

The search for truth, then, brought Christianity down to its spiritual essence, which of course was not susceptible to scientific refutation. "The stripping off of traditions has only brought into clearer relief the Divine Presence."[13] As Professor Francis W. Kelsey, in a lecture on "Primitive and Modern Christianity," put it, "The history of the church as a whole is an illustration of the law of the survival of the fittest. Christianity has shown a constant tendency to take the place of inferior beliefs. In its own inner life there has been a marked tendency to pass from lower to higher forms. . . . Christianity was not primarily a system of government, a ritual, or a theology; it was a life."[14]

The treatment of Christianity as a life and not a doctrine, as something caught more than taught, as "the Fatherhood of God and the brotherhood of man,"[15] resolved a multitude of problems. First of all, it was a genuinely grand moral vision, an attempt to recover and apply the selfless ethics of Jesus, which had often been obscured by theological dogma and ecclesiastical ambition. The grandeur of these ideals explained the otherwise intellectually embarrassing assertion of the superiority of Christianity to other religions, and hence the superiority of Western cultures to others which it was dominating. James Angell himself, who had served as the U. S. minister to China, made this the theme in one of his lectures, listing the ways in which Christian civilization was morally superior, especially in its regard for individuals, for charity, for international law, for the dignity of women, and for truth seeking.[16]

Justifying Christianity in Lincolnesque fashion solely by its moral teachings, which seemed to bring peace, freedom, and justice, resolved an even more trying problem which plagued almost every thinking Christian of the generation—was Christianity true? Particularly, could Christians still believe the Bible? The generation had been reared on the most profound reverence for the authority of the Bible, not only in doctrine, but also in history. In the pre–Civil War era, America's most advanced academic debates, those in the great theological journals, had been built on the premise of biblical authority and reliability. The next generation, especially the swelling numbers of academics who took their graduate work in Germany after 1860, found this premise almost impossible to accept.

The historical criticism of the Scriptures which these academics learned in Europe was already far advanced. While Cambridge and Scotland offered some models of more moderate criticism, Americans who studied in Germany seemed more often impressed by more radical continental views. Scholars such as Ernest Renan and David Friedrich Strauss had, in effect, demonstrated a flaw in the fusion of Enlightenment and evangelical Protestant ideals which seemed to have worked so well in America. If Christianity was supported and confirmed by objective science, then the Bible should be able to be subjected to the same historical analysis as the documents of any other religion. Scientific naturalism thus became the starting point for historical inquiry into the Bible. From that point of view, of course, the Scriptures looked very different than they did if viewed with the premise that they were revealed by God. The miracle stories, for instance, became embarrassments, rather than evidences. By modern critical standards historical reporting in Scripture looked inaccurate and fabricated. Particularly the Old Testament narratives, as well as many of the claims to authorship and dating, appeared implausible if the writings were viewed as simple products of the evolving faith of an ancient primitive people.

Darwinism, which appeared at about the same time and was built on the same purely naturalistic premises, only added a dramatic point to this more basic erosion of biblical authority. Darwinism reinforced already strong challenges to the historicity of the narratives of the early chapters of Genesis, which included not only the creation narratives, but also accounts of the Great Flood and the Tower of Babel. Darwinism was especially important in that it offered a plausible alternative to biblical creation accounts of how humans originated. The biblical accounts, rather than standing as the best answer to an otherwise unsolvable question, could be relegated to the realm of myth.

John Dewey, one of the stars on the Michigan faculty, took the new point of view as his starting point in his address on "Christianity and Democracy" to the Christian Association. Religious beliefs, he said, may appear to be in a special category of human experience. "Research into the origin and development of religion destroys the appearance," however. "It is shown that every religion has its source in the social and intellectual life of a community or race." Dewey did not mention that this outlook was the premise of the research as well as its conclusion. "Every religion," he said simply, "is an expression of the social relations of the community," to which he added somewhat more affirmatively, "its rites, its cult are a recognition of the sacred and divine significance of these relationships."[17]

Dewey is especially fascinating because his spiritual and intellectual journey, spanning the whole era of the rise of the American university, almost perfectly mirrors the changing dominant academic opinion. Born in Vermont in 1859 and reared in the evangelical Calvinism of his mother, Dewey soon learned moderate Calvinist theology from his pastor and as a student at the University of Vermont. In his early twenties he had a conversion experience and became an active member and frequent Sunday school teacher in the Congregational church. From 1882–1884

Dewey was a graduate student at Johns Hopkins University and, under the influence of the philosopher George Sylvester Morris, adapted his Christianity to Hegelianism. This put him in the camp of liberal "progressive orthodoxy" which was revolutionizing Congregationalism, most notably at Andover Theological Seminary.[18] During this era, especially among philosophers and theologians, a progressive philosophical idealism that could explain spiritual progress in divine terms, and was not dependent on the historical claims of Scripture, was the major academic substitute for the old biblically based dogmatics and history.

When Dewey spoke to the University of Michigan Christian Association in 1892 the Hegelian elements in his outlook still shone through. Nonetheless, even though he was still active in the local Congregational church, the distinctly Christian elements of his thought were eroding, an erosion covered in part by idealist rhetoric. God, said Dewey, is not the sort of being who makes certain fixed statements about himself. Rather, "The one claim that Christianity makes is that God is truth; that as truth He is love and reveals Himself fully to man, keeping back nothing of himself; that man is so one with the truth thus revealed that it is not so much revealed *to* him as *in* him; he is its incarnation." This is what Jesus meant by "The Kingdom of God is within us." God is therefore revealed in all search for truth in the human community. Democracy thus is an expression of God's spirit in that it allows freedom, including the freedom to search for the truth: "If God is, as Christ taught, at the root of life, incarnate in man, then democracy has a spiritual meaning which it behooves us not to pass by. Democracy is freedom. If truth is at the bottom of things, freedom means giving truth a chance to show itself, a chance to well up from the depths." This spirit of freedom and truth embodied in democracy provided not only intellectual freedom, but practical freedom in ending slavery and breaking down class and social barriers that were dividing humanity.[19]

Other speakers to the Michigan Christian Association in 1892 and 1893 suggested, as did Dewey, an emerging social gospel as yet another justification for the redefinition of Christianity as the highest democratic morality. Here was another immense set of challenges which the shift to the ethics of Jesus could address. Industrialization, powerful trusts, labor troubles, urbanization, and immigration all tested revived verities about economic and social relations. The new social sciences that were emerging out of the old unspecialized moral philosophy and political economy were attempts to address the far more complex and differentiated social and economic realities that were emerging. Christians, still inspired by millennial dreams of moral and material progress going hand in hand, hoped to temper social strife with an ethic of love. During the first generation of the rise of the social sciences many Christians, including many social scientists, assumed that the sciences would be allies of the faith.

So at Michigan, Professor Henry C. Adams, an economist, in his address on "Christianity as a Social Force," insisted that one "must assume the ethical teachings of Jesus as an unalterable premise in the discussion of every social, political, industrial, or personal question." Adams considered it blasphemy for some persons to quote Scripture to argue that in either national affairs or business one should look out only for one's own interests in disregard of the interests of others. Adams admitted this was "a hard saying" for those who wished to be competitive in American business. He argued that a person should work within the present rules of what the law calls honest but take "as the highest aim in life, the task of doing what he may to so change laws and modify customs that the old Christian conception of a just price, and the modern Christian conception of equal opportunities for all, may become a realized fact."[20]

Such social gospel views, not unusual among leading economists and sociologists of the generation, were not popular with some of the business supporters of the universities. In 1886, the year of the Haymarket riots, Adams himself had been denied a permanent professorship at Cornell because of the reaction of the university's conservative Christian benefactor, Henry W. Sage, to a prolabor speech in 1886. Adams's case was one of the first of such tests of academic freedom during the latter years of the century.[21]

James Angell, who, much more than Adams or Dewey, retained the conventional language of the New England theological tradition, nonetheless interpreted that heritage in a strongly ethical way, so that the example of Jesus was always a prominent theme.[22] In preaching to students he typically applied the ideals of Jesus in urging them to cultivate traits of personal character, such as chastity, honesty, purity, and self-control, but he also taught that the message of love had world-changing social implications with respect to the way one should treat strangers, outcasts, and the less fortunate.[23] Though Angell himself did not tread into social controversy, he was sympathetic to a social Christianity and clearly encouraged his faculty openly to express their Christian ideals.

In his 1890 essay on religion at state universities Angell celebrated the expansion of voluntary religion. "I doubt whether a really better state of religious life has ever existed in our principal colleges and universities than now exists." The recent remarkable response of students to Moody's call for missionaries, resulting in the Student Volunteer Movement, was evidence of this trend.[24] Keeping his hand on the religious pulse of the university, Angell conducted another survey of state universities in 1896 and gained further support for this claim. Of nearly five thousand students concerning whom he gained information at five state universities (Indiana, Kansas, Michigan, Washington, and West Virginia), 55 percent were church members and the total rose to nearly 90 percent if one included those who claimed to be afilliated with or to attend a church. The membership figures, also far above the national average, appeared to be rising,[25] perhaps because liberalized Protestant church membership was easier to attain. The universities were also overwhelmingly Protestant, far more than the nation as a whole. Only 165 students (or about 3 percent) were identified as Catholics and only 44 (less than 1 percent) were Jews.[26] A notable feature of these statistics that does not seem to have been much taken into account by historians of women in higher education is that everywhere the percentage of women students who were church members was substantially higher than the percentage of men. At Michigan, for instance, the figure was only 52 percent for men and 70 percent of women. Growing numbers of women students were a significant force in the growth of voluntary religion.[27]

It was another question, however, whether all this voluntary religion and all the solicitude from a pious president had much to do with how the academic life of the university was defined. The answer seems to be that it did not.[28] What made Michigan important was that it was a prototype of the state research university. In defining the research ideal Michigan ended up simply following the national standards established at Hopkins and elsewhere.[29]

Of course, concern for broader issues did not disappear immediately. Members of the transitional generation, dominated by liberal Protestants, often combined their religious-moral concerns with their scholarship. But they failed to apply these principles to *defining* the major components of the university. Even the proponents of Christianity had treated it as essentially a set of moral concerns, accentuating the trend already set by moral philosophy courses. A broadly Christian moral consensus could be presumed in academic life. As long as that was the case, there seemed little reason to provide it with formal institutional or intellectual supports.

Ironically what Angell and his generation of New Englanders achieved, often in the name of Christianity, was much like the Jeffersonian ideal for the university. In this respect, Michigan was not much different from the University of California. It was scientific at its center, open to broad humane ideals, and welcomed voluntary and sectarian religion on its periphery. The only difference was that Angell spoke more openly of the unifying philosophy as "Christian." Whatever Angell's personal beliefs, the type of Christianity that actually played a role in the conduct of the university would hardly have displeased Jefferson. It was an informally presented nonsectarian ethics of Jesus, combined with a total commitment to truth seeking and to the scientific method as an unassailable sacred enterprise. "We may learn from our Lord," said Angell, "that the quest after truth, after all truth, is justified. . . . So all learning, all science, is in its proper sense sacred."[30] Angell might emphasize that all such science must serve humanity,[31] but so had Jefferson. The specifics of science and philosophy had shifted in developmental and idealist directions, but the prevailing spirit was still that of a nation founded on Enlightenment principles. After a century of resistance from more traditional Christians, the dominant educational ideals were defined by a synthesis of Enlightenment ideals and an enlightened Christianity, or religion of humanity.

It was not a long step from such informal ethical Christianity to recognition that explicit Christianity was superfluous to the enterprise. Since Christianity was being defined by high moral ideals of a civilization dedicated to freedom, science, and service, why not state directly that these latter were practically your defining principles?

John Dewey saw this point presciently and thus became a leading spokesperson for the academic consensus of the next half century. At Michigan Dewey was on the verge of dropping both his philosophical idealism and his Christianity as unnecessary baggage. When he went to the University of Chicago in 1894 he let his church affiliation lapse. One of his last contributions to the University of Michigan was an essay that argued that "because science represents a method of truth to which so far as we can discover, no limits whatsoever can be put, . . . it is necessary for the church to reconstruct its doctrines of revelation and inspiration, and for the individual to reconstruct, within his own religious life, his conception of what spiritual truth is and the nature of its authority over him."[32]

In 1892, when speaking to the Michigan Christian Association, Dewey had anticipated these sentiments, ending his address with a stirring appeal to turn away from supposed revelation in "the older formulation, inherited from days when the organization of society was not democratic," to the scientific method of the university which will not "isolate religious thought and conduct from the common life of man." Dewey ended with almost an altar call to turn from past religion to a scientific future: "Remember Lot's wife, who looked back, and who, looking back, was fixed into a motionless pillar."[33]

Notes

1. "Dissolving View; Rev. Dr. Horton's Opinion of Unitarianism," *Oakland Tribune,* December 17, 1888, contrasts an atmosphere favorable to religion at Michigan to that at Berkeley. Horace Davis, the Unitarian president, also appealed to aspects of the Michigan model. Davis repeated Gilman's suggestion for denominational houses, citing a "Hobart House," founded by Episcopalians in Ann Arbor. *Occident,* September 11, 1888, and *San Leandro Advertiser,* September 8, 1888. From newspaper clippings book in university archives, Bancroft Library, University of California at Berkeley.

2. Bradley J. Longfield, "From Evangelicalism to Liberalism: Public Midwestern Universities in Nineteenth-Century America," in *The Secularization of the Academy,* George M. Marsden and Bradley J. Longfield, eds. (New York: Oxford University Press, 1992), 46–73.

3. George P. Fisher to E. C. Walker, July 28, 1869, in *From Vermont to Michigan: Correspondence of James Burrill Angell: 1869–1871,* Wilfred B. Shaw, ed. (Ann Arbor, 1936), 70–71. Angell had also taught modern languages and literature at Brown prior to the Civil War.

4. James Burrill Angell, "Inaugural Address, University of Michigan" (1871), *Selected Addresses* (New York, 1912), 29.

5. Victor R. Wilbee, "The Religious Dimensions of Three Presidencies in a State University: Presidents Tappan, Haven, and Angell at the University of Michigan," Ph.D. dissertation, University of Michigan, 1967, 198–200. Cf. Winton U. Solberg, "Religion and Secularism at the University of Illinois, 1867–1894," *American Quarterly* 18 (1966), 187.

6. Wilbee, "Religious Dimensions," 201–2.

7. Michigan Legislature, *Legislative Journal, Daily Proceedings* (Lansing, 1873), as quoted (without original page numbers) in Wilbee, "Religious Dimensions," Appendix A, 217–20. Concluding statement from *Journal,* 1775, quoted in Wilbee, 203.

8. Angell to Peter Collier, September 28, 1871, in Shaw, *From Vermont to Michigan,* 292–93. Wilbee, "Religious Dimensions," 179–82. Morning chapel services finally ended in 1894 and all services ended in 1901 or 1902.

9. Wilbee, "Religious Dimensions," 205–6.

10. Angell to D. C. Gilman, October 23, 1885, quoted in Laurence Veysey, *The Emergence of the American University* (Chicago: University of Chicago Press, 1965), 75.

11. Angell, "Religious Life in Our State Universities," *Andover Review* 13 (April 1890), 365–72. Cf. Clarence Prouty Shedd, *The Church Follows Its Students* (New Haven, 1938), 11.

12. "Editor's Note," *Religious Thought at the University of Michigan* (Ann Arbor, 1893), iv.

13. V. M. Spalding, "How Has Biological Research Modified Christian Conceptions?" in *Religious Thought at Michigan,* 96–109. Though the preponderant tone of the volume is liberal, some authors appear more conservative; e.g., W. J. Hardman defends biblical miracles and sees archaeological evidence as confirming historicity of Scripture. "The Methods of Science Applied to Christianity," 124–38.

14. Francis W. Kelsey, "Primitive and Modern Christianity," in *Religious Thought at Michigan,* 19.

15. H. C. Adams, "Christianity as a Social Force," in *Religious Thought at Michigan,* 53. Cf. Angell, "The Old and the New Ideal of Scholars," Baccalaureate Address, June 18, 1905 (Ann Arbor, 1905), 8.

16. Angell, "Christianity and Other Religions Judged by Their Fruits," in *Religious Thought at Michigan,* 3–14.

17. John Dewey, "Christianity and Democracy," in *Religious Thought at Michigan,* 60.

18. Bruce Kuklick, *The Rise of American Philosophy: Cambridge, Massachusetts, 1860–1930* (New Haven: Yale University Press, 1977), 230–53, provides a valuable account of Dewey's journey and it relation to earlier New England theology. Steven C. Rockefeller, *John Dewey: Religious Faith and Democratic Humanism* (New York: Columbia University Press, 1991) is also valuable.

19. Dewey, "Christianity and Democracy," 60–69.

20. Adams, "Christianity as a Social Force," 51–59.

21. Richard Hofstadter and Walter P. Metzger, *The Development of Academic Freedom in the United States* (New York: Columbia University Press, 1955), 411–67.

22. In "The Expanding Power of Christianity," for instance, Angell talks about God as "a beneficent moral governor of the universe," the need for special revelation, "the plan of redemption" (though declining to discuss any theories of the atonement), and "the hope for immortal life" (though he is vague as to

whether this is a quality of life or actual life after death. *Religious Thought at Michigan,* 141–50.

23. Ibid. See also several baccalaureate addresses, all published in Ann Arbor, "Lesson Suggested by Christ's Life to the Scholar" (1903), "The Old and the New Ideal of Scholars" (1905), and "The Age of Quickened Conscience" (1908).

24. Angell, "Religious Life," 368–69.

25. Wilbee reports a survey at Michigan in 1881 that showed that "seventy per cent of the students and thirty-nine per cent of the faculty were not professing Christians." "Religious Dimensions," 206. Other reports suggest a rise in Christian belief in colleges during this era, though such a large change would seem remarkable.

26. Frank W. Kelsey, "State Universities and Church Colleges," *Atlantic Monthly* 80 (December 1897), 827. Jews were listed among "church members."

27. Ibid., 828. At this time Michigan had in all its schools 2263 men and 662 women students. The surveys included all schools and typically showed the proportion of church members "somewhat greater in the collegiate department than in the professional schools." However, at Michigan the medical school had the highest percentage of church members, suggesting perhaps that the ethos of the Michigan elite was still substantially Christian.

28. Wilbee's "Religious Dimensions" likewise concludes that by the time Angell finally retired in 1909 the university was in essential respects a secular institution. See his abstract for summary.

29. See, for instance, James Turner, "The Prussian Road to University? German Models and the University of Michigan, 1837–c.1895," *Rackam Reports* (Ann Arbor: University of Michigan, 1989), 6–52, for an account of the unsuccessful effort at Michigan in the 1880s to define the standards for the Ph.D. degree in terms other than narrow specialization.

30. "Lessons Suggested by Christ's Life to the Scholar," Baccalaureate Address (Ann Arbor, 1903), 4–5. On the continuing New England influence, Samuel Haber, *Authority and Honor in the American Professions, 1750–1900* (Chicago: University of Chicago Press, 1991), 277, notes that, while the professoriate increased by four times from 1870 to 1900, it also became more predominantly of Congregational and Presbyterian background.

31. Ibid., 5. "But after all in every true scholar, the manhood is more than the scholarship. . . . It calls on the scholar as a man to dedicate all his powers and attainments to the good of his fellows." This passage suggests that "manhood" and "Manliness," so often used in this era, might have a connotation of the selflessness arising from recognizing one's common humanity. Angell illustrates this point with examples of service of women from the university.

32. John Dewey, "Reconstruction," *The Bulletin* 15 (May 1894), quoted in Wilbee, "Religious Dimensions," 207.

33. Dewey, "Christianity and Democracy," 68–69.

11

Harvard and the Religion of Humanity

Once we have seen the extent to which the rest of New England's higher education establishment moved in a functionally unitarian or even Jeffersonian direction as it adjusted to the demands and promises of a complex modern society, we can see one reason why by the end of the century Harvard could readily reclaim its national leadership. Of course its superior age and wealth, as well as the literary prominence of many of its graduates, guaranteed Harvard's eminence. During the first half of the nineteenth century, however, Harvard's Unitarianism had isolated it somewhat from the evangelicalism of national trends and by most measures it had fallen behind Yale and Princeton. But in the age of the university, as the winds of liberalism blew strong, the fact that Harvard had already tacked in the direction of liberal Christianity helped it to regain its position as a flagship setting the pace for a national educational ideology.

Nowhere was the metamorphosis from old-time religious college to modern university more rapid or more dramatic than at Harvard. To paraphrase Henry Adams, Harvard in 1850 was in many ways closer to the Middle Ages than to the Harvard of 1900.[1] At midcentury many of the forms of seventeenth-century Harvard—the tutors, the recitations, the discipline, the strong clerical presence, daily chapel, the classical curriculum—were still in place. The professoriate was largely Unitarian, drawn predominantly from the local eastern Massachusetts aristocracy and their descendants. By the final decade of the century only a fifth of the professoriate were Unitarian. Among the others, Catholics and Jews had at least token representation. Perhaps most significant, over a fourth were of no easily identifiable religious persuasion.[2] At turn-of-the-century Harvard, in the "golden age" of William James, Josiah Royce, George Santayana, Hugo Münsterberg, and others, religion could still be an issue, but old questions of orthodoxy seemed as far away as the Dark Ages.

It was not at all an accident that in Massachusetts, where the formal establishment of the church had lasted longest (until 1833) and the Puritan heritage had been most formidable, the reaction of dedication to freedom for liberal religious expression was most intense. California might be comparable in its openness, but there freedom prevailed largely because the area lacked a heritage of Protestant establishment and hence was open to pluralistic tolerance and indifference. At Harvard, on the other hand, acceptance of the ideal of individual freedom was the culmination of a longstanding crusade. Charles W. Eliot, Harvard's renowned president from 1869 to 1909, had a faith in self-development that was most clearly manifested in his insistence on a radical elective system that gave undergraduates virtually complete freedom to choose their own courses. A corresponding freedom from religious restraints facilitated Harvard's ability to prevail in late-nineteenth-century competition to assemble professional faculties. For a time it easily surpassed its longtime rivals.

Harvard's transition toward liberal Christianity had been going on since the revolutionary era. In 1805 with the election of Henry Ware as Hollis Professor of Divinity, the Unitarians wrested control of the college from the moderate Calvinists. Reeling from this defeat, Massachusetts Calvinists established Andover Theological Seminary, the first American divinity school, in 1808. The Andover charter went to considerable lengths to guarantee that in future generations liberals could never take it over. The guarantee could not hold liberalism back even for a century, however. In the early 1880s, Andover Seminary dramatically emerged as the center for Congregational liberalism of the sort we have seen in university leaders such as Gilman and Angell. Conservative efforts to halt the trend by dismissing a faculty member were blocked by a Massachusetts court. In 1908 Andover Seminary moved to Cambridge and affiliated with Harvard Divinity School.[3]

The early Massachusetts Unitarian liberalism, which emerged in the oldest and most cosmopolitan parts of Massachusetts during the revolutionary era, was an adaptation of the Puritan heritage to the demands of moderate Enlightenment ideology. Above all it was reasonable and moralistic. Without rejecting biblical revelation, it argued that the Bible should be interpreted in the light of modern rational standards of morality. Unitarians were optimistic about human abilities and hence were, even more than evangelical Protestants, enthusiasts for common sense, specifically for Scottish Common Sense epistemology and moral philosophy.[4]

During the first half of the nineteenth century, then, moral philosophy was as close to the essence of the collegiate mission at Harvard as it was anywhere in the country. The Harvard leadership was dedicated to study of the classics just as much as were their Connecticut counterparts who issued the Yale Report of 1828. This classicism, as Daniel Howe points out, helped liberate students from the lingering hold of Puritan orthodoxy and yet was fully compatible with the continuing legacy of moralism.[5] The goal above all else, as Henry Ware, Jr., put it in a highly successful 1831 tract, was shaping "Christian character" by internalizing habits of moral discipline that would contribute to the improvement of individuals and of society.[6] As in England in the early Victorian era, such virtues were increasingly recognized by the leadership in the emerging industrial societies as invaluable both to themselves and as a creed for all classes.

Having fought and largely won their battle with Calvinism, midcentury Unitarians thought of themselves as in the forefront of the human quest for intellectual freedom. Like other American Protestants they saw what they were doing as simply an extension of the Reformation. In the *History of Harvard University* (1840), President Josiah Quincy deplored the medieval times when "religion and learning were taught by the same masters." According to Quincy, "They enforced the dogmas of the former by the terrors of a future life, and taught the rudiments of the latter by corporeal terrors in the present." In 1840 everyone knew that you did not need to look nearly so far as the Middle Ages to find survivals of such practices, especially in the disciplinary attitudes at old-time colleges which, not incidentally for Bostonians, had some counterparts in contemporary Catholic education. In such a medieval system, said Quincy, "the mind was taught just as a man teaches inferior animals." The object was to bring the mind into subjection, rather than to excite the exercise of its full powers.

"After the Reformation," Quincy continued, "a more liberal system was introduced." Even so, the Protestant states did not progress far from the Church of Rome's traditional goal of bringing "the general mind into subjection through the instrumentality of education." Only in recent times were attempts being made "to rescue the general mind from the vassalage in which it has been held by sects in the church, and by parties in the state." Only as science and learning were recognized as community values in their own right was the mind beginning to be liberated from "subserviency to particular views in politics or religion."[7]

Harvard was the first American school to feel the impact of the ideal presented by the rising eminence of the German universities. Even before 1820 two of its graduates, Edward Everett and George Bancroft, as well as George Ticknor, who joined the Harvard faculty in 1819, had already led the way in what would later become a flood of American gentlemen-scholars studying in Germany. What the Harvard contingent, like their other American counterparts, brought back from Germany were not exact German models so much as admiration for German scholarship and increasing openness to idealist and romantic modes of thought. This new spirit added to the Americans' Enlightenment reverence for science a celebration of the life of the creative mind or the individual's intellectual quest. The "Copernican revolution" of Immanuel Kant in the eighteenth century had shifted the paradigm of human intellectual activity from a model of discovery of the fixed principles to a model of the intellect as an active agent imposing its categories on reality. Idealist philosophy recognized that this revolution made truth to some degree relative to the individual and to time and place and celebrated truth seeking as a process. Concern to understand historical development also began to emerge, but the accompanying romantic idealism insulated it against the negative implications of relativism. God and the entire universe could be understood in terms of the analogy of the mind progressing toward truth. The highest human activity was to participate in this ongoing, creative, self-fulfilling, and ultimately divine truth-seeking process. Intellectual inquiry was thus deified.[8]

The thousands of American scholars who studied in Germany during the nineteenth century typically did not assimilate fully the details of German philosophy. Nevertheless, Germany continued to provide them with powerful symbolic ideals with which to challenge conventional American practices. One of them was "the research ideal." Another was the practical freedom of students in Germany to regulate their own lives and to choose which lectures they would attend. Most pervasive of all, perhaps, were romantic ideals, growing in Germany and elsewhere, of cultivating character as the goal of humanistic education. Whatever their exact sources, during the nineteenth century such conceptions became standard belief among well-educated Americans, displacing Calvinist views of human nature that emphasized obedience to the Creator, rather than creative human development.

Before these new ideals had had much impact, Unitarian Harvard College was becoming isolated and parochial in the American setting. In 1821 Harvard had been the largest and the richest American college; by 1836 its graduating class was smaller than those at Yale, Union, Princeton, and Dartmouth.[9] Among other problems, the evangelical-Calvinist countermovement, which was plaguing Jefferson in the South, was having an impact even in Massachusetts. In 1825 Calvinists founded Amherst College in western Massachusetts as an orthodox alternative to Harvard. The next year Lyman Beecher arrived in Boston to challenge the Unitarian menace in its lair.

The evangelical-Calvinist counterattack, which effectively emphasized that religious liberalism was sectarian rather than pluralistic, helped keep Harvard local, isolated, and overwhelmingly dependent on its own Unitarian old-boy network. By 1845 the Harvard faculty, though still distinguished, was less impressive than that of 1821. One conspicuous exception to Unitarian uniformity was the brilliant young naturalist Asa Gray. Gray was a New School Presbyterian and his appointment in 1842 was the clearest case reflecting the growing sentiments of some faculty that the school should be moving toward purely professional criteria in hiring. It still had quite a way to go.[10]

At most other colleges Unitarians were viewed with suspicion. Despite some calls for letting professional achievements play a larger role in determining hiring, the vaunted nonsectarianism of midcentury schools frequently did not extend as far as Unitarians. Most such discrimination was, of course, informal. In 1851, however, at Columbia College in New York it came disturbingly into the open in the case of Oliver Wolcott Gibbs. When the chair of natural science at the then undistinguished college became vacant in 1851, some progressive trustees urged that they begin to make professional considerations paramount in hiring. They contrasted the amateurism at the American college with Göttingen, which had also been founded in one of the domains of George II a century before and was now a world-renowned university. At the least, Columbia should compete with Yale.[11] A first step in the proposed new regime was the nomination of Gibbs to the natural science post. Gibbs was a distinguished scientist teaching at what became the City College of New York. Though baptized Episcopalian, since his father's death he had attended a Unitarian church.

Columbia was still controlled by Episcopalians, with strong minority representation from Presbyterians and Dutch Reformed. When Gibbs's nomination was finally proposed late in 1853 the conservatives on the board, led by a number of clergy from the various denominations, opposed him on religious grounds. On the question of relating religion to science, Gibbs could answer conventionally that Nature too was part of God's revelation, but the Presbyterians were not satisfied with his views on "the divine plenary inspiration of the Scriptures." The real issue, however, clearly came down to Gibbs's Unitarianism.[12] When this issue surfaced, a predictable storm broke out on the closely divided board. If Columbia were a "church college," which it was not, said the progressives, religious views might be relevant to teaching church history or moral philosophy. But surely even at such a college religion would not be relevant to natural science. One of the dogmas of the Enlightenment was that science had no sects. Surely there were no Unitarian versus Trinitarian views of chemistry. More important, the attempt at exclusion was especially unconscionable because the state constitution expressly forbade any religious test for officers of colleges. In fact, one could see how outrageously new was the imposition of a sectarian test by noting that earlier in the century the board of trustees had included none other than Oliver Wolcott, a Unitarian, the grandfather of Wolcott Gibbs. The so-called conservatives were now proposing to restrict what had become an established obligation for a college to serve all the public.[13]

The conservatives, however, had just enough votes to win, thus for the time being keeping Columbia on its narrow track. They could argue, as they did when the case was tested in court, that even if the institution had no religious test, individual trustees were free to vote their consciences. As with most such efforts, however, the victory was largely pyrrhic. Much of public opinion was offended by the exclusion, which underscored the difficulties encountered by quasi-public institutions in finding an alternative to vague and informal religious tests. At Columbia, the progressives were strengthened in their resolve to turn the school into a university, which they began to do in subsequent decades. Gibbs also was eventually rewarded with a chair in chemistry at Harvard in 1863.[14]

The subsequent transformation of Harvard itself illustrated, perhaps even better than White's Cornell, the interaction of such ideological battles for the liberalization of religion with more practical concerns revolutionizing education. A liberalized ideology seemed almost essential for professionalization, for promoting research in the service of a modernizing economy, and for building an educational market that was responsive to new, diversified, and pluralistic educational demands.

All these pressures toward liberalizing religion were operative at Harvard as elsewhere, but at Harvard the ideological-religious revolution was more explicit and thoroughgoing than at most other institutions. The expansion of the definition of religion involved various ways of raising human creative achievements to primary religious significance, especially achievements through science and scientific method on the one hand and in art and romantic or idealistic thought on the other. This transformation of the meaning of Christianity also involved an acceleration of the tendency, long evident in evangelical moral philosophy as well, to subordinate the letter of traditional Christianity to its moral spirit.

The paradox of secularization that could be seen at most other American universities was nowhere better illustrated than at Harvard. From a traditionalist point of view what was happening at Harvard looked simply like the secularization of the college. Yet these developments were taking place not in the name of an attack on Christianity but under the banner of the expansion of its influence. At Harvard, in fact, this point was made in advance of other American schools. Already in 1866 the Rev. Frederic Henry Hedge of the Harvard Divinity School reassured an alumni group that, even though the college had shifted from its original emphasis on training clergy, "the secularization of the College is no violation of its motto, *'Christo et Ecclesiae.'* For, as I interpret those sacred ideas, the cause of Christ and the Church is advanced by whatever liberalizes and enriches and enlarges the mind."[15] In effect, Hedge was declaring that whatever Harvard does simply *is* Christian.

Charles Eliot and Freedom

Charles Eliot initiated practical reforms at Harvard as a means of implementing religious ideals. Eliot's religion, which has been well described as "Unitarianism raised to the *n*th degree,"[16] reflected his Unitarian background as modified by both the evolutionary-scientific and idealist-romantic ideological currents of his era. Harvard, because it was already free from the constraints of Calvinism and popular evangelicalism, could with little inhibition absorb the latest intellectual trends from abroad and translate them into an American context. At the same time in New England, even more than in the rest of the country, reform had to be justified by appeal to an ultimate ideal. That was what Eliot, thoroughly a son of Harvard, could provide. The cause of education was ultimately the cause of a higher religion.

In one sense Charles Eliot's career at Harvard might be seen as mobilizing the forces of professionalism and modern technique. He was chosen to the Harvard presidency because of his reputation as a practical man. Following his graduation in 1853 Eliot came back as a tutor in mathematics and in 1858 became an assistant professor of chemistry. His hopes for a Harvard professorship were thwarted, however, by the appointment in 1863 of Wolcott Gibbs, a case of the more qualified professional winning out against the gentleman insider. Eliot did receive a chemistry post at nearby M.I.T. in 1865 and was called back to Harvard partly because of his renown as an organizer. In his inaugural he announced his aspirations to apply to higher education the modern methods of technological organization, declaring: "The principle of divided and subordinate responsibilities, which rules in government bureaus, in manufactories, and all great companies, which makes a modern army a possibility, must be applied in the University."[17] By the latter part of his career, in the age of efficiency, he described himself as an apostle of "the expert."[18]

This theme of rational efficiency might be seen as reflecting the practical commercial-materialist side of the Unitarian heritage (Eliot's father was a businessman who had studied theology); but in Eliot, as for many in his generation, it was harmonized with an equally basic motif of romantic individualism. Eliot came of age in the era when young men and women of the Protestant elite, especially in Massachusetts, were enthralled by romantic Emersonian ideals of self-reliance and spiritual inspiration. Emerson provided an American version of the German idealist celebration of self and creativity.[19]

One did not have to adopt Transcendentalism wholesale, nor did one have to be an impractical romantic, to appropriate these inspiring ideals. Rather, Eliot's generation, of which he was so typical, resolved the tensions of modernity by allowing two themes to counterbalance each other. On the one hand they could have the passion for order, systematizing, efficiency, scientific principle, personal discipline necessary for modern warfare, business, or professional and social organization.[20] At the same time they filled the void left by the collapse of older theologies with their celebrations of a new idealism that not only ascribed redemptive qualities to the modernizing processes themselves, but at the same time deified individual freedom as the ultimate that justified modern progress.

Eliot's presidency is best remembered for the controversial elective system which by the 1880s allowed Harvard students free choice in course selection. The beginnings of an elective system were already evolving at Harvard and elsewhere at the time Eliot took office, but Eliot's reforms offered students virtually free rein. The new system was, of course, the quickest way to break the hold of old college traditions. One justification for the revolution was practical. Almost none of the two hundred courses offered at Harvard in 1885, Eliot pointed out, could have been offered in its present form at the beginning of the century, so it was impractical to say that a few timeless courses were essential for all. Growth, change, and development were fundamental categories for Eliot and his generation; so while he saw the necessity of keeping touch with the past, "not neglecting the ancient treasures of learning," one could not be bound to it, lest one miss what is important in the present.[21]

The more essential rationale, however, was moral. The moral purpose of the college of the new university, as that of the old colleges, was to build character. The theories of how that was best done, however, had evolved. Character was best shaped not by constraints from without, but voluntarily from within. Still there was continuity with the old mental and moral philosophy. Eliot, like his predecessors, talked about training the mental faculties. A major component of the rationale for the elective system, in fact, was that mental growth came through exercise of the mind, so that particular subjects did not matter a great deal. Learning the uplifting habits of freedom of thought gave this exercise a moral quality. One could meet great minds at work, seeing how they applied the principles of free inquiry, equally in any discipline.[22]

Preeminent among the faculties to be cultivated was the individual will, in which personal freedom was paramount. In the old colleges the pedagogical theories reflected still older ideals of constraint from without, or even trying to break the will; hence they were constantly contending with overt and covert rebellions of willful students. The nineteenth century, however, had put increasing emphasis on the freedom of the will as essential to what is human. So now freedom and choice were to be cultivated and turned toward the interests of effective pedagogy. As Eliot argued:

> The moral purpose of a university's policy should be to train young men to self-control and self-reliance through liberty. It is not the business of a university to train men for those functions in which implicit obedience is of the first importance. On the contrary, it should train men for those occupations in which self-government, independence, and originating power are preeminently needed.[23]

Some critics viewed Eliot's emphasis on student freedom as Germanizing; in fact it was at least as much homegrown.[24] Eliot did note in his 1885 defense of electives that Continental universities long had allowed student freedom in course selection and that Oxford and Cambridge recently had instituted it. Nonetheless, he also insisted, as he had put it earlier, "When the American university appears, it will not be a copy of foreign institutions, or a hot-bed plant, but the slow and natural outgrowth of American social and political habits."[25] Although the very idea of evolving ideals embodied in a national spirit reflected the influence of German idealism, even in this framework the American heritage was the only relevant one. So Eliot, while appropriating international intellectual trends, saw what he was doing as in continuity with the New England religious past, which in turn had contributed to American ideals of liberty. "The elective system," he proclaimed, "is in the first place, an outcome of the spirit of the Protestant Reformation. In the next place, it is an outcome of the spirit of political liberty."[26]

The counterpart to this vast expansion of the spirit of Protestantism was a constriction of its formal regime. At Harvard compulsory chapel was the principal issue. Eliot moved cautiously on this front, apparently motivated by an administrator's concern not to offend conservative opinion. Nonetheless, progressive sentiment was very much on the side of reform, coming from students and eventually even from the Board of Overseers. Phillips Brooks, the famous Episcopal preacher of Boston's Trinity Church, played a leading role. Earlier in the decade Brooks had turned down Eliot's offer to become the university preacher. Now he helped convince the overseers that voluntarism would be beneficial to religion. In 1886 they abandoned compulsion. Distinguished preachers including Brooks himself would address the continuing voluntary services, which in subsequent decades continued to be reasonably well attended. Eliot was pleased later to take credit for the arrangement.[27]

Freedom was the principle that tied everything else together. Evolutionary naturalism, which was one dimension of Eliot's outlook, may have seemed to rest on deterministic principles, but not if the highest product of evolution was the ideal of freedom itself. Similarly, the scientific method might have been thought to rest on deterministic premises, but on a higher plane it could be seen as teaching the lofty principles of free inquiry by which mind triumphed over matter. For the individual, freedom was the principle that allowed one to transcend local and parochial limitations and to reach one's full potential. And, of course, freedom was essential to American national spirit.

William James and the Freedom of the Will

Eliot's personal views paralleled those of his contemporary and most prominent faculty member, William James, who also developed a philosophy in which freedom of the will was central.

James, in turn, has to be understood in the framework of the impact of Darwinism. James was seventeen years old when Darwin's *Origins* was published and in 1861 he embarked on a scientific career, entering Harvard's Lawrence Scientific School, where Eliot taught. James was convinced early by Darwin and also saw the disturbing philosophical implications of Darwinism. At Harvard there was by no means unanimity on Darwin. Louis Agassiz, one of the university's two renowned naturalists, rejected development of species on the grounds of a philosophical idealism. Asa Gray, though an orthodox Congregationalist, was a correspondent of Darwin and one of America's earliest and most influential promoters of Darwin's views, though he argued against Darwin that randomness did not preclude providential design as to the eventual outcome. Harvard's leading philosopher, Francis Bowen, on the other hand, was philosophically typical of antebellum Common Sense moral philosophers who revered natural science as providing evidence in support of the argument from design. He accordingly rejected Darwinism as having removed "all proof of the incessant creative action of a designing mind, by reducing it to a blind mechanical process."[28]

Young William James continued studying science, mostly at the Harvard Medical School, but also abroad through most of the decade of the 1860s. James saw in Darwinism an abyss of determinism that would destroy individual freedom and meaning. The dread of this prospect was one of the causes of a profound personal crisis which reached its peak in 1870. James resolved this by adopting a variation on the Kantian view of the primacy of the active powers of the mind in supplying categories necessary to make reality meaningful. Hence free will could legitimately be a first principle, based on faith. So, as James wrote in his diary the day he resolved his crisis, "My first act of free will shall be to believe in free will."[29]

In 1872 Eliot hired James to teach at Harvard. During the next decades James led the way in developing the field of physiological psychology. At the same time James had strong philosophical interests and played a role in freeing American philosophy from theology. In its early stages modern American philosophy was the work of amateurs. Most important was a somewhat ironically titled Metaphysical Club, formed around 1870 by James and some of his Cambridge friends, including Oliver Wendell Holmes, Jr., Chauncey Wright, and Charles Peirce.[30] Since psychology was not yet clearly separated from philosophy James could develop his more speculative philosophical interests at Harvard, emerging by the end of the century as the leading exponent of pragmatism.

James's pragmatism was essentially an extension of his psychological work, taking the active powers of the human mind as the object of scientific inquiry. Since our minds provided the only access to reality and indeed structured what we knew, the proper philosophical questions were those such as "How does the mind come to hold the beliefs it does?" Or, given evolutionary premises, "What are the functions of the mind in adjusting us to reality?"

Although James rejected the prevalent systems of cosmic idealism as too speculative, his more down-to-earth emphasis on the creative powers of minds had a similar function, providing a generation with a basis for broad religious belief as an alternative to traditional Christianity on the one hand and materialism on the other. James was careful, therefore, in his famous analysis of *Varieties of Religious Experience* (1902), to affirm the reality of the "more" to which religious experience pointed, even if we could not know about it as exactly as most particular religions claimed.

Moreover, even though James disagreed with cosmic idealism, he was not entirely adverse to it. He was instrumental in bringing to Harvard in 1882 its other great philosopher and America's leading idealist, Josiah Royce, who became his next-door neighbor and close friend.

As Bruce Kuklick observes, in his definitive study of the rise of Harvard philosophy, philosophers like James and Royce played a mediating role in the era of transition in cultural authority from the minister to the scientist and the expert. At the beginning of their careers philosophers were still on the side of the clergy. By the end, in the early twentieth century, like everything else in the academy, philosophy was increasingly defined in terms of professional expertise.[31] James, in fact, late in his career, in 1903, lamented bitterly how the "Ph.D. octopus," or the demand of many colleges that every teacher, no matter how talented, must earn a Ph.D., was eliminating the creative amateur thinker. America, he thought, was in danger of suffering terribly from "the Mandarin disease" if this "grotesque tendency" continued.[32]

Ultimate Nonsectarianism

During this transitional era, philosophy was not the only contender to fill the spiritual and moral void created by the demise of moral philosophy and conventional Protestantism. Indeed virtually every major discipline could be seen as playing a part in this diversified effort. The moral earnestness of the early social sciences has already been noted. History too was a source of moral insight. Even the natural sciences were seen as sacred expressions of moral integrity and truth seeking. Under these circumstances Eliot's radical elective system seemed less threatening to the moral integrity of the college program.[33]

The emerging fields of literature and the arts were especially conspicuous in taking over a spiritual and moral role. Again Harvard was a pioneer. Henry Wadsworth Longfellow taught modern languages and belles lettres from 1836 to 1854 and was succeeded by James Russell Lowell. Countering the trend toward the imposition of scientific models, the study of literature began to shift from philological approaches toward a view of great literature both as a source of enduring moral insight and as part of an inspiring "liberal culture" into which every educated person ought to be initiated. Great literature, such as Homer, Dante, Chaucer, Shakespeare, and Milton, thus became the canon for a popular cultural idealism. Human spiritual growth in the highest culture could be a complement to or a substitute for the Christian drama of the biblical canon. By the latter decades of the century this inspiring view of "liberal culture," was the prevailing curricular ideal for literature.[34] Classical culture also took on a new life as a major component of this ideal heritage, a point that was underscored by the continuing dominance of classical architectural models for the expanding universities.

The fine arts also emerged as a significant curricular component of the new cult of high culture. Here again Harvard was in the forefront. In 1874 Eliot appointed his cousin Charles Eliot Norton to teach art history. During the next two and a half decades at Harvard Norton became the dominant spokesman and even symbol of American education's commitment to inspiring cultural ideals. As one student summarized Norton's influence, "Beauty became not aesthetic satisfaction merely but took her place high among Moralities."[35]

President Charles Eliot's views on religion in the university can be understood in this framework of liberating idealism, which provided the spiritual counterbalance to evolutionary naturalism. To Eliot the divine was simply the name we give to the essential spirit of the universe. As he wrote in 1886:

> If the universe, as science teaches, be an organism which has by slow degrees grown to its form of to-day on its way to its form of to-morrow, . . . then, as science also teaches, the life-principle or soul of that organism for which science has no better name than God, pervades and informs it so absolutely that there is no separating God from nature, or religion from science, or things sacred from things secular.[36]

Hence any entirely free and honest inquiry into any dimension of reality simply *was* part of true religion. Speaking at the inaugural of his friend Daniel Coit Gilman at Johns Hopkins, Eliot took the opportunity to meet head-on the issue of religious criticisms of the new universities. Some had spoken as though open-minded study of humans and of nature led to impiety. Eliot retorted:

> On the contrary, such study fills men with humility and awe, by bringing them on every hand face to face with inscrutable mystery and infinite power. The whole work of a university is uplifting, refining, and spiritualizing; it embraces
>
> Whatsoever touches life
> With upward impulse; be He nowhere else,
> God is in all that liberates and lifts,
> In all that humbles, sweetens, and consoles.[37]

These infinitely broad sentiments provide the context for understanding Eliot's most frequently quoted remark, which immediately followed: "A university cannot be built upon a sect. . . ." Just as Harvard served Christ and the church by doing anything that Harvard did, so universities were by definition the cathedrals of the most catholic of all religions, transcending every pettiness of sect.

True to his patriotism, Eliot framed this new universalism in terms of the nation. The complete sentence of his remark was: "A university cannot be built upon a sect, unless indeed, it be a sect which includes the whole of the educated portion of the nation." This in turn simply echoed a phrase from his own inaugural in 1869, "A university is built, not by a sect, but by a nation."[38] The sentiment was one that spoke to the post–Civil War generation. Nations must be united on the highest principles. In the new age nations would no longer have established churches; they would establish universal truths in other ways. Yet they must have a morally superior elite leadership who would bring unity out of diversity. Sectarian divisions among that class would be disastrous. Rather "the whole educated portion of the nation" should guide the nation intellectually. Though free individuals, they could speak with one voice because they were united by one divinely sanctioned scientific quest for truth. Thus they could be the ministers of unifying cultural ideals in an increasingly diverse nation.

Later in life, at the time of his retirement from Harvard in 1909, Eliot quite explicitly championed a "Religion of the Future" as an alternative to traditional Christianity. In this higher unifying religion "the best knowledge of God" quite simply "comes through knowledge of the best of the race."[39] At just about the same time, Eliot was induced by the publishing house of P. F. Collier and Son to lend Harvard's name and his own as editor of the Harvard Classics. "Dr. Eliot's five-foot book shelf" was highly promoted and vastly successful so that in his later years Eliot was renowned for having, in effect, provided middle-class America with a reassuring, if largely unread, new canon for the religion of humanity.[40]

Eliot's Harvard accentuated a theme that was apparent at other major universities as well. Complementing and compensating for professionalized, scientific, technological culture was a higher realm of ideals that included a new humanistic religion of humanity and high culture. Like most of the academic innovations it was conceived of by most of its proponents not so much in opposition to Christianity as an extension of its liberating and uplifting spirit.

Notes

1. This is more directly a paraphrase of Daniel Walker Howe, *The Unitarian Conscience* (Cambridge, Mass.: Harvard University Press, 1970), 300, alluding to comments in *The Education of Henry Adams* (1907).

2. Robert A. McCaughey, "The Transformation of American Academic Life: Harvard University, 1821–1892," in *Perspectives in American History,* Vol. VIII (1974), Appendix D, 327–32, provides a valuable profile of Harvard faculty from 1821 to 1892.

3. Daniel Day Williams, *The Andover Liberals: A Study in American Theology* (New York: Octagon Books, 1970 [1941]). Frank Hugh Foster, *Genetic History of New England Theology* (Chicago: University of Chicago Press, 1907).

4. See Howe, *Unitarian Conscience.*

5. Ibid., 263.

6. From Ware, *On the Formation of Christian Character,* as summarized in Howe, *Unitarian Conscience,* 106–7.

7. Josiah Quincy, *The History of Harvard University* (Cambridge, 1840), II:444–46, from excerpt in *American Higher Education: A Documentary History,* Richard Hofstadter and Wilson Smith, eds. (Chicago: University of Chicago Press, 1961), I:436.

8. This is an elaboration of points made in Richard Hofstadter and Walter P. Metzger, *The Development of Academic Freedom in the United States* (New York: Columbia University Press, 1955), 371–75.

9. McCaughey, "Transformation," 246–55. Howe, *Unitarian Conscience*, 261–69.

10. McCaughey, "Transformation," 255–63.

11. Hofstadter and Metzger, *Academic Freedom*, 271.

12. *The Diary of George Templeton Strong*, Allan Nevins and Milton Halsey Thomas, eds. (New York, 1952), from excerpt in Hofstadter and Smith, *Documentary History*, I:441–50.

13. These arguments are from Samuel B. Ruggles, *The Duty of Columbia College to the Community and its Rights to Exclude Unitarians from its Professorship of Physical Science, Considered by One of its Trustees* (New York, 1854), reprinted in Hofstadter and Smith, *Documentary History*, I:451–64, and were presumably voiced at the trustees' meeting.

14. Hofstadter and Metzger, *Academic Freedom*, 269–74.

15. Frederic Henry Hedge, "University Reform, An Address to the Alumni of Harvard, at Their Triennial Festival," *Atlantic Monthly* 18 (July 1866), 199–307, excerpt in Hofstadter and Metzger, *Academic Freedom*. Hofstadter and Smith, *Documentary History*, II:562–63.

Eliot said much the same in his "Inaugural Address as President of Harvard College" (1869): "The worthy fruit of academic culture is an open mind, trained in careful thinking, instructed in the methods of philosophical investigation, acquainted in a general way with the accumulated thought of past generations, and penetrated with humility. It is thus that the university in our day serves Christ and the church." Eliot, *Educational Reform: Essays and Address* (New York, 1898), 8.

16. Hugh Hawkins, *Between Harvard and America: The Educational Leadership of Charles W. Eliot* (New York: Oxford University Press, 1972), 38. My primary debt for the overview of Eliot that follows is to Hawkins. Also see Earl Hubert Brill, "Religion and the Rise of the University: A Study of the Secularization of American Higher Education, 1870–1910," Ph.D. dissertation, American University, 1969; and Laurence Veysey, *The Emergence of the American University* (Chicago: University of Chicago Press, 1965).

17. Eliot, *Educational Reform*, 34.

18. Hawkins, *Eliot*, 166.

19. Emerson, "The American Scholar" (1837).

20. McCaughey, "Transformation," presents a thorough analysis of the rise of professionalism at Harvard. He argues that Eliot did not fully move away from hiring Unitarian gentlemen scholars (like himself) until around the late 1870s, when he was forced by the competition from Johns Hopkins into adopting more professional criteria.

21. "Liberty in Education," (Debate with James McCosh before the Nineteenth Century Club of New York, 1885), Eliot, *Educational Reform*, 142–43.

22. Ibid., 144

23. Ibid., 148.

24. Laurence Veysey, "The Emergence of the American University," Ph.D. dissertation, University of California, Berkeley, 1961, 411.

25. Eliot, "New Education," *Atlantic Monthly*, 23:216, quoted in Hawkins, *Eliot*, 53.

26. Eliot, "Experience with a College Elective System" (1895), Eliot papers, quoted in Hawkins, *Eliot*, 94.

27. Brill, "Religion and the Rise of the University," 186–93, provides the best account of this.

28. Quoted in Bruce Kuklick, *The Rise of American Philosophy: Cambridge, Massachusetts, 1860–1930* (New Haven: Yale University Press, 1977), 41. I am most immediately dependent on Kuklick for most of this account.

29. Quoted in Kuklick, *Rise,* 161. See 161–62.

30. The comment of William's brother, Henry, the novelist, must not be omitted. Writing to his friend Charles Eliot Norton in 1872 he reported that William and "various other long-headed youths have combined to form a Metaphysical Club, where they wrangle grimly and stick to the question. It gives me a headache merely to know of it." Quoted in Kuklick, *Rise,* 47.

31. Kuklick, *Rise,* esp. 565.

32. William James, "The Ph.D. Octopus" (1903), in *Memories and Studies* (Westport, Conn.: Greenwood Press, 1971 [1941]), 334.

33. Perhaps it is significant that the free-floating elective system went out of favor after the turn of the century at the same time as fewer disciplines seemed to be playing this quasi-spiritual and moral role.

34. James Turner, "Secularization and Sacralization: Speculations on Some Religious Origins of the Secular Humanities Curriculum, 1850–1900," in *The Secularization of the Academy,* George M. Marsden and Bradley J. Longfield, eds. (New York: Oxford University Press, 1992), 74–106.

35. Quoted from Ellery Sedgwick in Turner, "Secularization," 87. This account is drawn from Turner.

36. Eliot, "What Place Should Religion Have in a College?" (unpublished reply to McCosh, 1886), Eliot papers, Harvard, quoted in Hawkins, *Eliot,* 129–30.

37. Eliot, Address at the Inauguration of Daniel C. Gilman as president of Johns Hopkins University, February 22, 1876, *Educational Reform,* 43.

38. Eliot, "Inaugural Address," 31.

39. Eliot, "The Religion of the Future" (1909), in *The Durable Satisfactions of Life* (New York, 1910), 172.

40. Hawkins, *Eliot,* 191–96. The distance that Eliot had moved from evangelical Christianity is suggested by the remark of Billy Sunday that Eliot was "so lowdown he would need an aeroplane to get into hell." Upton Sinclair, *The Goose-Step: A Study of American Education* (Pasadena, 1923), 103, quoted in Hawkins, 297.

12

Holding the Line at Princeton

At Harvard's 250th anniversary celebration in 1884, the aging Oliver Wendell Holmes, Sr., of "One-Hoss Shay" fame and one of the great debunkers of the Puritan heritage, read a poem exalting how "Harvard's beacon shed its unspent rays" to benefit other American colleges. Among Harvard's beneficiaries was the College of New Jersey: "O'er Princeton's sands the far reflections steal, Where mighty Edwards stamped his iron heel. . . . " According to the Harvard story, Princeton's president James McCosh left the festivities early in protest.[1] McCosh indeed admired Edwards and saw his own work as continuing that of his famous forerunner.[2] In any case Princetonians hardly welcomed being told that they needed Harvard's "unspent rays."

Princeton is especially significant to the present inquiry because if a more traditionalist Protestant intellectual alternative to the emerging definitions of American academia was to survive at any major school, Princeton was the foremost candidate. All the other leaders in shaping university education moved in essentially the same social orbit. The major university founders, such as White, Gilman, Angell, and Eliot, kept in close touch and sometimes vacationed in the same vicinity in Maine. Whatever their shades of differences, they were all progressive New Englanders. With the South eliminated and New England dominance established in the Midwest, such Mugwump reformers had almost a free hand in shaping American higher education to their tastes. Even conservative Yale was firmly enough set in the same orbit to ensure that it would soon be following the prevailing trends with only minor deviation. Princeton, on the other hand, was a different story. It had the wealth, the prestige, and the tradition to resist New England hegemony. Its presidents throughout the latter decades of the century were foreign born, McCosh from Scotland and his successor, Francis Patton, from Bermuda. Each would test whether there might be an alternative to the prevailing American agenda, especially on the religious questions.

James McCosh came from Scotland to the Princeton presidency in 1868, following the path taken by John Witherspoon a century earlier. Born in 1811, McCosh was the most distinguished academic to fill the college's presidency since Witherspoon, perhaps since Edwards. He had established himself as a significant interpreter of the central Scottish philosophical debates, while the tradition of Common Sense realism was being modified in a Kantian direction by William Hamilton and attacked by the empiricism of John Stuart Mill. Like many foreign-born intellectuals, McCosh was revered by Americans, who were still severely conscious of their provincial status. Unlike Noah Porter, McCosh could not be written off as a local reactionary. A leading philosophical realist, McCosh also did some work as a naturalist, kept up with the latest scientific ideas, and caused a mild sensation in American Presbyterian circles by being an early advocate of a theistic version of Darwinism. He was also a reformer, desirous of turning the College of New Jersey into a university.[3]

Despite these progressive credentials, McCosh had a heritage of Presbyterian polemicism that made him unlikely to give in to broad cultural trends without a fight. McCosh had come of age in Scotland in the midst of the bitter controversy between Moderates, who wished to adjust Scottish Presbyterianism to the spirit of the age, and Evangelicals, led by Thomas Chalmers, who resisted the Moderate trends. McCosh admired Chalmers and stood with the Evangelicals, who in 1843 left in protest to form the Free Church of Scotland. Unlike most of the New England educational leaders of his generation (and certainly unlike the reformers of the next generation), McCosh did not see himself as nonsectarian but was proud to have taken a costly stand on a doctrinal matter.[4]

Princetonians also had their reservations about the New England brand of nonsectarianism. Like most colleges of the late revolutionary era, the College of New Jersey had broadened its outlook during the early years of the century. Dissatisfaction with that trend led some of its conservative Presbyterian board members to establish Princeton Theological Seminary in 1812. Unlike the college, which was chartered by the state to serve the public but controlled by a predominantly Presbyterian board, the seminary was strictly an agency of the Presbyterian Church in the U.S.A. As at other colleges, the religious identity at Princeton grew stronger by midcentury. In Princeton's case, the seminary led the way. In the Presbyterian denominational division of 1837–1838, Princeton Seminary emerged as the leading voice of the confessionalist Old School denomination, a group with a sizable southern constituency. While the seminary and the college were formally separate, informally they were closely connected. During this era when the seminary's famed theologian, Charles Hodge (1797–1878), was principal editor of the formidable *Princeton Review,* the college stood in the intellectual shadow of the seminary. While the college continued to be a leading center for training American statesmen and jurists, it too had a strong hue of Presbyterian confessionalism. Beginning in 1854 the key professorship of mental and moral philosophy was held by Lyman Atwater, Hodge's right-hand polemicist on the *Princeton Review.* At the time that McCosh was called to the Princeton presidency, seven of the ten faculty members were clergy and all were strongly Calvinist.[5]

By 1868, however, the situation of the Old School Presbyterians had changed dramatically. The Civil War brought the exodus of southern churches to form their own denomination. The war also hurt the college, which had always had a strong southern constituency. Wartime patriotism had also removed some political differences with the New England–oriented New School. McCosh himself was known for his strong antislavery stance. The New School leaders were insisting on their Presbyterian orthodoxy. Even Lyman Atwater was convinced that some of them now "out Princeton Princeton itself." In 1869 the northern branches of the church reunited.[6]

McCosh's arrival at the College of New Jersey coincided then with a general effort to broaden its outlook so as to recapture its position of national leadership without abandoning its heritage of doctrinal vigilance. Like other academic reformers of the day, McCosh introduced more diversity into the faculty. During his first twelve years thirteen of the seventeen professors he brought in had no previous affiliation with the college or the seminary. At the same time, however, he affirmed that he would not appoint anyone who "is not known to be a decided Christian." While in fact there may have been a couple of exceptions,[7] McCosh was adamant that "religion is not to be abolished from College teaching." To reinforce the point, he added to the existing chapel and Sunday service requirements mandatory biblical instruction on Sunday afternoons, taught for years by himself, on which students were examined.[8] While McCosh was attempting to modernize the college, as in improving its science offerings and teaching, and even was eager to transform it into a full-fledged university,[9] he insisted that it would be a Christian university, in a traditional sense.

The theological conservatism of the McCosh era is illustrated by the appointment in 1884 of Francis L. Patton, a Presbyterian clergyman, to be Lyman Atwater's successor in the pivotal chair of ethics. Patton was every bit as militant as his predecessor. During the 1870s, Patton, a graduate of Princeton Theological Seminary, had created a national sensation by his efforts in Chicago to oust from the recently reunited Presbyterian denomination a popular Presbyterian pastor, David Swing. In 1881 Patton took a position at Princeton Theological Seminary. In 1883 he began teaching at the college as well and in 1884 accepted the position in ethics. The college trustees, who were solidly in the conservative camp, and even worried a little about McCosh, were particularly eager for Patton's appointment.[10]

At the time, one of Patton's recent opponents was Harvard's president Charles Eliot. Eliot had proposed changing the education of clergy from an authoritarian to a scientific basis. "The divine right of the minister," said Eliot, "is as dead among Protestants in our country as the divine right of kings." Like other progressives, Eliot in urging reform pointed to a changing national spirit. In the United States, "the people in these days question all things and all men, and accept nothing without examination." Ultimately this national spirit was expressed in the scientific ideal: "A new method, or spirit, of inquiry has been gradually developed, which is characterized by an absolute freedom on the part of the inquirer from the influence of prepossessions or desires as to the results." Clergy were suspected by laymen of violating this sacred rule if they relied on external authority or theological tradition.[11]

Patton, a skilled debater, responded that it was absurd to suggest, as Eliot had, that theology should be made to conform to the political system. Moreover, Americans did not seem often to apply the new spirit of inquiry that supposedly questioned everything to the work of lawyers, physicians, bankers, or scientists. The real conflict was not between a new spirit of honest inquiry and accepting authority. Rather it was between agnostic science and positive religion. "If men can oppose Christianity only by saying that we do not know whether anything is true and therefore do not know whether Christianity is true [or false], we need no modification of the minister's traditional training to remedy this condition of affairs."[12]

President McCosh remained Princeton's preeminent academic spokesman, and as the national debate over higher education was heating up and relations between Harvard and Princeton cooled, he was the leading choice of those who wished to hear a moderate alternative to Eliot's progressivism. In 1885 the Nineteenth Century Club in New York staged just such a gentlemanly showdown, inviting Presidents Eliot, McCosh, and Porter to participate in a three-way debate on the elective system. Noah Porter, who was not as effective a public debater as the other two, bowed out, leaving McCosh to defend the more conservative position. McCosh stood somewhere between Porter and Eliot, not identified as simply with the old-college classicist ideal as was the Yale president, open to curricular innovations, but still firmly opposed to Eliot's revolutionary philosophy of virtually total curricular freedom for undergraduates.[13]

In the widely publicized encounter, McCosh responded to Eliot's arguments for the elective system by asserting that freedom must always exist within limits. Just as in medicine or engineering there was a body of requisite foundational studies to be mastered, so also in the arts. It was absurd, said McCosh, to have a college curriculum in which a student might study music, French plays and novels, or whatever captured his fancies, but which omitted not only the classics but mathematics, logic, ethics, political economy, or the sciences. Particularly he was alarmed that one could gain a Harvard education without being taught anything of either morality or religion. Rumor had it that Harvard was close to giving up required chapel as well. McCosh culminated his presentation by suggesting that since the future of religion in colleges was such a crucial issue, a second debate should be held just on that subject.

The second debate, held before a large crowd on a stormy evening in February 1886, was also highly publicized in the newspapers. Eliot presented his arguments that a national college could not be founded on a sect. If it were, it would have the undesirable effect of dividing the educated classes so that they could not effectively stand together against materialism and hedonism. He thus alluded to a powerful motive for the liberalization of Protestantism: in an ethnically changing country, the dominant class should not be divided. Moreover, said Eliot, tolerance of all religion did not imply indifference. Voluntary religion should be encouraged both out of respect for family ties and because no one had found an effective way to teach morality without religion. Yet colleges could also teach catholicity, so that every classroom would point to the candid spirit that illustrated the unity of all truth seeking and that science was creating a truly spiritual idea of God.[14]

In reply McCosh argued first of all that the sectarian issue was a red herring. Princeton and most other religious colleges exempted students from religious instruction if it was a matter of conscience for their parents or (if they were of age) themselves. Hundreds of colleges had also demonstrated that one could have nonsectarian college worship. So it did not make sense to say that, because of alleged sectarianism, one of the greatest forces in the shaping of modern civilization should be excluded from higher education. At places like Harvard, McCosh suggested, the motto over the gates should read "All knowledge imparted here except religious."

Differing views of human nature separated the Calvinist from the Unitarian institution and McCosh felt that he had the empirical evidence on his side. "If religion is not honored in a college, any one acquainted with human nature," he alleged, "and with the present tendencies of opinion, can easily perceive what will be the prevailing spirit among the students." They will drift into "idleness or dissipation." Religion that is merely tolerated will soon come to be regarded as antiquated superstition and agnosticism will flourish. Students were asking, more earnestly than at any time since the declining days of the Roman empire, " 'Is life worth living?' " Harvard students were wrestling with this question, whether their president knew it or not. "Agnosticism has no answer to it, and I know that many a heart in consequence is crushed with anguish till feelings more bitter than tears are wrung from it."

Closing with a bit of rhetorical flourish, McCosh repeated several times with his own elaborations Eliot's remark that "nobody knows how to teach morality effectively without religion." It followed, did it not, that a college that neglected religion was neglecting morality?[15]

In rebuttal, Eliot observed that he meant something different by religion than did McCosh. What Eliot meant was the cosmic religion suggested in the phrases "In him we live and move and have our being" and "Beneath are the everlasting arms." Such religion, he affirmed, *was* taught at Harvard, and hence was the basis for a higher morality.

McCosh pressed what he sensed to be his advantage among those interested in the topic. He closed by urging that the two papers be published together. When Eliot declined McCosh published his own side of the debate, noting that Eliot had declined publication and that "unless

Christian sentiment arrest it, religion, without being noticed, will disappear from a number of our colleges, that is, from the education and training of many of our abler and promising young men."[16]

The Problem of Student Opinion

While McCosh could speak confidently of maintaining a strong religious presence, the College of New Jersey faced a number of major obstacles if it were to stay on that apparently high road.

Although in his farewell in 1888 McCosh could point to a high percentage of Christian profession among Princeton students,[17] he also had been coping with changing student expectations set by national trends. McCosh explicitly affirmed an in loco parentis attitude toward his students, a stance associated with some old-time Calvinist vigilance. With a student body still totaling only five or six hundred, the community could be treated like an extended family. Positively this meant that "no student passes through our College without his being addressed from time to time, in the most loving manner, as to the state of his soul."[18] More negatively, McCosh worried about things like students "collecting in each other's rooms and idling their times." For long Presbyterian Sabbath afternoons, he partly remedied the situation with Bible studies. Like most other Protestant leaders of the day, he also campaigned strenuously for temperance both on campus and by law in the surrounding community.

McCosh was not, however, a Puritan like Jonathan Edwards in his attitude toward students. Rather, as in other matters, he mixed the new with the old, attempting to retain the essential principles, while looking for whatever was good, or at least a matter of indifference, in modernity. Upon arrival at Princeton, for instance, he immediately endorsed building a gymnasium and in good British fashion encouraged collegiate sports. When he heard that students were gathering at a local billiard hall, he ordered three billiard tables for the gymnasium.[19]

Still, the price of retaining the in-loco-parentis stance of the old-time college seemed to be that of preserving the old-time campus disorders as well. During the 1880s McCosh and the faculty were plagued by student misdemeanors. Sports also were not the cure-all they were sometimes reputed to be. McCosh discovered to his dismay that emphasis on athletics, rather than promoting a gentlemanly balance of mind and body, was beginning to produce specialist athletes who did not concentrate on anything else. Worse, intercollegiate sports involved travel from campus. McCosh was especially appalled by events connected with a Princeton–Yale football game in 1885 held in New York City. Students had been entertained afterward by a special theater event and some, McCosh alleged, were seduced by actresses and prostitutes. That they had not attended church the next morning was taken as further evidence of their dissipation. McCosh's realistic view of human nature told him what would happen if young men spent the weekend in the city, and he determined not to let it happen again.[20]

McCosh, who was personally respected by most students, could still hope to keep things more or less in line by personal oversight. But the days of such control were numbered. Changing mores, increased mobility, and bigger colleges all signaled a new era. After McCosh's day, Princeton, like many schools, rapidly expanded, nearly doubling its undergraduate student body in the 1890s. Traditional Christianity's identification with strict Presbyterian mores was bound to lose out in a society in which elites increasingly expected control by personal choice.

The Problem of Science

On the intellectual front McCosh had likewise held his own in fostering an accommodation between tradition and modernity, but he left a situation in which his carefully crafted synthesis might prove merely transitional.

The Princetonians of McCosh's day were not lacking in intellectual firepower. McCosh was probably the most distinguished philosopher of his generation in America. Francis Patton and a number of impressive theologians at the seminary could hold their own with anyone in an argument. Although McCosh was more flexible of mind than they were and was always looking to separate the essential from the peripheral, he and they were in virtually the same intellectual camp. They were committed to an intellectual position and more basically to a theological outlook that could be adjusted to the dominant currents of the modern age only so far. With the new universities arising as the institutional loci for new definitions of what would be intellectually respectable, it was only a matter of time until Princeton traditionalists, whatever their prowess, would be regarded by the larger community as dinosaurs.

This problem of the limits of adjustability of the worldview is evident even regarding McCosh's most obvious short-term intellectual success at Princeton, his accommodation to biological evolution. When he arrived at Princeton in 1868 McCosh was hesitant about expressing his view that Darwin's developmental hypothesis had some merit, but he decided to do so in his student lectures. In 1871 he elaborated his views publicly in an important series of lectures presented at Union Theological Seminary in New York on "Christianity and Positivism." In 1855 McCosh had coauthored a book, *Typical Forms,* which recognized evolutionary progress in God's creation of nature, though without the Darwinian mechanism of natural selection. McCosh was therefore especially well positioned to appreciate the force of Darwin's arguments, which he saw as simply filling in our understanding of one of the mechanisms that God used in his creative work. He did not think it a threat to the faith to learn that if "a plant happens to get a thorn, or a beast a claw, it is more likely to live while others perish, and that it transmits its endowment to posterity."[21]

At Princeton, however, Charles Hodge of the seminary was an internationally known force to be contended with. Hodge argued that the answer to his title question in *What Is Darwinism?* (1873) was simple: "It is atheism." This was not the obscurantist dismissal that it is sometimes represented to be. Hodge admitted that in principle development in nature presented no theological problem, since God controlled all processes. He objected, however, to the philosophical assumptions behind Darwin's theory of development, assumptions both he and Darwin viewed as essential to the theory. Darwin, Hodge recognized, presupposed a universe of blind natural causes in which randomness, given enough time, could produce intelligence out of nonintelligence. Whatever lip service Darwin might give to a deity, his theory was indeed built on nontheistic assumptions.[22]

McCosh did not disagree with Hodge so much in principle as in emphasis. While Hodge judged Darwin's scientific theory by the philosophy that undergirded it, McCosh argued that Darwin's plausible theories about natural mechanisms of development could be separated from his bad philosophy. Thus in *Christianity and Positivism* McCosh set his discussions of Darwin in the context of an attack on positivism, as the crucial philosophical challenge of the day. McCosh's presentation took the conventional form of the many books of Christian evidences of the midcentury era, using science itself to defend the faith versus skepticism.

McCosh started by defending the argument from design, the very point that Darwin's philosophy rejected. "The argument is one and the same in all ages," said McCosh. " 'He that formed the eye, shall He not see?' is the way the Psalmist expresses it."[23] The only question was whether God used means or not. But discovering efficient causes did not in any way exclude the existence of final causes. The eye, for instance, was designed to see. The efficient causes or means by which God so fitted it to its environment were not incompatible with design. Rather, McCosh argued, evolution was simply the drawing out of potentialities that God built into the original creation. Every effect must have a sufficient cause. So the marvels that had developed in creation must come from a higher power, who designed the potentialities as well as the ends they would reach. Echoing William Paley's famous argument that the watch found on the beach was irrefutable evidence of a watchmaker, McCosh argued that "If man could construct . . . a watch which should produce other watches telling the hour through all time, our admiration of the skill of the artist would not be diminished."[24]

McCosh did draw the line, as did many at the time, at a purely evolutionary account of the origin of humans. "Religion," he affirmed, "is addressed to man, and she has to see that man's nature is not degraded and reduced to the same level as that of the brutes." Most important, McCosh was a biblicist. "There has been a special revelation made as to the origins and destiny of Man," he proclaimed, "and this we must uphold and defend."[25] In addition, there were a number of steps in the emergence of the world as we know it that McCosh thought could not be explained by natural causes alone. These included the origin of life, of intelligence, and of morality. Since, said McCosh, "no mundane power can produce them at first . . . [and] as evolution by physical causes cannot do it, we infer that God does it by an immediate fiat, even as he created matter and the forces which act in matter."[26] McCosh's view was thus a limited version of natural selection, punctuated by special creative interventions.

McCosh's openness to at least a limited version of biological evolution helped the Princeton community weather the sensation over Darwinism. McCosh's views were too solidly rooted in the traditional Presbyterian paradigm and his personal presence too impressive for him to be easily labeled a heretic. At the same time he kept the Princeton faculty from being written out of the scientific community. By about 1875 this stance was particularly important strategically, because it was becoming clear that almost all younger scientists, including many traditional Christians, saw merit in some form of biological evolution.[27] In that setting McCosh's view won support from many conservative Presbyterians at Princeton and elsewhere. The leading Princeton theologians of the generation that succeeded Charles Hodge, including Francis Patton, Benjamin B. Warfield, and Hodge's own son, Archibald Alexander Hodge, all accepted McCosh's viewpoint.[28]

Woodrow Wilson, who studied at Princeton in the 1870s, was just one of many students of his generation who were reassured in their faith by McCosh's accommodating views, and he remained a great admirer of McCosh. Wilson had a special interest in the subject as he had grown up in the South where there was much greater resistance to the new theory. Wilson's distinguished uncle, James Woodrow, had been appointed in 1861 as "Professor of Natural Science in Connection with Religion" at Columbia Theological Seminary of the Southern Presbyterian Church. During the 1870s Woodrow began teaching a limited version of Darwinism, which he reconciled, in a way very similar to McCosh's, to conservative readings of Scripture. Charges were brought against him in the Southern Presbyterian Church, however, and in 1886 he was removed from his seminary post. Woodrow Wilson was duly impressed with the ugliness of heresy hunting and remarked to his future wife, "If uncle J. is to be read out of the Seminary, Dr. McCosh ought to be driven out of the church, and all private members like myself ought to withdraw without waiting for the expulsion which should follow belief in evolution."[29]

Princeton and the northern Presbyterians never had such a purge, thanks largely to McCosh. Even Andrew Dickson White in his *History of the Warfare of Science with Theology* hailed the Scot as a deus ex machina who appeared at Princeton just in time to save it from the obscurantism of Charles Hodge and others.[30]

The Problem with the Bible

If the Princetonians had had to deal only with the issue of biological evolution, their position might have been able to survive within the new intellectual atmosphere. They might also have been able to withstand the assaults of positivism or skeptical scientific naturalism by pointing out how its assumptions begged the crucial questions. But these conflicts were inextricably tied to the even more basic question of the authority of Scripture, on which the defenders of the traditional evangelicalism of the antebellum era were losing ground at an astonishing rate in the intellectual community. This issue was far more immediately crucial to them than was biological evolution. Most questions concerning evolution as a scientific issue could be finessed if they could be defined as peripheral questions about mechanisms. Remove the authority of the Bible, however, and everything else in traditional definitions of Christianity, including its plan of salvation and the historical claims on which they rested, would collapse.

At Princeton this pivotal intellectual issue was debated more directly than at any of the other emerging universities. Because of the conservative Presbyterian confessionalism that dominated the community, combined with philosophical commitments that resisted romantic experiential definitions of Christianity, the Princetonians saw the debate over the Bible as a life-and-death struggle to preserve all the historic doctrines they held most dear.

Like almost all major American academic figures in the pre–Civil War era, the postwar Princetonians were committed to interpretation of Scripture as divinely inspired, largely literal history. They were able to accommodate their teachings to limited versions of biological evolution, but they all still believed that Adam and Eve were historical figures who at some point, whatever the pre-Adamite origins of their physical characteristics, were specially created as the first human beings with living souls. God breathed into these two the "breath of life" that made them humans. The Princetonians' basic view of science and the Bible was that the two sources of revelation could be reconciled. They continued, accordingly, to follow the gambit of the midcentury evangelical apologists, trying to beat the Enlightenment skeptics at their own game. Natural science, they affirmed in characteristic Common Sense fashion, was an objectively valid source of truth. What they were sure they could demonstrate, however, was that honest scientific inquiry would validate rather than undermine the Bible. Thus in 1888, the year of his retirement, McCosh was still arguing that the first chapter of Genesis was a marvelously concise anticipation of the sequences of creative development that modern geology had discovered. "Suppose," he suggested to a college audience, "that the opening chapter of Genesis, all unknown before, were discovered and published in our day, it would at once be denounced as a forgery, constructed by one who knows geological science, and who varies the record simply to keep the trick from being detected."[31] By this time such views in most of American universities were looking quaint.

Most of the essentials of the higher criticism of Scripture had been developed especially in Germany by the 1860s, but had little impact on American academic or ecclesiastical life until the following decades. This lack of acceptance was not because Americans were unacquainted with the German scholarship. Edward Everett, one of the first Americans to study in Germany in the late 1810s, had already translated Johann Gottfried Eichhorn's *Introduction to the Old Testament* (1783), which introduced the "documentary hypothesis" that the books attributed to Moses were compilations of earlier and later documents. Everett left academics for politics in 1825 and even at Harvard higher critical views would be accepted only cautiously during the next decades. Transcendentalists outside of academia, such as Theodore Parker and Ralph Waldo Emerson, eagerly accepted the new theories, but Andrews Norton, Harvard's leading biblical scholar until midcentury, adapted the new criticism only selectively to a more traditional view of biblical authority.[32]

Virtually everywhere else at American colleges and seminaries during the pre–Civil War era there was even more resistance to the new views than at Harvard. Especially in Congregational and Presbyterian circles where leading young men were making early pilgrimages to Germany, this resistance involved a great deal of scholarly discussion. At Andover Theological Seminary, set up to be the antidote to Harvard liberalism, two of the founders of American biblical scholarship, Moses Stuart and Edward Robinson, held the line for traditional views. Princeton was the other outstanding center for informed conservative viewpoints. Charles Hodge, who had a strong interest in biblical as well as theological issues, studied in Germany in the late 1820s and thereafter provided regular accounts of German developments in his *Biblical Repertory and Princeton Review*. During the 1850s about a third of the lengthy articles in this quarterly addressed issues regarding higher criticism.[33]

The astonishingly rapid acceptance of higher criticism by leading American academics after 1880 cannot be explained, then, simply by saying that a body of evidence and interpretations previously unknown was discovered and found to be objectively compelling.[34] There were some serious difficulties with the traditional views, particularly in literalistic attempts to impose modern historical canons on ancient biblical statements, so that the old approaches were vulnerable to the new scholarship. There were also some recent advances in criticism, like Julius Wellhausen's sophisticated version of the documentary hypothesis; but the new analyses were more accumulations of considerations that increasingly strained the old paradigm than dramatic breakthroughs. Wellhausen's views were an elaboration of principles suggested by Eichhorn. In New Testament studies the crucial patterns were established at least by 1835, the year of publication of David Friedrich Strauss's highly critical *Life of Jesus* and Ferdinand Christian Baur's criticism of the pastoral epistles, which classified them as late productions representing a Hegelian synthesis of Greek and Hebraic traditions.

The midcentury American academic resistance to higher critical views, and the sudden late-century acceptance of them, has to be explained at a number of levels. First of all, the German criticism arose in the framework of philosophical idealism which suggested that the divine could be seen in historical processes. So biblical criticism was unlikely to be widely accepted in the United States until idealism spread there. German idealism, with its interest in historical development, also fostered modern historical consciousness, which did not take firm hold in the United States until late in the century. Historical consciousness, well-developed in Germany by the early nineteenth century, shifted the emphasis in human thought from the perennial quest for timeless truths to explaining how human belief changes and progresses. Hence the study of history took on a new importance, an importance enhanced by the rise of scientifically critical historical methods aimed at determining, in the famous words of Leopold von Ranke, *wie es eigentlich gewesen,* or what actually was.[35]

What these methods meant for the Bible was that it would be treated, as was often said, just "like any other book." Once this initial move was made, of course, one was on a scholarly track that would yield conclusions consistent with the premise, namely, that the Bible was a cultural product just like any other book. In a setting where ecclesiastical interests were still strong, spiritualized idealism also made an important contribution by providing a way that the new views could be fit into a theological framework that described God as immanent in all historical processes, so that the humanized Scriptures could still be seen as an immensely important part of God's ongoing revelation.

While such philosophical views were common in Germany during the first half of the nineteenth century they did not spread widely in the United States until the second half, particularly during the later decades. The United States, which was born during the Enlightenment, still clung to philosophies that were concerned to discover fixed truths, applicable in all times and places, like the self-evident truths of the Declaration. In part such continuing interests reflected British, rather than continental, philosophical tendencies. Furthermore, because the United States was intellectually a province, its thinkers tended to hold on to older outlooks; hence the long-lasting impact of Scottish Common Sense philosophy. Whether in philosophy or religion, Americans in that era were still looking for fixed eternal truths. Conservatism on Bible questions was of a piece with that outlook. Enlightenment skeptics, like Jefferson and Paine, welcomed biblical criticism, but the orthodox could successfully answer them in kind on a piecemeal basis. Not until idealism prepared the way, however, could the more systematically radical criticism win a wide hearing within the dominant Protestant community.

Of course, the relationship between biblical criticism and idealist historicism was reciprocal. Many persons of the generation of university founders may have begun by finding it difficult to believe the traditional claims about the Bible on which they had been reared and then turned to Christianized idealism as a way of saving their faith. The traditional views of Scripture involved miraculous claims that might arouse skepticism in any era; such beliefs could be especially problematic in an elite Protestant community, which had demystified almost everything else about reality. Anti-Catholicism was strong and Protestants called Catholics superstitious for believing in extrabiblical miracles and accepting things on blind authority. Furthermore, advancing technique was rationalizing much of life. Holding on to a special corner of belief in a miraculous revelation of miraculous events seemed increasingly anomalous for those who prided themselves on open and scientific attitudes.

Popular romanticism also created strong pressures to escape from a worldview based on literal interpretations of Scripture. Rising sentiment especially among the middle classes placed increasing value on each individual life and on close family ties. At the same time the Civil War precipitated agonizing reflections on traditional biblical teachings that loved ones might be lost forever and suffering in hell. After the war a host of novelists, popular writers, preachers, and free thinkers joined in the chorus denouncing such literalistic readings of Scripture.[36]

Economic and cultural forces added to the pressures to abandon the old biblicist views specifically in higher education. The simple fact was that clerical and ecclesiastical control of the most advanced education threatened to hold the nation back economically. Such clerical control was legitimated in Protestantism by the belief that the Bible was the highest intellectual authority. At a time of immense economic and technological expansion, it was important to be free to expand education to meet economic needs. Whatever the weight of capitalism in shaping the culture, much of it was on the side of change from the older views, particularly for the dominant classes.

Furthermore, even with respect to less practical areas of learning, American economic expansion brought a new leisure class who formed an important part of the clientele for the new learning. Students, adopting new ideals of personal freedom, could now successfully demand to be free from clerical control. For all these reasons external pressures to get rid of the authority of the old restrictive biblicism and to adopt the newer critical outlooks was immense.

In strictly ecclesiastical settings the changes came more slowly than in other areas of public life and were more often successfully contested. After about 1880 the new views of Scripture became matters for intense public debate in major Protestant denominations and in theological seminaries. Among the Congregationalists, for example, Andover Theological Seminary, which had been designed to stand forever as a conservative alternative to Harvard, in the early 1880s was suddenly taken over by "progressive orthodoxy." Conservatives counterattacked and in 1885 E. C. Smyth, one of the "Andover liberals," lost his job for endorsing higher critical views. In 1892, however, Smyth was reinstated. In other denominations conservatives had longer lasting, but still temporary successes in holding back the new views. Into the first decade of the twentieth century northern Presbyterians and northern Methodists were still successfully restricting some theological teachers from questioning such traditional views as the Mosaic authorship of the Pentateuch. Critical views were virtually excluded throughout the South and in general theologians had to be circumspect in introducing the new outlooks.[37]

Nevertheless, by this time in most parts of the North at least, the division of labor between theological education and university education had been rather completely effected. Smaller colleges might be under closer ecclesiastical control and possible restraint. In most of the major emerging universities, however, by the 1880s higher critical views, or simple skepticism about traditional views, were generally accepted among the leading professors as a matter of course. Since Scripture was rarely part of the curriculum, the issues did not have to be addressed directly, though advanced views were implicit in many discussions of Darwinism.

Even at conservative Yale, evangelical piety was combined with openness to critical views. In 1886 Yale hired a brilliant thirty-year-old alumnus, William Rainey Harper, to be professor of Semitic languages. Soon Harper had introduced the study of the English Bible into the Yale College curriculum. This precipitated a national trend during the 1890s, reaching state universities such as Angell's Michigan and elsewhere. In 1892 Harper carried his zeal for critical biblical study into his new position as founding president of John D. Rockefeller's richly endowed Baptist school, the University of Chicago.[38]

Princeton was unusual, then, as an emerging university in which the leadership took a stand against higher critical views of Scripture. Moreover, if James McCosh, who was conservative on biblical and philosophical issues, had nonetheless projected a demeanor of moderation, the conservative trustees saw to it that his successor would not give even the appearance of compromise. In 1888 they appointed as president the militant, though personable, Francis Patton. During the next fourteen years Patton headed the college, carrying out among other things McCosh's desire to claim formal university status. (The name was officially changed from the College of New Jersey to Princeton University in 1896.)

During this entire era, from the later years of McCosh's administration and throughout that of Patton, the conservative Princetonians were also engaged in the most intense debates over the doctrine of Scripture in the Presbyterian Church in the U.S.A. Patton himself played a leading role in these controversies. While Patton did not insist on the strict biblicist and confessional standards for the college that he sought for the denomination, he did hope at least to reserve room for them. It is worth looking at how the champions of the older biblicist viewpoint defended their views and why in the modern university they were doomed to extinction.

The American Presbyterian debates on Scripture were sparked by the much publicized heresy trial of Robertson Smith in the Scottish Free Church (McCosh's former denomination). In 1881 Smith was dismissed from his position in Old Testament at the Free Church College in Aberdeen for advocating the higher critical views of Wellhausen and others. American conservatives, led by Princetonian theologians like Archibald Alexander Hodge and B. B. Warfield, insisted that the American Presbyterian denomination's standard be that Scripture is "inerrant" in its claims, including all its historical accounts. In 1892 the General Assembly of the Presbyterian Church in the U.S.A. adopted this standard of inerrancy, much to the chagrin of some advocates of higher criticism.[39]

Typical of the position of conservatives like Patton was their insistence that their biblicism rested on science and reason and not on any blind appeal to authority (like the recent affirmation of papal infallibility at Vatican I). This was Patton's stance in an important summary of the conservative position in 1883. "The rationality or rather the reasonableness of a belief is the condition of its credibility," he affirmed. "By this," Patton explained further, "is not meant that a belief must be capable of proof apart from Revelation, but that it is rational to believe in what is taught by Revelation." The difference between Protestants and Catholics, he continued, was that Protestants admitted that ultimately any belief had to rely on such private judgment. "We . . . are Protestants. The right of private judgement is part of our inheritance. It is not for us to abridge the franchises of any man, even though he should use his liberty to his own destruction. . . . We are certainly not required to submit to any authority when adequate reasons for doing so cannot be given."

The Princeton conservatives, then, accepted the same principle as their progressive critics, that Protestantism inevitably led to a spirit of free scientific inquiry. They believed, however, that in such a free debate biblical reliability could be sustained. All that was needed was a truly free inquiry. "It will be insisted on the one side that the critic shall not assume the impossibility of miracles, and with equal fairness it will be demanded on the other side, that evangelical critics shall not postulate plenary Inspiration." Then the issue could be settled by an "inductive investigation" that takes into account "all the facts."

The Bible was not getting a fair hearing, the Princetonians were convinced, because of naturalistic prejudices against it. Much of the attack on higher criticism, accordingly, was built around an attempt to undermine the presuppositions on which it was founded. "When, therefore," said Patton, "men deny the personality of God, or, being theists, nevertheless believe that all religious belief is the outcome of a process of development, they cannot help construing the history of Israel in the light of these naturalistic presuppositions." By contrast, "when evangelical critics confine themselves to the Old Testament facts without any naturalistic bias" they will find, for instance, that the Mosaic authorship of the Pentateuch is still a plausible explanation. The references of Jesus to Mosaic authorship, as well as the most ancient traditions of the Jews and the church, created a presumption in its favor, and there was no rational reason to give up the belief.[40]

Patton represented the case almost as though presuppositions were something that *other* people had. However, the Princetonians did recognize that they too had points of view that influenced their interpretations. Often they talked about their own position as "believing criticism" and acknowledged that their view of biblical inspiration was dependent on a wider set of religious beliefs: belief in God, morality, human sinfulness, the necessity of salvation, of a revelation, and so forth. Moreover, they believed that their recognition of the truths revealed in Scripture depended on the illumination of the Holy Spirit.[41] Still, they saw their own viewpoint as objective and that of their opponents as biased. In their view, the illumination of Holy Spirit helped remove from humans the blinding effects of sin, which kept them from seeing the truth of God's revelation. The general Christian worldview that led to a belief in divine inspiration of Scripture could therefore be established on a good set of arguments, such as those taught in the old-time college courses in evidences. Any unprejudiced person should be able to recognize their legitimacy. Hence the Princetonians could at once acknowledge that they had a point of view and hold that science, if unbiased, would yield results consistent with their claims.

Historicism and Common Sense

The Princetonians, like many of their early nineteenth-century predecessors, especially those who followed Scottish Common Sense philosophy, took for granted that the human mind possessed a fundamental and universal structure. One of the recurring phrases in the philosophical work of McCosh and other Scottish philosophers is that "the human mind is so constituted." That is, there are "Regulative Laws and Principles guiding the mind."[42] The Scottish philosophers attempted to analyze these laws of the mind inductively, believing that once individual differences and the influence of cultural customs were taken into account, they could establish universal principles of human thought.

Sensible as this project might be in itself, it tended to depend on an assumption that had prevailed in Western thought since at least the Greeks but was becoming problematic in the nineteenth century. That was the assumption that truth was a fixed entity and that the function of the mind was to discover it. This belief was particularly congenial to Presbyterians, who had been, like other Americans, strongly influenced by the Enlightenment. Not only were their religious beliefs defined dogmatically by the Westminster Confession of Faith, which they treated as a definitive doctrinal statement that should stand for all time, but they also had Enlightenment confidence in definitive scientific discovery. Fixed truths held their worldview together.

In the context of such an outlook, modern historicism was entirely alien. Historicism started with the post-Kantian premise that the human mind plays a creative role in defining what is reality and then added that various cultures, subcultures, and individuals each created their own definitions of truth, adapted to a particular time and place.

Inevitably, then, historicism became the focal point in the protracted Presbyterian controversies. This was particularly evident in the Princetonian debates with Charles Briggs, an Old Testament scholar at Union Theological Seminary in New York and their primary antagonist. Campaigning for a revision of the denomination's creed, the Westminster Confession of Faith, Briggs in 1889 issued a powerful and much noticed volume, entitled *Whither?*, expounding the implications of historical method for the Presbyterian tradition. Each form of Christianity that had developed, said Briggs, had been suited to a particular time and place. Each had flourished for a time, transformed a culture, but then had become "stereotyped in a dead orthodoxy that blocked the way of further progress." One could not expect then that one historical development of Christianity would be appropriate to everyone. The whole world was open to the Gospel, but "can we suppose that our Teutonic type of Christianity will be imposed upon the Oriental and African races? "Is there any prospect whatever that the Greek and Latin and Slavonic races will adopt the Teutonic type?" Rather than the imperialism of one culturally defined tradition, Briggs looked for the evolution of a higher Christianity. "The ultimate Christianity that will suit our race will be as much higher than Protestantism as Protestantism is higher than Romanism."[43]

James McCosh, recently retired from the Princeton presidency, was appalled at these developments in American Presbyterianism. Immediately he issued a rejoinder to Briggs, with the whimsical title *Whither? O Whither? Tell Me Where.* Although McCosh, with characteristic moderation, would allow minor revisions in the Presbyterian creed, he was solidly on the side of the Princeton theologians on the central issues.

"Whither are we drifting?" McCosh asked. He especially feared that the scholarly attacks on the credibility of the Bible would undermine the faith of a generation of young men. Briggs himself might be able to engage in criticism and still keep his faith. But like a cigar being smoked near inflammable materials; such criticism could easily set off a conflagration that had not been intended. Particularly dangerous, said McCosh, was that Briggs, like so many young Americans, had sold his soul to German scholarship. Churches were already declining in Germany and now the destructive underlying philosophy had become a major American import. McCosh was confident that the German critical views could be answered if their opponents were given a fair hearing. He referred readers to the authority of William Henry Green of Princeton Seminary, who was as accomplished a Hebrew scholar as anyone, and asked them dispassionately to assess Green's current debate with William Rainey Harper of Yale.

Nonetheless, McCosh was fearful that if the assumptions of impractical German professors prevailed, a whole generation could be led astray.[44]

The issue was, as McCosh lamented, the rush of American academics to embrace German philosophy. The corollary, which McCosh did not mention in so many words, was that they were turning just as rapidly from the Scottish philosophers. McCosh was nearly the last of a species. In 1889, the same year he answered Briggs, he had issued his last major philosophical work, *First and Fundamental Truths,* which he regarded as "the cope-stone of what I have been able to do in philosophy."[45] In it he reiterated the basic principles of the Scottish philosophy which he had taught through much of the century. In opposition to Immanuel Kant, he asserted that "we are so constituted as to behold things as they are. . . . [O]ur intuitions are not of the nature of Forms imposed on things by the mind." So humans can trust their basic intuitions, as actually they cannot help doing. Human knowledge was, of course, limited, imperfect, and subject to error. Nonetheless, our knowledge could be "correct so far as it goes" so that there were fundamental truths on which we could rely and on which, through careful scientific procedures, we could build a solid system of knowledge.[46]

McCosh was no longer, however, directly addressing the philosophical issues of the day.[47] In the age of Nietzsche and Freud or even of James and Dewey, his was a voice that could be ignored. It was not simply because of his biblicism, which overtly played only a small role in works like *First and Fundamental Truths.* It was an entire philosophical outlook that was being subverted by evolutionary, developmental, or historicist accounts of human consciousness. Ultimately, it was not a matter that could be settled simply by an appeal to "science." Rather, it was a set of naturalistic working assumptions about the nature of human experience, versus an outlook that assumed an essentially orderly and stable creation of God. Ironically, McCosh, who receives so much credit for his efforts to accommodate Christianity to biological evolution, could not by appealing to "science" stop the flood of the broader evolutionary worldview.

The Princetonian traditionalists went on fighting with flags flying. In their view they were the only ones still standing on solid epistemological ground and therefore they were confident that ultimately science must be on their side. This viewpoint was stated most starkly by Benjamin B. Warfield, a systematic theologian of Princeton Seminary after 1888. Warfield, a former protégé of McCosh and a close associate of Patton, would be for the next generation Princeton's most brilliant polemicist. Writing in 1903, he declared:

> It is the distinction of Christianity that it has come into the world clothed, with the mission to *reason* its way to its dominion. Other religions may appeal to the sword, or seek some other way to propagate themselves,. Christianity makes its appeal to right reason, and stands out among all religions, therefore, as distinctively "the Apologetic religion." It is solely

> by reasoning that it has come thus far on its way to its kingship. And it is solely by reasoning that it will put all its enemies under its feet.[48]

The context for such apparent intellectual bravado was not an attack on theological liberalism but a reaction to the suggestion of a fellow theological conservative, Abraham Kuyper of the Netherlands, that science might lead to different conclusions for Christians than it did for non-Christians. In 1898 the remarkable Dutch Calvinist theologian, newspaper editor, educator, and politician had been in Princeton to deliver the Stone Lectures at the seminary, and so he had gained some attention among American Calvinists. Kuyper is particularly relevant to our story in that in 1880 he founded the Free University of Amsterdam. Kuyper's philosophical outlook was thus part of a broader cultural experience that suggests an alternative to the American model. Kuyper, who served as prime minister of the Netherlands from 1901 to 1905, was the leader in a protracted and eventually successful effort to gain equality in tax support for multiple school systems, including those religiously defined. The Free University of Amsterdam correspondingly provided a confessionally based Calvinist alternative to the older state-controlled universities.

The intellectual basis for this rejection of the homogenization of academic life was Kuyper's rejection of the Enlightenment premise that there must be one science for all humanity. From a traditional Christian point of view, Kuyper wrote in his major theological treatise, there "are two kinds of people," regenerate and unregenerate, and hence "two kinds of science." Since Christians and non-Christians were working from differing frameworks of assumptions, they were building not one house of knowledge but two or more. Each would be equally scientific and many particular procedures and findings would be similar, but since the fundamental assumptions differed, ultimately each would "claim for himself the high and noble name of science, and withhold it from the other."

Warfield found this outlook outrageous. In his view science must be an objective, unified, and cumulative enterprise. "The human spirit," he insisted, "attains this . . . by slow accretions, won through many partial and erroneous constructions." So long as they were being truly scientific, "men of all sorts and of all grades work side by side at the common task, and the common edifice grows under their hands into ever full and truer outlines." This belief explained Warfield's immense confidence that science would vindicate Christianity. If Christianity was true, science would inevitably confirm it. "All minds are of the same essential structure; and the less illuminated will not be able permanently to resist or gainsay the determination of the more illuminated." Hence the reason of the regenerated, illuminated by the Holy Spirit, "shall ultimately conquer the whole race." In a fair competition, "it is the better science that in the end wins the victory."[49]

Warfield thus held essentially the same assumption about the triumph of one science for the race as other elite Protestant academics of the day.

He would not have to yield anything to Andrew Dickson White or Charles Eliot on that score. Each had a combination of Enlightenment heritage and virtually millennial expectation, anticipating the unification of the race on the basis of the triumph of a fully rational science. Even those American thinkers who had most thoroughly shifted from a pre-Kantian version to a post-Kantian version were still retaining the essential Enlightenment faith in a unifying science. So, for example, when Charles Peirce, the most sophisticated American philosopher of science of his day, stated as the essence of pragmatism that truth is "the opinion which is fated to be ultimately agreed to by all who investigate," he was expressing a point with which the most conservative Princeton theologians could agree.[50] The elements common to Peirce and Warfield are even more striking in Peirce's elaboration of his point:

> Different minds may set out with the most antagonistic views, but the progress of investigation carries them by a force outside of themselves to one and the same conclusion. This activity of thought by which we are carried, not where we wish, but to a fore-ordained goal, is like the operation of destiny. No modification of the point of view taken, no selection of other facts for study, no natural bent of man even, can enable a man to escape the predestinate opinion.

Common Sense philosophy and historicist pragmatism, despite their fundamental differences, were still American cousins. Both were descendents of the union of Protestantism and the Enlightenment. Strict biblicists committed to the Common Sense philosophy took for granted that one reasonable and unifying outlook must triumph in public life as much as did those who hailed scientific progress and a higher evolving religion. The stakes they thus set were remarkably high; in fact they were all or nothing. Unlike Abraham Kuyper, who in a setting of more stable European pluralism could provide an intellectual rationale for being one voice among many, the instincts of those who participated in the mainstream of American culture were almost always assimilationist. One view would win in public life and it would be winner take all. In such a setting, views such as strict biblicism that in practice were divisive (American Marxists sometimes had similar problems) had little chance of surviving in mainstream culture or in its elite higher education.

Notes

1. Samuel Eliot Morison, *Three Centuries of Harvard* (Cambridge, Mass., 1936), 362–63.

2. J. David Hoeveler, Jr., *James McCosh and the Scottish Intellectual Tradition: From Glasgow to Princeton* (Princeton: Princeton University Press, 1981), 64.

3. Ibid., passim.

4. Ibid., 88.

5. Ibid., 224.

6. On Atwater see George M. Marsden, *The Evangelical Mind and the New School Presbyterian Experience* (New Haven: Yale University Press, 1970), 217–19, 225–27. Atwater quotation, 226.

7. Hoeveler, *McCosh,* 239

8. Ibid., 252–53, quotation, 252, is addressed to the trustees in 1885. McCosh did eventually take the lead in eliminating evening prayers, thus reducing the chapel requirement to once daily.

9. E.g., McCosh, *What an American University Should Be* (New York, 1885).

10. On Patton I am indebted to the research of Paul Kemeny such as his "President Francis Landey Patton, Princeton University and Faculty Ferment," *American Presbyterianism: The Journal of the Presbyterian Historical Society* 69 (1991), 111–19. Cf. Hoeveler, *McCosh,* 332.

11. Eliot, "On the Education of Ministers," from the *Princeton Review,* May 1883, in Eliot, *Educational Reform: Essays and Address* (New York, 1898), 66–70.

12. Francis Patton, "On the Education of Ministers: A Reply to President Eliot," *Princeton Review,* 4th ser., 2 (July 1883), 48–66, quotations, 49 and 57.

13. Hoeveler, *McCosh,* 234–36.

14. From a substantial abstract in "Religion in Colleges, Discussions by Drs. McCosh and Eliot," *New York Daily Tribune,* February 4, 1886, 3.

15. McCosh, *Religion in A College: What Place it Should Have* (New York, 1886), 522, passim.

16. *New York Daily Tribune,* February 4, 1886, 3. McCosh, *Religion in A College,* Prefatory note, 3.

17. McCosh noted that two-thirds of Princeton students were church members, well over half belonged to the campus Christian association there had been revivals every two or three years during his presidency, and during his era "not above half a dozen out of our two thousand and more students have left us declaring that they had no religious belief." Likely McCosh's method of survey discouraged such declarations. McCosh, *Twenty Years of Princeton College* (New York, 1888).

At Harvard, in comparison, a postgraduation survey of the 184 members of the class of 1881 showed 25 undecided about religion, 15 declared agnostics, and another 23 classifying themselves in categories such as "non-sectarian," "rationalist," "deist," and "theist." Henry F. May, *Coming to Terms: A Study in Memory and History* (Berkeley: University of California Press, 1987), 94. May provides an engaging account of the religious quest of one member of the class who had an orthodox religious background.

18. Quoted in Hoeveler, *McCosh,* 253.

19. Ibid., 254–55.

20. This account closely follows Hoeveler, *McCosh,* 323–24.

21. McCosh, *Christianity and Positivism: A Series of Lectures to the Times on Natural Theology and Apologetics* (New York, 1875). Hoeveler, *McCosh,* 180–211, summarizes McCosh's view on natural science.

22. Charles Hodge, *What Is Darwinism?* (New York, 1874).

23. McCosh, *Christianity and Positivism,* 3.

24. Ibid. 38 and passim. Cf. McCosh, *The Religious Aspect of Evolution* (New York, 1888), 1–9.

25. McCosh, *Christianity and Positivism,* 43.

26. McCosh, *The Religious Aspect of Evolution,* 54.

27. Jon H. Roberts, *Darwinism and the Divine in America: Protestant Intellectuals and Organic Evolution, 1859–1900* (Madison: University of Wisconsin Press, 1988) presents a persuasive overview. James R. Moore, *The Post-Darwinian Controversies: A Study of the Protestant Struggle to Come to Terms with Darwin in Great Britain and America, 1870–1900* (Cambridge: Cambridge University Press, 1979) and Peter J. Bowler, *Evolution: The History of an Idea* (Berkeley: University of California Press, 1984) are particularly helpful among the many books on this topic.

28. Gary Scott Smith, *The Seeds of Secularization: Calvinism, Culture and Pluralism in America, 1870–1915* (Grand Rapids, Mich.: Christian University Press, 1985), 94–111, esp. 98. Also David N. Livingstone, *Darwin's Forgotten Defenders: The Encounter between Evangelical Theology and Evolutionary Thought* (Grand Rapids, Mich.: William B. Eerdmans, 1987).

29. Quoted from Arthur S. Link, ed., *The Papers of Woodrow Wilson* (Princeton, 1966–), 3:217, in Hoeveler, *McCosh,* 278.

30. Andrew Dickson White, *A History of the Warfare of Science with Theology in Christendom* (New York, 1896), I:80, cf. 412n. Cf. Hoeveler, *McCosh,* 278–79.

31. McCosh, *The Religious Aspect of Evolution,* 70.

32. For this summary, I am following most directly the useful overview of John W. Stewart, "The Tethered Theology: Biblical Criticism, Common Sense Philosophy, and the Princeton Theologians, 1812–1860," Ph.D. dissertation, University of Michigan, 1990, passim. The most complete survey is Jerry W. Brown, *The Rise of Biblical Criticism in America, 1800–1870* (Middletown, Conn.: Wesleyan University Press, 1969).

33. Stewart, "Tethered Theology," 202. Stewart points out that Ira Brown's article "Higher Criticism Comes to America, 1880–1890," *Journal of the Presbyterian Historical Society* 38 (1960): 193–212, has misled scholars by arguing that the "debate on historical criticism did not begin in America until after 1880" (96).

34. John Dillenberger and Claude Welch make a similar point: "This does not mean . . . that the new conception of the Bible which came to characterize Protestant liberalism originated simply as a reaction to the discoveries of historical criticism. In fact, the situation was more nearly the reverse. It was new conceptions of religious authority and of the meaning of revelation which made possible the development of biblical criticism." *Protestant Christianity: Interpreted through Its Development* (New York: Charles Scribner's Sons, 1954), 197.

35. See the summary in Mark A. Massa, *Charles Augustus Briggs and the Crisis of Historical Criticism* (Minneapolis: Fortress Press, 1990), 4–6. Peter Novick, *That Noble Dream: The "Objectivity Question" and the American Historical Profession* (Cambridge: Cambridge University Press, 1988), suggests that Ranke's phrase is better translated "as it essentially was" but in America it was understood as "as it actually was."

36. Paul A. Carter, *The Spiritual Crisis of the Gilded Age* (DeKalb: Northern Illinois University Press, 1971), 63–107.

37. Mark A. Noll, *Between Faith and Criticism: Evangelicals, Scholarship, and the Bible in America* (San Francisco: Harper & Row, 1986), 27–28. Noll provides an excellent overview of the developments.

38. James P. Wind, *The Bible and the University: The Messianic Vision of William Rainey Harper* (Atlanta: Scholars Press, 1987), esp. 46–48, 102–3.

39. Massa, *Briggs,* provides a valuable summary of these developments.

40. Francis Patton, "The Dogmatic Aspect of Pentateuchal Criticism," *Presbyterian Review* 14 (April 1883), 343, 344, 354, 375, and passim. Avowals of a Protes-

tant principle of freedom were, of course, difficult to reconcile with strict ecclesiastical limits on what one was free to say. Patton, for instance, was best known for his role in the recent David Swing heresy trial. Patton explained, however, that Presbyterian clergy, who had *voluntarily* taken their ordination vows, were also obliged to conform their views to the teachings of the creeds of the church. Patton admitted that the relationship of these two principles was "not easy to set forth" (356).

41. Noll, *Between Faith and Criticism,* 23–27. Cf. Archibald A. Hodge and Benjamin B. Warfield, "Inspiration," *Princeton Review* 2 (1881), 225–28, 241.

42. McCosh, *First and Fundamental Truths: Being a Treatise on Metaphysics* (New York, 1889), 12, cf. 28.

43. Charles Augustus Briggs, *Whither? A Theological Question for the Times* (New York, 1889), 16.

44. James McCosh, *Whither? O Whither? Tell Me Where* (New York, 1889), 1–47, passim.

45. McCosh, *First and Fundamental Truths,* i.

46. Ibid., 28, 327.

47. Cf. Hoeveler, *McCosh,* 321.

48. Benjamin B. Warfield, "Introduction" to Francis R. Beattie's *Apologetics* (Richmond, 1903), in *Selected Shorter Writings of Benjamin B. Warfield,* John E. Meeter, ed. (Nutley, N.J.: Presbyterian and Reformed, 1973), II:99–100.

49. Ibid., 103. In my *Understanding Fundamentalism and Evangelicalism* (Grand Rapids, Mich.: William B. Eerdmans, 1990), 122–52, I elaborate on these issues.

50. Quoted from Charles S. Peirce, "How to Make Our Ideas Clear" (1878), from Novick, *That Noble Dream,* 570–71.

13

Making the World Safe from the Traditionalist Establishment

Recognition of the commonalities shared by leading American Protestant educators in their assumptions that they should shape a unified national culture sets the stage for understanding Princeton during the very different administrations of Francis Patton (1888–1902) and Woodrow Wilson (1902–1910). Patton was every bit as triumphalistic as his friend Benjamin Warfield. "If Calvinism is true, Arminianism is false," Patton declared a few years before becoming president of the college. "If the Baptists are right Paedobaptists are wrong. The positions . . . being contradictory, we are shut up to one or the other of them. . . . Believing in Calvinism, we believe that if Christendom shall ever have a unanimous faith, it will be a Calvinistic faith, which was the faith of Augustine, which was the faith of Paul."[1]

One might well find it incredible that during the 1890s a respected American university would have a president who held such views.[2] It is less remarkable when one remembers, however, that Patton made a clear distinction between what was appropriate for the church and what was appropriate for the college, which, despite control by Presbyterian trustees, was not an agency of the church. At the time of his selection to the presidency in 1888 some of the alumni were suspicious of Patton because of his well-deserved ecclesiastical reputation as a heresy hunter. Patton had a winsome personal manner, however, and was an effective public speaker. In a dramatic speech at annual dinner of the Princeton Club in New York, he won the skeptical over. While affirming that "we must keep Princeton a Christian college," he made clear that he did not conceive of that task in a narrow way. At the end of the speech Patton received a rousing standing ovation. "Such a personal triumph I never witnessed before or since," one observer recalled. "He had converted his opponents and began his administration with the heartiest good wishes of all parties."[3]

Patton made the same point at his inaugural. While praising the nearby seminary, Patton argued that the college had a different purpose and insisted that it was to be free from political or theological sectarianism. On the other hand, he pointed out that freedom always took place within boundaries and that academic freedom was never unlimited. So just as an American university would not allow a Communist to teach political economy, "nor is it part of university freedom to open the halls of science and philosophy to men who teach atheism or belittle the Christian faith." As he had argued earlier, Patton believed that truth would flourish in an atmosphere of free inquiry; on the other hand, he feared that minds would be closed if teachings hostile to the faith were permitted.

Patton felt it necessary, therefore, to guarantee a place for theism, much as in the old-college traditions. "True philosophy," he declared in his inaugural, "has God as its postulate; true science reaches God as its conclusion." Hence at the college "there should be a distinct, earnest, purposeful effort to show every man who enters our College Halls the grounds for entertaining those fundamental religious beliefs that are the common heritage of the Christian world." This broadly Christian worldview, he was convinced, could be taught without sectarianism.[4]

Patton made sure his faculty were aware of their duties to present a broad Christian perspective in the classroom. When Patton wrote to Woodrow Wilson in 1890 informing him of his election to the Chair of Political Economy and Jurisprudence, he immediately let Wilson know that at Princeton he would have to be more explicit in his Christian concerns. Patton was concerned "that in your discussion of the origin of the State you minimize the supernatural, & make such unqualified application of the doctrine of naturalistic evolution & the genesis of the State as to leave the reader of your pages in a state of uncertainty as to your own position & the place you give to Divine Providence." In addition, Patton was concerned that Wilson gave too exclusive credit to the influences of Roman law in shaping modern civilization, yet "you are silent with respect to the forming & reforming influences of Christianity." The trustees of the college, Patton emphasized, were determined "to keep this College on the old ground of loyalty to the Christian religion," which meant that subjects such as Wilson's were "to be dealt with under theistic and Christian presuppositions: & they would not regard with favour such a conception of academic freedom or teaching as would leave in doubt the very direct bearing of historical Christianity as a revealed religion upon the great problems of civilization."[5]

Despite this rather blunt admonition that he would have to buck the academic trends, Wilson accepted the position at his alma mater. After a few months back at Princeton, Wilson wrote to a friend that Patton was "a man of most liberal outlook in his whole mental attitude, outside of church battles."[6] Similarly, James Mark Baldwin, professor of philosophy and psychology, recalled that Patton encouraged him to work on the evolutionary development of the mind. According to Baldwin, there were "two Pattons—a Calvinist of the most thorough stripe in the pulpit, but a person of immense charity among the 'sinners' of the world the rest of the week."[7]

Patton in fact proved himself something of a hero to those who wished to move the college out of the shadow of ecclesiastical scrutiny. In 1897 the Princeton academic community came under sharp attack from irate Presbyterians, because some Princeton faculty had joined in a successful petition to grant a liquor license to the Princeton Inn so that beer and wine could be served. They defended this on the grounds that it would promote temperance by allowing student drinking in a controlled environment, rather than in the local saloons. Total abstinence, however, was becoming a virtual article of faith in many denominations and some Presbyterians expressed outrage that Princeton was operating a "university rumshop" and leading students toward "the calamity of the cup."[8]

Francis Patton, at the center of the maelstrom, withstood the ecclesiastical pressure. Speaking to New York alumni at Delmonico's, he declared that "I know the law and the constitution of my Church and I know that much of what has lately been quoted as the law of that Church is not law and has no binding authority. But whether it has or not, I cannot consent to have the law of that Church, as such, imposed on Princeton University. . . . While I hold my place as the head of your alma mater I will do what in me lies to keep the hand of ecclesiasticism from resting on Princeton University."[9]

Patton and his conservative Presbyterian allies were holding on to a peculiar hybrid position. On the one hand, true to their Old School Presbyterian heritage, they made a sharper distinction between church and nation than did most Protestants. They resisted imposing strict church standards on public life, or on semipublic life like that of a university. On the other hand, they retained enough of the Protestant establishmentarian mentality to insist that a broad theism should be maintained in public affairs. They took the lead, for instance, in decrying efforts to exclude theism from the nation's public schools, having abandoned earlier Old School Presbyterian efforts to found a parochial school system.[10] They were thus attempting to maintain a national atmosphere congenial to Christian faith, without establishing particular Christian tenets. In effect, then, they were promoting for public life a sort of second-level national Christianity that would differ little from the views of a Jefferson or Franklin and would not in fact be much different from liberal Protestantism.

This ambiguity in conservative Presbyterianism between an exclusivist theological Christianity for the church and a functional unitarianism for public life helps explain the famous controversy that soured Woodrow Wilson on Princeton's Old Regime. In the fall of 1896 Wilson was negotiating on behalf of the university with Wisconsin's well-known historian, Frederick Jackson Turner, to join him as a colleague. When Turner asked about any religious tests at Princeton, Wilson replied, "I think I can say without qualification that no religious tests are applied here. The president and trustees are very anxious that every man they choose should be earnestly religious, but there are no doctrinal standards among us."[11] This was the standard Patton line and Wilson was no doubt convinced it applied in this case.

It proved otherwise with the Princeton board of trustees. At a first meeting in December there was simply an unexplained delay. Then Wilson learned that his colleague Andrew West was opposed to the appointment on the grounds that Turner was a Unitarian. Wilson surmised that this must be the difficulty for the conservative members of the board of trustees as well. He knew that some people were concerned that orthodox Presbyterian donors would be upset by a Unitarian appointment. In any case, in March the trustees turned down the appointment, alleging that the school could not afford to create a separate position in American history. Wilson could not prove that religion was the real issue, but he was outraged. To Turner he wrote, "I am probably at this writing the most chagrined fellow on this continent! . . . [I]t is no doubt just as well that I have not now a chance to go elsewhere."[12]

What the incident showed was that it was virtually impossible to have it both ways with two functioning levels of religious tests, as the conservative Presbyterians were proposing. If the college was to be considered a public institution, rather than an ecclesiastical one, then any doctrinal test would involve drawing a line that would prove offensive to those who were more liberal. And the attempt to make the test so broadly Christian that it could include Unitarians, as Patton had suggested the policy would be, was offensive to the ecclesiastical constituency. Patton himself was caught in the middle and ultimately went along, willingly or unwillingly, with the conservative Presbyterians. Orthodox Presbyterianism, however, could not much longer play any role in defining the ideological basis for Princeton's longstanding task of serving the nation by training its leaders. The result was an impossible ambiguity. With no clear principle to draw on, the conservatives could not much longer hold to an arbitrary line that was "nonsectarian" yet excluded Unitarians.

In the palace revolution that brought Patton's resignation in 1902 and his replacement by Wilson, the religious issue played little direct role, though it may have been a significant factor in the background. The immediate issue was Patton's demonstrated incompetence as administrator of a modern university. This does not seem to have been primarily a matter of laziness, as sometimes was alleged, as much as an inappropriate administrative style. Patton, a native of Bermuda who retained his British citizenship, lived as a gentleman. His gentlemanly manners were part of his personal charm and helped set the tone at Princeton, which was rapidly developing into an elite gentleman's club. Administratively, Patton's style seemed to be based on the principle that the university, being composed of free individuals, should run itself without much presidential interference or systematic planning. Patton, for instance, did not have an "office" but a "study." Before 1901 he did not even have a secretary. He answered the vast majority of his letters by hand and, in true gentlemanly manner, responded to even the most trivial inquiries.[13]

Patton could not be described as simply an old-time college president preserving the ideals of an earlier era. He often spoke out in favor of progress and, if he did little to advance his announced ideals, he also did little to oppose progress taking place under his presidency. While he continued to teach not only a required senior course in ethics and Christian evidences but also three semesters of New Testament studies for underclassmen, his resemblance to his old-time predecessors went only so far. Most conspicuously, Patton did not believe in rigorous student discipline, either socially or academically. Princeton, as much or more than other schools of the era, was in the grip of the cult of football. When it put on a lavish sesquicentennial celebration in 1896, a football match was a featured attraction. A faculty member later recalled that Patton was content with "the spectacle of the young barbarians all at play, and went so far as to believe that their friendship might in future years be a source of benefit to the university."[14]

The relative freedom that Patton encouraged among the students suited their increasingly conspicuous wealthy lifestyles. Forbidden on religious grounds from having fraternities, the students created members-only eating clubs which during Patton's years developed into an elaborate system of elitism that dominated campus social life. Patton was reputed to have boasted that he presided over the finest country club in America.[15]

The men's club atmosphere that Patton permitted might not have been offensive to the faculty had it not carried over to academics. At the turn of the century, as college education was increasingly becoming a status symbol in the emerging consumer culture, there were complaints at many leading schools of low levels of academic performance. Princeton was second to none in its lack of rigor. Patton frankly encouraged the trend. Patton wished Princeton to be based on an English model, which he regarded as implying the recognition that only a select few students would be truly serious about the life of the mind. To force others into such a commitment would be artificial. Students who chose to take the many "pipe" courses the college offered were free to do so.

Patton did as little for graduate education as he did for undergraduate rigor. He was eager to call the school a university and promised to transform Princeton's paltry graduate offerings into a true graduate school; but he never did anything to bring this about. In 1900, after years of frustration, the faculty took matters into its own hands and succeeded in getting the board to inaugurate a graduate school with a dean independent of the president's authority. Patton remained intransigent, however, regarding undergraduate reforms. Finally in 1902 a small group of faculty members, including Woodrow Wilson, suggested to the trustees that the school be run by an executive committee, with Patton as the nominal head. Patton rejected the plan and after being assured that his substantial salary and professorship would be continued offered his resignation. Always the gentleman, he immediately nominated Wilson to be his successor. Patton moved to the presidency of Princeton Theological Seminary.[16]

College Religion in the Nation's Service

Woodrow Wilson, who had been easily the most popular teacher during the preceding decade, as well as the most influential faculty leader, came to his new duties with a clearly thought out view of the proper role of religion in universities. Wilson himself was indelibly religious. His father was a leading Old School Southern Presbyterian minister. Being reared in such a home meant that Woodrow Wilson's essential categories for understanding himself and his duties were shaped in an atmosphere that was highly rigorous both intellectually and morally. Referring to the experiences of boyhood, Wilson later told Princeton students, "No one of you will ever shake off the personality he has now already made for himself,"[17] and Wilson remained committed to the essentials of a traditional Presbyterian faith. While he opposed ecclesiastical dogmatism of the Francis Patton sort or of the sort that hounded his uncle James Woodrow, he did not feel that his faith hinged on fending off all biblical criticism. Wilson revered the Bible as a rule for life and was essentially conservative in his Christian views. He believed, and often repeated, that humans were basically defective. Not only that; there was a God-ordained moral law which they had failed to obey. Christ was necessary to salvation, and the life-transforming commitment to Christ provided the motive necessary to be able to carry out one's duties of service to others. Ultimately society could be changed only by changing individuals.[18]

Wilson's views of religion in the university are best understood as a blending of his Old School principles with some of the prevailing currents of moral idealism. Most essential to his outlook was that like his Old School forebears and unlike his more liberal Protestant contemporaries, he made a sharp distinction between the church and society. So he was cool to the social gospel which advocated the church's direct involvement in political action and reflected the trend to identify the interests of the church with those of society. As he wrote to John R. Mott, the leader of the student missionary movement, in 1908,

> I have had the fear in recent years that the ministers of our churches, by becoming involved in all sorts of social activities . . . have too much diverted their attention from the effectual preaching of the Word. The danger seems to be that individual churches will become great philanthropic societies instead of being what it seems to me they ought to be, organizations from which go forth the spiritual stimulation which should guide all philanthropic effort.[19]

This view can be traced to Old School suspicion of pretenses to be a national church, which were especially accentuated in the Southern Presbyterian Church of which Joseph Wilson had been a founder in 1861. James H. Thornwell, the leading theologian of the Southern Presbyterians, articulated a longstanding Presbyterian distinction between the covenant of grace, which had to do with God's offer of salvation, and the covenant of nature, which established God's moral law for nations. To the Southern Presbyterians, who were resisting ecclesiastical pronouncements against slavery, this distinction meant that the church should confine itself to matters concerning the covenant of grace and not meddle in matters of the state. The state in the meantime was bound by God's moral law contained in the covenant of nature and nations would not be blessed if they did not obey God's moral law. Woodrow Wilson, for whom the covenant was a basic category of thought, held broadly the same view.[20]

For Wilson as an emerging professional academic during this era when many other intellectuals underwent a severe crisis of faith, one of the uses of this distinction was that in his scholarship he could keep his particular Presbyterian faith and his broader moral categories in more-or-less separate compartments. As a student of constitutional development, he could trace the natural forces that shaped the state and civil law, relating these broadly to moral concerns, without directly invoking Scripture or Providence in his writings in ways that would offend modern professional standards.[21]

A similar distinction was pivotal in Wilson's conception of the university. Wilson eloquently proclaimed his views in a famous speech, "Princeton in the Nation's Service," at Princeton's Sesquicentennial Celebration in 1896. Speaking to an international audience that included many dignitaries, the talented young orator rehearsed his version of the history of the college. Although the founders of the college were Presbyterian clergy who wished to train clergy for the church, Wilson observed, they were not under authority of the church and they founded a nonsectarian school. "They acted without ecclesiastical authority, as if under obligation to society rather than to the church." Central to sealing the character of the school, Wilson emphasized at length, was that it was shaped in the crucible of the American Revolution. The college was always a "school of duty" and its close ties to the revolutionary cause gave it a central role in its mission to the nation. Specifically, the college served the nation by training its leaders. It cultivated character and an ideal of service. Religion was important to this public task. "There is nothing that gives such pith to public service as religion. A God of truth is no mean prompter to the enlightened service of mankind; and character formed, as if in his eye, has always a fibre and sanction such as you shall not easily obtain for the ordinary man from the mild promptings of philosophy."

This public influence of religion, however, should come only indirectly from the churches. "Churches among us," Wilson declared, "as all the world knows, are free and voluntary societies, separated to be nurseries of belief, not suffered to become instruments of rule." Here was a crucial part of the Old School heritage. Churches were private societies set apart from societies as "nurseries of belief." Nobody had to join them and churches could have their own peculiar standards. By the same token they were not instruments to rule over people with differing standards.

Colleges, on the other hand, were defined by their mission to serve the public sphere.[22] Churches and universities were under different covenants, as it were, and hence had differing duties shaping their constitutions. The duties of the university, then, were discoverable on natural grounds by looking at the university's relationship to the larger constituted entity it served, the nation.

Wilson saw the particular duty of higher education as that of training a leadership in the highest ideals of a nation's heritage. Wilson's outlook thus resembled the national idealism of other university builders. "It is the business of a University," he proclaimed, "to train men in . . . the right thought of the world, the thought which it has tested and established, the principles which have stood through the seasons and become at length part of the immemorial wisdom of the race." Hence university study should be built around history and especially the best literature of the race. "In short," Wilson declaimed, "I believe that the catholic study of the world's literature as a record of spirit is the right preparation for leadership in the world's affairs, if you undertake it like a man and not like a pedant."

The most striking aspect of Wilson's oration, however, was its culmination in a stinging attack on the primacy of the scientific ideal in higher education. "I am much mistaken," he declared, "if the scientific spirit of the age is not doing us a great disservice, working in us a certain great degeneracy." Wilson duly lauded the benefits of scientific progress and hailed the large place in higher education for the study of natural science itself. "We have made a perilous mistake," he objected, however, "in giving it too great a preponderance in method in every other branch of study." Especially destructive, he said, was that in giving too much credit to the scientific method,

> we believe in the present and in the future more than in the past, and deem the newest theory of society the likeliest. This is the disservice scientific study has done us; it has given us agnosticism in the realm of philosophy, scientific anarchism in the field of politics. It has made the legislator confident that he can create and the philosopher sure that God cannot. Past experience is discredited and the laws of matter are supposed to apply to spirit and the makeup of society.

Even though Wilson argued his point on broadly theistic and public grounds, his skepticism of the scientific method was rooted in one strand of the heritage of Augustine, Luther, and Calvin with which he identified. The successes of applied science, he argued, had created an illusion that was leading many people to forget the defectiveness of human nature. Science, said Wilson, in what might be taken as a prophecy of the twentieth century,

> has not freed us from ourselves. It has not purged us of passion or disposed us to virtue. It has not made us less covetous or less ambitious or less self-indulgent. On the contrary, it may be suspected of having enhanced our passions by making wealth so quick to come, and so fickle to

> stay. It has wrought such instant, incredible improvement in all the physical setting of our life, that we have grown the more impatient of the unreformed condition of the part it has not touched or bettered, and we want to get at our spirits and reconstruct them in like radical fashion by like processes of experiment. We have broken with the past and have come into a new world.[23]

Mere knowledge, then, whether scientific or even humane, for that matter, could not be the ultimate goal of education; rather this had to be a transformation in moral character that would result in right action.[24] Religion, Wilson believed, was a great contributor to that goal; but in the public setting of a university, the religion he preached was a religion of moral action. Wilson, in fact, preached often at Princeton, at the student Philadelphian Society, at chapel, at Sunday services, and at baccalaureates. As president he also selected visiting preachers and essentially filled the role of "university pastor."[25] While he set his moral emphases in a general Christian framework and sometimes emphasized that selfless action must be a response to God's love, he preached moral ideals that would be unexceptionable among liberal Protestant preachers and not much different from what one would hear in other college chapels of the day.[26]

As president, Wilson essentially toned down the religious emphases that had prevailed under the Patton regime. He dropped the required Sunday afternoon service, though not the Sunday morning requirement or daily chapel. More dramatically, upon assuming the presidency, Wilson immediately terminated Bible instruction as part of the curriculum. Required introductory Bible courses had been offered by Francis Patton, who had recently hired his son George to supplement the offerings. George Patton was promoted to offering upper-level options in ethics, as his father continued to do also. After three years, electives in biblical studies were reintroduced under new auspices. The impetus for Wilson's resolution of the Patton problem as well as in terminating the Sunday afternoon service was apparently the desire to eliminate Presbyterian dogmatism from the curriculum. He also signaled the end of religious tests for the faculty by hiring the first Jew to teach at Princeton in 1904 and the first Roman Catholic in 1909. In 1906 he had the university formally declared nonsectarian.[27]

The Struggle for Community

Wilson was less successful in his positive program of substituting a much more broadly Christian community of character and service. It was one thing to preach ideals that inspired many individual students; it was another to change the fundamental social structures that had evolved at Princeton. Although the religious dimensions of the struggles of Wilson's presidency were seldom explicit, they nonetheless form an important part of the background of the familiar stories.

Wilson's first four years as president, which were devoted to strengthening the school academically, were extraordinarily successful. Following the English model, he established a system of preceptors to guide undergraduates' work. The New York *Evening Post* commented wryly that Wilson had "ruined what was universally admitted to be the most agreeable and aristocratic country club in America by transforming it into an institution of learning."[28]

In the spring of 1906 Wilson suffered a serious stroke. He spent the summer and much of the fall recuperating in England. He came back filled with high ideals as to what was necessary to make Princeton a model university. What he found particularly offensive in the way his university had evolved in the past decade was its extreme social elitism. Especially since 1897 when Grover Cleveland had retired to an estate at Princeton where he also served on the university board, Princeton had become preoccupied with social connections and was attracting some of the wealthiest students in the country. At the center of this social system were the lavishly endowed eating clubs with their closed memberships. Social success or failure at Princeton depended almost entirely upon election as an upperclassman to one of these clubs. The elite insider system for the best clubs reached back even to the prep schools, such as Lawrenceville and St. Paul's, that served as feeders to Princeton.

Wilson returned from his convalescence with a grand plan for reorganizing the university in a way that would end the influence of the clubs. This "Quad Plan," which he proposed to the board in December 1906, would establish residential colleges on the English model. Wilson presented the plan as a direct attack on the deleterious social influence of the eating clubs.

Wilson's proposal to reform the social life at Princeton grew directly out of his Christian vision. "The disintegration is taking place, a disintegration into atoms too small to hold the fine spirit of the college," he told the trustees in defense of the plan. "We must substitute for disintegration, a new organic process. The new body will have division, but all the parts will be organs of a common life. It is reintegration by more varied and abundant organic life." This image not only reflected the ideal, common in the era, of the healthy growing organism, but also was a paraphrase of the Apostle Paul's familiar depiction of the church as one body made up of many parts.[29] Like most other educational leaders of his day, Wilson fused such Christian ideals with his ideals for a national culture.

The most immediate problem for such attractive ideals at Princeton was that mainstream Protestants were running up against the realities of rapidly increasing wealth within their own constituency. Wilson, who had been politically conservative, was being forced toward some of the conclusions that liberal Christians and other progressive reformers had been proclaiming for some time. American ideals, he was beginning to see, were being subverted by the inequities created by moneyed power. Wilson was well aware of the corruptibility of human nature and in the opposition to his Quad Plan he perceived the forces of evil gathering round about him. The clubs were, of course, strongly represented by the wealthiest of the alumni and contributors, many of whom were outraged by Wilson's plan to destroy the social ideals they had built at Princeton. Wilson also handled the tactics of his proposal badly, presenting the plan without preparing support ahead of time and without consulting the faculty. Even some of Wilson's faculty friends deserted him. The more the opposition rose, however, the more Wilson (who seemed to have become more inflexible after his stroke) saw his cause as just. "The fight is on," he wrote to one ally, "and I regard it, not as a fight for the development, but for the Restoration of Princeton. My heart is in it more than it has been in anything else, because it is a scheme of salvation."[30]

The controversy, which dragged out through the last four years of Wilson's presidency, was complicated by a second and related issue. Princeton already had a small graduate school which had been established in 1900 as the result of the earlier faculty rebellion against Patton. Andrew Fleming West from the faculty had been named dean with powers largely independent of the president. Wilson and West agreed that the graduate program needed to be housed in an elegant residential graduate college, again on an English model. West, however, strongly opposed what he considered Wilson's highhanded manner in the Quad fight and soon a bitter struggle developed over the location of the graduate college. Wilson, true to his organic ideal, insisted that the graduate college should be in the midst of the university, so that scholars at all levels would be mutually stimulated and grow together. West insisted just as fervently that the graduate college be located by itself on the periphery of the university, near the golf course.

Wilson and West make an interesting comparison and contrast. Both were sons of Presbyterian ministers. West's father, Nathaniel West (1826–1906), was one of the progenitors of fundamentalism. He was an ardent premillennialist who interpreted biblical prophecies literally and depicted modern America as "Babylon" about to be destroyed.[31] Andrew West was of a far different stripe. While he took the conservative side on the Frederick Jackson Turner question,[32] he shared with Patton and some others of the Presbyterian conservatives a faith in the combination of traditional theology and comfortable living. West was a specimen of the portly Victorian Grover Cleveland type. In fact the former president named his Princeton home "Westland" in gratitude for West's help in bringing him there. West, perhaps compensating for the embarrassing intensity of his father's revivalistic pietism, was "a *bon vivant*, the perfect host who cultivated an atmosphere of gentility and breeding around him."[33]

West's ideal for the graduate school was quite frankly based on the gentleman's club model. A classicist himself, with little interest in scientific models, he wanted the school to be elegant and leisurely, signaling that it was not dominated by professionalism. "If the higher teachers of the nation," he later wrote, "should be trained in a place and society worthy of their calling, why should they not dwell in a beautiful, even in a stately home." The graduate school, he insisted, should resist the commercialization and specialization of higher education by being an interdisciplinary community. "More scholars," he argued, "fail in life because they do not understand their fellowmen than because they do not understand their subjects." The Ph.D. should not be a specialized union card, but a sign of broad cultivation. The school should also include gentlemen scholars who were not proposing permanent scholarly careers.[34] West had already established such an atmosphere at "Merwick," an estate near campus housing the graduate students, best known for its gentlemanly ambience, its broad humane approach to graduate studies, and regular sessions of bridge.[35]

Wilson and West shared essentially the same general theories about graduate education, which could be related to a broad Christian vision of the value of humane learning in community.[36] Both thought the danger lay in Germanic influences, fragmentation, and overreliance on the scientific method.[37] They differed rather on details. In the context of the Quad fight Wilson became convinced that West's differences were part of the problem of the plutocracy that was ruining the Princeton ideal. As the controversy became increasingly bitter, Wilson became more and more blunt. Speaking to a largely unsympathetic audience of some of the school's richest alumni at the New York Princeton Club in 1910, Wilson asked, "When the country is looking to us as men who prefer ideas even to money, are we going to withdraw and say, 'After all, we find we are mistaken: we prefer money to ideas?' "[38]

When Wilson failed to gain substantial support, he attacked the churches as well: "I believe that the churches of this country, at any rate the Protestant churches, have dissociated themselves from the people of this country. They are serving the classes and they are not serving the masses. They serve certain strata, certain uplifted strata, but they are not serving the men whose need is dire. The churches have more regard to their pew-rents than to the souls of men."[39] The more Wilson attacked, the more he became a lonely voice, at least so far as his Princeton constituency was concerned. Finally, he was dramatically defeated by an unexpected event. An alumnus who died in the spring of 1910 left a large estate to the Princeton graduate school and named West as executor of his will. Wilson realized he could do nothing and capitulated. Having won more admiration outside Princeton circles than within, Wilson stepped down into politics, successfully running in 1910 for the governorship of New Jersey.

The story of Patton and Wilson is a tale of the failure of conservative Protestantism to provide any viable way to resolve the fundamental issues involved in relating the inherited tradition to the modern university. First of all Wilson had felt it necessary to free the school from what he considered the sectarian narrowness that still persisted under Patton's regime.

The issue, he correctly noted, was that historically Princeton was more essentially a public institution than it was an agency of a church. Given Princeton's history of commitment to the public, the only solution seemed to be to adopt a broad religious-moral base that was functionally no different from liberal Protestantism, save in its lack of hostility to conservative Protestantism. Protestant theology was expected to be cultivated in the privacy of churches and seminaries.

Deepening the problem, however, was the fact that conservative Presbyterianism, despite its theory of the private character of the church, nonetheless had a social program. Historically it was closely connected with some of the wealthiest of the business and professional classes. Correspondingly, its social program was that churches should have no social program that would interfere with the benefits of respectable wealth and social class. This kind of Christianity became an obstacle to attacking one of the conspicuous moral problems associated with the emerging universities, the problem of social elitism. Older schools with church connections were least likely to be able to address such issues.

Thus while Wilson was able to reduce the theological influences at the university, he was thwarted in his efforts to build a model Christian and nation-serving educational community as an alternative. The elitism of the school, however, went much deeper even than that which Wilson addressed in the debates over the Quad and the graduate school. As John Mulder points out, Wilson did not alter the admissions policies, which perpetuated the school's dependence on a wealthy prep-school clientele.[40] During Wilson's later years, the handful of Jewish students increased slightly; but Jews who did attend were often unhappy. The club system especially was a source of "social humiliation," as one who transferred to the University of Pennsylvania explained to Wilson.[41] Until well after midcentury Princeton retained its reputation for anti-Semitism and was the least popular of the prestigious schools among Jewish applicants.[42] The one Jewish faculty member hired during Wilson's presidency, Horace Meyer Kallen, was an avowed unbeliever who apparently felt uncomfortable and stayed only one year.[43]

In deference to the school's strong southern constituency, Wilson discouraged African Americans from even applying to Princeton. Wilson, like many progressives, subscribed to the characteristic racist views of the day. He also faced virulent student pressures. According to one story, during the 1890s at a dinner at Princeton following a Harvard–Princeton football game, the Princeton team walked out when the Harvard team brought their black player along. Not until 1947 did an African American receive an undergraduate degree at Princeton.[44] Women undergraduates were excluded for another quarter century.

It is, of course, somewhat too easy for us to condemn persons of an earlier era for not taking a prophetic stand against all the prejudices of their day. Yet there was a larger point illustrated by Wilson's futile struggles to combat some of Princeton's prejudice. Protestantism in higher education was part of a religious establishment, and therefore inextricably intertwined with a conservative social establishment.

The issues were at least as much social as religious and there was no easy correlation of theological conservatism and social conservatism. Princeton, in fact, was losing its conservative Presbyterian character at the very time it was becoming more elitist. In 1890 two-thirds of the students were Presbyterians. By the end of the Wilson administration that number was down to a little over one-third. Much of the shift, however, came from an increase in the number of Episcopalian students, who were even more likely than Presbyterians to be socially elitist, and probably less likely to be strict in religious principle.[45] When it came to admitting African-American students, social considerations clearly triumphed over religious concerns. The theologically conservative Princeton Seminary, in fact, was far ahead of the religiously more diverse college, admitting African Americans at least as early as the 1870s and thereby providing them an avenue to take graduate courses at the college or university. When in 1876 undergraduate students protested to James McCosh about a black thus enrolled in his psychology course, the Scotsman suggested that the protesters were perfectly free to drop the course. Even McCosh, however, could not change the undergraduate admissions policies.[46]

The question of admitting Jews on the one hand and of admitting African Americans or women on the other had quite opposite religious components. Blacks and women were excluded from the college *despite* the close affinities of some to the traditional Protestant heritage. Jews, on the other hand, would be at best second-class citizens so long as the institution kept a strong Christian identity.

The issue of conservative religion and social elitism was far from simple; the overwhelming tendency, however, was for the conservative religious establishment to be on the side of social conservatism. Princeton was in this respect more like a southern school than any of the other major universities. As was true throughout the South, the conservative religious establishment was saddled with the millstone of a conservative social establishment.

Woodrow Wilson's Christian program for Princeton recapitulated much of the course that had been set by the New England university builders. Theological and sectarian concerns were put safely aside in a private sphere. Yet their intention was not to secularize except in the strict sense of reducing church influence. Princeton was to serve the public as a model Christian community, with Christianity in this context defined as a moral system based on high ideals. In principle this community should have been inclusivist. In fact, however, Wilson's difficulties at Princeton were a microcosm of what eventually proved to be the undoing of the moral leadership of dominant twentieth-century Protestantism. Despite sincere proclamations of unifying and egalitarian moral ideals as the essence of the Christian spirit, their ideals were belied by the realities of a social establishment that white male Protestants controlled. Later in the century very similar moral ideals would contribute to the breakup of the social establishment's monopoly and, paradoxically, help bring the near abandonment of reference to Protestantism or Christianity as a basis for doing so.

Notes

1. Francis Patton, *Christian Theology and Current Thought* (n.p., 1883[?]), 61–62, quoted in Laurence R. Veysey, *The Emergence of the American University* (Chicago: University of Chicago Press, 1965), 52.

2. "Incredible" is the word Veysey uses of Patton in quoting the statement cited in note 1. He adds, "Patton, though over thirty years younger than McCosh, frequently sounded centuries older." Ibid.

3. Francis L. Patton, *Speech . . . . at the Annual Dinner of the Princeton Club of New York, March 15, 1888,* 4–6, Alumni Alcove Speer Library, Princeton University and William Berryman Scott, *Some Memories of a Palaeontologist* (Princeton, 1939), 203, both quoted in Paul C. Kemeny, "President Francis Landey Patton, Princeton University and Faculty Ferment," *American Presbyterians: The Journal of the Presbyterian Historical Society* 69 (1991), 113.

4. Patton, *Inauguration . . . . as President of Princeton College* (New York, 1888), 42f–43, quoted in Kemeny, "Patton," 116.

5. Francis Landey Patton to Woodrow Wilson, February 18, 1890, in *The Papers of Woodrow Wilson.* Vol. VI, 1888–1890, Arthur S. Link et al., eds. (Princeton: Princeton University Press, 1969), 527 (hereafter cited as *Papers of WW*). This was not the first time Wilson faced such issues. When he was hired at Bryn Mawr, President James E. Rhoads wrote to Wilson after their interview in 1884, "I feel assured that the moral and religious lessons of History will in thy hands be used to fortify a wide and comprehensive yet well-defined faith in Christianity." James E. Rhoads to Woodrow Wilson, December 1, 1884, quoted in John M. Mulder, *Woodrow Wilson: The Years of Preparation* (Princeton: Princeton University Press, 1978), 91.

6. Wilson to Albert Shaw, November 3, 1890, *Papers of WW,* VII:62. Quoted in Kemeny, "Patton," 116.

7. James Mark Baldwin, *Between Two Wars, 1861–1921 being Memories, Opinions and Letters Received* (Boston, 1926), I:341. From Kemeny, unpublished draft of "Patton."

8. Thomas Jefferson Wertenbaker, *Princeton, 1746–1896* (Princeton: Princeton University Press, 1946), 374–75. This debate in part reflected a difference between the Old School and the New School Presbyterian heritages. The Old School thought that since consumption of alcohol was not forbidden in Scripture, such questions of personal behavior were matters of Christian liberty. Some of the seminary faculty joined in the petition for the liquor license. The complaints came primarily from former New School areas such as New York.

9. Patton, *New York Herald,* January 21, 1898, quoted in Wertenbaker, *Princeton,* 375.

10. G. S. Smith, 74–93. Archibald Alexander Hodge, "Religion in the Public Schools," *New Princeton Review* 2 (January 1887), 28–47, is particularly revealing in this regard.

11. Wilson to Frederick Jackson Turner, November 15, 1896, *Papers of WW,* X:53.

12. Wilson to Turner, March 31, 1897, *Papers of WW,* X:201. Cf. Wilson to Ellen Axson Wilson, February 16, 1897, *Papers of WW,* X:164. And see accounts in Kemeny, "Patton," and in Henry Wilkinson Bragdon, *Woodrow Wilson: The Academic Years* (Cambridge, Mass.: Harvard University Press, 1967), 226.

13. Kemeny, "Patton," 118.

14. Hardin Craig, *Woodrow Wilson at Princeton* (Norman: University of Oklahoma Press, 1960), 31. Quoted in Kemeny unpublished version of "Patton."

15. Bragdon, *Academic Years,* 272. Bragdon provides a helpful picture of changing campus life.

16. Ibid., 274–77.

17. Wilson, Baccalaureate Address, June 12, 1904, from photocopy of manuscript reproduced in Mulder, *Years of Preparation,* 181.

18. Mulder, *Years of Preparation,* provides by far the best analysis of Wilson's religious views. On his view of higher criticism, Winthrop M. Daniels says, "I remember once asking him flatly it he thought it possible to maintain the traditional view of inspiration of the Scriptures. He said frankly that it was impossible; but the admission he made did not seem either to interest or disturb him overmuch." *Recollections of Woodrow Wilson* (New Haven: Privately printed, 1944), 39–40.

19. Wilson to John R. Mott, May 1, 1908, quoted in Mulder, *Years of Preparation,* 255–56.

20. Ibid., 7–8, 107–8.

21. Ibid., 108 and passim.

22. "The service of institutions of learning is not private but public," Wilson said in his Inaugural Address. "Princeton for the Nation's Service," Inaugural Address, October 25, 1902, *Papers of WW,* XIV:170.

23. Wilson, "Princeton in the Nation's Service," A Commemorative Address, October 21, 1896, *Papers of WW,* X:11–31.

24. Wilson, "The 1905 Baccalaureate Sermon," reprinted in John M. Mulder, "Wilson the Preacher: The 1905 Baccalaureate Sermon," *Journal of Presbyterian History* 51 (1973), 275.

25. Quoted from Arthur Walworth, *Woodrow Wilson* (Boston, 1965), 84, in Mulder, *Years of Preparation,* 178.

26. Ibid., 176–82. Mulder, "Wilson the Preacher."

27. Kemeny, "Patton," 118.

28. Quoted from a letter of Ellen Axson Wilson to Anna Harris, February 12, 1907, in Mulder, *Years of Preparation,* 187.

29. Wilson, A Supplementary Report to the Trustees, c. December 13, 1906, *Papers of WW,* XVI:523, quoted in Mulder, *Years of Preparation,* 191. This account is dependent especially on Mulder, 187–228 and Bragdon, *Academic Years,* 312–83.

30. Wilson to Cleveland Dodge, July 1, 1907, quoted in Bragdon, *Academic Years,* 322.

31. See, for instance statements by West quoted in George Marsden, *Fundamentalism and American Culture* (New York: University Press, 1980), 57, 67.

32. He also had criticized Eliot's Harvard for its laxity concerning required religious practices. Andrew West, "What Is Academic Freedom?" *North American Review* 140 (1885), 432–44.

33. Mulder, *Years of Preparation,* 204; cf. Bragdon, *Academic Years,* 271.

34. Andrew F. West, *The Graduate College of Princeton: With Some Reflections on the Humanizing of Learning* (Princeton: Princeton University Press, 1913), 28, 22, and passim.

35. Willard Thorp, "When Merwick Was the University's 'Graduate House,' 1905–1913," *Princeton History* 1 (1971), 50–71. Cf. Mulder, *Years of Preparation,* 207–8.

36. West's *Graduate College of Princeton* emphasizes the humanizing aspects of higher culture and is careful not to introduce religion directly but rather refers to philosophy as the culmination of human learning and adds, "Any questions behind this belong to the ultimate problem of religion" (35). Princeton Graduate School retained a reputation for a leisurely and nonprofessional atmosphere until after World War II and was accordingly not highly regarded by the academic specialists.

37. Veysey, *Emergence,* 244–48.

38. Speech to the Princeton Club of New York, April 7, 1901, *Papers of WW,* XX:348, quoted in Mulder, *Years of Preparation,* 220.

39. From news reports April 17 and 20, 1901, quoted in Mulder, *Years of Preparation,* 221–22.

40. Ibid., 226.

41. Leon M. Levy to Wilson, June 25, 1907, *Papers oj WW,* XIV:9. Thanks to Paul Kemeny for this citation.

42. Marcia Graham Synnott, *The Half-Opened Door: Discrimination and Admissions at Harvard, Yale, and Princeton, 1900–1970* (Westport, Conn.: Greenwood Press, 1979), esp. 160–98. The numbers of Jews matriculating rose from about five annually early in Wilson's term to about ten at the end. The number of Catholics enrolling stayed at only about fifteen per year.

43. Mulder, *Years of Preparation,* 189, 177. Kallen, later a founder of the New School for Social Research, was alleged to have been dismissed because of his religious views, although Mulder finds no evidence to support the accusation (177n).

44. Synott, *Half-Opened Door,* 175.

45. By the end of Wilson's era, Episcopalians nearly equaled Presbyterians in numbers; by the 1920s, when the club system was at the height of its powers, they surpassed them. Ibid., 176–77.

46. Ibid., 175.

14

The Low-Church Idea of a University

All the trends in the formation of the university as a modern American institution were accelerated with the spectacular emergence of the University of Chicago in the 1890s and early 1900s. Armed with John D. Rockefeller money and the brilliant imagination of the former wunderkind President William Rainey Harper, Chicago came to epitomize American pragmatism and enterprise applied to higher education. Like the great World's Columbian Exposition that opened on the adjacent Midway in 1893 during the university's first academic year, the school that seemed to arise from nowhere on a south-side marsh signaled that anything was possible in the modern world. And like the city of Chicago itself, the university embodied the startling American principle that there was no advantage in being bound by tradition. As the imposing Gothic architecture suggested, one could buy the appearance of tradition and thus duly impress a midwestern constituency.[1] The university proved also that one could buy a first-rate faculty and immediately become a leading national institution. This was the American way.

William Rainey Harper added a passion for innovation. Although not all of his schemes worked, his university anticipated many of the traits of the twentieth-century multiversity. In addition to the Graduate School and Divinity School, the university in its early decades included a College of Commerce and Administration, a College of Education, a Medical College, a Law School, and a College of Religious and Social Service. The undergraduate program was divided into a Junior College and a Senior College and was to be fed by affiliated high schools and lower schools. The university also introduced a summer school and was widely known for conducting an elaborate extension and correspondence program to broaden the base of higher education. Moreover, it moved toward affiliation with existing colleges around the country that were to become part of the Chicago system.

The brash, enterprising ethos of the university drew its critics, and it became commonplace to make commercial comparisons, referring to Chicago as a "department store," "a factory," "Ye Rich Rockefeller University," or, of course, "Harper's Bazaar."[2] Thorstein Veblen, who had been a junior member of Harper's original faculty but was soon asked to resign because of poor teaching and unorthodox life-style, used Chicago as his number one example in *The Higher Learning in America: A Memorandum on the Conduct of Universities by Business Men.* Veblen drafted his polemic early in the century, but out of respect delayed publication until long after Harper's death from cancer at age fifty in 1906. Veblen's extended complaint was that the operation of universities by businessmen on business principles was corrupting higher education as much as had the tyranny of clerical control. "Captains of erudition," of whom Harper was the prototype, were creating huge bureaucratic structures, based on principles of efficiency and promoted by crass advertising. All the innovations were oriented toward the practical, which threatened to replace true learning and scholarship. "Business house" universities were designed to indoctrinate citizens with the spirit of capitalism. "Through indoctrination with utilitarian (pecuniary) ideals of earning and spending, as well as engendering spendthrift and sportsmanlike habits, such businesslike management diverts the undergraduate students from going in for the disinterested pursuit of knowledge."[3] Scholarship itself had been preempted by "matter-of-fact" specialization and had become primarily a means of advertising by which a university trumpeted its own prestige.

Upton Sinclair followed Veblen's bitter attack with a better documented and even more scathing critique of his own, *Goose-Step: A Study of American Education,* published in 1922. Sinclair pointed out that from his own socialist perspective the vaunted freedom of American universities was a hoax. University professors were free to say anything just so long as it did not offend the plutocratic business interests which ran the institution. "Interlocking directorates" of universities were indistinguishable from those of the businesses that financed them. "The University of Standard Oil" under Harper was only one of many such instances in Sinclair's account, and not the worst. Nonetheless, in Sinclair's view, Rockefeller represented the epitome of the plutocracy's "pathetic trust in education, as something you could buy ready made for cash, the same as a political machine or a state railroad commission." Rockefeller's university was "Education F.O.B. Chicago." According to Sinclair the worst hypocrites were those who claimed God was on the side of big business. While he did not single out Rockefeller and Harper on this score, he treated their religious expressions as purely superficial.[4]

Absent the socialist overtones, the image of Harper's Chicago as manifesting the application of business principles to universities has persisted. In Laurence Veysey's definitive *The Emergence of the American University* this framework provides the dominant interpretive grid. Veysey's interpretation is built around an important insight. The rise of the American university from 1865 to 1910, he points out, can be divided in two eras, the age of idealist pioneers, lasting until about 1890, followed by an era of rapid expansion, rising prestige for university education, correspondingly large business support, and proliferation of university-related structures.

The dominating theme of the later era is the bureaucratization of the enterprise, related to its expansion. Although only 4 percent of Americans in the appropriate age group were attending colleges or universities in 1900, the function of universities for socializing the northern European Protestant elite was becoming increasingly important. Moreover, the expanded and diversified universities were designed to serve a wider constituency and thus anticipated a time in the later twentieth century when academic policy would be even more openly market-driven. Dependent on social, economic, and market forces, universities soon became remarkably alike and could not be guided by abstract ideals. The alienated academic intellectual who still stood for humane values was an unhappy by-product of this inexorable American tendency to run a university like a successful department store. At the top of such enterprises emerged, inevitably, managers replacing the earlier presidents, who had been men of vision.[5]

This interpretation does much to clarify our understanding of the emergence of the American university, but in the process of telling a compelling story it imposes too many of the traits of the mid-twentieth century onto the decades at the turn of the century. Nowhere is this more evident than in Veysey's treatment of William Rainey Harper.[6]

According to Veysey, Harper epitomizes "charisma without ideology." Moreover, Harper is representative of the other managers. His personality "meaningfully if at times almost comically caricatures the traits of the rising new group of academic executives." He had a fondness for organizational charts and "structural embellishments," so that his university was "unmistakably *over*-organized during its early years." Harper's mind was "basically untouched by the power of abstract ideas," so that "Chicago never clearly 'stood for' anything in the sense that Cornell had stood for democracy and Johns Hopkins had stood for research." Though Veysey recognizes the strongly Baptist origin of the university, he dismisses it by pointing out that the dominating Baptist views were of a liberal sort, that the university had token representation of Jews on the board and faculty from the beginning, and that the administration did not want to emphasize "the Baptist side" of their work. More telling traits, according to Veysey, are revealed by observing that "the University of Chicago represented a blending of the small-town promotional spirit of the adolescent Middle West with big-city standards of sophistication." Although the university had a talented faculty that made it "one of the liveliest, most creative academic establishments of the day," it nonetheless "was indeed rather like a factory in many respects."[7]

Although this characterization accentuates one important side of the evolution of American universities, there is no reason to assume that building a more efficient or bureaucratic organization is incompatible with a religiously based idealism.[8] Harper was indeed a quintessential organizer in the turn-of-the-century age of efficiency.[9] He had the traits that Veysey describes. Harper himself early suggested to Rockefeller that the new university should be "an educational trust."[10] Nonetheless, we can better understand the obsessive energy behind this relentless preoccupation with organization if we see that it was driven not simply by personal ambition (though Harper himself recognized its role),[11] but by a religious mission.

So at the same time that we can correctly see Chicago as an early prototype of what eventually became the bureaucratic multiversity, we should also understand it as a quintessential *Protestant* institution. Not only was it Protestant, but more particularly it was *low-church* Protestant. This fact has to some extent been successfully obscured by Gothic or classical architecture. Nonetheless, the low-church Protestant background is a basic clue to why American universities took on some of their characteristic traits. In fact, we can generalize more broadly by observing that because the United States is the only modern nation in which the dominant culture was substantially shaped by low-church Protestantism, we should expect the institutions of that dominant culture to bear indelible marks of that heritage. So with respect to American universities, their pragmatism, their traditionlessness, their competitiveness, their dependence on the market, their resort to advertising, their emphasis on freedom as free enterprise for professors and individual choice for students, their anti-Catholicism, their scientific spirit, their congeniality to business interests, and their tendency to equate Christianity with democracy and service to the nation, all reflect substantial ties to their low-church Protestant past. Of course, Protestantism is not the sole source of any of these traits and the relationship between Protestantism and modernity is complex. Nonetheless, the low-church Protestant heritage is a most revealing clue for understanding the shape of American universities.

A Baptist University

The University of Chicago arose out of the concern of Baptists that they were falling behind in the educational race in the West. Congregationalists and Presbyterians had, of course, disproportionate influence in education, but even the Methodists, who had been rising socially at about the same rate as the Baptists, had twenty-one colleges outside the East and five times as many students as the Baptists. While the Methodists could point to their Northwestern University near Chicago, the Baptist effort to sustain its "University of Chicago," begun in 1857, had never amounted to anything and it finally closed its doors in 1886. Part of the problem was that care for the founding and support of Baptist colleges was directly under the auspices of the denomination's American Home Mission Society, which was preoccupied with evangelism and church extension and for whom colleges were a subsidiary concern. Chicago Baptists, eager to revive the university idea as well as support their local Morgan Park Theological Seminary, persuaded the denomination to establish in 1888 a separate American Baptist Education Association. Thus they followed the precedent of other denominations in having a separate agency for this branch of home missions.[12]

The immense breakthrough for the Chicagoans, of course, was convincing John D. Rockefeller, Sr., that their city was the place to build a great new university. Rockefeller, a pious Baptist layman of a traditional sort, in typical American fashion saw competitive individualism as an expression of Christian calling, and thus apparently had little trouble reconciling Standard Oil's ruthless business practices with his sincere Christian belief. Moreover, he professed to see his money as a trust given by God for Rockefeller to administer for the benefit of God and fellow humans. A Christian university was wonderfully suited to such altruistic ambitions. Using one's fortune for founding a university was in vogue, for example, at Cornell, Johns Hopkins, Vanderbilt, and, more recently, Stanford and Clark. Unlike the others, Rockefeller did not attach his family name to his money and apparently saw a university as a way to serve both the church and the society on a broad basis.[13]

In choosing William Rainey Harper to head the new university the Chicago Baptists of the American Education Society were looking to one of their own. Born in 1856, the son of an observant Presbyterian storekeeper in New Concord, Ohio, the precocious Harper graduated from the local Muskingum College, a Presbyterian institution, before he was fourteen. After three years at home during which he honed his phenomenal language skills, he entered Yale in 1873 and in 1875, at age eighteen, he received his Ph.D. in the study of ancient languages. In 1876 he began teaching at Denison University in Ohio, a Baptist college. Toward the end of that year he had a conversion experience at a Baptist prayer meeting and subsequently joined that denomination. In 1879 he took a position teaching Hebrew at the denomination's Morgan Park Theological Seminary in what was then suburban Chicago.

From that time on the teaching of Hebrew and Old Testament Studies became an overriding passion for Harper. Most important, he revolutionized the study of Hebrew by making it popular. In 1881 he organized a summer school in Hebrew that became so popular that he conducted it each summer in various American cities and supplemented it with a successful correspondence program.

In 1883 Harper's enthusiasm for popular education was united with the larger vision of the Chautauqua movement. Headed by a Methodist former circuit rider, the Rev. John Heyl Vincent, Chautauqua brought a broad program of lay education to Victorian Americans. Upgrading the Methodist camp meeting tradition and merging it with the new vogue of summer vacation made possible by railroad transit, Chautauqua offered seven-week courses in subjects that might be found in a modern college curriculum. Although biblical and theological studies were offered as part of the program, the whole enterprise was regarded as religious on the basis that "all knowledge, religious or secular, is sacred."[14]

By 1887 Harper's organizational talents and enthusiasm for the Chautauqua vision brought him to the position of principal of the College of Liberal Arts, in charge of the national Chautauqua curriculum. So strong was his commitment to the Chautauqua ideal that in 1892, the same year that he was organizing the University of Chicago, he ignored the advice of the other founders and took on the position of principal of the entire Chautauqua educational system. Only after his failure to bring part of the Chautauqua program under the auspices of the University of Chicago did Harper give up his administrative role in the lay summer institutes. Nevertheless, Harper's Chautauqua connection is indicative of part of his vision for the University of Chicago and helps explain many of its popular features.

At the center of Harper's vision for lay education was, as James P. Wind has shown, his enthusiasm for biblical study, not only as the subject of his own prodigious scholarship, but also as the key to the redemption of American life. In 1895 he added as a postscript to a letter to the president of Vassar College, "You understand that my special business in the world is stirring up people on the English Bible. The University of Chicago is entirely a second hand matter."[15] Though this may have been hyperbole, during his Chicago years Harper was indeed continuing prodigious work in organizing national biblical study. By the turn of the century he was directing programs through the American Institute of Sacred Literature, which involved some 10,000 students all over the world in various phases of the program, including correspondence study and a network of summer courses. He himself continued to teach not only in these programs but at the University of Chicago as well. He also edited the *Biblical World,* a semipopular scholarly journal that claimed a wide audience. All the while he continued to publish biblical study aids and commentaries. He championed reestablishing biblical studies in public schools and making them a regular part of college curricula. Lest there be any danger that he might relax on weekends, he presided over his own Hyde Park Baptist Church Sunday School. He also championed Sunday school reform, and wrote his own Sunday school lesson series. He further was a principal organizer of the Religious Education Association, designed to coordinate his educational reforms. In short, Harper was the leading figure in an influential national movement, sometimes known as "the Bible Renaissance," that tried to put the Bible at the center of American cultural life.[16] His biblicism was a manifestation of a pervasive impulse in nineteenth-century popular Protestantism to find the key to salvation through a return to the purity of the biblical word.[17]

Harper's mission to sanctify the nation through biblical principles involved both Baptist and Methodist motifs. They were low church like the Baptists, emphasizing individual moral responsibility, freedom from external or traditional intellectual authority, a general disdain of tradition, appeals to a universal primitive authority, the importance of lay involvement on a voluntary basis, and the ad hoc practical nature of institutions.

Methodism, with equal emphasis on the practical and on reaching the people, was also anti-elitist. Schools in these traditions were typically co-ed, as was Chicago. More directly than anything else Methodism brought a tradition of efficient organization. The Chautauqua network was an extension of Methodist technique. It often has been observed that the dominant culture in nineteenth-century America took on a Methodist hue; it might be added that the turn-of-the century cult of efficiency, of which Harper was such a conspicuous example, had some of its earliest precedents in the rise to dominance of Wesley's followers through efficient method.

In the low-church American Protestant tradition, the institutional church often had little standing except as a convenient pragmatic device to facilitate God's work in the individual heart and in the nation. For many American Protestants, these were the most interesting loci of God's work anyway. People outside the church could easily be shown the value of transformation in these self-evidently important areas. Liberal Protestantism like Harper's accentuated these tendencies. Individual salvation was not so much a dramatic shift from the lost to the saved as it was a matter of building individual character. The goals of the institutional church were hardly distinguishable from those of the nation. The national covenant was a matter of extending a combination of individualistic and unifying democratic ideals and thereby advancing the Kingdom of God.

The Bible was, as James Wind shows,[18] the pivotal link connecting all of Harper's ideals. He believed that his democratic and individualistic values were derived from the Bible and that a religious motive was necessary if these ideals were to be universally adopted. Moreover, his progressive understanding of the Bible was founded on the firm foundation of science, which in turn was dependent on freedom for the search for God's truth. To complete the circle, modern education at all levels, particularly when integrated with the teaching of modern scientific higher critical principles of biblical study, was the best path to truly Christian and democratic ideals.

The task of restoring the Bible to its foundational place in American life was a mission not primarily against paganism but against Christian superstition, particularly biblical superstition. Popular Protestantism's benighted prescientific readings of Scripture were discrediting Christianity and had brought it to the precipice of a vast cultural disaster. One of Harper's most frequently reiterated themes was that traditional Bible teaching was an embarrassment, unworthy of the faith of modern educated persons. Such naive "bibliolatry" opened up Christianity to "the sneers of an Ingersoll."[19] "It is the misinterpretation of the Bible that furnishes the occasion of all skepticism," he wrote in an editorial in the *Biblical World* in 1894. "The friends of the Bible have been its worst enemies. A faith in the Bible constructed upon a scientific basis will be acceptable to everyone who will take the pains to look at it."[20] So just as passionately as Harper advocated the integration of the new biblical study into all levels of American education, he insisted on the exclusion of the old.

"We may frankly acknowledge," he emphasized in 1904, "that the methods employed almost universally twenty-five years ago in connection with the study of the Scriptures—methods still in vogue in many quarters—were unworthy, not only of the subject itself, but of any place in an institution of higher learning."[21]

This outlook had evolved in the course of his own career as a biblical scholar. Harper was both reared in and converted to fairly traditional evangelicalism and in his earlier years as a biblical scholar he was in the camp of the moderate critics who attempted to preserve the essentials of traditional historical understandings of Scripture. During the 1880s, however, Harper was gradually persuaded by more radical views, especially by the influential new views of Julius Wellhausen, which dismantled any notion of the Mosaic authorship of the Pentateuch. In 1886 Harper went from Morgan Park to Yale. There in the more diverse atmosphere of the East, in the era of the Andover liberals, Harper openly became a champion of more liberal views. By the time he was called to Chicago, he hesitated in part over concern that the atmosphere might be too restricted for his higher critical outlook.[22]

At Yale Harper's popularity as a teacher as well as the liberal evangelical ethos of the school helped him in launching what became a national campaign to introduce the study of the Bible as a regular part of college curricula. For Harper this was but one part of his larger effort to make Bible study an integral part of American education at every level. Since Yale was still the model for many other schools, the cause gained national credibility with Harper's appointment in 1890 to the first chair of English Bible at Yale. A similar chair was instituted at the University of Michigan in 1893 and biblical courses entered the curriculum of many schools, across the country, both public and private. As president of Chicago Harper continued to teach, locating his Department of Old Testament and Semitic Studies in the university rather than the Divinity School.[23]

Harper shared with many of his contemporaries enthusiasm about the powers of "scientific study" to settle longstanding human debates in all areas. He accordingly justified the inclusion of the Bible and other distinctly religious subjects in the broadening university curriculum on the grounds that they could now be studied scientifically. There were "laws of religious life" just as there were laws of health and physical life. Yet "men and women of the highest intelligence in matters of life and thought are discovered to be cultivating a religious life far below the plane of their intellectual life." Advances in the scientific study of religion, not only in biblical studies, but notably also in the psychology of religion, now made possible a scientific approach to this part of life as much as any other.[24]

The addition of the Bible to the curriculum had ambiguous implications for the role of Christianity in universities. In the old-time colleges the authority of the Bible was simply taken for granted and implicitly related to much else that went on. Now the Bible would be studied as simply another subject alongside all the rest, if it was studied at all.

Harper did not see the scientific study of religion as at all opposed to true religious faith and practice. Scientific biblical studies, he believed, revealed the irreducibly supernatural and divine elements of Scripture, once the human elements were clearly discerned.[25] Religious education, furthermore, was analogous the physical education and should be included in the university curriculum for comparable reasons. Both sought to develop a crucial aspect of human experience that was now becoming much better understood through scientific study, but in which practice was essential. A similar analogy could be drawn to the study of medicine. There was room for pure research, but always with an eye to applications. Such an outlook fitted Harper's characteristic combination of the scientific and the practical. Though he revered the Johns Hopkins research ideal, he shared some of the suspicions of other turn-of-the-century critics regarding specialized research for its own sake. Practical applications were essential. So with respect to religion, he declared in 1904, "The university in its laboratory of practical religion should encourage the development of the altruistic spirit, for this is an essential part of the religious spirit. . . . In settlement work and in a thousand other ways, opportunity is open. This is a real part of the religious life which may not be neglected, and for which the university should make ample provision."[26]

In an age when dominant American Protestantism seemed to be taking on an activist methodistic hue, emphasizing practice over doctrinal traditionalism, Harper's practical piety, his activism, and his biblicism helped allay the suspicions of orthodox Baptist critics. In the early days of the University of Chicago, John D. Rockefeller's views were the biggest concern. Rockefeller had a conventional layperson's views of Scripture and some rivals of Harper attempted to capitalize on the biblical scholar's heterodoxy.[27] What assured Harper's acceptability, however, was that he was unquestionably a champion of the practical use of the Bible. While some orthodox theologians, including the Princetonians, attacked Harper's views, and rumors about liberal views of Scripture could be damaging, in the long run most practical Christians were not likely to quarrel long with so noble an enterprise. Harper, after all, was proposing to do with the new theology what the old theology could no longer do: put the Bible at the center of American cultural life.

Compared with other university benefactors such as Ezra Cornell, Jonas Clark, or the Stanfords, Rockefeller generally kept his distance from the direct governance of his university. Nonetheless, he did on occasion intervene, or at least express his concerns. Particularly he wanted to be sure that his enterprise was overtly Christian. Soon after the university opened in 1892, Harper responded to an inquiry with reassurances:

> We were all glad to learn anew of your deep personal interest in the religious condition of the university. . . . From the beginning . . . every possible effort has been made . . . to emphasize the fact that the institution is a Christian institution. Their first service was the chapel service. . . . The first general University lecture was a Bible lecture attended by hundreds. The first faculty meeting was opened with prayer, an order

> not customary even in our theological seminaries. . . . Every faculty meeting in every department has since then been opened in the same manner.[28]

Rockefeller occasionally also expressed concern about faculty mores, particularly public drinking and undignified speculation on the stock market.[29] He also told Harper in 1896 that he had "received many letters from many parts of the country complaining of the attitude which the university has seemed to take regarding the Bible," and he suggested that a proposed new theological journal be published by the Divinity School, where it could be under the purview of the denomination, rather than simply that of the university. Harper, however, consistent with his conviction that biblical study was central to the university itself, published the new *American Journal of Theology* under the name of the university with no mention of the Divinity School. Thus defiantly to ignore his benefactor's wishes and possibly to raise Rockefeller's ire was a substantial risk for so practical an administrator as Harper to take. So far as his major life's work was concerned, he was far from lacking ideology.[30]

It helped that Rockefeller apparently accepted the premise that a true university would have to allow freedom of expression and that this principle would have to apply to a Christian university as well. Although Rockefeller occasionally relayed complaints he had heard about supposedly radical remarks by progressive faculty members, he did so without much pressure, and the university was relatively free by the standards of the time.[31] A case that occurred in 1905 was especially revealing of the connections of this attitude to Christianity. Frederick T. Gates, Rockefeller's trusted personal secretary, who handled all his university business and correspondence, directly answered a complaint about a remark attributed to an anthropologist, Frederick Starr. After stating that he did not know anything about Starr or the alleged remarks and that he knew how upsetting radical opinions could be, just as conservative opinions must be upsetting to radicals, he added:

> I do not know of any way in the world by which we can arrive at the truth except by letting everybody speak out what he believes to be the truth within the limits of public morality. And it seems to me that there is no place on earth where this liberty of utterance should be so carefully guarded and cherished as in an institution of learning which at least pretends to be a place of impartial research. The fact that such an institution is founded by private money or denominational money seems to me to make no sort of difference and must not be allowed to interfere in the smallest degree with this freedom of inquiry, freedom of opinion, and freedom of utterance. Indeed, it seems to me to be one of the chief glories of the Christian religion and of the Baptist Church that it frankly dares to found precisely such an institution.[32]

Gates did restrict university freedom with the catchall qualifier, "within the limits of public morality," which meant that the dominant middle-class culture and especially the business community would take over the role of the church in defining an orthodoxy. For faculty who were essentially middle class in their outlooks, this allowed some latitude, although they could not openly advocate anarchism or alcohol. Carrying to the extreme the low-church Protestant tendency to undercut the authority of the institutional church, the ideals of the dominant society took over the role of setting moral boundaries. The ideals of the mainline Protestant churches merged with those of society, which was appropriate enough for the "nation with the soul of a church." So a "free" and "Christian" university made sense. On the other hand, leading Protestant educators viewed a "Catholic university" as an oxymoron and would apply the same principles to any ecclesiastical pretensions of their own denominations to set limits for academia.

William Rainey Harper was particularly explicit (though otherwise not widely different from his contemporary university builders) in attempting to build the university on principles of a broad new Christianity that was a way of life that permeated everything, rather than a narrow set of doctrines. The university conducted daily chapel services, but it soon made attendance voluntary, partly because of the lack of a place for all to assemble. Later in Harper's administration weekly chapel was required for various divisions of the university, including a Thursday chapel for graduate students. The massive Rockefeller Chapel was not built until the 1920s, one of the clearest cases of a building erected in memory of a fading religious spirit. During Harper's day, the situation was the opposite. A building was not a high priority because Christianity was not to be confined to one locus but was to pervade academic life.

The university itself was to be like a church community. Harper apparently regarded the YMCA and YWCA as too narrowly evangelical in 1892 and instead instituted a Christian Union. A remarkable and revealing aspect of this agency was that all members of the university were automatically nominal members of it. The original university faculty of about one hundred included three Jews, as well as a dozen without ecclesiastical ties, though no Roman Catholics.[33] The student body, although also overwhelmingly Protestant, included some Catholics and Jews as well.[34] The university chaplain, Charles R. Henderson, explained that although Christians led worship at university services, "this does not exclude other dialects of the common faith of the world, and the freedom to voice the deeper feelings of the soul in any form hallowed by reverence and family associations is permitted and encouraged."[35] In 1901 Christian Union membership was made voluntary, though it remained open to all.

Harper's zeal for community was reflected as well when in 1896 he added to the university governance a body known as the Congregation, composed not only of all administrators and faculty, but also of Ph.D.s of the university, various other alumni, and representatives of affiliated institutions. Major policy decisions were to be discussed by the Congregation, thus integrating the university community with the wider constituency it was to serve. Having no real authority, this unwieldy structure proved superfluous and faded from prominence.[36]

More significant in actually building community and more explicitly Christian was the role of sports. True to Harper's broad vision of twentieth-century education, intercollegiate athletics would be integrated into the university program. The rationale was, however, a typically Victorian moral one. Sports built character and community. In these respects sports were extensions of the practical work of the church. Consistent with this philosophy, Harper hired as his director of athletics, with full faculty status, the prototype of the Christian collegiate athlete, Amos Alonzo Stagg. When Harper had arrived at Yale, Stagg was in the midst of his collegiate career as a revered baseball star. Stagg also helped build Yale football dominance and was the central figure in the new cult of Yale athletics. At the same time, Stagg was also a leader in establishing the social prominence of the Yale YMCA, Dwight Hall. During a fifth year, Stagg served as student secretary of Dwight Hall and continued to play on the Yale teams. He was beginning divinity studies and had taken a course from Harper. He came to the conclusion, however, that he could do more to serve the cause of Christ in Christian athletics than in the ordained ministry. When he was invited to Chicago he feared that Harper might be too much of an intellectual to support sports, but he was immediately assured that the president saw the value of winning teams who could go "around the country and knock out all the colleges." His work, Stagg reflected, would not only create "college spirit," "best of all, it will give me such a fine chance to do Christian work among the boys who are sure to have the most influence. Win the athletes of any college for Christ, and you will have the strongest working element attainable in college life."[37]

Football could do for the universities much of what liberal Christianity hoped for. Much more effectively than chapel, it could bring the whole community together in one place and unite them in a cause. It could also serve better than the church for enlisting the loyalties of the surrounding community. It could be viewed also as a way, on a voluntary basis, to domesticate student rowdiness. Student uprisings did not entirely disappear, but football could be one way of channeling the energy in a voluntary society.[38] The problem, of course, was to keep football from making matters worse. The problem of violence on the field in the era before elaborate protective gear was a serious one and eventually had to be attacked. Moreover, the sports life could be associated with the vices that were a large part of the free and leisurely style that was so attractive in collegiate life. The abstemious Stagg (who lived to be one hundred) worked hard to clean up this image, encouraging athletes to shun smoking and drinking. He also helped invent and regulate modern football, bringing to the game innovations such as the forward pass, which helped his Chicago teams become major powers in the Big Ten.

Stagg viewed his calling, not just as coach but as head of the University of Chicago Department of Physical Culture and Athletics, as fully in sympathy with Harper's liberal Protestant vision. In his autobiography, Stagg quoted approvingly the great liberal preacher Lyman Abbot's summary of the Harper vision:

> The distinguishing characteristic of the German university is scholarship. The spirit of the English university is culture. President Harper has built a university in terms of service. The older college of the English type produces gentlemen. The newer college of the German type produces scholars; and doubtless the University of Chicago produces both. The scholarship which the first has regarded as a means and measure of self-development, and the second as an end in itself, the third has regarded as a preparation for active American life.[39]

As for many liberal Protestants, the United States was Harper's church. This was consistent with his ultra low-church principles. So in his Presidential Report of 1902, reviewing the first ten years, Harper could emphasize that "the position of the University of Chicago religiously has been definitely and professedly Christian." This was so, he noted, despite substantial Jewish contributions, and the presence of Jews on the board, on the faculty, and in the student body. Moreover, it did not make any difference that there were no religious tests and that the faculties were drawn from people of almost every religious communion, and "many who were not members of any church." Nonetheless, "as the country of which we are citizens is a Christian country, so the University of Chicago is a Christian institution."[40]

The University as Home Missionary Society

"All my work," William Rainey Harper wrote to a correspondent in 1905, "is in a very fundamental sense missionary work."[41] Consistent with his Chautauqua and low-church background and his programs in which the university took over functions of a church, Harper often made the missionary imperative explicit. Among most other university leaders of the era, the cultural mission was more implicit. Nonetheless, Harper's quite acceptable explicitness provides a revealing clue to a major motif of university building.

Harper's explicit talk of a Christian mission was acceptable to other leading educators, including even professors, because his Christianity was so thoroughly equated with American democracy. In a talk to Chicago students, "America as a Missionary Field," this equation was the major motif. World history, Harper proclaimed, is approaching "the American period." These would be "the best days for civilization," he affirmed with progressive and postmillennial overtones typical of the day. Later generations would recognize the insights of this age as "new revelations of God." Such insights would come through science, but especially through recognition of "the paramount dignity of the individual." Harper virtually equated individualism with Christianity.

> The question of individualism as a whole is still on trial; the real test of Christianity's success is still in the future. She cannot be said to have achieved final success until her founder Jesus Christ has been everywhere recognized. The arena in which the great trial shall be conducted is America. The old countries with their traditions and institutions which obstruct their performance of full human functions by the masses, cannot work at the problems that confront us.

Advanced Christianity and America, which was freed from "dead institutions and deadly traditions" (that is, Catholicism and monarchy), were both on trial. But traditional evangelicalism by itself would not meet the test. "The gospel as it is commonly understood . . . is not sufficient. It will free men from vice and impurity, but when thus freed the converts would better be permitted to die, unless they are provided with an education which will free them from narrowness, prejudice, and dishonesty." Traditional evangelization without education was worse than nothing. "Education will be the watchword [of] the new Christianity." Here was America's Christian mission to the world. "It is a call to establish here at home the foundations for the evangelization of the world; for if the world is to be evangelized, America must do it."[42]

Since the traits of democracy were, in Harper's views, easily interchanged with those of Christianity, he could as readily apply his missionary vision to state schools as to church-related ones. Such an equation was indeed prominent in his best known discourse on the nature and destiny of the university, "The University and Democracy," delivered at Founders' Day ceremonies at the University of California in 1899 and assigned first place in his 1905 collection, the *Trend in University Education.*

Drawing on his Old Testament studies and on an analogy to the familiar formula that Jesus Christ was a prophet, priest, and king, Harper summarized his message: "Democracy has been given a mission to the world, and it is of no uncertain character. I wish to show that the university is the prophet of this democracy, as well, its priest and its philosopher; that in other words, the university is the Messiah of the democracy, its to-be-expected deliverer."[43]

In Harper's view, universities were archetypical democratic institutions because they stood for freedom. "The three birth-marks of a university are, therefore, self-government, freedom from ecclesiastical control, and the right of free utterance." In other words the three marks of the university were—freedom, freedom, and freedom. "And these," Harper added in a sentiment sure to be as popular in California as it was important to him, had "given it the right to proclaim itself an institution of the people, an institution born of the democratic spirit." "The state," Harper elaborated, "has no more right than the church to interfere with the search for truth, or with its promulgation when found." States as well as churches might have their schools for indoctrination for special purposes, such as military schools or theological seminaries. "But such schools are not universities."[44]

A university's search for truth made it a holy place. No sacred ascription was too high in describing its service to Democracy's religion. So Harper elaborated in a virtual three-point sermon the analogies between the work of the university and the biblical service of prophet, priest, and philosopher. (The Old Testament expectation of a king "was only an adaptation to the monarchy," but when Jesus came, he was not the expected sort of king, but more a philosopher, "a democratic spirit.")

This democratic religion was frankly humanist, but still Christian. "Its god is mankind, humanity; its altar, home; its temple, country." It creed was "brotherhood," its ethics "righteousness." At the same time:

> In this religion there is much of Judaism, and likewise much of Christianity. This was to be expected, for it was Jeremiah of olden time who first preached the idea of individualism, the idea that later became the fundamental thought in the teaching of Jesus Christ, the world's greatest advocate of democracy; while the supplementary idea of solidarity, the corollary of individualism, was first preached by Ezekiel, and likewise later developed into Christianity.[45]

John Dewey and the Religion of Democracy

Once we notice Harper's tendency to conflate Christianity and democracy, it becomes apparent that his view was not functionally much different from that of John Dewey, eventually the best known of the early Chicago faculty members. When Dewey was being considered for the position for which he was to leave Michigan for Chicago in 1894, James F. Tufts, who had earlier made the same move, assured Harper in a letter of recommendation that Dewey was "a man of a religious nature, is a church member, and believes in working with the church. He is, moreover, actively interested in practical ethical activity, and is a valued friend at the Hull House in this city."[46] Dewey himself had proclaimed, in sentiments much like Harper's, that a democracy is "a society in which the distinction between the spiritual and the secular has ceased, and as in Greek theory, as in the Christian theory of the Kingdom of God, the church and the state, the divine and the human organization of society are one."[47] The major difference was that Dewey recognized earlier than most of his contemporaries that in such an equation the church was superfluous. So when he arrived in Chicago Dewey, who was also abandoning the Hegelianism that had sustained his theism, took the occasion to allow his church membership to lapse. At the same time, he was a board member of Jane Addams's Hull-House and, as Robert Crunden argues, Dewey like Addams was prototypic of that generation of progressives who, as their traditional theological beliefs receded, compensated with a corresponding increase in social idealism and activism.[48]

At the University of Chicago Dewey was the head both of the Department of Philosophy and of a new Department of Pedagogy (later Education) in which he established his experimental school, where he tested his progressive theories of education. Both in developing what became his instrumentalist philosophy and in his accompanying action-oriented educational theory, Dewey proved himself a kindred spirit to Harper. Dewey and Harper both believed in the redemptive functions of education. Dewey viewed the public schools as virtually the new established church, teaching the values of American democracy. Though Dewey had worked out the theory further than Harper, each believed that science was the key to finding unifying communitarian values, because only through science could one eliminate superstitions and sectarian differences and thus build an inclusivist "community of truth."[49] Dewey's talk, presented to the students at Michigan, "Christianity and Democracy," and Harper's "Democracy and the University," despite some obvious differences, were two of a kind.

In this context of mutual concern to build a democratic or Christian community, it made little practical difference that Dewey had jettisoned his own church life and at Chicago spoke less explicitly of the Christian side of the equation. Just as at the convention of the Progressive (Bull Moose) party as late as 1912 the delegates could unite to sing "Onward Christian Soldiers,"[50] regardless of their personal beliefs, so at the progressive University of Chicago, Christian service, not theology or church practice, was the test of faith.

Dewey had a falling out with Harper and left for Columbia in 1904; but the evidence does not support the later supposition that Dewey's turn from the church contributed to the rift. The problem at the time was that Harper had a tendency to promise more than he could deliver and Dewey felt constantly frustrated in implementing his grand vision, especially for his experimental school. The touchy question, which may easily have been decisive, of the employment of Dewey's wife, Alice, was also involved.[51] So far as religion is concerned, however, Harper was careful to emphasize, doubtless sincerely, that religious tests should have absolutely nothing to do with employment at the university. Even the Rockefellers, who were more traditional Baptists, apparently regarded Dewey highly and did not raise any question about his church life.[52] As for Harper, when he organized the Religious Education Association in 1903, he included Dewey as one of the speakers at the first convention, and so evidently regarded him as still more-or-less within the fold.[53]

Sociology as the Last Flowering of Moral Science

Although one could find the functional equivalent of Protestantism shaping nearly every academic discipline at the turn of the century, the academic field most closely matched to what the University of Chicago stood for was sociology. In fact, when it opened in 1892 Chicago was the first university to include sociology as a full-fledged separate discipline. To head the new field, Harper brought to Chicago Albion W. Small, president of Colby College in Maine. Small, who had studied at Johns Hopkins and in Germany, was the principal founder of the discipline of sociology in the United States. In 1896 he began the *American Journal of Sociology* and he secured Chicago's place as a leader in the discipline.

Small was a man after Harper's own heart. He was a serious Baptist with ministerial training and dedicated above all to establishing a practical Christianity.[54] His continuities with the ideals of the old moral philosophy were direct; he had taught "Mental and Moral Philosophy" to the seniors at Colby. Concerned to reach a larger audience, he readily involved himself in Chautauqua work, co-authoring his first book, *An Introduction to the Study of Sociology* (1894), with George E. Vincent, Chautauqua's founder, for use in the summer programs. Sociology for Small had a practical moral purpose and was a means of inspiring people to take part in understanding and resolving society's problems, especially through charitable institutions such as Hull-House. At the same time Small was eager to establish the discipline on a scientific basis. In Germany, where he married the daughter of a general, he acquired a taste, typical of the sociological reformers, for German versus the more conservative British classical economics approaches to understanding society. Small regarded the German views, based on evolutionary models of a progressing community of ideals, as more scientific than classical economics. Thus the high calling to research was of one piece with progressive moral reform. "The first commandment with promise for graduate schools," declared Small, mimicking the *Westminster Shorter Catechism* on the Sabbath commandment, "is: Remember the research ideal, to keep it holy!"[55]

Small, like so many of his academic contemporaries, thus combined moral idealism (often explicitly Christian idealism) with a positivist faith in scientific progress, based on an "objective" research ideal that would guide the evolution of society.[56] Dorothy Ross, in her account of the origins of American sociology, attributes its distinctive qualities to the need to justify American exceptionalism. Accepting Ross's insight, we should go one step further and recognize that at the heart of American exceptionalism for these elite men was their Protestantism. As the republican and Whig traditions of earlier eras had taught, what made the United States exceptional were traits of its Protestant heritage related to freedom, free inquiry, morality, individual and communal values, and democracy.[57]

The mentor of Small and of the cadre of like-minded Christian social scientists and progressive reformers was Richard T. Ely. Born in 1854 into a well-known family of New York Presbyterian controversialists, Ely joined the Episcopal Church, in which he could safely distance himself from Calvinist theology while championing a liberalized version of its ideal of Christian social transformation. After graduating from Columbia, he studied in Germany where he became interested in economics and was converted to the German historicist outlook. In 1881 he gained a position at Johns Hopkins and he remained there until 1892. During that time he taught a remarkable group of students and was particularly influential in shaping the views of a number of the founders of the American social sciences, including John R. Commons, Albion Small, Edward A. Ross, Albert Shaw, Thomas Nixon Carver, Frederic C. Howe, and Edward Bemis. Ely is well described, as his principal biographer puts it, as "a missionary and an evangelist to the American public."[58] He was a regular Chautauqua lecturer in the era when Harper was in charge and missed being on the first Chicago faculty only because some complicated negotiations broke down. In 1892 Frederick Jackson Turner, another former student, aided in bringing him to the University of Wisconsin, which Ely helped build into a center for Christian reformist views.

The Christian side of Ely's school of thought was controversial not so much because it was Christian as because it was mildly socialist. Ely, who was an early exponent of the social gospel and of most of the reforms that were implemented in the Progressive era, believed that the key to social progress was the Christian ideal of brotherhood. At the center of this ideal was love to neighbor, as taught in the Sermon on the Mount. The benefits of applying this principle to society, he believed, were better grounded on empirical evidence than were the "a priori" views of the British school. William Graham Sumner's defense of untrammeled free enterprise was the most objectionable example of the British method. The state, Ely believed, was the principal agency through which Christian moral principles should be implemented in modern times. In 1885 Ely was a principal organizer of the American Economics Association to promote his anti–laissez-faire views of a "practical Christianity." Ely also explicitly called for an alliance of church and state in promoting this application of advanced Christian principles to economic science.[59] Twenty of the original members of the AEA were either active or recently active clergy. From the outset some in the organization were uncomfortable with its Christian socialism. When in 1892 Ely, as the secretary, singlehandedly moved the annual meeting to Chautauqua, New York, near his home town, he precipitated a rebellion that alienated him from the organization. Those who called for a more professional atmosphere also stood for a more conservative economics.[60]

In the highly charged political atmosphere of the early 1890s, the question arose as to whether the reputedly radical views of Ely and his friends were appropriate to a university. Ely himself was one of the first to be attacked. In 1894 the Wisconsin superintendent of public instruction, an ex officio member of the Regents of the University of Wisconsin, publicly attacked Ely and brought charges against him to the regents. Wells claimed that Ely had personally encouraged striking printers in Madison in 1893, that he had threatened to participate in a boycott against a company, and that his works encouraged these subversive practices. The backlash against unions and strikes was so strong in 1894 that confirmation of a professor's activity in a strike would have cost him his job. Ely, who despite all his radicalism was a gentleman reformer (he was, after all, an Episcopalian), realized the gravity of the threat to his work. Since the charges were much overblown, he chose to center his defense on denying them rather than defending his right to participate in strikes. In fact, he conceded, had he indeed participated his removal would have been justified. Ely's defense was successful and he was exonerated by the regents.[61]

The University of Chicago got burned, or at least singed, by the fires of reaction to labor agitation. Edward W. Bemis, another one of Ely's students, who was teaching in the extension division, was not rehired by the university in 1895. Bemis had taken the side of labor during the tense days of the Pullman Strike and was vocal in criticizing the monopolistic tactics of the Gas Trust in the city of Chicago. Harper, who did criticize Bemis's views, denied that his teachings were the reason for the dismissal. Bemis was not attracting enough students in his extension work to pay his way. Bemis and his allies such as Richard T. Ely and Edward A. Ross, as well as a good bit of public opinion, were always convinced that was not the true reason.[62] The implications of the Bemis case were indecisive, however. Harper, who apparently had legitimate practical reasons for dropping the economist, was in general a defender of academic freedom, continued to invite Ely to Chautauqua, and was a close friend of Small. On the other hand, it is difficult to believe that Harper's expressed disagreement with Bemis's prolabor stance had nothing to do with the action.

Populism at Stanford

The most notorious case of direct external interference was that which brought the dismissal of another of the Ely circle, Edward A. Ross, from Stanford in 1900. The Leland Stanford Junior University, founded in 1885 and opened in 1891 as a memorial to the late son of the railroad tycoon, Leland Stanford, and his wife, Jane Lathrop Stanford, was widely perceived as a close parallel to Chicago. It differed, however, in that it cultivated a more genteel atmosphere that reflected the close paternalistic involvement of the founders. With the death of Leland, Sr., in 1893 this relationship became intensely maternalistic as Mrs. Stanford devoted her benevolent energies to the personal oversight of the memorial institution.

From its beginnings the religious stance at Stanford was the vaguely Christian nontheological, nonsectarian, theistic, romantic, moral idealism toward which most other institutions were moving. David Starr Jordan, whom the Stanfords brought from the presidency of Indiana University to be the founding president, was congenial to this outlook, occasionally attending a Unitarian church while at Stanford. Jordan, a zoologist, was even more than most of his generation enamored of the implications of evolutionary science. His positivism was so pronounced that he was capable of stating that "to say that the university is scientific is to say that it is genuine, that it is devoted to realities, not to make-believes and shams."[63] Nonetheless, Jordan described himself as a "Puritan moralist" and stood for high ideals, community, and a positive outlook, all of which Mrs. Stanford could approve.[64]

The religious stance of the Stanfords' university was expressed most vividly in its architecture. The designers rejected not only the medieval pretensions of the Gothic, but also the alternative massive classicism, which was adopted at the nearby Berkeley campus, for example, a few years later. Stanford's motif was Mediterranean, which suited the California setting. Fitting with the rest of the design was the central building, the Memorial Church, which was Byzantine, suggesting the more mystical Eastern piety. More revealing still was the mosaic on the chapel facade, which dominates the view as one approaches the university. There one sees an idyllic scene, reminiscent of the Sermon on the Mount, representing Christ welcoming the righteous into the Kingdon of God.

When conjoined with Jordan's statements regarding science, one could not find a better representation of the essence of the original conception of the American university. Though the business of the university rested on scientific realities, rising above were still higher principles of Christ's nonsectarian righteousness.

Edward Ross's outspoken populist radicalism, which favored the workers who actually lived in rural settings, did not fit Mrs. Stanford's view of righteousness. Her expectation for professors was that they would be Republican. That could be taken for granted of most professors almost as much as that they would be Protestant. Indeed, fifty Stanford professors took out an ad for McKinley in 1896. If someone were a Democrat, he should at least be a gentleman, meaning polite enough to be quiet about his politics. Ross, however, was one of the younger cadre who dared to violate such expectations. He had strong sympathies for labor and for rural populism and in 1896 spoke out vigorously for Bryan. Mrs. Stanford privately expressed to Jordan her opinion that Ross should be removed and in 1897, acting as the sole trustee, she banned any faculty participation in political campaigns. Jordan defended Ross and successfully sheltered him from Mrs. Stanford's attacks for several years (though he did not prevent her from effecting the removal in 1898 of another sociologist, H. H. Powers, after she had heard him at a student meeting give a pessimistic talk that belittled religious idealism). In 1900, however, Ross, who was determined not to have his academic freedom inhibited, again spoke out clearly on the labor side of issues.

This time Mrs. Stanford was not to be stopped and Jordan capitulated, preferring compromise of principle to loss of the university endowment. The American Economics Association meeting in 1900, in an action that anticipated the formation of the American Association of University Professors by some of the same people fifteen years later, appointed an investigating committee. This committee criticized Stanford's action, but its report had no force other than moral suasion. Nonetheless, in a chain reaction at Stanford seven additional professors resigned in protest over the Ross case. Mrs. Stanford never changed her views but gave up her sole trusteeship of the university in 1903. Ross eventually joined Ely at Wisconsin in 1906.[65] By this time, however, tensions between business supporters of that university and radical professors were beginning to subside. Already in the 1890s Ely and some of his disciples had distanced themselves from the more radical socialists and by the 1900s progressive reforms were becoming more popular among the dominant middle classes.[66] In *Sin and Society,* published in 1907, Ross included a vigorous letter of endorsement from the Republican president, Theodore Roosevelt.[67]

The revealing irony of the case of Ross at Stanford, which makes this subsequent convergence less surprising, is how close the two sides were in their underlying religious commitments. Like so many of the academic leaders, Ross had been brought up as a strict Presbyterian but had rebelled against theological sectarianism, adopting instead an evolutionary outlook that sought the realization of unifying moral ideals. To Ross, this was a vision of the Kingdon of God in America based on science as represented in the universities and on justice toward all who labored and were heavy laden. It was also a distinctly Protestant vision of a culture of assimilation into the highest ethical ideals. Thus in retrospect Ross looks unprogressive in his advocacy of immigration restrictions on "unassimilable" peoples, such as Asians, and Jews, Catholics, or Eastern Orthodox from eastern or southern Europe. Ross's populism was of the sort that championed the rural Protestant worker. Prohibition was one of the planks of his platform. All this, however, he saw, just as did Mrs. Stanford, as the means for building a harmonious society embodying the righteous of Jesus' teachings. Had Ross designed the Stanford mosaic, the righteous might have looked like sturdy Nordic laborers at a populist rally. Otherwise the vision was much the same. A unifying "higher religion" would replace "low or debased religion." *"Now for the first time,"* Ross wrote in his autobiography concerning the benefits of modern science to Christian missions, "*the Christianity carried to the 'heathen,' may be as spiritual as is the Sermon on the Mount.*"[68]

The Mission of Unifying a Democratic Community

Across the nation at the turn of the century, one could find academic leaders, both conservatives and progressives, who would not have been ashamed to view themselves as missionaries for the higher culture based on science and the unifying ethical ideals of Jesus.[69] Nowhere was the equivalent task being carried on more explicitly than at Chicago. Harper saw his calling as to help raise all of American higher education to a higher scientific, and hence higher religious, plane. True to his methodistic propensity to promote efficiency as well as uplift, one of Harper's projects was to use his university to improve collegiate education by standardizing it. The denominationally generated system of hundreds of competing small colleges was unproductive. Harper proposed that colleges, as well as high schools and preparatory academies, be affiliated with the university. His close friend Albion Small was in charge of the project. The struggling colleges would gain credibility through connection with the university, which would help set uniform standards. Though the Chicago affiliation for colleges never amounted to much, Harper did propose to Andrew Carnegie that he devote his resources to a similar goal. In 1906 Carnegie in fact set up the Carnegie Foundation, which among other things provided incentives for colleges to drop denominational affiliations.[70]

The missionary motif of uplift was present in Harper's collegiate concerns as in all that he did. In 1901, for example, Albion Small and Shailer Mathews of the Divinity School were sent to tour colleges in the American South. Mathews, who was then emerging as one of the leading proponents of Protestant liberal theology, wrote to Harper, "It is almost pathetic to see how the men in the faculties of these [southern] colleges want private talks with me. . . . The men are full of unrest, are open to conviction, but have no one who can put them on the track. . . . You understand it is not I they are interested in, but in a Christianity that asks no odds and claims to be honest in its investigations."[71] In America the primitive religion that the reformers had to replace with a higher Christianity was most often sectarian Protestantism.

In 1903 Harper established the Religious Education Association as a "clearing-house" for his educational reform efforts. The agency, which would promote religious education at every level from the family and the Sunday school to the university, would, said Harper, "make new contributions to the cause of religious and moral education, and this will be done through the light of scientific investigations." In addition to "the scientific spirit," the association would be controlled by "the universal spirit," which would forbid the distinctive or exclusive views of any one denomination.[72] Convention meetings featured numerous speakers, including distinguished educators like G. Stanley Hall and John Dewey, and a galaxy of liberal theologians, such as Shailer Mathews. Harper was particularly taken with the liberal educational theories of George E. Coe of Northwestern University. Coe celebrated that American public schools had "won freedom from ecclesiastical control." Secular education, Coe argued, only appeared secular when considered by the ecclesiastical standards of the past. From the point of view of "progressive Christianity," however, we could recognize that it embodied the attitude that "Jesus exhibits when, by living a human life, he shows us what God is." Jesus shows us that "the Christian life is to be an incarnation, a realization of divine purpose, presence, and communion in our everyday occupations."[73]

As Stephen A. Schmidt points out in his history of the Religious Education Association, one anomaly in the reformers' claim to an inclusive universality was that, according to its ideology, "Fundamentalists and Catholics were outside the fold of the democratic fellowship." So were African Americans.[74] Nonetheless, the vision of universality which proposed to assimilate all Americans was grand. As Harper put it in a typical statement: "Back of the awakening human sympathy that so distinguishes the thought of today, lies the reiteration of God's love, of the Golden Rule, of the teaching of man's brotherhood and God's fatherhood,—in a word, of the story of Jesus Christ. The need of today is simply that such Christian influence be exerted more avowedly and more scientifically."[75]

Albion Small, a confidant of Harper, was one of many who in either Christian or secular terms carried on the assimilationist vision of universal science and universal morality. Writing in the *American Journal of Sociology* he proclaimed to an audience of social scientists in 1915:

> My own Pillar of Fire and Pillar of Cloud, in this wandering toward the Kingdom, is a vision of *the American Religion*. . . . The Jew, the Catholic, and the Protestant might graft this religion each on the trunk of his peculiar faith. . . . Its polity is the concerted purpose of every American, from Eastport to San Diego, to join in a perpetual league for finding out the quality and program of life which gives sincerest heed to the spiritual possibilities in every one of us.[76]

Notes

1. "One gets this impression of antique dignity more powerfully from the campus and buildings of the University of Chicago," editorialized the *Chicago Herald*, "than from many an older institution of equal rank, Harvard for instance." Quoted from editorial of October 1915, in Thomas Wakefield Goodspeed, *A History of the University of Chicago* (Chicago: University of Chicago Press, 1916), 421.

2. For instance, Robert Herrick, *Chimes* (New York, 1926), 6; Richard J. Storr, *Harper's University: The Beginnings* (Chicago: University of Chicago Press, 1966), 210. Laurence Veysey, *The Emergence of the American University* (Chicago: University of Chicago Press, 1965), 31.

3. Thorstein Veblen, *The Higher Learning in America: A Memorandum on the Conduct of Universities by Business Men* (New York, 1935 [1918]), 225 and passim.

4. Upton Sinclair, *Goose-Step: A Study of American Education*, 2nd ed. (Pasadena, Cal., 1923 [1922]), 240–41. James P. Wind, *The Bible and the University* (Atlanta: Scholars Press, 1987), 147–61, helpfully summarizes these and a number of other assessments of the university.

5. Veysey, *Emergence*, 263–68, 342–56.

6. Henry F. May remarked that his researches have found the bureaucratic characterization also misleading regarding Benjamin Wheeler, president of the University of California during the first decades of the century. (Conversations, 1991.)

7. Veysey, *Emergence*, 368–79.

8. Wind, *The Bible and the University,* develops this point. I am much indebted to his insights. The tendency to eliminate religion as a major cultural interpreter appears already early in the twentieth century in the outlooks of observers such as Veblen and Sinclair. They were preoccupied with the important insight of business dominance, a way of looking at things that was reinforced (notably in Sinclair's case) by the vogue of Marxist interpretation.

9. Cf. Samuel Haber, *Efficiency and Uplift: Scientific Management in the Progressive Era, 1890–1920* (Chicago: University of Chicago Press, 1964). Max Weber's observations in *The Protestant Ethic and the Spirit of Capitalism* (1905) makes the point of the affinities of Protestantism and the spirit of compulsive efficiency.

10. Storr, *Harper's University,* 24.

11. See Storr's touching account of Harper's religious anxieties expressed on his deathbed to Ernest D. Burton and Albion W. Small. Ibid., 364.

12. Ibid., 3–15.

13. Ibid., 6–34.

14. Wind, *The Bible and the University,* 42, quoting Vincent in 1886. This account of Harper very closely follows Wind, 37–46, 105–9.

15. Quoted in Wind, *Bible,* 178.

16. My thanks to Lee Carter for his work on this point.

17. Nathan O. Hatch, *The Democratization of American Christianity* (New Haven: Yale University Press, 1989). Richard T. Hughes, ed., *The American Quest for the Primitive Church* (Urbana: University of Illinois Press, 1988).

18. Wind, *The Bible and the University,* passim.

19. Quoted in ibid., 58.

20. Harper, Editorial, *Biblical World* 3 (1894), 3, quoted in Stephen A. Schmidt, *A History of the Religious Education Association* (Birmingham: Religious Education Press, 1983), 11.

21. Harper, "The University and Religious Education," *The Trend in Higher Education* (Chicago, 1905), 56. Originally published in *Biblical World* 24 (November 1904).

22. Wind, *The Bible and the University,* 50–57. Storr, *Harper's University,* 49–51, re Harper's worries over his own heresy.

23. Wind, *The Bible and the University,* 75, 81–93.

24. Harper, "University and Religious Education," quotations on 60 and 61; cf. 57.

25. Wind, *The Bible and the University,* 63.

26. Harper, "University and Religious Education," 58, 74–75.

27. Storr, *Harper's University,* 49–51.

28. Harper to John D. Rockefeller, Sr., December 18, 1892, quoted in Barry H. Westfall, "The William Rainey Harper/John D. Rockefeller Correspondence: Religion and Economic Control at the University of Chicago, 1889–1905," *Vitae Scholasticae* 4 (Spring/Fall 1985), 112.

29. Laurence Veysey, "The Emergence of the American University," Ph.D. dissertation, University of California, Berkeley, 1961, 1116n. In Robert Herrick's novel *Chimes,* which draws on Herrick's experiences as a Chicago faculty member, both these issues are mentioned.

30. Westfall, "Correspondence," 115, quoting letter from Frederick T. Gates (Rockefeller's secretary, who handled his university affairs) and Harper, March 17, 1896. In a letter from Gates, January 2, 1897, Harper was told of Rockefeller's strong displeasure over the defiance.

31. Veysey, "Emergence," 1116n.

32. Frederick Gates to H. C. Mabie, enclosed in a letter from Gates to Harper, June 17, 1905, quoted in Storr, *Harper's University,* 98–99n.

33. Gates to Mrs. J. D. Rockefeller, December 22, 1892, from Veysey, *Emergence,* 373n. Baptists predominated, with twenty-four Congregationalists and ten Presbyterians. (It was required that two-thirds of the trustees be Baptist.)

34. By 1903 a graduating class of 142 included 10 Jews and 8 Roman Catholics. Storr, *Harper's University,* 110.

35. From a statement in a presidential report, 1902, quoted in Storr, *Harper's University,* 185. See his useful account of religion at the university from which the present account is drawn (183–89).

36. Ibid., 92–93. Goodspeed, *University of Chicago,* 395.

37. Amos Alonzo Stagg to his family, January 20, 1891, from Storr, *Harper's University,* 179. See Stagg and Wesley Stout, *Touchdown!* (New York, 1927), 110.

38. Veysey, *Emergence,* 276–77.

39. Stagg and Stout, *Touchdown,* 147.

40. Harper, Decennial Report, July 1, 1902, in *The Idea of the University of Chicago: Selections from the Papers of the First Eight Chief Executives of the University of Chicago from 1891 to 1975,* William Michael Murphy and D. J. R. Bruckner, eds. (Chicago: University of Chicago Press, 1976), 7. The quotation continues: "The drawing of a narrower line than this would be fatal to the growth of the University. Here lies the distinction between a college and a university. The one may be controlled by the ecclesiastical or political spirit; the other may not be. . . ."

41. Quoted in Wind, *The Bible and the University,* 178.

42. William Rainey Harper, "America as a Missionary Field," in *Religion and the Higher Life: Talks to Students* (Chicago: University of Chicago Press, 1904), 175–84.

43. Willian Rainey Harper, "The University and Democracy," in *Trend in Higher Education,* 12.

44. Ibid., 4, 8.

45. Ibid., 21; cf. 1–34 and passim.

46. Quoted (without precise citation) in Robert M. Crunden, *Ministers of Reform: The Progressives' Achievement in American Civilization, 1889–1920* (Urbana: University of Illinois Press, 1984), 58.

47. John Dewey, "The Ethics of Democracy" (1888) quoted in Dorothy Ross, *The Origins of American Social Science* (Cambridge: Cambridge University Press, 1991), 163.

48. Crunden, *Ministers of Reform.*

49. Jean B. Quandt, *From the Small Town to the Great Community: The Social Thought of Progressive Intellectuals* (New Brunswick, N.J.: Rutgers University Press, 1970), shows this ideal of community to be at the heart of the progressive vision (102–25 [on Dewey] and passim).

50. Cf. Crunden, *Ministers of Reform,* 200–224.

51. Storr, *Harper's University,* 339–41.

52. Westfall, "The William Rainey Harper/John D. Rockefeller Correspondence," attempts to lay to rest a later suggestion that religion was an issue

53. Dewey, "Religious Education as Conditioned by Modern Psychology and Pedagogy," in *The Religious Education Association: Proceedings of the First Annual Convention, Chicago, February 10–12, 1903* (Chicago, 1903), 60–66. Dewey, predictably, spoke of "bringing the child to appreciate the truly religious aspects of his own

growing life, not . . . inoculating him externally with beliefs and emotions which adults happen to have found serviceable to themselves." (61).

54. On Small's career see Vernon K. Dibble, *The Legacy of Albion Small* (Chicago: University of Chicago Press, 1975).

55. Small, "Research Ideals," *Record* 10 (October 1905), 87, quoted in Storr, *Harper's University,* 159.

56. Cf. Thomas L. Haskell's discussion of these and other tendencies in *The Emergence of Professional Social Science: The American Social Science Association and the Nineteenth-Century Crisis in Authority* (Urbana: University of Illinois Press, 1977), 1–23. Robert C. Bannister, *Sociology and Scientism: The American Quest for Objectivity, 1880–1940* (Chapel Hill: University of North Carolina Press, 1987), 32–63, provides a valuable discussion of Small's views, including his concept of objectivity. Cf. the discussion in Mary O. Furner, *Advocacy and Objectivity: A Crisis in the Professionalization of American Social Science, 1865–1905* (Lexington: University of Kentucky Press, 1975), 295–304. Also see Arthur J. Vidich and Sanford M. Lyman, *American Sociology: Worldly Rejections of Religion and Their Directions* (New Haven: Yale University Press, 1985), 178–94, for a strong version.

57. Ross, *Origins of American Social Science.* Ross acknowledges this connection in passing but misses the religious force of Protestant exceptionalism.

58. Benjamin G. Rader, *The Academic Mind and Reform: The Influence of Richard T. Ely in American Life* (Lexington: University of Kentucky Press, 1966), 2. See list of students, 26–27.

59. "Statement of Dr. Richard T. Ely," *Report of the Organization of the American Economics Association* (Baltimore, 1886), 18.

60. Rader, *Academic Mind,* passim. Crunden, *Ministers of Reform,* 69–73.

61. Rader, *Academic Mind,* 136–50.

62. Sinclair, *Goose-Step,* 244–45, quotes a letter containing Bemis's account. Storr, *Harper's University,* 83–85, argues for Harper's view. Richard Hofstadter and Walter P. Metzger, *The Development of Academic Freedom in the United States* (New York: Columbia University Press, 1955), 426–35, has a helpful analysis of conflicting interpretations.

63. Jordan, *The Care and Culture of Men* (San Francisco, 1896), quoted in Veysey, "Emergence," 479n. Veysey says this statement was typical of Jordan and cites several additional examples.

64. Veysey, "Emergence," 478–94.

65. The account of the Ross case is based on Veysey, *Emergence,* 400–406, and on Hofstadter and Metzger, *Academic Freedom,* 436–45.

66. Ross argues this general thesis. For her view of Small, see *Origins,* 136–37.

67. Edward Ross, *Sin and Society: An Analysis of Latter-Day Iniquity* (Boston, 1907), ix–xi.

68. Edward Ross, *Seventy Years of It: An Autobiography* (New York, 1936), 188, quoted in Vidich and Lyman, *American Sociology,* 157, cf. 157–61. Dorothy Ross, *Origins,* 230–40, paints a much more secular picture of Ross than do Vidich and Lyman. Julius Weinberg, *Edward Alsworth Ross and the Sociology of Progressivism* (Madison: State Historical Society of Wisconsin, 1972), points out, however, that although Edward Ross gave up his traditional Presbyterian belief, he also rejected naturalism and affirmed the moral ideals of Christianity. Naturalism, he said "cries struggle," a social view of religion cries "Bear ye one another's burdens." Edward Ross, *Social Control* (New York, 1901), 196–217, quoted in Weinberg, 85.

69. Several universities, including Yale, Syracuse, and Princeton, conducted

foreign missionary work as well by setting up colleges in China that would export Christian and American cultural and political ideals. See, for instance, Jeffrey Alan Trexler, "Education with the Soul of a Church: The Yale Foreign Missionary Society and the Democratic Ideal," Ph.D. dissertation, Duke University, 1991.

70. Storr, *Harper's University,* 211–22, 331.

71. Mathews to Harper, March 8, 1901, quoted in Storr, *Harper's University,* 222.

72. Harper, "The Scope and Purpose of the New Organization," in *The Religious Education Association: Proceedings of the First Annual Convention, Chicago, February 10–12, 1903* (Chicago, 1903), 231, 237, 239.

73. Coe, *The Religion of the Mature Mind* (New York, 1902), quoted in Schmidt, *A History of Religious Education Association,* 17–18.

74. Ibid., 45.

75. Harper, Editorial, *Biblical World* 5 (January 1895), 2.

76. Small, "What Is Americanism?" *American Journal of Sociology* 20 (1915), 682–83, quoted in Vidich and Lyman, *American Sociology,* 191.

III

WHEN THE TIE NO LONGER BINDS

Harper's Chicago represents the high-water mark of liberal Protestant university building in which Christianity played an explicit role. Harper was more outspoken in his statements of Christian purpose than were most other university leaders and he was a pioneer in giving the Bible a place in the curriculum. Yet his outlook had many parallels. Evangelical Yale of the 1890s, the Yale of Henry Sloane Coffin and Dwight L. Moody's missionary volunteers, was another claimant to be the model Christian university. And Harper did not differ greatly from his presidential peers in his broad Christian outlook. James Angell, who still presided at Michigan throughout Harper's Chicago years, was just as explicitly Christian. Woodrow Wilson was attempting to implement something comparable to Harper's ideals for university-as-community in the less expansive Princetonian context. Daniel Coit Gilman, though less often explicitly Christian in his academic rhetoric, paralleled Harper in many of his interests and motivations. Eliot at Harvard could be viewed as a broader counterpart. Even Andrew Dickson White saw Christian and national interests as one, if Christianity was properly understood. And none of these was proposing a program for the university that contradicted the proviso, popularized by White, that modern intellectual life must follow the dictates of value-free scientific inquiry. Christian moral ideals would supplement and counterbalance such demands for scientific professionalism, not undercut them.

Explicitly Christian rationales for these ideals for the American university did not long outlive William Rainey Harper. By the 1920s, such expressions would seem vestigial. The fatal weakness in conceiving of the university as a broadly Christian institution was its higher commitments to scientific and professional ideals and to the demands for a unified public life. In the light of such commitments academic expressions of Christianity seemed at best superfluous and at worst unscientific and unprofessional. Most of those associated with higher education were still Christian, but in academic life, as in so many other parts of modern life, religion would increasingly be confined to private spheres.

Surveying twentieth-century developments of American academic culture in the chapters that follow, we can identify the growing pressures against substantive religious reference in mainstream academic life. While some influential academics who were frankly secularists were important advocates of this change, their success was fostered by much larger forces. Broader cultural pressures were on their side. The American universities had already been so defined by their liberal Protestant founders that, in the presence of such forces, the near exclusion of religious perspectives appears almost inevitable. Few university leaders intended that result. In fact, twentieth-century university leaders often encouraged attempts to compensate for the secularizing trends. Yet in the long run the pressures pushing toward a standardized secular national academic culture prevailed. Mainline Protestantism, which as late as midcentury had hopes of providing an ecumenical basis for national consensus, found its own Christian identity an embarrassment. Nothing stood in the way of the elimination of almost all religious perspectives from dominant academia. The result was academic conformity with respect to religion, often supported in the name of diversity.

15

The Trouble with the Old-Time Religion

"Blasting at the Rock of Ages"

In May 1909 *Cosmopolitan* magazine published the first in an announced three-part series on what was being taught at American colleges. The sensationally written articles paid secondary attention to controversial economic views, but the revolution in religion was the major theme. The first of the essays, "Blasting at the Rock of Ages," immediately created a stir in pulpits around the country. The editors, sensing that they had hit on something, extended the series for two additional months, devoting the last two essays entirely to religious questions.

The author, Harold Bolce, followed the typical muckraking conventions. After visiting a number of campuses, sitting in on classes, and interviewing professors, he adopted an attitude of consternation in disclosing his discoveries. The editors, borrowing a number of Bolce's phrases, summarized both the content and the breathless tone of the message:

> Those who are in not in close touch with the great colleges of the country, will be astonished to learn the creeds being foisted by the faculties of our great universities. In hundreds of class-rooms it is being taught daily that the decalogue is no more sacred than a syllabus; that the home as an institution is doomed; that there are no absolute evils; that immorality is simply an act in contravention of society's accepted standards; that democracy is a failure and the Declaration of Independence only spectacular rhetoric; that the change from one religion to another is like getting a new hat; that moral precepts are passing shibboleths; that conceptions of right and wrong are as unstable as styles of dress; . . . and that there can be and are holier alliances without the marriage bond than within it.[1]

Despite the hyperbole, Bolce correctly identified the direction in which higher education was heading and the revolution that already had taken place regarding traditional Christianity. He acknowledged that by no means all professors agreed with the most progressive views; but he quoted many of the best known and most influential academics throughout the country—William James, Josiah Royce, George Howison, William Graham Sumner, Edward Ross, Albion Small, Shailer Mathews, Andrew

Dickson White, and many others. President David Starr Jordan of Stanford, who compared the way "men lose their reason and self-control" in a religious revival to drunkenness, was only one of many prominent figures who deplored conversionist evangelism. Even at Northwestern, a Methodist school, George A. Coe opposed most traditional evangelistic methods. At Syracuse, another Methodist school, Professor Edwin L. Earp taught that sociology showed that moral beliefs were evolutionary products of experience and it was therefore "unscientific and absurd to imagine that God ever turned stone mason and chiseled commandments on a rock." As for the University of Chicago, Bolce summarized: "This institution is nominally a religious seat of learning, but if it were dedicated to free thought and agnosticism it could not be more outspoken in its arraignment of many things in our orthodox theology." Chicago's Professor Herbert B. Willett, for instance, maintained that the Old Testament needed editing to raise its moral tone. At Syracuse, Chicago, and elsewhere, Bolce pointed out, teachings on the social origins of religion and morality led to the view that all moral rules were merely "mores" and that traditional institutions, particularly marriage, were not sacred.

Bolce was clear, however, that the progressive views seldom reflected mere secularism. Rather, he pointed out, although the professors to whom he listened thought orthodox Christianity unscientific and preposterous, they believed that "what is needed in this age is not less of God, but more." The professors, he correctly saw, "believe that the mightiest movement the world has witnessed is now under way—a movement destined to sweep away the mass of ritual which has kept man from a clear vision of God." Their views, which dominated all the leading philosophy departments, were evolutionary idealist, affirming scientific progress but opposing materialism. Bolce suggested an analogy between their views and those of Christian Science. Although the analogy was not exact, each indeed suggested a genteel and literate route to a new age of a higher religion and a higher morality. Each embodied a missionary zeal. "If we move our students," economist Simon Patten (a friend of Ely) of the University of Pennsylvania was quoted as saying, "we move the world."[2]

Orthodox clergy, including many in mainline Protestant pulpits, were disturbed by such revelations and in his fifth essay Bolce sympathetically recounted some of their reactions. Their consensus, according to Bolce, was that "no greater calamity could befall civilization than the academic destruction of the old gospel that there is but one name given among men whereby humanity can be saved." Whereas "the unequivocal teaching of orthodox Christianity" was that "man is ransomed by the blood of Christ," the college professors repudiated that doctrine, "declaring that the fall of man is a myth; that it was a Judean peasant, not a God, that was crucified on Calvary; and that shameful tragedy had absolutely nothing to do with remission of sins and the reconciliation of an erring race to an outraged God."[3]

Although Bolce was pointing out an ever-widening chasm between what was typically taught in America's pulpits and what was taught in its universities, only a minority of church people or even of clergy were ready to sound an alarm. The strength of American Protestantism was largely in its activism and elevating sentiments. Even though most American Christians formally adhered to traditional doctrines, most of that same rank and file agreed that the real tests of the faith were in one's sense of personal reverence for the deity and in living according to moral principles. Liberal Protestant theology said much the same and in doing so employed much traditional Christian language. Evolutionary idealism might be more theistic than Christian and pragmatism might base more action on scientific concerns alone, but all the positions could be blended together and united behind the high cause of a moral culture. In the dominant Anglo community of the mainline churches, the impulse was strong to emphasize commonalties with, not differences from, other Protestants.

Besides, those who were unhappy with the religion taught at the universities had other options. There were still hundreds of denominational colleges and in many of these traditional Christianity still played a prominent role. Approximately half of all undergraduates attended church-related schools. Although the better known colleges were reshaped by the same spirit that formed the universities, so that an Oberlin or an Amherst shifted dramatically from evangelical to progressive religion by the World War I era,[4] many more local and parochial colleges remained as havens for distinctive denominational emphases. So for those who remained strictly traditional in their religious sensibilities, the denominational colleges provided an important safety valve while the universities got on with advancing modern technical civilization.

Another factor mitigating criticism of the liberal trends was that most Americans did not go to college. By 1910 the total had risen to only about one in twenty.[5] For white middle-class Protestants, the percentage was much higher but was still a decided minority. Thus there was not as yet much of a social base for a religiously populist critique of university trends.

Most of what criticism there was could be deflected by universities by the standard pieties regarding their service to industry and to the nation, their contributions to building student character, and the freedom and opportunities they provided for students to worship as they chose. A survey of state university campuses in 1905 indicated that about 60 percent of students were church members and that the percentage had risen slightly since the previous decade. An estimated 35 to 50 percent of students attended churches on an average Sunday at state campuses and something like 20 percent of men and 50 percent of women belonged to the YMCA and YWCA respectively. It was still plausible to claim that "the atmosphere of our state universities is pre-eminently Christian."[6] Moreover, by the second decade of the century the much-discussed idea of denominational houses to offer varieties of ministries was at last being realized, increasing opportunities for voluntary religious expression.

For university administrators, of course, a major motive was to keep religion in its place and let the university get on with its business. This required enough openness to voluntary religion to satisfy conservative critics, while keeping religion away from the main work of the university where it would be not only divisive among diverse faculties but also a threat to good relations with constituents. In 1916, President Benjamin Ide Wheeler of the University of California wrote to Henry Morse Stephens, chair of the History Department, about Preserved Smith, a liberal Protestant interpreter of the Reformation. Wheeler wrote that, while he much admired Smith's work, "I am afraid it would never do to make him a professor in the University outright because of the very ticklish character of his subject. In spite of the utterly scientific method of his procedure, one denomination or another would surely take exception, if not to the facts, at least to his balance. . . . We are going on very comfortably now and perhaps it is better not to kick a slumbering dog."[7]

In addition to worries about the potential disruptiveness of specific Christian teachings, the ongoing pressure for professionalization helped steer the rapid university expansion away from religious concerns. By the early decades of the twentieth century professionalized standards for university hiring were so firmly in place that overt religious considerations were virtually precluded, so far as Protestants were concerned. Hiring was, of course, largely controlled by an old-boy network entrenched in an elite educational system that guaranteed a preponderance of birthright Protestants. Nonetheless, in the minds of those setting the standards, the "scientific" accomplishments of candidates, together with concerns regarding their "character," were the official criteria. At the same time, because the most lucrative function of the universities was their service to capitalist society in providing technical expertise, much of the expansion of programs would be in areas where religion was of little concern. The more technical competence would be the controlling criterion for building a university, the less religion would be a factor. In faculty hiring, the more professional competence was the overriding consideration, the more faculty loyalties would be shaped by the profession rather than by any particular heritage of their institutions.

All these forces, then, underscored the seriousness of the question that critics such as Harold Bolce were raising in sensational form. Were the universities essentially subversive of traditional Protestant belief? Was it even possible to maintain a true university that kept its traditional Christian identity?

Catholic Authoritarianism

There were, of course, many Catholic colleges and universities. These, however, were all small, having a total collegiate enrollment of less than seven thousand in 1907. The great majority were under complete clerical control and were run and staffed by members of religious orders. Prior to World War I the Catholic colleges still had not adjusted to American curricular patterns; rather they typically offered six- or seven-year courses, for boys only, combining preparatory and collegiate courses on a European gymnasium model. The curricula of these school resembled those of the American Protestant old-time colleges. They were built around readings of Greek and Latin classics, with a capstone year devoted to Thomistic philosophical studies. Graduate education generally was still limited to the M.A., which was a beefed-up B.A. awarded after two additional years of study. The most notable effort to bring Catholic education somewhat more in line with current American university trends was the founding of the Catholic University of America in 1889. Originally exclusively a theological school, Catholic University soon offered doctoral degrees under Catholic auspices in a variety of subjects.[8]

The founding of Catholic University[9] was, however, part of the ill-fated Americanist movement. The university's first rector, John Keane, was one of the principal leaders of that progressive Catholic movement. The outlook of the Catholic Americanists reflected an attempt to synthesize Catholic teachings with cautious versions of the attitudes typical of American university founders. Not radicals, the Americanists' would be far closer in their views to moderate traditionalist Protestants such as a James McCosh or a Woodrow Wilson, than to a William Rainey Harper or a George A. Coe. They could affirm traditional theology, but they wished to be open to reconciling it with modern science, reverent biblical criticism, and especially with the tolerance of liberal culture. These attitudes went hand in hand with a deep faith in American culture and American destiny and hence an eagerness to see Catholics assimilated into American life. One of the early professors at Catholic University, for example, argued against the common Catholic belief that in America the government was too un-Christian to offer acceptable public education. Rector Keane was an outspoken champion of the temperance crusade, a cause identified with the Protestant establishment. He also joined his liberal Protestant counterparts in participating in the Parliament of World Religions held in conjunction with the Columbian Exposition in Chicago in 1893. All this brought sharp criticism from conservatives, especially from Germans, who were more zealous than the Irish leadership to retain ethnic identity, Catholic schools, and Catholic theological distinctives.

The intra-American debates, however, were soon preempted by the pope, who had complete authority over the American church, still officially a missionary enterprise. Pope Leo XIII viewed the Americanist developments of the 1890s with increasing alarm. In 1895 he issued an encyclical addressed to the American church, warning that American separation of church and state should not be thought of as the desirable model for the church everywhere. The next year he fired a more forceful warning shot against the innovators by removing Keane from his rectorship of Catholic University.

The Americanizers' zeal for American political freedom went hand in hand with their faith in free inquiry. The most conspicuous issue was Darwinism. Conservative Catholics had condemned biological evolution as incompatible with Christian faith. In America, notably, the formidable Orestes Brownson, famed Catholic convert of the previous generation, had declared the Darwin doctrines in the *Descent of Man* irredeemably materialistic and incompatible with belief in a creator. A few progressive Catholic scholars, however, argued along with many Protestant counterparts that biological evolution need not be *necessarily* materialistic but could be guided by God's creative providence. Keane and Archbishop John Ireland attempted to appoint one of the best known of such theistic evolutionists, the British zoologist St. George Mivart, to a chair at Catholic University, but their efforts were blocked by conservatives in the American hierarchy. The progressives did appoint a lesser known defender of theistic evolution, Joseph Pohle.

The controversy came to its crisis in 1896 when John Zahm, professor of physics at Notre Dame in Indiana and a close ally of Keane, published *Evolution and Dogma,* detailing the compatibility of biological evolution, church teaching, and Scripture. In 1898 Zahm's volume was placed on the Index of Forbidden Books and he was forced to withdraw it from its publisher.[10] The tense situation was not helped by the American defeat of Catholic Spain in 1898 in which the Americanists supported their nation's cause. Early in 1899 Pope Leo issued another encyclical, this time directed against the heresy of "Americanism." Although the doctrines condemned may have gone beyond what the progressive American leaders actually held, the Vatican critics of American culture pointed out that American emphases on freedom as a central organizing cultural principle begged the question of "freedom for what" and opened the door for building social values around human material desires and interests alone. Moreover, the prevailing intellectual trends threatened the authority of Scripture, church tradition, and centralized church control. Confronted with the dominant outlook in American culture running counter to its interests, the principal solution that Rome had to offer was a heavy-handed one. Not only did it reassert its own authority over the entire church but it wedded itself to very conservative views in politics and especially in doctrine, preempting all progressive efforts to reconcile church teachings with the spirit of the age.

The Roman Catholic Church in America was thus forced to retain its identity and its distinctiveness, but at the price of accepting Roman authoritarianism and severe restraints on its intellectual life. During the following decade the limits of permissible Catholic inquiry became increasingly restricted. In 1906, much to the consternation of a number of Catholic biblical scholars, the Pontifical Biblical Commission declared that the settled church position was that Moses was the substantial author of the first five books of the Bible and that one could not teach otherwise. The next year Pope Pius X issued a sweeping condemnation of "modernism" directed at a wide variety of efforts to reconcile Catholic teaching on theology and Scripture and on society and politics with the assumptions of nineteenth-century historicist methodology.

The result in America was that a "siege mentality" and an "inquisitorial spirit" prevailed within the intellectual community.[11] At Catholic University a professor of Scripture, Henry A. Poels, was dismissed in 1910 because he held, contrary to the Biblical Commission's declaration, a multi-authorial view of the Pentateuch. A complicated controversy, extending over several years and involving direct intervention by the pope, came down to the point that Poels would be required to sign an oath stating not only that he would not *teach* views on the Pentateuch that contradicted those of the Biblical Commission, but that he did not *hold* contrary views. Poels could not sign such a statement in good conscience and his contract was not renewed. None of the influential Americanists, who in earlier years had spoken out for freedom, now took a strong stand in Poels's defense. Cardinal James Gibbons, for instance, was instrumental in his dismissal.[12] After the papal condemnation of modernism in 1907, in fact, other faculty members at the university who had endorsed positions that might have been interpreted as modernist quickly repudiated any such positions.[13]

In recent years a number of interpreters of the Americanist controversy have moved away from the earlier scholarly assumption that the Americanists in their original program of adjustment to American values were simply correct, representing enlightened progress versus benighted reaction, freedom versus oppression. Since the 1970s, disillusion with turn-of-the-century American triumphalism and with an assimilationist strategy that would have hastened the melting of ethnic identities has led critics to suggest that the Americanists' faith in the American way of life may have been, in its way, just as much a blind faith as was the support of conservative American Catholics for Roman authority.[14]

Much the same can be said of the intellectual crisis. Catholic conservatives, whatever the merits of their reasons, were among the few major groups in America to dissent substantially from assumptions of the virtuous neutrality of liberal American culture and of the inevitable universal triumph of such ideals under the rubric of "progress." They recognized, at least in selected areas, the fundamental materialism that underlay American claims to idealist progress. Moreover, they questioned whether philosophies that constantly celebrated innovation, openness, and individual choice could in fact provide the moral basis for a higher civilization, as was claimed by progressive Protestants and secularists. Most fundamentally, they questioned the claim that the application of modern scientific standards to all area of inquiry provided the basis of universally valid claims about the essential nature of reality.

The constructive counterpart to the restrictions on American Catholic intellectual life was the rise of neo-Thomist philosophy. This Thomist revival was almost entirely the result of an effort by the papacy to standardize Catholic thought and to provide it with a viable basis for resisting the inroads of modernity. In 1879 Leo XIII declared Thomism the official philosophy of the church. In America, where other philosophies had been taught, it took some time for Thomism to gain a foothold. At first the revival of Scholasticism appeared to some progressives as providing a basis for raising the level of Catholic intellectual life. At Catholic University a School of Philosophy was opened in 1895 dedicated to St. Thomas. The head of the school was Edward A. Pace, a well-trained Thomist but also a progressive, notable for bringing an experimental psychological laboratory to the university. With the papal reactions to Americanism and modernism, however, the shift toward Thomism became increasingly a method of maintaining papal control and a new conservatism. In 1914 Pius X admonished Catholic teachers of theology and philosophy that "if they deviated so much as a step from Aquinas, especially in metaphysics, they exposed themselves to grave risks."[15]

The strength of Thomism was that it provided a formidable alternative to prevailing twentieth-century naturalist and historicist assumptions, particularly in asserting an alternative basis for scientific knowledge grounded in divinely created natural law. It could thus counter contemporary claims that modern science established universally valid objective truths with its own version of the same claim. As Thomism was generally interpreted, the natural law philosophy provided the functional equivalent of an eighteenth-century Enlightenment claim for human ability to discover objective truth. An orderly universe with theistic origins was in fact presupposed, as it was by most Enlightenment thinkers, but science was presented as established based not on prior faith claims but on objective foundations discovered by reason. Thus a historicist positivism was countered with a natural law positivism, which within the Catholic community could hold the line in an era when the universal validity of science was widely taken for granted.[16]

In Europe the imposition of Thomism sparked something of a renaissance in Catholic thought, evidenced by such impressive scholars as Etienne Gilson, Jacques Maritain, and Christopher Dawson. In America the intellectual achievement was far more modest.[17] Near the end of the era of intellectual isolation Catholic scholars could assume, as John Tracy Ellis put it in 1955, "general agreement as to the impoverishment of Catholic scholarship in this country."[18]

Nonetheless, given impressive Catholic intellectual achievements abroad, this impoverishment appears to have had far more to do with massive problems inherent in the American immigrant Catholic situation than with the imposition of Thomism and the limits placed on academic freedom. As Ellis points out in his analysis of the situation, Catholics in America had no sustained intellectual tradition. When Catholic University was founded in 1889 John Keane, in recruiting his first faculty, hired six foreign-born and two American-born converts. With so much of the community consisting of first-generation immigrants of peasant origins, priorities were elsewhere, financial resources were limited, and anti-intellectualism was strong. Throughout the first half of the twentieth century Catholic colleges sent far smaller percentages of their students on to graduate school in either the sciences or the humanities than did their Protestant equivalents. Financial resources were limited as well. Catholic University at its founding received only two large gifts, one of $300,000 and another of $100,000. During its first sixty-six years it never received a donation of as much as a million dollars. As late as 1947 not one of the American Catholic hierarchy of bishops and archbishops had college-educated parents. Protestant prejudice and monopolies on America centers of power combined with the ongoing disadvantages of immigrant communities to perpetuate vastly disproportionate patterns of leadership in all aspects of American life. In 1927 *Who's Who in America* listed more than half again as many Unitarians as Catholics, even though Catholics outnumbered Unitarians three hundred to one in the general population.[19]

All this is not to argue that intellectual repression from abroad was not a contributor to the conspicuous limitations of Catholic colleges and universities during the first half of the twentieth century. Rather, it is to suggest that a significant tradeoff was involved. Catholic colleges and universities in fact made major gains by almost every measure during this era. The problem was that they also had a long way to go. The intellectual restrictions of neo-Thomism limited the range of their intellectual inquiry, but it also provided a base for building an alternative worldview by a community that was threatened with absorption into an alien culture with highly appealing claims.[20] Without dependency on European Catholic guidance, American Catholic intellectual life, impelled by a zeal to gain respectability, almost certainly would have developed a far greater dependency on the dictates of contemporary American intellectual fashion.[21] Whatever the weaknesses of Catholic higher education during this era, and they were many, Catholics emerged from this era with one thing Protestants did not: universities with substantial religious identities.[22]

In the short run, however, the Catholic repression combined with the second-class character of their universities confirmed all the worst Protestant prejudices. For mainstream Protestant universities, such authoritarian repression of academic freedom along with the seemingly medieval ethos of Vatican I Catholicism, which shaped its academic communities, was unthinkable. That is not at all to say that theologically defined boundaries were unthinkable in the Protestant context. Countless sectarian groups, immigrant groups, and conservatives in almost every denomination who were resisting absorption of their tradition into the larger national culture favored such restrictions and, when possible, imposed them on their colleges.[23] Most of the schools in the South, where sentiment never to yield to Yankee imperialism was still strong, routinely accepted formal and informal restraints regarding religious teaching. Where such repression was becoming unthinkable was, rather, among *mainstream* Protestants who aspired to shape and lead a unified, technologically advanced, and morally superior American culture. For them, the Catholic example underscored the point that any religiously defined university would be a contradiction in terms.

The Perils of Methodist Success

The development of Methodist universities provides a striking example of the difficulties in building a Christian university. Methodists, unlike other major Protestant denominations, founded numbers of significant universities. Schools with Methodist origins include Boston University, Drew, Duke, Emory, Northwestern, Southern California, Southern Methodist, Syracuse, and Vanderbilt. Several factors contributed to Methodism's greater propensity to university building. Older denominations, such as Congregationalist and Presbyterian, could point to distinguished universities that shared their heritage and concentrate any continuing efforts to preserve denominational identity on colleges. Methodists, however, were just emerging on the educational scene during the years of university building. By the Civil War era they had many colleges, but none was especially distinguished. Methodism's elaborate systematic organization also made it possible to build schools for whole regions, rather than being forced (as the Baptists, for instance, usually were) to rely on more local and more limited support.

Especially important for understanding the development of Methodist universities is that in the era following the Civil War Methodism was making the transition from the periphery to the center of dominant Protestant culture. In the early nineteenth century Methodists were regarded much as Pentecostals are in the twentieth century. However, the Methodists had become the largest Protestant denomination and already by the 1840s they had shed most of their sectarian image. By the post–Civil War era significant numbers of Methodists were culturally prominent. They were on their way up and eager to be competitive at all levels. At the same time, they were close enough to their sectarian roots to be proud of their heritage and of their distinctive doctrines and practices. They were beginning to be divided, however, over the issue of what of that heritage was essential to preserve as they were being absorbed into the cultural mainstream.

In higher education the most dramatic struggle was at Vanderbilt University. The Methodist Episcopal Church, South, which had separated from its northern counterpart in 1844, had been talking about establishing a university in Nashville since before the Civil War. In 1872 church leaders succeeded in chartering this "Central University," although its opening was contingent on raising considerable funds. The money would almost certainly have to come from the North, rather than the devastated South. Many northerners did, in fact, feel an obligation to help in reconstructing and uplifting the conquered territories. Southern Methodist

Bishop Holland McTyeire, one of the principals in the university project, had a connection with Cornelius Vanderbilt through the Commodore's young second wife, to whom the bishop was a cousin. In 1873 Bishop McTyeire managed a visit to the Vanderbilts' home in New York, where he spoke enthusiastically of his university project. Although Vanderbilt's young wife had a strongly Southern Methodist background, the Commodore himself was not a church member or much interested in such matters. Nonetheless, he saw an opportunity to endow not merely a university but, as Paul Conkin puts it, "an educational mission in a benighted land."[24] Vanderbilt offered half a million dollars, sufficient to allow the opening of the university in 1875, and brought his total contribution to approximately a million before his death in 1877.

Despite its financial advantages, Vanderbilt University during its first two decades was little more than an undistinguished Methodist college and a few fledgling professional schools. As both a Methodist and a regional school it had to contend with a lack of a well-developed educational tradition. Southern Methodists never offered much support financially and students were hard to find. In 1884–1885, a low point, there were only 176 students. Fifty of these were in the "Biblical Department," a separate school so named because of Methodist suspicion of professional theological training.

The college also ran into early suspicions that it would undermine orthodoxy. Alexander Winchell, a geologist, was the most accomplished member of the faculty and the only northerner. Winchell's credentials as a loyal Methodist were strong. In 1873 he had moved from a faculty post at the University of Michigan to Syracuse University, another new Methodist enterprise, where he had served briefly as chancellor. In 1875, not having found administration agreeable, he returned to Ann Arbor but took a part-time position lecturing each spring at Vanderbilt.

Winchell was among the pious defenders of Darwinism and in 1875 he published his efforts to reconcile evolution with traditional views of Scripture. Where he ran into difficulty was not with Darwinism as such but with his view, published in 1878, of races of humans who preceded the biblical Adam. This theory raised the sensitive question of the biological evolution of humans and also seemed to contradict the plain reading of Scripture. Though Winchell claimed the Bible did leave room for these unmentioned pre-Adamites, he was attacked in some Southern Methodist publications. Without mention of these issues, the Vanderbilt board meeting in the spring of 1878 summarily terminated Winchell's lectureship. They thereby eventually gained the dubious honor of being memorialized along with the opponents of Galileo and others in the final 1896 edition of Andrew Dickson White's *A History of the Warfare of Science with Theology in Christendom.*[25]

Early Vanderbilt remained in most respects a strict Methodist institution, much like an old-time college in its authoritarian style of government and strict ideas of discipline. In 1878 a popular professor of modern languages, Edward S. Joynes, an Episcopalian, was dismissed for drinking, though he claimed that the basis was only one much exaggerated incident several years earlier and he was not allowed a hearing or an appeal.[26]

The students, who were in a buyers market, were more difficult to keep under tight rein. The student body was predominantly Methodist but it was also all male and restless to free itself from strict Methodist social restrictions. Probably the most significant student victory was in establishing fraternities, despite administration efforts to ban them. By the mid-1880s fraternities dominated campus life and had defied Methodist mores by sponsoring dances and even, it was rumored, encouraging consumption of alcoholic beverages. During the same era, students had instituted intercollegiate sports teams despite some old Methodist opposition to such games as frivolous. As usual, the rise of the national student culture of volunteerism also brought with it an active YMCA on campus to supplement required chapel and Sunday services.[27]

By the 1890s Vanderbilt was beginning to look more like other fledgling American universities. This transition was effected particularly under the leadership of James Hampton Kirkland, who in 1893 began what was to be a lengthy chancellorship. Kirkland, the son of an upcountry Methodist itinerant, was a fully pedigreed 100 percent loyal Methodist. He was, however, typical of most of the turn-of-the-century leaders in higher education in holding to a broad view of what was essential to his denominational heritage. As Conklin observes, "He always tended to translate 'Methodist' into 'Christian.' " Moreover, he often translated Christian into "liberal Christian," or the "upbuilding of Christ's kingdom," a phrase that could encompass everything constructive in modern civilization.[28] Having taken his doctoral work in Germany, Kirkland also had modern views of scholarship and was determined to make Vanderbilt into a high-quality national institution.

Old-style Southern Methodists were not happy about this trend toward absorption of higher education into a national culture. They correctly recognized that their deeply held religious values would no longer be an influence. In 1901 came the first faint rumbling of what was to build into a massive controversy. Bishop Warren Candler was one of a number of archconservatives on the Vanderbilt board. In 1901 he introduced a resolution that the university should give preference to hiring Methodists, all else being equal. The motion passed without opposition, since this had in effect always been the position of the university. They would look for good Methodists but, since candidates were seldom equal, hire the best man from any Protestant denomination.

Three years later, however, the resolution became a serious issue when Candler nearly persuaded the board to postpone the appointment of Frederick W. Moore as academic dean. Moore was a devout Baptist. Chancellor Kirkland was irate and determined to end the bishops' dominance over the board, on which they served as ex officio members. One of Kirkland's motives was financial: since the Southern Methodists never provided much funding for Vanderbilt, he had to look to northern philanthropists if the university were to gain national standing. In that context denominational ties were an embarrassment. Kirkland was already working with the Rockefeller-funded General Education Board, which was not likely to be favorably impressed by the denial of an appointment to a Baptist. The next year, 1905, the issue became more acute with the establishment of the Carnegie Foundation, which offered attractive retirement programs for faculty members of colleges and universities, but only if the institutions were nonsectarian.[29] Kirkland stated the issue baldly:

> I say to you candidly, as I have said before, I have never found a man, be he Methodist or be he non-Methodist, willing to contribute to our work here who has not endorsed a liberal Christian policy in the administration of affairs. . . . I have never denied our Methodist allegiance, I have never denied our Methodist history, but I have maintained that, greater than Methodism was the cause of Christ and that the call for service in His name was greater than the call to the service of the church.[30]

At the 1905 board meeting Kirkland succeeded in reducing the governing role of the Methodist bishops. This action aroused the fury of another formidable conservative, Bishop Elijah Hoss, who upon returning from a trip to Brazil learned that he had been effectively removed from the board. Already for a decade Hoss had been using his editorship of the *Christian Advocate* to blast trends at Vanderbilt. Hoss thought the university was becoming too cosmopolitan and he deplored everything from the scandalous departures of students from Methodist mores to the frivolity of the football craze.[31]

The full-fledged warfare that broke out in 1905 dragged on for the next nine years. A commission of legal experts ruled essentially in favor of the bishops, establishing them as a board of visitors. Kirkland and the board, however, resisted efforts to restore total Methodist control. In 1910 the Southern Methodist General Conference claimed final say over the university, including the right to name board members as well as oversight by the bishop's board. Kirkland, meanwhile, was on the opposite course, more deeply involved than ever in courting northern philanthropists on the basis that Vanderbilt was nonsectarian. The Vanderbilt board, meeting in the summer of 1910, defied the General Conference and refused to seat new trustees elected by the conference. Noncompromise was no longer possible and the issue went to the courts. A lower court ruled in favor of the General Conference; but in 1914 the Tennessee Supreme Court reversed the decision. Amid great rejoicing among the student body and the faculty, Vanderbilt was declared entirely separate from the denomination.[32]

In the meantime, to take up the slack from the Vanderbilt defection conservatives established two new universities with theological seminaries, Southern Methodist in Dallas and Emory in Atlanta. The latter was funded by the Coca-Cola magnate Asa Candler, brother of the conservative bishop. Predictably, after a generation or so, these schools too drifted into the national mainstream.[33]

The developments at Vanderbilt differed from what was going on elsewhere at Protestant denominational universities only in explicitness and dramatic quality. Because Vanderbilt was located in the South, conservative church forces were strong enough to force a showdown. In the North the same forces were present but had less strength, so that traditionalists' efforts to restrain the trends collapsed earlier. For instance, at Northwestern University, the largest of the Northern Methodist institutions, Charles W. Pearson, a professor of English for thirty years, was dismissed in 1902 for publishing in a local newspaper an article that said the Bible contained myths and errors. Evanston, Illinois, had a large Methodist population and local residents demanded Pearson's resignation. The school was between presidents so the board handled the matter itself. In a rare case in which sanctions regarding religious views were brought against a professor outside a school of theology, the board supported the local sentiments. The firing, however, brought much negative national publicity and the incoming president made clear that he would steer a broader Christian course, even though he would steer carefully. "It is vitally important," he told the board in 1908, "that an institution like Northwestern should not be misrepresented in its character in such a way as to offend either the denomination which gave it birth or the great community which is becoming interested in it without respect to denominational considerations."[34]

Northern Methodist universities were all moving in similar direction, though with similar caution not to arouse a large, usually tolerant, conservative constituency. At Boston University, early in the century, charges of heresy were brought against two of its professors. One of these, Borden Parker Bowne, was the best known figure at the university. Bowne had served as head of the philosophy department and as dean of the graduate school. He was the principal progenitor of the philosophy that came to be known as Boston Personalism, one of the most influential efforts to counter the materialism of modern science by putting it into the framework of a theistic universe that was ultimately personal. Bowne's theology was by no means orthodox and he was accused of denying traditional views of the Trinity, of miracles, the Atonement, future life, and salvation. After a trial before a local Methodist conference, the charges were dismissed in 1904.

The case of Bowne's colleague, Old Testament professor Hinckley G. Mitchell, however, went much differently. One reason may have been that Mitchell was teaching in the School of Theology, where orthodoxy was regarded more a direct concern of the church. Moreover, since 1895 students had initiated several petitions complaining of Mitchell's teaching higher critical views of the Bible. Faculty appointments to the School of Theology were reviewed every five years by the bishops of the Methodist

Episcopal Church [North]. In 1900 Mitchell was reappointed with a warning not to violate church teachings. In 1905, however, his contract was not renewed. In the wake of the ensuing controversy over his dismissal, however, the Methodist General Conference of 1908 decided that the church bishops should no longer act as guardians against theological heresy, thus effectively removing the likelihood that the church would intervene in university affairs. Conservatives continued to complain bitterly for years; but the fact of the matter was that the leadership of the denomination was coming under the firm control of the more liberal party. In 1916 the General Conference abandoned a conservative test for membership and adopted a book list in its "Course of Study," used for training clergy, that included some decidedly more liberal texts than had previously been used. After that point, the issue of church control, so far as traditional Methodist theology was concerned, was moot. The denomination had followed its educational institutions on their liberal Christian path and hence was not likely to attempt a reversal.[35]

In the meantime the Methodist universities were being further pressured by almost all the forces shaping them to put aside their traditionalist ties. Many of these forces, such as technological concerns, broad ideological trends, and changing student mores, were informal. Others were more explicit.

The most dramatic explicit pressure came from the Carnegie Foundation for the Advancement of Teaching, founded in 1905. Andrew Carnegie, an immigrant from Scotland, had no traditional religious training and acquired his religious views eclectically. He was, in effect, an Emersonian. "It is a growing belief with me," he told theology students at St. Andrews University in 1902, "that in the not distant future increasing importance will be attached to one truth until it overshadows all others and proves the center around which religious sentiments will finally gather—the declaration of Christ, 'The Kingdom of Heaven is within you.' " This kind of religion taught that "the worship most acceptable to God is service to man" and had faith in "science which has revealed an illimitable, indestructible and constantly expanding universe under the reign of law, and also the divine law of his being which leads man ever steadily upward, thus assuring him that all is well, since all grows better."[36]

In setting up a foundation to benefit higher education Carnegie turned to Henry Smith Pritchett, president of the Massachusetts Institute of Technology (MIT). Pritchett, the son of a Missouri frontier Methodist preacher, held an essentially secular faith in the same things as did Carnegie. "His 'faith' was science," wrote historian Ellen Condliffe Lagemann, "his church the university; and, with the new power to know the natural order that science provided, he believed a new possibility existed for achieving human harmony." Secular and religious were not meaningful distinctions in the context of this faith in science and humanity. Pritchett was a close friend of President Charles Eliot, who was chair of the foundation board when it called Pritchett to its presidency in 1905.

Pritchett, perhaps true to his Methodist roots, was one of the leading proponents of the gospel of efficiency, so popular at the turn of the century. Not surprisingly William Rainey Harper, whose illness cut off his work with the new foundation, was one of those who strongly urged Pritchett to take its presidency. In his inaugural at MIT, Pritchett had talked about "The Educated Man and the State," emphasizing specialized training along with character and patriotism to serve the state.[37] As the United States was moving from its agricultural basis to become a leading industrial power, he proclaimed in a typical statement, "every human being should become an effective economic unit."[38] He brought similar goals for shaping a national higher education to the Carnegie Foundation. His goal, he wrote to Carnegie, was to make the foundation "one of the Great Agencies not only in dignifying the teacher's calling but also in standardizing American education."[39]

With the blessings of Carnegie and of a board made up of virtually every major university president, including Charles Eliot, Nicholas Murray Butler of Columbia, Arthur T. Hadley of Yale, David Starr Jordan, and Woodrow Wilson, Pritchett designed the Carnegie Pension Fund in 1906 with the explicit purpose of providing monetary leverage for standardizing American higher education.[40] Much as William Rainey Harper had been, Pritchett was concerned about the unregulated and often backward state of American higher education. Sectarian control was an obvious culprit. Accordingly, among the fund's earliest and most explicit goals was an effort to eliminate denominational affiliations whenever possible. To help do so, it set up a generous pension fund for college and university teachers, making it available only to those private institutions not owned or in any formal way controlled by a denomination and at which there were no denominational tests for trustees, students, or faculty and no "distinctly denominational tenets or doctrines [were] taught to students." In an initial survey of schools in the United States and Canada only fifty-one qualified.[41]

Pritchett, apparently not afraid to play the role of lion in a den of Christians, presented a strongly argued and revealing defense of the foundation's policy in a speech in Atlanta before the Conference on Education of the Methodist Episcopal Church, South, in 1908, when the Vanderbilt controversy was in full bloom. Pritchett offered four arguments against denominational control. First, he argued that the teaching of denominational tenets and practice simply made for bad education. To support this point he posited a fundamental distinction between religion as "a life springing up in the human soul which blossoms into forgetfulness of self and into service of God and of man" and particular denominational tenets. The latter, he suggested, were typically conveyed by methods of the Sunday school or the revival, appealing to emotions rather than to reason. In essence they were educationally unsound. "Methods which contravene the intellectual ideals of trained students, or which fail to meet their honest inquiries, have a doubtful effect in the development of their characters." Religious organizations might want to convert people, but educational institutions were not the place to do it. Moreover, to cling to a religious test "goes against the very spirit of intellectual freedom for which a college or university stands."

Prichett's second concern was the practical one that denominational competition was a major contributor to the sheer inefficiency of a nation supporting hundreds of colleges. Pritchett observed that there were nearly a thousand schools in the United States that called themselves colleges, though only about half were more than preparatory schools. Many of the rest, largely denominational schools, had shoddy standards and characteristically claimed they were more than they were, for instance, when smaller colleges called themselves "universities." Denominations typically scattered their resources among many schools rather than concentrating on a few. Though they claimed their schools were nonsectarian, they often set up their own institution in an area where another denomination already had an adequate school.

Pritchett's third line of argument was also an appeal to principles of efficiency. It was simply not good policy, he argued, to have an educational agency run by another agency for which education was not a primary concern. So it would be in churches' interests to support better education conducted by specialists. "If any branch of the Christian church is to grow in the efficiency of its religious leadership, it must draw into service in increasing proportions men whose education is sincere, thoro [*sic;* Pritchett also spelled words efficiently] and broad."

Pritchett's fourth concern pointed to the fundamental problem of Protestant colleges' claims to be public institutions. Denominations were free to conduct their own colleges for the purpose of propagating their faith, however benighted it might be to do that rather than to support teaching of broader religious truth. If denominations continued to insist on controlling educational institutions, then they should be willing to pay for them as well. While much of the public could be expected to favor religion, it could not be expected to promote purely denominational goals. "No denomination can in the future expect to control a college," Pritchett announced, "and at the same time call on the public to support it."[42]

Pritchett's strongest argument was that he controlled a lot of money, so that the foundation's policy was having the predicted result. Within the first four years of the Carnegie pension program twenty additional schools had severed their vestigial denominational ties and so qualified for the funding. Moreover, the Carnegie agents discovered that when those who did have denominational ties were asked what difference denominational affiliations made, they responded "almost without exception that such connection played little, if any, part in the religious or intellectual life of the student body."[43]

No one was more unhappy about his school being disqualified as "sectarian" by the Carnegie Foundation than was Chancellor James R. Day of

Syracuse University. Syracuse was founded as a Methodist university and the majority of university's trustees were named by Methodist conferences. On the other hand, already in 1872 its first chancellor, Alexander Winchell, had declared, "The University is not sectarian. It is an institution founded in the interest of truth, which knows no sect, no sex, no color, no contrasts."[44] Despite continued affirmations of its nonsectarianism, Syracuse had a reputation as a strongly religious school and the location was popularity known as "Piety Hill," a characterization that contrasted it with its longtime rival, Cornell.[45] When James Day assumed the chancellorship in 1894, he had been a successful Methodist preacher of the upwardly mobile sort. In a prominent New York City pulpit he had already gained a reputation for cultivating the wealthy. At Syracuse, where he presided for close to three decades, he was known for his powerful chapel preaching, for his domineering presence, his autocratic rule, and for raising the funds necessary to turn the school into a major university.

At Day's inaugural in 1894 he made the point that, although Syracuse was Methodist, it was

> to be far more Christian than denominational. . . . It will be a university Christian enough to make a Hebrew as much at home as a Christian, to afford equal facility to Catholic and Protestant. There is no creed in mathematics or in natural science. Syracuse University will be a brain manufactory, taking its material from all sources of usable brains. It will be Christian not by exclusion, but by inclusion; not by magnifying a sect, but by magnifying human learning and contributing to the same.[46]

The Carnegie Foundation's test, however, was not that of the spirit but of the letter of church control. In its initial evaluations the Carnegie Foundation first informed Day that since Syracuse "has stood so consistently and so vigorously before the country as a distinctly Methodist institution," it did not qualify for the pensions. Chancellor Day, however, would not take no for an answer and in an exchange of correspondence pressed the point that the Methodist conferences did not have to choose Methodists as trustees, that the chancellor did not have to be a Methodist, and that there were no denominational tests for faculty. Unable to convince the foundation by such arguments, Day explored whether it would help if the Methodist conferences chose only five of the thirty-three trustees. The foundation refused to draw such a line and replied that *any* church control constituted ineligibility. Day also protested to Pritchett against the presumption of the Carnegie Foundation in acting as an accrediting agency and publishing reports evaluating and comparing institutions. Finally, after years of fruitless protests, Day settled the matter in 1910 by publishing a bitter defense of Syracuse and denunciation of the foundation. He concluded:

> Other colleges may do as they please. If they wish to crawl in the dirt for such a price, that is their privilege. But no university can teach young people lofty ideals of manhood and forget its self respect and honor or

> sell its loyalty and faith for money that Judas flung away when in remorse he went out and hung himself. It is an insult for such a proposition to be made to a Christian institution. "The Money perish with thee," is the only answer to it.[47]

Chancellor Day's righteous indignation against mammon may have rung hollow to some observers, since he was known for his books and articles defending big business. Critics supposed that these were related to his zeal for fund-raising. He had attacked not only the muckrakers for their criticisms of business interests, but even President Theodore Roosevelt for attempting to break the trusts. Unrestrained capitalism, Day insisted, was the only source of the nation's prosperity and there was no reason for the pious to be worried about tainted money, a point he had put into practice by successfully cultivating the Rockefellers.[48]

Nor was he unwilling modify the relationship to the denomination when funding was involved. In 1919 when he was attempting to bring the New York State College of Forestry to the Syracuse campus, he was denied funding by the state on the grounds that the university was "sectarian." This time (as he had earlier proposed to the Carnegie Foundation) he did have the charter amended to ensure that the Methodist conferences could elect only a minority of board members. The strategy worked and the funding was granted.[49]

Chancellor Day was probably as much as any of the university builders attempting to steer a middle course and discovering how difficult that was. The Methodist and Christian identities were important to him, and he was not willing to abandon them entirely. At one point in 1913 in response to an alumni request to increase board representation he told the trustees, "This body is not sectarian, but it is important that some Christian body should be responsible for this organization. This [proposal] simply opens the way to throw this institution out of the hands of the church that founded it within five years. . . . We cannot afford that." Day thus recognized that there were deep problems in attempting to remain generically Christian. A year later he sent a communication to his dean regarding faculty appointments, noting that "we are running pretty largely to other denominations," and urging that no one forget that Syracuse was a "Methodist School." This was not precisely what he said to the foundations. To John D. Rockefeller, Jr., he wrote in 1916, "We know no man after flesh or sect or nation here. We welcome Jew, Gentile, Protestant and Catholic. We will not have atheists and free thinkers on our faculties to sow seeds of infidelity in young minds, but we are no sectarian propagandists."[50]

Despite his efforts to hold some balance, the effect of Day's chancellorship was to remove Syracuse from any effective Methodist control. This seemed almost essential to his goal of building a "great university." As one of his associates wrote of his work:

> Syracuse is like most of the church-founded institutions—each of them was forced to make a choice—either to remain a small denominational

college with formal religion very much in the foreground, or to endeavor to play a larger part in the intellectual world without great emphasis on the outward expressions of religious interest.

Chancellor Day made the choice for Syracuse and chose the latter course.[51]

James Day, like his counterparts elsewhere, led the university on the path to secularization in the name of Christianity; but he was particularly explicit in calling the university "Christian" and in invoking God as his ultimate guide. This stance, which might not have caused comment in a strictly ecclesiastical setting, invited criticism the more the school moved toward being a national institution. With respect to Day, the most biting criticism came near the time of his retirement in 1922, with the publication of Upton Sinclair's polemic *Goose-step.* According to Sinclair, Syracuse was the "University of Heaven." Its board members, of whom the president of Standard Oil was only the most conspicuous, was the most pure plutocracy in the nation. "Never has there been such a series of grand dukes and duchesses as at this university," wrote Sinclair. Chancellor Day, Sinclair claimed, apparently on the basis of conversations with faculty, ruled as a total autocrat, "unassisted save by God." For Sinclair, of course, Day was the chief of sinners because he had invoked God's name for the trusts and against strikes and labor unions. Sinclair alleged, however, that Day's disregard for workers extended to the faculty at the university as well. There was no faculty tenure, claimed Sinclair. Rather Day hired and fired people at will and sometimes for petty religious offenses, such as endorsing Sunday baseball, or deviations from doctrinal orthodoxy, such as denying the verbal inspiration of the Pentateuch. While acknowledging that scientists might teach evolution, Day told them at least to "be as pious as you can."[52]

Some of this, such as the charges concerning Sunday baseball and the Pentateuch, was probably apocryphal or exaggerated. Nonetheless, even the official history of the university reveals that Day was an autocrat, who had (as was still common at the time) his own way in hiring and firing. In 1916 he assured John D. Rockefeller, Jr., "We will allow no wild-eyed socialism in economics or kindred subjects, while giving liberty of investigation to sound minds." When he was accused in 1920 by a socialist of having had a bill introduced in the New York legislature to ensure that he could fire without redress, Day replied only that this was nonsense since the power already lay with the trustees, which was to say that the chancellor already had virtual control. The most notorious case at Syracuse had been back in 1899 when the position of John R. Commons, another of the Ely circle, was mysteriously terminated. Although Commons did not claim that he was fired specifically because of his progressive economic views, he did later remark that "it was not religion, it was capitalism that governed Christian colleges."[53]

Here was still another problem for those who would maintain an ex--

plicit Christian identity for a national university. Whatever one's views on political issues, unless vaguely in the middle, they would be taken as claims regarding God's will for the nation and thus offend constituencies with opposite views. The champions of Christian progressivism, such as Ely and his circle, of course had something of the same problem. But the problem was more severe for those who held power and who cultivated such power. Claiming God on the side of power was a perennial liability of national religious establishments. The informality of the American establishment did not make it an exception to this tendency. The alliance of Christianity, usually the more conservative Christianity of some of the wealthy, with political and economic power opened to criticism the whole enterprise of maintaining explicitly Christian institutions.

In the long run there was not so much difference between James Kirkland of Vanderbilt and James Day of Syracuse. Kirkland shepherded his university to independence from church ties while Day retained a formal relationship with Methodism but removed the possibility of formal church control. Each was insistent that his university not be classed with Roman Catholic or other close-minded schools. The simple fact was that once a college expanded its vision to become a university and to serve a broad middle-class constituency, the days were numbered when any substantive denominational tradition could survive. In the cases of Vanderbilt and Syracuse, the less the student body and then the alumni were predominantly Methodist, the less they would stand for Methodist traditions. Perhaps even more important, if the financial support for the university was to come from largely non-Methodist sources, as it did in each case, it was virtually inevitable that the religious stance of the school would be determined by a broader consensus of middle-class polite opinion, whether secular or religious. It was still appropriate on occasion to call this consensus "Christian," but as new generations took over and informal traditions of distinctiveness faded, that term took on an increasingly ceremonial function.

Notes

1. Editor's note, Harold Bolce, "Blasting at the Rock of Ages," *Cosmopolitan* 46 (May 1909), 665.

2. Ibid., 665–76; Bolce, "Avatars of the Almighty," *Cosmopolitan* 47 (July 1909), 209–18; and Bolce, "Christianity in the Crucible," *Cosmopolitan* 47 (August 1909), 310–19.

3. Bolce, "Rallying Round the Cross," *Cosmopolitan* 47 (September 1909), 492.

4. Valuable studies are Thomas H. A. LeDuc, *Piety and Intellect at Amherst College, 1865–1912* (New York: Columbia University Press, 1969); John Barnard, *From Evangelicalism to Progressivism at Oberlin College: 1866–1917* (Columbus: Ohio

State University Press, 1969); David B. Potts, *Wesleyan University, 1831–1910: Collegiate Enterprise in New England* (New Haven: Yale University Press, 1992); and Earl Hubert Brill, "Religion and the Rise of the University: A Study of the Secularization of American Higher Education, 1870–1910," Ph.D. dissertation, American University, 1969.

5. The U.S. Census figures for 1910 indicate 346,000 undergraduates (up from 232,000 in 1900) and 9000 graduate students at 951 institutions. The total number of students represents 5.12 percent of the U.S. population of 18 to 21 year olds (up from 4.01 percent in 1900). In 1910 degrees in higher education were granted to 30,716 men and 9,039 women. Of these, 399 were Ph.D.s for men and 44 for women. United States Bureau of the Census, *Historical Statistics of the United States, Colonial Times to 1957* (Washington, D.C.: Government Printing Office, 1960), 210–12.

6. William A. Scott, "The Religious Situation in State Universities," *Biblical World* 26 (July 1905), 25, cf. 20–24.

7. Wheeler to Stephens, February 22, 1916. Stephens Papers, University of California, Berkeley, in Henry F. May, "Two or Three Berkeleys: Competing Ideologies in the Wheeler Era, 1899–1919," paper presented to university history group, University of California, Berkeley, 1991, 10. I am grateful to May for pointing out this quotation and especially for much thoughtful advice and encouragement on this project.

8. This summary follows that of Philip Gleason, "American Catholic Higher Education: A Historical Perspective," in *The Shape of Catholic Higher Education,* Robert Hassenger, ed. (Chicago: University of Chicago Press, 1967), 15–53. Also valuable are the essays in Gleason, *Keeping the Faith: American Catholicism Past and Present* (Notre Dame, Ind.: University of Notre Dame Press, 1987).

9. Useful studies of this subject are John Tracy Ellis, *The Formative Years of the Catholic University of America* (Washington, D.C.: Catholic University of America Press, 1946); Patrick H. Ahern, *The Catholic University of America 1887–1896: The Rectorship of John J. Keane* (Washington, D.C.: Catholic University of America Press, 1948); and C. Joseph Nuesse, *The Catholic University of America: A Centennial History* (Washington, D.C.: Catholic University of America Press, 1900).

10. R. Scott Appleby, *"Church and Age Unite!" The Modernist Impulse in American Catholicism* (Notre Dame, Ind.: University of Notre Dame Press, 1992), offers a valuable account of Zahm as well as Catholic modernism generally.

11. Margaret Mary Reher, *Catholic Intellectual Life in America: A Historical Study of Persons and Movements* (New York: Macmillan, 1989), 95, 97. Gerald P. Fogarty, S.J., *The Vatican and the American Hierarchy from 1870 to 1965* (Collegeville, Minn.: Liturgical Press, 1982), who provides one of the most valuable accounts of the developments, heads his chapter: "Americanism Condemned: The End of Intellectual Life."

12. Gerald P. Fogarty, S.J., *American Catholic Biblical Scholarship: A History from the Early 'Republic to Vatican II* (San Francisco: Harper & Row, 1989), 83–116. Cf. Reher, *Catholic Intellectual Life,* 61–98.

13. Appleby, *"Church and Age Unite,"* 230.

14. R. Laurence Moore, *Religious Outsiders and the Making of Americans* (New York: Oxford University Press, 1986), 49–71, summarizes some of these critiques and adds to them. See also Reher, *Catholic Intellectual LIfe,* 86–87; David J. O'Brien, *The Renewal of American Catholicism* (New York: Oxford University Press, 1972); and Philip Gleason, "Immigrant Assimilation and the Crisis of Americanization" (1969), in Gleason, *Keeping the Faith,* 58–81.

15. Quoted from Pius X, *Doctoris Angelici* (1914), in William M. Halsey, *The Survival of American Innocence; Catholicism in an Era of Disillusionment, 1920–1940* (Notre Dame, Ind.: University of Notre Dame Press, 1980), 141; see account, 140–41.

16. Cf. Halsey, *Survival,* 5.

17. Halsey argues that there was something of a renaissance, however.

18. John Tracy Ellis, *American Catholics and the Intellectual Life* (Chicago: Heritage Foundation, 1956), 47.

19. Ibid., 24, 31, 34, 47. Episcopalians and Presbyterians each had five to six times as many *Who's Who* listings, even though total Catholic populations outnumbered them by about twenty and eight times, respectively.

20. Cf. Philip Gleason, "Neoscholasticism as Preconciliar Ideology," *CCICA Annual 1988* (Catholic Commission on Intellectual and Cultural Affairs), 15–25.

21. Gleason, "Immigrant Assimilation," argues that such Americanization happened very quickly after the dependency on Thomism was broken after the 1950s. "What happened, in short, was that a campaign which was intended to increase the number of Catholic intellectuals had reached the point of denying that there could be such a thing as a Catholic intellectual" (76).

22. William P. Leahy, S.J., *Adapting to America: Catholics, Jesuits, and Higher Education in the Twentieth Century* (Washington, D.C.: Georgetown University Press, 1991), provides a valuable account.

23. Thorstein Veblen, *The Higher Learning in America: A Memorandum on the Conduct of Universities by Business Men* (New York, 1935 [1918]), remarks that "none but the precarious class of schools made up of the lower-grade and smaller of these colleges, such as are content to save souls alive without exerting any effort on the current of civilization, are able to get along with faculties made up exclusively of God-fearing men" (149).

24. Paul K. Conkin, *Gone with the Ivy: A Biography of Vanderbilt University* (Knoxville: University of Tennessee Press, 1985), 32. This account and the subsequent account concerning Vanderbilt depend on Conkin, which is one of the very best and most thorough of the university histories and is especially distinguished for integrating the place of religion into the story.

25. Ibid., 50–51, 60–63.

26. Ibid., 59.

27. Ibid., 76–84.

28. Ibid., 94–154.

29. Ibid., 151–56.

30. Quoted in James Tunstead Burtchaell, "The Decline and Fall of the Christian College," *First Things* 12 (April 1991), 20. Cf. Burtchaell's account and reflections (16–29) and *First Things* 13 (May 1991), 30–38.

31. Conkin, *Vanderbilt,* 158–59.

32. Ibid., 157–84.

33. For example, at Emory, Candler's initial million-dollar gift came with special emphasis on providing a church-directed alternative to secular education. Nonetheless, to pick some minor but indicative instances, the first on-campus dance was allowed in 1941 and compulsory chapel was discontinued in 1958, although the university continued to affirm its "Christian heritage." Thomas H. English, *Emory University, 1915–1965: A Semicentennial History* (Atlanta: Emory University Press, 1966), 61, 104. On Asa Candler's intentions see, his letter of July 16, 1914, quoted in Henry Morton Bullock, *A History of Emory University* (Nashville, 1936), 285–88.

34. Harold F. Williamson and Payson S. Wild, *Northwestern University: A History 1850–1975* (Evanston, Ill.: Northwestern University Press, 1975), 110, cf. 103.

35. Harmon L. Smith, "Borden Parker Bowne: Heresy at Boston," in *American Religious Heretics: Formal and Informal Trials,* George H. Shriver, ed. (Nashville: Abingdon Press, 1966), 148–87; Stewart G. Cole, *The History of Fundamentalism* (Westport, Conn.: Greenwood Press, 1971 [1931]), 184–92; Robert E. Chiles, *Theological Transition in American Methodism: 1790–1935* (Nashville: Abingdon Press, 1965), 64–65, 70–71. For a conservative complaint, see L. W. Munhall, *Breakers! Methodism Adrift* (New York, 1913).

36. Andrew Carnegie, "A Confession of Religious Faith" (1902), quoted in Ellen Condliffe Lagemann, *Private Power for the Public Good: A History of the Carnegie Foundation for the Advancement of Teaching* (Middletown, Conn.: Wesleyan University Press, 1983), 11.

37. Henry S. Pritchett, "The Educated Man and the State," *Technology Review* 3 (1901), 41, quoted in Lagemann, *Private Power,* 29. Lagemann quotation characterizing Pritchett is from *Private Power,* 35.

38. Pritchett, "A Woman's Opportunity in Business and the Industries, An Address Given at the Second Annual Commencement of Simmons College, Boston, June 12, 1907," quoted in Lagemann, *Private Power,* 22.

39. Pritchett to Andrew Carnegie, November 16, 1905, quoted in Lagemann, *Private Power,* 37–38.

40. Lagemann, *Private Power,* 37–39.

41. Henry S. Pritchett, "The Policy of the Carnegie Foundation for the Advancement of Teaching," *Educational Review* 32 (June 1906), 86, 89. At that time there were listed 218 denominational schools with 2802 professors, 58 state institutions with 1461 professors, and 51 nondenominational with 1944 professors, which altogether included "about one-half of the entire number of so-called higher institutions" (86). Catholic schools were among those apparently not considered. See Richard Hofstadter and Walter P. Metzger, *The Development of Academic Freedom in the United States* (New York: Columbia University Press, 1955), 361–62.

42. Pritchett, "The Relations of Christian Denominations to Colleges," *Educational Review* 36 (October 1908), 217–41.

43. The Carnegie Foundation for the Advancement of Teaching, *Second Annual Report of the President and Treasurer* (1907), 53–54, quoted in Hofstadter and Metzger, *Academic Freedom,* 362.

44. Quoted in Richard Wilson, ed., *Syracuse University,* Vol. III, *The Critical Years* (Syracuse: Syracuse University Press, 1989), 349.

45. Ibid., 251.

46. Inaugural of James R. Day as chancellor, Syracuse University, June 27, 1894, reprinted in W. Freeman Galpin, *Syracuse University,* Vol. II, *The Growing Years* (Syracuse: Syracuse University Press, 1960), Appendix, 488.

47. Ibid., 411–14, quotations from 412 and 414. Lagemann, *Private Power* 185–86, quotes other protests from Day. See 180–83 on Josiah Royce's objections to Carnegie's efforts at standardization.

48. Galpin, *Syracuse,* II:469–77.

49. Ibid., 415–20.

50. These quotations are all cited without full references in Galpin, *Syracuse,* II:415n. Letter of Rockefeller is from December 11, 1916.

51. W. P. Graham to Frank Collins, January 1, 1942, from excerpt in Galpin, *Syracuse,* II:vi.

52. Upton Sinclair, *Goose-step: A Study of American Education,* 2nd ed. (Pasadena, Cal., 1923 [1922]), 277–87.

53. Quoted without exact citation in Galpin, *Syracuse,* II:25.

16

The Elusive Ideal of Academic Freedom

While concerns of the modern market, represented by business supporters, students, and public opinion, were sometimes blindly pushing emerging universities away from their distinctive Christian emphases, the persons most explicitly seeking a rationale for freedom from religious restraints were the progressive professors. By the early decades of the twentieth century professors were beginning to emerge from under the shadow of administrators and to set their own professional standards for academic culture.

The rumors were true that on matters religious the most prominent professors were also likely to be the most outspoken progressives at a university. What Harold Bolce had expressed with alarm to *Cosmopolitan* readers in 1909, James Leuba documented with approval in 1916. Leuba, a professor of psychology at Bryn Mawr College, had been a student of G. Stanley Hall, and his 1916 volume *The Belief in God and Immortality: A Psychological, Anthropological and Statistical Study* was both an early effort to apply the scientific uses of statistics and a pragmatist tract for scientifically created religion.

As a tract, Leuba's study may be seen as an early effort not only to bring out of the closet the widespread academic skepticism regarding traditional Christianity, but also to proclaim skepticism's intellectual superiority and domination. Leuba's essential thesis was that as intelligence and education increase traditional religious beliefs will inevitably decrease. This was a thesis that Thomas Paine, Thomas Cooper, or Thomas Jefferson would have subscribed to, but in the United States its proclamation had been muffled for nearly a century as evangelicals and their immediate heirs had held much of the field in academia. Now armed with the prestige of the new evolutionary sciences and with the reassuring idealist versions of a Jeffersonian Sermon-on-the-Mount civil religion, the cause could reemerge in an irrepressible form. Often hidden behind the pious and patriotic rhetoric of academic administrators, the renaissance of this enlightened skepticism was already well advanced. Much had happened even since the 1890s when the vestiges of orthodoxy had been routed in most leading schools. And if James Leuba's statistics meant anything, the future was bright for a new era guided by science and high ideals.

Perhaps Leuba's most striking findings, and those which told the most about the future, were the marked differences in attitudes toward traditional beliefs among those who were leaders in academic fields compared with the rank and file. Beginning with scientists, he chose randomly from *American Men of Science* three hundred in the ordinary listings and two hundred others who were categorized as "eminent" scientists. He sent each of these a brief survey, on which he received approximately 75 percent answered returns. The first set of three questions regarded belief in God and offered three choices:

1. I believe in a God to whom one may pray in the expectation of receiving an answer. *By "answer," I mean more than the subjective, psychological effect of prayer.*
2. I do not believe in a God *as defined above.*
3. I have no definite belief regarding this question.

Although Leuba recognized that this question about God was limited to a very specific dimension, he argued that this dimension of a personal relationship between God and humans was essential to a traditional Christian view. The point of so limiting the question was to find a very brief way to distinguish traditional Christian views from those views (often also called Christian) in which "the traditional Christian God is exchanged for a God-belief in agreement with present knowledge."[1]

A second set of questions attempted to make a similar discrimination by offering the same three choices regarding belief in personal immortality of persons in another world.

Of the "lesser" scientists answering, 45.5 percent affirmed belief in a God in the sense specified, nearly as many disbelieved, and the rest had no opinion. For the "greater" scientists, however, a startlingly lower number, only 27.7 percent, affirmed the belief, while just over half expressed disbelief, with the rest not sure. Regarding personal immortality the percentage of believers was 52.8 percent for "lesser" scientists, but only 35.2 percent for "greater" scientists.[2]

Leuba also conducted smaller surveys of other major fields. Philosophers, of course, could not be evaluated since they were unable to answer survey questions without adding their own provisos. Of the rest, Leuba found that historians were the most likely to affirm the beliefs in question, about half of them doing so. On the other hand, sociologists and psychologists were even more likely than biologists to be skeptics, only about a quarter of their whole number believing in a prayer-answering God (see figure). Leuba explained these differences by noting that physicists might "recognize the presence of invariable law in the inorganic world only," and that for historians, who still often see the hand of God in human affairs, "the reign of law is not so clearly revealed in the events with which history deals as in biology, economics, and psychology."[3]

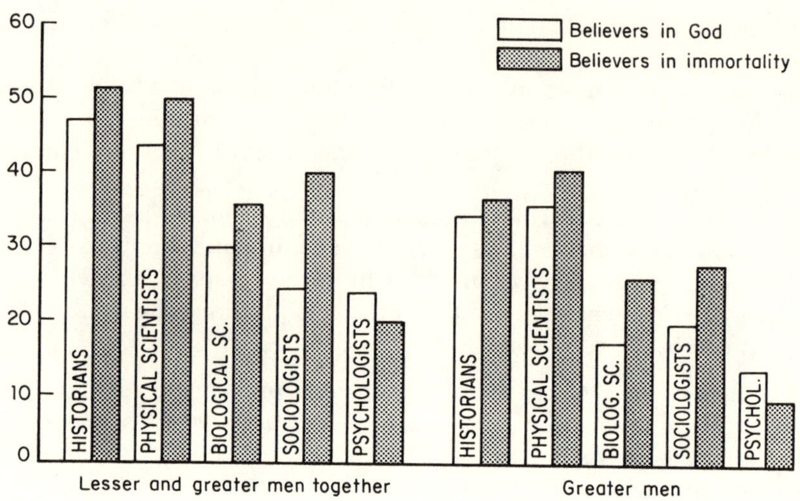

In each field, however, the surveys yielded similar patterns of greater skepticism among those who were identified as eminent in their fields than those were not. Leuba had a clear explanation. "I do not see any way to avoid the conclusion that disbelief in a personal God and in personal immortality is directly proportional to abilities making for success in the sciences in question."[4]

Whatever the assumptions behind Leuba's conclusion and the limits of his questions, he did seem to be finding striking differences between likelihood of belief among those most prominent in their fields compared with the less prominent. One explanation for this might be self-selecting mechanisms within disciplines in which persons with similar assumptions about the universal orderliness of things were controlling the disciplines and helping the likeminded rise to the top. In any case, Leuba was probably correct that something like these assumptions were correlated with academic success. His conclusion also was basically correct: "The essential problem facing organized Christianity is constituted by the wide-spread rejection of its two fundamental dogmas—a rejection apparently destined to extend parallel with the diffusion of knowledge and the intellectual and moral qualities that make for eminence in scholarly pursuits."[5]

Not surprisingly the beliefs of students were influenced by those of their mentors. To measure student responses Leuba had distributed to students at nine "colleges of high rank" and at one normal school (teacher's college), mostly in psychology classes, a short answer questionnaire concerning beliefs in God. The first question was "Do you think of God as a personal or impersonal being?" The subsequent three questions asked students to describe what difference belief in God, or nonbelief, made in their lives. Here the most striking finding was that men were far more likely to have accepted modern ideas of an impersonal God than were women, with 56 percent of men affirming belief in a personal God and 31 in an impersonal God. For women, however, 82 percent believed in a personal God and only 11 percent described God as impersonal. This finding fit with other surveys that consistently showed substantially higher rates of active church participation among college women than among college men or, for that matter, among American women generally, compared to American men. Leuba's interpretation was simply that, for whatever reasons, "during the years of adolescent self-affirmation the desires for intellectual freedom and for a rational organization of opinions and conduct are in young women more effectively balked than in young men by the tender ties of the home and the authority of the church."[6]

Since responses in these student surveys were short answers, they were difficult to classify neatly. Leuba did find that rate of belief was considerably higher in the one teacher's college than it was in the leading colleges, so he was tempted to throw out the data from the normal school. One of his general conclusions, nonetheless, was probably accurate enough, once we discount its overt bias. "The deepest impression left by these records is that, so far as religion is concerned, our students are groveling in the dark. Christianity, as a system of belief, has utterly broken down, and nothing definite, adequate, and convincing has taken its place."[7]

Leuba also documented, on the basis of a more limited sample, some change in students' religious beliefs through their college careers. Here he surveyed all the students at only "one college of high rank and moderate size," presumably Bryn Mawr. "The spirit of this institution," he observed, "is assuredly as religious as that of the average American college." This time he asked about belief in personal immortality and found 80 percent believers among freshmen, 76 percent among sophomores, 60 percent among juniors, and 70 percent among seniors. Leuba could not accept the greater belief of seniors compared with juniors as evidence of a pattern of "a return to a 'saner' view after a brief iconoclastic period." Rather, he was convinced by a suggestion, confirmed by several observers, of the "intellectual superiority of the junior class." This conclusion he thought was demanded, since his investigation of professors provided "incontrovertible evidence of a decrease of belief corresponding to an increase of general mental ability and, perhaps, of knowledge."[8]

Based on his larger student survey, Leuba felt that he could generalize that most young people enter college "possessed of the beliefs still accepted, more or less perfunctorily, in the average home of the land," but that at the better colleges about 40 to 45 percent had abandoned some cardinal Christian beliefs. This he attributed to the maturing of their mental powers, to achieving greater independence of thought, and (somewhat paradoxically) to "study under the influence of persons of high culture."[9]

A self-reliant, independent quality, Leuba affirmed, was the principal characteristic distinguishing eminent men of science in all fields from lesser persons in the field. The leaders had to be willing to break, sometimes even with a certain callousness, from family and social pressures that would otherwise control their opinions. Lesser professors, either temperamentally, or as a result of social constraints of local communities on local schools, less often achieved this independence. Greater academics were more often from more eminent families in which they were able to achieve habits of personal freedom earlier. Moreover, they could more often establish themselves in major academic communities in which "intellectual freedom is honored far above orthodoxy."[10]

Academic Freedom as a Sacred Concept

When the American Association of University Professors (AAUP) was organized in 1915, its founders proclaimed an ideal of academic freedom as essential to the definition of a university. At first some academic administrators resisted aspects of the due process in hiring and firing that the AAUP insisted their ideal implied; but within the next two decades academic freedom, more or less as the AAUP had defined it, was widely accepted. By 1940 when an important restatement of the AAUP principles was widely adopted, the ideal had become a standard assumption in American academic thought.[11] Certainly by the end of the era of McCarthyite repression of the early 1950s academic freedom had attained sacred status among the professoriate and was spoken of as though it were an ancient absolute, associated with universities since time immemorial.

The fact of the matter was that, although aspects of the concept of academic freedom could be found among the Jeffersonians and at nineteenth-century German universities, the phrase, as well as most of its twentieth-century applications, was hardly older than the century itself.[12] Some aspects of the modern concept, of course, had a longer history. Thomas Jefferson talked about liberty in education as the ideal for the University of Virginia, but at the time the American educated elite was sufficiently divided for his program to be widely recognized for what it was: a substitution of boundaries of inquiry consistent with Unitarian Christianity for the older conventional boundaries set by orthodox Protestantism.[13] By the late nineteenth century, however, an updated version of the Jeffersonian ideal of a neutral science had become sufficiently dominant in the academic community to rout the remaining opposition. In this regard the intellectual naiveté of faith in the neutrality of science now often attributed to the Enlightenment was much more prevalent in early twentieth-century America than it had been in the eighteenth or early nineteenth centuries.[14] Prevailing academic opinion now accepted, almost without dispute, that since a university was defined as a scientific institution it a was a neutral territory in which all views would have an even chance to be judged on their intellectual merits alone. Marxists, Catholics, conservative Protestants, and others who complained that their views did not get a fair hearing, were dismissed as of no intellectual merit.

The direct inspiration for the modern American conception of academic freedom came, however, from Germany, or at least from the romanticized impressions of Germany that the many thousands of American academics who studied there brought back with them. Particularly important for the American organizers of the academic profession after 1890 was the German *Lehrfreiheit,* referring to freedom for university professors. In Germany this freedom included, first, the rights for professors to teach whatever they chose with a minimum of administrative regulations and, second, the freedom to conduct one's research and to report one's findings in lectures and publications without external restraint. At the heart of *Lehrfreiheit,* as Americans typically understood it, was the modern ideal that truth is progressive and that for science to advance it must be freed from tradition and preconception. In nineteenth-century Germany this outlook was associated with the term *Wissenschaft,* which meant more than just the English word "science," suggesting instead the "sanctified" moral ideal of a scientific search for truth.[15] During the nineteenth century, German Protestant universities only gradually won full recognition of such professorial autonomy, including freedom from occasional ecclesiastical interference. Nonetheless, they were always far in advance of American schools and by the time of the establishment of the German empire *Lehrfreiheit* was solidly enshrined. The peculiarity of the German freedom, however, was that it was guaranteed by the autocratic state, which controlled the universities and so protected them from direct interference of other interests. In a society far more hierarchical and more conscious of status than the United States, *Lehrfreiheit* was not an extension of any general commitment to freedom for all citizens but one of the prerogatives of professorial status, suggesting the precedent of much more limited professorial immunities going back to the Middle Ages. Once the wider applications of modern *Lehrfreiheit* were accepted, however, they were proclaimed by their Protestant advocates as essential to any institution calling itself a "university."[16]

While the German ideals of *Wissenschaft* and *Lehrfreiheit* converged with and were translated into American Whig or republican ideals and so transformed had important influences as *ideals* for the academics who defined American universities, the Americans never followed German precedents very closely. In fact, the cases during the 1890s that precipitated the American formulations of "academic freedom" involved activities that went beyond what the German precedents would allow. The series of dismissals of politically progressive professors was overwhelmingly the leading issue that sparked the American discussions and the continuation of such concerns among academics led directly to the founding of the AAUP The major question of the 1890s, which was still not resolved late in the Progressive era at the time of the founding of the AAUP, was what rights professors had to speak *in public,* particularly on political issues. In Germany, professors were not assumed to have a right to take partisan political stands, especially if they favored socialism.[17] In the United States, however, when progressive professors with mildly socialist leanings were dismissed for political activities or public presentations of their views, an outcry was raised about freedom of speech. Could professors have less freedom than other American citizens? Freedom for public speech thus was a major component rolled into the American version of "academic freedom."

Since there were always severe limits both on what might be taught and on what might be advocated publicly, such as against obscene, scandalous, inflammatory, or revolutionary teachings, exact lines were hard to draw. Albion Small, implicitly defending his friend William Rainey Harper regarding the Bemis dismissal, insisted in 1899 that he had never seen a case in which professors of economics or sociology were not free to teach and publish views contrary to those of the business benefactors of the universities. Any demand for more freedom would go beyond true academic freedom since it would substitute partisanship for the open-mindedness of true science. "The American professor whose digestion is good and who has escaped brain-fag has all the freedom he wants. He knows that he could not have more without resorting to license that would place him among social quacks."[18]

Small's colleague John Dewey, subsequently became the first president of the AAUP and so was the leading early proponent of what became the orthodox view. Writing on "Academic Freedom" in 1902, he enunciated all the essentials of the standard twentieth-century American definition of a university. There are two types of institutions, he said. "An ecclesiastical, political or even economic corporation holding certain tenets," he affirmed, "certainly has a right to support an institution to maintain and propagate its creed." These "teaching bodies, called by whatever name" were not to be confused with "the university proper." While professors at partisan institutions might deplore the narrowness of such schools and work to speed their transformation into true universities, in the meantime they would have to accept that schools had a right to limit free inquiry, so long as their standards were clearly stated.

Universities, on the other hand, were constructed for the scientific investigation of the truth. "To investigate truth; critically to verify fact; to reach conclusions by means of the best methods at command, untrammeled by external fear or favor, to communicate this truth to the student; to interpret to him its bearing on the questions he will have to face in life—this is precisely the aim and object of the university."[19]

Dewey regarded this principle as beyond dispute but recognized problems in its application. The major one was that in many fields science had not yet reached the mature state it had attained in mathematics, astronomy, physics, and chemistry. In part this was simply a problem of lack of full public acceptance of scientific findings, as when popular prejudices limited teaching about biological evolution at some smaller colleges. In some other disciplines, such as sociology and psychology, and those aspects of history and literature having most to do with religion, the almost total public ignorance of the scientific character of such inquiries was compounded by some backwardness in the sciences themselves. This meant, on the one hand, that there must be total freedom to educate the public in the findings of these sciences. On the other hand, it demanded care on scholars' parts not to speak dogmatically on subjects on which they were not scientifically expert.

This latter point was an important proviso in the AAUP founders' early definitions of academic freedom. Freedom of expression was limited to areas of scientific competence. So Dewey quoted approvingly a statement of President Harper in 1900 that declared that professors abused academic freedom if they propounded opinions not accepted by the community of scientists, if they preempted scientific inquiry with partisan politics or sensational methods, or if they spoke on controversial issues beyond their subject or their competence. Dewey emphasized as well his enthusiasm for Harper's affirmation that enduring the dangers of abuse of such liberty "is not so great an evil as the restriction of such liberty." Even though Dewey welcomed Harper's reassurances on this crucial point, he saw dangers in the centralization that the expansion of the universities had brought. Presidents had assumed increasing power at the expense of faculties. This tendency should be systematically corrected.[20]

Ultimately the question for Dewey was how the university was to serve the public. Just as his New England predecessors of the John Adams ilk had seen the necessity of a natural aristocracy to check an unruly democracy, so Dewey believed that the cacophony of conflicting and nonsensical voices in modern America called for leadership of men of science. "There has never been a time in the history of the world," he wrote, "when the community so recognized its need of expert guidance as to-day. In spite of our intellectual chaos, in spite of the meaningless hullabaloo of opinion kept up so persistently about us by the daily press, there is a very genuine hunger and thirst after light. . . . With the decay of external and merely governmental forms of authority, the demand grows from the authority of wisdom and intelligence."[21]

In 1904 Dewey moved from the University of Chicago to Columbia in New York City, where Nicholas Murray Butler, another of the great academic entrepreneurs of the era, presided. Bringing Dewey to Columbia was part of Butler's program to build the New York school into a leading American university. Butler was conservative in many ways and his views may be taken as representative of the more cautious administrative opinion at the time the concept of academic freedom was emerging. In a succinct statement, published in the Philadelphia *Public Ledger* in 1914, Butler pointed out some necessary limits to academic freedom. These limitations were "those imposed by common morality, common sense, common loyalty, and a decent respect for the opinions of mankind." Most abuses of academic freedom, he observed, were cases in which mildly controversial opinions that might have been tolerated otherwise were combined with "lack of ordinary tact and judgment." At Columbia there was therefore one simple rule, "to behave like a gentleman." Being a gentleman meant to have due regard for the opinions of others, for the impressionability of the young, and for the wisdom of earlier eras. Despite urging such voluntary limits, Butler as much as the progressives accepted the standard formula that freedom from "shackles of political, religious, or scientific beliefs and opinions" was essential to the definition of a university. "If preconceived views must be taught and if certain preconceived opinions must be held, then the institution whose teachers are so restricted is not a university."[22]

As in the 1890s most of the controversies regarding academic freedom were political. Typically they involved accusations by political progressives and by increasing numbers of Socialists (Eugene Debs received nearly a million votes as the Socialist party candidate for the presidency in 1912) that academics were muzzled by the business interests who paid their bills. That big business would now be seen as the primary threat to free expression was understandable, not only because of the conspicuous power of vast wealth, but also because of the shift from clerical to lay control of higher education. In 1860–1861 nearly 40 percent of the board members of private colleges were clergymen, and these were often the most prominent, the best educated, and the most influential trustees. By 1900–1901 less than a quarter of board members were clergy, and for the first time they were outnumbered by businessmen and lawyers. The percentage of clergy representatives continued to drop precipitously, especially at schools without close church ties.[23] Clergy presidents might still be found at small colleges and at denominational schools but were becoming rare at major universities. At most of the leading schools overt restriction of religious belief was not an issue so long as one was a gentleman. Jews, of course, might be thought not very gentlemanly and were discriminated against in hiring, especially in the humanities, but that was only partly a question of religious belief. Pentecostals, Mormons, and unreconstructed Southern Baptists probably could not have been hired at most universities either. Despite these blind spots, the official policy was, as Nicholas Murray Butler put it in his 1914 article, that "the tenure of office of a university teacher must . . . be quite independent of his views on political, religious, or scientific subjects."[24]

Controversial religious views and most traditional theological views were also often excluded from universities by being either disparaged or ignored.[25] To the shapers of American universities, however, such exclusions were not seen as restrictions on academic freedom. Their positivist-progressive paradigm dictated that any decline in traditional religious privilege was an advance for freedom. Even if they did recognize that freedom for one thing always means exclusion of something else, they typically viewed the exclusion of religious restraints on intellectual inquiry as self-evidently justified.

Even if religious issues in teaching were residual at most universities, the battle was ongoing in academia as a whole. Many professors taught at church-related colleges where such questions were still very much alive. Questions of religious restrictions, moreover, had more to do with precipitating the founding of the AAUP than is recognized in the usual historical accounts. In fact, just at the time in January 1914 when the *Philadelphia Ledger* was publishing President Butler's views on academic freedom, the Philadelphia area was agitated by a controversial case of religious restraint. The question, fought bitterly at Lafayette College in Easton, Pennsylvania, was in effect whether the academic profession would any longer even tolerate old-time college religious standards in northern colleges that hoped to compete in the respectable mainstream. For the first time professional organizations of the professoriate played a major role in the controversy and the case was intimately involved with the organization of a professorial union.

Warfare at Lafayette

The president of Lafayette College was Ethelbert Warfield, who was probably best known as the younger brother of Benjamin Breckinridge Warfield, the leading conservative Presbyterian theologian of the era. The brothers were from the Union side of the famous Breckinridge family of Kentucky and were loyal to the rigorous Old School Presbyterianism in which they had been reared. Ethelbert had studied in Germany and at Oxford, practiced law briefly, and served as president of Miami University in Ohio before becoming president of Lafayette in 1891 at age thirty. Benjamin, who joined the faculty of Princeton Theological Seminary in 1887, had helped forge the Princeton formulation of the "inerrancy" of Scripture and had been a leading opponent of Charles Briggs for deviation from that standard. In 1899 Ethelbert was ordained to the Presbyterian ministry and in 1904 he became the president of the board of trustees of Princeton Theological Seminary, which remained a fortress of Presbyterian orthodoxy. Originally chartered in 1826, Lafayette College was a classic instance of a college founded, as its name suggested, under liberal auspices. The original charter stated clearly "That persons of every religious denomination shall be capable of being elected trustees, nor shall any person, either principal, professor, tutor or pupil, be refused admittance into said college or denied any of the privileges, immunities or advantages thereof for or on account of his sentiments in matters of religion." Nonetheless, as often happened to colleges of the mid-nineteenth century, Lafayette soon came under the sway of Presbyterian educational imperialism. Militant Old School Presbyterians were largely responsible for the early success of the college and in 1854 its charter was amended to give the Old School Synod of Philadelphia power to nominate or to dismiss trustees or faculty. In 1885, however the Synod's power was reduced to a nominal oversight that was commensurate with the Synod's lack of financial support for the college. During Warfield's presidency the catalogues stated that the school was "under the general direction of the Synod of Pennsylvania" and that the instruction was to be "within the lines of general acceptance among evangelical Christians."[26] Any more specific controls would be informal.

Before the case that came to the attention of the founders of the AAUP, President Warfield had been involved in an extreme, though aptly symbolic, illustration of the problem of lack of formal professorial recourse against autocratic presidents and their boards. In 1897 the position of George Herbert Stephens, a Princeton College and Seminary alumnus who taught logic and ethics, had not been renewed. Stephens responded by burning down the principal college building in hopes of thus discrediting Warfield. No ideological issue was overtly involved, and Stephens was judged mentally unstable.[27]

In 1905 Warfield filled a new endowed chair in the pivotal old-time college subject of mental and moral philosophy by turning to an outstanding young man, John Mecklin. From Warfield's perspective Mecklin had the correct pedigree. The son of an orthodox Presbyterian pastor from Mississippi, he had been educated in Presbyterian schools, had a degree from Princeton Theological Seminary, was distinguished by a German doctorate, yet remained solidly in the Presbyterian orbit.

Once at Lafayette, Mecklin very soon became absorbed with the pragmatism of William James as a philosophical guide. Warfield, who taught a brief senior course in Christian evidences, expected the chair in mental and moral philosophy to be used to defend traditional Christianity against the challenges of modern thought. Mecklin, however, was moving rapidly away from his strict Presbyterian heritage and saw philosophy as an ongoing and ever-changing human quest. His job, as he viewed it, was to reconcile the Christian heritage to modern thought. He did so, for instance, by suggesting that Jesus, Paul, Athanasius, and Augustine were all ultimately pragmatists who valued their experience of knowing and obeying God more than mere doctrine. Mecklin was an intellectual leader on the faculty and quickly became far more popular among the students than was Warfield himself.[28]

Despite repeated efforts by Warfield to have the board of trustees formally constrain Mecklin's teachings or the texts he was using (including John Dewey and James Tufts on ethics and a number of other pragmatists on psychology and psychology of religion), the young professor successfully defended himself on the grounds that he was only teaching students to *think* and that such honest intellectual inquiry could not be a threat to the faith. In the meantime, however, he was quite explicitly teaching that religious beliefs were products of social evolution and illustrating such views by references to higher critical interpretations of the Old Testament.[29]

The controversy between Warfield and his board versus Mecklin smoldered over a four-year period, finally bursting into flames in the spring of 1913. Mecklin sent Warfield copies of exams from his course on theism, which Mecklin apparently believed would reassure the president of the good he was doing. The exams had the opposite effect, confirming Warfield's suspicions that Mecklin's teachings were undermining traditional Protestantism. Warfield, like other conservative Princetonians, had no objection to biological evolution being taught in science classes, since that could be reconciled as a mode of divine Providence. On the other hand, he believed, quite correctly from his point of view, that theories of social evolution of religion were far more threatening to traditional Protestantism. Particularly, higher critical theories of the social evolution of Judaism and Christianity threatened the claim, foundational for biblicist Protestantism, that Christianity originated in divine revelations, supernaturally revealed in the Scriptures. While Warfield did not insist on inerrancy as a test of the faith at the college, he was convinced that theories of social evolution would destroy any version of the traditional Protestantism for which the college professed to stand.

At the June board meeting, just before commencement in 1913, Warfield finally persuaded most his board that Mecklin's views did indeed threaten the religious stance of the college. Calling Mecklin in, the board confronted him with the possibility of a vote on his dismissal. Sensing that there probably was no other recourse, Mecklin offered his resignation, which the board accepted.

The case, however, was far from closed. When the graduating seniors, gathered at a baseball game, heard of Mecklin's resignation they immediately demonstrated in protest. For years Warfield's star had been setting so far as popularity with the students was concerned. Dissent had been expressed most directly during daily chapel exercises when the students, all boys (as they were called—not always inappropriately), would regularly show disrespect any time Warfield or one of his sympathizers was speaking by simultaneous tapping, fits of coughing, or with standard chapel pranks such as setting a series of alarm clocks to go off during the service. At the graduation ceremony the day after Mecklin's resignation, the students behaved in a similar fashion, tapping loudly whenever Warfield spoke and falling silent otherwise. After the graduation ceremony the class marched to a commencement room chanting what they called their "pirate cheer," ending with a forceful "to hell with Warfield." After repeating their cheer three additional times at the door for the benefit of the assembled alumni and faculty, they entered the room, but when Warfield rose after the meal they gave a cheer for "Johnny Meck" and exited en masse. To add a little weight to their protest they adopted a formal petition stating that they were "thoroughly convinced that President Warfield has demonstrated his incapacity to fill the position of president of Lafayette College" and that they would withhold their class gift until there was a new administration. Needless to say, the board of trustees was alarmed by what looked like an old-time student rebellion, and they were worried about the threat to their student constituency. In a special meeting they appointed a committee to investigate.[30]

Thus far the story was not so different from that of the ouster of President Clapp from Yale, except that in the twentieth century the issues seemed anomalous, even if the behavior was somewhat tamer. In the eighteenth century, it would have been the students who burned down the college building.

The added twentieth-century feature, however, was the professionalization of the professoriate. Academics were already organized into professional societies and these provided annual meetings and journals for publicity and a base for further organization.

Mecklin sent letters to two professional journals explaining that it was not because his views were contrary to church standards, but because he used textbooks such as Dewey and Tufts on ethics and James R. Angell's *Psychology*. (Angell, son of Michigan's former president, was a Dewey student and later president of Yale.) These texts were used at some other Presbyterian colleges and their use was opposed only by the more conservative Presbyterians, not by the church as a whole. So, in Mecklin's view, the case boiled down to the question of "whether a well-meaning but misguided loyalty to outworn theological beliefs is to take precedence over loyalty to approved scientific methods and well-attested facts."[31]

The presidents of the American Philosophical Association and the American Psychological Association acted quickly in appointing a joint committee of inquiry, headed by Arthur O. Lovejoy of Johns Hopkins University. In November 1913 the committee addressed a letter to President Warfield inquiring via a lengthy list of questions as to the exact policies of the college and whether John Mecklin's published account was accurate. A month later they received an evasive reply from the executive committee of the board, not answering the specific questions but stating that the college was under the general direction of the Synod of Philadelphia and that the chair Mecklin occupied had been endowed with the express purpose of continuing Lafayette's tradition of providing "a foundation for conservative Christian thought and character."

Arthur Lovejoy responded on behalf of the committee pressing Warfield "to let the committee have, from yourself personally, some more specific statement" in response to the questions asked. To this Warfield took the ground that colleges were still autonomous associations of gentlemen whose affairs were not open to the public. "I trust you will pardon me," he responded curtly, "if I say that your committee has no relation to me personally which would justify my making a personal statement to you with regard to this matter." Citing the confidentiality of board affairs, he concluded with the hope that the committee would "on reflection perceive the impropriety" of his discussing private board affairs with outsiders.

Such a response could only raise the ire of the committee and speed them in their resolve to create an organization through which professorial rights could be heard. In the meantime they could resort only to publicizing their views.

Their conclusion, as published in the Journal of Philosophy, Psychology, and Scientific Methods, was that "American colleges and universities fall into two classes." Institutions of one type enjoyed virtually complete freedom of inquiry, while the others were "frankly instruments of denominational or political propaganda." Since it was inevitable that such propagandizing institutions should continue to exist, the professional societies should publicize which institutions were which. They should also investigate and expose instances at either type of school, in which freedom had been infringed beyond declared limits. Most important for the propagandizing schools, professors should demand that exact limits on freedom be declared to prospective teachers publicly and *in advance* of their employment. One of the objectionable features in the Mecklin case, the committee argued quite convincingly, was that, whatever the merits of the Lafayette board's position, everything in the college literature was phrased so ambiguously as to make it impossible to know what the doctrinal rules of the college in fact were.[32]

John Mecklin himself astutely pointed out the inherent contradiction in Lafayette's policy, which was the same contradiction found in every Protestant institution we have looked at. On the one hand, Warfield was determined to keep the school's teaching at least compatible with orthodox Presbyterian doctrine. On the other hand, the school's charter still carried the provision against religious discrimination. Moreover, while the catalogue declared that the aim of the school was "distinctly religious," and the school was under the "general" direction of the Synod of Pennsylvania, nonetheless it also assured that "religious instruction is carried on . . . within the lines of general acceptance among evangelical Christians, the points of agreement, rather than those of disagreement, being dwelt upon." The ambiguity was captured in a Synod visiting committee's report that recommended "this splendid institution as a safe and profitable one . . . for a liberal up-to-date education." According to Mecklin, "Our two-faced educational Janus said to the heretics, 'We offer you a liberal and up-to-date education.' To the minority of orthodox Presbyterians and so-called evangelicals this educational Janus said, 'Behold, I give your boys a safe and sound Christian education.' "[33]

In February 1914, within a few weeks of the publication of the findings of the investigators from the professional organizations, Warfield resigned his presidency at Lafayette. The Lafayette board, however, had been moving in the direction of seeking Warfield's resignation since before the intervention of the professional associations, and there is no way to measure the impact of the national publicity. John Mecklin was not restored to his position.[34]

The American Association of University Professors

The Lafayette case was directly tied to the organization of the AAUP. Already in the spring of 1913, in the spirit of progressive reform,[35] senior faculty members at Johns Hopkins University had issued a call for an organization of professors. Major universities sent representatives to a preliminary conference held in November 1913, which coincided with the efforts to investigate the Lafayette case. Arthur Lovejoy, chair of the Lafayette investigating committee, was the principal organizer and served as acting secretary. The group called for a larger gathering, which met January 1 and 2, 1915, and formed the AAUP. John Dewey was chosen president.[36]

In an opening address Dewey pointed out one of the major implications of professorial organization. National association provided a healthier atmosphere for the progress of science. Truth, he said in a line of thought that Charles Peirce had suggested and Dewey had popularized, was defined by the convergence of views of scientific observers. It was what objective investigators would eventually agree on. For such pragmatic views, as much as for their Baconian predecessors, it was therefore crucial that local and parochial interests not hinder agreement. "The best way to put educational principles where they belong—in the atmosphere of scientific discussion—" Dewey proclaimed, "is to disentangle them from the local circumstances with which they so easily get bound up in a given institution. The very moment we free our perplexities from their local setting they perforce fall into truer perspectives. Passion, prejudice, partisanship, cowardice and truculence alike tend to be eliminated, and impartial and objective considerations to come to the front."

Whatever the merits of such proposals, as cultural history we can see them as efforts to define and control a national culture at the expense of local cultures. Professional societies were already accomplishing this to a degree; they were creating loyalties and self-definitions based on the scientific standards of national organizations, and thus undermining loyalty to particular institutions and their traditions. The AAUP would foster this nationalizing trend. Its ideals would be the apotheosis of nonsectarianism. Local and parochial traditions would be eliminated, not immediately by a decree of a ministry of education, but in the more democratic way of the "expression of a public opinion based on ascertained facts."[37]

In such a modern world the experts would rule. The AAUP accordingly was formed among the professorial elite. Membership was initially limited to full professors and was by nomination only. The original core organizing committee had consisted of representatives of nine leading research universities. These in turn nominated men of full professorial rank in their own institution and within each of their disciplines. At the first gathering of these academic leaders the understanding was confirmed that "the association shall be composed of college and university teachers of recognized scholarship or scientific productivity."[38]

We can presume that such a gathering of America's academic elite would have had just about the attitudes toward traditional Christianity that James Leuba had discovered in his contemporaneous survey of "greater" men of science in all major disciplines. Enough of a distinguished minority of conservatives or those who had respect for conservatives would be present to ensure no frontal assault on traditional Christian education. Nonetheless, a disdain for the parochial past would be clearly visible as well.

This was the case in the classic Report of the Committee on Academic Freedom and Tenure presented at the end of 1915 and accepted and approved at the AAUP annual meeting. Following closely the formula of the report on Lafayette, the committee (which had two of the same members, including Lovejoy) noted that churches or businesses have a moral right to conduct a proprietary institution to be used "as an instrument of propaganda." "Concerning the desirability of the existence of such institutions," the committee remarked somewhat disingenuously, "the committee does not desire to express any opinion." Nonetheless, it was "manifestly important that they should not be permitted to sail under false colors." The hopeful sign, the committee suggested, was that "such institutions are rare, and are becoming ever more rare." Most denominational colleges were evolving toward uniform ideals of academic freedom in which their particular traditions did not substantially intrude.

Such institutions, the committee pointed out, were moving from a private proprietary status to being a "public trust." Consequently the defining characteristic of true institutions of higher learning was that they would serve the public, and academic service to the public was based on the premise that "education is the corner stone of the structure of society and progress in scientific knowledge is essential to civilization." Such a trust justified elevating the dignity of the professoriate, so that the best men would be attracted to it.

In serving the public the university had three major functions. First was "to promote inquiry and advance the sum of human knowledge." On this point the committee's allusion to religion was particularly revealing of the prevailing theory of knowledge. "In the spiritual life, and in the interpretation of the general meaning and ends of human existence and its relation to the universe, we are still far from a comprehension of the final truths, and from a universal agreement among all sincere and honest men." Such an assumption as to where all human knowledge would eventually lead demanded a freedom that by definition would preclude all claims to settled religious truths.

The second function of the university was "general instruction to students." Here freedom to say what one believed was essential to the integrity of teaching. At the same time the professoriate saw college education as disabusing students of outdated beliefs and recommended that, particularly for the immature students of the first two college years, "the instructor will introduce the student to the new conceptions gradually, with some consideration for the students' preconceptions and traditions." In general, however, it was "better for students to think about heresies than to not think at all."

The third function, to "develop experts for various branches of the public service," was likewise revealing of the underlying assumptions defining the modern academic profession. Here the document thoroughly reflected the spirit of progressive reforms. Democratic opinion needed to be guided by scientifically informed experts. Almost half the drafting committee were social scientists, including Richard T. Ely and the chair, Edwin R. A. Seligman of Columbia, another founder of the American Economics Association. Democracy, they pointed out, was both a check against tyranny and itself a potential source of tyranny through intolerant public opinion. Experts were desperately needed to keep democratic opinion from being swept by waves of irrationality. Such guardian experts must be free to examine and advocate positions contrary even to strongly prevailing opinion. Hence it was essential that the universities protect freedom of scientific investigation even when its conclusions were unpopular. Professors should have the same rights as other citizens to speak out in public and even to campaign on controversial issues. Science provided the means whereby democracy could be saved from itself and hence for the sake of society universities must be sacred preserves.

The theory was accompanied by proposals for needed practical reforms. The central idea that professors served the public and not private interests meant that college professors should no longer be treated as though they were simply employees. Faculty committees should participate in the processes of hiring and firing. Professors and associates should have permanent tenure. All faculty members should have rights to standardized judicial procedures involving peer review.

The AAUP committee recognized that academic freedom could not be unlimited but argued that there should always be a presumption in its favor, with no firm lines drawn around it. Restraints were sometimes necessary, of course, against extreme, scandalous, or irresponsible statements. But, as a rule, restraints should be voluntary.[39]

Critics were, of course, quick to point out difficulties in the revolutionary concept of freedom as a virtual absolute or presumption on which there were no formal restraints. Particularly what if such freedom undermined the stated goals of an institution? Chancellor Day, for instance, argued that if professors have rights of conscience, so should trustees have rights of conscience and freedom to fire.[40] The Association of American Colleges, an organization which college presidents founded in 1915 and which included representatives of many church-related institutions, spoke specifically to the religious issue in a 1917 report. "A man who accepts a position in a college which he has reason to believe is a Christian institution and who, further, may properly infer that the canons of good taste forbid, perhaps, the asking when the contract is made, of intimate personal questions about his own religious belief, can scarcely assume that freedom of speech includes either the right privately to undermine or publicly to attack Christianity."[41]

This line of defense pointed to a critical weakness in the Protestant establishment in higher education. As at Warfield's Lafayette, even the more liberal Protestant administrators wanted to have it both ways. On the one hand, as they were attempting to attain more professional scientific standards and to serve an increasingly pluralistic public, propriety forbade that they ask about professorial candidates' religious beliefs. Those were "intimate personal" matters. On the other hand, many of the schools were sufficiently connected to their denominations that they did in effect have an implied doctrinal test, at least that professors were not allowed publicly to attack Christianity. The AAUP was demanding, reasonably enough, that if Christian institutions had boundaries, they should state them clearly. Before very many years, schools that aspired to a national standing would have to concede that particular religious traditions could not have normative standing in shaping academic policies.[42]

Loyalty as a Limit on Freedom

On the other hand, the inherent limits of the AAUP's position on the larger point of proclaiming the sacredness of freedom as though it were an absolute became apparent very quickly when the United States entered World War I in the spring of 1917. Patriotic hysteria swept through the elite professoriate as much as any group in America. They were predominantly Anglo and saw the ideals of Anglo-democracy as their heritage, well worth fighting for. President Wilson, who predicted the hysteria but did not prevent it, was one of their number, university professor and president turned progressive reformer. If the highest morality—some would say the highest Christian morality—was to serve democratic society, then no calling was higher than for professors as well as universities to put themselves at the nation's service. This was not a conservative versus liberal issue, because many of the liberal reformers saw in the war the ultimate progressive cause and were as ready as any conservative to defend the flag. Often with unrestrained enthusiasm, they offered their services to university and local war committees. They wrote books and thousands of articles in the massive propaganda effort to vilify Germany and to represent the war as the ultimate crusade for all that humanity held dear. The National Security League, which later was accused of patriotic excess, included among its propaganda writers leading progressive professors and organizers of the AAUP such as Richard T. Ely and Arthur Lovejoy. Shailer Mathews of the University of Chicago Divinity School, a center where patriotism was especially fervid, served as chair of a Committee on Patriotic Service established by the AAUP.[43]

Of the organizers of the AAUP Arthur Lovejoy was particularly enthusiastic in support of the war effort, though others, like John Dewey, shared similar sentiments with only minor qualifications. Those such as Dewey, who had during the early stages of the European conflict urged rational pacific solutions, came around to support American intervention once they were convinced of the high moral justification that the survival of democracy was at stake. Professorial opinion, of course, covered a spectrum, and a small minority was pacifist, pro-German, or otherwise opposed to the American war effort. Across the country at least twenty academics were fired for disloyalty and the number whose contracts quietly were not renewed is impossible to estimate.[44]

At Columbia University AAUP leaders John Dewey and Edwin Seligman tried to play mediating roles as their university faculty was torn apart by the purge. The situation was aggravated by the allegedly dictatorial methods of President Nicholas Murray Butler. Already in 1916 the distinguished progressive historian Charles Beard, notorious for his irreverent *An Economic Interpretation of the Constitution* (1913), was accused of condoning a speaker who said "To Hell with the Flag." Beard survived the board's inquisition by denying that he condoned the statement. Once the United States entered the war the following April, heads began to roll. In October, after a protracted controversy, the trustees dismissed on the grounds of disloyalty two senior professors, J. McKeen Cattell and the pedigreed Henry Wadsworth Longfellow Dana. Within a week Charles Beard resigned, affirming his own support for the war but charging that the university "is really under the control of a small and active group of trustees who have no standing in the world of education, who are reactionary and visionless in politics, narrow and medieval in religion."[45]

While the AAUP leadership also deplored such unilateral procedures by trustees, they did not in principle oppose dismissals for disloyalty. In December 1917 the AAUP adopted a report on "Academic Freedom in Wartime," from a special three-man committee chaired by Arthur Lovejoy. The committee affirmed its own unqualified loyalty and that of the vast majority of academics to the American cause and deplored "the sinister forces which have involved humanity in the present unspeakable catastrophe." They further argued simply that freedom of speech and academic freedom had to be temporarily curtailed in wartime and that their only concern was that such necessities not be carried to extremes or allowed to subvert proper procedures in ways that would permanently threaten the very freedoms they were fighting for. Thus although they urged that universities not dismiss all conscientious objectors or German sympathizers, they found it perfectly justifiable to do so if anyone taught or advocated draft resistance or publicly questioned the moral legitimacy of the American cause. Professors with German heritages might be "so blinded to the moral aspects of the present conflict" as to support the land of their origins, but they should remain silent.[46]

American professors typically were chagrined by the way the professors of the German universities seemed to have sold out to the cause of barbarism. At the outset of the war in 1914 ninety-three of German's most renowned professors, including liberal theologian Adolf von Harnack, had issued a manifesto defending Germany's role in the war. Many American scholars were appalled by this blatantly partisan departure from a scientific stance and by what seemed to the Americans a denial of the plain facts. The unprofessional attitude of the German academics was particularly galling to many of the American elite who had studied in Germany, and in retrospect many recalled autocratic tendencies deep within the German character. Already in 1914, Arthur Lovejoy called the German professors' statement "a scandalous episode in the history of the scholar's profession" and approvingly quoted a statement that it was "the greatest moral tragedy of the war." In 1918, Richard T. Ely used stronger terms, linking the cause directly to that of Christian civilization. We are at war with Germany, he explained, "because Germany has embraced a false religion, worships a false tribal god and practices false tribal ethics."[47] Demonstrating his total loyalty to the American cause, Ely was a leader in organizing a petition in 1918 signed by 90 percent of the Wisconsin faculty deploring what they described as the virtually treasonous disloyalty of Wisconsin senator Robert LaFollette.[48]

The vast majority of the American professoriate, seeing the cause of science and the highest morality so self-evidently on the side of American patriotism, found it difficult to recognize that they were guided by a virtually religious loyalty to their own nation not far different in kind from that of their German counterparts. Both sides proclaimed a new age of science that would be at once objective and consistent with the highest ideals of civilization. Once contrary idealisms clashed, armed with the destructive power of the latest technology, the same intellectual world could not be put back together again.

The Sequel

After the war many American professors eventually became chastened about the degree of their wartime patriotism, but it is not clear that many appreciated the dimensions of the intellectual crisis that was facing the Western world. Even if they did, they did not see in it any lesson that would modify their prewar faith in science, which made it possible to speak of academic freedom as almost an absolute.[49] Rather, soon after the war there were signs of reconciliation between the Association of American Colleges (AAC) and the AAUP and by 1940 a widespread consensus on the subject led to a succinct restatement of the 1915 principles now jointly authored by representatives of the AAUP and the AAC and endorsed by many other academic associations. The 1940s report was thus canonized and became the basis for American case law regarding academic freedom.[50]

Academic freedom in the 1940 report was based, as in earlier formulations, on its being essential to "the common good."[51] Institutions that limited freedom for religious or other purposes could be exempted from the general rules so long as they stated in writing their restrictions as conditions for appointments.

What did not seem to be well recognized was that the ideal of the common good involved inbuilt restrictions on what one was free to say or teach. The blatant restrictions on academic freedom during World War I were simply accentuations of the sorts of limitations that always had prevailed. Ultimately it was not academic freedom but the common good that was the absolute. Freedom would be limited to that which was judged consistent with the prevailing concepts of the common good.

Who would judge what was the common good was another crucial question. In American academia it would be the elite professoriate. That group, as Leuba had shown, was more likely even than most other academics to be skeptical of traditional religious claims. Moreover, they typically were committed to the opinion that scientific viewpoints were the basis for finding the highest good in society and to the orthodoxy that freedom from preconceptions was essential to the scientific method. In the light of such beliefs, traditional religious viewpoints had a negative effect on "the common good." They could be tolerated, but only as exceptions to the rule. In the universities themselves, they would be like grandparents in an upwardly mobile family, tolerated and sometimes respected because of their service in the past, even given some nice quarters of their own and celebrated on holidays, but otherwise expected either to be supportive or to stay out of the way and not say anything embarrassing.

Notes

1. James Leuba, *The Belief in God and Immortality: A Psychological, Anthropological and Statistical Study* (Chicago, 1921 [1916]), 224, xviii.

2. Ibid., 252–53. These figures are from the second set of 500 questionnaires that Leuba sent to scientists. The first set, worded slightly differently, yielded somewhat higher levels of belief but similar difference between the two groups (51 percent for "lesser" and 35.7 percent for "greater" regarding God and 66.5 percent for "lesser" and 38.8 percent for "greater" regarding immortality). Leuba used the second set of questions in surveying those of other disciplines.

Leuba also compared the beliefs of biologists and physical scientists in these groups and discovered that biologists were substantially more likely to be skeptical, the most striking difference being that "greater" biologists were only about half as likely (16.9 percent) to affirm belief in a prayer-answering God as were the "greater" physicists (34.8 percent). Of "lesser" biologists, however, 39.1 percent affirmed this belief. These figures conflate the answers to the two surveys. Ibid., 255.

3. Ibid., 279. For sociologists Leuba compared academics to nonacademics in the field and found the nonacademics to be almost twice as likely as the academics to affirm the beliefs in question (263).

4. Ibid., 277.

5. Ibid., 280.
6. Ibid., 186, 201, 283–84.
7. Ibid., 212, cf. 185.
8. Ibid., 213, 215–16.
9. Ibid., 280, 282.
10. Ibid., 286–87.
11. Richard Hofstadter and Walter P. Metzger, *The Development of Academic Freedom in the United States* (New York: Columbia University Press, 1955), 468–90.
12. In the 1880s the debate on "academic freedom" had to do with the Charles Eliot's introduction of the elective system for students. Laurence Veysey, *The Emergence of the American University* (Chicago: University of Chicago Press, 1965), 384–85. Cf., for example, Andrew F. West's attack on Eliot's views in "What Is Academic Freedom?" *North American Review* 140 (1885), 432–44, reproduced in Walter P. Metzger, ed., *The American Concept of Academic Freedom: A Collection of Essays and Reports* (New York: Arno Press, 1977).
13. Richard Hofstadter recognizes this in Hofstadter and Metzger, *Academic Freedom,* 240–42. See also chapter 3 of the present work.
14. Charles D. Cashdollar, *The Transformation of Theology, 1830–1890: Positivism and Protestant Thought in Britain and America* (Princeton: Princeton University Press, 1989), traces the spread of Comtean positivism during the intervening era.
15. Metzger, in Hofstadter and Metzger, *Academic Freedom,* 373, uses the term "sanctified." Cf. his account of *Lernfreiheit* and *Lehrfreiheit,* 386–407, on which the present account principally depends. This interpretation is confirmed in Veysey, *Emergence,* 384–97; Charles E. McClelland, *State, Society and University in Germany, 1700–1914* (Cambridge: Cambridge University Press, 1980); and Fritz K. Ringer, *Education and Society in Modern Europe* (Bloomington: Indiana University Press, 1979). I am also indebted to Darryl G. Hart, my colleague on this project for a year, for his background work on this subject.
16. Hofstadter and Metzger, *Academic Freedom,* 387.
17. See ibid., 390, cf. 367–412 for discussion of similarities and differences.
18. Albion W. Small, "Academic Freedom" *The Arena* 22 (1899), 471, cf. 463–72, reproduced in Metzger, *American Concept.* Samuel Haber, *Authority and Honor in the American Professions, 1750–1900* (Chicago: University of Chicago Press, 1991), 288–92, has a helpful discussion of the ambiguities of academic freedom in the late nineteenth century.
19. John Dewey, "Academic Freedom" *Educational Review* 23 (1902), 1, 3, reproduced in Metzger, *American Concept.*
20. Ibid., 8–13.
21. Ibid., 13–14.
22. Nicholas Murray Butler, "Academic Freedom," *Educational Review* 47 (March 1914), 291–94, reproduced in Metzger, *American Concept.*
23. Hofstadter and Metzger, *Academic Freedom,* 352. The percentage of clerical board members was 39.1 percent in 1860–1861, 23 percent in 1900–1901, and 7.2 percent in 1930–1931.
24. Ibid., 291.
25. Remarkably, one of the few founders of modern academia to make this point and to recognize that the universities might not be as free as they claimed was Charles Eliot. Eliot was a rugged individualist of the mid-nineteenth-century type and hence had a more jaundiced view of modern organization than did most of the more entrepreneurial university presidents of the next generation. Speak-

ing to the Cornell Phi Beta Kappa society in 1907, Eliot pointed out the subtle censorship that could occur even at places like Cornell. "To be sure, there is another mode of preventing free teaching on dangerous subjects, which is quite as effective as persecution and much quieter, namely, the omission of all teaching on those subjects, and the elimination of reading matter bearing on them. Thus the supreme subject of theology has been banished from the state universities, and from many of the endowed universities; and in parts of the country the suppression of Bible-reading and prayer at the opening exercises of the schools, in deference to Roman Catholic objections, has resulted in the children's getting no direct ethical instruction whatsoever. A comical illustration of this control by omission is the recent suggestion that Shakespeare's 'Merchant of Venice' ought not to be read in any school where there are Jewish children, because it contains an unamiable and inaccurate representation of the character of a Jewish money lender." Charles W. Eliot, "Academic Freedom," *Science* 26 (July 5, 1907), 2, reproduced in Metzger, *American Concept.*

26. John Mecklin, *My Quest for Freedom* (New York: Scribners, 1945), 132–34. David Bishop Skillman, *The Biography of a College: Being the History of the First Century of the Life of Lafayette College* (Easton, Penn., 1932), II:49.

27. Skillman, *Biography of a College,* II:119–37.

28. Mecklin, *Quest,* 1–148. Skillman, *Biography of a College,* II:195.

29. Mecklin, *Quest,* 148–56. "The Case of Professor Mecklin: Report of the Committee of Inquiry of the American Philosophical Association and the American Psychological Association," *Journal of Philosophy, Psychology and Scientific Methods* 11 (January 1914), 75.

30. Mecklin *Quest,* 156–65. Skillman, *Biography of a College,* II:194–99.

31. Letter of John M. Mecklin, September 11, 1913, *Journal of Philosophy, Psychology, and Scientific Methods* 10 (September 1913), 559–60. He addressed a similar letter to *Science,* which also took a leading role in fostering the organization of the AAUP.

32. "The Case of Professor Mecklin," *Journal of Philosophy, Psychology, and Scientific Methods* 11 (January 1914), 67–81.

33. Mecklin, *Quest,* 133–34. Cf. "The Case of Professor Mecklin," 74.

34. Skillman, *Biography of a College,* II:198–203. In 1915 Warfield became president of Wilson College, a Presbyterian women's college in Chambersburg, Pennsylvania, where he served another lengthy tenure.

35. Hofstadter and Metzger, *Academic Freedom,* 472–74. The majority of cases had to do with dismissals that were alleged to be connected with a professor's political views. Religion cases, however, were the second leading concern. Among the half-dozen or so cases that were current at the time the AAUP was founded was one other having to do with religion in which a professor at Wesleyan University in Connecticut was dismissed, allegedly for remarks he made in a public speech opposing sabbatarianism. Ibid., 479.

36. Arthur O. Lovejoy, "Organization of the American Association of University Professors," *Science* 41 (January 29, 1915), 151–54.

37. John Dewey, "The American Association of University Professors: Introductory Address," *Science* 41 (January 29, 1915), 148–49.

38. Lovejoy, "Organization," 152; Dewey, "Introductory Address," 148.

39. "General Report of the Committee on Academic Freedom and Academic Tenure," presented at the Annual Meeting of the Association, December 31, 1915. Reproduced from *Bulletin of the American Association of University Professors* 1 (1915), 17–43, in Metzger, *American Concept.*

40. James Day, "The Professors's Union," quoted in *School and Society* 3 (January 29, 1916), 175. John Dewey dismissed such views as "literally appalling when they come from the head of a university, for, acted upon, they mean the death of American scholarship." Dewey, "Is the College Professor a 'Hired Man'?" *Literary Digest* 51 (July 10, 1915), 65. Both quoted in Hofstadter and Metzger, *Academic Freedom,* 482.

41. "Report," Committee on Academic Freedom and Tenure of Office, *Bulletin* (Association of American Colleges) 3 (April 1917), 49–50.

42. By 1922 the AAC's Academic Freedom Commission had conceded most points to the AAUP and in 1940 the AAC's approval was crucial to the canonization of the AAUP's 1940 report. Hofstadter and Metzger, *Academic Freedom,* 485–87.

43. Carol S. Gruber, "Mars and Minerva: World War I and the American Academic Man," Ph.D. dissertation, Columbia University, 1968, 96–101. Particularly revealing are attacks from the University of Chicago Divinity School on premillennial fundamentalists of Moody Bible Institute and elsewhere as unpatriotic. See George Marsden, *Fundamentalism and American Culture: The Shaping of American Evangelicalism 1870–1925* (New York: Oxford University Press, 1980), 146–48.

44. Gruber, "Mars and Minerva," 69–70, 80, 98, 106–9, 208.

45. Charles Beard to N. M. Butler, October 8, 1917, *Minutes of the Trustees of Columbia University* 38 (1917–1918), 89–90, reprinted in Richard Hofstadter and Wilson Smith, eds., *American Higher Education: A Documentary History,* II (Chicago: University of Chicago Press, 1961), 882. For accounts of the controversy see Gruber, "Mars and Minerva," 227–49, and Hofstadter and Metzger, *Academic Freedom,* 498–502. Two other Columbia professors resigned in the wake of the controversy.

46. AAUP, "Report of Committee on Academic Freedom in Wartime," 29–47, reproduced in Metzger, *American Concept.*

47. Lovejoy, letters to editor of *The Nation* 99 (September 24, 1914), 376, (November 5, 1914), 548, quoted in Gruber, "Mars and Minerva" 135. Ely, *The World War and Leadership in Democracy* (New York, 1918), ca. 18–34, quoted in Gruber, "Mars and Minerva," 116. For similar statements see Gruber, "Mars and Minerva," passim.

48. Gruber, "Mars and Minerva," 250–52. John R. Commons, another pioneer of American social science, was also an organizer of the petition drive.

49. For example, in the field of history Carl Becker and Charles Beard appreciated that the Enlightenment faith in objectivity could no longer be sustained, but they represented a minority in the field. See Peter Novick, *That Noble Dream: "The Objectivity Question" and the American Historical Profession* (Cambridge: Cambridge University Press, 1988). Furthermore, as progressive secularists, they were so much on the side of freedom that they were hardly going to challenge the Enlightenment basis for the recent definition of academic freedom.

Probably most representative of the rationale for academic freedom in the interwar era was Arthur O. Lovejoy's article on the topic in the *Encyclopedia of the Social Sciences,* (New York, 1930), I:384–88, reproduced in Metzger, *American Concept,* which is an eloquent appeal to the ideal of universal "unbiased investigation and thought" serving the cause of "the intellectual life of a civilized society." Societies with only religiously defined schools would lack "adequate provision for the advancement of science."

50. Walter P. Metzger, "The 1940 Statement of Principles on Academic Freedom and Tenure," *Law and Contemporary Problems* 53 (Summer 1990), 3–77. On the legal standing of academic freedom see the entire issue of *Law and Contempo-*

rary Problems and Walter P. Metzger, ed., *The Constitutional Status of Academic Freedom* (New York: Arno Press, 1977).

51. AAUP, "Academic Freedom and Tenure: 1940 Statement of Principles and [1970] Interpretive Comments," *AAUP Policy Documents and Reports* (Washington, D.C., 1973), reproduced in Metzger, *American Concept.*

17

The Fundamentalist Menace

Nothing did more to consolidate dominant academic opinion behind the cause of academic freedom than the fundamentalist attacks of the 1920s. While there might still be some religious traditionalists at major universities, almost no one, either administrator or faculty, would countenance the extreme demands of fundamentalists, which would have turned back the clock forty years.

Traditional teachings still prevailed in the vast majority of Protestant pulpits and traditional belief was even stronger in the pews. This meant that as immense cultural changes proceeded on other fronts, the potential for an explosive showdown steadily increased. Within each of the major denominations there had already been scrimmages and minor wars over this or that change, often centered, as we have seen, on educational institutions. Not until after World War I, however, were the conservative forces effectively organized into a national campaign.

The war itself was the immediate precipitant of the sense of a national religious crisis among Protestant conservatives. Promoted as a moral crusade, it heightened consciousness of the issue of national righteousness and made it everybody's business. Preserving doctrinal purity was therefore not just a church concern, but a national issue as well. Under Wilson's guidance the Puritan ideal of a national covenant had reemerged as a popular ideal. It was a mixed blessing. One unexpected consequence was that the heightened national moral consciousness immediately raised the question for Protestant conservatives of why the liberals were setting the terms. Moreover, the example of the perceived moral monstrosity in Germany suggested to conservatives what happened to civilizations that forsook their Christian foundations. It was an easy step from that observation to another that pointed out the formidable German influences on America's educational elite and especially how Protestant liberals had been importing German theology for years.[1]

Fundamentalists found confirmation of the alarming consequences of the German and Protestant liberal influences in the dramatic changes in mores that followed the war. The rebellion against Victorian culture had been building for some time, but it took the war to bring it into the open. Despite the triumph of the enactment of Prohibition, the last major cause on which the conservative and the moderate-liberal wings of Protestantism had agreed, the moral foundations of the nation seemed to conservatives to be eroding. Women's suffrage, and especially the breakdown of taboos regarding sexuality, seemed to threaten the family, the bedrock of the republic.[2] Young people were, of course, a particular cause for alarm. The jazz age and the dance craze, women smoking, new openness about sex, and the whole new phenomenon of a youth culture with its own standards signaled breakdown of traditional verities. Such behavior was the inevitable consequence of the spread of relativist and materialist philosophies and would undermine any Christian basis by which Americans could resist Godless and radical solutions to their problems. The foreign-inspired Bolshevism that sparked the Red Scare immediately after the war was one manifestation of the threat, but homegrown atheism and materialism were more subtle and would be equally destructive.

Crucial to the fundamentalist countermovement was to find an issue that got to the heart of the matter, rather than merely attacking symptoms, and at the same time would have a popular appeal. Bolshevism and the German threat soon became too distant, materialism was too subtle, admitted atheists were hard to find. The real culprits, after all, were those compromisers, the liberal Protestants, who in the name of Christianity had opened the doors to relativistic philosophies that ultimately would undermine Christian moral foundations.

Biological evolution proved to be the issue that tied everything together. Not only could Darwinism be shown to rest on materialist assumptions, but naturalistic evolutionary assumptions were part of every false philosophy of the day. Just as important, the hypothesis of the biological origins of humans could be contrasted to the Genesis account and thus raise the issue of the authority of the Bible. For Protestant conservatives, the displacement of the authority of the Bible was at the heart of the intellectual revolution of the past forty years. In the opinion-shaping centers of the culture the Bible was being judged and often discredited by evolutionary theories of cultural development and by supposedly higher moral ideals that had developed since biblical times. Most conservative Protestants saw the culture of the United States as implicitly Christian, resting on a moral foundation derived from the Bible. If the Bible's authority were undermined, as the Darwinist account of human origins seemed to them to do, then the very survival of American civilization was at stake.

What was more, the issue of biological evolution had a strong populist appeal, important for market-oriented American evangelicalism, which long had depended on popular support. At the democratic level the threat of Darwinism to the dignity of humans could be presented as the question of whether one's ancestors were apes and amoebas. In the South opinions on such issues were especially strong. One of the effects of World War I was to demonstrate that the South was coming back into the Union and to show that southern pride could be expressed in the form of American patriotism. Southern patriotism, however, had this twist:

concern for national morality still often translated into alarm at how secular culture imported from the North was corrupting Christian southern ways. All over the nation—in ethnic communities of the Midwest, for example, and in many religious communities with distinct identities—there were comparable pockets of resistance to the dominant ideals of emerging national culture.

Education was the most concrete area where almost everyone had to face the issues. Particularly important was the rise of the high school. In 1890 fewer than 300,000 Americans were attending high schools; by 1930 the number was 4,800,000, representing a sixteenfold increase.[3] Compulsory high school education was a new invention of an industrial society that was moving away from the countryside. No longer did the economy depend on youth employed at home. Rather, it needed more literate and commercially skilled citizens. High school also helped create an independent culture among youth. Its designers, however, saw it as a way of promoting the same set of assimilating national cultural ideals that had been shaping the new universities. The vast growth of high schools also increased the constituency for colleges and universities, which by the 1920s were also firmly established as an essential component of the cultural machinery. Formal education had thus emerged as a much more pervasive part of the culture than ever before. Compulsory education laws meant that almost everyone would have to contend with national cultural ideals. For many conservative Protestants, the teaching of biological evolution came to symbolize the sinister dimension of this trend.

All the campaign needed was organization and leadership. Organization came largely from evangelists who created various independent agencies to combat the new cultural and religious trends after the war. The World's Christian Fundamentals Association, founded in 1919 by premillennialist[4] Protestants who insisted on literal biblical interpretation, was a prototype. By 1920 antievolution had emerged as a leading issue in these circles, which were being tagged "fundamentalist." At a preconvention gathering of the new fundamentalist coalition in the Northern Baptist Convention, premillennialist leader A. C. Dixon eloquently tied evolution to all the evil trends of the day, from the triumph of the "might makes right" philosophy of Nietzsche in Germany, to Bolshevism, to the decline of the family and moral values at home. At the annual meeting of the Northern Baptist Convention itself, the fundamentalists succeeded in appointing a committee to investigate alleged infidelity at Baptist-supported schools.[5] In the meantime, T. T. Martin, secretary of the Anti-Evolution League (and soon well known as the author of *Hell and the High Schools: Christ or Evolution, Which?* [1923]), had created a furor in North Carolina early in 1920 with an attack on William Poteat, the distinguished president of Wake Forest College, for his endorsement of evolutionary views.[6]

During 1920 antievolution grew from what was largely a church issue into a national concern when William Jennings Bryan took up the crusade. In the fall of that year Bryan spoke on the evils of evolution to a

Sunday crowd of forty-five hundred at the University of Michigan. Some local clergy were outraged that Bryan was presenting false and simplistic alternatives that reopened an issue they thought had long since been resolved. Bryan responded by beefing up his argument and having five thousand copies of his speech printed and distributed. During the next two years controversy swirled around Bryan as he carried the antievolution torch on the Sunday school and lecture circuits.

Bryan was not a typical fundamentalist; he promoted a progressive social gospel that included women's rights as well as the literal interpretation of Scripture. His prominence and the dramatic character of the issues, however, depicted both by him and his opponents as the clash of two worlds, provided a field day for the press. The issue had practical importance as well. Bryan supported fundamentalist efforts to enact legislation prohibiting the teaching of biological evolution in states throughout the nation. He and his cohorts were especially threatening to state universities, which were the targets of such legislation. When early in 1922 Bryan used an invited speech at the University of Wisconsin to assail the teaching of evolution, President Edward A. Birge, a scientist himself, was furious. The two had a heated exchange after the speech and continued to hurl published polemics at each other for the next year and a half. Bryan suggested that the taxpayers should rid themselves of a president whose university undermined the majority of the people's Christian belief.[7]

Bryan's favorite evidence of the alarming state of universities and colleges was James Leuba's survey on belief in God and immortality among academics. Over half the prominent scientists and social scientists in fields dominated by evolutionary theory rejected traditional faith. "The evil influence of these Materialistic, Atheistic or Agnostic professors" was further disclosed by Leuba's studies of professorial influence on the beliefs of college students. Bryan reported stories he had been told of how professors at Wisconsin, Michigan, Columbia, Yale, and Wellesley taught classes in which they explicitly told students to give up their traditional beliefs about the Bible. A president of one of the largest state universities reportedly had told students that " 'if you cannot reconcile religion with the things taught in biology, in psychology, or in the other fields of study in this university, then you should throw your religion away.' " Such materialistic beliefs, Bryan warned, would undermine any basis for unselfish moral reform. The choice was between "Nietzsche's 'Superman' " and the biblical Prince of Peace. "If the Bible cannot be defended in these schools it should not be attacked, either directly or under the guise of philosophy of science."[8]

Essential to Bryan's argument was that there were only two choices, the Bible or evolution. "Theistic evolution," which especially in the North was supported by some prominent Protestant conservatives as well as by moderates and liberals, was in Bryan's representation "even more demoralizing than atheistic evolution." It might be true that "*some* believers in

Darwinism retain their belief in Christianity; some survive smallpox." Since Darwinism *"leads many astray,"* students should be protected from it. "Theistic evolution," Bryan said dramatically, "is an anesthetic; it deadens the pain while the Christian religion is being removed."[9]

Bryan recognized that the either–or choice was essential to his populist campaign. In private the Commoner acknowledged that evolution of species other than humans would be compatible with biblical theism;[10] in public he would admit only a simple dichotomy. There was, after all, enough truth in what he said to make a plausible case. Even if some form of biological evolution could be reconciled with biblical ideas of a creator, Darwinism *was* often used to undermine faith in literal interpretations of the Bible.[11] The pieties of theistic evolution tended to obscure that fact. Moreover, the assumption that made Darwinism's conjectures regarding evolutionary mechanisms so compelling in the scientific community—that there *had* to be a purely naturalistic explanation of how life-forms developed—was parallel to that shaping every scientific discipline. Everything *had* to have a purely naturalistic explanation and hence evolutionary theories were the best explanations of how change took place. Darwinism made it plausible to adopt this outlook as a universal view of things and Darwinism's prestige was an essential component in the growing prestige of purely naturalistic worldviews.

There were, then, some significant theoretical issues that might have been debated. The proposal simply to ban the teaching of the biological evolution of humans, however, made constructive debate virtually impossible. It turned the issue into a political debate and assured that what was a complex and subtle issue would be vastly oversimplified.

The Battle of North Carolina

Some of the most dramatic antievolution agitation and campaigns against a state university took place in North Carolina. There, as in most of the South, traditional evangelicalism seemed to be everywhere, and biblical literalism was often taken for granted. In 1924, the governor of the state, Cameron Morrison, personally intervened with the State Board of Education to ban two biology textbooks that taught the evolution of humans. Virtually every major antievolution crusader, including Bryan, Billy Sunday, T. T. Martin, evangelist Mordecai Ham, the World's Christian Fundamentals Association, and A. C. Dixon, a native son, campaigned in the state to promote legislation banning the teaching of biological evolution. The battle in North Carolina was particularly fierce, however, because the forces of the New South were strong as well, especially in some of the colleges and the University of North Carolina at Chapel Hill.

In 1920 T. T. Martin's attack on President William Poteat of Wake Forest had sparked a lengthy controversy among North Carolina Baptists. Nonetheless, Poteat was an impressive figure and his evident piety, together with some Baptist reluctance to enforce centralized control, helped him survive attacks in the North Carolina Baptist Convention.[12]

Among the Methodists, second in numbers to the Baptists, there was similar agitation against "unorthodox doctrines" taught in the denominational colleges. Of particular concern was Trinity College in Durham, headed by William Preston Few. Few was a pious Methodist, deeply committed to relating Christianity to higher education, but liberal in his theological leanings. He was also a champion of the New South, wanting to bring the South in general and Trinity in particular into the mainstream of American culture. Despite conservative Methodist opposition, Methodists accepted practical piety as a test of the faith and were reluctant to enforce doctrinal tests. When in 1924, in the midst of the controversies, James B. Duke endowed Trinity as Duke University, liberal piety was conspicuous. The bylaws of the act of endowment were a classic encapsulation of liberal Protestant educational ideals, opening with the words: "The Aims of Duke University are to assert a faith in the eternal union of knowledge and religion set forth in the teachings and character of Jesus Christ, the Son of God. . . ." Few had this statement inscribed on a plaque at the center of the campus facing the huge Gothic chapel that dominated the lavish architecture of the new university. A School of Religion, for the training of clergy, stood next to the chapel. Although the first dean, Edmund D. Soper, a comparative religionist from Northwestern, was accused of being a modernist, Duke University could hardly be faulted for neglect of Christian concerns.[13]

The Presbyterians, third largest denomination in the state, were the best organized against evolution. Since the dismissal of James Woodrow from the Presbyterians' Columbia Seminary in South Carolina in 1884, antievolution had been an article of faith among conservative Southern Presbyterians. William Jennings Bryan and Billy Sunday were Presbyterians, as was Governor Cameron. The Presbyterians' leading college, Davidson, was considered safe by the antievolution campaigners. The problem, however, was the University of North Carolina at Chapel Hill, in which the Presbyterians long had taken an informal proprietary interest.

In 1920 Harry W. Chase became the president of the University of North Carolina. Chase was from Massachusetts and had studied psychology with G. Stanley Hall. He titled his inaugural "The State University and the New South," thereby announcing a New South agenda to create a new civilization that synthesized "the best in both the old and the new." It did not help that Chase was a Yankee and that the university tolerated distinctly progressive views, including some on race. Nonetheless, Chase was making effective strides toward building the Chapel Hill school into being a respected institution by national standards.

By 1923 attacks on the university were building on several fronts. Late in 1922 A. C. Dixon had set off a new round of controversy in a well publicized antievolution sermon at the First Baptist Church in Raleigh. William Jennings Bryan made two visits to North Carolina in 1923, presenting his standard antievolution views, citing the evidence from the Leuba study. Bryan berated professors who belittled him on the basis of their mere guesses and noted that a professor in Kentucky who had attacked him was now out of a job. While Baptists were ambivalent about the intrusion of religion into state institutions because of their principles of the separation of church and state, conservative Presbyterians had fewer such compunctions. They saw the republic as voluntarily Christian; or as Governor Morrison put it to an Elks convention, North Carolina was an "old fashioned Christian state." Since 1921 Presbyterians had taken the lead in attempting to counter the secular drift with legislation that would have instituted Bible teaching, under church supervision, in public schools, including Bible offerings for credit at the colleges. President Chase was not adverse to courses on the Bible, but negotiations with the Presbyterians broke down in 1924 when it became clear that churches could not control how the Bible would be taught.

As efforts to guarantee positive Christian teachings in state schools faltered, the Presbyterians and their allies turned increasingly to the argument that had routed the Jeffersonians in the nineteenth century, namely, that teachings contrary to Christianity should not be taught either. The conservatives were particularly concerned about the McNair lectures, established in the nineteenth century by John Calvin McNair, a conservative Presbyterian, to address questions relating science to theology. Since 1915, the McNair lecturers had included John Dewey, Shailer Mathews, Roscoe Pound, and in 1922 Charles Dinsmore of Yale Divinity School, who had explicitly attacked conservative interpretations that taught the universe was only six thousand years old. William Poteat was announced as the lecturer for 1925. Although Poteat was a moderate and not a Yankee like the others, this again stirred up the cauldron of Baptist antievolution sentiments.[14]

In the meantime a storm of protest broke from conservatives in all the major white Protestant denominations in the state in response to what seemed an even more direct attack on traditional Christianity from the university. In January 1925 the *Journal of Social Forces,* edited by sociologist Howard W. Odum of the university and published by the university's press, published two articles that could not have better illustrated what the conservatives were warning about. The first, by L. L. Bernard of Cornell, on "The Development of the Concept of Progress," spoke of the gods "as having been created by the folk mind as the projection of their longing and desires," and included early Jewish belief in that category. Jesus, according to Bernard, suggested a more secular idea of progress, though he talked in mystical language; but he had been unable to formulate an abstract principle for social improvement without the "metaphysical and scientific categories yet to be developed." Harry Elmer Barnes of Smith College was even more blunt. Referring to the belief that ethical values were derived from divine commands, Barnes stated that "Hebrew and Christian history, together with biblical criticism, have, of course, proved that these ideas have been but the product of the folkways and mores of the primitive Hebrews."[15]

The journal was swamped with requests for the January issue, which was immediately attacked by religious periodicals all over the state. One sympathetic observer remarked, "What I have long feared at last has happened. Somebody has read the *Journal of Social Forces*." The journal was, among other things, conspicuous in promoting new views of race and made a point of including in its pages works of African-American scholars. Howard Odum, who knew the existence of the journal was threatened, was determined not to back down to the "Ku Kluxers" and antievolutionists. He wrote to one sympathizer that his Christian faith had survived two Ph.D.s at supposedly "infidel institutions," but that current scurrilous attacks in the name of Christianity were now severely shaking his belief.[16]

By now, however, Bryan and others had so often made the point that biological evolution lay at the root of all the other dangerous evolutionary views that the controversy could not be focused on anything else. This became especially true after early January 1925 when a state representative, David Scott Poole, introduced a bill in the state legislature prohibiting any official or teacher in a tax-supported school from teaching "as a fact either Darwinism or any other evolutionary hypothesis that links man in blood relationship with any lower forms of life."[17] This raised the controversy to a fever pitch over the next six weeks as the bill was considered. The threat was real, as the success of a parallel bill in Tennessee that same winter was to prove. President Chase saw the very essence of a university threatened by allowing popular opinion to dictate what might be taught. "A real university," he told the student body at Chapel Hill, "is an ideal. It is a spiritual thing . . . and those of us to whom the preservation and perpetuation of that ideal are . . . entrusted . . . are obliged to feel that it lives in the realm of principle, where consideration of expediency can not enter."[18]

Much to the relief of the progressives in the state, after much public debate, the Poole bill was defeated in February by a vote of sixty-seven to forty-six. The antievolution agitation, however, by no means ended. Poteat's lectures at the university in the summer of 1925 brought a new round of efforts by Baptists to oust him from Wake Forest. There was also an attempt to oust Chase from the university. In 1927 Poole introduced a second antievolution bill. All these efforts were defeated. Nonetheless, the fundamentalist gains were substantial. Some counties passed legislation banning the teaching of anything that called into question the inspiration of the Bible and on the local level most teachers were intimidated from teaching evolution. The universities, however, survived with their independence. Although North Carolina had one of the most heated controversies, its most progressive schools, at least, survived with renewed zeal to defend their independence.[19]

The National Debate Trivialized

Resolve for academic freedom was similarly steeled throughout the country. During the 1920s legislation banning the teaching of biological evolution was considered in twenty states and adopted in five, all more-or-less in the South. More important for higher education were the dismissals taking place over the issue. The AAUP, of course, took a strong stand. By the end of 1923 its president, Joseph V. Denny, noted a dozen or more dismissals, two at state universities. He declared that "fundamentalism is the most sinister force that has yet attacked freedom of teaching."[20] In Tennessee, for instance, a young professor of secondary education, J. W. Sprowls, was told that he should not use as a text James Harvey Robinson's *Mind in the Making* because of its evolutionary views. Sprowls objected bitterly, but the president of the university insisted on the grounds that anti-evolution legislation might be passed if the university should "soft pedal" the issue. At the end of the academic year 1922–1923, Sprowls was dismissed, ostensibly on grounds of incompetence as a director of field work. In the controversy that followed, six others of the university faculty were dismissed, largely for their role in defending Sprowls. The AAUP investigated and sharply criticized the university, primarily for its improper system for tenure and hearings. The investigating committee, however, did not find grounds for concluding that views on evolution or Protestant orthodoxy were at the heart of the issue, as some of the dismissed alleged, even though two of the dismissed were Unitarians and most of them were known for their liberal religious views.[21]

In the meantime many in the professoriate were looking with increasing alarm and disbelief at the antievolution campaigns across the country. The AAUP appointed a special committee on "Freedom of Teaching in Science," which reported early in 1925. The fundamentalist opposition, they observed, was "un-American" in that it attempted to control learning by popular vote, rather than relying on the leadership of qualified experts.[22] Significantly, the Association of American Colleges agreed. "The thing that America needs more than anything else from American colleges and universities," wrote one of their representatives with specific reference to religion, "is the type of leader who understands that the first requisite . . . is not the desire to know what the people want, but . . . to help the people want what they ought to have."[23] The Age of the Expert was dawning.

The consolidation of academic opinion was evidenced by a special gathering on Academic Freedom and Tenure held under the auspices of the American Council on Education, which included the AAUP, the American Association of Colleges, and several other higher education associations. The American Association of Colleges drafted a statement on academic freedom, which was slightly modified at the suggestion of the AAUP and then unanimously endorsed by all the representatives present. This statement, which in substance closely resembled the 1915 AAUP statement, represented a major step toward gaining almost universal recognition of the essential AAUP principles among the shapers of dominant American academia.[24]

The sequel to the dismissals at the University of Tennessee was, of course, the Scopes Trial of 1925. The two events were not unconnected. When John Scopes, a young high school teacher, was persuaded to test the state's new law banning the teaching of biological evolution, one of the dismissed professors, John R. Neal, from the university's Law School, was the first lawyer to volunteer his legal services.[25] Even though Scopes was convicted and prevented from effective appeal, the opponents of the law succeeded spectacularly in their objective of exposing it to public scrutiny. The huge publicity surrounding the trial's debates between Clarence Darrow and William Jennings Bryan solidified liberal opinion against Bryan's larger concerns. In the midst of Menckenesque ridicule, the serious issues that Bryan attempted to raise were widely dismissed.

Perhaps most important was that the populist attacks on biological evolution trivialized the old anti-Jeffersonian argument and thereby helped seal its doom. A central point in the campaigns for anti-evolution legislation was that if specifically Christian teachings were to be banned from tax-supported schools, then so also should teachings that attacked Christianity. Bryan, for instance, argued that

> in schools supported by taxation we should have a real neutrality wherever neutrality in religion is desired. If the Bible cannot be defended in these schools it should not be attacked, either directly or under the guise of philosophy or science. The neutrality which we now have is often but a sham; it carefully excludes the Christian religion but permits the use of the schoolrooms for the destruction of faith and for the teaching of materialistic doctrines.[26]

Bryan here correctly identified a major problem in American democracy. If Christianity was no longer going to be the established religion, either officially or unofficially, in the tax-supported schools, then what philosophy *would* be established? If doctrines of materialism prevailed and schools routinely taught that all religion was an illusory human creation, then irreligion would be established. Darwin's own version of Darwinism was materialistic, and philosophies built on evolutionary analogies increasingly were given a materialistic bent. Such philosophies, whatever their merits, Bryan was pointing out, should hardly be permitted to travel under the colors of neutrality toward religion, especially toward biblicist Protestantism.

William Allen White once said of Bryan that he was always right in diagnosis and always wrong in prescription.[27] Bryan's remedy for philosophical materialism was another case in point. Although Darwinism was sometimes indeed part of a materialistic worldview and sometimes used to promote such a view, the situation was far more complicated. Liberal

Protestants typically affirmed biological evolution as explaining the mechanics of creation but saw that as subordinate to a higher spiritual reality by which God was guiding the world toward establishing his kingdom. Consistent with this view, high school textbooks of the era typically pointed out that biological evolution did not preclude God's role in creation.[28] When the AAUP recommended that professors take into account the tender sensibilities of younger college students, it probably had in mind allowing room for similar reconciliations of science and religion. Some conservative Protestants made similar accommodations, although with concerns to fit in the essentials of the biblical narrative. Only the most literalistic biblicists (of whom, of course, there were many) regarded the issue, as Bryan did, as a clear choice: *either* biological evolution or the Bible.

So what might have been raised as a serious point of national educational policy was presented in such a narrow way that only true believers would be convinced by the argument. For others it could easily be held up for ridicule as obscurantist and antiscience. Populist fundamentalist campaigners guaranteed this interpretation of their efforts. T. T. Martin, for instance, speaking to a North Carolina audience in 1926, with a massive flag-draped portrait of the recently deceased Bryan in the background, asked the crowd how they would like it if the state demanded that they pay taxes to have their children drilled on Tom Paine's *Age of Reason* and then sold their property if they refused to pay. "That is exactly the issue, except that evolution is far worse than Tom Paine's *Age of Reason.* God's word says that God created great whales; evolution teaches that is a lie; that whales used to have legs and walked around on the earth and got to going into the water more and more and after millions of years evolved into whales; here it is in school books."[29]

Walter Lippmann, who attempted to step back from the immediate prejudices of the day, was one of the few mainline opinion makers to acknowledge the genuine dilemma involved. In *American Inquisitors: A Commentary on Dayton and Chicago,* given as the Barbour-Page Lectures at the University of Virginia, Lippmann pointed out that Jefferson's Bill for Establishing Religious Freedom, adopted in 1786, stated that "to compel a man to furnish contributions of money for the propagation of opinions which he disbelieves, is sinful and tyrannical." Bryan, he pointed out to the heirs to Jefferson's university, was fair enough in asking why, if it was wrong to compel citizens to pay for the teaching of Anglicanism, it was not wrong to compel them to pay for teaching agnosticism.

Yet such a Jeffersonian appeal to rights was too easily undercut by another Jeffersonian principle, majority rule. Lippmann constructed a "Dialogue on Olympus" to make this point. On the sacred mount, Socrates quizzed Jefferson and Bryan on their first principles. Bryan's appeal to people's prejudices, Socrates pointed out, showed the danger of assuming, as Jefferson had, that popular rule would promote the rule of reason. Jefferson had assumed that the dictates of reason were fixed and that eventually a free people would discover them. In the twentieth century, however, Socrates argued, the conclusions of sciences were constantly changing. The populace could not be relied on to follow the latest view. Hence, he implied, education must be guided by a class of disinterested experts. Certainly it could not be guided by popular whims.[30]

As Lippmann suggested, the threat of populist rule of intellectual life forced academicians to assert all the more the sacred authority of the scientific method. What Lippmann did not fully answer, however, was how to deal with the other issue Bryan had recognized, the danger of the establishment of agnosticism. Dominant American educational practice was based on the long-held assumption that science would lead to a unified set of truths on which all persons should be in essential agreement. Whether Jeffersonian, "nonsectarian" evangelical, liberal Protestant, or twentieth-century agnostic, the educational system had been defined on the presumption that a single set of such reasonable ideals should guide American education. Even the twentieth-century idea that truth was fluid presumed that scientific inquiry would lead to a progressive consensus on which all right-thinking people should agree. This principle that science provided the grounds for an informed social consensus on truth was instituted in the monolithic public school establishments and was extended to state universities. Private universities were built on similar assumptions. Liberal Christians and agnostics might disagree on various points, but the underlying assumption was that their common commitment to the scientific method assured that they were moving in the same direction. Thus any lingering sense of alarm that there might be cultural warfare between Christianity and irreligion was lulled by the assurance of cultural harmony.

The fundamentalists' insistence that there was warfare and their attacks on biological evolution only strengthened the resolve of the dominant parties to insist that the issues could be resolved peacefully. Liberal Protestantism had been the principal buffer against the spread of militant agnosticism in universities. Until the 1920s it had successfully countered trends toward materialism fostered by scientific naturalism with the argument that higher spiritual and moral ideals, often specifically Christian, must provide the higher framework in which science operates. Mainline church leaders continued to look for ways to address those concerns. At the same time, however, the rise of populist fundamentalism inevitably drove liberal and moderate Protestants to the defense of the freedom to teach agnosticism. Fundamentalists, after all, placed agnostics and liberal Protestants in the same camp. Defending themselves meant defending a strong principle of freedom from religious restraint, based on the authority of science. Hence any liberal or moderate Protestant dissent from the growing academic consensus on such points was to be muffled. Liberal Protestantism was now a buffer primarily against fundamentalism.

The *Christian Century*, a mainline Protestant journal, for instance, professed astonishment that repression, encouraged by Mr. Bryan, was occurring "outside the ranks of the Roman Catholic teaching fraternity, where dogmatic control of learning was supposed to have its sole abode." For Protestant America to turn in a similar direction, the *Century* warned, would be disastrous to American cultural progress. "The backwardness under the Roman Catholic system is a commonplace. The effect of a similar policy in the United States will be none the less pronounced if state universities or denominational colleges are not allowed a perfectly free quest for truth."[31]

Thus the fundamentalists pushed the mainline Protestants toward unqualified tolerance. Meanwhile, their attack on biological evolution did not get at the constitutional issue in a clear way. The line it drew did not simply divide Bible believers from agnostics. It also divided one major group of Christians from another. In effect it gave preferential standing to fundamentalist views of the Bible at the expense of modernist Christian views, and it could be construed as establishing the fundamentalist interpretation.[32] From the fundamentalist point of view, this was fair enough, as the liberal Protestant view was already established. Nevertheless, this division between the two major groups of Christians obscured the constitutional question concerning established religions and other ideologies in public education. Ultimately the problem lay in the premise that American public schools should all teach the same ideology. Each side assumed that its views were compatible with universal American public ideology and that such an ideology should be established for all. As Sidney E. Mead later observed: "The public schools in the United States took over one of the basic responsibilities that traditionally was always assumed by an established church. In this sense the public school system of the United States *is* its established church."[33] The problem was whose religion or ideology would be established.

Another way of understanding the issue was, as Walter Lippmann also pointed out, that the division between the two parties reflected two very different sets of underlying assumptions about the nature of education. The older ideal, which until recently had been almost universal, was that the purpose of education was for the younger generation to learn the wisdom of the elders. Fundamentalists still held this view. While they professed to revere science, they did so within a framework of higher fixed truths that science was not allowed to challenge. Modernists, by which Lippmann meant people committed to the dominant modern outlook, on the other hand, gave their ultimate intellectual allegiance to the scientific *method* as the essence of true education. The higher truth was an ever-progressing ideal toward which the human community of scientific inquirers always moved, yet never reached. Since truth was by definition always changing, the only thing ultimately sacred was the means of pursuing it. No religious or other dogmatic claim could be allowed to stand in its way. Hence, as Lippmann pointed out, free inquiry involved an inherent limit. "Reason and free inquiry can be neutral and tolerant only of those opinions which submit to the test of reason and free inquiry." Two irreconcilable views of truth and education were at issue.[34] In the midst of fundamentalist threats and liberal reactions, however, meaningful discussion of these differences was seldom heard.

Notes

1. See George Marsden, *Fundamentalism and American Culture* (New York: Oxford University Press, 1992), 141–64.

2. Betty A. DeBerg, *Ungodly Women: Gender and the First Wave of American Fundamentalism* (Minneapolis: Fortress Press, 1990), emphasizes this theme.

3. "Education," *The Encyclopedia Americana, International Edition* (New York: Americana Corporation, 1963), IX:635.

4. Premillennialists, who had much to do with organizing fundamentalism, believed that Jesus would soon return to judge corrupt civilization. See Marsden, *Fundamentalism,* 43–71.

5. "The Conference on Fundamentals," *Watchman-Examiner* (July 1, 1920), 839–40. Cf. Marsden, *Fundamentalism* 161–67. The committee's mandate, however, was weak and its report, returned in 1921, essentially exonerated the schools and suggested that their doctrinal purity be secured by boards of trustees or by local Baptists and not by the convention. Agitation from the more extreme fundamentalists continued, however. Robert A. Ashworth, "The Fundamentalist Movement among the Baptists," *Journal of Religion* 4 (November 1924), 613–21.

6. Willard B. Gatewood, Jr., *Preachers, Pedagogues and Politicians: The Evolution Controversy in North Carolina, 1920–1927* (Chapel Hill: University of North Carolina Press, 1966), 30–37.

7. Ferenc Morton Szasz, *The Divided Mind of Protestant America, 1880–1930* (University: University of Alabama Press, 1982), 110–11.

8. William Jennings Bryan, *In His Image* (New York, 1923), 118–21, 133, 122, and passim.

9. Ibid., 122. Bryan, "The Fundamentals," *The Forum* 70 (July 1923), from excerpt in Willard B. Gatewood, ed., *Controversy in the Twenties: Fundamentalism, Modernism, and Evolution* (Nashville: Vanderbilt University Press, 1969), 136.

10. Ronald L. Numbers, *The Creationists* (New York: Knopf, 1991), 43.

11. Numbers's valuable account of these developments in *The Creationists* notes that such attacks often helped motivate fundamentalists.

12. Gatewood, *Preachers,* 30–37, 59–75.

13. On the history of religion at Duke I am grateful to have the benefit of Bradley J. Longfield, " *'Eruditio et Religio':* Religion at Duke between the World Wars," and a chapter by Robert Durden, "Theological Training at Duke University, 1925–1950," each of which was being prepared for publication. See also Gatewood, *Preachers,* 77–79, 193, 197–98..

14. Gatewood, *Preachers,* 1–128, passim, esp. 17, 87, 100, 103–4, 108, 111.

15. L. L. Bernard, "The Development of the Concept of Progress," *Journal of Social Forces* 3 (January 1925), 209, 212; Harry Elmer Barnes, "Sociology and Ethics: A Genetic View of the Theory of Conduct," *Journal of Social Forces* 3 (January 1925), 214. Cf. Gatewood, *Preachers,* 114–15.

16. Gatewood, *Preachers,* 119n, 119.

17. Quoted in Gatewood, *Preachers,* 127.

18. W. H. Chase, "Address to Student Body," February 1925, University Papers. Quoted in Gatewood, *Preachers,* 137.

19. Gatewood, *Preachers,* 146–233 passim.

20. Joseph V. Denney, Presidential Address, *Bulletin of the American Association of University Professors* 10 (February 1924), 26–28, reprinted in Gatewood, *Preachers,* 270–72.

21. "Report on the University of Tennessee," *Bulletin of the AAUP* 10 (April 1924), 21–68. Cf. *Bulletin of the AAUP* 11 (February 1925), 70. James Riley Montgomery, Stanley J. Folmsbee, and Lee Seifert Greene, *To Foster Knowledge: A History of the University of Tennessee, 1794–1970* (Knoxville: University of Tennessee Press, 1984), 186–88.

22. Report of Committee M, "Freedom of Teaching in Science," *Bulletin of the AAUP* 11 (February 1925), 93–95.

23. C. M. Richmond, "The Place of Religion in Higher Education in America," *Bulletin of the Association of American Colleges,* reprinted in *Bulletin of the AAUP* 11 (March–April 1925), 174.

24. Report on American Council on Education," *Bulletin of the AAUP* 11 (February 1925), 99–109.

25. Montgomery et al., *To Foster Knowledge,* 188.

26. Bryan, *In His Image,* 122.

27. Szasz, *Divided Mind,* 122–23.

28. W. W. Campbell, "Evolution in Education in California," *Science* 61 (April 3, 1925), reprinted in Gatewood, *Preachers,* 249.

29. Quoted in Gatewood, *Preachers,* 192. Cf. 191.

30. Lippmann, *American Inquisitors: A Commentary on Dayton and Chicago* (New York, 1928), 12–22, 37–49.

31. Editorial, "Academic Freedom not Yet Achieved," *Christian Century* 40 (March 8, 1923), 292.

32. Cf. William Waller, "The Constitutionality of the Tennessee Anti-Evolution Act," *Yale Law Journal* 35 (1925), 198, reprinted in Walter P. Metzger, ed., *The Constitutional Status of Academic Freedom* (New York: Arno Press, 1977).

33. Sidney E. Mead, *The Lively Experiment: The Shaping of Christianity in America* (New York: Harper & Row, 1963), 68. Robert T. Handy observes that Mead's comment may be an overstatement, but "his remark does fit the opening decades of the twentieth century, when many Protestants—and some other Americans—viewed the common schools with religious and patriotic fervor because they filled a gap in an increasingly pluralistic culture and provided a unifying force." *Undermined Establishment: Church–State Relations in America, 1880–1920* (Princeton: Princeton University Press, 1991), 138.

34. Lippmann, *American Inquisitors,* 85 and passim. I have restated Lippmann's points slightly. On the fundamentalist view of science see Marsden, *Fundamentalism,* esp. 212–21.

18

The Obstacles to a Christian Presence

Protestantism's New Initiatives

Despite their resolve not to sound like fundamentalists, moderate and liberal Protestant church leaders of the 1920s, including some university administrators, were still concerned with the most general question raised by the fundamentalists. Where was the place for Christianity in modern higher education? From their own experience, mainline Protestant church leaders were acutely aware of the massive revolution that had taken place in education over the past forty years. By the mid-1920s, moreover, it was much more difficult to be sanguine about these changes than it had been even fifteen years earlier. Staid liberal Protestants had almost as much reason as fundamentalists to be alarmed about the flappers, the dance craze, jazz, the automobile, bobbed hair, short skirts, women smoking, and both sexes drinking to excess in defiance of the recent Protestant triumph in the enactment of Prohibition. The consumer economy had produced a youth culture with its own rules, language, entertainments, and mores. As high school education expanded, college attendance also took a sudden upswing. Undergraduate enrollments tripled from 1910 to 1930 so that by the latter date the equivalent of one in every eight eighteen to twenty-one years olds was in college.[1] The burgeoning college campuses became leading loci for declarations of youthful independence.[2]

The most perplexing question was how to maintain some countervailing Christian influence at state universities. While all higher education was expanding, state education was growing at a faster rate than was private education and by 1930 was threatening to displace private education as the dominant force on the university scene. This most tangible manifestation of secularization presented especially perplexing challenges to Protestant leaders because of the ambiguous relationship between Christianity and government. Arrangements varied from state to state. Not only were lines between church and state variously drawn, but the much more ambiguous issue of the relationship of Christianity to the state was not at all settled.

Not surprisingly, thinking on the legal issues of relating Christianity to civil government paralleled the trends we have already seen in higher education. Until about the 1890s it was common to give open legal recognition to the preferential position of Christianity in American life. In 1892, for instance, Associate Justice Brewer, in presenting a unanimous decision of the Supreme Court, argued that the acceptance of Sabbath laws, prayers in government assemblies, legal oaths in the name of God, and simply the vast public support for Christian activities, indicated that the United States "is a Christian nation." Much mainline Protestant opinion supported this conclusion.[3]

At the same time many states during the era following the Civil War adopted legislation or constitutional provisions banning sectarian religious tests, sectarian instruction, sectarian books in classes or libraries in public schools, and use of state money for sectarian instruction.[4] The complex motives for such laws were largely related to the massive rise in Catholic population. On the one hand, the increasing Catholic presence fostered a growing recognition, sparked by Catholic protests, of the problems of Protestant privilege and control of public education. At the same time one of the principal motives for erecting a wall between Christianity and the state was fear that otherwise tax moneys might fall into Catholic hands in areas where Catholics were dominant.[5] With respect to higher education, some states, such as Wisconsin, attempted to be scrupulous in keeping sectarian teachings out of state colleges and universities, while others, such as Iowa, were more sympathetic toward explicitly Christian teachings. In the South, where the Catholic presence was the least, changes came most slowly. The University of South Carolina's revised statutes of 1873 provided for a moral philosophy course including "evidences of Christianity" and in 1890 an act of the state legislature declared that the president could not be an atheist or an infidel.[6] Into the early decades of the twentieth century most southern state-supported schools had required chapel, whereas in the North chapel at state colleges was becoming more rare, though not unknown, especially at smaller schools and teachers' colleges.

In some places in the North, however, legislators and administrators had become sensitive to public outcry concerning anything that might appear to use tax money to support a particular religious viewpoint. The 1919 case in which it was ruled that the New York state school of forestry could not be on the Syracuse University campus because Syracuse was a "sectarian" institution illustrates the ambiguities of the situation. When Chancellor Day had the university's charter amended so that the Methodist Conferences would control the naming of only a minority of the trustees, the state was satisfied. In northern state universities, the general disposition of administrators seems to have been to avoid the subject of religion, citing separation of church and state, except occasionally to issue reassuring statements about religion's importance on a voluntary basis.[7] There was no doubt, however, that by the early 1920s studies of religious subjects had become only a minute part of the curriculum.[8] Religious perspectives were absent from the vast majority of the courses students took and study about religion was marginal in the mainstream of academia. It was not regarded as one of the humanities and although often a topic of investigation by psychologists and sociologists, much of that attention had become hostile toward any belief in the supernatural.[9] The only place for substantial sympathetic academic study of Christianity was in theological seminaries.

While these pressures toward secularization of public life were rapidly increasing, so were concerns that Christianity retain at least some representation. The ambivalence of the national mood during the first decades of the twentieth century may be seen in the contradictory patterns of legislation concerning Bible reading in public schools. Between 1900 and the early 1920s five states joined Wisconsin in banning Bible reading or morning prayers in public schools. In the meantime, however, eleven states had joined Massachusetts in *requiring* such religious exercises.[10] At the university level there were comparably widespread concerns to find some way to retain a place for Christianity, or at least for a more general civic religion, without violating either principles of separation of church and state or academic canons.

At the turn of the century William Rainey Harper's campaign to include academic study of the Bible in liberal arts curricula had borne some fruit, so that at least a few courses in the Bible were available at most of the better schools, including the state universities. Protestant leaders, however, regarded the offerings as woefully inadequate, since the vast majority of students did not elect these courses.[11]

The growth of the state universities in the early decades of the century was the principal factor in convincing the major Protestant denominations that they must change their strategy regarding higher education. Maintaining their own colleges was still important, but they increasingly realized that in addition they would have to minister to their many students on state campuses. As state university enrollments began reaching into the thousands, it was not unusual for the total Methodist, Baptist, or Presbyterian population of such a university to outnumber the respective denomination's constituency at one of its own colleges nearby. Through the first decade of the twentieth century, most of the work of campus ministry had been left to the Christian Associations (YMCA and YWCA). Denominations had welcomed such work and continued to do so. Nonetheless, by early in the century the major denominations were becoming convinced that they should take matters into their own hands and by the second decade of the century they were rapidly building major networks of campus ministries.

The pattern soon became familiar at state universities. Each major denomination appointed a minister to the university. In an early recommendation the Presbyterians, for instance, compared the need as similar to that for military chaplains.[12] Methodists, Baptists, Congregationalists, Lutherans, Episcopalians, and Disciples adopted similar programs in a movement that accelerated around 1910. Denominational chaplains or university pastors typically would be associated with a denomination's church near the campus and would oversee a student center as headquarters for student religious activities. Modeled after the houses established by Presbyterians and others at the University of Michigan in the 1890s, these were centers for regular religious meetings, special lectures, and social activities that provided structures for ministering to students of each major denomination during their college years. While designed on the one hand to encourage denominational loyalties, these ministries reflected an ecumenical spirit as well. Most of the campus ministries were established in the era just following the founding of the Federal Council of Churches in 1908 and embodied a similar activist zeal for using denominations to mobilize a transdenominational Protestant activism. Roman Catholics' establishment of their own Newman Centers near university campuses closely paralleled the Protestant developments.[13] After 1920 the B'nai B'rith began establishing Hillel Foundations as well.

A major question for these early campus ministries was how they might compensate for the lack of opportunity for substantial religious training within the curriculum of the modern university. Typically the response was for the denominational centers to offer supplemental courses of study, especially in the Bible. One of the most promising solutions was for denominations to endow "Bible chairs" at their centers so that men with adequate academic credentials could offer courses in the Bible. The Disciples of Christ, whose tradition was especially strong on relying on "the Bible alone," were the early leaders in this movement and already by 1909 had established chairs at five state universities, Michigan, Virginia, Texas, Kansas, and Missouri. Other denominations followed suit, establishing additional chairs, often on an interdenominational basis. In the best cases, so far as the campus ministries were concerned, university administrations would be persuaded to grant academic credit for such courses when offered by academically qualified personnel. Eventually at least twelve state universities were giving credit for such church-sponsored courses. Elsewhere courses were offered on a noncredit basis.[14] Though such efforts were peripheral to the main business of the universities, they did represent a version of the Jeffersonian solution and helped reassure religious leaders and concerned constituencies that at least some state universities would not exclude religious voices entirely.

By the 1920s, the Bible chair ideal was expanding in some states into larger efforts to establish schools of religion within or associated with the universities. In 1922 Charles Foster Kent of Yale (which retained some its zeal for educational missions) established a National Council of Schools of Religion (changed in 1924 to the National Council on Religion and Higher Education) to promote such enterprises. Kent was a leading liberal biblical scholar, eager to reestablish a substantial place for religion in the university curriculum. He saw schools of religion as the answer. His greatest success, partially realized before his death in 1925, was in helping to establish a model for such schools in the School of Religion at the University of Iowa. As early as 1908, responding to pressures from religious groups, the University of Iowa had begun offering credit courses in religion. The rationale was that, since the Northwest Ordinance of 1787 had declared that "religion, morality, and knowledge" were necessary to good government, "Public education was by this organic act to be Christian education." In 1924, inspired by ideas promoted by Kent and others, local religious leaders succeeded in persuading the State Board of Education to establish a School of Religion. The school, which opened in 1927, was financed in part by John D. Rockefeller, Jr. Mainline Protestants, Catholics, and Jews were each allowed to nominate and finance a professor for the university program. During the next years the school offered a wide variety of courses on religious topics. In 1930 it also instituted a Commission on Religious Activities to coordinate campus religious programs of all campus ministries. The original purpose of the school was not simply the academic study of religion. Rather the school was also explicitly to promote religious interests, to foster sympathy for religion among students, and to encourage students to go into religious vocations. In 1938 the university took over the full administrative costs of the school.[15]

Despite a great deal of talk about the schools of religion movement in the 1920s, no other school of religion emulated the Iowa model. The National Council of Religion in Higher Education did see the beginnings of schools of religion in ten other state universities in the region from Indiana to Montana;[16] typically these schools simply represented the coordination of efforts of campus ministries offering courses at their student centers. Some of these programs were recognized for credit at the universities, and others were purely voluntary.[17]

One of the more successful programs was started at the University of Illinois. There in 1919 clergy representing the campus ministries of the Methodists, Disciples, and Roman Catholics petitioned to have university credit offered for courses taught at their campus houses. Despite some faculty resistance, permission was granted and course offerings began in 1920. By 1936–1937 nine courses were being offered each semester under Catholic, Jewish, and combined Protestant auspices, enrolling some three hundred students per semester.[18]

Despite some such successes, the school of religion idea began to recede during the 1930s. Part of the rationale for the program had been that it would promote the development of "a scientific attitude and method in the study of religion."[19] This ideal not only suited the liberal Protestant agenda but also could justify religion courses to university colleges and administrations. In fact, the very success of the campaign to promote the academic study of religion was making sponsorship by outside religious groups superfluous. Increasing numbers of colleges and universities were now offering courses in religion and establishing their own departments of religion. When university administrators were responsive, as they often were, to demands for offerings in religion, it was in their interest to offer such courses within the university as scientific or literary studies, rather than have them administered by denominations whose primary purpose was to promote a religious cause. The result was a hybrid field that typically had Christian form and implicitly Christian direction, but in which specific Christian purposes were subdued.

The case at the University of North Carolina is illustrative. In 1923, as the antievolution furor was heating up in the state, Presbyterian and Methodist leaders petitioned the university for permission to offer courses that would be financed and staffed by the cooperating religious groups but recognized for credit by the university. A university committee considered the proposal but turned it down. Their reasons were revealing. First, they declared, "A state university . . . cannot owe its primary allegiance to anything less than the State: to any class, party, locality, or creed within its borders." Hence, they reasoned, "Men who give accredited instruction . . . cannot from the very nature of the case be men whose primary loyalties are to one or another special cause, no matter how worthy that cause may be." Furthermore, though they recognized the ambiguity surrounding separation of church and state, their own view was that Bible instruction by church employees was a matter for church colleges. The university, on the other hand, might offer courses on the Bible "from the literary or historical point of view." At the time however, the antievolution agitation involving the university was gaining in intensity and the proposed courses were not immediately forthcoming. Finally, in 1926, after lengthy agitation, the major Protestant ministries in Chapel Hill joined together to form their own School of Religion. When in 1928 students from this school petitioned to receive credit for their courses, the faculty responded by instituting its own program. The course offerings as they actually developed had a broadly Christian orientation, some dealing specifically with Christian ethics or theology or the Bible itself as these bore on the search for God in the modern world. At the same time they were presented in academic frameworks that would soften partisanship.[20]

By 1940 not only did virtually all church-related colleges have departments of religion, but so did the vast majority of private colleges and universities, and even 30 percent of state universities (excluding teachers' and technical schools) had departments. Only 27 percent of nationally accredited colleges had no formal offerings on religious topics. So great was the increase, especially after 1930, that Clarence Shedd of Yale, one of the leaders in the movement, could declare confidently in 1941 that "state universities are more concerned today about religion than they have been at any other time during the present century."[21] Although these gains appeared considerable, the statistics that Shedd reported could have been interpreted in a much more sobering light. In a typical year, only about one in twenty-five students at public universities was taking a religion course.[22]

Merrimon Cuninggim, a protégé of Shedd who shared his mentor's enthusiasms in interpreting the trends, nonetheless acknowledged that courses in religion were not all they might be intellectually. In many colleges they were considered "snaps" or "cribs," suitable especially for football players. As a writer observed in a 1941 *Collier's* essay, "How to Keep Football Stars in College," the "beef" had to be guided to courses such as Bible, Psychology I, Astronomy, and Music Appreciation. "All were 'cripples' of the purest ray. Bible was taught by a lovable old gentleman who delivered lofty lectures and never bothered his sleeping class with details like questions or examinations." After quoting this passage, Cuninggim remarked that "at the present time the major problem concerning religious instruction is not, as in earlier days, to secure its introduction into the curriculum but rather to improve its quality."[23]

In the post–World War I era, those concerned to keep at least some religious presence in the universities had been working on a number of fronts. Charles Foster Kent, for instance, in 1923 instituted through his National Council a program to appoint "Council Fellows." Typically these were to be first-rate graduate students concerned to relate religion to their academic vocations. By 1941 the council could point to 202 of these fellows, including 31 women, 5 blacks, 3 Catholics, and 3 Jews, most of whom had become professors or administrators at colleges, universities, and divinity schools, including many of the best throughout the nation.[24] Furthermore, a number of mainline Protestant organizations, including the Religious Education Association, founded by William Rainey Harper in 1903, the Council of Church Boards of Education, and the National Association of Bible Instructors, provided a steady stream of literature encouraging the movement to bring more religion to higher education. So did other organizations with broader focuses, such as the American Council on Education and the Association of American Colleges. The AAC was a particularly significant forum for religious discussion and during this period college administrators affirmed the place of religion in higher education.[25] The YMCA continued to play a prominent role, though it was now only one of many organizations that sponsored major national conferences on the theme. Financial support was not a significant problem either. Rockefeller money had long been a major sustainer of the mainline Protestant establishment. Also important was the Edward W. Hazen Foundation, founded in 1925 and centered in New Haven, which supported many religious causes.[26] Religion in higher education was not going to disappear for lack of resourceful leadership.

The Larger Picture

The problems, however, ran much deeper. While the numerous campaigns of the interwar era succeeded in keeping and sometimes even building religious options in undergraduate liberal arts curricula, these very successes may have hidden the extent to which substantive aspects of Christianity were losing ground at the heart of the university enterprise.[27]

The great growth of higher education, including the doubling of the student population during the 1920s,[28] did not reflect a sudden upsurge in the love of learning among Americans, but rather that higher education had at last become a major arbiter of success in modern America.[29] World War I gave a dramatic impetus to the idea that an increasingly complex society demanded trained experts and specialists. The growth of higher education therefore largely took directions that would fill practical needs. While curricula were relatively coherent and traditional by later standards and at the better colleges subjects touching on the larger meanings of life were sure to be part of an education, increasing numbers of students concentrated in practical areas that such concerns would not touch.[30] One evidence of this trend was the growth of junior colleges. In 1918 fewer than one in fifty college students attended a junior college. By 1938 more than one in six did.[31] Approximately two-thirds of these were public institutions. Often they were commuter colleges without the religious support surrounding residential schools. Moreover, fewer could afford the luxury of religion courses compared to the larger four-year schools. Normal schools for teacher training were being transformed into regular liberal arts schools during this era. Nonetheless, they were also directed toward practical preparation and religion offerings were relatively rare, as they were in state agricultural and technical schools, where practical concerns also prevailed.[32]

Even in the largest schools with strong liberal arts offerings, where the campaigns for religion courses had their greatest success, expansion in other areas rendered such gains peripheral to the larger enterprise of the university. The expansion of professional schools, especially of medicine, law, and business, had virtually no religious dimension. This division of labor reflected long traditions, but it was also reinforced by the liberal Protestant belief that the technical dimensions of life had rules of their own to which religion might be added as a higher option. Just as the news magazines that first appeared in this era included a religion page somewhere in the back, so should a university keep a place for the option. At a dozen or so major private universities, divinity school provided a relatively substantial manifestation of this option, even if one that did not counter the effective irrelevance of Christianity to all but a small portion of the rest of the enterprise.

If the heart of an institution can be located by looking at its budget, the peripheral role of Christianity is apparent. During the era from 1900 to 1940, the budgetary story of the leading universities, aside from growth related to the vast increase in students and of buildings to care for them, was the comparably vast increase in funding of research. By the interwar years, leading universities, including California, Chicago, Columbia, Harvard, Illinois, and Michigan, were spending more than two million dollars per year on research, at a time when their yearly incomes were typically five to eight million dollars.[33] The principal special funding for such research, in this era before much federal government support, came from private foundations, particularly the network of Rockefeller agencies.[34]

How could Christianity relate to such institutions? The universities increasingly were becoming conglomerations of loosely related practical concerns without any particular center. They were "a collection of disparate interests held together by a common plumbing system."[35] Student bodies still seldom numbered over five thousand, but at the larger schools where the point had been passed the overall enterprise had a more-or-less unified rationale. Each unit was designed to serve the interests of business and society, thus endowing everything with a vague moral justification. Nonetheless, as elsewhere in American society, the effectiveness of the schools was associated with the absence of strong centralized control or a clear ideological center. Rather, universities flourished by allowing disparate interests to pursue independent initiatives.[36] In such a setting the specifics of Christianity seemed relevant to only one segment of university life, undergraduate education, and only to a fragment of that.

One compensatory strategy in the private universities was architectural. During this era when universities were particularly dependent on major business support,[37] business leaders were in the forefront in donating impressive chapels. Sometimes, as in the case of the Rockefellers, those who supported the diversified research also financed the unifying symbol, most notably the Rockefeller Chapel at the University of Chicago, completed in 1928. Although such buildings fostered important opportunities for worship and inspiration for parts of the communities and provided centers where the university itself might be worshiped on its high holy days, they were also monuments to a disappearing Christian ideal.

The Indifferent Generation

Another major obstacle to those who wanted to build a substantial Christian outlook in the universities was a lack of student support. For one thing, as student populations burgeoned they became (as the next chapter shows) more diverse. Even where they remained largely homogeneous and of predominantly Protestant stock, a more strongly secular spirit was apparent by the early 1920s. Popular magazines were filled with articles, often alarmist in tone, on the new youth culture and its departures from the mores of earlier years.[38] F. Scott Fitzgerald's *This Side of Paradise,* published in 1920, had an important effect on popular conceptions of the new college life. Set in prewar Princeton, it suggested how far youth culture had moved from Presbyterian (or in Fitzgerald's case, Catholic) mores. Fast cars, heavy drinking, and petting parties were the order of the day. Students sat late into the night "talking of every side of life with an air half of earnestness, half of mockery, yet with a furtive excitement." "The cities between New York and Chicago," Fitzgerald's protagonist discovered, were "one vast juvenile intrigue."[39] Fitzgerald's image caught the imagination of the new college-oriented generation and the image helped promote the reality. The place for Christianity in such an emerging youth culture was, to say the least, problematic.

As early as 1923 James Bissett Pratt of Williams College published a perceptive analysis of the widespread belief that the characteristic attitudes toward religion of college young people were far different from those of a generation earlier. The mood of the dominant groups of young people, who set the tone for most others, was not skepticism toward religion, but indifference. It was only a little exaggeration, Pratt explained, to say of today's generation that "their grandfathers believed the Creed; their fathers a little doubted the Creed; they have never read it." As a teacher of the history of religions for twenty years, Pratt reported that early in the century he had approached with great caution the comparisons between the Old Testament and the ancient religions of China, India, and Persia, lest he raise too many doubts about traditional Christianity. "Never a year went by," he reported, "but some of my students came to me after sleepless nights, wearied with inner struggle, sometimes with indignant voices to talk out, after class, the implications involved in Higher Criticism and in the attempt to deal with the Hebrew religion in the same historical light as we had studied Hinduism and Buddhism. All this is changed now."

The students of the 1920s, Pratt reported, were "as far removed from heresy as from orthodoxy." They did not worry about inspiration because they did not care about the Bible and in fact were largely ignorant of it. Recently, Pratt reported, a student had written that the ancient Hebrews were fairly moral considering their times, " 'hough of course they did not have our Ten Commandments.' "

Looking back twenty years to the William Rainey Harper era, Pratt observed there had been "glowing promises which we of the liberal movement made to ourselves . . . of a rationalized and newly vitalized Christian faith which should fill the masses with more spiritual religion and take the place of the old bondage of the letter." Instead, liberal religion had removed not only bondage to the letter of Scripture, but most of the reasons for paying attention to the Bible in the first place.[40]

Such new attitudes were not confined to New England, even if there the generational changes were most dramatic. In 1928 Robert Cooley Angell, a young sociologist at the University of Michigan, published *The Campus: A Study of Contemporary Undergraduate Life in the American University*. Based on his own close observations at the University of Michigan over a ten-year period, Angell's account provided the most astute portrait of the university student life of the era. On the subject of religion, he found himself in almost complete agreement with Pratt's more impressionistic observations.

While a majority of Michigan students were church members, that figure was deceiving. Only 20 to 25 percent, Angell estimated, attended church on Sunday. In Angell's judgment, most of these did so not because "of acceptance of unscientific dogma, but rather of whole-hearted participation in an institution which they believe to have value both for themselves and for society at large." While most students leaned in the direction of belief in a Supreme Being, only about a third had religious or philosophical views sufficiently formulated to provide a stable outlook that might shape their lives. A few more had attempted to find a guiding faith and failed. The majority, however, had not even attempted it. Perhaps a third of the students, Angell estimated, prayed; but many of these did so no more than about once a week. Regular reading of Scripture or adherence to an institutional creed was a rarity.

Nor did religious beliefs have much to do with student behavior on campus. "Young people, for instance, will dance or not dance according as their experiences of life suggest that dancing is good or bad. The fact that it is allowed or forbidden by their churches has almost no influence, except for a very small group."[41]

Campus drinking most conspicuously accentuated the gap between the students and their church heritages. Drinking on campus was increasingly a problem and did not seem to be appreciably slowed by the presence of large numbers of students who were at least nominally members of Protestant churches that supported Prohibition. More often, as Angell observed, Prohibition had "lent a glamour to drinking formerly quite unknown," and because liquor was sometimes scarce a common view was that it should be readily used whenever it was available. As was commonly said, Prohibition seemed to reinforce the younger generation's attitude of disrespect for rules formulated by their elders. Even at a liberal Protestant bastion like Yale, a straw ballot taken in 1926 showed almost three out of four students favored repeal of the Volstead Act. Three-fourths said they thought there was no less drinking on campus since Prohibition. The only place on campus where the survey found almost universal sentiment for enforcement of the law was at the Divinity School.[42] At Methodist schools like Duke and the University of Southern Carolina, students not only enjoyed the heightened pleasures of illegal drinking but agitated for the schools to abandon vestigial Methodist rules that banned dancing on campus as well.[43]

According to Robert Angell, a virtual holiday atmosphere was the prevailing spirit of campus life. On almost every campus, this mood was sustained by the dominance of fraternities and sororities. Though Greek letter houses had been common on American college campuses since the mid-nineteenth century, they reached their heyday in the 1920s. The numbers of fraternities and sororities grew dramatically. At Michigan over a third of the students belonged. As elite societies that chose potential campus leaders, the societies wielded influence disproportionate to their size. They were by far the best guarantees of social success on campus, they were prominent in sports and extracurricular activities, and they were recognized as steppingstones to success later in life.[44] Fraternities and sororities had always provided students with bases for resistance against some college (and hence sometimes church) control. In the 1920s they especially flourished since they were ideally situated as independent fortresses that could sustain independent youth culture in the emerging consumer society.

Fraternities and sororities also performed surrogate religious functions. Christian denominations had often spoken of having residential houses near campuses to serve their students, but nothing much ever came of such suggestions. In the meantime Greek letter houses provided churchlike functions as centers for brotherhood or sisterhood to which one gave a primary allegiance. Quasi-religious initiation rites and pledges of lifelong fraternal or sororital loyalty made the analogy explicit. Just as the Masonic order has long functioned quietly as a religious reality in American society, supposedly supplemental to Christianity but often superseding the churches by building alternative major loyalties, so fraternities and sororities helped guarantee youth cultures virtual independence to establish loyalties of their own. Although the societies might profess to be friendly toward Christianity, in fact they were functionally Deist and in effect discouraged strong loyalty to a traditional religion.

Fraternities and sororities, of course, represented only one segment of campus life; there were a number of other substantial subgroups. "Independents" might remain outside of fraternities either by choice or because of failure to be selected. Poorer students who had to earn their way through college were less likely to be fraternity members and were also more likely to be regular church attendees.[45] "Grinds," or those who actually viewed college as an academic activity, were another largely outsider group. Jewish students were often put in the same class with grinds and discrimination against them was taken for granted by the Greek letter houses. Otherwise religious distinctions were usually not as conspicuous as social distinctions on campus. In retrospect, both in personal memoirs and in academic studies, campus life of the era was typically recalled as though religion had not been present at all.[46]

At the time, observers who were old enough to recall prewar days often commented on the changes. The decline of the YMCAs was the most dramatic. In the prewar era they had been a major force in campus life. By 1921 the YMCAs reached their numerical peak with 731 chapters on the approximately 1,000 campuses in the country; they had enrolled well over 90,000 members, or about one in seven in a student population of about 600,000. By 1940 the number of institutions had climbed to 1,700, with 1.5 million students, but the number of Y's had fallen to 480 and their enrollments had dropped to some 50,000, or about one in thirty. Y activities were changing dramatically also. During the peak year in the Bible study movement, 1908, a typical Y chapter could expect to enroll one-fourth of the men on campus in Bible studies, and the total national enrollment was some 50,000. In 1920 the enrollments (always larger than numbers of regular participants) were still at 30,000; by 1930 the number had plummeted to 5,000.[47]

In the meantime the YMCAs were rapidly adjusting their emphasis from evangelism to the social gospel. This was partly in response to changing student interests. Before the war the Y's had been closely associated with the Student Volunteer Movement and between 1899 and 1915 over three thousand of the American missionaries who sailed had been products of the YMCAS or the YWCAS. Shortly after the war, student interest in missions as in Bible studies dropped precipitously. By the end of the 1920s, student chapters were taking the lead in making social service the principal emphasis of the YMCAS. C. Howard Hopkins, historian of the movement, compared the disappearance of the old evangelistic theology and methods of the movements to the collapse of "The Wonderful One-Hoss Shay." In 1931 the YMCA dropped its evangelical basis altogether, describing itself rather as "a world-wide fellowship of men and boys united by a common loyalty to Jesus Christ for the purpose of building Christian personality and a Christian society."[48]

Despite the sacrificial efforts of many Y members in volunteer welfare work, the organization, which of course was "dry," was out of step with the self-indulgent spirit of the dominant student culture. Most students at the University of Michigan, Robert Angell explained, vaguely resented the YMCA's "holier than thou" attitude. While they thought Y activities were worthy, they did not think there should be a special class of people who were known for their good deeds. "There is also a subtle feeling," Angell added, "that a person who is meek, gentle, and unusually religious is in some sense effeminate and unfit to cope with the problems of full-blooded men." By contrast, he observed, "women generally look with more favor on the YWCA, probably because service has been felt in our civilization to be a peculiarly feminine function."[49] In fact, campus women remained more active in their religious practice and slightly more conservative in their religious and social views; but in the emerging hedonistic student culture men's dominance was still widely assumed, so that men were seen as setting the trends.[50]

In 1926 and 1927 the student department of the YMCAS for the midwestern states commissioned a scientific study which confirmed that the influence of Y's on campuses was declining precipitously. "There is a serious trend toward failure and breakdown and even a complete wash-out of student YMCA's across the region," the report warned. Students were not clear on whether the Y's were supposed to be religious or social agencies, and in several schools students were "distinctly unfriendly to the Y." Some were put off by the fundamentalist-versus-modernist controversies. Others simply found the meetings unappealing. "I do not go to the Y. meetings," said one ex-attendee. "They sing the same unlucky thirteen hymns every time and I know in advance the brand of moralizing piffle the speaker will spout."[51]

Required chapel services were under attack for similar reasons. The chapel tradition, which had been integral to university life since the Middle Ages, had persisted into the interwar era. Clearly at church-related and private institutions administrations had an interest in retaining this symbol of a venerable heritage, which ensured at least one place for

Christianity in official university life. Even in 1940 the prevalence of chapel in the nation's colleges could seem reassuring. Of schools accredited by the Association of American Universities, 48 percent still had compulsory chapel, 20 percent had voluntary chapel, and only 32 percent had none. Even among state schools 27 percent still had chapel, usually voluntary. Smaller colleges were particularly likely to have chapel, and at schools for African Americans chapel was the rule, even in those that were not denominational.[52]

Nonetheless, religious observance had some relationship to social class and at many of the wealthiest and most influential private schools required chapel had yielded to student assaults, particularly during the mid-1920s. Within a few years Amherst, Brown, Chicago, Dartmouth, Vassar, Williams, and Yale all yielded to demands for voluntary worship.[53]

The case of Yale, still a bellwether school, was typical. When in 1921 Arthur Twining Hadley, Yale's first lay president since 1899, retired, the Rev. Anson Phelps Stokes, secretary of the Yale Corporation since 1899, was a strong candidate to replace him. The fact that he was an Episcopal clergyman, however, closely identified with Dwight Hall, counted against him among some influential alumni. Another insider, the Rev. Henry Sloane Coffin, was rejected on similar grounds. Instead the corporation turned to not merely a layperson but a non-Yale graduate, James Rowland Angell. Angell, the son of Michigan's former president, was a leader in the field of psychology at the University of Chicago. His thought had been influenced by James and Dewey but incorporated aspects of the liberal Protestantism of his upbringing as well.[54]

Yale's Dwight Hall heritage still ensured a strong representation of liberal evangelicalism on the faculty, but by the 1920s the definition of Christianity at Yale was increasingly emphasizing its formal functions.[55] From the 1890s until about 1910, Yale had been noted for its evangelical piety.[56] After that, however, Bible study and private piety had declined precipitously. Moreover, the younger generation did not seem to share the prewar generation's enthusiasm for sacrificial public service.

By the mid-1920s required chapel had become one of the victims of the new climate. In 1925 the *Yale Daily* led a persistent campaign against compulsion and through straw polls established overwhelming student and faculty opposition. Student editorials, of course, argued that religion would be healthier if it were voluntary; but the true sentiments of most may have been captured in a bit of doggerel titled "A Hymn: To Dear Old Mother Battell," referring to the venerable Battell chapel building and including such sentiments as:

Though we're grown you still confine us
Close beneath your musty wind,
And with nosey voice you whine us
Sappy songs you always sing.[57]

In bowing to student pressures, the Yale Corporation reassured concerned constituents that the shift to voluntary chapel was just an adjustment to the spirit of the times and would not lessen the university's intention to "uphold and propagate the Christian protestant religion."[58] President Angell likewise affirmed that the university remained in close contiguity with its religious heritage. "While the theological views of our generations are in many respects quite different from those of the founders of Yale and the later founders of the Church of Christ in Yale," he told the *Yale Daily* in 1927, "all are alike characterized by allegiance to the essential teachings of Jesus and to the promotion of those fundamental attitudes in private and public life which we call Christian."[59]

In the later years of his presidency, during the mid-1930s, Angell had to admit that at Yale, as elsewhere among American youth, "complete indifference to religion, colored at times with acrimonious hostility and ignorant contempt, is an altogether too common phenomenon." Nonetheless, he claimed comfort in other "large and influential groups of students" who showed "a deep and serious concern . . . for the essential religious and ethical values in life." In 1936 in one of his last baccalaureate services, Angell called for "a moral and spiritual renaissance." This awakening, however, would not be of "superstitions" or "outworn creeds" but instead "a vital reverence for the highest values in human life."[60]

Whatever the degree of genuine sympathy for the Christian heritage such statements indicated, even among its supporters religion was being reduced to vague platitudes. This was true not only of administrators, of whom such equivocation was to be expected. They after all had to communicate with a wide public and also prepare baccalaureates and other occasional remarks in which they had to say something pious yet offend no one. What is more telling is that such tendencies were increasingly typical of mainline Protestantism as a whole, especially when it addressed a wider public. The religious professionals most interested in restoring a place for Christianity on campuses were conspicuous in constructing a religion of no offense.

Searching for a Message

During the interwar era there was no lack of discussions, studies, symposia, journals, conferences, and programs about the restoration of Christianity to a place on campus. In almost all of these, however, one gets the impression that by the early 1920s the leadership in the Protestant establishment was desperately attempting to find a message that would reach the youth culture. One thing they were firmly convinced of was that they could not say anything that would make them sound like fundamentalists. The independent and rebellious mood of the youth, as they saw it—perhaps correctly—was in part a reaction against fundamentalism, or Puritanism, or outworn prescientific creeds. In response they attempted to articulate a broader version of Christianity that would appeal to a more modern mentality. Unfortunately, among many youth in the 1920s such religious idealism was also passé. It was high-sounding rhetoric; the problem was that most of the young were going to regard it as just that, the platitudinous ideals of an older generation that, aside from Prohibition, lacked much of a substantive agenda.

A 1924 symposium on "The Place of Religion in Higher Education," conducted by the Association of American Colleges, provides a typical example. Throughout the era, the AAC published in its *Bulletin* discussions of the importance of retaining a place for religion in higher education, sometimes recognizing how difficult was the task. The transcript of the opening remarks in the symposium by the president of the AAC, President C. A. Richmond of Union University, reveals the changed atmosphere of the day. Apologizing that he was a minister who was a college president, Richmond quipped,

> Some of you may have found that the office of minister, and college president—are often incompatible (laughter), at least, in the popular imagination they are supposed to be so, and when you ask a college president to talk about religion, well, it is like asking Mr. Bryan to talk about evolution. (Laughter). He is supposed to be unembarrassed by any knowledge of the subject. (Laughter).

The most substantive discussion of the issues on this occasion was provided by President Marion L. Burton of the University of Michigan, in remarks considered noteworthy enough to be reprinted in part in the *Bulletin of the American Association of University Professors.*[61] While universities were successful in teaching their students of advances in science, President Burton observed, they had failed to convey the advances to religion brought by scientific knowledge:

> Christ is no longer the center of metaphysical discussions about His person, but all of our thought, political, commercial, and economic, is increasingly Christlike. Man is no longer the wreck and ruin of a once perfect harmony, but he is a chaos, not yet reduced to order. Sin is not merely a taint of the past, but selfishness, pure and simple. Salvation is not saving the sinful soul from the fires of Hell, but the making of all men into good ones here and now. All things are not true, because they are in the Bible, but they are in the Bible because they are true.

Yet the problem, said Burton, was that there was a "deep, abysmal, unfathomable darkness about religion" on college campuses as elsewhere in the nation. When people thought of religion, they still thought of categories from the Dark Ages. What was needed was a religion that dealt with "character." They must, Burton concluded, "send out a generation of students who understand religion in its largest terms, and know that we can only build a life with an inner reality which matches the stern ineradicable order of truth that life gives us."[62]

"Character" was the most prominent word in the literature on the role of religion in higher education, since that was a worthy ideal to which religion could contribute without offending modern sensibilities. Moreover, in an age when the typical ambition of young people was to move from four years of hedonism in college to the life of business profit, building character seemed an especially urgent educational task.[63]

In *Christian Education,* published by the interdenominational Council of Church Boards of Education in the United States of America, a symposium on "Character Education" was headed by John D. Rockefeller, Jr., who spoke out for honesty in business, obedience to law, and clean living. The standard formula for how to influence college students was enunciated by another speaker: "Character is caught, rather than taught."[64] The more common version was voiced by Henry Sloane Coffin at a conference of leading eastern educators held at Princeton in 1928: "Religion is caught—not taught." The meaning was precisely the same. The consensus was that the key to conveying religious ideals in colleges was for leading persons, from administrators to professors, to be persons of high Christian character. Of course, as Coffin was quick to add, doctrinal tests were entirely out of bounds. Nonetheless, schools could informally provide worthy Christian models.[65]

With both popular magazines and fundamentalists making as much of a sensation as they could out of the alleged laxity in morals on campuses, the liberal Protestant establishment more often affirmed that things were not really so bad after all. In a 1926 survey of college and university presidents, conducted by *Literary Digest,* the not surprising result was an almost unanimous belief that drinking was down since Prohibition, at least on their own campuses. An editorial in the *Christian Century,* "Are College Girls Bad?," acknowledged that changes in mores were taking place at a bewildering speed. Women smoking openly on campuses, for instance, was causing a great deal of consternation at the moment. Changes in sexual mores were particularly rapid. "The changes are sudden, but are they bad?," asked the *Century.*

> Everybody knows that an interpretation of conduct obtains in college class rooms from which the fixed absolutes of a generation ago have been eliminated. Is there any better word to say than that we are going from an old world to a new and that we may trust human nature—in our girls as well as in our boys and grown-ups—to right itself upon its own keel? We can trust it, if, with our trust, we lend them the support which sympathy and understanding and faith can give and which distrust and dark suspicions cannot give.

The key phrase was that "we may trust human nature."[66] While liberal Protestants might sometimes express alarm about campus trends, their principal strategy was to sympathize and offer supportive guidance. They recognized correctly that the student attitudes were in many ways only extensions of their own principles. They represented confidence in human nature and hence confidence that increased freedom would lead toward the good.[67] The counterpart was that they stood against authoritarianism. So did the students. There would be a period of adjustment; but with some spiritual guidance, there was little need to worry. Human progress was assured.

Faith in God, humanity, and moral progress were all rooted in confidence in the scientific method as the great revealer. To the question "What are the ruling concepts in modern education?" the *Christian Century* responded in a 1931 essay: "The ruling concepts of modern education are freedom of the individual from disciplines and patterns of conduct based solely upon tradition, the right of the individual to realize his own possibilities and to discover the best means of realization by his own experience, and the duty of both individuals and society to bring all codes and commands and prohibitions to the experimental test." This "application of the scientific spirit to the matters which most deeply concern human life" had the danger, the *Century* conceded—presumably with Prohibition in mind—that experiments sometimes went wrong. Nonetheless, most people thought the benefits were worth the risks. Advances might bring periods of confusion and painful adjustment. Yet that was not too high a price to pay for "the transition from a morality of accepted codes and ipse-dixit rules to a morality based on a scientific study of the observable results of conduct."[68]

At the end of the 1930s religious liberalism was sometimes chastened by postliberal or neo-orthodox theological trends, which challenged their close identification with the culture. That theological critique of culture had little impact, however, on the largely positive assessments of what was happening on campuses. For one thing, the international threat of totalitarianism in the 1930s reinforced the point that Protestant colleges in America must stand first of all for freedom. Given this political context, it would indeed be difficult to deny that the very openness of campuses to diverse opinions, even to those antithetical to Christianity, were signs of health in a world of contagious absolutism.[69] Calls to strengthen Christian identity or separate the church from the world, therefore, would be inappropriate to campuses, even church-related campuses, since they would involve more restrictions, in contradiction to the quintessential cultural watchword of freedom. While Christian ministries saw themselves in a struggle against crass materialism, what they offered was nonetheless not confrontation with American culture but a voluntarily chosen spiritual dimension that could provide divine grounding for highest cultural ideals.

On these terms it was still plausible, even at the end of the 1930s, to give an optimistic account of religion on campuses. So, for instance, T. T. Brumbaugh after a tour of twenty-two colleges and universities concluded: "I am ready to state unhesitatingly not only that there is a growing concern for religion as such among students in this country but that in administrative circles in tax-supported and other schools there is enhanced appreciation of the spiritual interpretation of existence which is the specific province of religion." Brumbaugh cited the development of schools of religion and cooperative campus ministries, often encouraged by school administrations. Nonetheless, such ministries had to learn that "public institutions of learning can go no farther than to place due emphasis of learning upon the spiritual interpretations of life and the commonly acknowledged moral values implicit therein."[70]

Similarly, Merrimon Cuninggim, after extensive study of campuses just prior to World War II, could describe the forces of religion as gaining dramatically. On the one hand, he acknowledged that "the prevailing atmosphere in higher education today is secular," defining secularity as an "emphasis upon the material to the exclusion or denial of the intangible and upon nature to the disparagement of the supernatural." Nonetheless, Cuninggim, who had been a campus religious worker at Duke, saw the contest as more a friendly "two-sided game" than a warfare. "That it [higher education] has dealt so many cards to religion in recent years has made the game close, but has not yet made religion the victor. Secularism is too widespread for one to be able glibly to conclude that colleges are more Christian in attitude than in 1900."

What made such optimism was possible was a broad definition of religion. Religion, said Cuninggim, is

> a knowledge of high values in living. It is, moreover, an appreciation of and a personal commitment to those values, a search for the eternal verities, a faith in God. A student may be said to "have religion" when, for example, he possesses personal integrity and, what is more, knows why; or when he respects selfhood in those around him, the rights and needs and joys of others; or when through personal experience he knows reverence and sympathy and goodness; or when he is sensitive to his obligation to society and acts upon it.[71]

When religion was defined in more traditional ways, however, then it was clear that it was on the periphery of student life and consciousness. Ruth Davies, a professor of English literature at Ohio Wesleyan University, observed in 1939 that she was often asked the question "Are students losing their religion?" She responded that students "cannot lose what they do not have." The realistic view was that "the average student today has very little religion of the type meant by the people who ask the question," that is, not religion as just a broad idealism but "the conventional conception of religion which has found expression in the creeds and practices of the church in America." As modern activities were increasingly defined by mechanism, Davies observed, "religion is simply not on the boards in the theater of modern American life." People talk about "religious consciousness," but "religious unconsciousness" might be the more appropriate term. "Generally speaking, we seem spiritually to be under the influence of an anesthetic."[72]

Notes

1. United State Bureau of the Census, *Historical Statistics of the United States, Colonial Times to 1957* (Washington, D.C.: Government Printing Office, 1960), 210–11.

2. See, e.g., Paula S. Fass, *The Damned and the Beautiful: American Youth in the 1920s* (New York: Oxford University Press, 1977), 13–52.

3. *Church of the Holy Trinity v. United States,* 143 U.S. 457 (1892) at 471. In 1905 Brewer published his addresses as *The United States as a Christian Nation* (Philadelphia, 1905). Quotation from Robert T. Handy, *Undermined Establishment: Church–State Relations in America, 1880–1920* (Princeton: Princeton University Press, 1991), 13 and passim.

4. Burton Confrey, "Secularism in American Higher Education," *Catholic University of America Educational Research Monographs* 6 (January 15, 1931), 47–127, provides a compilation of "Constitutional Provisions, Statutes, and Legal Decisions Relating to the Secularization of Public Schools in the United States."

5. Handy, *Undermined Establishment,* 15–16, 45–48, 136–37.

6. Anson Phelps Stokes, *Church and State in the United States* (New York: Harper & Bros., 1950), II:621–22. Stokes reports that at Wisconsin there was even a serious debate in the Board of Regents in 1942 on the propriety of the university press publishing a book titled *The Religious Availability of God* (621).

7. Merrimon Cuninggim, *The College Seeks Religion* (New Haven: Yale University Press, 1947), 79–86.

8. Robert S. Shepard, *God's People in the Ivory Tower: Religion in the Early American University* (Brooklyn: Carlson, 1991), shows that the field of comparative religion, despite some fanfare around the turn of the century, did not catch on in colleges or universities. To the extent the subject was taught at all, it was usually under the auspices of theological seminaries. See below on academic study of the Bible, which fared somewhat better.

9. Cf. Darryl G. Hart, "American Learning and the Problem of Religious Studies," in *The Secularization of the Academy,* in George M. Marsden and Bradley J. Longfield, eds. (New York: Oxford University Press, 1992), 202–3.

10. Handy, *Undermined Establishment,* 160. Confrey, "Secularism," provides a chart summarizing these and related provisions.

11. Charles Foster Kent, "The Undergraduate Courses in Religion at the Tax-Supported Colleges and Universities of America," *Bulletin of the National Council on Religion in Higher Education* 4 (1924), 1–34, presents the results of a survey conducted in 1922–1923 showing that typically a few courses in Bible were offered at state universities, enrolling from 5 to 10 percent of the student bodies. However, only 20 to 30 percent of teachers' colleges and agricultural colleges had any courses in religion, and municipal colleges and universities were even less likely to offer such courses. Only seven of the forty-eight states had no tax-supported institution offering courses in religion.

Another survey of twenty-one state universities and colleges (presumably of all varieties) in 1923–1924 showed that six offered undergraduate courses in Bible and religion, though none at the graduate level. Edward S. Boyer, "Religious Education in Colleges, Universities and Schools of Religion," *Christian Education* 11 (October 1927), 38.

12. From a 1904-committee report to the General Assembly of the Presbyterian Church in the U.S.A., cited in Clarence Prouty Shedd, *The Church Follows Its Students* (New Haven, 1938). 14. Shedd surveys these development and is the principal immediate source for the present account.

13. John Whitney Evans, *The Newman Movement: Roman Catholics in American Higher Education, 1883–1971* (Notre Dame, Ind.: University of Notre Dame Press, 1980) is a valuable study of this work.

14. Shedd, *Church Follows Its Students,* 16, 26. Cuninggim, *College Seeks Religion,*

147. Cf. Mont Whitson, *The Work of a Bible Chair* (Lubbock, Tex.: College Christian Press, 1954); Charles Foster Kent, "Religion at a Great State University: Based on the University of Illinois Survey," *Bulletin of the National Council of Schools of Religion* 3 (1923); and Winton U. Solberg, "The Catholic Presence at the University of Illinois," *Catholic Historical Review* 76 (October 1990), 765–812. In 1937 Presbyterians reported receiving credit for courses at twenty-two of their fifty-one centers at all universities. Methodist Wesley Foundations were receiving credit at fourteen of their forty-six foundations. Shedd, *Church Follows Its Students, 130–31.*

15. *Shedd, Church Follows Its Students,* 190–95. On Kent's role see Seymour A. Smith, *Religious Cooperation in State Universities: An Historical Sketch* (n.p., 1957), 28, and Bradley Longfield, " 'For God, for Country and for Yale': Yale, Religion and Higher Education between the World Wars," in Marsden and Longfield, *Secularization of the Academy,* 146–69. Milton D. McLean and Henry H. Kimber, *Teaching of Religion in State Universities: Descriptions of Programs in Twenty-Five Institutions* (Ann Arbor: University of Michigan Press, 1960), 109–13, has a useful summary of the evolution of the school and its gradual absorption into the university and the redefinition of its goals ca. 1950 to general study and appreciation of religious values in human culture.

16. "Two Decades: The Story of the National Council on Religion in Higher Education (Founded by Charles Foster Kent), 1922–1941," *The Bulletin* 11 (May 1941), 12–13. The journals *Christian Education* and *Religious Education* published numerous articles on religion at state universities during this era.

17. Probably the most novel arrangement was at the University of North Dakota, which provided a variation on the Iowa arrangement but with only one denomination involved. There the Wesley Foundation started its own School of Religion and during the 1920s was recognized as essentially a college of the university. The school was run by the Methodist Episcopal Church, financed by voluntary contributions, yet its courses, which had the announced purpose of "the cultivation of religious idealism," were granted university credit and listed in the university catalogue. In 1922–1923 Wesley College was offering nine courses enrolling about 145 in a university of 1500 students. Herbert Leon Searles, "The Study of Religion in State Universities," *University of Iowa Studies in Character* 1 (ca. 1928), 86–87. Kent, "Undergraduate Courses," 12.

North Dakota was thus following a Canadian model in which some church colleges and theological schools were affiliated with state-supported universities. See D. C. Masters, *Protestant Church Colleges in Canada: A History* (Toronto: University of Toronto Press, 1966). According to Masters, this arrangement did not do much to forestall secularization of Canadian universities because the theological positions of the church colleges liberalized in the twentieth century (209–11). Theological colleges are still affiliated, however, with some major Canadian universities, notably the University of Toronto.

18. Shedd, *Church Follows Its Students,* 205–11. Solberg, "Catholic Presence."

19. Searles, "Study of Religion," 16, indicates that this was the ideal at Iowa and in the movement generally.

20. McLean and Kimber, *Teaching of Religion,* 102–9. See their list of course offerings for 1957–1958, which have a strongly Christian tone (32–36).

21. Shedd, "Religion in State Universities," *Journal of Higher Education* 12 (November 1941), 408, quoted in Cuninggim, *College Seeks Religion,* 88. Statistics are from Cuninggim, 146–47, 298–306. Among black colleges, 81 percent of private schools had departments of religion, but only two of sixteen of state schools had such offerings (304).

22. Shedd, *Church Follows Its Students,* 131, reporting that 10,245 of 279,802 students in tax-supported schools enrolled in religion courses in 1936.

23. Cuninggim, *College Seeks Religion,* 149. Quotation from William B. Huie, "How to Keep Football Stars in College," *Collier's* 107 (January 4, 1941), 20 (ibid.).

24. "Two Decades," 15, 36–37.

25. Cuninggim, *College Seeks Religion,* 94, and passim on administrative support. On the AAC, see Hart, "Religious Studies," 205–6. See also journals of these organizations such as *Religious Education, Christian Education,* the *Journal of Bible and Religion,* and the *Bulletin of the Association of American Colleges,* which are rich in materials on religion in higher education.

26. *The Edward W. Hazen Foundation 1925–1950* (New Haven: Hazen Foundation, 1950).

27. During this era there was relatively little talk of relating Christianity to academic disciplines, although presumably that is one of the things Kent scholars were supposed to be doing. One exception is Charles Ellwood, who was brought to head the Sociology Department at the new Duke University after thirty years of teaching at Missouri. Ellwood saw sociology as a Christian mission for the benefit of democratic society. His views were thus much like those typical of leading figures in the field at the turn of the century. Under its founding president, William Preston Few, Duke University (formerly Trinity College), which had Methodist connections, was more explicit in its liberal Christian ideals than were most universities in the North. I am indebted to my colleague on this project, Bradley J. Longfield, for his " '*Eruditio et Religio*': Religion at Duke between the World Wars" (unpublished manuscript).

28. Robert L. Geiger, *To Advance Knowledge: The Growth of American Research Universities: 1900–1940* (New York: Oxford University Press, 1986), 108.

29. This is the major thesis of David O. Levine, *The American College and the Culture of Aspiration, 1915–1940 (Ithaca: Cornell University Press, 1986).*

30. Cf. Frederick Rudolph, *Curriculum: A History of the American Undergraduate Course of Study since 1636* (San Francisco: Jossey-Bass, 1977), 245–55.

31. Levine, *American College,* 162.

32. Cuninggim, *College Seeks Religion,* 303–5. Kent, "Undergraduate Courses in Religion," 26.

33. Geiger, *To Advance Knowledge,* 232, 263.

34. Ibid., 166.

35. Robert L. Church, "Knowledge and Power: American Higher Education in the Twentieth Century: A Review Essay," *History of Education Annual* 7 (1987), 99. This remark is usually attributed to Robert Maynard Hutchins. On Hutchins, see chapter 20.

36. Geiger, *To Advance Knowledge,* argues that this pragmatic character is a source of the vitality of American universities that contributed to their gaining world leadership in the twentieth century.

37. By 1930 the percentage of clergy on the boards of private institutions had dropped to 7, down from 30 in 1860. William Clyde DeVane, *Higher Education in Twentieth-Century America* (Cambridge, Mass.: Harvard University Press, 1965), 79.

38. Fass, *The Damned and the Beautiful,* 17–25.

39. F. Scott Fitzgerald, *This Side of Paradise* (New York: Charles Scribner's Sons, 1948 [1920]), 58–59, as summarized and quoted in Helen Lefkowitz Horowitz, *Campus Life: Undergraduate Cultures from the End of the Eighteenth Century to the Present* (Chicago: University of Chicago Press, 1987), 125. Cf. Fass, *The Damned and the Beautiful,* 25–29.

40. James Bissett Pratt, "Religion and the Younger Generation," *Yale Review* 12 (1923), 594–96, 610.

41. Robert Cooley Angell, *The Campus: A Study of Contemporary Undergraduate Life in the American University* (New York: D. Appleton and Co., 1928), esp. 185–88. In an in-depth survey of seniors from the limited population of Reed College in Oregon, Helen Chambers Griffin summarized the following conclusions: "About four phases of religious thought there was little or no disagreement. First, Jesus is considered only human, but a great thinker and teacher. Second, the Bible is thought of in terms of historical and literary criticism. Third, these students believe that the miracles recorded in the Bible either did not happen, or they had natural causes. Fourth, to them no one religion contains all the elements of beauty and truth." "Changes in the Religious Attitudes of College Students," *Religious Education* 24 (February 1929), 160.

42. Angell, *Campus,* 162–63. *Yale Daily News,* April 21, 1926, 1.

43. For the latter see *Trinity Chronicle,* editorials, April 21, 1926, 2, and December 12, 1926, 2.

44. Angell, *Campus,* 2, 66–89.

45. "Religion on the Campus," *Christian Century* 42 (March 19, 1925), 370, found regular graduations in the correlations between wealth and lack of church attendance among students at the University of Michigan.

46. Horowitz, *Campus Life,* is particularly good in pointing out the diversities of subgroups on campuses. At the same time, her account of the interwar era is written as though religion was no presence on campuses, except in the distinction between Christians and Jews.

47. C. Howard Hopkins, *History of the Y.M.C.A. in North America* (New York: Association Press, 1951), 628, 645–46.

48. Ibid., 629, 521, 590. The YWCAs were more decentralized and apparently did not typically give up their evangelicalism quite so soon. I am grateful to Kathy Long for her work on this point.

49. Angell, *Campus,* 200–210.

50. "Religion on the Campus," 370. Horowitz, *Campus Life,* 118, 204, cf. 193–219.

51. News report, "Finds Student Y in Perilous Position," *Christian Century* 44 (June 23, 1927), 787–88.

52. Cuninggim, *College Seeks Religion,* 136.

53. Ibid., 134.

54. Longfield, " 'For God, for Country, and for Yale,' " 147.

55. I am indebted to Jeffrey Trexler for making this point and providing documentation of it. See Jeffrey Alan Trexler, "Education with the Soul of a Church: The Yale Foreign Missionary Society and the Democratic Ideal," Ph.D. dissertation, Duke University, 1991.

56. We get a mixed picture of the impact of extracurricular religion at Yale by contrasting two volumes, Mrs. Howard Taylor's *Borden of Yale '09* (London, 1927) and Owen Johnson's *Stover at Yale* (Boston, 1933 [1911]). *Borden of Yale* is a sentimentalized biography of William Whiting Borden (1887–1913, who gave up a million-dollar inheritance to become a foreign missionary but died en route to the field. Borden is a conservative religiously and complains of the liberalism of many of the chapel speakers, though approving of guests such as missionary promoters Robert Speer and John R. Mott. He was active in Dwight Hall and appreciative of a faculty-led Bible study. He also notes that the YMCA vice president was tapped to head Skull and Bones. At the same time he complains to

his mother of the students: "The great majority smoke, go to the theater Saturday night and do their studying on Sunday. Rather a hopeless state of affairs!" (89).

Stover at Yale, a fictional account of turn-of-the-century Yale, published in 1911, depicts a Yale in which religion is virtually absent. Dink Stover undergoes various "tests of manhood," which prove to be character building while helping him become a football hero and get into Skull and Bones.

57. *Yale Daily News,* November 2, 1925, 2. The editorials are summarized in Longfield, " 'For God, for Country, and for Yale.' "

58. Quoted in Ralph H. Gabriel, *Religion and Learning at Yale: The Church of Christ in the College and University, 1757–1957* (New Haven: Yale University Press, 1958), 2.

59. *Yale Daily News,* October 26, 1927, 1.

60. *Report of the President of Yale University for the Academic Year 1933–1934* (New Haven, 1934), 49, and James R. Angell, *American Education: Addresses and Articles* (New Haven 1937), 231–32, both quoted in Longfield, " 'For God, for Country, and for Yale,' " 157–58.

61. *Bulletin of the American Association of University Professors* 11 (January 1925), 172–74. This excerpt was incorrectly attributed to Richmond.

62. Charles A. Richmond and Marion L. Burton, "The Place of Religion in Higher Education," *Bulletin of the American Association of Colleges* 10 (1924), 90, 103–6.

63. See, for instance, "Character Education in American Colleges and Universities," in *1925–26 Year Book of the National Council on Religion in Higher Education* (Ithaca, 1926). The University of Iowa School of Religion had an Institute of Character Research and in the later 1920s was publishing a periodical, *University of Iowa Studies in Character.*

64. John D. Rockefeller, Jr., "Character," *Christian Education* 11 (April 1928), 417–20. John R. Hart, Jr., "Methods of Developing Character in College," *Christian Education* 11 (April 1928), 426.

65. Henry Sloane Coffin, "Pillars of Religion in the Colleges," in *Religion in the Colleges,* Galen M. Fisher, ed. (New York: Association Press, 1928), 23. Cf. Galen M. Fisher, "An Appraisal of the Conference," *ibid.* x.

66. "College Heads Say Drinking Declines," *Christian Century* 43 (July 29, 1926), 1100; "Are College Girls Bad?" *Christian Century* 43 (September 30, 1926), 1189–90. Similarly, a report in the *Christian Century* on a late 1926 student conference on religion on campuses observed that the ethics of sex life was not discussed in student conventions a decade earlier but assured that "this does not mean that sex morality is at a lower ebb than hitherto. . . . The emancipation of woman and the freer association of the sexes has indeed complicated an age-old problem; but whatever the perils that may come out of this freedom, they are more than balanced by the greater measure of sincerity with which young men and women face the problem of establishing a wholesome family life." "The Religion of the Campus," 44 (January 13, 1927), 37.

67. By 1928, for instance, most major leaders concerned for religion on campuses had joined student opinion in being "strongly opposed to compulsory chapel." Fisher, *Religion in the Colleges,* xi.

68. "What Are Education's Ruling Concepts?" *Christian Century* 48 (February 11, 1931), 197–98.

69. E.g., William F. Anderson, "The Church College—Battleground of Freedom," *Christian Century* 51 (September 5, 1934), 1115–57; "Shackles for Scholars,"

Christian Century 51 (May 8, 1935), 293–94; "Liberalism Has a Citadel in the Universities," *Christian Century* 53 (July 1, 1936), 924.

70. T. T. Brumbaugh, "Religion Returns to the Campus," *Christian Century* 55 (April 20, 1938), 493–95.

71. Cuninggim, *College Seeks Religion,* 250, 259, 247.

72. Ruth Davies, "Are Students Losing Their Religion?" *Christian Century* 56 (June 14, 1939), 767–69. Dan Gilbert, *Crucifying Christ in Our Colleges* (San Francisco, 1933), offer a fundamentalist view of the situation. Including documented accounts of what was taught in college texts, Gilbert presented case studies of students whose lives had been ruined by following the advice of Nietzsche or of contemporaries such as Bertrand Russell, who taught that humans were essentially animals. Such critiques apparently had negligible impact outside fundamentalist and perhaps Catholic circles.

19

Outsiders

Despite attempts to define the university in terms of the inclusivist ideal of liberal Protestantism, some significant groups were in fact being left out. For the pre–World War I generation who believed in the advance of both science and a higher Christianity, such exclusion might be represented as only temporary, since education would surely eventually eliminate most parochialism and prejudice. By the interwar era, such a view was increasingly problematic.

Groups were underrepresented in the leading institutions of the dominant culture for two major reasons. At one end of the spectrum were those who chose to maintain their own cultural identity, usually supported by strong religious convictions. At the other end were those who, while cultivating cultural identities with religious roots, nonetheless aspired to become part of the mainstream. Most religious groups, however, fell somewhere in between, exhibiting various mixes of both tendencies.

Roman Catholics were the largest group whose outsider status had a large voluntary component. They maintained their own parochial school system, an extensive network of colleges, and a few modest universities. So while Catholics' 5 to 10 percent representation among student bodies and faculties of non-Catholic universities was much less than their representation in the population generally, the difference was attributable more to choice and social class than overt religious discrimination. Even at prestigious schools of the East there was little evidence of overt discrimination against Catholics, although there was always strong discrimination based on social class.[1]

Even a 5 to 10 percent representation in the nation's major universities spoke of Catholic division on the question of separation from the dominant culture. A Catholic, after all, had been a viable candidate for the U.S. presidency in 1928 and many Catholics were pushing to become part of the mainstream. Even at Notre Dame, though Thomas Aquinas might be preeminent in philosophy and theology, Knute Rockne's preeminence on Saturdays suggested another side of Catholic culture that aspired to be 100 percent American.

At the University of Illinois, the Catholic Foundation sparked a protracted controversy within the church. The Rev. John O'Brien, an able scholar and colorful personality, was the pastor and chaplain to Catholic students. He had been instrumental in instituting courses, taught under his auspices, for which the university agreed in 1919 to offer academic credit. A few years later O'Brien launched an ambitious campaign to build a magnificent building for the Catholic Foundation. He pointed out that there were more Catholics enrolled at the university than in all the Catholic colleges in the state and that the foundation presented a marvelous new educational and missionary opportunity.

O'Brien's campaign soon aroused stiff opposition. Influential members of the Illinois church hierarchy, supported strongly by the Jesuits all over the world, argued that O'Brien's ministry was an attack on Catholic universities. If O'Brien's scheme succeeded, it would only encourage more Catholic students to attend state universities. O'Brien retorted that many of the best students were attending state universities anyway, and that his foundation was playing an essential role in training Catholic lay leaders for the next generation. Finally the controversy became so bitter that the Vatican stepped in and brought it to an end. O'Brien continued his work on the Catholic Foundation, but he had to scale down his plans because the opposition had weakened his sources of financial support.[2] The Catholic leadership that opposed O'Brien was asserting an ideal of Catholic separateness. O'Brien, on the other hand, was responding to the reality that, no matter what the church said, Catholics were being served and shaped by secular American institutions at least as much as by the church.

Protestants were also divided as to whether university culture should be regarded as a threat to the faith. In most mainstream denominations there were three major positions on this question. The largest group were those so used to Protestant hegemony that they could hardly conceive of a conflict between church and culture; as a matter of course they sent their children to universities without thought for their religious stances. Another sizable constituency supported the hundreds of denominational colleges. These offered a variety of religious outlooks, but the most common was a serious-minded evangelical liberalism, supported by required chapel, Bible courses, and restrictive campus moral regulations which preserved something of the Protestant mores that had been dominant before World War I. Rather than seeing themselves at war with the university culture, mainline denominational colleges saw themselves as offering the invaluable option of an added spiritual dimension.

The third group were the fundamentalists, who militantly opposed the cultural trends, were building their own institutions, and in some cases were seceding from the major denominations. After the mid-1920s, however, militant fundamentalism declined sharply in northern churches and now seemed marginal so far as those denominations were concerned. In fact, however, new networks were developing to support Protestant higher education outside the mainstream. Fundamentalist breakaway groups joined many other sectarian groups, such as those in pentecostal and holiness traditions, each of which supported its own institutions. Such groups founded more than a hundred Bible institutes, often patterned on the Moody Bible Institute in Chicago, which offered training in basic skills oriented toward learning to witness to the truths of biblicist Christianity in evangelism at home and in missions abroad.[3] Sectarian groups also supported many smaller four-year colleges. Protestant immigrant groups, such as the Missouri Synod Lutherans and the Christian Reformed, also founded their own colleges and cultivated a militant sense of separateness. Much of the white Protestantism of the South also had a mentality much like that of a separate ethnic group and many of their colleges, especially those of Southern Baptists and Southern Presbyterians, were determined to preserve conservative theological and cultural views.[4]

Women's colleges presented an ambiguous case with respect to the insider–outsider question and religion. Women were excluded from undergraduate admission at some of the most prestigious eastern universities. Elite institutions for women tended to be a shade more traditional in their religious observances than were their all-male counterparts.[5] Denominational women's colleges also emphasized religion a bit more than did men's schools and were certainly more protective regarding social behavior. In North Carolina even the state women's college at Greensboro had required chapel services into the 1940s, a decade after chapel requirements had been abandoned at the University of North Carolina at Chapel Hill. The conventional association of women with domesticity and religion contributed to a slight lag in secularization at women's colleges. Correspondingly, the most thoroughly secular parts of the university were those that were most defined by the scientific and professional ideals associated with male dominance.

Far less ambiguous was the situation of African Americans. Formally or informally discriminated against in most American universities, they were largely left to make the best of poorly funded black colleges. After World War I, the number of blacks attending college increased dramatically, though by 1927 the total had reached only some fifteen thousand, nine-tenths of whom were at colleges with all-black student bodies. At predominantly white schools, blacks faced numerous obstacles. At Yale, which had a long record of support for education of African Americans, a few were admitted, though they faced informal racial discrimination, which was growing during this era.[6] At Harvard in the early 1920s a major stir was caused when President Lawrence Abbot Lowell ruled that African Americans would not be admitted to freshman dorms. Although alumni protest led the trustees to modify the rule, blacks still could be admitted to the dorms only if they could afford a single room or find a black roommate. At Princeton, which always had strong southern ties, blacks were not admitted as undergraduates until after World War II, though they were admitted to the independent and theologically much more conservative Princeton Theological Seminary.[7] Qualified blacks could gain admission to state universities and, if they could afford it, to many private colleges in the North; but everywhere they faced social discrimination.

In most black colleges, biblicist Christianity played a major role. This emphasis was in part a reflection of the centrality of the churches in the black community. A survey conducted by Benjamin E. Mays in 1940 showed that an overwhelming majority of students at black colleges, usually well over 90 percent, were church members, and most professed conservative beliefs about God, prayer, and the Bible. Evidence of actual religious practice was, of course, mixed. One survey in 1945 showed that while 90 percent of black students attended church at least twice a month, only a third considered their classmates to be religious. Mays noted that black college students (like their white counterparts) often resented compulsory chapel and few attended when chapel services were made voluntary.[8]

Institutional support for Christianity was also strong at most black colleges. Over two-thirds were private colleges, most founded by northern white missionary organizations or by churches. Most of these had compulsory chapel, as did even some of the state schools.[9] In this respect they did not differ much from all-white colleges in the South.

The persistence of biblicist Christian patterns was deeply mixed with the questions of African-American identity in America. From one point of view the continuation of traditional Christian patterns, often with relatively strict social regulation of students, could be seen as a form of white control, since most black schools were still administered by whites. This issue was dramatically illustrated at Fisk University, where in the 1920s a strict disciplinary code was brought down by student protests. Fisk was considered academically the best of the black colleges. It was founded by the American Missionary Association and still had a white president. So the attack on the disciplinary code was in part an attack on white paternalism. On the other hand, the black community was divided just as was the white over how strict its colleges should be. Fisk's code was not as severe as that at Wilberforce, the first black school controlled by blacks, but which was run by the African Methodist Episcopal Church and hence had strict Methodist mores.[10]

Howard University, the only school for African Americans that was truly a university, with professional schools in law, medicine, and theology, presents an interesting case of the ambiguities of the role of religion. Howard was founded in Washington, D.C., after the Civil War with support from the Freedmen's Bureau and various church groups. By the 1920s, when its some two thousand students represented almost one-sixth of all blacks receiving higher education, its principal support came from yearly congressional appropriations.[11] Originally the school required evangelical church membership for faculty members. At the end of the nineteenth century attendance had been required at daily chapel services and at Sunday Bible classes and preaching services. The 1898–1899 catalogue stated: "This institution is always emphatically Christian. Its instructors believe in Christianity as the only basis of true culture; but pupils here are given no denominational bias and no ecclesiastical or denominational instruction is given in any department."[12]

Like some other colleges of the era Howard experienced revivals among its students into early decades of the twentieth century.[13] By the 1920s the collegiate atmosphere had begun to change. The college catalogue still described the school as "distinctly Christian in its spirit and work,"[14] and the president, James Stanley Durkee, one of a long succession of white Congregational clergymen to head the school, still described the purpose of the chapel as to encourage "life surrender to Christ."[15] Compulsory chapel, however, was becoming controversial at Howard, as elsewhere. Protests initiated by students in 1922 eventually resulted in capitulation to voluntary chapel in 1925. The variation at Howard from the pattern elsewhere, however, was that the chapel controversy was only one part of growing black student unrest about racism. Howard was not as strictly regulated as most of the smaller black colleges, but its regulations sparked broader protests. Students demanded the end of white control. Finally, in 1926, after enduring protracted criticism, President Durkee resigned to accept a pastorate. The trustees choose as its next president Mordecai W. Johnson, a young black Baptist pastor, who began a presidency that was to last until 1960.[16]

Under Johnson and his successors the process of secularization at Howard followed just about the same pattern as in mainline denominational colleges. The catalogue statement that Howard was "distinctly Christian" remained until the 1960s, but the formal definitions of Christianity broadened. Since then the university has become essentially secular, although it still has a Christian divinity school.[17]

Christianity, then, played an ambiguous role in the outsider status of black schools. To some extent Christianity was used as a means of social regulation and was an expression of white control. On the other hand, Christianity played an even greater role in African-American protests against white domination, and the demand for social justice was not a demand for secularization. As at denominational colleges of the era, there was some feeling that the religious character of the black colleges and universities was holding them back academically. E. Franklin Frazier, a Howard graduate of 1916 and later one of its most distinguished faculty members, encapsulated the problem in his famous remark that at black colleges there was "too much inspiration and too little information."[18] Other black educational leaders said the same. The fact of the matter was that in the dominant culture the great majority of those universities and scholars considered to be the best were those who dropped any reference to religion. Whatever the value of Christianity to the black community, the message they were being sent was the same that was being sent to denominational colleges everywhere: if they wanted to be part of the serious educational enterprise, Christianity would have to go. Since there were compelling economic and social reasons for blacks to strive for full acceptance in the dominant culture, it was unlikely they were going to question its essential assumptions except on the matter of race itself.

Judaism, Christianity, and Higher Education

Discrimination against Jews in the academy, though involving something of this same dynamic, had much more explicit implications regarding the place of religion.

From the point of view of our theme, a remarkable dimension of the Jewish experience in America is the paucity of explicitly Jewish institutions of higher learning. By the late nineteenth century, Reform, Conservative, and Orthodox Jews had established centers for the training of rabbis. Only in 1928, however, with the organization of Yeshiva College in New York as an Orthodox school that included teaching of secular subjects, was there opportunity for collegiate education from a Jewish religious perspective.[19] The founding of Yeshiva aroused considerable opposition from American Jews, who deplored any voluntary Jewish segregation and the criticism of dominant American institutions that a Jewish college implied. After World War II Brandeis University in Waltham, Massachusetts, was founded on a broader basis as a "Jewish-sponsored secular university." Brandeis followed a pattern much like that of denominationally related universities of the era. While providing a strong Jewish presence and opportunities for Jewish observance, Brandeis was careful to be nondiscriminatory, so that its initially strong Jewish identity was maintained primarily by self-selection and hence almost bound to fade.[20]

The nature of Judaism as an ethnic as well as a religious identity, its long history of being discriminated against and persecuted in Christian societies, and the dynamic of seeking acceptance and opportunity in American society all contributed to the predominant Jewish tendency to accept American higher education on its own terms. The most relevant question was how to get in. Jews were getting the same message from the universities that was being sent to outsider Christians, but it was underscored by religious differences. If persons were to be fully accepted in the academic community they would have to keep their traditional religion out of the picture. Hence American Jewish academics in the twentieth century were typically persons who had been reared in traditional Jewish practice but had abandoned their earlier religious practice and were ardent champions of thoroughly secular academic outlooks.[21]

On the other side, discrimination against Jews presented an embarrassing challenge to the broadly liberal Protestant self-definition of the American university that had emerged by the World War I era. Essential to the definition of the universities was that they stood for a universal cultural ideal to which everyone could be assimilated—at least in principle. The universal claims of science, together with the moral ideals of liberal democratic culture, provided a basis for this assumption. After World War I, such claims were less often identified explicitly with Christian civilization. During the 1920s and 1930s even foreign missionaries in the liberal Protestant camp were becoming reluctant to challenge other world religions in the name of Christianity and were talking rather about mutual learning of one religion from another. Yet at the same time that Christianity was being disestablished as the presumed highest religion of American culture, discrimination against Jews was on the rise. Such discrimination was particularly awkward to explain in the universities, which claimed to stand for freedom. Whether they still defined themselves as centers for promoting broad "spiritual value," or whether they spoke of themselves in more secular terms as essentially scientific, universities were still supposed to be inclusive.

A number of practical factors help explain why discrimination against Jews became a major issue in universities after 1920. The most immediate was that before the upsurge in popularity of collegiate education after World War I college admission had seldom been selective; even the best colleges took virtually anyone who applied and met the sometimes considerable entrance requirements. Jews, who made up only about 3.5 percent of the population, were disproportionately represented in student bodies. In 1918–1919 a survey of over a hundred institutions showed that Jewish students made up nearly 10 percent of total number of students. The percentage was considerably higher in some eastern schools and in New York City ran from one-third at a number of institutions to over two-thirds at the College of the City of New York.[22]

At the same time, although Jews were still only 3.5 percent of the total American population, that figure represented an immense increase over the past several decades—in 1881 Jews had numbered only a little over one half of one percent of Americans. By far the largest part of this increase had come from eastern European immigration. The character of the American Jewish population changed from predominantly German and relatively well-to-do to a predominantly foreign-born, Yiddish-speaking, initially poor immigrant population with all the problems that attend any such cultural transition. So the upsurge in the size and character of the Jewish population contributed to increasing anti-Semitism, which, of course, had always been present to a degree. Moreover, this was a time of a worldwide increase in anti-Semitism and racism. In the United States such attitudes were reflected in the post–World War I resurgence of the nativism that led to restrictions on immigration. Many clubs, resorts, neighborhoods, and jobs were closed to Jews. American universities, although by no means as discriminatory as many other areas of American life, were nonetheless touched by these sentiments.

Most notorious in this respect were the elite Ivy League schools, which in the early 1920s devised various ways to set admissions criteria other than sheer academic ability so as to limit the percentage of Jewish students. At Harvard and Yale the percentage was kept at about 10 percent.

The theory at these and other eastern colleges was that higher numbers of Jewish students would change the character of the student body. Lingering ideals of the Christian establishment, that colleges were to cultivate Christian spiritual values and character, had something to do with this sentiment, and these schools were still occasionally spoken of as essentially "Christian" institutions. The stronger cause, however, was the social snobbishness of the elite schools, which would have been much more directly threatened by a predominance of any group of students without WASP pedigrees.[23]

Princeton offers an especially interesting case of the mix of these motives. During the first half of the twentieth century Princeton was notorious as the prestige university least hospitable to Jewish students. The percentage of Jewish students there was always much lower than at other eastern universities and Jews who did survive the selection process had to brave ongoing social discrimination.[24] During this era Princeton, unlike Yale and Harvard, continued to require chapel attendance and displayed a slightly more serious desire to maintain a Christian ethos. Nonetheless, the concern to preserve a preferential place for the Christian religion in the communal life at Princeton seems only a secondary factor in accounting for anti-Jewish discrimination. As Woodrow Wilson learned, nowhere was social elitism more firmly entrenched than at Princeton. Such elitism had something to do with Christianity, but so did much of the opposition to it. So it would be difficult to interpret the discrimination as reflecting specifically religious concerns nearly so much as social ones.

It is difficult to isolate specifically religious factors in the growth of American anti-Semitism in the interwar era. So far as colleges and universities are concerned, it is an intriguing irony that discrimination against Jews increased after 1920 as traditional Protestantism was rapidly disappearing at leading schools to be replaced by liberal Protestant and secular alternatives. Perhaps the timing reflects only the coincidence of social prejudices and traditional religious decline. At least it does not seem right to blame anti-Semitism on liberal Protestantism. At Yale the college chaplain, Sidney Lovett, in the 1930s took the lead in ministering to Jewish students, encouraging their own religious practice, and inviting a rabbi to preach each year in Battell Chapel.[25] What the record indicates is not that liberal Christian teaching promoted anti-Semitism, but rather that church leadership did not have a major influence one way or the other in the universities when social and economic issues were at stake.

The role of religious discrimination in faculty hiring was similar but more subtle. From the late nineteenth century, most leading universities were not entirely closed to hiring Jewish faculty members, whose numbers gradually increased in the subsequent eras. However, Jews were much more likely to be hired in the sciences than in the humanities, and in professional schools rather than in undergraduate programs. This was the pattern at Yale, for instance. While Jews had some representation on the scientific, professional, and graduate faculties, and occasionally held junior positions at the college, before World War II no Jew received tenure on the Yale College faculty.[26] Only after the Holocaust was the anti-Semitism that was taken for granted in Western culture widely perceived as an embarrassment to the claims of liberal culture.

It was a telling symptom of the pattern of discrimination that at Yale, as at some other private colleges with Protestant lineage, the field of English literature was virtually closed to Jews until after World War II. This seems to have had something to do with the vestigial spirit, if not the substance, of the religious heritage. As James Turner has suggested, when traditional Protestantism faded in the late nineteenth century, English literature was one of the manifestation of a sacral ideal that arose to take its place.[27] This was one expression of a growing tendency to treat Western civilization as the bearer of the Christian heritage, broadly conceived. It was sometimes suggested that because this heritage of literature in Christendom grew in part out of the New Testament, it was inappropriate for Jews to teach it.[28] As literature was an important locus for teaching "character," it may have also been an area in which it was thought particularly appropriate to find the right sort of gentlemen, preferably those who used a familial middle name.

As much as any other factor, the continuance of anti-Semitism points to one of the deepest problems in maintaining a Christian identity at liberal Protestant institutions. As has been a persistent theme in this history, such schools had long viewed themselves both as Christian institutions and as serving the whole American public. During the nineteenth century they resolved this dilemma by declaring themselves "nonsectarian" even while discriminating against Catholics and other smaller religious groups, like the Jews. In the twentieth century this nonsectarianism was broadened into the moral ideals of liberalism or democracy and of Western civilization. Protestant leaders saw such ideals as perfectly compatible with their efforts after World War I to reinstate an explicitly Christian presence at universities and colleges. At the same time that such efforts were gaining ground, however, so were the realities of a pluralistic culture. How could they promote ever-widening inclusivist liberal ideals and at the same time reassert an explicitly Christian identity?

In the years following the Holocaust, the logic of the commitment to inclusivism eventually made it necessary for explicit Christianity to go. For most major institutions, it was not much of an issue, since Christianity played only a vestigial role anyway. At schools with stronger ties to their explicitly Christian heritage, the pressure was greatly increased to so broaden the definition of Christianity as to not exclude anyone. During the 1950s this broadening typically was accomplished by talking about the "Judeo-Christian" heritage as representing the highest ideals of Western civilization, which both liberal education and religious people "of all faiths" could stand for.

The logic of this broad definition of the Judeo-Christian Western heritage was that *no* particular religious tradition, especially not Christianity, could any longer play a substantive role in it. So long as universities were serving liberal cultural ideals, they could not give preferential treatment to one religious group at the expense of others. Because liberal Christianity had already largely resolved itself into concerns about character, democratic ideals, and service, this religious equity was accomplished, not by giving representation to a multiplicity of religious points of view, but by completing the process of the merger of the Christian heritage into nonsectarian, or perhaps "interfaith," liberal cultural ideals.[29] This elimination of substantive religion was augmented by growing support in some of the disciplines for objectivist or positivist standards for scholarship which declared religious perspectives illicit or simply nonsensical.

So far as most of the major groups of outsiders were concerned, soon after World War II they were welcomed into the academy—but only if they played by its rules. The academy was defined as a scientific enterprise that might be complemented by higher humanistic ideals. These ideals might be associated with organized religion, but in that case, except for some of their moral teachings, they should be regarded as private and kept from interfering with the main business of the university. Those from other than mainline Protestant cultural and religious heritages were welcome, then, so long as they checked the particularities of their beliefs at the door.

Notes

1. Marcia Graham Synnott, *The Half-Opened Door: Discrimination and Admissions at Harvard, Yale, and Princeton, 1900–1970* (Westport, Conn.: Greenwood Press, 1979), 130–33. Dan A. Oren, *Joining the Club: A History of Jews at Yale* (New Haven: Yale University Press, 1985), suggests relatively good acceptance of Catholics at Yale and no evidence of admissions quotas. Nonetheless, Catholics were much underrepresented in the most prestigious secret societies and fraternities. Synnott shows that Princeton was admitting about 5 to 10 percent Catholics in the interwar era, (195). This is about the same percentage found at state universities. A survey in 1923–1924 showed about 5 percent of students self-identified as Catholics at state universities. Edward S. Boyer, "Religious Education in Colleges, Universities and Schools of Religion," *Christian Education* 11 (October 1927), 27. Presumably that percentage grew during the interwar era.

2. Winton U. Solberg, "The Catholic Presence at the University of Illinois," *Catholic Historical Review* 76 (October 1990), 765–812.

3. Virginia Lieson Brereton, *Training God's Army: The American Bible School, 1880–1940* (Bloomington: Indiana University Press, 1990).

4. William C. Ringenberg, *The Christian College: A History of Protestant Higher Education in America* (Grand Rapids, Mich.: Christian University Press, 1984), provides a valuable overview of these developments.

5. Ibid., 138. At Wellesley, for instance, it had only been since 1912 that students had been allowed to travel on railroads or street cars on Sundays without special permission and in the 1920s Sunday mornings were to be observed as a quiet time. *Wellesley College News,* April 29, 1926, 5. Wellesley, perhaps because of its strong tradition of voluntary evangelicalism, had voluntary morning chapel. In

1922, in response to declining attendance, students debated whether to make it compulsory, but that plan was defeated. *Wellesley College News,* March 2 to March 23, passim. The college, however, continued to have required courses on the Bible into the 1960s.

6. Raymond Wolters, *The New Negro on Campus* (Princeton: Princeton University Press, 1975), 313.

7. Synnott, *Half-Opened Door,* 83–84, 91, 133–35, 174–75, and passim.

8. Benjamin E. Mays, "The Religious Life and Needs of Negro Students," *Journal of Negro Education* 9 (July 1940), 332–36. Ringenberg, *Christian College,* 138.

9. Walter R. Chivers, "Religion in Negro Colleges," *Journal of Negro Education* 9 (January 1940), 5–12. Cf. Richard I. McKinney, "Religion in Negro Colleges," *Journal of Negro Education* 13 (Fall 1944), 509–18.

10. Wolters, *New Negro,* 29–69, 293–313.

11. Ibid., 70–71. The ratio is for 1925. The number of blacks attending colleges was expanding very rapidly in the 1920s, so that this ratio was changing.

12. *Howard University Catalogue 1898–99,* 57, 58–59.

13. Rayford W. Logan, *Howard University, 1867–1967* (New York: New York University Press, 1969), 151.

14. "The Howard University Self-Study," June 30, 1966 (unpublished university document), 50.

15. Wolters, *New Negro,* 73.

16. Ibid., 70–136.

17. I am indebted to Paul Kemeny for his work in charting the secularization of Howard, particularly in its formal statements, such as presidential inaugurals, and in internal reports.

18. Quoted in Wolters, *New Negro,* 83. Christopher Jencks and David Riesman, *The Academic Revolution* (Chicago: University of Chicago Press, 1977 [1968]), 406–79, provides a critical look at the state of African-American higher education in the 1960s.

19. Gilbert Klaperman, *The Story of Yeshiva University: The First Jewish University in America* (London: Macmillan, 1969).

20. Israel Goldstein, *Brandeis University: Chapter of Its Founding* (New York: Bloch, 1951), provides the revealing perspectives of one of its founders. Goldstein also provides a summary of other efforts at Jewish higher education (1–5). Jencks and Riesman, *Academic Revolution,* 318–210, make some astute remarks about the similarities between dominant Jewish views and mainline Protestant views of higher education. Brandeis, they point out, aspired to be "separate but identical" (319). Edward S. Shapiro, *A Time for Healing: American Jewry since World War II* (Baltimore: Johns Hopkins Press, 1992), 71–76, discusses the criticisms of Yeshiva College and more recent debates regarding Brandeis's identity.

21. Susanne Klingenstein, *Jews in the American Academy 1900–1940: The Dynamics of Intellectual Assimilation* (New Haven: Yale University Press, 1991), illustrates this point, though she is asking a different set of questions.

22. Synnott, *Half-Opened Door,* 15–16.

23. Levine, *American College,* 136–61. Synnott, *Half-Opened Door,* passim.

24. Synnott, *Half-Opened Door,* 160–98, 218–25.

25. Oren, *Joining the Club,* 105–9. Even among fundamentalists, although there are clear instances of Christian religious justifications for anti-Semitism, there is also much evidence that dispensationalist teaching regarding the role of the Jews in the last days tempered grassroots anti-Semitism in America.

26. Ibid., 118–22. No Catholic held a full professorship at Yale College in this

era, though after 1929 one of the graduate faculty did teach French at the college (357). Cf. Klingenstein, *Jews in the American Academy,* 102–3, for a slightly wider summary of trends.

27. James M. Turner, "Secularization and Sacralization: Speculations on Some Religious Origins of the Secular Humanities Curriculum, 1850–1900," in *The Secularization of the Academy,* George M. Marsden and Bradley J. Longfield, eds. (New York: Oxford University Press, 1992), 74–106.

28. Oren, *Joining the Club,* 121–22.

29. This is, of course, a broad generalization that, while summarizing the dominant tendencies, does not do justice to many nuances in the ways mainline Protestants conserve some of the particularities of the Christian heritage. See chapter 21.

20

Searching for a Soul

In the interwar years American cultural leaders faced a new crisis of faith, not simply concerning Christianity but concerning liberal Western culture itself. This intellectual crisis, which emerged in the 1920s and heightened during the 1930s and the war years, undercut the ideological rationale for the universities as servants of democratic civilization. The universities were unreservedly committed to two things: science and the highest ideals of Western culture. Now a distressing realization began to dawn, although only a few prophets were willing to face its full implications, that these two ideals might be incompatible.

This crisis of cultural faith was sharply intensified by the general crisis of Western culture. By the early 1930s Americans were becoming aware of the dimensions of the worldwide crisis and at the same time facing the severest domestic challenges since the Civil War. The failure of democracies abroad and the rise of totalitarianism underscored the revived question of whether the American experiment would long endure. The unprecedented economic depression changed what had been previously a theoretical question into an engrossing concern, impossible to ignore. People were bound to ask what held American society together, or, for that matter, what would hold together any democracy. Was a democracy merely a pragmatic arrangement or did it require a body of shared ideas in order to function?

American universities, which only recently had emerged as major players in the national culture, mirrored the national crisis. The painful economic constraints of the depression era were, of course, the most immediate concern, but the questions debated at universities went deeper. Many of those who were used to looking for underlying explanations were becoming acutely aware that the cultural upheaval of the past half-century had undermined what had been thought to be the very foundations of Western civilization. Having been among the major promoters of these changes, intellectual leaders in the university had to face the question of whether the new culture for which they spoke had anything to offer in place of, or at least to shore up, the old verities.

For humanists, who were most likely to be debating such issues, the fear of losing moral compass was exacerbated by recognition that the dominant forces shaping the universities were functional and mundane.

Universities had been built to serve the needs of modern industrial society.[1] Much of their money came from corporate America, which controlled their boards. Despite the sincerity of their professions to stand first of all for the humane, in fact university organizations had far more to do with the insatiable demands of technological society. American universities succeeded in large part because they made themselves centers for scientific and technological research. In fact their organizations were modeled throughout on the technological principle of looking for the most rational and efficient way to get the job done.[2] Academic life, accordingly, was compartmentalized. Rewards were given for increasingly specialized and technical research. In most fields this imitation of the principles of practical technique extended to the embrace of an objectivist scientific ideology as the highest road to truth. Courses in great literature and in Western civilization could be inserted as counterweights to the mundane trends, but the effort was remedial. It did not take a prophet to see that ultimately the practical would overwhelm whatever stood in its way. Ironically it was after 1929, when industry could no longer do its job efficiently, that the conflict of these ideals become most apparent. No longer could the theoretical questions be put aside on the ground that the system works.

The broadest goal of the university, as Theodore Francis Jones, New York University's centennial historian, put it in 1933, was to "spiritualize the machine created by an earlier age." By the 1930s, however, an urban university such as NYU was hard pressed to sustain such idealist rhetoric. To celebrate the NYU centennial in 1932, Chancellor Elmer Ellsworth Brown sponsored an academic conference on "The Obligation of Universities to the Social Order."[3] As historian David Hollinger describes it, the conference revealed the divided mind of the university. Much of the conference was "resoundingly technocratic and progressive: social engineering, it was said, must go forward immediately, casting aside anachronistic traditions."[4] Yet Chancellor Brown also included a section on "The University and Spiritual Values." Here the idealist themes continued to be sounded. President James Rowland Angell of Yale, while averring (former protégé of Dewey that he was) that universities must advance by constant adjustments to social and economic needs, at the same time affirmed the counterbalance of a tradition of gentility. The most advanced conception of the universities had "arisen in response to deep-seated social impulses seeking to integrate the highest institution of learning with the life of the people in ways which shall inspire and elevate and refine."[5] Or perhaps most revealing were the reflections of John Campbell Merriam, president of the Carnegie Institution, on "Spiritual Values" in relation to the sciences. "In addition to consideration of realities, their analysis and synthesis by scientific and other methods," Merriam declared, "the university must present the world of ideals, comprising the highest attainments of human faculties." Spiritual values, which had to do with ideals such as beauty and art and development of individual character, were thus contrasted by Merriam to "realities."[6]

The most troubling question of the day, however, was whether the "realities" of modern science were even compatible with the higher ideals that were supposed to complement them. Mainline Protestant theologians, university administrators, and most humanists affirmed that the naturalistic science and high ideals were compatible, but not all observers agreed. Literary figures such as Ezra Pound, the early T. S. Eliot, F. Scott Fitzgerald, Gertrude Stein, and Ernest Hemingway, instead of fostering lofty ideals, were exploring the implications of living in a morally empty universe. Joseph Wood Krutch, a journalist, expressed the underlying point well in his widely read *The Modern Temper* (1929). If one took seriously the pure naturalism of modern science, then the only honest view, said Krutch, was that "nature, in her blind thirst for life, has filled every possible cranny of the rotting earth with some sort of fantastic creature, and among them man is but one." It followed that all the high ideals of human religion, philosophy, or literature, including the belief that there were real distinctions between right and wrong, were illusions. Of the beings on the evolutionary ladder, the human was "perhaps the most miserable of all, because he is the only one in whom the instinct of life falters long enough to enable it to ask the question 'Why?' " "Both our practical morality and our emotional lives," Krutch summarized, "are adjusted to a world which no longer exists."[7]

Scholars on the cutting edge of the sciences and of related academic disciplines, as much as literary figures, were dynamiting the foundations of Victorian idealism and morality.[8] Whatever the field, the premise and the problem were the same: in a naturalistic universe, human beings were on their own. Human intellect was an evolutionary mechanism for survival, but it came with no guarantees. There was no reason to presume that its dictates corresponded to anything other than changing human perceptions of human needs. For many leading philosophers the only question left was, as one influential title put it, "The Meaning of Meaning." In such a universe "good" as a moral term had only an "emotive use."[9] Such conclusions were later canonized for a time in British and American academic thought in A. J. Ayer's *Language, Truth and Logic* (1936). Metaphysical as well as ethical statements were, strictly speaking, meaningless.[10]

In a series of brilliant lectures delivered at the Yale Law School in 1931 and published as *The Heavenly City of the Eighteenth-Century Philosophers,* historian Carl Becker summarized the implications of the outlook of the intellectual avant garde. "Edit and interpret the conclusions of modern science as tenderly as we like," Becker declared,

> it is still quite impossible for us to regard man as the child of God for whom the earth was created as a temporary habitation. Rather must we regard him as little more than a chance deposit on the surface of the

> world, carelessly thrown up between two ice ages by the same forces that rust iron and ripen corn, a sentient organism endowed by some happy or unhappy accident with intelligence indeed, but with an intelligence that is conditioned by the very forces that it seeks to understand and to control. . . . What is man that the electron should be mindful of him!

Given this bleak portrait of the true implications of modern thought, Becker could argue his startling central thesis: that the Enlightenment was in fact closer to the outlook of the Christian Middle Ages than it was to modernity. "The *Philosophies* demolished the Heavenly City of St. Augustine only to rebuild it with more up-to-date materials." Enlightenment thinkers had indeed debunked the Christian superstitions of their predecessors; yet they themselves had an equally naive faith that in a universe governed only by the laws of nature human reason would be able to find meaning beyond what they themselves constructed.[11]

Carl Becker's intellectual development provides a paradigm of the crises of faith of the most progressive academics of his generation. Born in 1873, Becker grew up in a serious Methodist family in Iowa. One year at Cornell College, a Methodist school in his home state, was all he could take before he transferred to the University of Wisconsin. There in his undergraduate years he abandoned the miraculous aspects of Christianity but still attended church. Becker eventually completed his Ph.D. at Wisconsin, where his mentors included Richard T. Ely and Frederick Jackson Turner. He emerged a fairly typical progressive during the years preceding World War I. Although sometimes cynical about organized religion, he maintained a requisite faith in America and democracy. In 1917 Becker moved to Cornell University, where he remained until his retirement in 1941. By the 1920s his aversion to traditional Christianity had reached Menckenesque proportions. "If Methodism is slowly dying in Iowa," he wrote to a friend in 1928, "there is still hope for the world."[12] Such views were not uncommon among sophisticated academics of the era. What Becker added was the firm conviction that all substitute faiths, even those that claimed the authority of science and reason, rested on equally flimsy grounds.

For Becker, the principal acid of modernity, which dissolved even recent verities, was historicism. In all truly modern views, the world was in flux; change was the only constant. Meaning was only whatever interpretations humans, themselves the products of this flux, assigned to their experiences. Such historicist sensibilities, once their full implications were faced, placed an insurmountable gulf between twentieth-century thought and that of the era of the nation's founders.

In what became the best known presidential address of the American Historical Association, Becker in 1931 made another major contribution to spelling out the academic implications of modernity. Giving his speech the title "Everyman His Own Historian," Becker argued that there no longer was any basis for viewing academic study as a scientific investigation of "the facts." Strictly speaking, he declared, "facts do not exist." All we have is interpretations. Historians thus did not have access to George Washington but only to interpretations about him, interpretations in the documents from his time refracted further through interpretations of the historians themselves. Such interpretations were controlled by the interests of the interpreters so that ultimately the job of historians was "the keeping of the useful myths" of a society.[13]

Relatively few academics followed Becker all the way in facing the implications of the purely naturalistic universe of modernity (which would come into academic vogue in their "postmodern" garb a half century later). Many clung to scientific objectivism on the one hand and a wistful practical idealism on the other. Among historians, for instance, Becker and some kindred spirits, notably Charles Beard, were widely heralded but seldom followed to the bitter end of relativism. Comparatively few historians were philosophically minded, and few of them were ready to abandon the recently won authority of a discipline that used scientific methodology to sort out fact from mythology. Practical assumptions regarding objectivism persisted.[14]

In the social sciences, meanwhile, faith in the scientific method as definitive was hardly shaken at all. What Becker and the prophets of modernity in other fields did, however, was point out the deep internal flaws of modern intellectual life. Many intellectuals could recognize that the Enlightenment pillars on which their institutions rested were irreparably cracked and on the verge of collapse. Most, however, had little choice but to go on with business as usual.

Some looked for alternative scientific faith in the face of the internal contradictions of liberalism and its inability to guide modern life in any authoritative direction. For some forward-looking and secular academics of the 1930s Marxism seemed a promising and humane alternative. Marxism was another version of Enlightenment and nineteenth-century faith in science, but it at least took historicism and historical development into account. Claiming the authority of science, it offered a powerful explanation of why all other ideologies should be regarded as mythologies, constructed as legitimations of class and economic interest. For a generation reared on the hopeful idealism of the pre–World War I era, but now too sophisticated to accept the myths of Main Street, Marxism offered something in which to believe.

Protestant neo-orthodoxy offered quite a different sort of option, one that promised a way to reconstruct a chastened idealism. Like other movements responding to the widespread sense of cultural and intellectual crisis, neo-orthodoxy began to catch on among American theologians during the early 1930s. In the United States the best known form was that articulated by the Niebuhr brothers, H. Richard and Reinhold. The leading American neo-orthodox spokesmen were not nearly as interested in the recovery of orthodox theological categories and biblicism as was the European progenitor of the movement, Karl Barth. What united the Americans was their rejection of modernist theologies which they felt had been compromised with liberal cultural ideals. By reviving some traditional Christian categories, such as original sin or divine revelation, such theologians could wage an attack on the naive faith in humanity inherent in liberalism. So far as academic life was concerned, however, neo-orthodoxy had no program to offer. During the next several decades it inspired the thinking of important individual academics here and there, but its outlook did not systematically challenge the essential scientific definitions of the academic disciplines as havens immune from theological critique.[15]

It was far more common for American academics to recognize the problem of relativism, but nonetheless to retain a faith in progress based on scientific achievement.[16] Representative of this outlook was Ruth Benedict's *Patterns of Culture,* published in 1934 and gaining a firm place in the academic canon during the next quarter century. Benedict was one of a number of remarkable protégés of Columbia's Franz Boas, who set the standards for anthropology in America. Benedict saw less complex cultures, such as the Zuñi and the Kwakiutl, as ideal laboratories for studying varieties of cultural adjustment which have separated humans from the beasts. To study such cultures scientifically, the elementary first step, she argued, was to abandon our illusions of cultural superiority. Every culture, we should recognize, makes such claims, and typically supports them with religious teachings. Today, however, we should recognize that human achievement is not dependent on any force external to human culture. "If we inhabit one chance planet out of a myriad solar systems, so much the greater glory" for humans.

Modern persons, Benedict agreed with her readers, might feel a "justified superiority" over nineteenth-century Westerners who had assumed religious superiority in viewing other cultures. By now, she said, "we have accepted the study of comparative religion." At the same time, since Western culture was plagued by the irrationalities of race prejudice and nationalism, "we are justified in a little skepticism as to whether our sophistication in the matter of religion is due to the fact that we have outgrown naïve childishness, or simply to the fact that religion is no longer the area of life in which the important modern battles are staged."

The overriding moral theme for Benedict was that the study of anthropology would encourage mutual tolerance and discourage racism. Once we saw that the widest human differences were social constructions we would have little reason to claim superior heredity. We could also learn to accept differing cultural mores, a point implicitly important for a pioneer in demonstrating that women need not be excluded from the scientific scholarship of universities.

Benedict's important concerns provided additional impetus for opposition to traditional Christianity, which was typically associated both with retaining traditional mores and with claims to cultural superiority. For the modern anthropologist or enlightened academic, the rule that all cultures should be treated equally did not apply to Western cultures that showed intolerance. The American Puritans were the most common symbol for such intolerance and indeed the Puritans came in for Benedict's most scathing criticism. "To a modern observer," she wrote, "it is they, not the confused and tormented women they put to death as witches, who were the psychoneurotics of Puritan New England. A sense of guilt as extreme as they portrayed and demanded both in their own conversion experiences and in those of their converts is found in a slightly saner civilization only in institutions for mental diseases."[17]

The troublesome problem for a secular liberal society, however, was how to establish the grounds on which the citizenry should accept progressive moral ideals. The answer, especially for those influenced by the social sciences, was to invest science with supreme cultural authority. Thus reform-minded social scientists could speak, as Benedict did, as though science itself legitimated a worldview that all educated modern people would accept. Fundamentalists and others would disappear once education based on scientific principles was sufficiently widespread. John Dewey was the high priest of this faith. As he argued in his Terry Lectures at Yale, published in 1934 as *A Common Faith,* universal education could foster a rational humanistic religion dedicated to the healthy adjustment of humans to their social environments so as to promote "goods—the values of art in all its forms, of knowledge, of effort and of rest after striving, of education, and fellowship, of friendship and love, of growth in mind and body."[18]

The solutions offered by thinkers like Benedict and Dewey still left a major question unanswered. In a world where there were no longer self-evident first principles based on God-created natural laws, what happened when allegedly scientific definitions of the "good" conflicted? How could one argue, for instance, that all humans "are created equal" if one denied that humans were created?[19] In a world falling into totalitarianism, where "science" was rapidly being turned into an engine for propaganda, was there any court of appeal? Was American faith in science, social science, and experimentation just whistling in the dark of an empty universe?

Asking Hard Questions

The person who most successfully raised such issues and in fact made them the basis for national debate on the nature of universities was Robert Maynard Hutchins of the University of Chicago. Inaugurated in 1929 at age thirty as the fifth president of the university, Hutchins's meteoric rise in some ways resembled that of the school's founder, William Rainey Harper. Both were reared in Ohio, attended local colleges there, and came to Chicago after youthful successes at Yale. There were vast differences, however, so much so that Hutchins's career at Chicago may be seen as an effort to thwart the forces which Harper had set in motion.

One difference was that whereas Harper's father had been a storekeeper, Hutchins was the scion of pure-bred New Englander clergy. Both his grandfather and his father were Presbyterian ministers. The grandfather, Robert Grosvenor Hutchins, had been an abolitionist whose emotional evangelical style of preaching repelled his grandson. The father, Will Hutchins, on the other hand, was a model of the socially progressive evangelical liberalism of the early twentieth century. A graduate of Yale College and of Union Theological Seminary, Will Hutchins was an eloquent and well-known preacher, who in 1907 became professor of homiletics at the Oberlin School of Theology. Oberlin at that time had just completed its transition from the revivalist evangelicalism of the Charles Finney era to a socially concerned liberalism.[20] Young Robert Maynard Hutchins attended Oberlin College for two years before joining the Army Ambulance Corp to serve in World War I. Oberlin at the time must have been at that seemingly idyllic (though transitory) stage at which a college has dropped many of the restrictive aspects of evangelical theology and piety yet retains an ethos in which it is still widely assumed that education involves relating eternal truths to contemporary concerns. Although Hutchins completed his college work at Yale after the war, he seemed to retain an assumption that true education should be something like what went on at prewar Oberlin.[21]

Hutchins went on to Yale Law School, from which he graduated in 1925. Only two years later, while still in his twenties, he was named dean of the Law School. Hutchins's reputation as one of the most brilliant men of the era was made. While at the Yale Law School Hutchins was enamored of the legal realism which dominated that institution. Following roughly the principles of Justice Oliver Wendell Holmes, Jr., realism taught that the law should be regarded pragmatically as whatever the courts decide and so must be studied in the primary context of the social sciences, rather than with the illusory assumption that it reflected fixed truths.[22]

Hutchins's flirtation with the pragmatic social scientific spirit of the age was not to last long. By the time he arrived at Chicago in 1929 a deep reaction was setting in. This reaction was inspired primarily by his friendship with Mortimer Adler, a young Jewish philosopher who held the very unstylish view that philosophy should deal with questions of truth. Adler, whom Hutchins soon brought to Chicago, was a champion of the "Great Books" of the Western world, which he saw as revealing human thought at its best. Particularly, Adler was a champion of the tradition of natural law and human rationality as represented by Plato, Aristotle, and Aquinas. With them, Adler affirmed that true rationality pointed toward God.[23]

While Hutchins's new views resembled Adler's in his respect for natural law and human rationality in the tradition of the great thinkers, his idea of God remained vague. At the time of Hutchins's appointment, the chairman Chicago's trustees, Harold Swift, still maintained that, although the university had dropped its Baptist affiliations, its president should be a member of a Protestant church since "it is the purpose of the board to insure the continuance of the University forever as a Christian institution." In his interviews Hutchins was quizzed at length by Swift and by Charles W. Gilkey, dean of Rockefeller Chapel. Swift was most concerned with his youth; Gilkey with his religion. "You will be surprised to learn," he wrote to his parents, "that I was able to give more satisfactory answers to Gilkey than to Swift. There is no answer to the charge of youth. You can lie about your religion."[24]

When he came to Chicago, Hutchins was still a Presbyterian church member and regularly attended Rockefeller Chapel for Sunday morning services. Hutchins had heard liberal Protestant preaching all of his life, some of the best of it from his father. He had an accordingly low tolerance when it lapsed into platitudes. The last straw was one Sunday when Gilkey opened his sermon, "Yesterday I was on the golf course and as I teed off I was reminded that we must follow through in life." After that, said Hutchins, he "acquired a weekend hideaway and never reappeared in the chapel of the University of Chicago."[25]

Although Hutchins's scathing attacks on modern conceptions of the university were directed primarily against its dependence on scientific, technological, and practical vocational models, he also excoriated the bland religious-moral ideals which he regarded as palliatives used to make mindless pursuit of scientific models seem acceptable. In his convocation address in December 1933, which Hutchins used as a declaration of war on the current state of the university, he summarized with his typical cutting wit: "The three worst words in education are character, personality, and facts. Facts are the core of an anti-intellectual curriculum. Personality is the qualification we look for in an anti-intellectual teacher. Character is what we expect to produce in the student by the combination of a teacher of personality and a curriculum of facts."[26]

Those most outraged by the attacks were, of course, the champions of social scientific, empirical, and pragmatic ideologies who had built the University of Chicago into the nation's leading center for such outlooks. The new social science building at Chicago, completed in 1929, actually had the viewpoint of empiricist philosophy inscribed in stone over the entryway: WHATEVER EXISTS AT ALL EXISTS IN SOME AMOUNT.[27] Hutchins did his best to offend those who thus turned a methodology into a limiting worldview. "The gadgeteers and data collectors, masquerading as scientists, have threatened to become the supreme chieftains of the scholarly world," he declared in the 1933 convocation address. At a dinner for faculty and trustees a month or so later, Hutchins elaborated on the "anti-intellectual philosophy" that has "no principles." "The world is in a flux of events. We cannot hope to understand it. All we can do is to watch it. This is the conclusion of the leading anti-intellectuals of our time, William James and John Dewey."

The resulting furor, which divided the faculty, was highlighted by a dramatic debate between Anton J. Carlson, a noted physiologist, who defended empiricism and scientific naturalism, and Mortimer Adler, who insisted that for science to help humanity it must be located within a framework of metaphysical truths discovered by human rationality.[28] Hutchins and Adler were, however, swimming against the tide. Hutchins's attempt to institute major curricular revisions that would reflect his trust in the centrality of the great books was defeated in the spring of 1934, the first of a series of setbacks.

Undaunted, Hutchins next went to the public. In 1936 he published *The Higher Learning in America,* which became easily the most widely discussed book in higher education for the next decade. Combining his usual acerbic wit with keen analysis, Hutchins exposed the trends that were shaping the American university and driving it away from the search for truth. One of the most basic problems, he pointed out, was economic: "The people love money and think that education is a way of getting it. They think too that democracy means that every child should be permitted to acquire the educational insignia that will be helpful in making money. They do not believe in the cultivation of the intellect for its own sake."

American universities were thus constantly being distracted by the vocational. They were constantly pressured by a "service station mentality," which had led to the idea that "a state university must help the farmers look after their cows." Vocational concerns dwarfed everything else at private schools as well. Suggestions to establish schools of journalism, business, library science, social service, education, dentistry, nursing, forestry, diplomacy, pharmacy, veterinary surgery, and public administration typically were quickly implemented. Even in undergraduate work, it was becoming increasingly common to devote the last two years to preprofessional training. Most of university education was thus increasingly geared toward learning "tricks of the trade" that would soon be out of date.

Blindly following scientific models, universities had become organized into a bewildering array of specialized disciplines and subdisciplines with nothing to relate them. The result was that "the chief characteristic of higher learning is disorder." At the same time, freedom was urged as an end in itself. But utter freedom of choice could result only in "anarchy and the dissolution of the whole." The many sciences would turn up a myriad of facts; but universities provided no way of distinguishing the trivial from the timeless.

Hutchins's solution was to get rid of departments, provide only general education for the first two undergraduate years, and then divide university education into three parts: metaphysics or the science of first principles, social science, and practical sciences. Even in the latter two domains emphasis would be on a hierarchy of truths starting with the first principles regarding human relations or relations of humans to nature, especially as these had been discussed through the ages, and only then proceeding to more recent observations.

Metaphysics would thus be the heart of the enterprise. Theology had once served that purpose but could no longer. "We are a faithless generation and take no stock in revelation," wrote Hutchins. "Theology implies orthodoxy and an orthodox church. We have neither. To look to theology to unify the modern university is futile and vain." Therefore, as the ancient Greeks had done in the era of Plato and Aristotle, or as Thomas Aquinas had done insofar as he was a neo-Aristotelian metaphysician, we must use reason to determine the highest principles on which our civilization should be based. Otherwise our civilization would rush blindly after false ideas of progress and utility, guided only by our love of money and of things. A rationally ordered society, guided by rationally ordered universities, was our only hope.[29]

Like so many books of cultural criticism, Hutchins's tract gained wide attention on the strength of a compelling diagnosis, even while few were ready to follow its prescription. Some reviewers conceded that he had put his finger on some deep problems in American society and hence its universities, particularly the widespread love of money and attendant anti-intellectualism. On the other hand, except for the circle of Adler-Hutchins devotees, few were to find the solution plausible, let alone persuasive.[30] As Glenn Frank remarked in the *Yale Review,* "The metaphysics, which Mr. Hutchins substitutes for theology as the integrating force in the modern university, would, I fear, become but a secularized and denatured theology, a search for absolutes without revelation."[31]

The affinities of Hutchins's views to Catholicism were also a major strike against him. Catholics were in the midst of their own neo-Thomist revival and were offering critiques of American education similar to those of Hutchins. While wishing that Hutchins would allow more room for revelation and theology, Catholic thinkers were likely to hail his critique. His proposals for a return to Aristotelian-Thomist metaphysics could be read as a sign of a cultural swing in their direction.[32] Catholic thinkers, however, were seldom given a serious voice in mainstream American intellectual culture and most of those who controlled that culture were ready to dismiss Hutchins's views just because of their parallels to Catholicism. For secular progressive thinkers, the principal heirs to the old Whig rhetoric of freedom, older animosities were revived by the association of Catholicism with fascism. Catholic support of Franco in the Spanish Civil War aggravated such associations. Attacks on Catholicism by progressive intellectuals accordingly increased in the late 1930s. The *New Republic,* for instance, ran a series of articles in 1938 warning of Catholicism's characteristic opposition to political freedom. Sidney Hook, heir-apparent to Dewey as the leading philosopher of secular progressivism, in a typical statement of the era, wrote in the *Partisan Review* that Catholicism was "the oldest and greatest totalitarian movement in history."[33] Even if Hutchins disclaimed any interest in theology or the Roman Catholic Church, his views could still be dismissed as "medievalism."

As might have been expected, John Dewey himself was one of Hutchins's most severe critics. Dewey found Hutchins's underlying assumptions incredible in the modern era. Hutchins, he pointed out, believed in fixed truth " 'the same at any time and place' " and in a fixed human nature that included an intellect to discover these truths. Hutchins was thus proposing to revive a concept of intellect divorced from experience. Hutchins's concept of a hierarchical set of first principles, already known, within which science should operate, said Dewey, was "authoritarian." "I would not intimate that the author has any sympathy with fascism," Dewey remarked. "But basically his idea as to the proper course to be taken is akin to the distrust of freedom and the consequent appeal to *some* fixed authority that is now overrunning the world." Rather than following the authority of Plato, Aristotle, and Aquinas and thus retreating to "monastic seclusion," higher learning, said Dewey, must come to grip with the science and society of our own age as Plato, Aristotle, and Aquinas had with theirs.

In his reply, Hutchins denied that he was advocating a simple return to the authority of the past or that he thought that truths were "fixed and eternal." Rather than arguing for any particular metaphysical system, said Hutchins, he was arguing that education should center around the quest for first principles and that these should be pursued by the most rational means possible. University curricula centering around such metaphysics were inherently no more authoritarian than those that studied and taught only the natural and social sciences. As for fascism, it was "a consequence of the absence of philosophy. It is possible only in the context of the disorganization of analysis and the disruption of the intellectual tradition and intellectual discipline through the pressure of immediate practical concerns."[34]

Can This Civilization Be Saved?

Under the increasingly dark clouds of fascism the debates over first principles in American higher education took on an intensity and a seriousness they had never had before. Especially with the outbreak of World War II in Europe in 1939, many American intellectuals, as well as religious leaders, sought desperately for some cultural alternative to offer to the Western world.

The intensity of the feelings were dramatically illustrated in a storm that broke over a remark of Mortimer Adler in 1940. The setting was an auspicious gathering of leading American intellectuals supplemented by distinguished refugees from Europe. Initiated by Rabbi Louis Finkelstein, and held at the Jewish Theological Seminary in New York in September 1940, the conference was called by group of Jewish, Protestant, and Catholic leaders as the first of a series annual meetings to discuss the topic of "Science, Philosophy and Religion." The seventy-nine founding members included Franz Boas, Henry Sloane Coffin, Albert Einstein, Enrico Fermi, Harry Emerson Fosdick, William E. Hocking, Robert Hutchins, Douglas

MacIntosh, John Mackay, Jacques Maritain, A. J. Muste, Allan Nevins, Pitirim Sorokin, and Paul Tillich. Van Wyck Brooks in the introduction to the published volume wrote that the conference

> recognizes that our failure to integrate science, philosophy and religion, in relation to traditional ethical values and the democratic way of life, has been catastrophic for civilization. We are aware of the perils that beset democracy, not only the obvious peril of national and racial despotisms, but the more insidious danger arising from the instability of our culture. We see the passing of ancient sanctions and the collapse of traditional loyalties. Having no basis for agreement regarding causes and remedies, we recognize these signs of cultural weakness.

In the face of such dire challenges, he concluded, "we are under a special constraint at the moment to realize a unity of thought and effort because of the growing threat to our way of life."

The conference agenda accordingly was, in effect, an extension of the liberal Protestant, interfaith, democratic outlook that would dominate much of American public thought during the next two decades. As Van Wyck Brooks explained it,

> It means that mankind is one, admitting of no fragmentation. Regarding this unity, the Conference seeks to bring out not only its negative basis, the fact that the freedom of the scientific spirit and of every philosophy and faith is threatened by totalitarianism, but also its positive basis, the belief in the value of personality, in the creative endeavour or unregimented culture, in the brotherhood of man, and in the democratic way of life as a necessary means of sustaining these spiritual values.[35]

Mortimer Adler, a founding member of the conference, asked to present one of the papers at its first meeting. Adler agreed generally with the agenda of the conference but was convinced that its efforts would be undercut if it was essentially like other scholarly conferences in which people read papers to each other and there was no systematic effort to achieve consensus. When his efforts to establish a more unified agenda failed, Adler attempted to withdraw. He was finally dissuaded from doing so by Jacques Maritain and others and took the suggestion of Rabbi Finkelstein that he should present the essence of his critique to the conference.

Adler's paper, "God and the Professors," was a scathing attack on the American professoriate. The conference, Adler prophesied, was certain to fail because American professors were too inflexible to change their minds. This was proved by Robert Hutchins's "glorious, Quixotic failure" to achieve the reforms he sought at the University of Chicago. Had he succeeded, there would be no need for such a conference. The problem was that the great majority of American professors were positivists and naturalists. Their fragmented approach to learning, based on their illusions about the value of scientific models, prevented them from addressing questions of ultimate truth.

All this might have contributed to serious debate about the Adler-Hutchins agenda had not Adler been carried away by the logic of his own analysis. So convinced was he that a civilization could not survive without a way of searching for the truth and hence that the real danger was from within that Adler reiterated his point with the most inappropriate hyperbole. "The most serious threat to Democracy," he declared, "is the positivism of the professors, which dominates every aspect of modern education and is the central corruption of modern culture. Democracy has much more to fear from the mentality of its teachers than from the nihilism of Hitler."[36]

This was an astonishing thing to say at Jewish Theological Seminary in New York in 1940. That Adler was Jewish added to the incongruity. As he himself recalled, the audience received the remainder of the speech with icy stares. The press jumped on the unfortunate remark and gave it wide publicity. His serious points were forgotten. Adler had provided his progressive-positivist opponents an opening to discredit his campaign. Sidney Hook, for instance, made the most of the opportunity in an essay in the *New Republic* on "The New Medievalism."[37] The tag would be hard to shake.

As the remark illustrated all too well, the trust of Adler and Hutchins in intellect as the route to discover a metaphysical basis for modern civilization *was* quixotic. They had (as Dewey's attack on Hutchins in effect pointed out) much the same problem as did Dewey and Hook in establishing a scientific basis for civilization. In a pluralistic world, was there any adequate court of appeal to settle the questions of "Whose science?" or "Whose metaphysics?"

As America faced the prospect of a world at war, however, Adler and Hutchins versus Hook and Dewey represented only two of the major options in American intellectual life. Even among those who agreed on the responsibility of intellectual and religious leadership to find a basis for cultural consensus, only limited consensus was forthcoming. At the 1940 conference on "Science, Philosophy and Religion," almost every speaker took it as a premise that democracy was in danger of extinction unless some compelling rationale were provided to underwrite its basic values. Nevertheless, the points of view represented clearly contradicted each other. Rabbi Finkelstein, for instance, could approvingly quote Etienne Gilson to the effect that we must return to medieval concepts of the oneness of truth. Harvard sociologist Pitirim A. Sorokin, who had just issued his telling critique of modern "sensate" culture in *The Crisis of Our Age,* and Jacques Maritain could recommend similarly sharp critiques of modernity and the need to return to faith in God. Albert Einstein, on the other hand, suggested that the conflict between science and religion could not be resolved, and hence true unity cannot be achieved unless religious people give up the idea of a personal God and "avail themselves of those forces which are capable of cultivating the Good, the True, and the Beautiful in humanity itself." Liberal Protestant theologians, on the other hand, argued that such ideals were not incompatible with belief in a personal God. Throughout the war years the conferences on "Science, Philosophy and Religion" and similar themes continued annually, thus contributing to a degree of Protestant–Catholic–Jewish solidarity during and after the war, even if the intellectual and religious problems of finding a single ideological basis for the culture could not be resolved.[38]

Many secularist intellectuals were alarmed about this attempt to put religion into the same equation as science and philosophy. In 1940 and 1941, just about the time of the blow-up over Adler, the New York intellectual and religious communities had been heated to a fever pitch over precisely such a point. Bertrand Russell, widely criticized in conservative circles for his criticisms of Christianity but especially for his open views on sexuality, was offered a visiting professorship to teach logic and mathematics at the College of the City of New York. City College was run by the city government, which Russell later described as "virtually a satellite of the Vatican."[39] Russell's appointment was sharply attacked by Episcopal Bishop William T. Manning, who long had been warning New Yorkers of the dangers of Russell's views. After considerable furor, Russell's appointment was sustained by the Board of Higher Education. Not satisfied, a layperson brought a civil suit. At the hearing Russell was described in one rhetorical flourish as "lecherous, salacious, libidinous, lustful, venerous, erotomaniac, aphrodisiac, atheistic, irreverent, narrow-minded, bigoted, and untruthful." The judge, a Catholic, ruled that Russell was morally unfit for the position and revoked the appointment.[40]

Many intellectuals, including some theists as well as nontheists, were outraged. A group of predominantly Jewish scholars, who were understandably alarmed at the ability of clerics to stir up popular animosity toward intellectuals, issued a scathing volume entitled *The Bertrand Russell Case* in 1941. John Dewey, co-editor with Horace Kallen, compared it to the *Dred Scott* decision. Kallen evoked all the cases cited in Andrew Dickson White's *Warfare,* lamented Catholic prejudice, and deplored the zeal of clergy, with some Protestant exceptions, to "persecute."[41]

Such academics clearly felt beleaguered as World War II brought increasing talk of the importance of religion to civilization. In 1943 and 1944, progressive secularists, including many of the defenders of Russell, organized their own conferences. The first was titled similarly to its rival as "The Scientific Spirit and Democratic Faith." Its spokespersons directed their strongest polemics against the "new authoritarianism." Especially objectionable, participants insisted, was the claim that supernatural revelation provided the only proper foundation for the democratic way of life. They saw an ominous coalition emerging in the wartime religious revival. "The élite intellectuals with fine educational backgrounds" and great influence in the sphere of education were at the head of this coalition, the secularists warned, but the numbers of the supernaturalists were swelled by fundamentalists and Catholics. Max Otto, professor of philosophy at the University of Wisconsin, noted a passage by Jacques Maritain depicting civilization as locked in a struggle between God and the Devil and deplored that this passage was "not written by an untutored fundamentalist, but by one who is called the outstanding Christian philosopher of our time." Brand Blanshard, a philosopher at Swarthmore College, quoted a passage from Cardinal Newman and observed that the objection to Catholicism and to other authoritarian religions was that their loyalties to democracy were expressly limited by a higher faith. Such loyalties, Blanshard suggested, led ultimately to the logic of the Inquisition.[42]

The title of the second such conference, held in New York in 1944, "The Authoritarian Attempt to Capture Education," made sure that nobody missed the point. John Dewey and Sidney Hook headed the list of speakers. Viewing education as more than just what happened in schools, several presenters decried what they saw as a conservative bias in the press and radio. In formal education itself, said Hook, the views of Monsignor Fulton Sheen, Robert Hutchins, Mortimer Adler, and others, were particularly dangerous; further, the conservative press was all too ready to buy their line that the denial of eternal principles would lead inevitably to totalitarianism. The conference participants were convinced of just the opposite. The genius of American democracy was a spirit of freedom and tolerance. Authoritarianism, especially religious authoritarianism, was not only a superstitious denial of free inquiry but ultimately incompatible with true tolerance. If the religious authoritarians gained control, the United States would be well on its way to its own brand of totalitarianism.[43]

Notes

1. See Clyde W. Barrow, *Universities and the Capitalist State: Corporate Liberalism and the Reconstruction of American Higher Education, 1894–1928* (Madison: University of Wisconsin Press, 1990), for a Marxist version of this point.

2. On the force of such principles in shaping modern institutions see Jacques Ellul, *The Technological Society* (New York: Vintage, 1964 [1954]). On the specifics see Roger L. Geiger, *To Advance Knowledge: The Growth of American Research Universities, 1900–1940* (New York: Oxford University Press, 1986).

3. Theodore Francis Jones, *New York University 1832–1932* (New York, 1933), 220–21, 193, quoted in David A. Hollinger, "Two NYUs and 'The Obligation of Universities to the Social Order' in the Great Depression," in *The University and the City,* Thomas Bender, ed. (New York: Oxford University Press, 1988), 254–55.

4. Hollinger, "Two NYUs," 251. This summary of the conference follows the themes of Hollinger's more detailed analysis.

5. James Rowland Angell, "The University Today: Its Aims and Province," in *The Obligation of Universities to the Social Order* (New York: New York University Press, 1933), 20.

6. John Campbell Merriam, "Spiritual Values and the Constructive Life," in *Obligation of Universities,* 322, 327, 329.

7. Joseph Wood Krutch, *The Modern Temper: A Study and a Confession* (New York: Harcourt, Brace, & World, 1956 [1929]), 7, 16.

8. This image is borrowed from Henry F. May's monumental account of the beginnings of this intellectual revolution, just before World War I, *The End of American Innocence: A Study of the First Years of Our Time, 1912–1917* (New York: Knopf, 1959).

9. C. K. Ogden and I. A. Richards, *The Meaning of Meaning: A Study of the Influence of Language upon Thought and of the Science of Symbolism* (London, 1923), 228, quoted in Edward A. Purcell, Jr., *The Crisis of Democratic Theory: Scientific Naturalism and the Problem of Value* (Lexington: University of Kentucky Press, 1973), 48.

Another very valuable summary of these trends is found in Douglas Sloan, "The Teaching of Ethics in the American Undergraduate Curriculum, 1876–1976," in *Education and Values*, Douglas Sloan, ed. (New York: Teachers College Press, 1980), 191–254. Sloan documents, for instance, how in *The Psychological Index* the subject of Ethics has disappeared as a heading and such topics are subsumed under "Social Functions of the Individual" (207n).

10. Einstein's relativity theory and Werner Heisenberg's uncertainty principle contributed to the sense that even common sense was unreliable. At the same time logicians demonstrated that even the most fundamental principles of Aristotelian logic, such as the law of noncontradiction or of the excluded middle, could be construed as merely assumptions and other consistent logics could be constructed from alternative premises. Geometers likewise demonstrated that there could be non-Euclidean geometries that were as consistent with their premises as was classical geometry. Even the most obvious axioms of rationality were thus mere human constructions. Innovative social scientists were soon speaking of "non-Euclidean" social or political theories, which became a useful metaphor for challenging any verity. Purcell, *Crisis*, 49–59.

11. Carl L. Becker, *The Heavenly City of the Eighteenth-Century Philosophers* (New Haven: Yale University Press, 1932), 14–15, 32, and passim.

12. Quoted in Burleigh Taylor Wilkins, *Carl Becker: A Biographical Study in American Intellectual History* (Cambridge, Mass.: M.I.T. Press, 1961), 13. This summary of Becker's outlook is taken most immediately from Wilkins, passim.

13. Carl Becker, *Everyman His Own Historian: Essays on History and Politics* (Chicago: Quadrangle Books, 1966 [1935]), 233–35, 251.

14. Peter Novick, *That Noble Dream: The "Objectivity Question" and the American Historical Profession* (Cambridge: Cambridge University Press, 1988).

15. This point is developed persuasively in Douglas Sloan, *Faith and Knowledge: Mainline Protestantism and Twentieth-Century American Higher Education* (Philadelphia: Westminster Press, 1994) (forthcoming).

16. Carl Becker himself offers a version of this in *Progress and Power* (New York: Random House, 1949 [1936]).

17. Ruth Benedict, *Patterns of Culture* (New York: Mentor Books, 1946 [1934]), 2, 8, 255, and passim.

18. John Dewey, *A Common Faith* (New Haven: Yale University Press, 1934), 51.

19. For this concise phrasing of the modern (and postmodern) moral predicament, I am indebted to Phillip E. Johnson, "The Creationist and the Sociobiologist: Two Stories about Illiberal Education," *California Law Review* 80 (July 1992), 1089.

20. John Barnard, *From Evangelicalism to Progressivism at Oberlin College: 1866–1917* (Columbus: Ohio State University Press, 1969).

21. Mary Ann Dzuback, *Robert M. Hutchins: Portrait of an Educator* (Chicago: University of Chicago Press, 1991), 3–20 and passim, argues this point.

22. Purcell, *Crisis,* 140–41. See also relevant sections of Dzuback, *Hutchins,* and Harry S. Ashmore, *Unseasonable Truths: The Life of Robert Maynard Hutchins* (Boston: Little, Brown, 1989).

23. See, for instance, Mortimer J. Adler, *Philosopher at Large: An Intellectual Autobiography* (New York: Macmillan, 1977).

24. Quotations from Ashmore, *Unseasonable Truths,* 58, 59.

25. Ibid., 89. In a 1973 interview, from which this quotation is taken, Hutchins also remarked that he believed it was possible to maintain "those habits of having faith in one God, the Creator, or having faith in the immortality of the soul or any of the other central doctrines of religion" (idem). Neither of his recent biographers, Dzuback and Ashmore, provides any sustained account of his religious views during his years as university president.

26. Quoted from excerpt in Adler, *Philosopher at Large,* 162.

27. Purcell, *Crisis,* 31.

28. Adler, *Philosopher at Large,* 163–66, quotation from excerpt (163). Purcell, *Crisis,* 3.

29. Robert Maynard Hutchins, *The Higher Learning in America* (New Haven: Yale University Press, 1936), 31, 34–35, 48, 94–95, 106–7, 97, 119, and passim.

30. E.g., Henry Seidel Canby, "A Call for Aristotle," *Saturday Review* 14 (October 24, 1936), 10–11. Cf. Dzuback, *Hutchins,* 187.

31. Glenn Frank, "Toward an Ordered Learning," *Yale Review* 26 (December 1936), 393.

32. William M. Halsey, *The Survival of American Innocence: Catholicism in an Era of Disillusionment, 1920–1940* (Notre Dame, Ind.: University of Notre Dame Press, 1980), 15–117.

33. Sidney Hook, *Social Myths and Democracy* (New York, 1966), 76, originally published in *Partisan Review,* ca. 1938, quoted in Purcell, *Crisis,* 203. Purcell provides an excellent summary of the debates (esp. 117–58, 197–217). Merrimon Cuninggim, *The College Seeks Religion* (New Haven: Yale University Press, 1947), had a useful summary (96–122). R. Freeman Butts, *The College Charts Its Course: Historical Conceptions and Current Proposals* (New York: McGraw-Hill, 1939), 253–426, provides a contemporary summary from a progressive perspective.

34. *John Dewey: The Later Works, 1925–1953,* Vol. II, *1935–1937,* Jo Ann Boydston, ed. (Carbondale: Southern Illinois University Press, 1987), 392, 400, 401, 596. This exchange originally appeared in *Social Frontier* 3 as follows: John Dewey, "Rationality in Education" (December 1936), 71–73; Dewey, "President Hutchins' Proposals to Remake Higher Education" (January 1937), 103–4; Robert Maynard Hutchins, "Grammar, Rhetoric, and Mr. Dewey" (February 1937), 137–39; Dewey, "The Higher Learning in America" (March 1937), 167–69.

35. Van Wyck Brooks, "Conference on Science, Philosophy and Religion in Their Relation to the Democratic Way of Life," in *Science, Philosophy and Religion: A Symposium* (New York: Conference on Science, Philosophy and Religion . . . Inc., 1941), 1–4. Brooks's remarks echoed some of the same concerns expressed in the much-discussed recent essay by Archibald MacLeish, "The Irresponsibles," *The Nation,* May 18, 1940, also in MacLeish, *The Irresponsibles* (New York: Duell, Sloan and Pearce, 1940), 3–34.

36. Mortimer J. Adler, "God and the Professors," in *Science, Philosophy and Religion,* 120–49.

37. Sidney Hook, "The New Medievalism," *New Republic* 103 (October 28, 1940), 602–3.

38. *Science, Philosophy and Religion,* esp. 19, 90–119, 162–83, 213, 56–75. After three annual conferences on "Science, Philosophy and Religion" conferences were held more or less annually through most of the 1950s, with subsequent gatherings in 1960 and 1966.

39. *The Autobiography of Bertrand Russell, 1914–1944* (Boston: Little, Brown, 1951), 348.

40. Barry Feinberg and Ronald Kasrils, *Bertrand Russell's America, 1896–1945* (New York: Viking Press, 1973), 135–67. Quotation (153) from attorney Joseph Goldstein, Supreme Court, New York County, Appellate Division, *Papers on Appeal from Order,* in the matter of the application of Jean Kay against the Board of Higher Education of the City of New York, 40.

41. John Dewey and Horace M. Kallen, eds., *The Bertrand Russell Case* (New York: Da Capo Press, 1972 [1941]), 9, 38, and passim.

42. *The Scientific Spirit and Democratic Faith: Papers from the Conference on the Scientific Spirit and the Democratic Faith: Held in New York City, May, 1943* (New York: King's Crown Press, 1944): Edward C. Lindeman, "Introduction," x; Max C. Otto, "Authoritarianism and Supernaturalism," 18; Brand Blanshard, "Theology and the Individual," 76. Fundamentalists were mentioned several times as a threat, but unlike Catholic authors, they were not taken seriously enough to quote even for purposes of refutation.

43. *The Authoritarian Attempt to Capture Education: Papers from the 2d Conference on the Scientific Spirit and Democratic Faith* (New York: King's Crown Press, 1945): Sidney Hook, "Democracy and Education: Introduction," 10–12; Harry D. Gideonse, "Can Free Communication Be Achieved? Introduction," 31–34; Bruce Bliven, "Problems of the Press," 34–40; Bernard B. Smith, "Problems of the Radio," 40–49 and passim.

21

A Church with the Soul of a Nation

The Spirit of Protestantism

The urgent wartime debates on the relation of educational philosophy to the survival of democracy[1] had their counterparts in institutional reassessments of what colleges and universities stood for. Many schools drafted a new statement of their purpose,[2] though, as usual, these typically considered broad goals for their undergraduate programs only. By far the most influential such statement was the Harvard Report of 1945, *General Education in a Free Society*. Written by some of the best known scholars in the country, this two hundred–page volume set the standard for those seeking a middle ground among the contentious partisans.

The Harvard Report suggested that Americans had not yet faced up to their educational revolution. Between 1870 and 1940 the American population tripled, but the number of students enrolled in secondary schools increased ninety times and those in colleges thirty times. The day was long past when higher education could be directed simply toward producing gentlemen and ladies; it would now have to be geared toward educating the democratic masses. This tremendous growth, along with the increasing social diversity of the groups being served and the vast expansion and fragmentation of knowledge complicated immensely the problem of reaching a consensus on the educational task.

The Harvard committee took for granted that higher education should serve democratic or free society but was acutely aware of the lack of a center for this enterprise. In fact, the committee pointed out, the ideal of a free democratic society accentuated the dilemma. How could a democracy promote both loyalty and liberty? "A free society . . . cherishes both toleration and conviction," the committee reflected. "Yet the two seem incompatible." Could they promote democracy without resorting to indoctrination that would undermine the very freedom that democracies held sacred?

The Harvard professors considered and rejected four possible models for filling the "supreme need of American education . . . for a unifying purpose and idea." Religiously based education was the first of these. The others were great books education, education organized around contemporary problems, and education based on pragmatic scientific method.

Each of these proposals had some merit, but each was inadequate by itself. The Harvard solution was to balance some elements from each.

The religious dimension of higher education was the most difficult for Harvard professors to incorporate into their proposals. Adopting a developmental view of society, they emphasized continuity with tradition, especially classical tradition, while affirming the need to serve contemporary democracy with current scientific method. The affirmation of tradition meant that they had to deal with the issue of the religious heritage. Accordingly, they noted that Protestant colleges until less than a century before had found unity through sectarian education. This was still the approach of Roman Catholic colleges. This solution, however, "is out of the question in publicly supported colleges and is practically, if not legally, impossible in most others." "Given the American scene with its varieties of faith and even of unfaith," Harvard did not feel justified in proposing religious instruction as such as part of an undergraduate curriculum.

Nevertheless, the committee hoped to keep the curriculum open to the benefits of religion through a back door. Acknowledging that "much of the best tradition of the West is to be found in the distillations of the prophets, in the homilies and allegories of an earlier age, and in Biblical injunctions," Harvard could retain the "moral guidance" of this heritage through the humanities. So the core curriculum that the committee proposed would include a humanities course on "Great Texts in Literature," including religious texts. Definitions of humanism they advised, should be "careful . . . not exclude the religious ideal."

A canon of great books, the committee observed, "can be looked at as a secular continuation of the spirit of Protestantism." As Protestantism had rejected the authority of the medieval church, so Harvard was "rejecting the unique authority of the Scriptures" and placing "reliance on the reading of those books which are taken to represent the fullest revelation of the Western mind." The committee was satisfied that when thus oriented toward both human dignity and duty "the goal of education is not in conflict with but largely includes the goals of religious education, education in the Western tradition, and education in modern democracy."[3]

The Harvard reporters thus summarized the religious implications of one of the major curricular trends of the past half century. In effect they were recommending a liberal Protestantism with the explicit Christianity removed. They were affirming, as liberal Protestantism had done, the religious value of the best in Western culture itself. If the culture defined the highest ideals, then the specifically religious dimensions were expendable. Though the Harvard Report tended to emphasize the humanities rather than empirical social sciences, from a religious perspective the committee's position was similar to John Dewey's. If religion was valued primarily for its civilizing moral ideals, then one could identify those moral ideals and determine how to promote them without directly resorting to Christianity.

This outlook was consistent with Harvard's own religious heritage, dating back to the days of Charles Eliot.

The Harvard Report reflected a curricular trend toward "general education" that had been developing for several decades. To counter the fragmentation of modern learning, educators had been searching for a way to establish a common core of beliefs for the dominant culture. The curricular expression of this ideal was a set of core requirements highlighted by some broad surveys. In the social sciences, for instance, the Harvard committee recommended a course called "Western Thought and Institutions," which would be a survey of the evolution of Western institutions with readings of selections from major Western thinkers including, for example, "Aquinas, Machiavelli, Luther, Bodin, Locke, Montesquieu, Rousseau, Adam Smith, Bentham, and Mill." This course was explicitly patterned after a "Contemporary Civilization" course originated at Columbia during World War I as a "War Aims" course and very successfully taught there to freshmen ever since. Such proposals did not go as far as a curriculum based entirely on "great books," such as Adler and Hutchins had proposed and was implemented at St. John's College in Maryland. Rather, the Harvard plan followed the much wider trend toward requiring a general core of subjects such as "Western Civilization," and surveys of sciences and social sciences, great literature and the arts, that would thus establish at least a minimal evolving Western canon.[4]

Planning the Technocratic Order

Such quasi-religious humanistic ideals probably reached the peak of their influence in the post–World War II era. Even then, however, they were being surpassed by other trends that were advancing even faster. American higher education was once again expanding at a phenomenal rate. In the decade following World War II the college and university student population doubled.[5] One implication was that the ethnically Protestant establishment that dominated the universities and provided the social basis for any consensus was in its latter days. During the 1950s there was much talk of expanding the establishment into a Protestant–Catholic–Jewish consensus, but the fact was that the United States was much more complicated than that. A further major implication of the vast higher education expansion was an increasing orientation toward the practical and the vocational. Influential elite birthright Protestants plus a few allies could still successfully promote literate humane values in many institutions. Nevertheless, that was not the direction in which American higher education was headed.

The most revealing barometer of the dominant cultural and intellectual pressures that were reshaping American higher education was the influential and widely discussed Report of the President's Commission on Education. Appointed by President Truman in 1946, the commission issued a multi-volume statement at the end of 1947, significantly titled *Higher Education for American Democracy.*

One of the revolutions that the commission was announcing was the end of higher education as an elite enterprise. The Harvard Report had said the same thing, but the president's commission meant it. The commission repeatedly contrasted the democratic education it proposed to "aristocratic" education that would be "the instrument for producing an intellectual elite." From 1900 to 1940 the percentage of eighteen to twenty-one year olds attending college had risen from 4 to 16 percent. By 1947, with the huge influx of veterans aided by the G.I. Bill, enrollments were well on their way to doubling again. Startlingly, the commission proposed to promote this postwar expansion to the maximum. It estimated that about half the American population was qualified to complete at least two years of college and proposed that by 1960 the educational system be expanded, including both four-year and many new community two-year colleges, so that everyone who wanted a college education could receive one. Federal and state funds should be used to remove all financial barriers to such education. Moreover, racial barriers, especially the massive discrimination against blacks and quotas for Jews, should be eliminated.[6]

Together with this unreserved promotion of mass education came a pragmatic problem-centered educational philosophy. The commission called for "education adjusted to needs," advised that leaders should "agree on common objectives," emphasized above all "the social role of education," and education as an "instrument for social transition." The content of education should be "directly relevant to the demands of contemporary society."[7] The spirit of John Dewey was evident on almost every page.

Robert Hutchins was, as one might expect, appalled. Speaking for many humanists, his wit was at its best: "Every cliché and every slogan of contemporary educational discussion appear once more. Much of the report reads like a Fourth-of-July oration in pedaguese. It skirts the edge of illiteracy, and sometimes falls over the brink. And when the battle has ended, the field is strewn with the corpses of straw men the Commission has slain." Moreover, said Hutchins, "the Commission never misses a chance to communicate the news that our educational institutions are far too intellectual." It attacked, for instance, "the present orientation of higher education towards verbal skills and intellectual interests." Though the commission disclaimed any intention of subverting the liberal arts, it called for higher education to do so many other things that such intellectual life would almost be incidental. Given the fragmentation already present among disciplines, said Hutchins, the commission's advice to diversify was like telling a drowning man to drink lots of water.[8]

The report, reflecting the operating principles that were reshaping American education, revealed the realistic prospects for religion in higher education in the second half of the century. Despite the presence on the commission of clergy from the three major faiths (meaning a liberal Protestant, a non-Orthodox Jew, and a Catholic), religion was hardly mentioned. When it was, it was in the context of values that would make democracy work. Morality, said the commission in defining the first of eleven desired "basic outcomes," had been neglected in recent decades, as higher education had been too exclusively concerned with intellect. Yet "in these troubled times" people urgently needed "soundly based values," especially those of mutual trust and tolerance. Where such values would come from the commission was not quite sure, so it resorted to vagueness and use of the passive voice in relation to religion:

> Ethical principles that will induce this faith need not be based on any single sanction or be authoritarian in origin, nor need finality be claimed for them. Some persons will find the satisfactory basis for a moral code in the democratic creed itself, some in philosophy, some in religion. Religion is held to be a major force in creating the system of human values on which democracy is predicated, and many derive from one or another of its varieties a deepened sense of human worth and a strengthened concern for the rights of others.[9]

Throughout the report the "democratic creed" was the absolute by which all else was to be tested, just as the function of religion was to underscore democratic values of a sense of human worth and concern for the rights of others.[10]

According to the commission, loyalty to the democratic principle must qualify all other loyalties:

> Nor can any *group* in our society, organized or non-organized, pursue purely private ends and seek to promote its own welfare without regard to the social consequences of its activities. Business, industry, labor, agriculture, medicine, law, engineering, education . . . all these modes of association call for the voluntary development of codes of conduct . . . to harmonize the special interests of the group with the general welfare.[11]

Religious groups were not mentioned in this list, but their educational institutions certainly would be included. T. R. McConnell, chancellor of the University of Buffalo and a commission member, responding to the frequent criticism that the report had neglected religion, quoted with approval: "The church-related colleges of America in the twentieth century must not be led down the path of authoritarianism as opposed to freedom, nor up to the heights of revelation as opposed to scientific knowledge. . . . They must not separate themselves from the great goals of the society of which they are a part."[12]

Many Catholic educators were incensed by the report and by its philosophy. They claimed it implicitly attacked some basic principles of Catholic education, which usually was still frankly authoritarian. Two of the Catholic members of the commission issued a Statement of Dissent, appended to the report, objecting strongly to the recommendation that private schools be excluded from the proposed funding of educational opportunity.[13] According to Allan P. Farrell, education editor of the Catholic magazine *America,* "almost everybody agrees" that the tone of the report was to say "Farewell" to private education and to announce the era of government control of education. Even more fundamentally, Farrell, along with many other critics, was dismayed by the thoroughgoing secularism of the report. Its underlying philosophy, said Farrell, was that youth should be trained for the democratic state and that "the democratic state is a sort of religion, with public education as its church."[14]

Sociologist Robert S. Lynd, a secular critic from the left, essentially agreed. "We non-Catholics," he wrote, "worry about the case of education forced to operate within the political goals of the organization ramifying from the Vatican. But we do not, in the main and in public, recognize the possibility that there are other constraints upon education no less coercive and determined to have their way within our own cultural system."[15]

The President's commission argued from the premise that democratic values were self-evident principles, both everlasting and evolving. These principles, they maintained, should form the basis for a cultural consensus, based especially on equality of opportunity and mutual tolerance. "It is imperative," they affirmed, "that American education develop a 'democratic dynamic' that will inspire faith in the democratic way of life."[16] In the wake of World War II, neither the left nor the right was to be allowed much of a voice in questioning the ideals of democracy for which so many had died. In such a setting the ideals themselves did not have to be placed on a rational basis. So, for instance, while the commission propounded democratic values as though they were self-evident, it denied that ethical principles needed to be final or based on any authority. Moreover, while the commission placed a premium on freedom for a diversity of opinions, it still wanted everyone to agree on democracy.

The President's commission was a prophetic voice announcing the advent of an era in which the federal government would be a major force in making the educational wilderness bloom through technique. During the war the universities had made an important contribution to national defense. Perhaps the most telling sign of the times was that the most momentous development during Robert Hutchins's tenure at the University of Chicago was not anything having to do with discussion of the humanities or natural law; it was that in 1942, under the Amos Alonzo Stagg football field, scientists at the university split the atom. That secret work was the iceberg of which many other university government contracts were the tip. The attitudes that emanated from such successful cooperation grew into a conviction among government leaders that the universities should continue to play a vital role in national defense during the Cold War era. By 1960 federal expenditures for university research had reached $760 million ($20 million each if distributed equally among thirty-eight top schools). Moreover, the National Defense Education Act of 1958 declared that "the security of the Nation requires the fullest development of mental resources and technical skills of its young men and women." Accordingly, "This requires programs that will give assurance that no student of ability will be denied an opportunity for higher education because of financial need."[17]

While the American Protestant establishment could hardly be entirely pleased to see so much energy going into higher educational activities that had little direct relationship to their religious or humane goal, they had little ground for complaint about the premise on which such activities were based. Since at least Woodrow Wilson's day liberal Protestantism had been putting democracy and service to the nation first, in effect making the nation its church. During the first four decades of the century service to the nation had translated largely as service to the business community, which supplied most of the funds for the new universities. Some of the old classicist ideal of training for "citizenship" survived, but most of what was new in the universities was based on the technological model and students were learning skills to be leaders in business or the supporting professions.

Now with World War II, "serving the nation" came to include, as in World War I, an additional commitment to national defense. Furthermore, rather than demobilizing after World War II, throughout the Cold War the nation retained its military basis. The military draft was made virtually permanent, though the importance of college training was recognized by allowing for college exemptions. The G.I. Bill, which brought so many veterans to colleges after the war, was a sign of the government's interest in universities as a source of national strength. The federal government thus was a major player not only in financing universities during the Cold War but in determining who attended them and when.

The educational establishment, still vestigially Protestant, raised few objections to this new development. Not only did the government's role ensure a healthy share of Cold War prosperity, but the ideal of service to the nation was already so deeply ingrained that there was little ground for objection to expansion of that ideal. The humanists and the seriously religious might worry about some of its implications, but they had little reason to question the premise. Neither did those who were more secular, most of whom had nothing besides "democracy" to commit to.

The Revival of Campus Religion and Its Limits

Already in the years just before World War II, as Merrimon Cuninggim documented, there had been signs of growing religious interest on campuses. By the years after the war it was apparent that a national religious revival was gaining momentum, a momentum that reached its peak in the mid-1950s. The national revival covered a wide spectrum from sawdust trail healing evangelists to the platitudinous pieties of the Eisenhower White House. Billy Graham rose to fame during this time, as did Norman Vincent Peale, Bishop Fulton J. Sheen, and Martin Luther King. Reinhold

Niebuhr was practically the national theologian. Campuses were no exception to the religious resurgence. Campus ministries flourished. It was a sort of golden age for mainline campus ministries and insurgent evangelical groups such as InterVarsity Christian Fellowship or Campus Crusade for Christ were gaining increasing influence. The college educated were as likely as other Americans to evidence religious commitments.[18]

Part of what made the revival seem nationally significant was that it was more respectable than it had been in the previous decades to discuss religious questions in public places such as campuses. The highlight of this discussion was the publication in 1949 by the English Student Christian Movement of Sir Walter Moberly's eloquent *The Crisis in the University.* Moberly, an Oxford philosopher highly placed in English academic life, argued that modern universities had become at least implicitly hostile to Christianity, because of their reverence for the supposedly value-free scientific method, from which followed their prejudice against religion and neglect of higher human values. Christians, he said, had two alternatives. Either they could resign themselves to being "a small Christian enclave within a predominantly pagan university," or, as he strongly advocated, they could play the role of a "creative minority," and win enough respect to restore at least a general sympathy to Christianity. The broadly Christian contours of the cultural heritage would be of aid in this task.[19]

Moberly's book, widely heralded on both sides of the Atlantic, was only the best known of an extensive literature on the topic during the postwar decade. Many writers followed Moberly in describing the Christian's task as intellectual. It became common to speak, as Moberly had, of challenging the underlying presuppositions of the universities and their pretensions to neutrality. The exponents of these views were part of a rapidly growing movement to reestablish a place for Christianity in the intellectual life of universities. Student ministries were expanding and denominational and interdenominational agencies were building campus centers for religious activities at unprecedented rates. A number of research centers, such as the Christian Faith and Higher Education Center at Michigan State University, were founded. The National Council of Churches in 1953 established a Department of Campus Christian Life, which in turn created the Faculty Christian Fellowship and an attractive new journal, the *Christian Scholar.*[20] The numbers of religion departments, typically with an orientation to Christian theological and ethical concerns, continued to grow throughout this era.[21] Clarence P. Shedd of Yale Divinity School, who had long worked for such causes, may have been correct when he wrote in 1951, "Never in this century has there been so much serious and creative discussion of the problems of religion in higher education as during the past decade."[22]

This revival and the enthusiasm and activities it engendered were like a candle starved for oxygen, which burns more brightly before it flickers out. For the time being the gains were real and illuminating for many individuals involved, but they could not get to the source of the problem.[23] The commitment of mainline religion to "freedom" made any such gains necessarily dependent on the momentum generated by the revival of interest in things religious. Outside the churches themselves and their agencies, there were few institutional supports to sustain that momentum. Only in superficial ways could the renewed religious interests touch the structures of universities or redirect the dominant forces shaping those structures.

Clearly if Christianity was to have a significant role in universities it would have to be at least an option in the curricula; yet even in the most humane programs Christianity as such played no more than a token role. This was well documented in a study sponsored by the Edward W. Hazen Foundation, an agency that during and after World War II searched for ways to reestablish mainline Protestantism as a leading player in higher education. In 1948 the foundation issued *College Reading and Religion,* a collection of essays by some of the nation's top scholars—including Gordon Allport in psychology, Peter Bertocci in philosophy, Robert Calhoun in the history of philosophy, and Margaret Mead in anthropology—analyzing the treatment of religion in college texts normally assigned in each of their fields.[24]

The treatment of religion in the texts, the scholars found, ranged from indifference to implicit hostility. Several noted the power of what the editors called "the religion of science" and deplored the "materialist assumptions" of so much of modern academic writing. In the history of philosophy, texts could be dated according to their views of religion. Those written before World War I offered "critical appreciation"; those written between the wars reflected "active disparagement." Since World War II the treatment had brightened somewhat, although the most positive development, outside of Catholic publications, surprisingly, was a history by Bertrand Russell, who at least treated theology fairly. If Russell was on the positive side of the ledger, Christianity had indeed fallen on hard times in the world of scholarship. In American literature, a telling example was Vernon L. Parrington's popular three-volume *Main Currents in American Thought,* which gave lots of coverage to Puritan religion but with an unmistakably negative tone, valuing it as "merely one of the stages toward the growth of a secular democracy." Parrington's last volume, on the modern era, did not discuss religion at all. In the social sciences religion was usually ignored or, as in anthropology, seen as an aspect of "social mechanics." Social scientists, said one author, typically have only childish memories of religion, which they then contrast with the supposed "maturity and objectivity of the trained intellect" and conclude that religion should best be eliminated from modern life.[25]

One problem evident from the study was that the evaluating scholars themselves did not agree on what "religion" was and what role it ought to have in colleges. Theodore Spencer, writing on English literature, quoting an article by Margaret Mead in which the anthropologist had commentedon the blandness of America's generalized religion and suggested that the quality of American religion was the source of its weakness within academia. More "impartial" teaching of religion would only be a sign of secularization, not an answer to it. Spencer contrasted the general texts to those written for Catholic colleges, in which religiously based viewpoints actually made a difference. One reputable Catholic anthology stated frankly that one of its themes was "a cordial hatred of the bourgeois ideal and a corresponding love of the spiritual."[26]

Here was one of the most troubling problems for those who worked for a return of religious influences in higher education. With many religious groups vying for influence, and with these groups representing vastly different and often opposed definitions of religion, it was difficult to see how religion could provide a basis for unifying culture. This was particularly so given that one of the highest goods for the Protestant establishment was that whatever religious influence there was must be entirely free. The Hazen Foundation, for instance, hailed "the liberal ideal" in higher education and ruled out coercion from any quarter, including the churches.[27]

The proportions of the impasse may be gauged by the inability of one of the most astute of mainline Protestants leaders, Reinhold Niebuhr, to find a way around it. Niebuhr in 1945 wrote *The Contribution of Religion to Cultural Unity* for the Hazen series on higher education. Niebuhr's statement is particularly significant because he was the chief spokesperson for the American neo-orthodox movement. While not rejecting the liberal Protestant commitment to science or to liberal democracy, Niebuhr advocated recovery of aspects of the Christian heritage that would temper any celebration of mere intellectual or cultural achievement. Particularly, Niebuhr emphasized that the Christian doctrine of original sin should chasten human celebrations even of such ideals as freedom and creativity, since the highest human achievements so often led to the greatest vices. During the postwar era, Niebuhr's "realistic" message became widely popular among intellectuals as an alternative to more optimistic religious liberalism and to unthinking celebrations of the American way.

Niebuhr started in his reflections on higher education in typically prophetic style: "The religious problem is the ultimate issue in education." Religion deals with "the meaning of the whole," so that attempting to find meaning to life in anything less than the divine amounts to the idolatry of promoting a partial interest or perspective as ultimate. This was the problem with the sciences. Making even democracy the center of education was idolatrous, because if democracy were an end it itself, that would amount to a political religion.

But what were the alternatives? The "orthodox portion of American Protestantism," especially as found in the South, Midwest, and West, was "culturally obscurantist" and "so irrelevant to religion in higher education that no policy in the academic program can hope to overcome that irrelevance. " Liberal Protestantism, on the other hand, had been so anxious on college campuses "to prove itself intellectually respectable, that the total depth of life and experience, as apprehended in the Christian faith, was sacrificed to the flatness of modern culture." What it offered were vapid and self-defeating religion courses that taught only "a Christian naturalism or humanism" or the Bible as "literature." What was needed then were religion courses that without proselytizing taught "the positive meaning of the Christian faith" and led to "commitment."

At this point, however, Niebuhr simply sidestepped a major problem. How would schools find teachers who would tread this fine line between proselytizing and inspiring? Particularly, how was this going to happen if, as Niebuhr also made a point of emphasizing, there should be no religious test for faculty?

For Niebuhr, as for virtually every other Protestant writer on higher education, academic freedom was a sacred nonnegotiable. Moreover, he argued, such freedom was essential to Protestant Christianity. Protestant Christianity supported liberal culture in the best sense by insisting on criticism and self-criticism of the culture itself. However, as soon as the faith became official or dogmatic, the critical perspective so necessary to the faith itself was undermined. "While Catholicism may regard a secular culture as inimical to the highest values of Christianity, Protestantism at its best cannot make such an estimate of our liberal-democratic culture. Protestantism believes that faith must be achieved in freedom."[28]

Here surely was the Achilles heel of the mainline Protestant view of higher education, even when it was at its best in distinguishing between itself and the culture. The liberal ideal of freedom had become so essential to the faith that there was absolutely no way for the distinctive aspects of the faith to survive in the public institutions of a free society once the momentum of cultural dominance gave out. Christian realism of the Niebuhrian type had no plan for dealing with this concession to modern cultural ideals. Less critical liberal Protestantism did not even always see the problem.

The corollary of the commitment to freedom was a commitment to science. Niebuhr was often sharply critical of the Deweyan reverence for scientific method as a basis for social planning. Niebuhr saw such faith in science as a typical example of the human tendency to turn a virtue into a vice. Nonetheless, as Douglas Sloan has tellingly demonstrated, Niebuhr and his mainline cohorts were so thoroughly committed to the academic scientific ideals that they could provide no alternative to the scientific and technical models that were increasingly shaping most academic disciplines. Granted, they did offer a transcendent perspective that would challenge human tendencies to absolutize the relative. As valuable as such perspectives might be, they would not deflect the scientific-technological juggernaut. According to Sloan, they hardly challenged it.[29]

The Limits of Freedom

The limits of the commitment to freedom in both the educational and religious establishments were painfully evident in their mixed reactions to McCarthyism and anticommunism. On the one hand, university and mainline Protestant leadership overwhelmingly denounced the extremes of McCarthyism. Educational institutions and the Protestant National Council of Churches (which succeeded the Federal Council of Churches in 1949) were favorite targets of the right wing, for whom anything liberal was pink and anything pink was Red. Representatives of the accused groups were naturally outraged by the accusations, and they sharply denounced the McCarthyite tactics of guilt by association as well as the assumption that those who had sympathized with communism when that was in style in the 1930s, but had since renounced it, should be treated as though they were communists.

The counterbalance to liberal outrage over McCarthyite tactics was the liberals' own militant anticommunism. In the dangerous Cold War setting Communist party membership involved not only authoritarian beliefs but allegiance to a threatening and secretive international movement. Dedicated civil libertarians might defend rights for active party members, but much liberal opinion now saw the party as a threat to liberalism itself. Leaders of the American Association of University Professors, for instance, typically saw membership in the Communist party as an exception to the rule that political affiliations should not be an academic concern. The reason was, as Arthur Lovejoy explained in 1949, that "the Communist Party has already extinguished academic freedom in many countries," so "no one who desires to maintain academic freedom in American can consistently favor" accepting as faculty members "persons who have voluntarily adhered to an organization one of whose aims is to abolish academic freedom." Sidney Hook, who in 1932 had signed a petition in favor of the Communist party presidential candidate, now strongly concurred. Party members were committed to professional misconduct, said Hook in "What Shall We Do about Communist Teachers?," an essay appearing in 1949 in the *Saturday Evening Post.*

President James Bryant Conant of Harvard said much the same thing, as did his peers across the nation: "In this period of a cold war, I do not believe the usual rule as to political parties applies to the Communist Party." Since members of the Communist party were committed to secrecy, dedicated to indoctrination, and subservient to foreign powers, said Conant, they were not so much a political party, as "something more akin to a fanatic religious movement."[30]

In line with such sentiments, the dominant academic leadership offered little opposition to efforts to formalize the anticommunist dimension of academia's commitment to the republic. Administrations routinely gave assurances that no Communist activities would be permitted on campus, speaker policies were tightened, and radical student organizations virtually disappeared. Almost every state passed laws requiring teachers at universities to sign loyalty oaths. Even when, at the University of California at Berkeley, some thirty liberal professors were dismissed for taking a stand and refusing on principle to sign California's oath in 1949, the AAUP did not take effective action. While academic opinion eventually stood solidly against the worst excesses of McCarthyism, it did so within the framework of a basic anticommunism that remained the order of the day.[31]

Whatever its merits, liberal American anticommunism illustrated the point that liberalism's attachment to freedom was always limited by higher allegiances, of which the highest was the survival of the American version of liberal culture itself. A real and present danger of overthrowing the government would, of course, necessitate some limit on freedom. Beyond that, however, the logic of American liberalism invited another limitation on freedom. Tolerance, above all, seemed necessary to make democracy work in a pluralistic setting. The one thing that could not be tolerated was intolerance. To many leaders of academic opinion, dogmatism of any sort appeared a threat to democratic institutions. In the debates between the pragmatists and the proponents of eternal verities, the pragmatists seemed to have captured the field. The genius of America, it seemed to many, was in its antidogmatism, a point reinforced by the widely admired pragmatism of New Deal politics.[32] Stalinist communism was heretical because it denied this principle. Although it was difficult to explain how severe restrictions of communist expressions were consistent with "freedom" or with "academic freedom," these measures were consistent if freedom was defined as the freedom to deny anything but freedom.

The appeal of this position obscured another paradox. This enforced antidogmatism in the name of national welfare was itself dogmatic. Of course proponents of religious or political dogmatism were free to live in their own enclaves in America and their free speech was largely protected. One area, however, into which such protections did not fully extend was public or quasi-public education, including those institutions of higher learning that most celebrated their "academic freedom." Such institutions were considered so essential to the national welfare that they were inevitably limited by the dominant national viewpoints. Groups that were excluded, such as Marxists and fundamentalists, often raised the point that they were being excluded by liberal dogmatism, but they were seldom heard. In academic institutions where "free inquiry" was considered the very basis of the enterprise—the holy grail itself—the point that freedom always operates in a dogmatic framework was not often acknowledged.

The Trouble with Catholics

The relationship of the intense commitment to freedom to the Protestant heritage of the liberal community that dominated American universities is most evident in the close parallel between postwar attitudes toward Catholicism and communism.[33] Totalitarianism of the right was to be deplored as much as totalitarianism of the left. Although Catholicism was far less plausibly a foreign threat than was the Communist party, the Roman Catholic Church remained the chief candidate for a takeover from the right. Nor were such fears exclusively the property of Protestant fundamentalists. In the outbreak of anti-Catholicism that grew out of the war, secularists and mainline Protestants took the lead. The 1944 conference on "The Authoritarian Attempt to Capture Education," which issued in dark warnings of the Roman threat, was sponsored by secularists and civil libertarians. Paul Blanshard's bestseller, *American Freedom and Catholic Power* (1949), which popularized fears of a Catholic takeover and warned that education would be the first thing to fall, was excerpted in *The Nation.*[34] *The Nation* also financed Blanshard's research for a second volume, *Communism, Democracy and Catholic Power,* which detailed the parallels between the two types of "totalitarianism."[35]

Attitudes toward Catholicism, of course, varied but many of the most prominent leaders of mainline Protestantism joined in the liberal chorus of scathing attacks on Catholic intolerance and imperialism. Bishop G. Bromley Oxnam, for instance, perhaps the most influential Methodist leader of the era and a proponent of strengthening Christian identity in higher education, was a militant opponent of Catholicism. A person who takes his "religious thought from an authoritarian hierarch," Oxnam declared in one of his many postwar polemics, "is likely to be so conditioned that he may be willing to take his political thought from a dictator or his economic thought from a party." A close parallel could be drawn. "The American Catholic hierarchy," the Methodist bishop pontificated, "as well as the American Communist Party, is bound by directives from a foreign capital."[36]

The *Christian Century,* the leading journal of Protestant liberalism, was a major voice in mobilizing anti-Catholic sentiment. In late 1944 and early 1945 it ran an eight-part series by Harold E. Fey, titled "Can Catholicism Win America?," which warned of the menace of Catholic "totalitarianism." The series was then widely circulated as a pamphlet, advertised thus in the *Christian Century:* "Here is a carefully wrought study of the strategy by which Rome, weakened in Europe, hopes to make America a Catholic province, capturing Middletown, controlling the press, winning the Negro, courting the workers, invading rural America, and centralizing its power in Washington."[37]

Longtime *Christian Century* editor Charles Clayton Morrison followed up the Fey series with one of his own, which he expanded into a book, *Can Protestantism Win America?* (1948). Morrison warned that "three major forces are now bidding for ascendancy in the cultural and spiritual life of America." These were Protestantism, Roman Catholicism, and Secularism. Most Protestants, he felt, were complacent, taking their dominance for granted and not recognizing the urgency of the present cultural and spiritual crisis.[38] Such sentiments were one factor in strengthening mainline Protestant solidarity with the formation of the National Council of Churches in 1950.[39]

The most immediately alarming trend, according to the anti-Catholic authors, was Catholic inroads in education. One of their greatest fears, it seemed, was that public funds might be used to support Catholic schools. Court cases on such subjects were sending mixed signals. Oxnam and Morrison were among the leading founders of a movement to block any Catholic gains, "Protestants and Other Americans United for the Separation of Church and State," established in 1948.[40]

Paradoxically, this revival of anti-Catholicism took place at a time when there was much call among the dominant voices in America for an end to bigotry. The revelations of the horrors of the Holocaust steeled resolve to end any discrimination against Jews. Antiracist sentiments similarly had made great gains since the war and there were calls for ending the segregation of African Americans. Anti-Catholicism thus placed Protestant and secular liberal leadership in an awkward position. Many prominent leaders accordingly were more reserved in their anti-Catholic expressions than were Oxnam and Morrison. Henry Sloane Coffin, for instance, was among a group of Protestant leaders who were concerned with the Catholic threat but explicitly wanted to avoid the appearance of "bigotry" that might come with association with Protestants United.[41] While Protestant leaders might deplore the dogmatic and authoritarian Catholicism which in their eyes had contributed to European fascism, they were also cultivating "the right sort" of Catholics for "three-faith" pluralism that included Protestants, Catholics, and Jews. This tame united front, however, would be established on Protestant terms. The price of full acceptance in American public life would be that Catholicism and Judaism would have to act like denominations; that is, claims to be the true church or a chosen people could make no difference in their behavior.[42]

The watchword for this attempted resolution was "pluralism." As Philip Gleason has shown, pluralism had already taken on the meaning that is still current, a verbal celebration of American diversity, but with an insistence that this diversity be limited by accepting basic American values. In other words, pluralism was a new name for the old melting-pot ideal. This was the message being sent to postwar Roman Catholics.[43] They were welcomed to America with open arms. Their unquestioned patriotism was deeply appreciated. Nonetheless, they should not expect something as un-American as their parochial school system to be accepted on equal terms with other forms of education in America. It was not just that Catholic schools were different. Rather the religious authoritarianism at the heart of the enterprise was antithetical to free inquiry, which was the very basis of American education.[44] Paul Blanshard quoted a remark by John Dewey: "It is essential that this basic issue be seen for what it is—namely the encouragement of a powerful reactionary world organization in the most vital realm of democratic life with the resulting promulgation of principles inimical to democracy."[45] Harvard's president James Bryant Conant made the point a bit more politely. Contrasting America's education system favorably to those of England, Scotland, Australia, and New Zealand, Conant deplored the growth of American Catholic high schools. Public schools, he affirmed, were essential to unified national life. Religiously based criticisms of them were misplaced since "our tax-supported schools have had as a great and continuing purpose the development of moral and spiritual values."[46]

God and Buckley Revisited at Yale

In this atmosphere we can understand better the explosive reaction to Buckley's critique of Yale.[47] At the height of a revival of interest in religion, Buckley dared to say that university education was essentially not congenial to Christianity. Henry Sloane Coffin's committee was only echoing what leading religious educators were saying when it affirmed that "religious life at Yale is deeper and richer than it has been in many years." Compared with most front-rank schools Yale was relatively open to religious interests. Among themselves, Protestant leaders might admit that the situation was far from ideal. The Hazen volume on *College Texts and Religion,* published in New Haven, for instance, had recently documented the overwhelmingly secular slant of textbooks. Mainline Protestant speakers routinely decried the secularism, materialism, and scientism of universities. Yet when a Catholic pointed out the same things it was deeply offensive. To have a representative of their oldest ideological rival point out that the best of Protestant higher education was failing in its religious task was painful, especially so because the criticisms were largely accurate. As a number of the reactions suggested, his polemic against his alma mater was all the more outrageous because Buckley was a guest, one of the very beneficiaries of Protestant openness.

Buckley's dogmatic definition of Christianity was also offensive and deepened the inability of the two sides to communicate. Much of what the Protestant leadership long had counted as broadly Christian values Buckley regarded as wrongly baptized secularism.[48] Moreover, while the traditional Christianity for which Buckley spoke distinguished sharply between those who were in the church and those who were not, the Christianity believed suitable to a university centered on values that would bring people together. Ultimately, the Christianity that had survived at Yale, though it retained significant transcendent dimensions, had to meet the test of serving democracy.

Ironically, Buckley himself shared some of the premises that had helped define what religion would be tolerated in universities. He too had an establishmentarian's assumption that Christianity essentially involved a plan for a free American social order. Hence his prescription for a return to God at Yale was inextricably wed to a social and economic agenda built around free enterprise. Buckley was not proposing to get rid of the American religious establishment but to refurbish it with conservative religion and economics.

Because Buckley's combination of religious and economic views differed so radically from those acceptable to the Protestant establishment, he was able to point out forcefully that their claims to "academic freedom" were "superstitions." Here was a point on which the Protestant establishment was most vulnerable, even on its own terms. What a believing Catholic could see clearly, but the Protestant elite were loath to admit, was that the Protestant establishment *was* an establishment. By weakening the distinction between church and nation it had claimed the whole nation as its church. Although its doctrines were thus blended with and often subordinated to the liberal ideals of the republic, they were still doctrines. Moreover, they were doctrines with a distinctly *Protestant* heritage.[49]

Notes

1. Merrimon Cuninggim, *The College Seeks Religion* (New Haven: Yale University Press, 1947), 120–22, provides a bibliography of some of these works.

2. Ibid., 110–19, summarizes some of these.

3. *General Education in a Free Society: Report of the Harvard Committee* (Cambridge, Mass.: Harvard University Press, 1945), 71, 43, 39, 76, 174, 205, 76, 44, and 95.

4. Ibid., 216–17. Laurence Veysey, "Stability and Experiment in the American Undergraduate Curriculum," in *Content and Context: Essays on College Education* (New York: McGraw-Hill, 1973), esp. 50–53. Veysey points out that, rather than being invented at Columbia as is sometimes suggested, the concepts of great book and of Western civilization courses date back to before World War I and seem to have been pioneered at Berkeley (51).

Douglas Sloan, "The Teaching of Ethics in the American Undergraduate Curriculum, 1876–1976," in *Education and Values,* Douglas Sloan, ed. (New York: Teachers College Press, 1980), 237–48, presents a very valuable account of this "General Education" movement, its inability to agree on the basis for the common values it was supposed to teach, and its decline by the late 1950s.

5. United States Bureau of the Census, *Historical Statistics of the United States, Colonial Times to 1957* (Washington, D.C.: Government Printing Office, 1960), 210. By 1954 some 30 percent of the eighteen to twenty-one year olds were attending college.

6. *Higher Education for American Democracy, A Report of the President's Commission on Higher Education,* (Washington, D.C.: Government Printing Office, 1947), I:101, 25–36.

7. Ibid., 67, 49, and passim.

8. Robert M. Hutchins, "Double Trouble: Are More Studies, More Facilities, More Money the Key for Better Education?" *Educational Record* 39 (April 1948), 107–22. Reprinted in *Saturday Review of Literature,* July 17, 1948, under this title, reprinted in *Education for Democracy: The Debate over the Report of the President's Commission on Higher Education,* Gail Kennedy, ed. (Boston: D.C. Heath, 1952), 81–89.

9. *Higher Education,* I:50.

10. Cf. Hutchins, "Double Trouble," 84.

11. *Higher Education,* I:10.

12. T. R. McConnell, "A Reply to the Critics," in Kennedy, *Education for Democracy,* 110, quoting from C. J. Turk, "The Immediate Goals of Higher Education in America," *College and Church* 13 (1948), 13–16.

13. *Higher Education,* V: 65–68.

14. Allan P. Farrell, "Report of the President's Commission: A Critical Appraisal," *Journal of Educational Sociology* 22 (April 1949), 508–22, reprinted in Kennedy, *Education for Democracy,* 97–104, esp. 101–2. This article refers to several other of the Catholic critiques.

15. Robert S. Lynd, "Who Calls the Tune?" *Journal of Higher Education* 19 (April 1948), 163–74, reprinted in Kennedy, *Education for Democracy,* 52–61, esp. 55.

16. *Higher Education,* I:102.

17. William Clyde DeVane, *Higher Education in Twentieth-Century America* (Cambridge, Mass.: Harvard University Press, 1965), 127, 130.

18. Robert Wuthnow, *The Struggle for America's Soul: Evangelicals, Liberals, and Secularism* (Grand Rapids, Mich.: William B. Eerdmans, 1989), 34–35. Cuninggim, *College Seeks Religion.* Keith Hunt and Gladys Hunt, *For Christ and the University: The Study of InterVarsity Christian Fellowship of the U.S.A., 1940–1990* (Downers Grove, Ill.: Intervarsity Press, 1991).

19. Sir Walter Moberly, *The Crisis in the University* (London: SCM Press, 1949), 300–301 and passim. On the parallel between British and American developments see David Bebbington, "The Secularization of British Universities since the Mid-Nineteenth Century," in *The Secularization of the Academy,* George M. Marsden and Bradley J. Longfield, eds. (New York: Oxford University Press, 1992), 259–77.

20. Another source that, like the *Christian Scholar,* is filled with discussions of religion and higher education during this period is *Church and College,* the educational news bulletin of the Commission on Christian Higher Education of the Association of American Colleges.

21. These and other developments are documented in Douglas Sloan, *Faith and Knowledge: Mainline Protestantism and Twentieth-Century American Higher Education* (Philadelphia: Westminster Press, 1994) (forthcoming).

See also Erich A. Walter, ed., *Religion and the State University* (Ann Arbor; University of Michigan Press, 1958), which provides very intelligent discussions concerning many of the developments and challenges involved and itself is a mark of the high-water point reached in these campaigns.

22. In Foreword to R. H. Edwin Espy, *The Religion of College Teachers: The Beliefs, Practice, and Religious Preparation of Faculty Members in Church-Related Colleges* (New York: Association Press, 1951), vii.

23. Sloan, *Faith and Knowledge,* documents the temporary character of the revival.

24. *College Reading and Religion: A Survey of College Reading Materials* (New Haven: Yale University Press, 1948). *The Edward W. Hazen Foundation 1925–1950* (New Haven: Hazen Foundation, 1950).

25. *College Reading,* vi, ix; Robert L. Calhoun, "History of Philosophy," Ibid. 1–27; Theodore Spencer, "English Literature," Ibid. 172–73; Margaret Mead and Jean Rhys, "Cultural Anthropology," Ibid. 296; William A. Orton, "Economics," Ibid. 261.

26. Spencer, "English Literature," 181–82, cf. 165–66, referring to Margaret

Mean, "How Religion Has Fared in the Melting Pot," in *Religion and Our Racial Tensions,* Willard L. Sperry, ed. (Cambridge, Mass.: Harvard University Press, 1945), 61–81.

27. *The Hazen Foundation,* 31–32.

28. Reinhold Niebuhr, *The Contribution of Religion to Cultural Unity* (New Haven: Hazen Pamphlets, 1945), 3–15.

29. Sloan's analysis in *Faith and Knowledge* is a most important one and complements the present account.

30. Ellen W. Schrecker, *No Ivory Tower: McCarthyism and the Universities* (New York: Oxford University Press, 1986), 104, 106, 111, cf. 31, 379, and passim.

31. Ibid., 117–25, 323–25.

32. Purcell, *Crisis,* 235–66.

33. That Catholicism was sometimes associated with the extreme forms of anticommunism only reinforced the point that Catholicism might threaten liberal culture. On McCarthyism and the Catholic connection see Donald F. Crosby, *God, Church, and Flag: Senator Joseph R. McCarthy and the Catholic Church, 1950–1957* (Chapel Hill: University of North Carolina Press, 1978).

34. Paul Blanshard, *American Freedom and Catholic Power* (Boston: Beacon Press, 1949), 85 and passim.

35. Paul Blanshard, *Communism, Democracy and Catholic Power* (Boston: Beacon Press, 1951), ix–x.

36. Quoted in Robert Moats Miller, *Bishop G. Bromley Oxnam: Paladin of Liberal Protestantism* (Nashville: Abingdon Press, 1990), 408.

37. Ad in *Christian Century* 62 (February 28, 1945), 287, quoted in Philip Gleason, "Pluralism, Democracy, and Catholicism in the Era of World War II," *Review of Politics* 49 (Spring 1987), 226n. Cf. Gleason's account, 211–14.

38. Charles Clayton Morrison, *Can Protestantism Win America?* (New York: Harper & Bros., 1948), 1, vii.

39. Gleason, "Pluralism," 226n.

40. Miller, *Oxnam,* 405.

41. Ibid., 404–5.

42. John Murray Cuddihy, *No Offense: Civil Religion and Protestant Taste* (New York: Seabury Press, 1978), argues this point impressively.

43. Gleason, "Pluralism," esp. 215. Cf. Gleason, "Pluralism and Assimilation: A Conceptual History," in *Linguistic Minorities, Policies and Pluralism,* John Edwards, ed. (London: Academic Press, 1984), 221–57; and Gleason, "American Identity and Americanization," in *Harvard Encyclopedia of American Ethnic Groups,* Stephan Thernstrom et al., eds. (Cambridge, Mass.: Belknap Press, 1980), 43–46.

44. Blanshard, "American Freedom," 59–106.

45. Quoted from Dewey, *The Nation's Schools* (without further citation) in Blanshard, *American Freedom,* 106.

46. Conant, *Education and Liberty* (Cambridge, Mass.: Harvard University Press, 1953), 86. Cf. Gleason, "Pluralism," 216.

47. A comparable controversy took place at Princeton in 1954 when the Roman Catholic director of the Aquinas Foundation severely criticized the character of the Princeton departments of philosophy and religion. The Aquinas Foundation had been established at Princeton in 1952 with the avowed goal of "the rebirth of Christian culture in university life and thought," a goal that caused resentment among those who felt that "it presupposes a lack of Christian culture in Princeton University." George W. Elderkin, *The Roman Catholic Controversy on the*

Campus of Princeton University (n.p., 1955–1958), in four parts. Quotations from Part I, 5.

The controversy at Harvard in the late 1940s over the ultraconservative claims of Leonard Feeney, S.J., recounted in Cuddihy, *No Offense,* 49–64, also suggests some parallels.

48. Will Herberg, a Jewish scholar, presented a milder version of this point in a 1952 symposium in response to Margaret M. Wiley. Wiley, noting that twenty-five years earlier no one "could have predicted that by mid-century religion would have become a vital issue in higher education," was unhappy with the Christian biases of the religious revival and advocated finding the "spiritual underpinning for One World" through great literature. Herberg countered that, if anything, the leading promoters of religion in higher education were more in danger "of falling into formlessness and shallow eclecticism rather than flaunting a rigid and exclusive dogmatism." What the modern world needed was more particularistic biblical religion. Modern people, he argued, were prone to "demonic idolatries," especially totalitarianism. Is this country the danger was the idolatry of "secular humanism" in which "man becomes the measure of all things." Such philosophy, which talked of relativism but made humanity an absolute, was what "permeates so much of contemporary higher education." "Religion in Higher Education: A Journal Symposium," *Journal of Higher Education* 23 (October 1952), 350–58, 365–67.

49. Cf. Cuddihy, *No Offense,* esp. 11–23, where they are described as extensions of Protestant tendencies to insist that no institution should define a person's relationship to God.

22

Liberal Protestantism without Protestantism

In 1951 Robert Maynard Hutchins resigned as chancellor of the University of Chicago after years of frustration. Weary of having many of his most cherished proposals blocked by recalcitrant faculty Hutchins determined that he could do more for his educational ideals as an associate director of the Ford Foundation. Hutchins was, next to John Dewey, the best known American educator of the era. Twice he was honored with the closest thing to canonization by the American hierarchy, a cover appearance on *Time* magazine. His resignation, however, may be taken as a signal that even a person of immense prestige and ability could not deflect the educational stream that was by now so firmly set in its course. As Hutchins put it, "The academic administrators of America remind one of the French Revolutionist who said, 'The mob is in the streets. I must find out where they are going, for I am their leader.' "[1]

"Civilization is doomed," Hutchins wrote in the *Journal of Higher Education* in 1947, "unless the hearts and minds of men can be changed, and unless we can bring about a moral, intellectual and spiritual reformation."[2] Modern Americans were never more open to such a reformation than in the postwar years. Western civilization had just survived the nightmare of Nazism and was faced totalitarian Stalinism. Religious leaders of all stripes were calling for return to first principles. Had there been a realistic hope for such a return to first principles in academic life, Hutchins's first principles should have been prime candidates. They appealed to the authority of reason and thus were more broadly based than appeals to particular religious traditions, yet they allowed room for theological expression.[3] They could thus plausibly meet the necessary academic criterion of being "nonsectarian."

Yet even at this moment before the effects of mass education had been felt there was no prospect for establishing a metaphysical basis for "truth" that would serve the whole public. There could be no return to an American commonsense philosophy based on natural law. Hutchins grew up at Oberlin, only a generation away from the time when such philosophy was intact and when there was still an ethos that might allow a consensus to be built around the best of New England Protestant reforming ideals.

Americans still professed many high ideals, but these evolved haphazardly and were constantly reshaped by practical, rather than theoretical concerns. The pragmatists only articulated and systematized what most American educators already did anyway, which was to follow the trends. In Hutchins's view, almost all of American education was "not merely anthropocentric; it centers upon those aspects of human life least likely to elevate and ennoble the human spirit."[4] Hutchins himself turned his hopes for educational reform increasingly toward the "Great Books" series, which he hope would give adults a unified education in the Western tradition that universities could not provide.

Hutchins's example is important a half century later; it should remind us that the solution to the apparent directionlessness of American higher education is not simply a return to a simpler era that many can still recall. Even then, when higher education was controlled by a much smaller and much more homogeneous elite, a simple return to a Western civilization core, in the hope that it would somehow generate a consensus of shared values, was impractical.

The Problems of the Residual Establishment

The same applies to those who would attempt to correct academia's current aversion to substantive religion simply by renewing programs that were attempted in the 1950s. There were at that time some impressive programs, sometimes well-funded. In addition to active campus ministries and opportunities for student worship and service, there was funding to encourage students to study for the ministry, increased interest in building religion departments and strengthening divinity schools, and an immense literature on how to promote religion on campus. Particularly there was widespread concern that higher education promote higher values that would reflect the best in the Judeo-Christian and American heritages.[5]

While all these programs were valuable to many people at the time, they were superficial in their address to the question of the role that religion would play in the universities. Because American academic life was defined and structured as it was, there was no way to get at the heart of the issue simply by *adding* religious activities. For a time such activities might thrive, but only as long as there was a residual Protestant consensus, which in the 1950s was extended to include Catholics and Jews. Once interest in religion faded among the classes who supported the universities, so did the added religious activities.[6]

One dimension of the problem had to do with the character of the dominant Protestant religious tradition that goes back to at least the eighteenth century. Again a Catholic observer helps us see what is distinctly Protestant. In 1845 John Henry Newman joined the Roman Catholic Church, a move that forced him to give up a position at his beloved Oxford University. Newman's renunciation of Protestantism was based in part on his perception of tendencies in it that he thought ultimately would undermine the intentions of the Protestant reformers. These tendencies were evident in the evangelical Protestantism of Newman's day and apparent in Protestant ideas of university education. Specifically they were tendencies to see the essence of Christianity as religious sentiment and practical morality. These emphases were suited to the public establishment of Christianity, as in higher education, since they moved any exclusive claims of Christianity, particularly theological claims, away from intellectual life. Christianity in academia was located either in the subjective lives of individuals or in ideals of service to humanity with which no one was likely to quarrel.

In contrast to the American trends, in Newman's *Idea of a University,* enunciated for his Catholic University of Ireland, of which he became the founding rector in 1852, theology was at the center. This did not mean that the university would be primarily a school of theology, but rather that theology should have an integral place among the other sciences. Since universities claimed to teach universal knowledge and theology was a branch of knowledge it did not make sense to exclude theology from the main business of the university as was being done in England. The tendency of each discipline is to aggrandize its approach to understanding reality. If theology were not guaranteed its own domain among the sciences, the other sciences would soon deny its relevance. The result would be attempts of the other sciences to understand reality without taking into account one of its most essential components.[7]

In American Protestant higher education the trends militated against keeping theological principles part of the educational enterprise. Already in the eighteenth century, moral philosophy had begun to emerge as the central locus of Christianity in the curriculum, supplemented by periodic revivals intended to enlist student Christian commitment. Morality and sentiment, emphases that Newman criticized in Protestantism, were thus already prominent. Some reference to theological principles nonetheless persisted until the age of the universities. Early in that era, however, with many pressures working against theology and no formal provision for maintaining its presence, it was quickly banished to divinity schools, if not simply banished. Newman was correct that this development fit the logic of modernizing Protestantism. Protestants were in the process of declaring the whole nation their church, and with no institutional church in the picture the primary locations for Christianity lay in individual experience and in public morality. Neither of these provided any institutional basis for maintaining distinctive Christian theological principles as a factor in education.

However astute Newman's analysis may have been, in the American mainline Protestant setting his prescriptions were unthinkable.[8] By the twentieth century the nonsectarian logic of the American Protestant establishment was so deeply antitheological that there was no way to retrace the steps and even begin to go back to a time when theological principles had something to do with mainstream higher education. That was, in effect, one of the things that the post–World War II religious revival proved. Sometimes the will was there to retrieve some role for distinctly Christian teaachings, but the logic of the Protestant–Catholic–Jewish establishment would soon block anything substantive in such a move.

We can see this point in one notable example both of the extent and the limits of the renewed interest in religion. In 1953 Harvard inaugurated as its president Nathan M. Pusey, a devout Episcopalian. One of the first things Pusey did was accept an invitation to address the opening convocation of the Harvard Divinity School in 1953. Pusey noted that the last time the university's president had participated in Divinity School exercise had been in 1909 when Charles Eliot had delivered what became a well-known address, "The Religion of the Future." Eliot had proclaimed that the religion of the future would be, in effect, all that is good, whether in performing surgery, building better schools or playgrounds, or cleaning up a slum. Pusey, in his own address, which was reprinted in *Harper's, Christian Century,* and other journals, took Eliot to task for thus reducing religion to social service. Pusey objected that Eliot falsely contrasted such good with metaphysical Christianity, which made traditional claims about God and Christ. Harvard's new president could even sound like at least a distant echo of Newman: "It is my very sincere hope therefore that theological studies can here be given a fresh impetus and a new life within this University. . . . Theology should not be thought of as a minor intellectual exercise among other intellectual exercises; certainly not only this. It is expected to carry an answer to our deepest hungers and needs." Having said that, however, Pusey closed with words that would have confirmed Newman's darkest suspicions of Protestantism. Quoting a Harvard Divinity School faculty member, Pusey affirmed that what was desperately needed was more of " 'faith [that] is the consciousness that moral values and spiritual experiences have sacred character.' "[9]

While Pusey did strengthen the Harvard Divinity School, he also was light years away from Newman in having no way of reintegrating Divinity with the rest of the university. Even his efforts to hire more committed theologians in the Divinity School met opposition from other Harvard faculty.[10]

A dramatic confrontation brought out how difficult it was for the religious revival to make any headway if it was to involve anything distinctly Christian. In the spring of 1958 opponents of Pusey's efforts to strengthen Christianity at Harvard brought attention to the university's policy of regarding Memorial Chapel as a Christian place of worship and not allowing other faiths to hold services or even weddings there.[11] The policy itself was a remarkable example of one of the principal problems faced by champions of the religious renewal. Any strengthening of the place of Christianity on campus would be a strengthening of a residual cultural establishment[12] and hence was liable to attack simply on grounds of equity. The Memorial Chapel had been built in the early 1930s as a memorial to Harvard students who had died in World War I. Opponents of the Christians-only policy pointed out those who had died represented many faiths and perhaps none at all. A sharp controversy ensued, culminating in a distinguished group of faculty, including Perry Miller, Mark DeWolfe Howe, Jr., I. Bernard Cohen, John H. Finley, Jr., and Morton G. White, personally presenting Pusey a petition demanding that the chapel be open to all faiths. Perry Miller, an agnostic who thought that current Christianity at Harvard was a pale shadow of that of the Puritan founders, reportedly was outraged at the thought that he might not be buried from the chapel of his own university. The next week the corporation capitulated to the realities of Harvard pluralism and declared the chapel open to private services of all religious faiths.[13]

Pluralism was one of the major roadblocks whenever thoughtful religious leaders proposed ways of providing a substantive place for Christianity, or other religions, within university education. Will Herberg, a Jewish scholar and the era's most respected analyst of America's "three-faith" pluralism, observed in 1958 that "virtually all Americans who have given any thought to the matter are thoroughly dissatisfied with the present state of the relations between religion and education, particularly public education." Moreover, said Herberg, "the place that is granted to religion in the university scheme of things, at least on most campuses, does not correspond either to a sound conception of higher education or to the essential requirements of American religious pluralism."

Herberg backed his remark with a perceptive encapsulation of American educational history. "Nonsectarianism" of the nineteenth century had been translated into "nonreligious." Thus American schools were not neutral with respect to religion but had opened the door for the dominance of "ideological secularism." Such "secularistic pseudo-religion, usually some brand of naturalism or positivism . . . soon began to acquire almost official status." In the meantime, "Catholics established their own institutions, and the Jews of the first or second generation who aspired to a higher education were even more secularist-minded than the rest." Few voices spoke for a genuine religious pluralism. "Pluralism" that welcomed religion only when it was another bland version of the "American Way of Life" was not a true pluralism. Religious philosophies, if they were to be treated fairly, would "be given the same rights and privileges in the academic world as are the secularist philosophies."[14]

Catholic social philosopher John Courtney Murray offered a parallel critique. Liberal society, he said, presented a "genteel picture" of itself as a peaceful development. This was particularly true of the universities, which claimed to be the havens of dispassionate reason. The fact of the matter was that the modern world had always been engaged in active ideological conflict, often having to doing with religious questions about the fundamental nature of reality. The university should therefore "recognize its own spiritual and intellectual situation. The university would succumb to a special type of neurotic disorder if it were to cultivate an inflated image of itself as somehow standing in all serenity 'above' the religious wars that rage beneath the surface of modern life and somehow privileged to disregard these conflicts as irrelevant to its 'search for truth.' " To present this "genteel picture" of itself would be "to indulge in a flight from reality." American universities, rather, should be places where a student is free to "explore the full intellectual dimensions of the religious faith to which he is committed."[15]

Protestant observers, despite the rhetoric of some of their number, were inclined to hesitate if anything but mainstream Protestantism was thus related to the intellectual life of universities. Representing "the Protestant view" in the same forum addressed by Herberg and Murray, church historian Roland Bainton of Yale, for instance, saw a "quest for truth" as essential to the self-definition of modern universities. Bainton wondered, therefore, how Roman Catholics, fundamentalist Protestants, or Orthodox Jews could fully participate in the intellectual life of the university, as long as they held to the authority of sacred revelations that closed many intellectual questions. How could a Catholic fully participate in the intellectual community of biologists when the pope had ruled that Adam was a real person? "One may wonder whether Catholicism can be genuinely at home in any university other than a Catholic university."[16]

William Frankena, chair of philosophy at the University of Michigan, which hosted the conference, pointed out the particular problems of substantive religious teaching at a state university. Frankena, who was a more traditional Protestant than Bainton (a Quaker), pointed out that Herberg's proposal of separate ideologically oriented courses from the viewpoint of the three major faiths was itself a compromise, since American faiths were much more diverse than that. While apologizing for maintaining a "liberal" view when both Herberg and Murray were speaking of a "postmodern" age more open to religion, Frankena quoted approvingly John Stuart Mill's remarks: "The proper business of an University is . . . not to tell us from authority what we ought to believe, and make us accept the belief as a duty, but to give us information and training, and help us to form our own belief in a manner worthy of intelligent beings, who seek for truth." Frankena thus accepted the orthodox definition of a university established in America in the early twentieth century. Given this definition, yet agreeing with Herberg and Murray that mainstream Protestants were only confusing the issue by teaching the "bogus irenicisms [of] religions of the common denominator," Frankena concluded that at a state university one could do little more than teach *about* religion. The most that might be done would be to teach sympathetically, so as to suggest that such issues might be of personal importance to students. Specific religious teaching, however, was the responsibility of homes, churches, and religious ministries to universities, this could not be the business of the university as such. Frankena recognized that doctrinaire secularism might gain an advantage in the liberal university, but he saw no realistic way to promote religion within the boundaries of the public university itself.[17]

Despite the ambiguity as to their real purpose, the growth of religion departments during this era acted as a palliative that helped hide the inability to address the deeper issues. By 1950 some 60 percent of state universities and land grant colleges were offering courses in religion, and during the next decades the field continued to grow. For instance, more than three times as many doctoral degrees were granted during the 1950s than in the 1940s. Much of the immediate postwar growth was justified on the same grounds that sparked the general education movement to strengthen the humanities. As one of the humanities, religion was an important value-shaping dimension of the Western heritage. Religion department offerings in universities generally resembled the offerings at Protestant divinity schools,[18] where in fact many of the professors had been trained. Care could be taken to avoid indoctrination, especially at state schools, but in general the study *about* religion could be conducted in an atmosphere encouraging to religious practice.[19]

During the 1960s, however, the predominant outlook in the field changed rapidly. Most important was the impulse to professionalize religious studies. Because of its ties to the residual Protestant establishment, its staffing by seminary graduates, and its associations with Bible requirements at church-related school, the academic field of religion was often regarded as a second-class discipline and seldom taken seriously among the humanities. The response was to define the field increasingly in scientific terms. Thus religious studies would have a methodology more like the social sciences. The new trend was to study religion "phenomenologically," so that the object of study was the abstraction "religion," the common traits of which could be exemplified by looking at particular religions. Another manifestation of the professionalizing impulse was the formation in 1964 of the American Academy of Religion, which grew principally out of the National Association of Bible Instructors (which had long lived with this less professional name). While the AAR embraced both the humanistic and the social scientific impulse, the latter signaled the dominant direction for the future.[20]

A most important parallel was a growing consciousness of the legal difficulty of maintaining a residual Protestant establishment, even of the blandest sort. In 1963, in a landmark ruling, *Abington Township School District v. Schempp,* the Supreme Court outlawed formal religious exercises in public schools. At the same time, however, the majority of the court proposed a way for dealing with the touchy issue of religion in public education. Religion should be studied with objective detachment. In fact, said Associate Justice Tom Clark in his majority opinion, "It might well be said that one's education is not complete without a study of comparative religion or the history of religion and its relationship to the advancement of civilization." Such sentiment cleared the way for accelerating the expansion of the study of religion in higher education during the next decade.[21]

By this time the field of religious studies was also being changed by counterculture critiques of Western civilization, Western values, and hence Western religion, thus adding impetus to the trend away from the dominance of the liberal Protestant heritage. During the anti-Vietnam War era many liberal Protestant academics largely sympathized with such critiques and became sensitized toward intruding into their work anything that might be construed as establishmentarian. One result was that religion programs increasingly provided a place for nonWestern religions and increasingly looked for nontraditional ways to study Western religions.

Catch-22

These changes reflected an increasing uneasiness within the liberal Protestant community about asserting a distinctly Christian identity at all. One strong sensibility that had developed by the 1950s was fear of any appearance of cultural imperialism. Immediate postwar concern to strengthen the Western heritage soon was overwhelmed by the new phenomenon of American internationalism. Educated Americans, including much of mainline Protestant leadership, increasingly warned against claims of Western superiority. For mainline Protestants such concerns accelerated the trends already growing by the 1930s, to question the whole idea of traditional Christian missions, premised as they were on the assumption of Christian superiority.[22]

Much the same was happening in the face of increasing sensitivity to the challenges of pluralism at home. During the late 1950s and the 1960s the overwhelming social preoccupation of the mainline Protestant churches was the attack on racial discrimination. Thus committed to an integrationist society, churches' public stances naturally gravitated toward opposition to discrimination of any sort, including religious discrimination. The fact that, among white Americans, more traditional religious views often correlated with racist views underscored the point that in public places religious privilege was dangerous. Hence developed the Catch-22 of liberal Protestantism: the more it identified itself with a social mission the less prominent should be its own identifiable social influence.

This was apparent in traditionally Protestant colleges. Having defined themselves increasingly in terms of their service to the public, they were now rapidly divesting themselves of the specifics of their Christian heritage. The reasons for this were a mix of principle and necessity. One important factor was economic. In the era of expansion, smaller colleges were having difficulties keeping up. One solution was to broaden constituencies. Inevitably this meant toning down religious emphases. Furthermore, such colleges were under pressure to conform to national academic standards if they were to retain prestige or even respect. David Riesman in 1956 described American academia as a "snakelike" procession, in which parts that were behind the leader, especially those in the middle, constantly try to follow the changing direction of the head.[23] Keeping up meant hiring faculty with loyalties to national academic standards more than to church concerns. It also meant dropping anything that might be interpreted as religious indoctrination. Measures of academic success emphasized evidence that students were being taught to think for themselves, as opposed to "conformism" or submission to "authoritarianism."[24] All these factors added to the impulse for mainline church-related colleges to define themselves in terms less and less distinct from their secular counterparts.

During the 1960s a number of well-funded studies examined what church-relatedness meant for a college.[25] As David Riesman and Christopher Jencks commented in 1968, "Organizations like the National Council of Churches as well as individual denominations are constantly commissioning investigations aimed at defining a unique mission for those colleges which remain Protestant, but the very idea that such questions require research is a tribute to the triumph of academic over clerical values." They concluded "Very few Protestant colleges admit that the substance of what they teach is influenced by ideological considerations."[26] By the end of the 1960s, mainline Protestantism's own studies were saying little more than that their colleges should learn from the universities.[27]

Much the same trends were influencing Christian faculty at secular institutions. While during the 1950s a number of significant voices were still talking about the role of the Christian in the university, by the mid-1960s such concerns were sounding passé. The history of the *Christian Scholar* exemplifies the changing times. In 1953 the Commission on Higher Education of the National Council of Churches launched a Faculty Christian Fellowship and established the *Christian Scholar,* a well-edited and attractive journal. In its inaugural issue the *Christian Scholar* affirmed the remarkable claim that "the twentieth century is the greatest age in theology since the thirteenth." The journal would explore the whole range of academic implications of Christian faith, in the context of this theological renaissance. "*The Christian Scholar,*" it avowed confidently, "will be motivated by the assumption that Christian faith is not only relevant to, but actually indispensable for, the tasks of the academic community and the vocations of those who serve within it in their common search for meaning and truth."[28]

In 1967 the *Christian Scholar* announced its impending demise. The problem was not primarily financial, but ideological. The Department of Higher Education of the National Council of Churches no longer thought such a journal appropriate. Subscribers would receive a new journal, *Soundings: A Journal of Interdisciplinary Studies.* While this journal was published by the Society for Religion and Higher Education, the closest its initial announcement got to suggesting a religious perspective was that it would fill the gap of discussion regarding "engagement of the Scholar with issues of value, meaning and purpose." "The focus will be on themes of genuine relevance to scholars both as academicians and as men engaged by the common human concerns of our day." The Faculty Christian Fellowship was officially declared dead a few years later.[29]

The dramatic shift toward dropping distinctive Christian identity had an ideological counterpart in the popularity during the mid-1960s of "secular" theologies. While the "Death-of-God" slogan of a few of this movement's theologians drew some sensational attention, a more typical expression of the mood of mainline Protestant spokespersons was Harvey Cox's widely popular *The Secular City.* Within less than a year of its publication in 1965 it had already sold over a quarter million copies. Cox, a professor at the Harvard Divinity School, had initially designed his book as lectures to the National Student Christian Federation, an alliance of mainline campus ministries. In a chapter on "The Church and the Secular University," Cox celebrated the secularization of the university and pronounced the attacks on secularization during the 1950s, when books like Moberly's were popular, to have been "a mistake."

Cox's most biting criticism was reserved for any vestigial idea of Christian higher education. The churches' first response to the rise of secular universities was to establish its own colleges and universities.

> This of course is medievalism. The whole idea of a "Christian" college or university after the breaking apart of the medieval synthesis has little meaning. The term *Christian* is not one that can be used to refer to universities any more than to observatories or laboratories. No one of the so-called Christian colleges that now dot our Midwest is able to give a very plausible theological basis for retaining the equivocal phrase *Christian college* in its catalogue.

What Cox was attacking was primarily what he characterized, accurately enough, as the vestigial establishmentarianism of mainline Protestantism in American higher education. The mainline campus ministries were, in his view, hardly any better than the so-called Christian colleges. The whole effort to keep a Christian presence in higher education was a "cumulative catastrophe." Established Protestantism was so entrenched socially that, despite the intentions of some of its leaders, it was essentially conservative in its cultural views and hence unable to facilitate real change. In contrast, Cox especially admired the YMCA and YWCA, which, in dropping their distinctive Christian heritage in favor of broader social concerns, had anticipated Dietrich Bonhoeffer's theology of "religionless man." Even though Y's were dying off as campus ministries, they had during the 1950s at least "survived the acute period of psychopathic confessionalism."

Cox's alternative to fighting the secularism of the university was to join it. The task of the Christians was "to discern where God's reconciliation is breaking in and to identify themselves with it." The church was not testifying to "some kind of common world view" or even to one worldview among many. Rather the Gospel taught reconciliation in the world. "It frees people to live with each other *despite* radically conflicting ideologies, theologies, and politics, as men with men." Affirming that the "religious" stage of history had come to an end, Cox proclaimed that "man must now assume the responsibility for his world. He can no longer shove it off on some religious power."[30]

Leading mainline Protestants were thus already beating a retreat for their conventional ministries when the counterculture arrived on the scene.[31] Their own principals of dedication to serving the best interests of society meant, ironically, that they must abandon some of the very institutions through which they had attempted to influence society. Nowhere was this more true than in higher education, where demands to keep up with the latest cultural trends were becoming overwhelming.

In the short run, the new stance could be seen not as a retreat at all, but as an advance. As Dorothy Bass points out, already by the early 1960s campus student organizations were increasingly turning to politics, particularly to issues of racial justice. With the eruption of the Free Speech movement in 1964, ever-deepening involvement in Vietnam, and increasingly violent urban disorders, politics overwhelmed everything else. Moreover, the imperative if churches were to "stay where the action is" was increasingly radical. Opposition to "the establishment" became a political fundamental. The comfortable campus ministry buildings with which religious groups had surrounded the universities were now an embarrassment when the poor were crying out for justice. Theological discussion was a cop-out if it did not lead to action. Traditional worship smacked of the staid and complacent middle class that was now so much despised. Even the guitars, balloons, and informality of the early sixties could hardly keep pace with the experiential standards of antiestablishment campus culture of the end of the decade.[32]

Politics was all there was, and even on that front it was impossible to keep up. In 1966 the ecumenical National Student Christian Federation reorganized as the University Christian Movement (UCM). During its initial year the UCM president sent a "fraternal" letter to the radical Students for Democratic Society (SDS) pledging to stand in solidarity for equality and justice. The UCM was still funded by the Danforth Foundation, headed by Merrimon Cuninggim, and still the principal promoter of much of the work in religion in higher education. The UCM itself became increasingly radical. Its expressed purpose was "to work for the termination of American economic and cultural exploitation at home and abroad." Early in 1969 the meeting of the General Committee of the UCM broke down in acrimonious debate over a task force recommendation to work "only in terms of total dismantlement of that [American] society." With matters already at a seemingly hopeless impasse, members of the black caucus demanded that in the name of justice the UCM should turn over $50,000—most of the UCM budget—to their control. The next morning the UCM leadership voted the organization out of existence.[33]

The story of the University Christian Movement is an especially dramatic instance of what was happening to ecumenical and mainline denominational ministries generally. Committed to international and social justice, looking for God's action in what was happening in the secular society, they instinctively responded to the counterculture movement by trying to keep up with it. That, however, was becoming increasingly difficult as the counterculture became more fragmented and divided between ideals of reforming society and simply dropping out. Protestant leaders could still call for a prophetic political voice, as Kenneth Underwood did in a major Danforth study of campus ministries published in 1969. The difficulty, however, was that by 1969 there was little reason for students to think of campus ministries if they were looking for political advice.[34]

However justifiable the stance for peace and justice and the attack on the establishment may have been in the short run, in the long run there was little left of the mainline and ecumenical campus ministries by the 1970s. Once the war was gone as a unifying cause, the radical political movements fragmented even further into special interest groups. With the political issues changed and interest in political questions waning, there was little basis for retrieving a student constituency. The mainline Protestant churches were experiencing alarming numerical declines, attributable especially to their inability to retain the loyalty of the younger generation. By the 1970s a substantial gap had developed between Americans who had gone to college and those who had not with respect to religious belief and practice. In the 1950s surveys had found no significant correlation between college education and religious belief. By the 1970s the college educated were far less likely than other Americans to attend religious services regularly or to hold traditional Christian views.[35]

The Soul of the Multiversity

As for the universities themselves, whatever their myriad concerns, religion was very low on the list. The 1960s was another era of huge growth. The vast majority of this growth came in state-sponsored education. Whereas in 1950 private four-year institutions enrolled slightly more students than did public ones, by 1970 the enrollments at public schools outnumbered the private by well over two to one.[36] Virtually none of this growth, furthermore, had anything directly to do with religion, although an increase in the study *about* it, even at state schools, may have allayed potential complaints. So much else was happening to the universities, however, that the mainline Protestant withdrawal was hardly noticed. The university had become, as California Chancellor Clark Kerr had characterized it in 1963, a "multiversity."[37] Increasingly looking to the government for funding, its technical and research concerns were expanding in bewildering ways, so that any hopes to find a center to the enterprise were increasingly illusory. Expansion was also fueled by the cultural revolution that has been described as the shift from "mass to universal higher education."[38] With higher education now regarded as a right available to virtually anyone who desired it, further proliferation of programs oriented toward preparation for the job market contributed to the decentralized ethos.[39]

In modern America, technological expansion has always been accompanied by countermovements demanding more concern for human values. In the 1960s the most effective voices making such counterdemands were students at the multiversities. They attacked the depersonalization of the technological society and established alternative lifestyles. The intellectual counterpart was what Theodore Roszak well characterized as the attack on "the myth of objective consciousness," the premise, on which university education had been built, that detached observation was the most accurate and effective way of looking at things.[40]

Students also questioned the basic premises of American politics and economics, especially the partnership of business and government in technical, commercial, and international (and hence military) expansion. In pointing out that the universities served the political needs of the society, they were saying nothing new; but with the Vietnam draft hanging over the heads of many, students were not inclined to honor the idea of education as *preparation* for service. In local campus insurrections they briefly brought the educational process to a stop; henceforth change in university policy would be most effectively initiated by organized interest groups who could threaten to paralyze the rest of the enterprise if their demands were not heard.

While the counterculture movement was too diverse to characterize neatly, one thing that was often noted at the time was that the student demands had characteristics of a religious quest.[41] Part of the impulse was a demand for meaning in universities and a society that had little to offer on that front. Search for experiential and spiritual fulfillment in an otherwise depersonalized environment was a major part of the impulse as well. Eastern religions, new religions, and the occult gained unprecedented followings as well. Such movements, as well as the drug, communal, and rock cultures, provided alternatives, or complements, to political activism. The rise of the Jesus People movement by the early 1970s provided a Christian alternative, as did a broader resurgence of campus evangelicalism generally.

The principal responses of the universities were on the political front. American universities had always in some sense been political entities, but more than ever they would have to be directly responsible to their constituency. Or perhaps it would be more accurate to say that they would have to be responsive to a wider set of constituencies. On the one hand, their dedication to producing knowledge for industry and government persisted; on the other, their stated goals now had to include strong counterbalancing affirmations concerning social justice.

Perhaps typical of the thinking about the university that emerged from the 1960s were the conclusions of the Carnegie Commission on Higher Education and the Carnegie Council on Policy Studies in Higher Education arrived at after extensive studies between 1967 and 1979. In 1980

Clark Kerr summarized the findings of the many Carnegie reports, emphasizing that the main point that had given universities credibility was that they were *"oriented toward the national welfare first and the welfare of all of higher education second."* In other words, "they were aimed at the advancement of American society through higher education and not the other way around." With this in mind the commission had identified five goals for higher education:

> (1) . . . the education of the individual student and the provision of a constructive environment for developmental growth; (2) advancing human capability in society at large through finding and training talent, developing new ideas, and enhancing understanding; (3) educational justice for the postsecondary age group; (4) pure learning—by supporting intellectual and artistic creativity; and (5) evaluation of society for renewal through individual thought and persuasion.[42]

Such statements would be duplicated many times over with little variation in particular institutions' definitions of their missions. They speak of educating students first, add the production and dissemination of knowledge, and emphasize ethical ideas of inclusive justice and of service to the community.

A typical formulation is the "mission statement" of Duke University formulated for its self-study in 1988. Duke (which is appreciatively acknowledged as the primary venue for the present work) is an institution well attuned to contemporary university trends, particularly since it has been self-consciously moving away from the more regional and parochial aspects of its heritage toward establishing itself as a major national university. Its stated goals thus express a characteristic set of contemporary university ideals:

> Duke University shall endeavor to accomplish these missions: to educate students for meaningful, ethical and productive lives, to discover and interpret significant new knowledge; to promote the spirit of free inquiry on moral and intellectual issues; to foster the exchange of ideas and information within and across traditional disciplinary boundaries; to enrich the lives of the residents of our region by producing a variety of educational, medical, cultural and recreational services; and to support diversity and mutual tolerance throughout the university.

Duke's statement, however, offers a small uncharacteristic variation alluding to the Protestant heritage that in the South still needs to be acknowledged. After a paragraph elaborating on the goals already enumerated, the report adds: "Duke cherishes its historic ties with the United Methodist Church and the religious faith of its founders, while remaining nonsectarian."[43]

This delicately stated formulation suggests that, so far as the university's purposes are concerned, Christianity (not mentioned by name) is a thing of the past; yet at the same time the church connection is to be revered. In fact, the university has a predominantly Methodist and distinctly Christian Divinity School, privileges regular Christian services in its chapel, and retains pro forma ties between its board and the North Carolina United Methodist Conference. At the same time, as the statement of purpose indicates, Christianity as such is peripheral to the main business of the university.

The role of Christianity in Duke's 1988 mission statement contrasts strikingly with that adopted in its founding bylaws in 1924, only two generations earlier. That mission statement begins: "The aims of Duke University are to assert a faith in the eternal union of knowledge and religion set forth in the teachings and character of Jesus Christ, the Son of God."[44]

One implication of this study, however, is that these two statements are more closely connected than they might seem. The 1924 statement, originally drafted earlier in the century for Duke's predecessor, Trinity College, is a classic example of the liberal Protestant vision of a unified culture under Christ. Knowledge and religion are united in the ethics of Jesus. The implication is that all the university's goals are expressions of that unifying ethic. These goals are, the statement continues, "to advance learning in all lines of truth; to defend scholarship against all false notions and ideals; to develop a Christian love of freedom and truth; to promote a sincere spirit of tolerance; to discourage all partisan and sectarian strife; and to reach the largest permanent service to the individual, the state, the nation, and the church. Unto these ends shall the affairs of this university always be administered."

The ideals that universities typically proclaim today are much the same as these; the only difference is that the references to the ethics of Jesus and to the church have become superfluous. Liberal Protestant theology had already located salvation primarily in social advance and so had removed any basis of maintaining a distinction between church and society. The rest of the twentieth century worked out the inevitable implication of that fusion. Public life could get along just as well, perhaps better, without the Protestant churches claiming to be at the center.

The universities are left with ideals of service to society and of enriching human life. These are high ideals and liberal Protestantism should receive credit for being among their progenitors. Critics, of course, might question how extensively universities are driven by the ideals that are promulgated in their catalogues and on university holy days. Much of university policy can be explained, for instance, as responsiveness to the market. Nonetheless, university constituencies demand, among other things, idealism. Although they would be loath to admit it, even many of the most persistent critics of the white, male, Protestant, Eurocentric traditions in the universities have themselves been shaped by interpretive traditions regarding humanity that have a substantial Protestant heritage and are difficult to find outside the West. Even if under new auspices, the traditions of moral idealism and service to humanity, designed to be the counterbalance to science in defining nineteenth-century universities, persist among the forces shaping academic culture today.

Moreover, it should be said that in many respects contemporary universities *do* do a fine job of serving society. Often that service comes in the form of very practical contributions to technological advance. Jaroslav Pelikan describes the twentieth-century challenges to which universities have responded as the Four Horsemen of the Apocalypse—war, famine, disease, and death—to which he adds a fifth, ignorance.[45] Any complete account of American universities would have to include credit for the immense contributions of their medical schools and hospitals. Moreover, much of university expansion over the past half century has been in technological areas, specialized research, and practical training, providing services that we sometimes fail to appreciate because we take them so much for granted. In many such areas, American universities are the best in the world.

Nonetheless, as many recent critics have noted, the universities, despite many practical accomplishments and continued professions of high ideals, are in the midst of a moral crisis. The nature of the crisis is suggested by the character of the ideals themselves. Aside from the catchall ideal of service, the one ethical issue on which universities have consistently taken a stand since the 1960s is "diversity and mutual tolerance." On the face of it, this seems a wholly laudable ideal. Yet it would be more laudable if its meaning were clearer.

The problem, as many critics have pointed out, is that tolerance and diversity do not by themselves define a coherent ethical stance. In practice tolerance and diversity always work within definite limits. This has been well illustrated in many of the recent debates concerning "political correctness." Politically conservative and traditional liberal critics complain that political establishments on many campuses that campaign under the banner of diversity and tolerance are really intolerant.[46] What is being disputed is not so much whether one group favors tolerance and freedom more than another, but what are the interests of society that properly should limit speech and action. Here, of course, is where the problems arise, since there is no agreed-upon court of appeal for such disputes. In fact, such questions are likely to be settled by contending interest groups. Often those who have prevailed have been backed by financial power. Since the 1960s, however, they have frequently been overtly political groups. Contemporary campuses have become particularly susceptible to organized factions that threaten to disrupt academic activities if their voices are not heard. Policy has often been written by the crowd on the quadrangle.

Universities would, of course, like to think that unlike parts of society where political forces prevail, they are havens where rationality should govern, particularly in identifying the social interests the universities are to serve. To some extent, of course, that is the case. Nevertheless, such definitions of what universities stand for, exemplified by the early AAUP's assumption that experts would provide a check on democratic irrationality, have become increasingly problematic as traditional rationality itself has been under attack. Postmodern ideals, *au courant* among many academics, have prompted withering attacks on the authority of the Enlightenment "scientific" standards that originally shaped American universities. Conventional standards of objectivity based on scientific models no longer have any prospect for claiming universal authority. Nor is there an adequate basis for establishing a consensus of moral values. The hermeneutics of suspicion can effectively dismantle any substantial claim by looking at the interests it serves. Even the most popular moral ideals of justice and equality propounded by campus progressives are not exempt from such critiques. The heirs to the liberal Protestant universities still equate all good with the social good. Yet all they have left is campus politics.

Notes

1. Quoted from *Time,* November 21, 1949, in Harry S. Ashmore, *Unseasonable Truths: The Life of Robert Maynard Hutchins* (Boston: Little, Brown, 1989), 300.

2. Hutchins, "The Spiritual Need for the Times," *Journal of Higher Education* 18 (May 1947), 325.

3. Speaking at the inauguration of the Federated Theological Faculty of the University of Chicago in 1943, Hutchins proclaimed, "Theology and the theological school are at the apex of the university because they seek to supply the answers to ultimate questions about the most fundamental matters with the university is concerned." "The Place of Theological Education in a University, *Christian Education* 27 (1943–44), 98. However, it was the quest for truth, rather than any particular theology, in which Hutchins was interested.

4. Ibid., 101.

5. Douglas Sloan, "The Teaching of Ethics in the American Undergraduate Curriculum, 1876–1976," in *Education and Values,* Douglas Sloan, ed. (New York: Teachers College Press, 1980), 191–254, provides a valuable summary of these trends as well as an analysis of their limits. For instance, Sloan documents that by 1950 sixty percent of state university and land grant colleges were offering academic credit for instruction in religion and that number continued to grow for the next decade and a half. Such programs were the principal loci for teaching ethics in the curriculum during that era. By the 1970s, however, pressures to professionalize the academic study of religion had led to a reduction of its ethical concerns (248–51). Cf. D. G. Hart, "American Learning and the Problem of Religious Studies," in *The Secularization of the Academy,* George M. Marsden and Bradley J. Longfield, eds. (New York: Oxford University Press, 1992), 195–233.

R. Laurence Moore, "Secularization: Religion and the Social Sciences," in *Between the Times: The Travail of the Protestant Establishment in America, 1900–1960,* William R. Hutchison, ed. (Cambridge: Cambridge University Press, 1989), 233–52, presents a valuable account of renewed concerns to relate ethical values to the study of social sciences during and after World War II. He concludes, however, that these efforts had little lasting impact and did not stem the tide of secularization.

An interesting statement of the problem at the time is found in the title essay of Morton White, *Religion, Politics, and the Higher Learning* (Cambridge, Mass.: Harvard University Press, 1959), 93. White suggests "that any educational effort to nourish religious feeling or to stimulate religious action by trying to present an abstract essence of religion, conceived as the life of feeling and willing (as opposed to knowing), will fail. From this I conclude that we should not make the effort in colleges which are not religious institutions, and that we become frankly sectarian in our teaching of religion and therefore limit higher religious instruction to the divinity schools; since divinity schools are more properly devoted to the *study and the propagation* of religions conceived as total ways of life, knowledge, emotion, and action."

6. Dean R. Hoge, *Commitment on Campus Changes in Religion and Values over Five Decades* (Philadelphia: Westminster Press, 1974), passim, esp. 41 and 90, beginning with the Leuba survey, finds that levels of religious orthodoxy and interest fluctuated over the decades. There was a decline between the 1910s and the 1930s and an apparent rise between the late 1940s and early 1950s, with the peak being reached between about 1952 and 1955. By 1954 many of the measures suggested return to levels of belief close to those of 1914.

7. John Henry Newman, *The Idea of a University* (Notre Dame, Ind.: University of Notre Dame Press, 1982 [1873, 1852]), 14–74.

8. A striking example is how little is said of theology in Jaroslav Pelikan's *The Idea of the University: A Reexamination* (New Haven: Yale University Press, 1992), even though Pelikan is a theologian and frames the book as a dialogue with Newman. Cf. my review essay, "Christian Schooling: Beyond the Multiversity," *Christian Century* 109 (October 7, 1992), 873–75.

9. Nathan M. Pusey, "A Faith for These Times," in *The Age of the Scholar: Observations on Education in a Troubled Decade* (Cambridge, Mass.: Harvard University Press, 1963), 7–8.

10. "Pusey's Divinity School Policy Criticized," letter to the editor, *Harvard Crimson,* March 3, 1956, 4. "Panel Disagrees on 'Commitment' of Faculty in 'Secular' University," *Harvard Crimson,* April 29, 1958, 1.

11. Nathan M. Pusey, "The Christian Tradition," letter to the editor, *Harvard Crimson,* April 98, 1958, 2.

12. At Harvard and elsewhere during the 1950s there was some controversy when athletic teams began to disregard the Protestant tradition of not playing or practicing on Sundays.

13. *Harvard Crimson,* April 18, 1958, 1; April 23, 1958, 1. Miller's viewpoint is based on his writing and oral tradition, consistent with the evidence. Other *Crimson* articles on the controversy can be found in the following issues from 1958: March 28, April 8, 9, 10, 11, 12, 14, 15, 16, 17, 18, 19, 21, 23, 26, 29, May 19, 20, and June 9. An approximate survey of religious affiliations of Harvard undergraduates for 1956 showed 25 percent Jewish, 14 percent Catholic, 40 percent Protestant (Episcopal with the largest representation, 14.5 percent), 10 percent other, and 11 percent none. *Harvard Crimson,* March 28, 1958, 5.

14. Will Herberg, "The Making of a Pluralistic Society—A Jewish View," in *Religion and the State University,* Erich A. Walter, ed. (Ann Arbor: University of Michigan Press, 1958), 37–40.

15. John Courtney Murray, S.J., "The Making of a Pluralistic Society—A Catholic View," in Walter, *Religion,* 16, 22.

16. Roland H. Bainton, "The Making of a Pluralistic Society—A Protestant View," in Walter, *Religion,* 47.

17. William K. Frankena, "A Point of View for the Future," in Walter, *Religion,* 299, 305, and 295–309 passim. Mill quotation from his inaugural address as rector of St. Andrews University (299).

18. This is evident in Milton D. McLean and Harry H. Kimber, *Teaching of Religion in State Universities: Description of Programs in Twenty-five Institutions* (Ann Arbor: Office of Religious Affairs, University of Michigan, 1960).

19. This account depends largely on D. G. Hart, "Problem of Religious Studies," in Marsden and Longfield, *Secularization of the Academy,* 194–233. Also see Sloan, "The Teaching of Ethics," 248–51.

20. Hart, "Religious Studies." For valuable contemporary assessments of the trend see Paul Ramsey and John F. Wilson, eds., *The Study of Religion in Colleges and Universities* (Princeton: Princeton University Press, 1970). The acronym of the National Association of Bible Instructors (NABI) was a play on the Hebrew word for prophet.

21. Dorothy C. Bass, "Revolutions, Quiet and Otherwise: Protestants and Higher Education during the 1960s," in *Caring for the Commonweal: Education for Religious and Public Life,* Parker J. Palmer et al., eds. (Macon, Ga.: Mercer University Press, 1990), 222.

22. Cf. Grant Wacker, "A Plural World: The Protestant Awakening to World Religions," in Hutchison, *Between the Times,* 253–77. One sign of the times, for instance, was that the "Yale-in-China" program, which since early in the century had maintained a Christian college on the mainland as part of its educatinal mission, now reopened in Hong Kong on a purely secular basis. At home, the Yale board still included some of the men who had been shaped by pre–World War I missionary enthusiasm. Now, however, they were convinced that the Christian spirit of their cultural mission for international understanding was best expressed by dropping explicit reference to Christianity. Jeffrey Alan Trexler, "Education with the Soul of a Church: The Yale Foreign Missionary Society and the Democratic Ideal," Ph.D. dissertation, Duke University, 1991.

23. David Riesman, *Constraint and Variety in American Education* (Lincoln: University of Nebraska Press, 1956), 25–52.

24. Philip E. Jacob, *Changing Values in College: An Exploratory Study of the Impact of College Teaching* (New York: Harper & Brothers, 1957), helped fuel the worry over conformism of college students during this time. Cf. the response of Allen H. Barton, *Studying the Effects of College Education: A Methodological Examination of Changing Values in College* (New Haven: Hazen Foundation, 1959). Barton quotes approvingly the concern of Theodore M. Greene, *Liberal Education Reexamined* (New York: Harper, 1943), regarding provincialism of students: "A person is provincial in his thinking if his outlook is restricted, either historically or systematically or geographically" (17). Kenneth A. Feldman and Theodore M. Newcomb, *The Impact of College on Students* (San Francisco: Jossey-Bass, 1969), another follow-up to Jacobs, develops a negative "authoritarian category that would include traditional religion" (I:30–31). Theodore W. Adorno et al. *The Authoritarian Personality* (New York: Harper & Brothers, 1950), developed an "F-scale" on authoritarianism used in some studies of college students. Cf. Barton, *Effects,* 86–87.

25. The most comprehensive of these was manning M. Pattillo, Jr., and Donald M. MacKenzie, *Church-Sponsored Higher Education in the United States,* Report of the Danforth Commission (Washington, D.C.: American Council on Education, 1966).

26. Christopher Jencks and David Riesman, *The Academic Revolution* (Chicago: University of Chicago Press, 1968), 327, 332.

27. This is the conclusion of Bass, "Revolutions," 214–15, and of Robert Wood Lynn, " 'The Survival of Recognizably Protestant Colleges,' " in Marsden and Longfield, *Secularization of the Academy,* 170–94, esp. 183, regarding Kenneth

Underwood, *The Church , the University, and Social Policy: The Danforth Study of Campus Ministries* (Middletown, Conn.: Wesleyan University Press, 1969).

Douglas Sloan, "The American Theological Renaissance," (an early draft of *Faith and Knowledge: Mainline Protestantism and Twentieth-Century Higher Education* [Philadelphia: Westminster Press, 1994 (forthcoming)]), 61–69, comes to a similar conclusion. By the late 1960s, he says, the slogan of three decades in the Student Christian Movement, "Let the University be the University," had shifted from a challenge to include Christian concerns to mean "Let the university be the university—as it is."

28. J. Edward Dirks, "About the Journal" (Editor's Preface). *Christian Scholar* 36 (1953), 3, 4. The first quotation is from J. V. Langmead Casserley, *The Retreat from Christianity in the Modern World* (London: Longmans, Green, 1952), 91. The *Christian Scholar* succeeded *Christian Education.* Cf. Sloan, "American Theological Renaissance," 1, 26.

29. "An Ending Not an End," *Christian Scholar* 50 (Winter 1967), 341, and "Announcing: SOUNDINGS: A Journal of Interdisciplinary Studies," *Christian Scholar* 50 (Winter 1967). Cf. Sloan, "American Theological Renaissance," 1, 26.

30. Harvey Cox, *The Secular City: Secularization and Urbanization in Theological Perspective,* rev. ed. (New York: Macmillan, 1965), 193–94, 217–37.

31. Such theological trends were already strong by the time Cox wrote. See Bass, "Revolutions," 209.

32. For a critical view of these developments see Leonard I. Sweet, "The 1960s: The Crises of Liberal Christianity and the Public Emergence of Evangelicalism," in *Evangelicalism and Modern America,* George Marsden, ed. (Grand Rapids, Mich.: Wm. B. Eerdmans, 1984), 29–45.

33. This account follows closely that of Bass, "Revolutions," esp. 218–19, from which the quotations are taken.

34. I am grateful to Sloan, "American Theological Renaissance," 64–65, for this insight.

35. Robert Wuthnow, *The Struggle for America's Soul: Evangelicals, Liberals, and Secularism* (Grand Rapids, Mich.: William B. Eerdmans, 1989), 34–35.

36. *1986–87 Fact Book on Higher Education,* Cecilia A. Ottinger, comp. (New York: American Council on Education, 1987), chart 73.

37. Cf. Bass, "Revolutions," 212, and Clark Kerr, *The Uses of the University* (New York: Harper & Row, 1963).

38. Martin Trow, "Reflections on the Transition from Mass to Universal Higher Education," in *The Embattled University,* Stephen R. Graubard and Geno Ballotti, eds. (New York: George Braziller, 1970), 1–42.

39. Francis Oakley, *Community of Learning: The American College and the Liberal Arts Tradition* (New York: Oxford University Press, 1992), 73–104, offers revealing statistics documenting government expansion and vast increases in two-year colleges, community colleges, and higher education outside the humanities since the 1960s. For instance, in 1960 one in six faculty members taught at a liberal arts college, whereas by 1980 only one in twelve did (98).

40. Theodore Roszak, *The Making of a Counter Culture: Reflections on the Technocratic Society and Its Youthful Opposition* (Garden City, N.Y.: Doubleday, 1969), 205–38.

41. For example, Jill Conway, "Styles of Academic Culture," in Graubard and Ballotti, *Embattled University,* 43–55.

42. Clark Kerr, "The Carnegie Policy Series, 1967–1979: Concerns, Approaches, Reconsiderations, Results," in *The Carnegie Council on Policy Studies in*

Higher Education: A Summary of Reports and Recommendations (San Francisco: Jossey-Bass, 1980), 2–3.

43. *Crossing Boundaries: Interdisciplinary Planning for the Nineties: Duke University Self-Study* (1988), 3–4.

44. This statement is found on a plaque at the center of the West Campus, Duke University.

45. Pelikan, *The Idea of the University,* 15–21. Cf. Francis Oakley's *Community of Learning,* in which the president of Williams College provides a positive assessment of current liberal arts education.

46. E.g., Dinesh D'Souza, *Illiberal Education: The Politics of Race and Sex on Campus* (New York: Free Press, 1991). Also C. Vann Woodward, "Freedom and the Universities" (review of D'Souza), *New York Review of Books,* July 18, 1991, 32–37. Stanley Fish in a sense concedes the point in "There's No Such Thing as Free Speech and It's a Good Thing Too," *Boston Review,* February 1992, 3–4, 23–26, which argues very persuasively that questions of free speech on campus can be reduced to issues of political power. David Bromwich, *Politics by Other Means: Higher Education and Group Thinking* (New Haven: Yale University Press, 1992), levels a critique against both the left and the right.

Concluding Unscientific Postscript

Discrimination against Traditional Religion Reconsidered

Since no historical interpretation lacks an agenda, it is appropriate to elaborate how this history bears on some current issues in the light of my own interests. Such explicit prescription has, of course, the danger that readers who do not share my viewpoint may be so distracted by their disagreements as to discount the historical argument. Nonetheless, I must ask their indulgence to consider my concerns which, at the least , should be illuminating regarding why I asked of the historical materials the questions that I did. As stated at the outset, the preeminent evaluative question is whether, in the light of the reasons why American higher education has been defined as it has, there are compelling reasons for perpetuating such strong prejudices against traditional religious viewpoints. I think there are not.

Intellectual Grounds

The widespread current critiques of scientific objectivity provide a context for reconsidering the near exclusion of religious perspectives from the academic life of American universities of Protestant heritage. Initially the relegation of religion to the periphery of American universities was justified on essentially Enlightenment grounds. Religious viewpoints, at least traditional ones, were considered both unscientific and socially disruptive. A unified and universal science would provide an objective basis for a united society. Universities would provide leadership in such a society. The liberal Protestant establishment endorsed this ideal, which had the added attraction of effectively excluding from the front ranks of American education its two most numerous religious rivals, Catholics and more traditional Protestants.

Liberal Protestants justified these exclusions not only on the negative grounds that traditional Christian beliefs were unscientific, but also by the positive rationale that cultural development advanced the Kingdom of God. Moreover, a broad idealism expressed especially in the humanities, the arts, and the social sciences (as originally conceived) could balance the scientific enterprises with those that built moral character. Formal religious practice would be provided in chapel that emphasized nonsectarian moral ideals and through neighboring churches on the periphery.

Throughout the first sixty years of the twentieth century, as prevailing intellectual ideals became less friendly to religious concerns and the dominance of the mainline Protestant ethos receded, Protestant leaders became increasingly uneasy with this original arrangement. They realized that in academic life itself it favored purely naturalistic and materialistic worldviews. In response, they added campus ministries, schools of religion, chaplains, impressive chapel buildings, student programs, and literature to promote religious concerns. They had limited success, however, in challenging the original definitions of academic life, and with the cultural upheavals of the 1960s, such efforts declined as well. Academic life remained a haven largely freed from religious perspectives.

In the decades that followed, however, the original intellectual rationales for excluding religious perspectives were much weakened. Few academics believed in neutral objective science any more and most would admit that everyone's intellectual inquiry takes place in a framework of communities that shape prior commitments. Such prior commitments might be arrived at on formal religious grounds or in some more informal way, but they were prior commitments nonetheless. Hence there is little reason to exclude a priori all religiously based claims on the grounds that they are unscientific.

One way to describe the current state of affairs, however, is that, in effect, the only points of view that are allowed full academic credence are those that presuppose purely naturalistic worldviews. Advocates of postmodernist viewpoints have, as a rule, been just as committed to exclusively naturalist premises for understanding human belief and behavior as were their turn-of-the-century predecessors who established evolutionary naturalism as normative for academic life.[1] One must wonder, however, whether there are adequate grounds for most academics to insist on naturalistic premises that ignore the possibility of fruitful religious perspectives.

Originally liberal Protestantism allowed scientific naturalism free rein in much of the intellectual life of American universities on the grounds that scientific truth would not contradict philosophical and religious truth but could be complemented by it. By the 1930s, however, it was becoming apparent that while the assumptions of scientific naturalism could provide a broad practical basis for shaping most academic disciplines, philosophical idealism and liberal Protestantism were no longer able to command a comparable consensus. Despite counterefforts to restore religious perspectives in the 1950s, naturalism and pragmatism held the field academically. The postmodernist intellectual crisis may thus be understood as a crisis within the naturalistic community. Given a purely naturalistic evolutionary and radically historicist set of premises, finding any rational grounds for building a consensus on any significant human question becomes problematic. Consistent application of the hermeneutics of suspicion reduces everything to the interests of individuals or groups. Even one's own moral claims, for example, regarding equality or justice, are vulnerable to such critiques. Old-style liberal opponents of such relativism have no place to stand in establishing a basis for their moral claims. Appeals to natural law have far less chance of commanding a consensus than they did even in Robert Hutchins's day. Yet the alternative of liberal pragmatism has led, much as Hutchins predicted, to postmodern relativism.

It is, of course, conceivable that a pure naturalism provides the best account of reality that we humans can have. There is no way, however, to demonstrate that it does. It is not a conclusion of modern scientific thought, but rather an often useful methodological premise. As a claim about reality, however, exclusivist naturalism is unsubstantiated and unfalsifiable. The question arises then why we should virtually prohibit any but that restrictive premise to play a role in the intellectual life of our universities.

This is not to say that in a more open university just anything would pass muster academically. What might be called procedural rationality is still necessary. Even when the foundations for a definitive rationality have crumbled, each discipline finds that it must nonetheless honor some basic rules of evidence and argument.[2] The same rules would apply to religious as to nonreligious perspectives. In each case, much nonsense would be precluded. Religious perspectives may be particularly prone to anti-intellectual dogmatism (although the history of the twentieth century proves that secular viewpoints can give them a hard run for that distinction). Especially in pluralistic academic settings, claims to private revelations or other religious attitudes that preempt intellectual inquiry are particularly problematic. Yet while the procedural rules of academia may preclude some extreme religious attitudes and viewpoints, there is no reason why it should be a rule of academia that *no* religious viewpoint shall receive serious consideration.

Some might argue, of course, that any claim to religious revelation is nonsense. That, however, is simply to revert to the dubious premise of pure naturalism.[3] Ultimately there seems no intellectually valid reason to exclude religiously based perspectives that have strong academic credentials on all other grounds. One test is whether a religious perspective, taken as a whole, rather than preempting intellectual life, has proven itself a starting point for further intellectual inquiry.[4] Some very traditional religious viewpoints would qualify on this score. For example, just looking at the Western world, the traditions associated with Augustine, Maimonides, Averröes, Aquinas, Dante, Luther, Calvin, Milton, Pascal, Edwards, and Newman (to name only a few) have proven themselves intellectually as elegant[5] and fruitful as any in history. It would seem then that such traditions, all of which have capable twentieth-century representatives, ought to have the same rights academically as viewpoints based on nonreligious starting points. The same should be true for comparable viewpoints in other religious traditions.

Pluralism

Once the intellectual reasons for excluding such formidable religious perspectives from respectable academia have failed, the reasons that remain have to do with universities' commitments to society. In the interest of social harmony, the tendency has been to exclude from academic life all but the blandest religious views. Some religious views, of course, *are* disruptive beyond what a society might be expected to tolerate. Religious viewpoints that demand political violence or are presented so dogmatically and aggressively as not to be accommodated within the procedural rules of pluralistic academia could be excluded on the same grounds as comparable secular viewpoints. Nonetheless, if one is talking about advocates of religious viewpoints who are willing to operate intellectually within the procedural rules of universities, showing respect for those with whom they disagree, there is little ground for regarding such viewpoints as inherently more disruptive than nonreligious outlooks.

One of the strongest current motives for discriminating in academia even against traditional religious viewpoints that play within the procedural rules of universities is that many advocates of such viewpoints are prone to be conservative politically and to hold views regarding lifestyle, the family, or sexuality that may be offensive to powerful groups on campuses. Hence in the name of tolerance, pluralism, and diversity academic expressions of such religious perspectives may be discriminated against.

The incoherence of such widely current ideas concerning the meaning of tolerance, pluralism, and diversity is readily apparent. Tolerance, one might think, ought to include tolerance of religious viewpoints, including religious viewpoints in academic life. Pluralism, one might likewise suppose, would encourage first-class citizenship within universities for the widest feasible variety of cultural expressions. Since religion is integral to most cultures, one might expect that a commitment to diversity would entail the encouragement of intellectual expressions of a variety of religious perspectives. The presence of strongly held differences of belief on campuses should be dealt with by enforcement of rules of civility, not by intolerance toward and exclusion of a whole class of viewpoints.[6]

Pluralism as it is often conceived of today seems to be almost a code word for its opposite, a new expression of the melting-pot ideal. Persons from a wide variety of races and cultures are welcomed into the university, but only on the condition that they think more-or-less alike. Though the leadership may no longer be all northern European male, the establishmentarian impulse toward homogenization still prevails. Religious viewpoints that do not blend into the multicultural melting pot are excluded.[7]

Academic Freedom

Prejudice against academic expressions of religious viewpoints has also flown under the banner academic freedom. The crucial 1940 statement on academic freedom grounded the principle in "the common good." That means that academic freedom is in fact limited by whatever are the prevailing ideals of the common good. This point was amply illustrated during the McCarthyite era when the AAUP did relatively little about the dismissals. Nonetheless, the McCarthy episodes also sparked extensive academic attention to strengthening principles of academic freedom, so that by the late 1950s academic freedom was more than ever a cornerstone of academic orthodoxy.

In this orthodoxy, religious and political conservatism were often conflated and assumed to be equally repressive. One center for this antireligious interpretation was the American Academic Freedom Project at Columbia University. In *Academic Freedom in Our Time* (1955), Robert M. MacIver, director of that project, wrote:

> Those who advocate that the university should take a definitely religious stand are in their proselytizing zeal committing themselves to a total perversion of the function of the university. They would revert to the intellectual confusion of earlier times, when a superimposed prior "truth" retarded the advance of knowledge and thus tended to imprison the inquiring mind. To make the university a center for the propagation of any creed, of any system of values that divides group from group, is to destroy the special quality and the unique mission of the university as a center for the free pursuit of knowledge wherever it may lead.[8]

Richard Hofstadter was also associated with the Columbia project and together with his associate Walter Metzger provided the most influential history of American academic freedom. Hofstadter was also a major contributor to the attack on religious conservatism. In his *Anti-Intellectualism in American Life* (1962), for instance, Hofstadter made evangelical Protestantism the number one example of the American impulse toward intellectual repression.

The events of the 1960s, however, revealed a deep problem in the sort of consensual academic viewpoint for which scholars such as MacIver and Hofstadter stood. The uprisings on campuses across the country could be seen as, among other things, demands for the universities to live up to their own proclamations of academic freedom as an absolute. As the free speech and counterculture critics pointed out, academic freedom was limited to "the common good," as defined by the predominantly white male Anglo establishment who had always run the universities.

Since then control of the universities has been diversified to include representatives of other groups, who often have been equally insistent that *they* are the true champions of freedom. In fact, as has often been suggested in the recent debates over "political correctness," the "freedom" such groups advocate is equally bounded by a limiting, even if somewhat different version of "the common good."

The intellectual crisis of the past quarter century underscores the problem with continuing to use academic freedom as a basis for discrimination against religious viewpoints. Academic freedom as originally defined in the United States assumed a universal science that required only open-minded free inquiry to flourish. It also assumed a universal moral ideal of higher civilization which experts informed by such science would serve. These ideals were conceived of as the apogee of nonsectarianism.

Today, however, the idea of such objective science no longer seems viable and many critics have pointed out the community-relative character of moral ideals, including those that limit academic freedom.[9] In the present context it seems much more plausible to view all ideals for the social good as sectarian and the sciences that serve those ideals as equally so. There is little basis for sustaining the illusion that "academic freedom" is part and parcel of an open-minded scientific search for truth that ought to exclude the substantial influence of all religious viewpoints.

This is not to suggest that academic freedom is not a high academic ideal, important to the advancement of knowledge. To enhance the creativity of a community, academics should be as free as possible within the framework of their other higher commitments to explore and communicate even unpopular and unconventional ideas. A presumption of freedom within defined limits is an immensely valuable way of defining academic life.

That is all the more reason to emphasize that institutions which are going to define themselves on the basis of religious perspectives should be required to state their limiting standards publicly. Early in the century, as in the case involving Lafayette College, the AAUP made the telling point that if there were functional creedal limits on employment, schools should state them openly in advance.[10] The same principle should apply to secular institutions. If, for instance, the operative academic boundaries of an institution are defined by certain conceptions of humanity as ultimate, or by insistence that only purely naturalistic viewpoints are to be taught, then it would be consistent to demand that these limits be frankly stated.

Questions of academic freedom and religion should be considered in different terms at the end of the twentieth century than they were at its beginning when an informal Christian establishment was still in place. Religious establishments had been part of the history of universities since their beginning and at the time of the rise of American universities were forces to be contended with. In the interests of guaranteeing freedom for certain types of academic inquiry, academic freedom was defined at that time in such a way as to defend against preemptive religious restrictions on inquiry. Since the 1960s, however, there is scarcely any danger in leading American universities of a dominant religious belief leading to the imposition of general restrictions on free inquiry. So the reasons for discrimination against religious outlooks in academia are greatly reduced. Persons who work from religious perspectives, after all, do so voluntarily. The same is true of people who choose to teach at institutions that set some religious boundaries. Since their guiding viewpoints are held voluntarily, their freedom is hardly infringed by choosing to work within those restrictions.

Church and State

Many people believe that the Constitution of the United States precludes religious perspectives at institutions that depend on government funding. That interpretation of the American tradition, however, does not fit the actual practice in academia at any point in American history. Some religious perspectives have always been tolerated legally and even today there are a fair number of individual exceptions to the prevailing academic rules. Persons with strong academic credentials who respect standards of academic civility and who honor other points of view in fact have the legal right to speak from religious perspectives.[11] To prohibit them would involve very strained interpretations of academic freedom and of free exercise of religion. Moreover, as is often pointed out, attempts at exclusions of all identifiable religious perspectives privilege nonreligious perspectives.

The relationship between government and organized religion in the United States cannot be settled by any simple formula such as "separation of church and state." Rather, the First Amendment prohibits the *establishment* of religion. How that prohibition is to be interpreted has been sharply contested. It seems clear enough that the state should not establish any one religion in public life. It is much disputed whether that should imply the government may not establish nonreligious views either. Furthermore, it is far from clear that the best way to prevent the establishment of religion is to attempt to exclude *all* public religious expression. The problem, of course, is that exclusion of all religious expression infringes on the other half of the First Amendment provision concerning religion. The government should not interfere with the free exercise of religion. If *this* constitutional principle is taken seriously, nonestablishment might seem better accomplished by encouraging *varieties* of religious expressions, rather than discouraging them.

As is true regarding academic freedom, questions of church and state ought to be reconsidered in the light of the demise of the mainline Protestant religious establishment since the 1960s. While the overwhelming numbers of professed Christians in the population seems to provide potential for establishing undue privilege for one religious view, that danger is almost nonexistent in dominant American higher academia today. Especially since Christians are sharply divided among themselves, encouraging a *wider* variety of religious viewpoints than has ever been allowed in higher academia involves little danger of reintroducing a virtual establishment.

Is There Room for Institutional Pluralism?

Though the present story has centered on pace-setting American universities with a Protestant heritage, some of its most important implications may be applicable to those institutions that have been outsiders to the dominant academic culture. Throughout the era since the rise of American universities, pressure has come from many directions for institutions to conform to the homogenized national ideal. Many small colleges that long retained a more distinctive heritage eventually conformed and lost their identity.[12] Today, in addition to confronting an intellectual climate that penalizes anything but pure naturalism, they face practical pressures arising from concerns for pluralism, academic freedom, and church–state issues that parallel those just considered regarding universities.

Pluralism remains a basis for imposing uniformity. Accrediting agencies sometimes attempt to penalize institutions for having a distinctive religious heritage. While the general rule for accrediting agencies has been that institutions should be allowed to define their own goals and then be accredited on that basis, accreditors sometime exert pressure against distinctive religious and cultural traditions. In 1990, for instance, the Middle State Association of Colleges and Schools deferred accreditation of Baruch College of the City University of New York on the grounds that it had a "paucity of minority representation on the faculty and in administration." While this institution with a considerable Jewish constituency already had 18 percent representation of "minorities" on its full-time faculty, the accrediting agency considered this percentage insufficient, since minorities constituted 70 percent of the student body. While Baruch capitulated to the demands of the accreditors, its president, Joe Segall, later wrote, "It is hard to decide whether higher education has entered a new era of McCarthyism or a Kafkaesque trial process." Particularly offensive, said Segall, were the accreditors' accusations of "racism" if a school was reluctant to accede to their quotas. The Baruch case as well as Middle Atlantic pressure against conservative Westminster Theological Seminary, which required that its board members be ordained clergy or elders and was committed to church law that forbade ordination of women, led in 1991 to a delay in government reauthorization of the Middle States Association itself. Lamar Alexander, then Secretary of Education, in a strongly worded statement, questioned whether imposition of affirmative action policies was appropriate to the evaluation of an institution's educational quality.[13]

Robert H. Atwell, president of the American Council on Education, responded with a classic endorsement of academic homogeneity promoted in the name of diversity. Responding to the question "*Will the application of Middle States' standards force some institutions to change their educational mission, thus imposing an undesirable uniformity?*," Atwell wrote:

> Such a fear is totally unfounded. The regional accrediting bodies are made up of widely varying colleges and universities, which are quite vigorous in defending and maintaining their distinct identities and missions.
>
> However, diversity among institutions does not satisfy the need for diversity *within* institutions. . . . [M]any people in higher education . . . have come to understand the critical importance of recognizing and cultivating the diversity that exists among the various cultures that compose the United States. Applying this concept to higher education requires a comprehensive approach that encompasses the makeup of the faculty, student body, and staff; the curriculum offered by the institution; and the climate of the campus itself.[14]

In other words, regardless of religious traditions, uniformity would be imposed. Atwell simply considered it a *desirable* uniformity.

"Academic freedom" continues to be another favorite watchword for those who would bring pressure on religiously defined schools to abandon their heritages.[15] In the early twentieth century, while the AAUP affirmed the *right* of religiously defined schools to exist, its literature implied the undesirability of such schools. Such institutions, the AAUP suggested, were inferior exceptions to a universal rule and could never be full-fledged institutions of higher learning. In its 1970 Interpretive Comments on the definitive 1940 declaration on academic freeedom the AAUP stated: "Most church-related institutions no longer need or desire the departure from the principle of academic freedom implied in the 1940 Statement, and we do not now endorse such a departure." This view is still prevalent in the AAUP and within American academia generally. As late as 1988 a subcommittee of an AAUP committee on freedom and tenure recommended that because the 1940 statement made full academic freedom normative, a "necessary consequence" of the choice of religious institutions to remain as exceptions to this principle is their forfeiture of "the moral right to proclaim themselves as authentic seats of higher learning." In the opinion of the subcommittee, an "institution has no 'right' under the 1940 Statement simultaneously to invoke the Limitations Clause and to claim that it is an institution of learning to be classed with institutions that impose no such restriction." Though this recommendation was not adopted, the fact that such a proposal could get as far as it did reveals the continuing tendency to regard religiously based institutions as inherently backward and second-class.[16]

Similarly, the Phi Beta Kappa Society has denied chapters to the overwhelming majority of the hundreds of Catholic colleges and universities. Until the late 1930s no Catholic school was admitted to the prestigious honor society and only two were included before the 1960s. As late as 1989 only a dozen Catholic schools had been granted such recognition. Catholic institutions that have been otherwise academically qualified have been excluded on the grounds that their religious stance inhibits academic freedom.[17] Even the best of the many liberal arts colleges of the Christian College Coalition are denied membership on the same grounds.[18]

Government agencies and the courts have often shown similar prejudice toward religiously defined education, although they have typically sent mixed messages. The tensions are nicely illustrated by the impact of the "Bundy aid" laws in New York State, named for the recommendations of a state commission headed by (William F. Buckley's erstwhile adversary) McGeorge Bundy. On the one hand, the 1968 report of the committee, which signaled the waning of anti-Catholicism, recognized the increased necessity for state funds if private colleges were to survive and argued strongly that religiously affiliated colleges should be eligible for state aid. The New York State Constitution contained the so-called Blaine Amendment (recalling the senator of "Rum, Romanism, and Rebellion" fame), which prohibited state aid to any school "wholly or in part under the control or direction of any religious denomination, or in which any denominational tenet or doctrine is taught." The Bundy Commission advocated that this amendment be changed or reinterpreted to allow state aid to religiously affiliated colleges. On the other hand, the commission opposed "any assistance to institutions whose central purpose is the teaching of religious belief." To decide eligibility, the commission suggested that the state determine whether a school "is primarily a religious institution or primarily an institution of higher education." As a result of legislation implementing the Bundy proposals, the State Education Department withheld aid from religiously affiliated colleges until they furnished satisfactory evidence that religious considerations were secondary to defining the tasks of the college. Such pressures as well as those growing out of parallel court decisions of the era sped the processes of secularization for many colleges, particularly Catholic colleges that were already reassessing the meaning of their Catholic affiliations. A few colleges resisted such pressures. Those that wanted state or federal aid, however, typically did all they could to demonstrate that their religious commitments made no real difference in how they taught their subjects.[19]

One implication of the present study is that the prevalent view that "religious institutions" cannot also be "institutions of higher learning," or that any institution with a strong religious mission must inhibit higher learning, stands on shaky ground. This attitudes reflects the dominant standards set by American universities of Protestant heritage in the late nineteenth and early twentieth centuries and the characteristic assumptions of that time. There is no reason to take such standards as though they were normative for all time. As we enter the twenty-first century, colleges, universities, or aspiring universities that still have substantial religious commitments ought to be free to continue to do so. Those in which religious commitment has eroded ought to feel free to attempt to preserve and cultivate what is left.[20]

Restoring a place for religious perspectives in higher learning will require movement on several fronts. As has been argued here, there should be room, even in America's leading universities, for varieties of intellectual expressions, including religious ones. A first step is that religiously committed scholars who are already present at many universities will have to overcome their own longstanding inhibitions about relating faith to scholarship and establish academic credibility for expressed religious viewpoints. Other faculty members, in turn, should be receptive to the ideas of individual scholars whose religious perspectives may frankly influence aspects of their work, especially in the humanities and social sciences. Religiously based perspectives need not be any more tendentious than other perspectives. Moreover, truth in advertising suggests that scholars and teachers should reveal their viewpoints. Universities might also include religiously shaped research institutes or affiliated colleges, following British or Canadian models.

So long, however, as the deep-rooted prejudice against substantive religious viewpoints in formerly Protestant universities persists, Americans should also be building pluralism *among* institutions of highest learning. There is no necessity that so vital a part of society as its highest intellectual life should be pressured to fit one monolithic mold into which all subtraditions are poured. Rather, it seems there ought to be *encouragement* of institutional variety, including variety based on substantive religious concerns. Instead of following the pattern of having nonsectarian national standards set by a dominant establishment and then classing dissenting religious perspectives as at best second-rate, it should be recognized that religiously defined points of view can be intellectually as responsible as nonreligious ones.[21] It follows that religiously defined colleges and universities should have the right, if all else be equal, to be regarded as excellent.

In twentieth-century America religiously defined higher education often has been dismissed by stereotypes based on its worst exemplars. Mention of Christian education sparks in many people's minds images of fundamentalism or of repressive Catholic authoritarianism and that is the end of the matter. Such critics fail to take into account that religiously committed scholarship and institutions come in many varieties. Like other American groups, religiously committed scholars and institution should not be discriminated against on the basis of cultural stereotypes. Rather, once the origins of the intolerance are identified, attitudes might be revised on the merits of particular cases.

As should be apparent by now, this prescription for American higher education is not a call for a return to the past. Rather it is a call to understand and to appreciate the forces that have shaped American education, while questioning one important dimension of the results. There are many reasons to appreciate, for example, the American impulse to build a unified national culture, especially if we consider the alternative of ethnoreligious warfare seen in much of the rest of the world. The American alternative that places so much emphasis on mutual tolerance is to be greatly valued. Suspicions of religiously based intolerance are often well grounded. Nonetheless, it does not follow that in order for these values to be preserved in academia an entire class of intellectual perspectives and a whole class of institutions must be discriminated against.

Similarly, the demands of a technological society, which more than anything else give universities their shape, are in many respects valuable or at least inescapable. So are many of the attendant features of a technological society, such as rules of procedural rationality and standards of professionalization guaranteeing such academic practices as tenure and academic freedom within declared boundaries. Yet again, we may ask whether these values could not be just as well preserved without infringing on the rights of legitimate academic viewpoints that are informed by religious perspectives.

In many of the American colonies all the citizens were taxed for the support of the established religious group, regardless of the citizens' religious affiliations. In the nineteenth century the Protestant establishment became informal and declared itself nonsectarian. Today nonsectarianism has come to mean the exclusion of all religious concerns. In effect, only purely naturalistic viewpoints are allowed a serious academic hearing. As in earlier establishments, groups who do not match the current national ideological norms are forced to fend for themselves outside of the major spheres of cultural influence. Today, almost all religious groups, no matter what their academic credentials, are on the outside of this educational establishment, or soon will be, if present trends continue. Americans who are concerned for justice ought to be open to considering alternatives.

Notes

1. It is on this crucial point that I most fundamentally part ways with postmodernists, although I think they are correct in their critique of scientific objectivity. If one starts with the premises of the purely naturalistic worldviews that usually define the permissible limits of academic inquiry, then postmodernist skepticism about both normative scientific and moral claims seems to me to be the most consistent conclusion. If, on the other hand, one believes, as I do, that humans are not the primary creators of reality, then, while one may acknowledge the impact of community interests on science and especially on morality, belief in a creator who has created both us and reality throws into an entirely different context questions concerning epistemology, science, and the superiority of some human beliefs to others.

2. Pluralistic academic communities are possible because persons from various subcommunities can agree upon common sets of procedural rules of inquiry. This explains why wide agreement is often possible, particularly in the physical sciences and on standards of excellence in most other disciplines. Discrimination

against religious perspectives arises, however, when the rules of the artificially constructed academic community are in effect absolutized and universalized (particularly the claim that only naturalistic explanations of reality are valid) so as to exclude academically constructive viewpoints of some subcommunities.

3. Jon D. Levenson, "The Bible: Unexamined Commitments of Criticism," *First Things,* February 1993, 24–33, writing from the perspective of traditional Judaism, makes some telling points on this topic with respect to biblical scholarship itself.

4. I do not mean here to reinstitute the rule that prevailed during the first two-thirds of the twentieth century, that the only views that might qualify in highest academia would be liberal religious outlooks that regard all religious beliefs as part of a quest. Such views should, of course, have a place in the academy. However, so also should firmly held theological views which may be important stimuli to creative intellectual life in many academic inquiries.

5. Today in fields such as mathematics and many of the sciences, intellectual elegance or beauty is a major criterion determining the attractiveness of a theory. The same standard might be applied to religiously based views.

6. Alasdair MacIntyre, *Three Rival Versions of Moral Enquiry* (Notre Dame, Ind.: University of Notre Dame Press, 1990), provides a powerful philosophical analysis that parallels much in the present work. Looking especially at Scottish models, MacIntyre also notes that those who defined modern universities in the late nineteenth century understandably regarded the residual religious tests in the dominant universities of their day as unjust. They incorrectly concluded, however, that the resultant freedom, which defined their idea of proper science, would guarantee intellectual progress. The collapse of these late nineteenth-century assumptions, especially regarding science, has left universities in disarray. However, pressures to exclude religious traditions in the name of science still remain strong. MacIntyre proposes that universities be characterized as places for "constrained disagreements" in which those informed by religious traditions are permitted to participate. See especially 216–36.

7. It can be argued, of course, that the present situation in the universities is not as detrimental to religious interests as it might first appear. While religious perspectives may be largely absent from intellectual life, campus religious organizations still provide a wide variety of religious options for students. Mainline Protestant campus work may have declined since the 1950s, but it is still present; in the meantime, evangelical campus organizations such as Campus Crusade and InterVarsity Christian Fellowship have flourished. Catholic and Jewish campus ministries, as well as those of other major religions, have been active as well and are treated with equity. Hence it might be argued that the present arrangement is an optimal one. Religion is kept out of public intellectual life yet remains a private option.

While the work of campus ministries may provide invaluable compensation for the religious poverty of the rest of the universities, it seems shortsighted for persons with religious perspectives to be content with such arrangements. The primary problem, of course, is that as long as the prevailing intellectual outlook of universities is built on community standards antithetical to most traditional religious belief, what goes on in the classrooms will be undermining the outlooks presented in campus religious meetings. Moreover, since universities train the next generation of academics, such attitudes are perpetuated across the generations and carry into the leadership positions of the entire society. Campus ministries help many individuals yet, as presently constructed, hardly touch the antireligious heart of modern academia.

In recent years there have been a number of proposals to build stronger intellectual components into campus ministries or to build academic ministries, such as study centers, specialized academic institutes, or even religiously oriented colleges or graduate institutes associated with universities. These are, I think, alternatives worth pursuing.

Many observers of American religion in recent decades have complained of the "privatization" of American religion. It seems odd, however, that many such observers are academics who have seemed quite content with the privatization of religion in so vital a part of national life as the university.

8. Robert M. MacIver, *Academic Freedom in Our Time* (New York: Columbia University Press, 1955), 138.

9. For a helpful discussion of the problems inherent in the concept of academic freedom see Edmund L. Pincoffs, ed., *The Concept of Academic Freedom* (Austin: University of Texas Press, 1972). Pincoffs remarks in his introduction, "When a professor or a student claims that he is entitled to academic freedom he is generally understood to be claiming the right to *pursue the truth unhindered.* This understanding is nearly as vague and full of difficulties as the general understanding that the *summum bonum* is happiness" (viii).

10. It is also essential that due process be protected. This is particularly important at strongly religious colleges where dictatorial rule is particularly common.

11. The courts have not always been consistent about this, however, particularly when less established teachers might be considered to be proselytizing for unpopular views. See, for instance, Phillip E. Johnson, "The Creationist and the Sociobiologist: Two Stories about Illiberal Education," *California Law Review* 80 (1992), 1071–90. See the summary of a case of a leading quantum chemist who was allowed more freedom to express his religious views than was a lesser known teacher whose case is described (1071–80, esp. 1076, n.26).

12. Bradley J. Longfield and George M. Marsden, "Presbyterian Colleges in Twentieth-Century America," in Milton J. Coalter, John M. Mulder, and Louis B. Weeks, *The Pluralistic Vision: Presbyterians and Mainstream Protestant Education and Leadership* (Louisville: Westminster/John Knox Press, 1992), 99–125.

13. Joe Segall, "When Academic Quality Is Beside the Point," *Wall Street Journal,* October 29, 1990 (Segall had resigned the Baruch presidency by the time of writing this guest editorial); "Accrediting Boards Court Diversity and Controversy," *USA Today,* May 14, 1991, 8D; "Education Chief Challenges Rule on Campus Mix," *New York Times,* April 13, 1991, 1, 10; "Presbyterian Seminary Faces Catch-22 on Accreditation," *Washington Post,* April 20, 1991, G11. The Middle States Association had applied its diversity standard in twenty-seven cases. President Samuel T. Logan, Jr., of Westminster Theological Seminary commented on the issues in "Academic Freedom at Christian Institutions," *Christian Scholar's Review* 21 (December 1991), 164–74.

14. Robert H. Atwell, "The Dangers of U.S. Intervention in Accreditation," *Chronicle of Higher Education,* November 20, 1991, A52 (italics in original).

15. In his plurality U.S. Supreme Court opinion on the 1971 case of *Tilton v. Richardson* involving funding for buildings at Catholic colleges, Chief Justice Warren Burger wrote that one reason why the funding was permissible was that the colleges involved were "characterized by an atmosphere of academic freedom rather than religious indoctrination." Quoted in Joseph Richard Preville, "Catholic

Colleges, the Courts, and the Constitution: A Tale of Two Cases," *Church History* 58 (June 1989), 209.

16. Michael W. McConnell, "Academic Freedom in Religious Colleges and Universities," *Law and Contemporary Problems* 53 (Summer 1990), 308–10.

17. Richard Nelson Current, *Phi Beta Kappa in American Life: The First Two Hundred Years* (New York: Oxford University Press, 1990), 210–18, provides a very frank account of such policies. Loyola University of Chicago, which had been judged to be otherwise qualified, was turned down in 1985 because of objections to a statement in its faculty handbook that forbade faculty members from "attacking and ridiculing authoritative Catholic teachings" when speaking as representatives of the university. Based on telephone interviews with Joyce Wexler, March 5, 1993, and Frank Fennell, March 16, 1993, and *Faculty Handbook* (Loyola University of Chicago, 1983), 30.

18. Brigham Young University is another example. In 1992 Phi Beta Kappa for the third time turned down its application for membership, citing the Mormon university's mission statement, which says: "Any education is inadequate if it does not emphasize that His [Jesus Christ's] is the only name given under heaven whereby mankind may be saved." Douglas W. Foard, secretary of Phi Beta Kappa, commented: "That's a limitation on academic freedom. What Phi Beta Kappa is about is the quest of excellence and open-ended inquiry." *Chronicle of Higher Education,* June 3, 1992, A4.

19. *New York State and Private Higher Education: Report of the Select Committee on the Future of Private and Independent Higher Education in New York State* (January 1968) (Albany: State Education Department, 1968), 47, 49. Maureen Manion, "The Impact of State Aid on Sectarian Higher Education: The Case of New York State," *Review of Politics* 48 (Spring 1986), 264–88. The secularizing impact of these cases is closely paralleled by that of cases culminating in the 1971 Supreme Court decision *Tilton v. Richardson* (which also permitted aid for facilities at four Catholic colleges after they had satisfied the Court that the facilities would not be used for religious purposes and that the colleges were "characterized by an atmosphere of academic freedom rather than religious indoctrination"). Preville, "Catholic Colleges," 209, from Chief Justice Warren Burger's plurality opinion. Preville documents faculty members' testimony that Catholic doctrine made no difference in their teaching. For a discussion of the impact of the pressures at the time see Walter Gellhorn and R. Kent Greenawalt, *The Sectarian College and the Public Purse: Fordham—A Case Study* (Dobbs Ferry, N.Y.: Oceana Publications, 1970).

20. Rebuilding a strong religious identity is more problematic. As this history has shown, once a college or university makes a commitment to serve primarily the whole public, it acquires obligations to a wide variety of constituencies and eventually is shaped in the image of those constituencies. Keeping a strong religious identity typically has required that ideals such as academic freedom be defined in the context of commitment to a church or religious community which qualify commitments to the whole society. Shifting, however from a concept of academic freedom defined primarily by public standards to one defined primarily by a church or religious group is extraordinarily difficult, especially when it comes to questions of faculty hiring or retention. Church-related schools that seek to strengthen residual religious identity should consider seeking religiously committed faculty for affirmative action add-on positions that would not threaten the status of current faculty.

21. For discussion of why, everything else being equal, religious viewpoints should be regarded as equally rational as nonreligious ones see Alvin Plantinga and Nicholas Wolterstorff, eds., *Faith and Rationality: Reason and Belief in God* (Notre Dame, Ind.: University of Notre Dame Press, 1983). Plantinga and Wolterstorff and others associated with the Society of Christian Philosophers have further advanced the discussion since that time. Some of my own reflections on the difference that a Christian viewpoint might make in scholarship and on the relation of Christian to non-Christian scholarship are found in "Common Sense and a Spiritual Vision of History," in *History and Historical Understanding,* C. T. McIntire and Ronald A. Wells, eds. (Grand Rapids, Mich.: Wm. B. Eerdmans, 1984), 55–68; "Evangelicals, History and Modernity," in *Evangelicalism and Modern America,* George Marsden, ed. (Grand Rapids, Mich.: Wm. B. Eerdmans, 1984), 94–102; and my contribution to a forum, "The Decade Ahead in Scholarship," *Religion and American Culture* 3 (Winter 1993), 9–15.

Index